Al-Kafi

Volume 8 of 8

English Translation

Al-Kafi
Volume 8 of 8
(al-Rawdah min al-Kafi)

English Translation

Second Edition

Compiled by
Thiqatu al-Islam, Abu Ja'far Muhammad
ibn Ya'qub al-Kulayni

Translated by
Muhammad Sarwar

Published by
The Islamic Seminary Inc.
www.theislamicseminary.org

The Islamic Seminary Inc., New York
© 2015 by The Islamic Seminary Inc.
All rights reserved
Second Edition 2015
Printed in the United States of America.

ISBN: 978-1-943081-00-4

Al-Kafi, Volume 8 of 8. English Translation – 2nd ed.
Sha'ban 1436
June 2015

Note to Readers

Dear respected readers, please note the following:

The English translation of this volume from Kitab al-Kafi is now, by the will of Allah, in your hands. It was only because of the beauty of the words of Ahl al-Bayt *'Alayhim al-Salam* that made it all possible. The magnitude of this project had become quite large and complex due to two language texts and it was sometimes difficult to handle.

All comments, suggestions and corrections will be very much appreciated. In fact it will be your participation in the good cause and rewarding in the sight of Allah, most Majestic, most Glorious. Please e-mail your comments, suggestions or corrections to: info@theislamicseminary.org.

With thanks,

The Islamic Seminary
www.theislamicseminary.org

Contents

The Book of al-Rawdah (Garden of Flowers (Hadith))

An Outline of the Number of Volumes, Sections and Subdivisions of Kitab al-Kafi

Part 1 - Al-'Usul (Principles)

Volume 1

This part of the book consists of *Ahadith* on the principles of beliefs and it is called 'Usul (principles) in *al-Kafi*.

The sections or chapters in volume 1 are as follows:

1. The Book of Intelligence and Ignorance (*Kitab al-'Aql wa al-Jahl*)
2. The Book of the Excellence of Knowledge (*Kitabu Fad al-'Ilm*)
3. The Book on Oneness of Allah (*Kitab al-Tawhid*)
4. The Book about the people who possess Divine Authority (*Kitab al-Hujja*)

Volume 2

Sections or Chapters in Volume 2:

5. The Book on Belief and Disbelief (*Kitab al-'Iman wa al-Kufr*)
6. The Book on Prayers (*Kitab al-Du'a'*)
7. The Book on the Excellence of the Holy Quran (*Kitabu Fadl al-Quran*)
8. The Book of Social Discipline (*Kitab al-'Ishra*)

PART 2 - Al-*Furu'* (Branches)

Volumes 3-7

This part consists of *Ahadith* on Islamic practical laws such as:

> The acts of worship (*'Ibadat*)

> Business transactions (*mu'amalat*)

> Judicial laws (*al-Qada'*)

Furu' al-Kafi (volume 3 – 7): The rules of conduct, the practical laws of the Islamic system, consists of the following:

9. The Book of Laws of Cleanliness (*Kitab al-Tahara*)
10. The Book of Laws of Menstruation (*Kitab al-Hayd*)
11. The Book of Laws about the dying people and their burials (*Kitab al-Jana'iz*)
12. The Book of Laws of Prayer (*Kitab al-Salat*)
13. The Book of Laws of Charities, Taxes (*Kitab al-Zakat*)
14. The Book of Laws of Fasting (*Kitab al-Siyam*)

15. The Book of Laws of Pilgrimage (*Kitab al- Hajj*)
16. The Book of Laws of Defense (*Kitab al-Jihad*)
17. The Book of Laws of Business (*Kitab al-Ma'ishah*)
18. The Book of Laws of Marriage (*Kitab al-Nikah*)
19. The Book of Laws about New-born (*Kitab al-'Aqiqa*)
20. The Book of Laws of Divorce (*Kitab al-Talaq*)
21. The Book of Laws of Emancipation of Slaves (*Kitab al-'Itq wa al-Tadbir wa al-Mukataba*)
22. The Book of Laws of Hunting (*Kitab al-Sayd*)
23. The Book of Laws of Slaughtering Animals for food (*Kitab al-Dhaba'ih*)
24. The Book of Laws of Foods (*Kitab al-At'imah*)
25. The Book of Laws of Drinks (*Kitab al-Ashriba*)
26. The Book of Laws of Dresses, Beautifying and the Ideal of Manhood (*Kitab al-Zay wa al-Tajammul*)
27. The Book of Laws of Animal Farming and Poultry (*Kitab al-Dawajin*)
28. The Book of Laws of Wills (*Kitab al-Wasaya'*)
29. The Book of Laws of Inheritances (*Kitab al-Mawarith*)
30. The Book of Laws of Penalties (*Kitab al-Hudud*)
31. The Book of Laws of Restitution for Bodily Injuries (*Kitab al-Diyat*)
32. The Book of Laws of Testimony and Witnessing (*Kitab al-Shahadat*)
33. The Book of Judicial Laws (*Kitab al-Qada' wa al-Ahkam*)
34. The Book of Laws of Oaths, Vows and Expiation (*Kitab al-'Ayman wa al-Nudbur wa al-Kaffarat*)

PART 3 - Al-Rawdah (Garden of Flowers (Hadith))

Volume 8

This part consists of miscellaneous *Ahadith* of both the *'Usul* and *Furu'* of *al-Kafi*. The topics are not arranged and organized as in the other volumes. The chapters are not in alphabetical order of *Ahadith* or narrators.

This volume comprises about six hundred *Hadith* on various topics and is a treasure of knowledge of the matters of belief, spiritual discipline, interpretations of many verses of the Holy Quran, accounts of the noble manners of the Holy Prophet and infallible members of his family and information about the system of this and the next life.

In the Name of Allah, the Beneficient, the Merciful

The Book of al-Rawdah
(Garden of Flowers (Hadith))

The letter of Abu 'Abd Allah, *'Alayhim al-Salam*, to a group of Shi'ah

H 14449, h 1

Muhammad ibn Ya'qub al-Kulayni has narrated that narrated to me, Ali ibn Ibrahim from his father from ibn Faddal from Hafs al-Mu'adhdhin from abu 'Abd Allah, *'Alayhi al-Salam*, and Muhammad ibn 'Isma'il ibn Bazi' from Muhammad ibn Sinan from 'Isma'il ibn Jabir who has narrated the following:

"Abu 'Abd Allah, *'Alayhi al-Salam*, wrote this letter to his companions and commanded them to study, think about its contents and continue to practice them in their daily lives. They, thereafter, would keep it in the places of their *Salat* (prayer) in their homes and after their *Salat* (prayer) would read it.

Narrated to me (Ibrahim ibn Hashim) al-Hassan ibn Muhammad from Ja'far ibn Muhammad ibn Malik al-Kufiy from al-Qasim ibn al-Rabi' al-Sahhaf from 'Isma'il ibn Mukhallad al-Sarraj from abu 'Abd Allah, *'Alayhi al-Salam*, who has narrated the following:

"This letter from abu 'Abd Allah, *'Alayhi al-Salam*, was addressed to his companions:

"In the name of Allah, the Beneficent, the Merciful

"Thereafter (after saying, 'In the name of Allah, the Beneficent, the Merciful') I advise that you must ask your Lord to grant you good health. You must maintain peacefulness, dignity and serenity. You must maintain bashfulness, keep yourselves clear, and clean (from sins) as the virtuous people before you have done. You must maintain courteous manners when dealing with people of falsehood. You may suffer because of their injustice but you must avoid indignantly disputing with them. You must remain within the limits of the religion both of you follow. When you associate, sit, come and go with them or express differences, it must be within the limit of *taqiyah* (piety and fear) of violating the laws or suffering losses. (It is a manner) that Allah has commanded you to observe when dealing among yourselves. When you face a difficult condition with them, they harm you and you can observe signs of hatred in their faces. If Allah, most High, would not dispel them away from you, they attack you. What is in their heart of hatred and anger is more than what you can see from them. Your gathering place and their gathering place are the same but your spirits are different and unharmonious. You can never love them and they will never love you. Allah, most High has honored you with the Truth and He has

1

shown it to you. He has not made them of the people of Truth. Be polite and courteous to them and exercise patience. They do not have polite manners or patience in anything. Their resource is inducing temptation in each other. The enemies of Allah bar you from the Truth if they can and Allah saves you from such plots.

"You must remain pious before Allah and hold back your tongue except from that which is good.

"You must not allow your tongue to slip away with false words, accusations, sins and animosity. Holding back your tongue from what Allah dislikes such as the matters He has prohibited you to do, is better for you in the sight of your Lord than the slipping of your tongue into what He dislikes. The slipping away of the tongue into what Allah dislikes and has prohibited is destruction for a servant in the sight of Allah; it brings hatred from Allah. It brings disgrace deafness, blindness and muteness which will remain attached to one on the Day of Judgment and then one will become as Allah has said, 'They are deaf, mute and blind and they cannot return', (2:18) which means that they cannot speak and 'permission will not be given to them to present any good excuse.' (77:36)

"You must remain on your guard against what Allah has prohibited you to do. You must remain silent except in what Allah will benefit you thereby in the matters of your next life and will grant you rewards. You must say a great many times *Tahlil*, (no one deserves worship except Allah), speak of His Holiness, *Tasbih* (Allah is free of all defects) and of praise of Allah. You must remain humble before Him and interested in what is with Him of the good for which there is no measuring tool available to measure and no one can reach its end.

"You must keep your tongue occupied in such matters to avoid committing what Allah has prohibited of false words which gives the speakers, as a consequence, eternal fire if one dies upon such words without repentance, return to Allah but does not separate thereof. You must pray and appeal before Allah. The Muslims cannot achieve success in finding their wishes to come true by any other means other than prayer and being inclined to Him, appealing before Allah and asking from Him.

"You must remain interested in what Allah has encouraged you to achieve and answer Allah to what He calls you, so you can achieve success and protection against the suffering and punishment from Allah. You must remain on your guard against the greed of your souls that wants to achieve what Allah has made unlawful for you. One who violates what Allah has made unlawful in this world, Allah blocks him from the garden (paradise) and its bounties, joys and honors that remain forever for the people of the garden (paradise).

"You must take notice that it is the worst misfortune when one exposes himself to the risk of disobeying Allah and to transgress against what Allah has made unlawful in matters of worldly pleasures which go away from the hands of its

2

people. (Such risk may amount to) costing one the everlasting bounties of the garden (paradise), its pleasures and honor for the people of the garden (paradise). Woe is on those who suffer such loss and will face the worst failure before their Lord on the Day of Judgment. You must ask Allah for protection against such a miserable condition and against a suffering like their suffering which they will face. We have no power as well as you without Him.

"You must remain pious before Allah, O group of salvation. If Allah, by means of what He has granted you, completes (your religion) for you then you must keep in mind that it does not become complete until you experience what virtuous people before you experienced. That you face a trial in matters of your souls and assets so much so that you will hear from the enemies of Allah a great deal of painful words. You must remain patient and bear it upon your side (back) even though they humiliate and hate you and place injustice on you which you must bear to seek thereby the pleasure of Allah, the house of the next life, until you curb and control your intense anger in suffering for the cause of Allah, most Majestic, most Glorious. They may incriminate you and call you liars about the truth, treat you as their enemies and hate you but you must remain patient with them. Such examples are all in the book of Allah which Jibril, *'Alayhi al-Salam*, brought to your Prophet, *O Allah grant compensation to Muhammad and his family worthy of their services to Your cause*. You have heard the words of Allah, most Majestic, most Glorious, to your Prophet, *O Allah grant compensation to Muhammad and his family worthy of their services to Your cause*, '. . . you must bear patience as the messengers of firm determination bore patience and do not be impatient about them.' (46:35)

"He then has said, '. . . if they call you a liar, messengers before you were called liars also and they exercised patience against their calling them liars and they were harmed.' (6:35) The Prophet of Allah and the messengers before him suffered much harm and people called them liars about the truth. If the command of Allah (gives you pleasure because of your being with *Ahl al-Bayt*) you must also bear in mind that He created them at the beginning of creation, the origin of the creation from disbelief that was in the knowledge of Allah, to create them originally of those whom He has mentioned in His book in His words, '. . . We made from among them *'A'immah* (leaders) who call to the fire.' (28:41) You must think about this to understand it and must not remain ignorant of this fact. One who remains ignorant of this and similar issues that Allah has made obligatory in His book in the form of command and prohibition, he disregards the religion of Allah. Such poeple continue in sin and disobedience, which subject them to the anger of Allah Who throws them in the fire on their face.

"He (the Imam) said, 'O the blessed, sussessful group who has achieved salvation, Allah has completed for you what has come to you of the good. You must take notice that it is not in the knowledge of Allah and it is not of His command that any of His creatures follow His religion based on their desires, opinions and their analogizing. Allah has revealed the Quran and has placed in it the explanation for everything; He has assigned for Quran and for teaching the Quran a people. The people with knowledge of Quran, which Allah has given to them, cannot take it according to their desires, opinions or analogizing because Allah has made them needless of following such manners; He has given them its knowledge, has made them special people in this issue, placed it with them as an honor from Allah to honor them thereby. They are the people of *al-Dhikr* (al-Quran, knowledge) about whom Allah has commanded this nation to ask them and they are the ones who ask them (command them). It has already passed in the knowledge of Allah that it is necessary to acknowledge them and follow their path. He guided and granted them of the knowledge of Quran enough to guide to Allah by His permission and to all good paths. They are the ones from whom no one turns away in asking for guidance and of their knowledge with which Allah has honored them and has placed it with them, except those who in the knowledge of Allah have wickedness and misfortune as their share in the origin of the creation under the shadow.

"They are the ones who turn away from asking the people of *al-Dhikr* to whom Allah has given the knowledge of Quran, placed it with them and has commanded people to ask them. Such people take (the religion of Allah) based on their desires, opinions and analogizing until Satan enters in them. They have considered the people of belief, according to the knowledge of Quran before Allah, of the unbelievers and the people of misguidance, according to knowledge of Quran before Allah, of the believing ones. They have made the lawful matters of Allah, in many cases unlawful. What Allah has made unlawful, in many cases they have made them as lawful. For this reason, the origin of the fruit is their desire. The Messenger of Allah, *O Allah grant compensation to Muhammad and his family worthy of their services to Your cause*, commanded them before his death. They, however, said that after Allah, most Majestic, most Glorious, takes away His Messenger, *O Allah grant compensation to Muhammad and his family worthy of their services to Your cause*, we can follow (and practice issues of Shari'ah) on such basis upon which people's opinions have come together. They did so despite his command and covenant that he left with us and commanded us thereby; it was against Allah and His Messenger, *O Allah grant compensation to Muhammad and his family worthy of their services to Your cause.*

"There is no one more daring against Allah with clearer misguidance than one who takes such daring steps and thinks that he can do it. By Allah people owed to Allah to obey Him and follow His command in the lifetime of Muhammad, *O Allah grant compensation to Muhammad and his family worthy of their services to Your cause*, and after his death. Can these enemies of Allah who think that one who has become a Muslim with Muhammad, *O Allah grant compensation to Muhammad and his family worthy of their services to Your cause*, has the authority to take (issues of Shari'ah) on the basis of his word, opinion and analogizing? If one says yes, he has lied against Allah and has gone in misguidance far away. If one says, 'No, one cannot take (issues of Shari'ah) based on his word, opinion and analogizing' then he has acknowledged the real

Authority against his own soul. He is of those who believe that Allah must be obeyed, His command must be followed after He (Allah) took away His Messenger, *O Allah grant compensation to Muhammad and his family worthy of their services to Your cause*. Allah has said, and His words are true, 'Muhammad is only a messenger before whom other messengers lived. If he dies or is killed, will you then turn back on your heels to (ignorance)? Those who turn back on their heels can never harm Allah by anything and Allah grants reward to those who are thankful.' (3:144) They must know that it was obligatory to obey the commands of Allah and He was obeyed in the lifetime of Muhammad, *O Allah grant compensation to Muhammad and his family worthy of their services to Your cause*. At the time of Muhammad, no one of the people had the right to take (issues of Shari'ah) based on his desires, opinion and analogizing, against the command of Muhammad. Also no one after Muhammad, *O Allah grant compensation to Muhammad and his family worthy of their services to Your cause*, has the right to take (issues of Shari'ah) on the basis of his desire, opinion and analogizing.

"He (the Imam) said, 'You can ignore raising your hands in *Salat* (prayer) except once in the beginning of *Salat* (prayer) because people may defame you therefor. Allah is the Supporter and there is no means and power except the means and power of Allah.

"He (the Imam) said, 'You must pray to Allah a great many times, because Allah loves those among His believing servants who pray to Him and Allah has promised His believing servants to accept their prayers. Allah is the One Who on the Day of Judgment will turn their prayers into such deeds that will increase for them in the garden (paradise). So you must speak of Allah as much as you can in all hours of the day and night because Allah has commanded to speak of (and remember) Him and Allah speaks of those of the believing people who speak of Him. You must take notice that whoever of the believing servants speaks of (remembers) Him, He speaks of him with goodness. Therefore, you must show your hard work and striving in obedience to Allah. No one of the good things with Allah can be achieved without obedience to Him and keeping away from what He has made unlawful according to the apparent meaning of al-Quran as well as its hidden meaning.

"Allah, most Blessed, most High, has said in His book and His words are true: 'You must keep away from the apparent and hidden sins . . .' (6:120) You must take notice that whatever Allah has commanded to keep away from, He has made it unlawful. You must follow the footprints of the Messenger of Allah, *O Allah grant compensation to Muhammad and his family worthy of their services to Your cause*, and his *Sunnah* (tradition) and accept it. Do not follow your desires and opinions lest you become misguided; the ones who lose the most in the sight of Allah are the ones who follow their desires and opinions without guidance from Allah. You must do good to yourselves as much as you can. If you do good, it is for your own soul and if you do evil things, it is against your own soul. You must deal with people courteously and do not carry them on your necks (make them dominant) and in so doing you will be obeying your Lord as well.

"You must never blaspheme the enemies of Allah when they can hear you to make them to blaspheme Allah in animosity without knowledge. It is very proper for you to know the penalty for blaspheming Allah and how wicked it is. Whoever blasphemes the friends of Allah (people who possess divine authority) has committed a great violation regarding blaspheming Allah. No one is more unjust in the sight of Allah than the one who causes others to blaspheme Allah or friends of Allah (people who possess divine authority), and you must never ever do so. You must follow the commandments of Allah. There is no means and power without the means and power of Allah.

"He (the Imam) said, 'O group of people whose affairs Allah has protected for them, you must follow in the footprints of the Messenger of Allah, *O Allah grant compensation to Muhammad and his family worthy of their services to Your cause*. You must follow his *Sunnah* (tradition) and the footprints of the *'A'immah* of guidance from the family of the Messenger of Allah, *O Allah grant compensation to Muhammad and his family worthy of their services to Your cause*, after him (the Messenger of Allah) and their *Sunnah* (tradition). Whoever adopts this finds guidance and those who ignore it are lost and misguided. Allah has commanded and has made it obligatory to obey and acknowledge the *Wilayah* (divine authority and power) of *'A'immah* from the family of His Messenger.

"Our great grandfather, the Messenger of Allah, *O Allah grant compensation to Muhammad and his family worthy of their services to Your cause*, has said this: 'To continue one's deeds according to the laws and the *Sunnah* (tradition) even if it is small in quantity is more pleasing to Allah. It is more beneficial in consequences than wallowing in heresy and following one's base desires. Following the desires and heresy without guidance from Allah is misguidance and all misguidance is heresy and all heresy is in the fire.'

"Nothing of the good with Allah is achievable without obedience, patience and acceptance. Patience and acceptance are of obedience to Allah.

"You must take notice that a servant of the servants of Allah does not become a believing one until he accepts from Allah what He has done for him and with him in all that he likes or dislikes. Allah never does anything to someone, who is patient and accepting from Allah, other than what is worthy of Him and it is for his good of the matters that he likes or dislikes. You must protect your *Salat* (prayer), especially the middle *Salat* (prayer) and stand up for the sake of Allah supplicating as Allah has commanded the believing people, in His book to do, before you. You must be aware of the fact that you must like the destitute Muslim people; those who consider them lowly in their arrogance have slipped away from the religion of Allah Who makes them lowly and hated.

6

"Our great grandfather, the Messenger of Allah, *O Allah grant compensation to Muhammad and his family worthy of their services to Your cause*, has said, 'My Lord has commanded me to love the destitute Muslim people.' You must take notice that whoever considers any of the Muslims lowly, Allah throws hatred on him and lowliness. People hate him and Allah hates him more intensely. You must remain pious before Allah regarding your Muslim brothers who are destitute. They have a right on you which is to love them and Allah has commanded His Messenger, *O Allah grant compensation to Muhammad and his family worthy of their services to Your cause*, to love them, so those who do not love the ones about whom Allah has commanded to be loved have disobeyed Allah and His Messenger. One who disobeys Allah and His Messenger and dies in such condition has died as a lost transgressor.

"You must never claim greatness and glory because glory is the gown of Allah, most Majestic, most Glorious, and one who disputes Allah about His gown, Allah breaks him down and humiliates him on the Day of Judgment. You must never transgress against each other; it is not of the quality of the virtuous ones. One who commits transgression, Allah turns his transgression against his own self and Allah's support goes in favor of the one against whom transgression is committed and one who receives help from Allah defeats his opponent triumphantly by the help of Allah.

"You must never be jealous toward each other because jealousy is the origin and root of disbelief. You must never provide help against an oppressed Muslim; he will pray before Allah against you and his prayer is answered.

"Our great grandfather, the Messenger of Allah, *O Allah grant compensation to Muhammad and his family worthy of their services to Your cause*, would say, 'The prayer of an oppressed Muslim is accepted.' You must help each other because our great grandfather, the Messenger of Allah, *O Allah grant compensation to Muhammad and his family worthy of their services to Your cause*, would say, 'Providing assistance to the Muslim is better and of the greater reward than fasting for one month and performing *'I'tikaf* in *Masjid al-Haram* (the Sacred area).'

"You must not give a hard time to your Muslim brother for something that he may owe to you when he has difficulty to pay. Our great grandfather, the Messenger of Allah, *O Allah grant compensation to Muhammad and his family worthy of their services to Your cause*, has said this: 'A Muslim must not give another Muslim a hard time and one who gives time (respite) to one who has difficulty to pay his dues, Allah provides shadow (shelter and protection) for him from His own shadow on the day when there will be no shadow except His shadow.

"You must remain on your guard, O group of forgiven and preferred ones over the others, against withholding the rights of Allah with you for a day after a day, for an hour after an hour. One who quickly pays the right of Allah must take notice that Allah is more powerful to double quickly the good for him immediately or later on. One who delays payment of the right of Allah, which he owes, must take notice that Allah is more powerful to delay providing his sustenance. One whose sustenance Allah withholds cannot find it by himself. You must pay to Allah His rights out of what He has granted to you so that Allah will make the remaining more pleasant for you, so that He completes for you what He has promised to you in double and in multiples of which no one has the knowledge in terms of numbers and origins of its excellence except Allah, the Cherisher of the worlds.

"He (the Imam) said, 'Remain pious before Allah, O special group, and do not allow, if you can, yourselves to be an embarrassment for the Imam. One who causes embarrassment for the Imam is he who discredits people of good services of the followers of the Imam of the Muslims because of his excellence, who exercise patience in paying his rights and who acknowledge his sanctity. You must take notice that one who reaches such a stage (to discredit meritorious people), it is an embarrassment for the Imam. If he does it before the Imam, he (the Imam) is embarrassed not to condemn the discredited ones who are people of good deeds among his followers, submissive before him (the Imam) because of his excellence, patient in paying his rights and well aware of his sanctity. When he (the Imam) condemns them because of the embarrassment caused by the enemies of Allah the condemnation becomes a blessing for them from Allah and the condemnation from Allah, the angels and the messengers take them (the ones causing embarrassment) as its subject.

"You must take notice, O group (of my followers), that the *Sunnah* (tradition) from Allah has been set in the case of the people of good deeds before. He (the Imam) said, 'Those who like to meet Allah, as believing persons in the true sense, must love Allah, His Messenger and the believing people and must disown their enemies before Allah. They must accept what they have learned of their excellence because their excellence is not fully comprehensible even by the angels with high position before Allah or the messengers of great determination or those of lower positions. Have you not heard of the excellence of the followers of the Imam of guidance, who are of the believing people , '. . . they are with those to whom Allah has granted bounties, such as Prophets, the truthful ones, the martyrs and people of good deeds and they are very good companions.' (4:69)

"This is one aspect of the excellence of the followers of *'A'immah*; then how can one fully explain the excellence of the *'A'immah* themselves? If one likes that Allah complete for him his belief so that he can be a believing person in the real sense then he must remain steadfast with the condition, which Allah has placed on the believing people. The condition that He has set is to accept and acknowledge His guardianship, the guardianship of His Messenger and the guardianship of *'A'immah* of the believing people, performing *Salat* (prayer), payment of *Zakat*, providing good loans to Allah and in keeping away from indecent activities, those apparent as well as those hidden. Not a single matter of the detail of what Allah has made lawful and unlawful remains untold without being included in one sentence of his words. It says, 'If one follows a religion between himself and Allah sincerely just for Allah and does not allow his soul to ignore any one item, he in the sight of Allah is of members of the triumphant party of Allah. He is of the believing people in the real sense.'

"You must never insist on doing what Allah has prohibited and has made unlawful in the apparent meaning of al-Quran or in its hidden meaning. Allah, most Blessed, most High, has said, '. . . and they do not persist knowingly on what they have done.'" (3:135) [To this point is the narration of al-Qasim ibn al-Rabi'.] "It means that the believing people before you when forgetting something of the condition Allah had set on them in His book would come to know eventually that they have disobeyed Allah. They would abandon that thing, ask forgiveness from Allah and would not repeat, as it is indicated in the words of Allah '. . . they do not knowingly persist on what they have done.' (3:135)

"You must take notice that there are commandments and prohibitions so that obedience to the commands and keeping away from what is prohibited can come into being. Those who follow His commands have obeyed Him and find all that is good with Him and those who do not keep away from what Allah has prohibited, they have disobeyed Him and if they die with disobedience, Allah will throw them on their face in the fire.

"You must take notice that there is no other thing between Allah and anyone of His creatures, angels of high position, a Prophet commissioned or less important creature of His creatures all of them except obedience to Him. Therefore, you must strive hard in obedience to Allah, if you like to be of the believing people in the real sense. There is no power except the power of Allah.

"He (the Imam) said, 'You must remain obedient to your Lord as much as you can; Allah is your Lord, the Cherisher. You must take notice that Islam is submission and submission is Islam. One who submits has accepted Islam and one who does not submit has no Islam. One who likes to do a favor to his soul, he must obey Allah because one who obeys Allah has done a favor to his own soul. You must remain on your guard against disobedience to Allah. If one transgresses and disobeys Allah, one has done something extremely bad to his soul and there is no third choice between good and bad. For the people of good deeds with their Lord there is the garden (paradise) and for the people of bad deeds with their Lord there is the fire. You must act in obedience to Allah and keep away from disobeying Him. You must take notice that no one of the creatures of Allah can make one independent of Allah, regardless if he is an angel of high position, or a Prophet messenger or a less important creature. If one likes that the intercession of those who intercede benefit him before Allah, he must plead before Allah to be happy with him. You must take notice that no one of the creatures of Allah can make Him to be pleased with him without being obedient to Him, to His Messenger and to those who possess *Wilayah* (divine authority and power) from the family of Muhammad. *O Allah grant compensation to Muhammad and his family worthy of their services to Your cause.* Disobedience to them is disobedience to Allah. One must not deny any of their merits and excellence, small or great.

"You must take notice, those who deny are those who call a fact a lie and such people are hypocrites about whom Allah, most Majestic, most Glorious, has said and His words are indeed true, 'The hypocrites will be placed in the lowest level of the fire and you can never find for them any helper.' (4:145) No one among you who has made obedience to Allah and humility before Him binding upon himself should fear those whom Allah has taken away from the quality of truthfulness. One must not fear those whom He has not made of the people of truth; those whom Allah has not made of the people with the quality of truth are of the *Shayatin* (Satans) in the form of man and Jinn. Satans in the form of man plot, trick, deceive and seduce each other in their effort, if they can, to divert the people of Truth from the fact with which Allah has honored them. These Satans try to divert them from thinking about the religion of Allah. Allah has excluded the Satans of mankind and of Jinn from being of His followers, because of His will not to make the enemies of Allah equal to the people of Truth, in matters of doubts, denials and refutation so they all become equal. Allah, most High, has said in His book, 'They wish you to become unbelievers as they themselves are...' (4:89) Allah, then, has prohibited the people of truth to take the enemies of Allah as guardians and helpers. The plots of Satans of man and their plots in your affairs must not frighten you or turn you away from the help of the Truth with which Allah has favored you. You must dispel evil with good from among yourselves and from them for the sake of your Lord and in obedience to Him. However, there is nothing good in them. It is not lawful for you to make public to them anything of the principles of religion of Allah because if they hear from you anything they become your enemy in that matter, take it against you, seek to destroy you, show you what you detest. They will not behave toward you with justice in the dominion of the sinful rulers. You must remain aware of your position among yourselves and the people of falsehood. It is not proper for the people of Truth to step in the place of the people of falsehood. The reason for this is found in the words of Allah in His book when He says, 'Do We consider the righteously striving believers equal to the evil-doers in the land? Are the pious ones equal to those who openly commit sin? (38:28) You must remain dignified and keep away from the people of falsehood. You must not make Allah, most Blessed, most High, Whose example is most High; your Imam and your religion, which you follow, to be used as a means of plotting by the people of falsehood; you will make Allah angry with you and you will become destroyed. You must remain on your guard, O people of good deeds, do not abandon the commandments of Allah and the commandments of the one which Allah has made obligatory on you to follow, otherwise, Allah changes His blessing with you. Love for the sake of Allah those who possess your quality and hate for the sake of Allah those who oppose you. You must make your love and advice available [to those who have your quality] and do not bestow it upon those who turn away from belief, deal with you in animosity and transgression and commit theft.

"Such is our discipline with which Allah has disciplined us and you must adopt it, understand, comprehend it and do not throw it away behind your backs. You must accept whatever agrees with your guidance and throw away whatever agrees with your desires. You must remain on guard against arrogance toward Allah and you must take notice that a servant is not afflicted with arrogance toward Allah except that he is arrogant toward the religion of Allah. You must remain upright for the sake of Allah and do not turn back to misguidance to come back as losers, may Allah grant us protection as well as you against arrogance toward Allah and there is no power for us and for you except the power of Allah."

"He (the Imam) said, 'If Allah has created a servant originally, in the original creation, as a believing person, he does not die until Allah makes him to detest evil and keeps him away from it. One whom Allah has made to detest evil and has kept him away from it, Allah grants him a cure for his sickness of arrogance and remaining sick with it, thus, his nature remains soft and flexible, his moral behavior pleasant, his face open and bright. The dignity of Islam flows in him as well as its serenity, humbleness and restraint from what Allah has made unlawful. He keeps away from causing His anger and Allah places in his heart the ability to love people and be courteous with them, not to keep away from them or dispute with them. He is not a disputing one neither is he of the disputing people in anything.

"If a servant whom Allah has created, in the origin of the creation - original creation - was as an unbeliever he will not die until he begins to love evil matters and keep close to it. When evil is made beloved to him and is kept close to it he suffers from the sickness of arrogance and pride, thus, he becomes hard hearted, his moral behaviors deteriorate, his face thickens, his obscenity becomes apparent and his bashfulness diminishes. Allah opens up his privacy and he commits unlawful deeds all the time. He disobeys Allah, hates to obey Him and those who obey Allah, thus there is a great distance between the condition of a believing person and an unbeliever.

"You must ask Allah for good health and try to find it with Him. There is no means and power except with Allah. You must train the soul to learn exercising patience by means of trial (hardships) in this world. Continued trial and intense obedience to Allah, His guardianship and the guardianship of those whose *Wilayah* (divine authority and power) He has commanded to acknowledge and accept is of the best consequences before Allah in the hereafter compared to the worldly kingdom. It is better than the worldly kingdom even if the bounties of the worldly kingdom continue with its blossoming affluent lifestyle in disobedience to Allah and under the guardianship of those whose guardianship Allah has prohibited to accept as well as obedience to them. Allah has commanded to acknowledge and accept the guardianship and *Wilayah* (divine

11

authority and power) of those whom He has spoken of in His book in His words. '. . . We have made them *'A'immah* (leaders) by our command.' (21:73) They are the ones whose *Wilayah* (divine authority and power) Allah has made obligatory to acknowledge and accept. The guardianship and obedience that Allah has prohibited to follow and accept is the guardianship and obedience to the *'A'immah* (leaders) of misguidance. Allah has allowed to this kind of leaders to establish their dominion in this world against His friends (people who possess divine authority), *'A'immah* from the family of Muhammad. They work in their domain in disobedience to Allah and in disobedience to His Messenger, *O Allah grant compensation to Muhammad and his family worthy of their services to Your cause*; so that the word of suffering comes true upon them and so that you can be with the Prophet of Allah, Muhammad, *O Allah grant compensation to Muhammad and his family worthy of their services to Your cause*, and the messengers before him.

"You must think about what Allah has stated for you in His book of the trials with which He tested His Prophets and the believing people of their followers. You must appeal before Allah to grant you patience against hardships in peacetime and in time of war, in difficulties and in ease like that which He had granted to them (believing people of the past).

"You must remain on guard against disputations with the people of falsehood. You must follow the guidance of the virtuous people, their dignified manners, serenity, forbearance, humbleness, their restraint and their keeping away from that which Allah has made unlawful. You must follow their truthfulness, loyalty, hard work for the sake of Allah, in working according to His commandments; if you did not do so, you, in the sight of your Lord, will not be placed in the ranks of the virtuous people who lived before you.

"You must take notice that when Allah wants good for a servant He opens up his chest for Islam and when He grants him this He then makes his tongue to speak with truth, and binds his heart upon the same, thus he acts accordingly. When Allah brings it all together, for him his Islam becomes complete and he will truly be of the Muslims, if he dies in that condition. If Allah does not want good for a servant, He leaves him to his own self and his chest becomes narrow and constricted. If truth comes through his tongue, his heart does not believe in it and when his heart does not believe in it, Allah does not give him the chance to act according to such truth. When this comes upon him, he, until the time of his death, remains in that condition. He, then, in the sight of Allah is one of the hypocrites. The truth has passed through his tongue but Allah did not grant him the chance to believe in it and he did not act accordingly. It then will become an argument against him on the Day of Judgment. You must remain pious before Allah and plead before Him to open your chest for Islam and make your tongues speak with truth until the time of your death to remain in that condition and make your return like the return of the virtuous people who lived before you. There is no power except the power of Allah, and all praise belongs to Allah, Lord of the worlds.

"If one likes to know whether Allah loves him, he must act according to the commandments of Allah and follow us. Has he not heard the words of Allah, most Majestic, most Glorious, to His Prophet, *O Allah grant compensation to Muhammad and his family worthy of their services to Your cause*, 'Say, if you love Allah then follow me. Allah will love you and forgive your sins.' (3:31) By Allah, no one obeys Allah ever except that He includes in his obeying Him to follow us as well. It is a fact, by Allah, whoever of the servants ever disobeys us, it is because he hates us. No, by Allah, no one ever hates us but that he disobeys Allah and one who dies disobeying Allah, Allah brings him low and throws him on his face in the fire; all praise belongs to Allah, Lord of the worlds.'"

The *Sahifa* of Ali ibn al-Husayn, *'Alayhi al-Salam*, and his words on restraint from unlawful matters

H 14450, h 2

Muhammad ibn Yahya has narrated from Ahmad ibn Muhammad ibn 'Isa and Ali ibn Ibrahim has narrated from his father all from al-Hassan ibn Mahbub from Malik ibn 'Atiyyah from abu Hamzah who has narrated the following:

"I never heard of anyone as pious as Ali ibn al-Husayn, *'Alayhi al-Salam*, except what I had heard about Ali ibn abu Talib, *'Alayhi al-Salam*. Abu Hamzah has said, 'When Imam Ali ibn al-Husayn, *'Alayhi al-Salam*, would speak about restraint from unlawful matters and preach, people present would weep.' Abu Hamzah has said, 'I read a document on restraint from unlawful matters in the words of Ali ibn al-Husayn, *'Alayhi al-Salam*, and copied it down entirely, then I went to Ali ibn al-Husayn, *'Alayhi al-Salam*, presented it before him (the Imam). He recognized it and made certain corrections in it:

"In the name of Allah, the Beneficent, the Merciful

"I pray to Allah to grant us sufficient support against the plots of the unjust ones, the transgression of the jealous ones and the threats of tyrant ones. O believing people, do not allow the transgressors and their followers who are attracted to the worldly matters and inclined to it, who are deceived by the same who approach it and its abandoned ruins, its left-over straws that will be no more tomorrow, to deceive you. You must remain on guard against what Allah has commanded you to do and exercise restraint against what Allah has prohibited you to do. Do not rely on the worldly things like those who have taken it as their permanent dwelling and residence. By Allah what is in it is proof of warning against its changing days and conditions, its hardships, its childish playfulness and that it raises the failing and fails the honorable ones, and that it sends many people to the fire of tomorrow. In it, there is a lesson, an experience, an admonishing and a warning. The matters that you face every day and night from the dark mischievous ones, the heretical happenings and unjust traditions, the noisiness of the time, threats of the rulers, the temptations of Satan, all slow down the heart. They slow it down in learning awareness, weaken it in finding guidance and recognizing the people of the Truth except a very few people whom Allah has protected. No one is able to recognize its changing days, conditions and the consequences of harmfulness of its mischievous matters except those whom Allah protects, makes to walk on the path of right guidance, and on the road of fairness. Those who restrain from unlawful matters, think frequently, get advice from patience to notice the warning, restrain from quickly vanishing delights of the worldly matters. They keep away from its pleasures, remain interested in the eternal bounties of the hereafter, and strive to achieve them with the required efforts. They watch, keep vigil, for the approach of death and the hateful life with the unjust ones. He then looks at the worldly matters with clear eyes and sharp sightedness. He looks at the mischievous happenings, misguidance, heresies and the injustice of the kings of the world with meaningful insight. By my life, you have left behind the transitory matters of the past days in the form of intense mischief and entanglement, which show you how to keep aside from the transgressing heretics and from their transgression and destruction of the land with no right to do so. You must seek help and support from Allah, return to His obedience and obedience to those who deserve obedience of those who are followed and obeyed.

"You must remain on guard before you regret and lament on arriving before Allah and when standing before Him. By Allah no one for disobedience has gone anywhere other than in the suffering which Allah has prepared. Whoever of the people has given preference to this world over the next world, their return has been bad and their journey bad. Knowledge about Allah and good deeds are two harmonious matters. One who has come to know Allah, fears Him and his fear encourages him to work in obedience to Allah. People of knowledge and their followers who have come to know Allah and who act in obedience to Him, those who are interested in what is with Him, are the ones about whom Allah has said, 'Only Allah's knowledgeable servants fear Him. Allah is Majestic and All-pardoning.' (35:28) You cannot seek anything of this world through disobedience to Allah. You must work in this world in obedience to Allah, make the best use of its opportunities and work hard in things that will save you tomorrow from the suffering that Allah has prepared. This (safety from suffering tomorrow) is of the least harmful consequence and the minimum form of excuse and of greater hope for deliverance. You must give the first priority, above all affairs, to the obedience of command of Allah and the commandments of those obedience to whom Allah has made obligatory. Do not give priority to matters that come upon you from the command of the tyrants about the worldly blossoms over and above being in the presence of Allah, obedience to Him and obedience to those who have control over your affairs with *Wilayah* (divine authority and power). You must take notice that you are servants of Allah and we are with you. A Ruling Master will rule, over us all, tomorrow. He will stop you and will question you so you must prepare the answer before you are stopped and questioned and presented before the Cherisher of the worlds. On that day, no one can speak without His permission.

"You must take notice, on that day Allah will not make a liar truthful, will not reject the excuse of the deserving and will not excuse those who have no excuse. He has the right argument against His creatures through His Messengers, and the

Executors of the wills after the Messengers. You must remain pious before Allah, O servants of Allah, move forward to reform your own selves, obey Allah and those whom you have accepted as your guardian with divine authority. Perhaps the regretful may regret for their excessive behavior toward Allah and destroying His rights, ask forgiveness from Allah, return to Him with repentance; He accepts the return and repentance of those who repent, forgives the sins and knows what you do. You must never join the disobedient one; support the unjust and associate with the sinners. You must remain on guard against their mischief and keep away from their location. You must take notice that those who oppose friends of Allah (people who possess divine authority) or follow a religion other than the religion of Allah, dictate their commands without the command of friends of Allah (people who possess divine authority) will be in the blazing fire. It is a blazing fire, which consumes bodies from which the spirit has departed and whose misfortune has overpowered them. They are dead because they do not feel the heat of the fire. Had they been living they would feel the pain caused by the heat of the fire. You must learn a lesson, O people of understanding, and praise Allah for granting you guidance. You must take notice that you cannot move out of the reach of the power of Allah. Allah as well as His Messenger will see your deeds. You will then be brought before Him, so benefit from good advice and discipline yourselves with the discipline of the virtuous people.'"

Advice of 'Amir al-Mu'minin to his companions

H 14451, h 3

Ahmad ibn Muhammad has narrated from Ahmad al-Kufiy who is al-'Asemiy from 'Abd al-Wahid ibn al-Sawwaf from Muhammad ibn 'Isma'il al-Hamadaniy who has narrated the following:

"Abu al-Hassan, Musa, *'Alayhi al-Salam*, has said that 'Amir al-Mu'minin, Ali, *'Alayhi al-Salam*, would give good advice to his companions and say, 'I ask you to remain pious before Allah, because it is the bliss for a hopeful seeker of Truth and the shackle for a runaway refugee. You must realize piety with an inner realization and speak of Allah purely and sincerely so you can live the best life and follow with it the road of salvation. Look at the world with the look of those who maintain restraint against committing sins who leave it for good. This world dislodges the established status and causes pain to the affluent and protected. (You must be like) one who does not expect from it the return of those who have gone and does not know what it will bring, for which one may patiently wait. Misfortune and comfort in it are connected and living in it is destruction, thus happiness in it is blurred with sadness and living in it moves to weakness and fragility. It is like a garden, in which the pasture is dense and has attracted onlookers. Its drink is sweet, its soil is fine, and roots pressing into the soil are excited inside. Its branches drip moisture until the herbs reach their due time and its fingers level, winds get excited under the leaves and frightens what is in good order and passes the day as Allah has said, '(Muhammad) , say to them, "The worldly life resembles the (seasonal) plants of earth that blossom by the help of the water which Allah sends from the sky. After a short time all of them fade away and the winds scatter them (and turn them into dust). Allah has power over all things.' (18:46) Think about the world and about the many things that attract you and the scarcity of that which benefit you.'"

The sermon of 'Amir al-Mu'minin, Ali, *'Alayhi al-Salam,* called the Sermon of Means and Connections

H 14452, h 4

Muhammad ibn Ali ibn Mu'ammar has narrated from Muhammad ibn Ali ibn 'Ukayah al-Tamimiy from al-Husayn ibn al-Nadr al-Fihriy from abu 'Amr al-Awza'iy from 'Amr ibn Shimr from Jabir ibn Yazid who has narrated the following:

"I once went to visit abu Ja'far, *'Alayhi al-Salam,* and I said, 'O child of the Messenger of Allah, *O Allah grant compensation to Muhammad and his family worthy of their services to Your cause,* the differences among the Shi'ah in their religion causes for me a great pain.' He (the Imam) then said, 'O Jabir do you want that I inform you about their differences from where they emerge and in which aspect they separate?' I said, 'Yes, O child of the Messenger of Allah, *O Allah grant compensation to Muhammad and his family worthy of their services to Your cause,* I like to know.' He (the Imam) said, 'You, then, must not differ if they did. One who denies people who possess divine authority is like those who denied the Messenger of Allah, *O Allah grant compensation to Muhammad and his family worthy of their services to Your cause,* in his time. O Jabir listen attentively.' I then said, 'As you like, I will listen attentively.' He (the Imam) said, 'Listen, pay attention and preach wherever your stumper will take you. Amir al-Mu'minin, Ali, *'Alayhi al-Salam,* once addressed people in al-Madinah, seven days after the death of the Messenger of Allah, *O Allah grant compensation to Muhammad and his family worthy of their services to Your cause,* and it was after his collecting and completely compiling al-Quran. He ('Amir al-Mu'minin, Ali) said, "All praise belongs to Allah who has prevented imaginations to reach Him except His existence. He has veiled reason from imagining His entity because of the impossibility of the existence of similarity of any shape with Him. In fact, He is the one in whose entity there is no difference and does not become in parts by numerical division due to His perfection. He is separate from things not in the sense of difference in places. He exists and is found in places but not in the manner of being mixed. He knows places but not by certain means and tools. Knowledge about places is not without the tools. Other's knowledge does not exist between His knowledge and the object of His knowledge (He has not learned from others). He possesses the knowledge of the object of His knowledge.

"If it is said that He existed, it is in the sense of interpreting the existence in eternal sense and if it is said that He will always exist it is in the sense of interpreting the negation of non-existence. Allah is free of all defects, most High and above the words of those who worship things other than Him and have taken a deity other than Him. Allah is most High and Great.

"We praise Him with a praise that He accepts from His creatures and has made it necessary for Him to accept. I testify that no one deserves worship except

Allah alone who has no partners and I testify that Muhammad is His servant and His Messenger. The two testimonies take the words high and increase (good) deeds. The balance from which they (testimonies) are taken away remains light and the balance on which they are placed remains heavy. With them is success to achieve the garden (paradise) and safety from the fire and securely passing the bridge. With the testament of belief, you can enter in the garden (paradise); with *Salat* (prayer), you can receive blessings. You must ask a great degree of compensation from Allah for your Holy Prophet, 'Allah and His angels send *Salat* on the Holy Prophet. O believing people, ask Allah to grant compensation to Muhammad worthy of his services to His cause, with peace and a great deal of peace.' O Allah grant compensation to Muhammad and his family worthy of their services to Your cause and peace.

"O people, no other nobility is higher than Islam, and no other honor is dearer than piety, no other protective means is a better protection than restraint from committing sins. No other intercessor is more useful than repentance, no garment is more beautiful than good health, no protection is more preventive than well-being, no wealth is more effectively dispelling of poverty than contentment and no treasure is richer than being satisfied. One who lives with basic necessities has provided comfort and brought home the ease of peacefulness. Craving is the key for fatigue, hoarding leads to a snare and ambush, jealousy is a disease for one's religion, greed leads to indulging in sins and it is the cause of deprivation. Transgression drives to destruction and yearning attracts the worst forms of disgrace. Certain forms of greed lead to failure, to false longing, a hope that leads to dispossession and a trade that turns into losses. O yes, one who is entangled in an affair without looking into its consequences is exposed to disastrous dishonor. The worst necklace is the necklace of sin for a believing person.

"O people, you must take notice that no other treasure is more beneficial than knowledge, no other prestige is higher than forbearance, and no other social outstanding position is more effective than proper moral discipline. No other snare is meaner than anger, no other beauty is more decorative than reason, no other disgraceful matter is worse than lying, no other protector is more safe and sound than silence and no other absentee is closer than death.

"O people, whoever looks into the deficiencies of his own soul does not bother the others, one who agrees with the sustenance of Allah does not regret for what is in the hands of the others. One who unsheathes the sword of transgression is himself killed therewith, one who digs a well for his brother himself falls in it and one who violates other's privacies, the privacies of his own house will be exposed. One who forgets his own slips sees other's slips as very great. One who is attracted to his own point of view is lost, one who thinks his reason is sufficient, slips, one who is arrogant toward people is humiliated, one who behaves dimwittedly among people is reviled, one who associates with scoundrels, becomes worthless and one who carries what one cannot afford fails.

"O people, no belonging is more beneficial than reason, no poverty is more intense than ignorance, and no adviser is a better preacher than advising about one's well being. No reasoning is better than contemplation, no worship is like thinking, no supporter is stronger than consultation, no alienation is more severe than conceit, no restraint from sin is better than keeping away from unlawful matters, and no forbearing is like patience and remaining silent.

"O people, there are ten qualities in a man which his tongue makes public. It is a witness of the inside. It is a ruler for settling the speech, and a speaker to provide response. It is an intercession that provides one's need, and an introducer that identifies things. It is a commander so it commands to do good. It is a preacher so it prohibits from indecent matters and it provides solace in sadness. It is a speaker so it clears malice. It is an articulator so it gives pleasure to the ears.

"O people, there is nothing good in remaining silent and not to judge and there is nothing good in the words spoken out of ignorance. O people, you must take notice that one who cannot control his tongue regrets. One who does not want to know remains ignorant. One who does not pretend to be forbearing cannot become forbearing. One who does not prevent does not understand, one who does not understand is insulted, and one who is insulted is not respected. One who is not respected is censured. One who earns an asset without the right to earn spends without a reward and one who does not desist when he is praiseworthy will desist from committing evil when he is blamed. One who does not give when he is sitting is denied when he asks when standing. One who seeks glory without the right to do so is humiliated, one who overpowers by injustice is overpowered, one who is hostile to the truth becomes weak, one who thinks for understanding becomes dignified, one who is arrogant is disgraced and one who does not do good is not praised.

"O people, death is better before the coming of lowliness, endurance before laziness, accounting before penalty and the grave is better than poverty, casting down one's eyes is better than looking a great deal, in an eon, one day is for you and one day against you. When it is for you do not be excited and when it is against you bear it with patience; in both ways you are tested – in another copy it is said, 'both things will be examined'.

"O people, you must take notice that the most amazing thing in man is his heart; in his heart there are matters of wisdom and their opposite ones. When he has the chance to live with ease of hope, greed humiliates him, when greediness stirs him up, desires destroy him, when despair overpowers him regret kills him. When he is angry his condition becomes tense, when he is fortunate and happy, he forgets to conserve. When fear seizes him, caution preoccupies him, when he is in peace glory makes him lazy [glory takes him over], when he finds new bounties glory dominates him. If he earns an asset, richness makes him to transgress, when poverty bites him misfortune preoccupies him [weeping makes him to strive], when he is afflicted with hardship impatience disgraces him, when hunger presses him hard weakness grounds him down. If he is excessive in eating, indigestion makes him upset, thus, every shortcoming is harmful to him and every excessive behavior destroys him.

"O people, you must take notice that one who reduces (generosity) becomes humiliated and one who is generous becomes the master, one who increases takes the lead and one whose forbearance increases becomes noble. One who denies the existence of Allah becomes a heretic. One who does something many times becomes known thereby. One who jokes very often is taken lightly; one who laughs very much, his solemnity goes away. One's social position is ruined because of the lack of his moral discipline. The best deed is protecting one's honor by means of wealth. One who sits with badmouthing ignorant ones, is not reasonable, one who sits with an ignorant one should become ready for a great deal of verbal exchanges. No rich person escapes death because of his wealth or a poor one because of his poverty.

"O people, you must take notice that if death could have been purchased, a nice and honorable one would buy it as well as a wicked and greedy person.

"O people, you must take notice that there are several witnesses in favor of the heart that can pull the soul back from the steps of excessive behavior. There is the insight for understanding the good advice, which calls the soul to remain cautious against danger. There are also the memories about the desires, thus reason gives warning, admonishing and prohibition. Experience is a renewed form of knowledge and learning lessons leads to right guidance. It is a good form of discipline for your soul to avoid what you do not like to happen to people other than you. You owe to your believing brother; likewise, he owes to you. One who considers his own opinion sufficient has endangered himself. Thinking and planning are needed before action because it saves from regretting. One who welcomes all kinds of opinions learns where mistakes have taken place. One who keeps away from useless matters, his opinion balances the reasons. One who keeps his carnal desires within lawful limits, his respect is saved. One who holds back his tongue, his people trust him and he finds his wishes fulfilled. In changing conditions, the substance of men comes to light. Passing of days explains for you the hidden secrets. One spark of lightening does not provide enough benefit for one who travels in the dark. One who becomes known for wisdom, eyes look to him with respect and veneration. The most noble of riches is abandoning longings. Patience is a shield against poverty. Greed is a sign of poverty. Stinginess is the gown of destitution. Loving is like a benevolent relative. Being a poor relative who maintains good relation is better than a wealthy one who cuts off good relations. Religious preaching is a protective stronghold for one who listens to it attentively. One who leaves his looks free, his regrets increase. Time has made it obligatory on those who find their wishes coming true to thank Him. Very little is fairness of the tongue in publicizing good or bad issues. Constriction of one's moral behavior tires down his family. One who achieves seeks domination. Very few of the wishes come true. Humbleness clothes one with reverence. Vastness of moral discipline is the treasure of sustenance. There are many who remain engaged in their sins until the end of their lives. One who chooses bashfulness for his dress his defects remain hidden from people. You must apply moderation to the words (you speak); one who seeks moderation incurs less expenses. In opposing, the soul is the right guidance for you. One who recognizes the days, he lives well prepared. With every sip there is (the possibility for) choking and with every morsel there is heartache. Bounties are not achievable without the vanishing of other bounties. For every living, there is sustenance, for every grain there is a consumer and your consumer is death.

"O people you must take notice that whoever walks on earth will end up in its belly. The day and night quarrel over [compete] destroying the establishments of lifespan.

"O people you must take notice that disregard of bounty is wickedness. Association with the ignorant is bad luck. It is noble to speak softly, make worshipping expressions audible and proliferating the greeting of peace. You must never become treacherous because it is a wicked moral behavior. Not every seeker succeeds in his quest and not every absent person comes back. Do not form interest in one who abstains from you. Many far away can be much closer than close. Ask about a travel mate before the journey and of the neighbor before buying a house. One who travels faster finds the place for a siesta. Keep the secrecy of the privacy of your brother, as you know them to be of the privacies for you. Forgive the slips of your friend for the day your enemy may dominate you. One who becomes angry with one whom he cannot harm, his sadness prolongs and it tortures his soul. One who is afraid of his Lord, he withholds his injustice. [One who is afraid of his Lord has sufficiently prevented his suffering]. One who does not deviate in his speech shows his pride. One who cannot distinguish between good and bad is like the animals. It is of destruction to lose the supplies. How small is the hardship in this life compared to the great poverty tomorrow (on the Day of Judgment); they by no means are comparable. You have ignored this fact only because of your disobedience and sins. Comfort is very close to fatigue and misery to bounties. An evil is not an evil where after there is the garden (paradise) and a good is not good where after is the fire. Every bounty less than the garden (paradise) is of very little value and every hardship less than the fire is good health. When the conscience is cleared, great sins appear. Purifying the deed is harder than performing the deed, making an intention sincere from invalidity is more difficult for the doer of deeds than prolonged struggle (jihad). It is a matter far away, however, had it not been because of piety, I would have been the most cunning one among the Arabs.

"O people you must take notice that Allah, most High, has promised to His Prophet Muhammad, *O Allah grant compensation to Muhammad and his family worthy of their services to Your cause,* the means and has promised him the Truth and Allah does not disregard His promise. It is certain that the means on the steps of the garden (paradise), the peak of the mane of nearness, the end and purpose of security (peace) has one thousand ladders and stairs. From one stair to the other, there is a distance of the running of a fine horse for one hundred years. It is between the stairs of pearls to the stairs of gems. It is between the stairs of *zabarjad* (chrysolite) to the stairs of pearls, to the stairs of ruby, to the stairs of *zamarrud* (emerald), to the stairs of corals, to the stairs of camphor, to the stairs of ambergris, to the stairs of aloe to the stairs of gold to the stairs of clouds, to the stairs of the air, to the stairs of light, (Stairs are references to the level of the positions of the people of the garden (paradise)) which has gone beyond all of the garden (paradise). The Messenger of Allah, *O Allah grant compensation to Muhammad and his family worthy of their services to Your cause*, on that day will be sitting on it wearing two fine garments. One of the garments will be of the kindness of Allah and one from the light of Allah with the crown of prophet-hood and the garland of messenger-ship, by the light of which the whole station will be filled with light. I on that day will be at a high position, lower than his position, wearing two fine garments of red light and a garment of camphor. The Messengers and Prophets will be standing on the stairs with the flags of the times and authorities of eons and duration (Executor of the will of the Prophets and Messengers) will be on our right, with glory of the garment of light and honor. Every angel of high position and messenger Prophet will be astonished and amazed because of our brightness and glory.

"On the right side of *al-Wasilah* (means) on the right side of the Messenger of Allah, *O Allah grant compensation to Muhammad and his family worthy of their services to Your cause*, there will be a cloud as far as the eye can see. An announcement whereof will be made. "O people on the station, goodness is with those who loved the executor of the will, believed in the Holy Prophet, of *'Ummiy al-Arabiy* and those who rejected him, their destination is the fire." On the left of *al-Wasilah* and on the left side of the Messenger of Allah, *O Allah grant compensation to Muhammad and his family worthy of their services to Your cause*, there will be a shadow. From this shadow, an announcement will be made. "O people of the station, goodness is with those who loved the executor of the will and believed in the Holy Prophet, *al-'Ummiy* to whom the high kingdom belongs. Success, happiness and the garden (paradise) are not possible for anyone other than those who comes before his Creator with sincerity to the two of them and following the stars (*'A'immah*) after the two of them. People under the guardianship of Allah, you must remain certain that your faces will be white, your seats prestigious, your return honorable and successful, sitting on this day on seats facing each other. O people of deviation and blocking the path, you must remain certain that your faces will be black and there will be anger toward you as recompense for what you had done. Every Messenger and Prophet of the past had informed his people about the Messenger coming after him and of the good news about the Messenger of Allah, *O Allah grant compensation to Muhammad and his family worthy of their services to Your cause*. Every Prophet made a will to his nation, to follow him, with a complete description of him so that they could recognize him by means of his qualities to follow him in matters of his *Shari'ah* (laws), so that they will not be misled about him after their messenger and that people face their destruction and misguidance only after the presentation to them of good reason and warning about the proof of the designation of the people who possess divine authority.

The nations lived with hopes about the Messengers and the coming of the Prophets. If they found themselves in the absence of the Prophet in their great suffering and hardships, they had the chance to hope for relief. No other hardship was as great as the hardship and suffering of the Messenger of Allah, *O Allah grant compensation to Muhammad and his family worthy of their services to Your cause.* Allah completed the system of warning and presentation of proofs with him (the Messenger of Allah) and stopped arguing about and providing proof of the status of His friends who possess divine authority among His creatures. He made him the door to Himself between Himself and His servants with a domain without which no other thing is acceptable. Getting closeness to Him without obeying him (the Messenger of Allah) does not exist. He has said it clearly in His book, "One who obeys the Messenger has certainly obeyed Allah. You have not been sent to watch over those who turn away from you." (4:80) He made obedience to Himself alongside of obedience to him, disobedience to Himself alongside disobedience to him and it is proof of giving him great authority and a witness over those who follow or disobey him which He has stated in many places of His great book. He, most Blessed, most High, in encouraging to follow him and exhortation to confirm the truthfulness of his mission and accepting his call has said, "Say to them that if you love Allah then follow me, Allah will love you and will forgive your sins." (3:31) Following him (the Messenger of Allah) brings the love of Allah and His pleasure is forgiving sins. Complete success is becoming of the garden (paradise) obligatory and allotted to one. Turning away from him (the Messenger of Allah) and disregarding him is animosity toward Allah, facing His anger, His dislike and being far from Him is dwelling in the fire as it is stated in His words, "Whoever of the parties reject him, the fire will be his dwelling place." (11:17) Rejecting him is equal to disbelieving and disobeying him.

"Allah, most High, has put to test His servants by means of me, killed His opposition through my hand, annihilated by my sword those who rejected Him and made me to be a means of seeking closeness to Allah for the believing people, the ground of death for the tyrants and His sword on the criminal. He supported through me His Messenger, honored me with his support, privileged me with his knowledge, bestowed his laws upon me, granted me priority as executor of his will and chose me to succeed him among his followers. He (the Messenger of Allah), *O Allah grant compensation to Muhammad and his family worthy of their services to Your cause,* said it in the crowd of al-Muhajir and al-Ansar (people of al-Madinah) among the throngs in gathering places, "O people, Ali's relationship with me is like the relationship of Harun to Musa except that there will be no Prophet after me." The believing people understood it well that the speech of the Messenger was from Allah because they knew that I was not his brother from his father and mother as was the case with Harun, brother of Musa, who was from his father and mother and I was not a Prophet because the number of Prophets was already complete. It however, was his appointing me as his successor just as Musa appointed Harun as his successor. Musa had said, "Be my successor in my people, do the reform work and do not follow the path of those who spread destruction." (7:142)

"There are also the words of the Messenger of Allah, *O Allah grant compensation to Muhammad and his family worthy of their services to Your cause*, when a group spoke saying, "We are the *Mawali* of the Messenger of Allah, *O Allah grant compensation to Muhammad and his family worthy of their services to Your cause*." The Messenger of Allah, *O Allah grant compensation to Muhammad and his family worthy of their services to Your cause*, left for the farewell al-Hajj then arrived at Ghadir Khum and commanded to prepare for him something like a pulpit. He then stood on it, held my arm, and raised it until his underarms appeared, raising his voice, then said in the gathering, "Whoever's *mawla* I am, Ali is his *mawla*, O Lord, love those who love him and treat as an enemy those who treat him as an enemy. . ." Thus over my *Wilayah* (divine authority and power) was the *Wilayah* authority of Allah and having animosity toward me was animosity toward Allah, most Majestic, most Glorious. On that day He sent this verse, "Today I have completed for you your religion; I have completed my bounty on you and accepted Islam as your religion." (5:3) My *Wilayah* (divine authority and power) was equal to completion of religion and the pleasure of Allah, most Majestic is whose mention. Allah, most Blessed, most High, as a special favor to me and honoring me gifted it to me for the greatness and excellence of the Messenger of Allah, *O Allah grant compensation to Muhammad and his family worthy of their services to Your cause*, granted it to me. This is said in His words stating, "Then return to your *mawla* in truth. Certainly to Him belongs judgment and He is the quickest in counting." (6:62) There are facts in my praise that if I mention, the height becomes great and listening lengthy. Those who dressed up for this position before me were no one other than the two unfortunate ones who disputed with me in what was not for them in truth but they took it over in misguidance and tied it down in ignorance. How evil is where they have landed and how evil is it as a cradle for their souls. They revile each other in their homes and each one disowns his other friend saying to his close friend when they meet, "I wish there was a distance as far as east and west between me and you." How bad is the associate! The more unfortunate one then answers in his ragged condition, "I wish I had not taken you as my friend. You misled me from *Dhikr* (good advice) that had come to me." Satan fails human beings. The good advice for him is a reference to me, which he had lost along with the path from which he deviated, belief that rejected, al-Quran that he departed, the religion that he called a lie, the path from which they veered off and debris they used as short-lived pasture and deceitful temptation of the temporal worldly attractions.

"They in their position (as rulers) were only at the brink of the pit of the fire prepared for them, in the most wicked arrival, in the most failing delegation, to the most condemned destination, shouting at each other with reviles and howling in regret. They will have no comfort or relief from suffering. The people continued worshipping statues as custodians of idols for which they performed rituals, designated for them certain offerings to seek nearness thereby. They designated *al-Bahirah; al-Wasilah, al-Sa'ibah* and *al-Ham* (titles given to camels and sheep after giving birth several times) and distributed them by means of casting a lottery using arrows of a certain shape and wondering about Allah,

Majestic is Whose mention. They were lost in matters of right guidance, ran away from the mercy of Allah, dominated by Satan, overwhelmed by the darkness of the age of ignorance, breastfed by illiteracy and weaned in misguidance. Allah brought us out as mercy for them and raised us over them with kindness. With us He removed the barriers before the light for those who sought it and as a favor to those who followed, (we became) support for those who acknowledged us, thus, they gained glory after lowliness, in increasing numbers after being very few so much so that hearts and eyes felt reverence for them and the powerful and tribes obeyed them. Thus, they became people of wealth, well spoken of and attained honor with ease, peace after fear and of a great number after being just a few. Through us prestige for Mu'd ibn 'Adnan became known and it made possible for them to enter the door of guidance and the house of peace. We collected them in the fabric of belief. Thus, through us, they became successful in the world and in the time of the Messenger, the days of virtuous people appeared before them through the efforts of hard working defenders and worshipping supplicants, performers of *I'tikaf*, who restrained from sins. They who preserved the trust to receive the reward (from Allah) until Allah, most Majestic, most Glorious, called His Holy Prophet back, and raised him to Himself. All of this soon after him took no more than a glance of an eye or a flap of a wing or a spark of lightening that they turned back on their heels. They turned backward behind them to seek revenge by forming armed battalions. They blocked the door (gate of knowledge), destroyed the towns, and changed the traditions of the Messenger of Allah, *O Allah grant compensation to Muhammad and his family worthy of their services to Your cause*. They disregarded his laws, moved far away from his light, and replaced his successor with an alternate that they found in which case they were unjust. They considered the one they had selected from the family of Quhafah a more deserving successor to the Messenger of Allah, *O Allah grant compensation to Muhammad and his family worthy of their services to Your cause*. They said that he is more qualified than the one the Messenger of Allah, *O Allah grant compensation to Muhammad and his family worthy of their services to Your cause*, had appointed as his successor. They assumed that the immigrant of the family of Quhafah whom they had selected was better than the immigrants of al-Ansar (people of al-Madinah), who were devoted to worshipping the Lord and who were of the sacred essence of Hashim ibn 'Abd Munaf. It is certain that the first false testimony, which came in public in Islam, was their testimony in favor of their companion. It said that he was the successor of the Messenger of Allah, *O Allah grant compensation to Muhammad and his family worthy of their services to Your cause*. The issue of Sa'd ibn 'Ubadah appeared the way it did. They took their words back and said, "The Messenger of Allah, *O Allah grant compensation to Muhammad and his family worthy of their services to Your cause*, passed away and did not appoint any successor." The Messenger of Allah, *O Allah grant compensation to Muhammad and his family worthy of their services to Your cause*, who was the blessed healer, provider of cure for all kinds of illness, was the first one in Islam against whom false testimony was presented. After very short time, they were to find out the evil consequences of the basis, the first ones established. Even though, it is a fact that, they had the option, the chance and respite to recover from the illness. They had enough space to return, to come out of the gradual grip of temptation, in a comfortable condition. They found certain of their wishes to have come true, then it also is certain that Allah, most Majestic, most Glorious, gave time to Shaddad ibn 'Ad, Thamud ibn 'Abud and to Bal'am ibn Ba'ur. He made the apparent and hidden bounties pleasant for them, extended their wealth, the duration of their lives and the land to provide them with it bounties so they might remember the bounties of Allah and learn how to come back to Him, return to Him and give up arrogance. They, however, could not complete the time and finish the morsel before Allah, most Majestic, most Glorious, cut them down. Certain ones of them were destroyed by sandstorm; others by thunder, yet others because of darkness, still others because of a quake and others were sucked in the ground. Allah did not do injustice to them but they themselves were unjust to their own selves. For everyone, indeed, there is a book, a document. When the time of the book and document ends it comes to light, to what kind of destination the unjust ones are headed and the losers have arrived. You will then run to Allah, most Majestic, most Glorious, away from what they had been involved in and to which they proceed.

"I among you, indeed, am like Harun among the people of the pharaoh and like the door of Hittah in the Israelites and like the ark of Noah. I am 'the great news' (78:2) and the great truthful. Very shortly, you will learn about what you were promised with. It is no more than a morsel of food and a sip of drink, short slumbers where after they will come in the grip of extreme suffering and failure in this world, and on the Day of Judgment they will turn into the most intense suffering. Allah is well-aware of what they have done. What then is the penalty for one who deviates from the authority (of Allah), rejects it, opposes His guides, turns away from His light, enters into darkness, gives up water in exchange for phantoms, bounties for suffering, success for misfortune, poverty for prosperity, happiness for hardships, affluence for constraints, anything other than what he has sown and its evil consequences. You must be certain of the promise made and about its reality and rest assured about the materialization of the promise. "There will come a day when they will hear the thunder strike in all truth, that will be the time to come out. We bring the dead to life and to Us is the destination. On the day when the earth is cut open from above them . . .""" (50:42-44)

The Sermon of al-Talutiyah

H 14453, h 5

Muhammad ibn Ali ibn Mu'ammar has narrated from Muhammad ibn Ali who has said that narrated to us 'Abd Allah ibn Ayyub al-Ash'ariy from 'Umar al-Awza'iy from 'Amr ibn Shimr from Salmah ibn Kuhayl from abu al-Haytham ibn al-Tayyihan who has narrated the following:

"'Amir al-Mu'minin, Ali, *'Alayhi al-Salam*, addressed people in al-Madinah and said, 'All praise belongs to Allah other than Whom no one deserves worship. He lived without condition. He did not have any condition and for His being, there was no condition. He was not in any place and He was not in anything. He was not on anything. He did not invent any place for His being. He did not become stronger after creating anything or weak before bringing anything into being. He was not lonely before inventing anything. He is not similar to anything. He was not without possession before inventing a thing and He will not remain without possession after the vanishing of all things. He was the Lord and lived without life. He was the owner before inventing anything and the Owner after inventing all beings. Allah does not have any quality, place, limit whereby to be defined. Nothing is similar to Him and He does not become old because of living for a long time; He does not become weak because of loneliness and does not become afraid as His creatures become afraid because of something. He is hearing without ears, seeing without eyes, powerful without power from His creatures. The glance of onlookers cannot catch Him and the ears of listeners cannot sense Him. If He wants to do something, He does it without consultation, support or experimentation and does not ask any of His creatures which He wants to create. Eyes cannot comprehend Him but He catches all eyes. He is subtle and well-Aware. I testify that only Allah deserves worship, He is one and has no partners and I testify that Muhammad is His servant and Messenger whom He has sent with guidance and the true religion to dominate all religions even though the pagans dislike it. He preached his message and outlined the manner of guidance, *O Allah grant compensation to Muhammad and his family worthy of their services to Your cause.*

"(I address you), O nation, who was deceived, suffered deceit and came under the deception of one who deceived it but persisted in what it had found to be so. The nation that followed certain desires, continued in dim-sightedness in misguidance when the Truth had become clear but the nation refused to follow the guidance. Even though the path was clear this nation deviated therefrom. I swear by the One Who opens the seed and carves the fetus into (a certain) shape, had you sought knowledge from its source, drank the water with its sweetness, preserved the good in its proper place, taken the clear path, followed the program of Truth according to its system, you would have the genuine curriculum. The signs would become manifest to you, Islam would become bright and you would then live with ease. No one would suffer poverty, and injustice would not be done to any Muslim or any allies. You walked on the dark path so your world became dark with its vastness. The doors of knowledge became close to you so you spoke from your desires. You faced differences in your religion so you gave fatwas in the religion of Allah without knowledge. You followed the transgressors who misled you, you abandoned the 'A'immah who abandoned you. So you began to judge according to your desires when faced with an issue, you asked the (one of the) people of *Dhikr* (knowledge) and when he gave you a fatwa, you said that he is (the essence of) knowledge exactly. Why then had you abandoned him, neglected and opposed him? Just wait, very shortly, you will harvest all that you had planted and sown and find the evil consequences of unwholesome deeds you have committed and what you have acquired. I swear by the One who opens the grain of seed and carves the fetus into shape, you knew well that I was your companion (master) obedience to whose command was obligatory on you. You knew well that I was your scholar in whose knowledge was your salvation, Executor of the Will of your Prophet, the chosen one by your Lord, the tongue of your light and the scholar of what is for your good. Very shortly, what you were told about will come upon you and that which came upon the nations before you. Allah, most Majestic, most Glorious, will ask you about your *'A'immah* (leaders) with whom you will be raised together and to Allah, most Majestic, most Glorious, tomorrow will be your destination. I swear by Allah that if I had as much supporters as Talut did or as much as the people of Badr who were your enemies, I would strike with the sword until you returned to the Truth repentantly in favor of the Truth. It would have been more suitable and mending for the rift and a more friendly dealing. O Lord, judge among us with truth, You are the best judge.'

"He (the narrator) has said that he (the Imam) then passed by a barn with about thirty sheep inside it. He (the Imam) then said, 'I swear by Allah, if I had a number of men, equal to the number of these sheep, who worked for the sake of Allah, most Majestic, most Glorious, and His Messenger I would have removed the son of the woman who ate unwholesome things from His kingdom.

"He (the narrator) has said that in the evening three hundred sixty people offered their allegiance to him (the Imam) with commitment to die in his support and 'Amir al-Mu'minin, Ali, *'Alayhi al-Salam*, told them to come to him at Ahjar of al-Zayt, (name of a place) with their heads shaved. 'Amir al-Mu'minin, Ali, *'Alayhi al-Salam*, shaved his head but no one of the people kept his promise except abu Dhar, al-Miqdad, Hudhyfah ibn al-Yaman, 'Ammar ibn Yasir and Salman among the people. He (the Imam) then raised his hand to the sky and said, 'O Lord, the people have weakened me just as the Israelites weakened Harun. O Lord, You know what we hide or show and things are not hidden from You in the earth or the sky, make me die a Muslim and join me with the virtuous ones. I swear by the House (al-Ka'bah) and the one who touched the House (the Holy Prophet) [by al-Muzdalifah and walking to throwing pebbles], had it not been because of my commitment with the Holy Prophet, the *'Ummiy, O Allah grant compensation to Muhammad and his family worthy of their services to Your cause*, I would have sent the opposing ones to the gulf of their death. I could send on them sparks of the thunder of death, but very shortly they will find out.'"

Excellence of Shi'ah and their prominent positions

H 14454, h 6
A number of our people have narrated from Sahl ibn Ziyad from Muhammad ibn Sulayman from his father who has narrated the following:

"Once I was with abu 'Abd Allah, *'Alayhi al-Salam*, when abu Basir came breathing fast. He took his seat, and abu 'Abd Allah, *'Alayhi al-Salam*, asked, 'O abu Muhammad, why are you breathing so high?' He said, 'I pray to Allah to keep my soul in service for your cause, O child of the Messenger of Allah, it is because of my old age, weaker bones, nearing of the time of my death and besides I do not know where I will end up in the hereafter.' Abu 'Abd Allah, *'Alayhi al-Salam*, said, 'O abu Muhammad is it you saying such words?' He replied, 'I pray to Allah to keep my soul in service for your cause, why should I not say so?' He (the Imam) said, 'O abu Muhammad, did you not know that Allah honors the young ones of you and is bashful with the old ones among you?' I (abu Basir) then asked, 'I pray to Allah to keep my soul in service for your cause, how does He honor the young one and is bashful with the old ones?' He (the Imam) said, 'Allah honors the young ones by not making them to suffer and is bashful with the old ones to bring them into accounting.' I then asked, 'I pray to Allah to keep my soul in service for your cause, is this just for us or it is for those who believe in Oneness of Allah?' He (the Imam) said, 'No, it is just for you of all the people in the world.' I then said, 'I pray to Allah to keep my soul in service for your cause, we are called with a nickname which breaks our backs and deadens our hearts. The ruling ones consider shedding of our blood lawful because of a Hadith that their scholars of law narrate for them.' Abu 'Abd Allah, *'Alayhi al-Salam*, asked, 'Is it *al-Rafidah* (rejecters)?' I replied, 'Yes, that is correct.' He (the Imam) said, 'No, by Allah, they are not the ones who have given you this name. Allah has given you this name. Have you not noticed, O abu Muhammad, that seventy people from the Israelites rejected the pharaoh and his people when they learned that they were misguided and they joined Musa, *'Alayhi al-Salam*, when they found out that he had the right guidance. In the army of Musa, they were named *al-Rafidah* (rejecters) because they had rejected the pharaoh and they were the ones with intense worship and love for Musa, *'Alayhi al-Salam*, and Harun and their offspring. Allah, most Majestic, most Glorious, sent revelation to Musa and told him to keep this name for them in the Torah and I have named them as such and have given it to them as a gift. Musa then recorded this name for them, then Allah, most Majestic, most Glorious, reserved this name for you to give it as a gift to you. O abu Muhammad, they rejected the truth but you have rejected the evil. People turned into sects and in branches. You branched with the family of your Holy Prophet, *O Allah grant compensation to Muhammad and his family worthy of their services to Your cause*, and went wherever they went, chose what Allah had chosen for you and you wanted those whom Allah had wanted for you. It is glad and happy news for you. You by Allah are the forgiven ones, good deeds of whose virtuous ones are accepted and the sins of their sinful ones are forgiven. Whoever will come to Allah, most Majestic, most Glorious, on the Day of Judgment without what you believe in, his good deeds will not be accepted and their sins will not be forgiven. O abu Muhammad does this make you happy?' I then asked, 'I pray to Allah to keep my soul in service for your cause, honor me with more good news.' He (the Imam) said, 'O abu Muhammad, Allah, most Majestic, most Glorious, has such angels who remove sins from the backs of our Shi'ah just as the wind makes the leaves fall off of a tree in fall season. This is the meaning of the words of Allah, most Majestic, most Glorious, 'Those who carry the throne and those who are around it say *Tasbih* (Allah is free of all defects), believe in Him and ask forgiveness for those who have believed.' (40:7) Their asking forgiveness by Allah is for you of all these creatures. O abu

Muhammad, does this make you happy?' I then asked, 'I pray to Allah to keep my soul in service for your cause, honor me with more glad news.' He (the Imam) said, 'O abu Muhammad, Allah has spoken of you in His book saying, "Of the believing people are those who remain true to their covenant with Allah, certain ones of them have passed away, others are still waiting and they have not changed at all." (33:23) You have remained loyal to the covenant that Allah had made with you about our *Wilayah* (divine authority and power). You have not exchanged us at all with others, had you changed your loyalty to your covenant Allah would reproach you as He has reproached them saying, "We did not find any loyalty on their part to their covenant but We found many of them as sinful ones." (7:102) O abu Muhammad, did I make you happy?' I said, 'I pray to Allah to keep my soul in service for your cause, I request for more.' He (the Imam) said, 'O abu Muhammad, Allah has mentioned you in His book and has said, ". . . as brothers sitting face to face." (16:47) By Allah, He has not willed it to apply to anyone except to you. O abu Muhammad, did I make you happy?' I said, 'I pray to Allah to keep my soul in service for your cause, I request for more.' He (the Imam) said, 'O abu Muhammad, "All intimate friends on that day will become each other's enemies except for the pious..." (43:67) By Allah He has not intended it to apply to anyone except you. O abu Muhammad, did I make you happy?' I said, 'I pray to Allah to keep my soul in service for your cause, I request for more.' He (the Imam) said, 'O abu Muhammad, Allah, most Majestic, most Glorious, has spoken of us and our followers and of our enemies in a verse of His book and He, most Majestic, most Glorious, has said, ". . . Are those who know equal to those who do not know? Only the people of reason take heed." (39:9) We are the people who know, our enemies are those who do not know and our flowers are the people of reason. O abu Muhammad, did I make you happy?' I said, 'I pray to Allah to keep my soul in service for your cause, I request for more.' He (the Imam) said, 'O abu Muhammad, Allah, most Majestic, most Glorious, has not made an exception about anyone of the executor of the wills of the Prophets and their followers except 'Amir al-Mu'minin, Ali, *'Alayhi al-Salam*, and his followers. In His book He has said and His words are true, ". . . on the day when no friend can be of any help to his friend and they will not be helped, except those to whom Allah will grant mercy." (44:42-43) He has meant it to apply to Ali, *'Alayhi al-Salam*, and his followers. O abu Muhammad, did I make you happy?' I said, 'I pray to Allah to keep my soul in service for your cause, I request for more.' He (the Imam) said, 'O abu Muhammad, Allah, the most Blessed, the most High, has spoken of you in His book saying, ". . . O my servants, who have acted excessively against their souls, do not despair from the mercy of Allah, Allah forgives the sins and He is forgiving and merciful." (39:53) By Allah, He has not willed it to apply to anyone except you. O abu Muhammad, did I make you happy?' I said, 'I pray to Allah to keep my soul in service for your cause, I request for more.' He (the Imam) said, 'O Muhammad, Allah, the most Blessed, the most High, has also spoken of you in His book saying, ". . . and you have no authority over My servants..." (15:42) By Allah, He has not intended it to apply to anyone except *'A'immah, 'Alayhim al-Salam*, and their followers. O abu Muhammad, did I make you happy?' I said, 'I pray to Allah to keep my soul in service for your cause, I request for more.'

He (the Imam) said, 'O Muhammad, Allah, the most Blessed, the most High, has spoken of you in His book as He has said, ". . . they will be with those to whom Allah has granted bounties of the Prophets, the truthful ones, the martyrs, the virtuous ones and they are very good friends." (4:69) Prophets stands for the Messenger of Allah, *O Allah grant compensation to Muhammad and his family worthy of their services to Your cause*, in this verse, we are the truthful ones and the martyrs and you are the virtuous ones, so you must take this name as Allah, most Majestic, most Glorious, has named you by this name (virtuous). O abu Muhammad, did I make you happy?' I said, 'I pray to Allah to keep my soul in service for your cause, I request for more.' He (the Imam) said, 'O abu Muhammad, Allah has spoken of you when He has quoted your enemies in the fire as He has said, ". . . why is it that we do not see the men whom we would count of the evil ones? We would mock at them. Have the eyes strayed away from them?" (38:62-63) By Allah, He has not meant it to apply to anyone other than you. In the eyes of the people of this world you seem as the evil ones, but in the garden (paradise) you will be honored and will be made to enjoy but in the fire, they will look to find you. O abu Muhammad, did I make you happy?' I said, 'I pray to Allah to keep my soul in service for your cause, I request for more.' He (the Imam) said, 'O abu Muhammad, every verse of al-Quran that is revealed and it leads to the garden (paradise) or speaks of its people with goodness, such verse applies only to us and to our followers. Every verse, which is revealed, and it speaks of the evil people or points to the fire, it applies to our enemies and to those who oppose us. O abu Muhammad, did I make you happy?' I said, 'I pray to Allah to keep my soul in service for your cause, I request for more.' He (the Imam) said, 'O abu Muhammad, No one follows the community of Ibrahim except we and our followers. Other people are far away from it. O abu Muhammad, did I make you happy?' In another Hadith it is said that he replied, 'Yes, it is sufficient for me.'"

Hadith of Abu 'Abd Allah, *'Alayhi al-Salam*, with al-Mansur in his procession

H 14455, h 7

Muhammad ibn Yahya has narrated from Ahmad ibn Muhammad from certain persons of his people and Ali ibn Ibrahim has narrated from his father from ibn abu 'Umayr all from Muhammad ibn abu Hamzah from Humran who has narrated the following:

"Abu 'Abd Allah, *'Alayhi al-Salam*, once said, when these people mentioned before him (the Imam) the difficult condition of the Shi'ah, 'I once was with abu Ja'far, al-Mansur (the Abbaside ruler) in his procession. He was on a horse, with a group of people on horses before and after him and I was riding a donkey on his side. He said to me, "O abu 'Abd Allah, it is proper for you to be happy with what Allah has granted us of power, victory and glory. You must not tell people that you have a greater degree of right to the position of ruler-ship as well as your family to provoke us against yourself and against them." He (the Imam) has said, 'I then said that whoever has said as such to you has not spoken the truth.' He then said, 'Will you take an oath about what you just said?' I said, 'People are like magicians which means that they love to destroy your feeling about me. You must not allow your ears to listen to them. We need you more than you need us.' He (al-Mansur) then asked, 'Do you remember the day I asked if we can have a kingdom and you replied, 'Yes, very vast, for a very long time and strong. You will continue in such chance of the worldly domain until you will shed blood against the law in a sacred month in al-Haram (the sacred area)?' I then noticed that he has remembered the Hadith. I then said, 'Perhaps Allah will save you and I do not apply this to you especially. I narrated a Hadith. Maybe someone else from your family will be in control of the government. He then remained quiet. On my return to my home certain ones of our friends came and said, 'I pray to Allah to keep my soul in service for your cause, by Allah, I saw you in the procession of abu Ja'far (al-Mansur) when you were riding a donkey. He was riding a horse as dominant above you and speaking to you as a supervisor does. I then said to myself that this is a friend of Allah (a man who possesses divine authority) over the people and the person in charge of the high authority in religion who must be followed and the other one acts unjustly, kills the descendents of the Prophets, causes bloodshed on earth in a way that Allah does not like. He is in his procession but he is riding a donkey. I nearly doubted in my religion and in my soul.' I then said to him, 'Had you seen those who were around me, before, behind, on my right and left of the angels you would despise him as well as those around him.' He then said, 'Now my heart has gained comfort. He then asked, 'For how long these people will remain in power and when we will find relief from their domination?' I then said, 'Do you not know that for everything there is an appointed time?' He replied, 'Yes, that is true.' I then said, 'Will knowing it help you? If it comes, it will be faster than a blinking of an eye. If you like to know their condition before Allah, most Majestic, most Glorious, and how it is you would hate them intensely. Had you and the people of the earth struggled to make it more difficult for them than what they are already in, you could not do so, thus do not allow Satan to incite you. Glory belongs to Allah, His Messenger and the believing people but the hypocrites do not know. You must take notice that those who wait for our cause to materialize and bear patience in facing the hardships and fear, tomorrow they will be along with us. There will come a time when you see the Truth has died, the people of truth have gone, injustice has covered the land, al-Quran is considered to have become old, heresy is invented about it when it was not there. A time will come when you see of religion remaining not anything more than a name like a bowl of water turned upside down. A time will come when you see the people of falsehood achieve high positions above the people of the Truth, evil has become apparent and no one prohibits it, instead they do not blame them, when you see sinfulness apparent, men satisfy themselves with men and women with women. A time will come when you see the believing remain silent and his words are not accepted. You will see the sinful speak lies and his lies and fabrications are not refuted. You will see small ones insult the grown up, when you see good relations with relatives are cut off, when you see when one is praised for his sinful ways he laughs, he is not stopped and his words are not rejected. A time will come when you will see the boy yield as women do, and women marry women. A time will come when you see admirations increased, when you see a man spend assets in something other than in obedience to Allah, he is not prohibited and his hand is not held back. A time will come when you will see the onlookers seek refuge with Allah because of what they see a believing person do and strive. You will find neighbors trouble neighbors and no one will stop them. You will see an unbeliever rejoice for what (problems) he finds with the believing people, and is cheerful because of the spreading of sinfulness in the land. A time will come when you see wine is used in public in the gatherings without fear of Allah, most Majestic, most Glorious, when you see commanding people to do good is called undignified, and the sinful ones in doing what Allah dislikes are thought of as great and praised. A time will come when you will see people of great signs are despised as well as those who like them, when you see goodness is stopped and the evil ways are adopted. You will see the house of Allah is neglected and ignoring it is commanded and you find men say what they do not do. You will see men use oil (to beautify) for men and women for women. You will see men earn through homosexuality, and women through prostitution. You will see women sit in gatherings like men do, when you see feminine signs apparent in the offspring of al-'Abbas and their using dyes and combs as women use for their husbands and men for their sexual organs and compete for men and men's feeling jealous over him. A time will come when the wealthy will be considered more important than the believing people will, when taking unlawful become public without blame, when women are praised because of fornication, when a woman does a favor to her man for his homosexuality. You will see most people and the best houses are considered the ones that help women in their sinful acts. You will see the believing people feel sad, despised and humiliated. You will see heresy and fornication have become apparent, people argue their case with the help of false testimony, the lawful is made unlawful and the unlawful as lawful. A time will come when you will see religion is taken by personal opinions, and the laws of the book are neglected. You will see people do not wait for the darkness of the night to cover their acts against Allah, and you will see believing ones cannot do more than rejecting in their hearts. A time will come when you will see great amounts of wealth are spent for what Allah, most Majestic, most Glorious, becomes angry. You will see the rulers become close to people of disbelief and stay away from the people of goodness, and you will see the rulers accept bribes to issue judgments. A time will come when you will see governing is contracted with those who give more, when you see incest take place and is taken as sufficient, when you see a man is killed for false accusation and surmising and jealousy is exercised over the man who gives his self and assets. You will see women overpower their husbands and work for what he will like and spend for her. You will see man hire his woman, his slave-girl and agree with worthless food and drink. You will see belief in Allah, most Majestic, most Glorious, is a great deal on false basis, when you will see gambling is apparent, wine is sold publicly without obstacles, and women give themselves to unbelievers. A time will come when you will see useless games have become apparent, people pass by but no one stops it and no one will dare to do so. You will see people of dignity are humble before those from whose domination they are afraid, when you will see the closest to rulers are those who are praised because of their reviling us, the *Ahl al-Bayt*. A time will come when you will see people compete over false words, when you see listening to al-Quran is heavy on people but their listening to falsehood becomes easy. You will see a neighbor respect a neighbor because of fear from his tongue, when you see laws of penalty are neglected and they are used according to desires. You will see Masjids are decorated, when you will see the most truthful person is the one who fabricates the most. You will see evil has become apparent as well as tale-bearing. You will see transgression is widespread, backbiting is made likeable and people give it as glad news to each other. You will see al-Hajj and Jihad are sought for things other than the pleasure of Allah and the sultans humiliate believing people for the sake of unbelievers. You will see destruction more than construction, a man's earning come from cheating in measurement and bloodshed will be taken lightly. A time will come when you see a man seek leadership for the sake of the worldly matters to make himself famous through bad-mouthing so he will be feared and affairs depend on him. You will see *Salat* (prayer) taken lightly, a man will possess a great wealth but will not pay *Zakat* at all. A time will come when you will see the dead exhumed from his grave, harmed and the shroud is sold. You will see anarchy rampant, a man in the evening elated and in the morning intoxicated and carefree of what people will face. You will see animals are used for indecent acts, animals kill (ride) each other, a man go out to the place of his *Salat* (prayer) and come back without any of his clothes on him. You will see people's hearts become hard and their eyes solid and speaking of Allah becomes heavy on them. You will see unlawful and filthy earning become apparent and contested. You will see one perform *Salat* (prayer) only to show off, when you will see a scholar of fiqh learn for the sake of something other than religion, seek worldly gains and leadership. You will see people are with those who overpower others, when you see those who seek lawful matters are reproached and rebuked and those who seek unlawful matters are praised with greatness, when you see acts that Allah does not like are committed in the two al-Haram (the sacred areas). A time will come when you will see a man who will speak of truth, command to do good and forbid the doing of evil; one will stand up and say that this is not your responsibility. You will see people emulate each other and follow people of evil. A time will come when you will see the path of goodness and its road empty on which no one will walk. You will see every year evil and heresy is invented more than in the year before. You will see people and gatherings do not follow someone other than the rich. You will see the needy receive help so that others laugh at his condition, and sympathy for reasons other than for the sake of Allah. You will see signs appearing in the sky are not feared, people engage in sexual acts like animals and no one expresses dislike because of fear from people. You will see the man squander a great deal, which is not for the sake of Allah but he denies the little in obedience to Allah. You will see disrespect to parents become apparent and they will be mistreated as being the worst ones of the people to the children who become happy for people's accusing their parents. You will see women dominant in a kingdom and on all rulers who do not act against what they dislike. You will see the son of a man accuse his father; present claims against his parents and become happy for their death. You will see a man who passes a day without committing a great sin like cheating in measurements, committing unlawful act, drinking wine, sad and depressed and counts that day as a day lost in his life. You will see the Sultan hoard food; you will see the assets of relatives distributed in falsehood and gambled with to drink wine. You will see wine is used as medicine, prescribed by the physicians. You will see people consider commanding to do good, to forbid evil and neglecting religion all the same. You will see people of hypocrisy and hypocrites on the rise and people of truth do not move, when you see *Adhan* and *Salat* (prayer) for wages, when you see a Masjid full of those who do not fear Allah, gather there for backbiting, consuming the flesh of the people of truth, and prescribe wine and intoxicants. You will see a drunken man lead *Salat* (prayer) with no understanding. However, people will not show any dislike for his being drunk. When he is drunk he is respected, feared and ignoring him is feared, he is not punished nor is executed for being drunk. A time will come when you will see those who consume assets of orphans will receive praise as virtuous ones. You will see the judges judge against the commandments of Allah, the rules trust the treacherous ones for greed, the rulers designate legacy for the sinful people and the daring against Allah who take from them and leave in what they desire. You will see piety preached from the pulpits but the preacher will not practice, you will see *Salat* (prayer) taken lightly as well as its times, you will see charity given through intercession but not for the sake of Allah. It is given because of people's demand and pleasure. You will see what matter to people will be their stomach and sexual desires, paying attention to what they eat or drink and the world will come to them. You see the signs of truth have become old then you must remain cautious and seek safety from Allah, most Majestic, most Glorious. You must take notice that Allah, most Majestic, most Glorious, is angry with people and He only gives them time for a matter for which He wants them. Remain watchful and strive, so that Allah, most Majestic, most Glorious, will see you in what is against what they do. If penalty falls on them when you are there, you can move quickly to the mercy of Allah. If you delay, they become afflicted; you must have come out of what they are in of their daring against Allah, most Majestic, most Glorious. You must take notice that Allah does not allow the rewards of the people of good deeds to become invalidated, the mercy of Allah is close to those who do good deeds.'"

Hadith of Musa, *'Alayhi al-Salam*

H 14456, h 8

Ali ibn Ibrahim has narrated from his father from 'Amr ibn 'Uthman from Ali ibn 'Isa in a marfu' manner who has narrated the following:

"He (the Imam), *'Alayhi al-Salam*, has said that once, when Musa *'Alayhi al-Salam*, was speaking secretly to Allah, most Blessed, most High, He said, 'O

Musa, you must not keep long-lasting hopes for the world. It hardens your heart and hardhearted people are far away from Me. O Musa, be like my happiness in you, if my happiness is obeyed, then I am not disobeyed. You must make your heart (the negative aspect of the soul) die by anxiety (fear of Allah) and allow your clothes to be old but your heart new, you will remain hidden to the people of earth but well known to the people of the heaven. You must spread the homes with the lamp of the night, plead and pray before Me like the pleading of those who bear patience. You must sob before Me because of a great many sins like the sobbing of a runaway sinner from his enemy and seek support from Me about it because I am the best helper and the best supporter. O Musa, I am Allah above the servants, the servants are below Me, and all things are helpless before Me. You must accuse your soul for doing wrong against your own soul. Do not trust your son about your religion unless your son is like you, loving the virtuous ones. O Musa, wash and take Ghusl (bath) and become close to My virtuous servants. O Musa, be their Imam in their *Salat* (prayer) and their Imam in their disputes, judge among them by what I have sent down to you; I have sent it as clear rules and bright proofs and as light that speaks about what was with the previous generations and what will exist with the later generations. I advise you, O Musa, as a kindhearted and compassionate adviser about the son of al-Batul (Virgin), Jesus, son of Mary, owner of donkey and hooded gown, oil and olive and prayer ark. I advise you thereafter about the owner of the red camel, the fine, clean and purified, whose example in the book is the believing dominant over all books. The one who performs *Ruku'* (bowing down on one's knees) and *Sujud* (prostrations), who is interested, (in the bounties of Allah) fearful, brother of the destitute, and whose helpers are from other people. In his time, there will be hardships, quakes, killing, and shortages of assets. His name is Ahmad, Muhammad the trusted above the others of the remainders of the previous generations, who believes in all books, confirms all Messengers, and testifies sincerely in favor of all Prophets. His followers are forgiven, blessed with whatever remains in the religion in its reality, for there are certain hours in which they perform *Salat* (prayer) as servants do for their master optionally, acknowledge him and follow his path; he is your brother. O Musa, he is *'Ummy* and a true servant. On whatever he places his hand it becomes a blessing for him and a blessing for it. This is how it is in My knowledge and as such I have created him and with him I will open the hour and with his followers I will seal the keys to the world; so command the unjust of the Israelites not to forget his name or betray him but they will do so. Loving him is a good deed before Me; I am with him, I am of his party, he is of My party and their party is victorious. My words are complete and I will make his religion dominant over all religions. I will be worshipped in all places. I will send to him al-Quran as a means to distinguish right from wrong, and as a cure for that which is in the chests. It, al-Quran, will serve as protection against the blows of Satan. You must ask compensation for him, O son of 'Imran, because I as well as My angels say, *O Allah grant compensation to Muhammad and his family worthy of their services to Your cause.*

35

"O Musa, you are My servant and I Am your Lord, you must not disparage a despicable poor person and do not deem a rich person fortunate for very little. You must be humble when speaking of Me, when reciting My *Dhikr* have hope in My mercy and allow Me to hear the recital of the Torah in a pleasant manner with a heartfelt sad voice. You must be comfortable when speaking of Me and remind of Me whoever becomes comfortable with Me, worship Me and do not take other things as My partner. You must seek My happiness; I Am the great master. I have created you from a despicable fluid seed from clay, which I took out from a lowly mixed land. It was a human being and I made him into a creature. Blessed, is My face. Holy is My craft. There is no other thing like Me and I Am ever living without failure.

"O Musa, when you pray to Me be fearful, anxious and afraid. You must rub your face on the ground for My sake, perform *Sajdah* (prostration) with the noble parts of your body and plead before Me when standing. You must speak to Me secretly when you speak to Me privately with an anxious and fearful heart and revive by My Torah in life, teach the ignorant My praises, remind them of My bounties and blessings and say to them not to continue in their transgression in which they live; My hold is painful and intense.

"O Musa, when My rope is cutoff it does not connect to the rope of others, so worship Me and stand before Me in the position of a lowly poor servant. You must blame your soul because it deserves more blame and do not dominate the Israelites by My book; it is sufficient advice for your heart and enlightenment. It is the words of the Cherisher of the worlds, most Majestic, most Glorious.

"O Musa, whenever you pray to Me with hope, I will soon forgive you for what may have taken place from you. The sky says *Tasbih* (Allah is free of all defects) fearfully, the angels are afraid and anxious, the earth says *Tasbih* (Allah is free of all defects) and all creatures say *Tasbih* (Allah is free of all defects) with humbleness. You must perform *Salat* (prayer) because of its important position with Me. Its covenant is firm before Me and I join with it that which is for it (the reward). *Zakat* provides nearness with clean assets and food; I do not accept anything other than clean whereby my pleasure is sought. Keep it connected with maintaining good relation with relatives; I Am Allah, the Beneficent, the Merciful. I have created the womb (means of relationship) from the extra from My mercy by which the servants can sympathize with each other. Before Me, it has a sultan (dominating power) in the return (hereafter) and it cuts off those who cut it off and connects those who maintain it connected. In this way, I will deal with those who lose My command.

"O Musa, be generous to one who asks for help from you with honorable words and giving a little to help because he comes to you who is not from man or Jinn. Angels of the most Beneficent come to test you to see how you deal with things in your possession and how you cooperate by means of that with which I have given preference to you over others, be anxious toward Me in pleading with ululation with the reading from the book. You must take notice that I call you as a master calls his servant to make him reach the honorable position and this is of My favor toward you and to your ancestors in the past.

"O Musa, do not forget Me in all conditions and do not be very happy due to the abundance of wealth because forgetting Me hardens the heart and with the abundance of wealth sins increase. The earth is obedient, the sky is obedient and the oceans are obedient. Disobedience is misfortune for both the heavy groups (man and Jinn) and I am the Beneficent, the Merciful. I am Beneficent in all times. I bring hardship after ease and comfort after hardship. I bring kings after kings and My kingdom is permanently established which does not go away. Nothing is hidden from Me in the earth or in the sky and how can that which is commenced by Myself remain hidden and how can your ambition not be centered on what is with Me when you will inevitably return to Me?

"O Musa, you must designate Me as your Protector, preserve your treasure of good deeds with Me and have fear from Me and not from the others; toward Me is the destination. O Musa, be kind to those below you among the creatures and do not be envious toward those who are above you; envy consumes good deeds just as fire consumes firewood.

"O Musa, the two sons of Adam, *'Alayhi al-Salam*, expressed humbleness at a stage to receive My favor and mercy so they offered offerings but I accept the offerings of the pious ones only. Their condition was as it happened of which you came to know. After this how can you trust the brother or a vizier?

"O Musa, give up arrogance and pride and remember that you will be a dweller of the grave and it must prevent you from indulging in desires. O Musa, be quick to repent and postpone sins, spend time to wait before Me in *Salat* (prayer) and do not keep any hope in anyone other than Me, designate Me as a shield for yourself in hardships and a fortress in catastrophic circumstances.

"O Musa, how can a creature become anxious who does not know My favors to him? How can it learn about My favors to it when it is not looking to it, how can it look to it when it does not believe in it, how can it believe in it when it does not have any hope in receiving any reward? How can it have hopes in receiving rewards when it is satisfied with the worldly matters and has taken it as a refuge? The unjust ones have depended on it. O Musa, compete in goodness with the people of goodness because goodness is like its name and leave evil for those who love it.

"O Musa, keep your tongue behind your heart; you will remain safe and speak of Me during the day and night; you will gain and do not allow sins follow sins so you will regret and the fire is the promised place for the sins.

"O Musa, seek to speak to those who have given up sins, be one of their associates, designate them as brothers in your absence and strive with them, they will strive for you. O Musa, death will inevitably approach you so prepare your supplies as those who are certain of the sufficiency of their supplies to reach their destination.

"O Musa, something with which My pleasure is sought, its smaller amount is a great deal and whatever with which someone other than Me is sought, even its great deal is a small amount. You must reform for your days, which are ahead of you and see which day is it and prepare the answer for it; it is where one is stopped and questioned. Learn your lesson from the eon and those who lived before because a long eon is short, its shorter duration is long, and all things are mortal, so you must act as if you see the reward for your deeds, so you will be more interested in the hereafter inevitably. Whatever is left of the world is like what is passed. Every worker works with awareness and examples. You must habituate your soul, O son of 'Imran; perhaps you will succeed tomorrow on the day of questioning where people of falsehood fail.

"O Musa, extend your palms in humbleness before Me like a pleading slave before his master; if you do so you will receive mercy and I am the most generous of the powerful ones.

"O Musa, ask Me for My favor and mercy; they are in My hand and no one else possesses them and when asking Me, see how your interest is in what is with Me. Every worker receives wages and even the ungrateful is rewarded for what he strives.

"O Musa, do not be concerned about the world and keep aside thereof; it is not for you and you do not own it. It is the home of the unjust. However, one who does good deeds, in his case it is the best home.

"O Musa, whatever I command, you must listen and do when you see, keep the facts of the Torah in your chest and remain awake with them during the hours of the day and night and do not allow the sons of the worldly people to turn your chest into a nest like the nest of birds.

"O Musa, the worldly sons and its people are means of trial for each other. So everyone decorates what belongs to him and the believing is one for whom the hereafter is beautified. Therefore, he looks at them and does not feel tired or weak. His desires for the beautiful matters of the hereafter veil him from the joy of worldly life. The beauty of the matters of the hereafter makes him to journey in the early hours of the morning like the traveler who drives to his destination tired and sad but how good it is for him if the curtain is moved aside and what he can examine of the joyful matters!

"O Musa, the world is a seed and it is not the reward for the believing or penalty for the sinful ones. Great and long awfulness is for those who sell the reward of their day of return in exchange for a small morsel that vanishes and a sip that does not continue. Thus, you must be as I command you to be and all of My commands are guidance.

"O Musa, when you see wealth coming to you, you must say that it is a sin for which suffering approaches quicker and when you see poverty coming to you, you must say welcome to it and say that it is the way of life of the virtuous ones. You must not become a tyrant unjust and do not remain close to the unjust.

"O Musa, lifetime is insignificant, if it prolongs its end becomes despicable and what goes away from you is not harmful for you if you remain grateful for its absence. O Musa, the book has spoken loudly about the destination to which you are headed. How can, then, the eyes sleep, or a people find the joy of life? It is because of the danger of continued neglect, following misfortune and desire that the truthful ones live restless.

"O Musa, command My servants to pray to Me in whatever condition they are, after they acknowledge that I Am the most Merciful of the merciful ones, listen to the helpless, remove evil, change the time, bring comfort, appreciate the little, reward a great deal, make the poor wealthy and that I am forever Majestic and Powerful. If one comes to you seeking protection, you must move close to those who have committed sins and say to them, 'You are welcome. The courtyard of the Cherisher of the worlds is vast.' Ask forgiveness for them and be with them like one of them, do not dominate them because of My granting you a favor and tell them to pray to Me for My favors and mercy, no one other than Me owns them and I Am the Great and Generous one. How good it is, O Musa, for you to be a protection for the sinful ones, sit with the helpless ones and ask forgiveness for the sinful ones! Your position with Me is agreeable, so call Me with a clean heart, truthful tongue, be as I have commanded you to be, obey my command and do not dominate My servants by means of that which has not started from you. Seek nearness to Me because I am near you. I do not ask for a thing, which harms you because of its weight to carry. I only ask you to pray and I will answer your prayer. Ask Me and I will give you, seek nearness to Me by means of what you have received from Me, its interpretation and it is up to Me to complete sending.

"O Musa, look to the earth, very soon it will be your grave, raise your eyes to the sky above you, there is a great angel. Weep for your soul as long as you are in the world and be afraid of destruction and of destructive matters. Do not allow the worldly attraction to deceive you or its blossoms. You must not agree with injustice. You must not be unjust because I survey the unjust until I will give victory over him to the oppressed.

"O Musa, good deeds are rewarded tenfold and only one sin is destructive, do not take anything as My partner, it is not lawful for you to take anything as My partner, seek nearness and remain firm, pray like one greedy for and interested in what is with Me, and be like a regretful one for what he has done. Just as the blackness of the night deletes the day so also does sins to good deeds. The darkness of night moves over the light of the day, so also does moving of the sins over the glorious good deeds and turns it black.'"

Advice of Abu 'Abd Allah, *'Alayhim al-Salam*

H 14457, h 9

Ali ibn Muhammad has narrated from those whom he has mentioned from Muhammad ibn al-Husayn and Humayd ibn Ziyad from al-Hassan ibn Muhammad al-Kindiy all from Ahmad ibn Muhammad from ibn al-Hassan al-Haythamiy from a man of his people who has narrated the following:

"I once read the answer from abu 'Abd Allah, *'Alayhi al-Salam*, to one of his companions. It said, 'Thereafter, (after praising Allah) I advise you to remain pious before Allah, Allah has guaranteed those who observe piety to turn them away from what they dislike to what they love and provides them sustenance from an unexpected source. You must not become of such servants who are feared for their affecting others by their sins but they themselves feel safe from suffering because of their sins; Allah, most Majestic, most Glorious, cannot be deceived about His garden (paradise) and what is with Him cannot be achieved without obedience to Him, by the will of Allah.'"

Seven marks of excellence for Banu Hashim

H 14458, h 10

A number of our people have narrated from Sahl ibn Ziyad from Muhammad ibn Sulayman from 'Aytham ibn 'Ushaym from Mu'awiyah ibn 'Ammar who has narrated the following:

"Abu 'Abd Allah, *'Alayhi al-Salam*, has said that once the Holy Prophet, *O Allah grant compensation to Muhammad and his family worthy of their services to Your cause*, came out happy and laughed because of joy. People said, 'May Allah grant you more happiness and laughing.' The Messenger of Allah, *O Allah grant compensation to Muhammad and his family worthy of their services to Your cause*, said, 'Every night and every day Allah grants to me a gift. Today Allah has granted me a gift the like of which He had not given to me before. Jibril came to me, conveyed to me the greeting of peace from the Lord and said, "O Muhammad, Allah, most Majestic, most Glorious, has chosen from banu Hashim seven people the like of whom He has not created in the people of the past and He will not create in future. O Messenger of Allah, you are the master of the messengers. Ali ibn abu Talib, the executor of your will, is the master of the executors of the wills. Al-Hassan and al-Husayn, your grandsons are the masters of the grandsons, Hamzah; your uncle is the master of the martyrs. Ja'far, the son of your uncle, the flier in the garden (paradise) flies with the angels where he likes and from you is al-Qa'im (the one who will rise with divine authority and power). Jesus, son of Mary will perform *Salat* (prayer), behind him, when Allah will send him down to the earth. He is of the descendents of Ali and Fatimah, from the children of al-Husayn, *'Alayhim al-Salam*."'"

This Book speaks to you in all truth

H 14459, h 11

Sahl ibn Ziyad has narrated from Muhammad ibn Sulayman al-Daylamiy al-Misriy from his father from abu Basir who has narrated the following:

"I once asked abu 'Abd Allah, *'Alayhi al-Salam*, about the meaning of the words of Allah, '. . . this Our book speaks to you in all truth.' (45:29) He (the Imam) said, 'The book did not speak and will never speak, however, the Messenger of Allah, *O Allah grant compensation to Muhammad and his family worthy of their services to Your cause*, spoke with the book. Allah, most Majestic, most Glorious, has said, ". . . this Our book (scribe) is speaking to you in all truth." I then said, 'I pray to Allah to keep my soul in service for your cause, we do not read it as such.' He (the Imam) said, 'This is by Allah how Jibril brought it to Muhammad, *O Allah grant compensation to Muhammad and his family worthy of their services to Your cause*, but it is of the vocation in the book of Allah.'"

About the words of Allah 'By the midday sun'

H 14460, h 12

A group has narrated from Sahl from Muhammad from his father [from abu Muhammad] who has narrated the following:

"I once asked abu 'Abd Allah, *'Alayhi al-Salam*, about the meaning of the words of Allah, '. . . by the sun and its brightness.' (91:1) He (the Imam) said, 'The sun stands for the Messenger of Allah, *O Allah grant compensation to Muhammad and his family worthy of their services to Your cause*, through whom Allah, most Majestic, most Glorious, clarified for the people their religion.' I then asked, '. . . by the moon when it follows the sun.' He (the Imam) said, 'This is a reference to 'Amir al-Mu'minin, Ali, *'Alayhi al-Salam*, who followed the Messenger of Allah, *O Allah grant compensation to Muhammad and his family worthy of their services to Your cause*, and who inspired him with knowledge with powerful inspiration.' I then asked, '. . . by the night when it covers the sun.' He (the Imam) said, 'This is a reference to the *'A'immah* of injustice who took over arbitrarily the task after the Messenger of Allah, *O Allah grant compensation to Muhammad and his family worthy of their services to Your cause*. They sat in a place which the Messenger had given to the one who was more deserving than them but they covered the religion of Allah with injustice and Allah has referred to their deeds saying, '. . . by the night when it covers the sun.' I then asked, '. . . by the day when it becomes bright.' He (the Imam) said, 'This is a reference to the Imam from the descendents of Fatimah, *'Alayha al-Salam*, who is asked about the religion of the Messenger of Allah, *O Allah grant compensation to Muhammad and his family worthy of their services to Your cause*, and he clarifies it for those who ask. Allah, most Majestic, most Glorious, has mentioned in His words, '. . . by the day when it brightens.'"

About the words of Allah 'Has the story of the overwhelming come to you . . .'

H 14461, h 13

Sahl has narrated from Muhammad from his father who has narrated the following:

"I once asked abu 'Abd Allah, *'Alayhi al-Salam*, about the meaning of the words of Allah, '. . . have you heard the story of al-Ghashiyah?' (88:1) He (the Imam) said, 'Al-Qa'im (the one who rises with divine authority and power) will overwhelm them by the sword.' I then asked, '. . . certain faces on that day will be humble.' He (the Imam) said, 'They will be so humble that they will not be able to bear denial.' I then asked, '. . . working.' He (the Imam) said, 'Worked without following what Allah had revealed.' I then asked, '. . . appointed.' He (the Imam) said, 'People other than those who possessed divine authority were appointed.' I then asked, '. . . the faces feel the heat of the fire.' He (the Imam) said, 'The faces will feel the heat of war in this world in the time of al-Qa'im (the one who rises with divine authority and power) and in the next life will feel the heat of the hellfire.'"

About the words of Allah 'They swear to Allah earnestly...'

H 14462, h 14

Sahl has narrated from Muhammad from his father from abu Basir who has narrated the following:

"I once asked abu 'Abd Allah, *'Alayhi al-Salam*, about the meaning of the words of Allah, most Blessed, most High, '. . . they swear by Allah in all earnestness that Allah will not raise again those who die. This is a true promise but most people do not know.' (16:41) He (the Imam) asked, 'What do you say about this verse?' I said that the pagans think and swear about the case of the Messenger of Allah, *O Allah grant compensation to Muhammad and his family worthy of their services to Your cause*, that Allah will not raise the dead. He (the Imam) said, 'May destruction fall on those who say so. Ask them, "Did the pagans swear by Allah or by al-Lat and al-'Uzza?"' I then said, 'I pray to Allah to keep my soul in service for your cause, enlighten me about it.' He (the Imam) said to me, 'O abu Basir, when our al-Qa'im (the one who rises with divine authority and power) will rise, Allah will raise a people of our followers. They will appear holding the hilt of their swords placed on their shoulders and a group of our followers who will be living will say, "So and so is raised from their graves and they are with al-Qa'im." The news will reach our enemies who will say. "O the community of Shi'ah, what kind of liars you are! You speak lies. It is your government and you speak lies. No, by Allah they did not live and will not live until the Day of Judgment." Allah has quoted them saying, ". . . they swear in all earnestness that Allah will not raise again those who die. This is a true promise but most people do not know."'"

About the words of Allah 'When they sensed the power of our anger. . .'

H 14463, h 15

Ali ibn Ibrahim has narrated from his father from ibn Faddal from Tha'labah' ibn Maymun from Badr ibn al-Khalil al-Asadiy who has narrated the following:

"I once heard abu Ja'far, *'Alayhi al-Salam*, speak about the meaning of the words of Allah, most Majestic, most Glorious, '. . . when they sensed Our power they began to run away. (They will be told) do not run but return to what you had enjoyed and your homes, perhaps you will be asked questions.' (21:13) He (the Imam) said, 'When al-Qa'im (the one who rises with divine authority and power) will rise and he will send for the Amawides in Syria, they will run away to Rome. The Romans will say to them, "We will not allow you until you convert to Christianity." They will hang crosses on their necks and allow them to enter. When the people of al-Qa'im will arrive, they will ask for amnesty and peace. The people of al-Qa'im will say, "We do not agree until you hand over to us those who are with you from us." They will hand them over and that is the meaning of His words, "Do not run but return to what you enjoyed and your home, perhaps you will be questioned."' He (the Imam) said, 'He will ask them about the treasures but he (the Imam) knows better.' He (the Imam) said that they would say, 'Woe is on us! We were unjust.' They will say it until we make them mowed down for good.'"

The letter of Abu Ja'far, *'Alayhi al-Salam*, to Sa'd al-Khayr

H 14464, h 16

Muhammad ibn Yahya has narrated from Muhammad ibn al-Husayn from Muhammad ibn 'Isma'il ibn Bazi' from his uncle Hamzah ibn Bazi' and al-Husayn ibn Muhammad al-Ash'ariy from Ahmad ibn Muhammad from ibn 'Abd Allah from Yazid ibn 'Abd Allah from the one who narrated to him who has narrated the following:

"Abu Ja'far, *'Alayhi al-Salam*, wrote to Sa'd al-Khayr:

"In the name of Allah, the Beneficent, the Merciful and thereafter, (commencing with the name of Allah) I advise you to remain pious before Allah; it is safety from loss and it is the good gain when returning to Allah, most Majestic, most Glorious. Piety is protection for a servant in whatever his reason leaves in oblivion. By means of piety his blindness and ignorance is made bright, by means of piety Noah, *'Alayhi al-Salam*, and those with him in the ark made it to safety, Salih, *'Alayhi al-Salam*, and those with him remained safe from the storm. By means of piety, the groups who exercised patience succeeded and remained safe from all the dangers and they have brothers in that path of seeking excellence. They have kept away from transgression and from indulging in desires because of that which has reached them from the book of lessons. They praise their Lord for what He has granted to them and He is the One who deserves all praise. They blamed their souls for the excess and they (souls dictating temptations) were the ones who deserved to be blamed. They took notice that Allah, most Blessed, most High, is forbearing, and all-knowing. He is angry only on those who do not accept what pleases Him and He withholds only from those who do not accept His favors. Only those who do not follow His guidance go astray. People of evil ways and sins are capable of turning to repentance and changing their evil deed to perform good deeds. He has called His servants in His book to this fact with a loud voice, has not cut it off, and has not prevented the call (prayer) of His servants.

"He has condemned those who hide what Allah has revealed and has made it obligatory on Himself to be merciful, His mercy comes before His anger, and it (His mercy) is complete in truth and justice. He does not begin when dealing with the servants with anger before they make Him angry and this is of knowledge in the form of certainty and knowledge of piety. Every nation from whom the knowledge of the book was taken away, it was only after they threw it behind their backs and made their enemy to rule them; only after they had taken those (enemies) as their friends. Of their throwing the book behind their backs was that they kept its letters and changed its limits (laws), thus they narrated it but did not practice its rules. The ignorant ones like their preserving the narration and the scholars become sad for their neglecting proper maintenance. Of the matters they have thrown of the book behind their backs is that people who do not have sufficient knowledge rule them and they take them where their desire leads and then take them out to ruination. They change the strongholds of religion, then leave it as legacy in dimwittedness and childish manner. The nation follows the command of people, instead of the command of Allah, most Blessed, most High, which is otherwise, and by their command, they are ruled. It indeed is an evil exchange by the unjust, the exchange of *Wilayah* (authority and power) of people in place of the *Wilayah* (authority and power) of Allah, the reward from people instead of (guarantee of) reward from Allah, the pleasure of people instead of the pleasure of Allah. This is how the nations have begun to live when among them there are hardworking ones in worship, in such condition of misguidance, attracted and deceived. Their worship is a mischief for them and those who follow them, when in the messengers there was a reminder for the worshippers. One of the Prophets who was perfectly obedient then only in one case disobeyed Allah, most Blessed, most High, he was then taken out of the garden (paradise), thrown in the belly of the fish and He did not save him until he repented and acknowledged. You must take notice that there are people similar to al-Ahbar and al-Ruhban who continued denying the book and forged, their trade did not gain and they did not find guidance. You must take notice of similar people in this nation who keep the letters of the book but change its limits (laws). They are with the great masters and when the leaders of desires scatter, they remain with those who possess more of the worldly things and this is how much knowledge they possess. They continue in such nature and greed, and the voice of Satan is heard through their tongue with falsehood a great deal. The scholars exercise patience in the harm they suffer from them and in violence but they blame and scold the scholars for burdening them. The scholars themselves are disloyal if they hide the good advice when they see a lost and misled one and do not guide him or a dead person without reviving him. How evil is what they do! Allah, most Blessed, most High, has made a covenant with them in the book that they must command people to do the good and prohibit them from committing sins and to cooperate with each other in pious and virtuous matters but not in sin and in animosity. The scholars suffer because of the ignorant ones and they struggle. If they (scholars) give good advice, they (people) say that they have transgressed and if they learn the truth, which they have left, they say that they have opposed and if they remain aside, they say that they (scholars) have departed the nation. If they ask to present proof in support of what they say, they say that they have become hypocrites and if they obey them they say that Allah, most Majestic, most Glorious, is disobeyed. The ignorant ones are destroyed in what they do not know; they are unlettered in what they read. They acknowledge the book when it is defined and they reject it (book) when it is changed (they accepted the changed one and reject the original), thus they do not reject it (the change). They are similar to al-Ahbar and al-Ruhban, leaders in matters of desires and masters in ruination and others of them are sitting between misguidance and guidance. They do not distinguish one from the other. They say that people did not know this and did know what it was. They say the right thing. The Messenger of Allah, *O Allah grant compensation to Muhammad and his family worthy of their services to Your cause*, left them on a clean and bright path (Shari'ah) in its night and its day. No heresy had appeared and no *Sunnah* was changed. There were no differences among them, but when people moved into the darkness of sins they became two Imams, one calling to Allah, most Blessed, most High, and one calling to the fire. At that time Satan spoke and raised his voice through the tongues of his friends, his horsemen became many as well as his foot soldiers, he shared them in assets and children and those who shared him acted in heresy, neglected the book and *Sunnah*. The friends of Allah spoke with authority and followed the book with wisdom. From that day, the people of truth became different from the people of falsehood and the people of guidance were betrayed and insulted. The people of misguidance cooperated with each other until they became a group with so and so and people similar to him. You must take notice of this kind and the other kind and look at them with the eyes of noble ones and remain firm with them until you arrive among your people. The losers lose their souls and people on the Day of Judgment and that indeed is a clear failure.

"This much is the narration of al-Husayn. In the narration of Muhammad ibn Yahya, there is an addition: 'They (people of truth) know the path. If there is suffering, do not hold it against them. If near them there is inequity because of the unfair ones, humiliation among them and suffering which ends, they will live in ease. You must take notice that trustworthy ones are brothers and the savings for each other. Had it not been because of the concern that surmising and guessing may take you away from me I would clarify for you certain things about the truth, which I have covered, and I would make public certain matters of the truth that I have kept hidden but I protect you and want you to live. One who does not observe caution to protect someone is not forbearing, when it is the condition to observe caution. Forbearance is the garment of the scholar, so you must not remain naked of such garment. With Salam.'"

Another letter to him from him (the Imam) also

H 14465, h 17

Muhammad ibn Yahya has narrated from Muhammad ibn al-Husayn from Muhammad ibn 'Isma'il ibn Bazi' from his uncle Hamzah ibn Bazi' who has narrated the following:

Abu Ja'far, *'Alayhi al-Salam*, wrote to Sa'd al-Khayr:

"In the name of Allah, the Beneficent, the Merciful and thereafter, I have received your letter in which you have mentioned about how much is obligatory to learn and obedience to the one whose happiness is the happiness of Allah. You then said to yourself that your soul is not held responsible if you ignored it. You are amazed about the fact that the happiness of Allah, obedience to Him and His advice are not accepted, found and recognized except in neglected people. The people who are away from people and people take them in ridicule because of what they ascribe to them of detestable matters so much so that it was said that a believing person is not a believing person unless he is the most hated among people like the carrion of a donkey. If you face the kind of suffering which we have faced then you must not consider the mischief caused by people like the suffering made by Allah – I ask Allah to protect you and us from such things – then you would near your destination even though it is a long distance.

"You must take notice, may Allah grant you mercy that the love of Allah cannot be achieved except by hating many people (their deeds). In addition, *Wilayah* (authority and power) of Allah cannot be achieved except by animosity toward many people, losing it (friendship with such people) is insignificant compared to gaining that (*Wilayah*) from Allah to the people of knowledge.

"O brother, Allah, most Majestic, most Glorious, has kept for every messenger a remainder (successor) of the people of knowledge who guide from misguidance to guidance and bear patience with them in suffering, who answer the call of Allah and call to Allah. You must look to find them, may Allah grant you mercy, because they are in a high position even though in the world it may seem low. They give life to the dead by the book of Allah, they see by the light of Allah in dark conditions. How many are the dead because of Satan whom they (people of knowledge) have given life again and how many are the lost ones whom they have guided. They sacrifice their lives to save the servants (of Allah) and how good is its effect on the servants (of Allah) and how bad the effects (unjust manners) of people are on them.'"

'Amir al-Mu'minin, *'Alayhi al-Salam*, was similar to Jesus, *'Alayhi al-Salam*

H 14466, h 18
A number of our people have narrated from Sahl ibn Ziyad from Muhammad ibn Sulayman from his father from abu Basir who has narrated the following:

"He (the Imam), *'Alayhi al-Salam*, has said that one day the Messenger of Allah, *O Allah grant compensation to Muhammad and his family worthy of their services to Your cause*, was sitting when 'Amir al-Mu'minin, Ali, *'Alayhi al-Salam*, came. The Messenger of Allah, *O Allah grant compensation to Muhammad and his family worthy of their services to Your cause*, said, 'You are similar to Jesus son of Mary. Was I not afraid of certain people's saying about you what the Christians said about Jesus son of Mary I would have said it about you and people would then strive to take the dust from under your feet to seek blessings thereby.' He (the Imam) said that two Arabs and al-Mughirah ibn Shu'bah became angry as well as a number of people of Quraysh along with them and they said, 'He did not become satisfied until he gave an example of Jesus for the son of his uncle.' Allah then sent this to His Holy Prophet, '. . . when the son of Mary is mentioned as an example, a group of your people

46

blocks it. They say, "Are our gods better or he is better? They mention it only to dispute with you; they are a quarrelsome hostile people. He was our servant to whom We granted bounties and made an example for the Israelites. Had we wanted, We would have made from you (banu Hashim) angels on earth as successors." (43:57-60) He (the Imam) said that al-Harith ibn 'Amr al-Fihriy became angry and said, 'O Allah, if this is truly from You that banu Hashim will inherit Heraclius after Heraclius then rain down on us stones from the sky or bring on us painful torment.' Allah then sent to him (the Messenger of Allah) the quotation from al-Harith and this verse was revealed. 'Allah does not want to punish them when you are among them and Allah does not punish them when they ask forgiveness.' (8:33) He (the Messenger of Allah) then said, 'O ibn 'Amr you must repent or leave.' He then said, 'O Muhammad, you must leave something for Quraysh of what is in your hand because banu Hashim has taken away the honor of Arabs and non-Arabs.' The Messenger of Allah, *O Allah grant compensation to Muhammad and his family worthy of their services to Your cause*, said, 'That is not up to me, it is up to Allah, most Blessed, most High.' He then said, 'O Muhammad, my heart does not follow me to repent but I would rather leave you. He then asked for his stumper and mounted it and when he arrived behind al-Madinah, a stone fell on him and crushed his skull, then revelation came to the Holy Prophet that said, 'Someone asked for torment to take place. For the unbelievers [in *Wilayah* (divine authority and power) of Ali, *'Alayhi al-Salam*] there is no protector from Allah, most Glorious.' (70:1-3) I (the narrator) then said, 'I pray to Allah to keep my soul in service for your cause, we do not read it as such.' He (the Imam) said, 'This is how, by Allah, Jibril had brought it to Muhammad, *O Allah grant compensation to Muhammad and his family worthy of their services to Your cause*, and this is how it is in Mushaf of Fatimah, *'Alayha al-Salam*.' The Messenger of Allah, *O Allah grant compensation to Muhammad and his family worthy of their services to Your cause*, then told them, 'Go to see your fellow. What he asked for has approached him and Allah, most Majestic, most Glorious, has said, 'They asked for it and all despotic hostile ones have failed.'" (14:15)

About the words of Allah 'Mischief has spread over the land. . .'

H 14467, h 19

Muhammad ibn Yahya has narrated from Muhammad ibn al-Husayn, from Ali ibn al-Nu'man from ibn Muskan from Muhammad ibn Muslim who has narrated the following:

"About the meaning of the words of Allah, most Majestic, most Glorious, 'Evil has spread over the land and the sea because of human...' (30:41) abu Ja'far, *'Alayhi al-Salam*, has said, 'This by Allah, happened when al-Ansar (people of al-Madinah) said, 'Allow us to have our own commander and you will have your own commander.'"

About the words of Allah '. . . Do not spread mischief in the land. . .'

H 14468, h 20

It is narrated from the narrator of the previous Hadith from Muhammad ibn Ali from ibn Muskan from Muyassir who has narrated the following:

"I once asked abu Ja'far, *'Alayhi al-Salam*, about the meaning of the words of Allah, most Majestic, most Glorious, '. . . do not spread destruction in the land after that it has been reformed.' (7:56) He (the Imam) said, 'O Muyassir, the land was ruined and Allah, most Majestic, most Glorious, brought reform in it through His Prophet, *O Allah grant compensation to Muhammad and his family worthy of their services to Your cause*, then He said, '. . . do not spread destruction in the land after that it has been reformed.'"

The Sermon of 'Amir al-Mu'minin, Ali, *'Alayhi al-Salam*

H 14469, h 21

Ali ibn Ibrahim has narrated from his father from Hammad ibn 'Isa from 'Uthman from Sulaym ibn Qays al-Hilaliy who has narrated the following:

"'Amir al-Mu'minin, Ali, *'Alayhi al-Salam*, once delivered this sermon. He (the Imam) praised Allah and spoke of His glory then asked, *'O Allah grant compensation to Muhammad and his family worthy of their services to Your cause*, then said, 'What I fear for you the most are two characteristics: following desires and long term worldly hopes. Following desires blocks one from the truth and long term worldly hope makes one to forget the hereafter. This world has moved backward and the hereafter has moved coming forward but sons of both worlds are the same. You therefore must become of the sons of the hereafter and you must not become of the sons of this world. Today is work without reward and tomorrow there will be accounting and no work.

"Commencement of mischief comes from the desires which are followed, and rules invented by which the rules of Allah are opposed. In this way, people take other people as their guardian. Had truth been pure no difference would take place. Had falsehood been pure there would have been no fear about people of reason. Certain amount is taken from this and certain amount is taken from that, then they are mixed. Here is where Satan dominates his friends but those about whom goodness from Allah has happened remain protected. I heard the Messenger of Allah, *O Allah grant compensation to Muhammad and his family worthy of their services to Your cause*, say, 'How will you behave when mischief will become your garment in which the small ones will grow up and the grown up become old? People will live in it and take it as a *Sunnah*. An evil thing comes on people, then the affliction becomes stronger. The offspring become captives and mischief will batter them just as fire batters firewood or just as grinding stones rub against each other. They learn fiqh (law of Shari'ah) but not for the sake of Allah and gain knowledge but not for good deeds and they seek the worldly gains by the deeds for the hereafter.'

"He then turned around to people of his family and the special ones of the Shi'ah. He (the Imam) said, 'The rulers before me acted as such that their actions were against the Messenger of Allah, *O Allah grant compensation to Muhammad and his family worthy of their services to Your cause*, willingly to oppose him (the Messenger of Allah), disregarding their covenant with him and changed his *Sunnah*. If I make people to abandon such acts and change their places as originally they were in the time of the Messenger of Allah, *O Allah grant compensation to Muhammad and his family worthy of their services to Your cause*, my army will scatter away from me. I will be left alone or just with a few of my Shi'ah who have acknowledged my virtue and excellence. Following my *Imamat* (leadership with divine authority and power) is obligatory because of the book of Allah, most Majestic, most Glorious, and the *Sunnah* of the Messenger of Allah, *O Allah grant compensation to Muhammad and his family worthy of their services to Your cause*.

"Consider, what will happen if I command to place the station of Ibrahim back where it was placed by the Messenger of Allah, *O Allah grant compensation to Muhammad and his family worthy of their services to Your cause*, returned Fadak (the gardens and land) to the heirs of Fatimah, *'Alayha al-Salam*. What will happen if I bring back the Sa' of the Messenger of Allah, *O Allah grant compensation to Muhammad and his family worthy of their services to Your cause*? What will happen if I approve treaties and contracts that the Messenger of Allah, *O Allah grant compensation to Muhammad and his family worthy of their services to Your cause*, had made with certain people but were not approved and executed? If I return the house of Ja'far to his heirs, break it away from the Masjid, reverse certain unjust judgments in certain cases, separate certain women who are under certain men without right and return them to their husbands and turn around the rules about it in matters of matrimony and relatives? What will happen if I make it lawful to take the offspring of banu Taghlib as captives, return the land of Khaybar, which was distributed, delete the list of gifts to be given to certain people? What will happen if I make the distribution of grants as it was in the time of the Messenger of Allah, *O Allah grant compensation to Muhammad and his family worthy of their services to Your cause*, in equal portions? What will happen if I do not allow it to become the wealth and government of the rich, drop the al-Musahah (a certain unit of measurement) of currency, make the system of marriage to take place in equitable manner? What will happen if I enforce the one-fifth (*khums*, tax due on net savings) of the Messenger as Allah, most Majestic, most Glorious, has made obligatory, return the Masjid of the Messenger of Allah, *O Allah grant compensation to Muhammad and his family worthy of their services to Your cause*, as it was? What will happen if I close the doors opened to it and open whatever is closed, make wiping on *al-khuff* (shoe) unlawful, execute the penalty for drinking *al-Nabidh* (a certain kind of wine)? What will happen if I command to consider the two *al-Mut'ah* (advantages) lawful, command to say five *Takbir* (Allah is great beyond description) in *Salat* (prayer) for the dead people, make people to recite the phrase, 'In the name of Allah, the Beneficent, the Merciful' aloud? What will happen if I take out those who are placed with the Messenger of Allah, *O Allah grant compensation to Muhammad and his family worthy of their services to Your cause*, in his Masjid? What will happen if I place therein whatever the Messenger of Allah, *O Allah grant compensation to Muhammad and his family worthy of their services to Your cause*, had placed there? What will happen if I make people to follow al-Quran and in matters of divorce according to *Sunnah*, distribute charity on its recipients and limits? What will happen if I return the manner of wudu and Ghusl (bath) and *Salat* (prayer) to their timings, common ground and places, and return people of Najran to their places? What will happen if I return the captives from Persia and other nations to the book of Allah and the *Sunnah* of His Holy Prophet, *O Allah grant compensation to Muhammad and his family worthy of their services to Your cause*? If I do such things, they scatter away from me. By Allah, I commanded people not to come together in the month of Ramadan except for obligatory *Salat* (prayer) and informed them that their congregation in optional *Salat* (prayer) is heresy, then certain ones of my army who fought against our enemy with me called, "O people of Islam, the *Sunnah* of 'Umar is changed. He prohibits us from *Salat* (prayer) in the month of Ramadan as optional *Salat* (prayer)." I became afraid of their revolting in a corner of my army because of what I have faced from this nation of sectarian issues due to following the *'A'immah* of misguidance and those calling to the fire. If I pay the share of the relatives about which Allah, most Majestic, most Glorious, has said, '. . . if you believe in Allah and what We have revealed to our servant on the day of distinction and on the day the two armies met.' (8:41) *Dhil qurba* (relatives) by Allah applies to us, which Allah has mentioned very close to His self and with the Messenger of Allah, *O Allah grant compensation to Muhammad and his family worthy of their services to Your cause*. He has said, '. . . for Allah, for the messenger, for the relatives, and the orphans, the destitute, those who remain on the road without supplies, [is especially about us] so that it does not become the wealth of the rich among you. What the messenger brings to you, you must follow and what he prohibits then desist thereof, have fear of Allah, [in being unjust to the family of Muhammad] Allah is firm in executing penalty', (59:7) against those who do injustice to them. It is because of His kindness to us and His granting to us self-sufficiency. He gave such commandment to His Holy Prophet, *O Allah grant compensation to Muhammad and his family worthy of their services to Your cause*. He did not designate anything in charity for us as an honor for the Messenger of Allah, and as an honor to *Ahl al-Bayt* instead of feeding us from the filth of the hands of people. They rejected Allah and His Messenger, denied the book of Allah which speaks in our favor and they refused to give us our rights which Allah had made obligatory. If they had not done what they did, the family of the Holy Prophet, would not face from his followers and what we faced after our Holy Prophet, but Allah is (our) supporter against their injustice to us, there is no means and no power without the power of Allah, most High, most Great."

A Sermon of 'Amir al-Mu'minin, Ali, *'Alayhi al-Salam*

H 14470, h 22

Ahmad ibn Muhammad al-Kufiy has narrated from Ja'far ibn 'Abd Allah al-Muhammadiy from abu Ruh, Fraj ibn Qurrah from Ja'far ibn 'Abd Allah from Mas'adah ibn Sadaqah who has narrated the following:

"Once 'Amir al-Mu'minin, Ali, *'Alayhi al-Salam*, addressed people in al-Madinah, praised Allah, spoke of His glory. He (the Imam) asked Allah to grant compensation to Muhammad and his family worthy of their services to His cause, then said, 'Thereafter, Allah, most Blessed, most High, did not crush the backs of the tyrants except only after sufficient respite to them and ease. He did not mend the broken bones of any nation except only after its suffering hardships and misfortune. O people, with every damaging matter that you faced and with every mishap whereby you suffered a setback, there is a lesson, but not everyone with a heart is intelligent, not everyone who has an ear listens, not everyone who has an eye sees.

'O servants of Allah, you must pay proper attention to what is important to you. Thereafter look at what is left of the dominions, the open land of those whom Allah through His knowledge subjected to equitable retaliation who followed the traditions of the pharaohs, people who possessed gardens, fountains, farms and gracious dwellings, then look at how Allah brought them to their end after their enjoying delightfulness and pleasure, commands and prohibition.

'For those of you who bear patience there is the end in the garden (paradise) of Allah to live in forever. In the hand of Allah indeed is the end of all things. It is astonishing and why should I not be astonished by the mistakes of these groups with all of their arguments in favor of their religion without maintaining the traditions of any Prophet or following in the footsteps of the executor of the will or believing in an unseen. They do not forgive any shortcoming. Fairness to them is what they know, prohibited for them is what they dislike. Every one of them is his own Imam (leader). They (these groups) hold firm to what they know of it (their religion as such) by their firm grips and strong means. They continue with injustice and do not increase in anything except wrong, do not gain any nearness and do not add to anything except in farness from Allah, most Majestic, most Glorious. They are comfortable with each other and acknowledge each other. It is all because of their fear from the legacy of the *'Ummiy* Prophet, *O Allah grant compensation to Muhammad and his family worthy of their services to Your cause*. It is because of their dislike of the news and information given by the Originator of the skies and earth regarding the case of the people who regret for (what they have done). It is because of the news about the people who are like caves of doubts, people of desires, of straying and doubts of those whom Allah has left to their own souls and desires. Those who are ignorant about him trust him and those who do not know him do not accuse him. How similar are they with the animals from which the shepherd is absent!

'How regrettable are the deeds of my Shi'ah after me even after the nearness of their love today? How they will humiliate each other after me and how they will kill each other, in a scattered condition tomorrow, despite their being from one origin with the branch, with hope to find victory from a direction that is not its direction. Every party holds to a branch thereof. Wherever the branch leans, they lean in the same direction. This will be the case along with the fact that Allah, to Whom belongs all praise, will gather them together for the worst day for banu 'Umayyah as they will be like scattered pieces of clouds in a fall day.

'Allah will place harmony among them then condense them as condensed clouds, thereafter will open them as flood gates upon the main source of their power (power of banu 'Umayyah) like the flood of the two gardens, which were hit, by the roaring flood that was because of the damage caused by efforts of a mouse. Thus, the hill could not withstand it (the flood) and its paths could not compensate for the damage of the rocks that were made to roll down the valleys. Thereafter made them to move in the land as fountains, restoring thereby the rights of a people and gave domination through them to a people over the lands of a people to expel and banish banu 'Umayyah thereof so that they would not usurp what they had usurped.

'Allah shook through them a pillar, threw them (banu 'Umayyah) through them (banu al-'Abbas) with the boulders of Eram, and filled with them the valleys of olives.

'I swear by the One who opens the seed and carves the fetus into shape this will indeed happen. It is as if I hear the whinnying of their horses and the humming of their men. I swear by Allah that what is in their hand, after their rise and domination over the lands will melt like the melting of a piece of fat over the fire. Those who die of them will die as lost and to Allah, most Majestic, most Glorious, will be left those of them who return and those of them who will repent before Allah, most Majestic, most Glorious. Perhaps Allah will bring together my Shi'ah after being scattered in a day which will be the worst day for them but no one has a choice before Allah, most Glorious is Whose name and Allah is the One Who has the command and choices all together.

'O people, those who undertake the task of an Imam (leader) but are not proper for it are many. If you do not accept a defeat due to the straightforwardness of the truth and do not languish by the weak and sapping falsehood, the ones who are not like you will not dare against you. Those who show you power will not be able to overpower you to achieve unjust obedience and remove it from those who are rightful in it. However, you are lost as the Israelites did in the time of Musa [son of 'Imran]. By my life, your wandering will increase after me in multiples of the wandering of the Israelites. By my life, if you after me will complete the duration of the domination of banu 'Umayyah you will come together around a ruler who calls to misguidance. You will revive falsehood and leave the truth behind your backs, cut off good relations with the near ones of the people of Badr and maintain good relations with the far away people of the sons of warriors against the Messenger of Allah, *O Allah grant compensation to Muhammad and his family worthy of their services to Your cause.* I swear by my life, when what is in their hands will melt away, purifying for the reward will draw closer. The appointed time will reach nearby, the duration will complete, the appearance of two-tailed-star from the east will take place. The bright moon will shine for you: at such time you must repent and you must take notice that if you will follow the one rising from the east, he will make you to follow the path of the Messenger of Allah, *O Allah grant compensation to Muhammad and his family worthy of their services to Your cause.* You will then find a cure for blindness, for deafness, speechlessness, and you will be made self-sufficient again with justice restored and you will cast aside the heavy, the backbreaking burden from your necks. Allah is not far away except from those who refuse and act unjustly and unfairly and take what does not belong to them. '. . . The unjust ones will soon take notice of the kind of destination to which they are returned.'" (26:227)

A Sermon of 'Amir al-Mu'minin, Ali, *'Alayhi al-Salam*

H 14471, h 23
Ali ibn Ibrahim has narrated from his father from ibn Mahbub from ibn Ri'ab and answer ibn al-Sarraj who has narrated the following:

"Abu 'Abd Allah, *'Alayhi al-Salam*, has said that 'Amir al-Mu'minin, Ali, *'Alayhi al-Salam*, when people pledged allegiance to him after the death of 'Uthman, climbed on the pulpit and said, 'All praise belongs to Allah who is high thus He took possession, He is near thus He is exalted. He has risen above all things that can be seen. I testify that only Allah deserves worship, He is One and has no partners and I testify that Muhammad is His servant and Messenger, the seal of the Prophets, the authority of Allah over the worlds. He confirmed the truthfulness of the messengers of the past, who was kind and merciful to the believing people, thus Allah and the angels said, 'O Allah grant compensation to Muhammad and his family worthy of their services to Your cause.'

'Thereafter, O people, you must take notice that transgression (indecency) drives the transgressors to the fire. The first one who transgressed (committed indecency) against Allah, glorious is Whose name was 'Unaq, daughter of Adam, *'Alayhi al-Salam*, and the first one whom Allah killed was 'Unaq. The place that she occupied when sitting on the ground measured one square Jarib (about one acre of land). She had twenty fingers with two fingernails on each finger like two sickles. Allah, most Majestic, most Glorious, sent on her a lion of the size of an elephant and a wolf of the size of a camel and a vulture of the size of a mule who killed her.

'Allah had killed the tyrants in their best conditions and granted safety to those who existed. He made Haman to die, destroyed the pharaohs and He killed 'Uthman. Your misfortune has come back in the same shape as it was on the day Allah sent His Holy Prophet, *O Allah grant compensation to Muhammad and his family worthy of their services to Your cause.* By the One who sent him (the

Messenger of Allah) in all truth, you will face strong turmoil and will be sifted thoroughly, stirred and turned as the contents of a cooking pan until your upper side is turned into your underside. Certain ones who had shortcomings will become the forerunners and certain ones who were forerunners will become of people with shortcomings.

'By Allah, I have not kept hidden any word and have not spoken any lies. I was foretold about this very position and this day. Sins are recalcitrant horses, which carry its people with their harness left loose to plunge with them in the fire. Piety certainly is a gentle transporting means that carries its people with its rein left alone and takes them to the garden (paradise). Its doors will open wide and they will sense its fragrance and goodness and it will be said to them, '. . . you can enter the garden (paradise) in peace and safety.

'People whom I do not consider qualified had advanced to possess this issue, the position of (*Wilayah*, leadership with divine authority and power). I did not give it to them because of their having no chance in it unless being a Prophet sent as such, when, in fact, there is no Prophet after Muhammad, *O Allah grant compensation to Muhammad and his family worthy of their services to Your cause.* He stood because of taking over the post of (*Wilayah*, leadership with divine authority and power) at the nearly crumbling brink of the fire. It falls right into the hellfire. There is truth and falsehood each with its people. The issue of falsehood existed from the ancient times and it was active. If truth is less (obeyed) it is because of 'if' and 'perhaps'.

'It is very rare that things turning back can come forward. If your government is returned to you, you are fortunate and I will try as best as I can. I am afraid that after a while, you will not have your enthusiasm with me whereby you will not be praiseworthy in your opinion before me and if I like I can say, 'Allah forgives the past.' Two men advanced for this issue post of (*Wilayah*, leadership with divine authority and power) and stood for it, the third like a crow whose ambitions were centered on its belly. Woe upon it, it would have been better if its (crow's) wings would have been trimmed and its head cut off. It is held back from the garden (paradise) and the fire is in front of it. Three and two equal to five and there is not a sixth (kinds of responsible creatures). (1) An angel flies with his wing and (2) a Prophet whose both shoulders receive support from Allah. There is (3) one striving and hardworking, (4) a seeker with hopes and (5) an intentionally falling-short person who is in the fire. The right and left are misguidance and the middle of the way path is the path upon which the book and the traditions of the Prophet have come. Destroyed is one who claims (something without right) and failing is one who fabricates against the truth. Allah has disciplined this nation with the sword and whip and there is no choice left for the Imam (leader) other than to execute (the law). You must remain covered in your homes, mend your relations among yourselves, repentance is behind you and one who exposes his cheek (opposes) to the truth is destroyed.' "

Hadith of Ali ibn al-Husayn, *'Alayhi al-Salam*

H 14472, h 24

Muhammad ibn Yahya has narrated from Ahmad ibn Muhammad ibn 'Isa fm al-Hassan ibn Mahbub from Hilal ibn 'Atiyyah from abu Hamzah who has narrated the following:

"He (the Imam), *'Alayhi al-Salam*, would say, 'The most beloved among you in the sight of Allah, most Majestic, most Glorious, is one who has the best deeds and the most great among you in the sight of Allah is the one with the greatest degree of interest in what is with Allah. The one among you who is most protected against suffering from Allah is the one who is the most anxious toward Allah. The nearest among you to Allah is one with the vastest degree of good moral discipline and the one with whom Allah is most pleased is one who provides the greatest degree of comfort for his family and most excellent among you in the sight of Allah is the most pious one among you.'"

Signs of the coming of the end of the world

H 14473, h 25

Muhamily from 'Abd Allah ibn Sulayman who has narrated the following:

"Abu 'Abd Allah, *'Alayhi al-Salam*, has said that 'Amir al-Mu'minin, Ali, *'Alayhi al-Salam*, has said, 'A time will come upon people when the most sinful is considered most graceful, nearness is sought with the most shameless ones and people of fairness are weakened.' He (the Imam) said that he (the Imam) was asked, 'When such things will happen O 'Amir al-Mu'minin?' He (the Imam) said, 'It will happen when trust is considered a gain, *Zakat* is considered a loss, worship a means of domination and good relation with relatives a favor.' He (the Imam) then was asked, 'When such things will happen, O 'Amir al-Mu'minin?' He (the Imam) said, 'It will take place when women will become dominant, slave-girls rule and children command.'"

Dealings of 'Amir al-Mu'minin, *'Alayhi al-Salam*, equitably among muslims

H 14474, h 26

'Uqbq' in a marfu' manner who has narrated the following:

"Once 'Amir al-Mu'minin, Ali, *'Alayhi al-Salam*, gave a sermon. He praised Allah and spoke of His glory and then said, 'O people, Adam, *'Alayhi al-Salam*, did not give birth to slaves and slave-girls. All people are free; however, He has made you as each other's friends. If one has a certain misfortune and bears patience in good manners, he must not consider it a favor to Allah, most Majestic, most Glorious. There is something in which we are all equal, black or red.' Marwan then said to Talhah and al-Zubayr, 'He has not meant thereby anyone other than you.' He (the narrator) has said that to each one of them he (the Imam) gave three dinars, to a man from al-Ansar (people of al-Madinah) he gave three dinars and thereafter to a black slave he gave three dinars. The man from al-Ansar (people of al-Madinah) said, 'O 'Amir al-Mu'minin, this is a slave whom I freed yesterday, and you consider both of us equal.' He (the

Imam) said, 'I looked in the book of Allah and did not find the sons of 'Isma'il to be more excellent than the sons of Ishaq.'"

Hadith of the Holy Prophet, *O Allah grant compensation to Muhammad and his family worthy of their services to Your cause*, when horses were presented before him

H 14475, h 27

Abu Ali al-Ash'ariy has narrated from Muhammad ibn Salim and Ali ibn Ibrahim has narrated from his father all from Ahmad ibn al-Nadr and Muhammad ibn Yahya from Muhammad ibn abu al-Qasim from al-Husayn ibn abu Qatadah all from ibn Muhammad from 'Amr ibn Shimr from Jabir who has narrated the following:

"Once the Messenger of Allah, *O Allah grant compensation to Muhammad and his family worthy of their services to Your cause*, came out to examine the horses and he passed by the grave of abu 'Uhayhah. Abu Bakr said, 'Allah has condemned the person in this grave. By Allah he would block the path to Allah and reject the Messenger of Allah, *O Allah grant compensation to Muhammad and his family worthy of their services to Your cause.*' Khalid his son then said, 'Allah has condemned abu Quhafah because he would not serve any guest or fight the enemy. Thus Allah condemns that one of them who is more worthless to the tribe.' The Messenger of Allah, *O Allah grant compensation to Muhammad and his family worthy of their services to Your cause*, placed the rein of his stumper on its neck and said, 'When you take on the pagans you must speak of them in general and do not speak of anyone of them in particular to anger his son.' The horses were presented before him (the Messenger of Allah) and when one horse passed by 'Uyaynah ibn Hesn said, 'This horse had such and such stories.' The Messenger of Allah, *O Allah grant compensation to Muhammad and his family worthy of their services to Your cause*, said, 'Hold it, I know more about horses than you do.' 'Uyaynah said, 'I know more about man than you do.' The Messenger of Allah, *O Allah grant compensation to Muhammad and his family worthy of their services to Your cause*, became angry so much so that his face turned red. He (the Messenger of Allah) then asked, 'Which man is more excellent?' 'Uyaynah ibn Hesn replied, 'Men of Najd who place their swords on their shoulders and their spears on the saddle of their horses then march with them step by step.'

"The Messenger of Allah, *O Allah grant compensation to Muhammad and his family worthy of their services to Your cause*, said, 'You have spoken a lie. In fact, men of Yemen are excellent. Belief is in Yemen and wisdom is in Yemen. Had it not been because of Hijrah I would have been of the people of Yemen. Injustice and hardheartedness is found in people being loud, the people of wool, Rabi'ah and Mudar and from the place the horn of the sun appears, and Mudhaj who more than others enter in the garden (paradise). Hadramut is better than 'Amir ibn Sa'sa'ah – others have narrated, 'better than al-Harith ibn Mu'awiyah – and Bajaliyah is better than Ri'al and Dhakwan. If Lihyan is destroyed I would not mind.' He (the Messenger of Allah) then said, 'Allah has condemned the four kings, Jamad, Makhwas, Mashrah, Abda'ah and 'Ukhtam al-'Amradah.

Allah has condemned al-Muhalil (one who legalizes woman for her previous husband after three divorces). He has condemned one for whom she is made lawful, one who finds a guardian other than his guardians and one who claims ancestors who are not known. He has condemned men who want to be similar to women, women who want to be similar to men, one who creates a heresy in Islam or accommodates a heretic. He has condemned one who kills someone other than his killer or beats up someone other than the one who has beaten him and one who condemns his parents.' A man then said, 'O Messenger of Allah, is there anyone who would condemn his parents?' He (the Messenger of Allah) replied, 'Yes, those who condemn the fathers of men and their mothers they then condemn his parents. Allah has condemned, Ri'al, Dhakwan, 'Adl, Lihyan, al-Mujdhamin of Asad, Ghatafan, abu Sufyan ibn Harb, Shahbala al-Asnan, two sons of Malikah ibn Jazim, Marwan, Hawdhah and Hawnah.'"

Advice of 'Amir al-Mu'minin, *'Alayhi al-Salam,* to his servant

H 14476, h 28

Ali ibn Ibrahim has narrated from Muhammad ibn 'Isa from Yunus from certain persons of his people who has narrated the following:

"Abu 'Abd Allah, *'Alayhi al-Salam,* has said that once one of the *Mawla* (slave) of 'Amir al-Mu'minin, Ali, *'Alayhi al-Salam,* asked him for a certain amount of assets. He (the Imam) said, 'When my share comes I will share it with you.' He said, 'That is not enough.' He left for Sham to see Mu'awiyah who gave him (what he wanted). He then wrote to 'Amir al-Mu'minin, Ali, *'Alayhi al-Salam,* informing him about the asset that he had received. 'Amir al-Mu'minin, Ali, wrote back to him and said, 'Thereafter, whatever asset is in your hand had owners before you and it will move to its owners after you. Your share in it is what you can prepare for the next life, so you must give preference to the well-being of yourself before the well-being of your children. What you collect is for one of the two kinds of men. One is a man who works with it in obedience to Allah so he becomes fortunate with something, which has given you misfortune, or he is a man who works with it in disobedience to Allah. He becomes unfortunate by what you collected for him and no one of these deserve your giving preference over your own self, therefore, you must not place a burden on your back. You must have hope in the mercy of Allah about the past and trust in the remaining of sustenance of Allah.' "

A speech of Ali ibn al-Husayn, *'Alayhi al-Salam*

H 14477, h 29

Narrated to me Muhammad ibn Yahya has narrated from Ahmad ibn Muhammad ibn 'Isa from his father from al-Hassan ibn Mahbub from 'Abd Allah ibn Ghalib al-Asadiy from his father from Sa'id ibn al-Musayyib who has narrated the following:

"Ali ibn al-Husayn, *'Alayhi al-Salam,* would speak to give good advice to people and about maintaining restraint from sins in this world, encourage them to become interested in good deeds for the next life. He (the Imam) gave such speeches every Friday in the Masjid of the Messenger of Allah, *O Allah grant compensation to Muhammad and his family worthy of their services to Your cause*, which then were preserved and written down. He (the Imam), would say, 'O people, you must remain pious before Allah and take notice that you will all return to Him. Every soul will then find whatever it has done in this world in the form of available good deeds or the evil and bad ones. He will find them even if a long time may have passed. Allah warns you about His self.

"Woe is on you O sons of Adam who are neglectful about themselves but are not neglected. O sons of Adam, the approaching of the time of your death is the fastest thing moving toward you and is moving to you quietly to seek you. It may approach you very soon when your lifespan is complete, when the angel of death will take your spirit away from your body and you are moved to your grave where you will remain alone; then your spirit is returned to you. Two angels called Na'kir and Nakir will enter on you to ask you questions and severely test you. The first thing they will ask will be about your Lord whom you worshipped, about your Prophet who was sent to you, about your religion by which you lived, about your book which you would recite and about your Imam whom you loved. They then will ask you for what you spent your life, about your assets, about how you earned them and on what you spent them. You must remain cautious, think about yourself and prepare the answer before the examination, questioning and test. If you are a believing and knowledgeable person in your religion, following the truthful ones, loving the friends of Allah, Allah will dictate to you your argument, make your tongue to speak right, your answer will be good and you will receive good news of happiness and the garden (paradise) from Allah, most Majestic, most Glorious. The angels will say welcome to you with the joyful spirits. If you will not be as such, your tongue will stutter, your argument will fail and you remain unable to answer, you will receive the news about the fire and the angel of torment will come before you to take you for a descent to the heat and feeling the heat of hell.

'You must take notice, O son of Adam, that what is hereafter is greater, shocking and painful for the heart on the Day of Judgment. It is the day of resurrection of all people and it will be the day of presence, when Allah, most Majestic, most Glorious, will bring together all the people of the past and the people of the later generations. On that day, the trumpet will sound and graves will be made open. That will be the day of the quake when the hearts will come up to the throat under stress and that will be the day when slips will not be reduced and no ransom will be accepted from anyone or any excuses accepted and there will be no repentance for anyone. It will be only reward for the good deeds or recompense for the bad deeds. Those who were of the believing people in this world will see their deeds of the size of an atom as well as their bad deeds of the size of an atom.

"You must remain cautious, O people about sins and disobedience in what Allah has prohibited and has told you to be cautious in His book of truth, the speaking statements. You must not feel safe from the dislike of Allah and His warnings and threats when Satan, the condemned one would call you to the short-living desires and pleasures in this world because Allah, most Majestic, most Glorious, has said, 'When a Satanic thought starts to bother the pious ones, they understand and see the light.' (7:201) Your hearts must feel fear of Allah and remember what Allah has promised you on your return to Him of the reward as well as fear from the severe suffering. One who is afraid of anything, he keeps away and abandons it. You must not remain of the neglectful ones who are inclined to the blossoms of the worldly things and who make evil plots. Allah has said in His book, 'Can they who have devised evil plans expect to be safe from the command of Allah to the earth to swallow them up, or from a torment which might strike them from an unexpected direction? (16:45) Are they confident that Allah will not seize them while they are on a journey because they cannot be defeated?' (16:46) You must remain cautious about what Allah has cautioned you and of what He has done to the unjust ones in His book. You must not feel safe from the coming of something with which the unjust ones were threatened in the book of Allah.

"By Allah, Allah has given you good advice in His book by giving examples about others. Fortunate is one who learns a lesson from the experience of others. Allah has made you to listen in His book what He has done to the unjust people of the towns before you as He has said, '. . . how many were the towns that We crushed because of their injustice.' 'Town' is a reference to the people of the town as He has said, '. . . thereafter We established other people.' He, most Majestic, most Glorious, has said, 'When they found Our torment approaching them they started to run away from the town. (21:12) We told them, "Do not run away. Come back to your luxuries and your houses so that you can be questioned." (21:13) [When suffering seized them] they said, "Woe to us! We have been unjust." (21:14) Such was what they continued to say until We mowed them down and made them completely extinct. (21:15) By Allah, it is an advice for you and a warning if you only learn a lesson to have fear of the warning.

"About the sinful and disobedient people the book of Allah, most Majestic, most Glorious, has said, '. . . if a blow of the penalty of your Lord touches them they say, "Woe is on us; we had been unjust." (21:46) If you, O people, say that Allah, most Majestic, most Glorious, has addressed thereby the pagans then why does He say, 'We shall maintain proper justice on the Day of Judgment. No soul will be wronged the least. For a deed even as small as a mustard seed one will be duly recompensed. We are efficient in maintaining the account.' (21:47) O servants (of Allah), you must take notice that no balance of fairness will be set up for the pagans and nothing as the record of the deeds will be published. They will be driven to hell in groups all together. Balance and record of deeds will be arranged only for the people of Islam. You must have fear of Allah, O servants (of Allah), and you must take notice that Allah, most Majestic, most Glorious, does not love the blossoms of the world and its short-lived matters for His friends and does not encourage them in such matters of short-lived blossoms and superficial delight. He has created the world and its inhabitants to put them to the test and see who is of good deeds for his hereafter. By Allah He has presented in it examples and signs for the people of understanding and there is no power without Allah. You must restrain from whatever Allah, most Majestic, most Glorious, has instructed you to exercise restraint in short-lived matters of the world. Allah, most Majestic, most Glorious, has said and He speaks the truth, 'The example of the worldly life is like the water sent down from the sky which becomes mixed with the earth's produce that people and cattle consume. When the land becomes fertile and pleasant, people think that they have control over it. At Our command during the night or day, the land becomes as barren as if it had no richness the day before. Thus, do We explain the evidence (of the truth) for the people who reflect.' (10:24)

"O servants (of Allah), you must live like the people of understanding who think and you must not depend on the world. Allah, most Majestic, most Glorious, has said to Muhammad, *O Allah grant compensation to Muhammad and his family worthy of their services to Your cause*, '. . . you must not depend on the unjust ones because the fire will touch you.' (11:113) You must not depend on blossoms of the world and on whatever is therein like those who have taken it as a permanent dwelling and residence. It is a dwelling of subsistence, a shabby home and the house of deeds. You must prepare your supplies with virtuous deeds, before its days are scattered and before Allah announces its departure and ruination. The one who first established it destroyed and commenced it is its guardian and heir. I ask Allah for support for us and for you in providing our supplies by means of piety and restraint from sins in this world. May Allah make you and us of the people who restrain themselves in the short-lived blossoming of the worldly life, who are interested in the rewards of the hereafter; we are by His power and for Him. *O Allah grant compensation to Muhammad and his family worthy of their services to Your cause*, greeting of peace for you as well as the mercy and blessings of Allah.'"

Hadith of the Shaykh with al-Baqir, *'Alayhi al-Salam*

H 14478, h 30

Muhammad ibn Yahya has narrated from Ahmad ibn Muhammad ibn 'Isa from Muhammad ibn Sinan from Ishaq ibn 'Ammar who has said that a man of our people narrated from al-Hakam ibn 'Utaybah who has narrated the following:

"Once I was with abu Ja'far, *'Alayhi al-Salam*, in a house filled with people, when an old man supporting himself with his staff came in, stood at the door and said, 'I offer greeting of peace to you, O child of the Messenger of Allah, and ask Allah to grant you from His mercy and blessings.' He then remained quiet. Abu Ja'far, *'Alayhi al-Salam*, said this. 'I offer greeting of peace to you also, and ask Allah to grant you from His mercy and blessings.' The old man then turned to the people in the house and said, 'I offer greeting of peace to you all.' He then remained quiet until all of the people in the house responded to him with greeting of peace. He then turned his face to abu Ja'far, *'Alayhi al-Salam*, and said, 'O child of the Messenger of Allah, allow me to come closer to you. I pray to Allah to keep my soul in service for your cause. I by Allah, love you, love those who love you and by Allah I do not love you and those who love you for any worldly interest. [By Allah], I hate your enemies and denounce them. I, by Allah, do not hate them and denounce them because of spilt blood between us. By Allah, I consider lawful what you make lawful and prohibit what you have prohibited and I wait for the establishment of your government. Is my condition hopeful in your view, I pray to Allah to keep my soul in service for your cause?' Abu Ja'far, *'Alayhi al-Salam*, called him to come closer and closer to him until he (the Imam) made him to sit on his side. He (the Imam) then said, 'O Shaykh, once a man came to my father, Ali ibn al-Husayn, *'Alayhim al-Salam*. He asked him just what you have asked me and my father said to him, "If you die you will arrive where the Messenger of Allah, Ali, al-Hassan, al-Husayn and Ali ibn al-Husayn, *'Alayhim al-Salam*, are. Your heart will feel (joyful) like being on ice in a scorching hot day and elated, your eyes delighted and the spirit and fragrance with honorable scribes will welcome, and greet you. If your soul will reach here – pointing with his hand to his throat – and if you live, you will see something whereby Allah will bring delight to your eyes and you will be with us in the exalted high place.' The old man then asked, 'What did you say, O abu Ja'far it is?' He (the Imam) repeated for him his words. The Shaykh said, '*Takbir* (Allah is great beyond description), O abu Ja'far, will I arrive where the Messenger of Allah, Ali, al-Hassan, al-Husayn and Ali ibn al-Husayn, *'Alayhim al-Salam*, are? Then my eyes will be delighted, my heart will feel (joyful) like being on ice in a scorching hot day and elated? Will the spirit and the fragrance along with honorable scribes say welcome to me if my soul will reach here? If I will live I will see something with which Allah will give delight to my eyes and then I will be with you in the exalted high place?' The old man then began to sob like a child in desperation '*ha, ha, ha*,' until he was flat on the ground and the people of the house sobbed and cried on seeing the condition of the old man. Abu Ja'far, wiped his tears with his finger from his eyelids then shook them away. The old man then raised his head and said to Abu Ja'far, 'O child of the Messenger of Allah, allow me to hold your hand.' He (the Imam) allowed him to hold his hand which he placed on his eye and cheek, then he placed his hand on his chest and belly, then stood up and said, '*Salamun Alaykum* (I offer greeting of peace to you).' Abu Ja'far, then turned and looked at him as he was leaving and said, to the people, 'If one loves to look at a person from the garden (paradise) he must look at this man.' Al-Hakam ibn 'Utaybah has said, 'I had never seen such a gathering of mourners like that one.'"

The story of the oil seller

H 14479, h 31

It is narrated from the narrator of the previous Hadith from Ahmad ibn Muhammad ibn 'Isa from Ali ibn al-Hakam from certain persons of our people who has narrated the following:

"Abu 'Abd Allah, *'Alayhi al-Salam*, has said that there was a man who sold oil and loved the Messenger of Allah, *O Allah grant compensation to Muhammad and his family worthy of their services to Your cause*, a great deal. Before going to work, he would first look at the Messenger of Allah. It had become noticeable. He would come and stretch himself to become taller so he could see him (the Messenger of Allah). One day he came and stretched his height to see him (the Messenger of Allah), then left and quickly came back. The Messenger of Allah saw him and made a hand gesture to call him closer, told him to sit nearby and asked, 'Why did you do today what you did?' He replied, 'O Messenger of Allah, by the One who has sent you as His Holy Prophet in all truth, my memory about you overwhelmed my heart and I could not go to work until I came back to you. He (the Messenger of Allah) prayed for him and spoke to him for his wellbeing. The Messenger of Allah, for a few days not seeing him, asked about him and he was told that they (people) also had not seen him. The Messenger of Allah wore his shoes and others of his companions followed him until they came to the market of oil sellers and found his shop empty, without any shopkeeper. He (the Messenger of Allah) asked about him from his neighbors and they said, 'O Messenger of Allah, he has died. He was a trusted and truthful man among us but he had one characteristic.' He (the Messenger of Allah) asked about what it was and they said that he followed women a great deal. The Messenger of Allah, said, 'May Allah grant him mercy, he loved me a great deal. Even if he had been a seller of slaves Allah would forgive him.'" (Perhaps meaning thereby seller of free people)

The excellence of Shi'ah

H 14480, h 32

Ali ibn Muhammad has narrated from Ahmad ibn abu 'Abd Allah from 'Uthman ibn 'Isa from Muyassir who has narrated the following:

"Abu 'Abd Allah, *'Alayhi al-Salam*, once asked me, 'How are your companions?' I replied, 'I pray to Allah to keep my soul in service for your cause, we are worse than the Jews, Christians, Zoroastrian and the pagans before them.' He (the Imam) was leaning, he then sat up straight and said, 'By Allah, not two of you will go to hell, no, by Allah not even one of you will go to hell. By Allah, you are the ones about whom Allah, most Majestic, most Glorious, has said, '. . . why is it that we cannot see men whom we had considered as wicked (38:62) and whom we mocked? Have they been rescued or can our eyes not find them?" (38:63) Such disputes will certainly take place among the dwellers of hellfire.' (38:64) He (the Imam) said, 'They will search for you in the fire but will find not even one person.'"

The advice of the Holy Prophet to 'Amir al-Mu'minin, Ali, *'Alayhima al-Salam*

H 14481, h 33

Muhammad ibn Yahya has narrated from Ahmad ibn Muhammad ibn 'Isa from Ali ibn al-Nu'man from Mu'awiyah ibn 'Ammar who has narrated the following:

"I once heard abu 'Abd Allah, *'Alayhi al-Salam*, say that the Holy Prophet, advised Ali, *'Alayhi al-Salam*, and said, 'O Ali, I advise you about certain characteristics that you must preserve from me.' He (the Messenger of Allah) then said, 'O Allah help him. The first one is speaking the truth and you must never allow any lie to come out of your mouth. Secondly, you must maintain restraint from sins and never dare to act disloyally. Thirdly, you must have fear of Allah, majestic is whose name, as if you see Him. Fourthly, you must weep because of feeling anxious toward Allah. For every drop of your tears, one thousand homes will be built in the garden (paradise). Fifth is spending your assets and blood for your religion. Sixth is holding to my *Sunnah*, in *Salat* (prayer), fasting and my charity. *Salat* (prayer) consists of fifty Rak'at (every day), fasting is three days every month, the first Thursday, the middle of the month Wednesday and the last Thursday of every month. The charity is up to your efforts until you say that you have given excessively but it is not excessive. You must perform the nightly *Salat* (prayer), perform *Salat* (prayer) at noon, perform *Salat* (prayer) at noon and you must perform *Salat* (prayer) at noon. You must recite al-Quran in all conditions. You must raise your hands in your *Salat* (prayer) and turn them. You must brush your teeth every time you take wudu, observe moral excellence to possess them, and remain away from evil moral manners. If you did not do so then do not blame anyone except yourself.'"

Criteria of a man's excellence

H 14482, h 34

A number of our people have narrated from Sahl ibn Ziyad from Bakr ibn Salih from al-Hassan ibn Ali from 'Abd Allah ibn al-Mughirah who has said that narrated to me Ja'far ibn Ibrahim [ibn Muhammad ibn Ali ibn 'Abd Allah ibn Ja'far al-Tayyar] who has narrated the following:

"Abu Ja'far, *'Alayhi al-Salam*, has said that the Messenger of Allah, *O Allah grant compensation to Muhammad and his family worthy of their services to Your cause*, has said, 'The status of a man consists of his kindness, reason, nobility, beauty, honor and piety.'"

Religion is no other thing than love

H 14483, h 35

It narrated from them from Sahl ibn Ziyad from al-Hassan ibn Ali from Ali ibn Faddal from Ali ibn 'Uqbah and Thalabah ibn Maymun and Ghalib ibn 'Uthman and Harun ibn Muslim from Burayd ibn Mu'awiyah who has narrated the following:

"Once I was with abu Ja'far, *'Alayhi al-Salam*, in his tent in Mina when he (the Imam) looked at Ziyad al-Aswad with his foot badly hurt, thus he (the Imam) expressed sadness about it and asked, 'What has happened to your feet that have become as such?' He replied, 'I came with a weak stumper and most of the way I walked.' He (the Imam) expressed more sadness then Ziyad said, 'I collected sins until I was afraid for my destruction. I then remembered your love which gives me hope for my salvation and it brightened my dark condition.' Abu Ja'far, *'Alayhi al-Salam*, then said, 'Is religion anything other than love?' Allah, the most High, has said, 'He has made belief beloved to you and has beautified it in your hearts.' (49:7) He has said, 'If you were to love Allah then follow me Allah will love you.' (3:31) He has said, '. . . they love those who migrate to you.' (59:9) Once a man came to the Messenger of Allah, *O Allah grant compensation to Muhammad and his family worthy of their services to Your cause*, and said, 'O Messenger of Allah, I love people who perform *Salat* (prayer) but I do not perform it, I love people who fast but I do not fast.' The Messenger of Allah, said, 'You are with those whom you love and to you belongs what you have earned.' He (the Messenger of Allah) has said, 'What you are seeking to find is where you will arrive. It is certain that if a shocking thing may come from the sky every people will seek protection in their safe places and we seek protection with our Holy Prophet, and you will seek protection with us.'"

The excellence of *Ahl al-Bayt*, *'Alayhim al-Salam*, and their Shi'ah

H 14484, h 36

Sahl ibn Ziyad has narrated from ibn Faddal from Ali ibn 'Uqbah and 'Abd Allah ibn Bukayr from Sa'id ibn Yasar who has narrated the following:

"I once heard abu 'Abd Allah, *'Alayhi al-Salam*, say, 'All praise belongs to Allah. It became a Murji'ah sect, a Harawriyah sect, a Qadriyah sect and you are called al-Turabiyah sect and Shi'ah of Ali. By Allah, there is only Allah who has no partners and His Messenger, *O Allah grant compensation to Muhammad and his family worthy of their services to Your cause*, and the followers of the family of the Messenger of Allah, *O Allah grant compensation to Muhammad and his family worthy of their services to Your cause*. These are the only people. Ali, *'Alayhi al-Salam*, was the most excellent person after the Messenger of Allah, *O Allah grant compensation to Muhammad and his family worthy of their services to Your cause*, and the most preferred person by him (the Messenger of Allah).' He (the Imam) said it three times.'"

Reviving the cause of *Ahl al-Bayt*, *'Alayhim al-Salam*

H 14485, h 37

It is narrated from the narrator of the previous Hadith from ibn Faddal from Ali ibn 'Uqbah from 'Umar ibn Aban al-Kalbiy from 'Abd al-Hamid al-Wasitiy who has narrated the following:

"I once said to abu Ja'far, *'Alayhi al-Salam*, 'I pray to Allah to keep you well, we have left our markets waiting for this matter, al-Qa'im (the one who rises with divine authority and power). A man from us is almost to commence begging.' He (the Imam) said, 'O abu 'Abd al-Hamid, do you think one who holds his breath for Allah, Allah will not find a way out for him? Yes, by Allah, He finds a way out for him. May Allah grant kindness to a servant (of Allah) who revives our cause.' I then said, 'I pray to Allah to keep you well, al-Murji'ah says that we were not supposed to be as we are until he comes. You (the opposition) will not be able to say that we and you were the same.' He (the Imam) said, 'O abu 'Abd al-Hamid, they have spoken the truth. If one repents, Allah accepts his repentance and one who hides hypocrisy, Allah rubs his nose on the ground. One, who publicizes our cause, Allah spills his blood. Allah slaughters them on Islam just as a butcher slaughters a sheep.' I then said, 'Will we and people be the same on the day of the rise of al-Qa'im?' He (the Imam) said, 'No, you on that day will be the pinnacle of the earth and its rulers. In our religion that is how it is.' I then said, 'What happens if I die before the time of al-Qa'im?' He (the Imam) said, 'One of you, who says, 'If I will live in the time of al-Qa'im of the family of Muhammad, I will help him, he is like one who strikes with his sword along with him and martyrdom with him is martyrdom twice.'"

Excellence of Shi'ah

H 14486, h 38
It is narrated from the narrator of the previous Hadith from al-Hassan ibn Ali from 'Abd Allah ibn al-Walid al-Kindiy who has narrated the following:

"Once during the time of Marwan we visited abu 'Abd Allah, *'Alayhi al-Salam*, and he (the Imam) asked, 'Who are you?' We replied that we were from al-Kufah.' He (the Imam) said, 'There is no town among the towns with more people who love us as the town of al-Kufah, especially this group. Allah, Glorious is whose mention has guided you to a matter of which others are ignorant. You have answered our call when people hate us, you have followed us when people oppose us, and you have acknowledged us when people reject us. Allah gives you life the way He has given life to us. He makes you die in the manner we die. I testify in favor of my father who would say, "The only thing between one of you and the delight that Allah will grant to your eyes and satisfaction is the reaching of your soul to here [the Imam pointed to his throat], and Allah, most Majestic, most Glorious, in His book has said, '. . . We sent messengers before you and made for them spouses and offspring.' (13:38) We are the offspring of the Messenger of Allah. *O Allah grant compensation to Muhammad and his family worthy of their services to Your cause.*'"

The wicked is wicked in his mother's womb

H 14487, h 39
Humayd ibn Ziyad has narrated from al-Hassan ibn Muhammad al-Kindiy from Ahmad ibn 'Udays from Aban from 'Uthman from abu al-Sabbah who has narrated the following:

"I heard certain words that are narrated from the Holy Prophet, *O Allah grant compensation to Muhammad and his family worthy of their services to Your cause*, and from 'Amir al-Mu'minin, Ali, *'Alayhi al-Salam*, and from ibn Masud. I presented it before abu 'Abd Allah, *'Alayhi al-Salam*, and he said, 'It is the word of the Messenger of Allah, *O Allah grant compensation to Muhammad and his family worthy of their services to Your cause*, which I recognize.' The Messenger of Allah, *O Allah grant compensation to Muhammad and his family worthy of their services to Your cause*, has said, 'A wicked one is wicked in the womb of his mother. A fortunate one is the one who learns a lesson because of others. The most intelligent among the intelligent ones is he who is pious. The most dimwitted one of the dimwitted ones is he who is involved in indecent acts. The worst narrator is the narrator of lies, the most wicked of the affairs is the heretical one. The worst blindness is blindness of the heart, the worst regret is the regret on the Day of Judgment. The greatest sin before Allah is the lying tongue, the worst earning is earning of unlawful interest, the worst food is the assets of orphans. The best beautification for a man is his good manners with faith, the manners that control and organize his affairs and his consequences. One who speaks to show off, Allah makes him to hear lies, one who persist in following the worldly matters fails, one who recognizes misfortune, he bears with patience, one who does not recognize it remains afraid. Doubt is disbelief, one who assumes arrogance, Allah humiliates him, one who follows Satan disobeys Allah and one who disobeys Allah faces suffering. One who thanks receives increase from Allah, one who bears patience in hardships Allah supports him and one who places his trust in Allah, Allah helps him sufficiently. You must not make Allah angry by making a creature happy, do not become close to a creature, which moves you away from Allah. Allah, most Majestic, most Glorious, grants good or removes evil from someone only because of his being obedient to Him and following His pleasure. Obedience to Allah is success in all goodness that is sought, and safety from all evil, which is avoided. Allah, most Majestic is whose mention protects one who obeys Him and one who disobeys Him does not seek protection with Him. A runaway from Allah cannot find any refuge, the command of Allah inevitably comes even if all creatures dislike. Every oncoming is near, what Allah wants takes place and what He does not want cannot happen. You must cooperate in piety and you must not cooperate in sin and animosity. You must remain pious before Allah because the punishment of Allah is intense.'"

About the words of Allah '. . . all people were one nation'

H 14488, h 40

Through the same chain of narrators as that of the previous Hadith, the following is narrated from Aban from Ya'qub ibn Shu'ayb who has narrated the following:

"Once abu 'Abd Allah, *'Alayhi al-Salam*, was asked about the meaning of the words of Allah, '. . . all people were one nation.' (2:213) He (the Imam) said, 'Before Noah, *'Alayhi al-Salam*, people were a misguided nation. Allah changed it, then sent messengers and it is not as they say that it is as such all the time. They have spoken a lie. In the night of al-Qadr, Allah differentiates hardships and ease or rain by the degree Allah, most Majestic, most Glorious, wants until the next similar night.'"

Hadith of the ocean with the sun

H 14489, h 41

(The following Hadith seems mutashabih (unclear) if it is meant to explain sun and moon eclipses in this manner for that time or it is about the working of the solar system and beyond. In addition, one person among its narrators, al-Hakam al-Mustawrid, is unknown, which leaves the possibility of addition or omission in its wordings. Unclear Hadith like unclear verses of al-Quran are left to the author to explain)

Ali ibn Ibrahim has narrated from his father from ibn Mahbub from 'Abd Allah ibn Sinan from Ma'ruf ibn Kharbudh from al-Hakam al-Mustawrid who has narrated the following:

"Ali ibn al-Husayn, *'Alayhi al-Salam*, has said that of the sustenance that Allah has determined for people in what they need is the ocean which Allah, most Majestic, most Glorious, has created between the sky and earth. He (the Imam) said, 'In the sky Allah has determined pathway of the sun, moon, stars and planets. He has put in position all of these on a group. Over the group, He has appointed an angel with whom there are seventy thousand angels. They move the group. When they turn it, the sun, moon, stars, and planets turn with it and descend in their position which Allah, most Majestic, most Glorious, has determined for its day and night. When sins of servants (of Allah) increase, Allah, most Blessed, most High, then decides to reprove them with a sign of signs. He commands the guard-angel to remove the group on which the pathway of the sun, moon, stars, and planets are positioned. The supervising angel commands the seventy thousand angels to remove it from its pathway.' He (the Imam) said, 'They remove it, then the sun turns in that ocean which moves in the group.' He (the Imam) said, 'Its light is wiped and its color changes. When Allah, most Majestic, most Glorious, wants to magnify the sign He wipes the sun in the ocean as Allah likes to warn His creatures by the sign.' He (the Imam) said, 'This is when there is an eclipse of the sun.' He (the Imam) said, 'The same thing happens to the moon. When Allah wants to brighten it He commands the guard angel to return the group in its pathway, the group returns it and the sun also returns to its line.' He (the Imam) said, 'It comes out of the water as dim.' He (the Imam) said, 'The moon is the same.' He (the narrator) has said that Ali ibn al-Husayn, *'Alayhi al-Salam*, said, 'No one feels anxious because of these two signs except our Shi'ah. When this happens you must express anxiety before Allah, most Majestic, most Glorious, and then return to Him.'"

In every family Allah places His proof

H 14490, h 42

Ali ibn Ibrahim has narrated from his father from Muhammad ibn Sulayman from al-Fadl ibn 'Isma'il al-Hashimiy from his father who has narrated the following:

"I once complained before abu 'Abd Allah, *'Alayhi al-Salam*, against my family because of their taking religion lightly. He (the Imam) said, 'O 'Isma'il, do not dislike that about your family because Allah, most Blessed, most High, has designated in every family a proof, an authority and a good argument who will be presented against them on the Day of Judgment. It will be asked from them, "Did you not see so and so among you? Did you not see his guidance among you? Did you not see his *Salat* (prayer) among you? Did you not see his religion? Why did you not follow him?" He will be an authority and a firm argument against them on the Day of Judgment?'"

Proof of Allah in every town

H 14491, h 43

It is narrated from the narrator of the previous Hadith from his father from Muhammad ibn 'Aytham al-Nakhkhas from Mu'awiyah ibn 'Ammar who has narrated the following:

"I once heard abu 'Abd Allah, *'Alayhi al-Salam*, say, 'One of you lives in a town and Allah, most Majestic, most Glorious, will present him on the Day of Judgment as good argument against his neighbors and it will be said to them, "Was so and so not among you? Did you not hear his words? Did you not hear his weeping in the night?" So he will be the authority and argument of Allah against them.'"

About the words of Allah '. . . He sent upon them swallows...'

H 14492, h 44

Muhammad ibn Yahya has narrated from Ahmad ibn Muhammad ibn 'Isa from al-Hassan ibn Mahbub from Jamil ibn Salih from abu Maryam who has narrated the following:

"I once asked abu Ja'far, *'Alayhi al-Salam*, about the meaning of the words of Allah, most Majestic, most Glorious, '. . . He sent on them swallows who shot them with marked stones.' (105:3-4) He (the Imam) said, 'They were birds flying close to the ground which came from the side of the sea with their heads like the heads of predators and claws like the claws of predator birds. Each one carried three stones, one stone in each claw and one in their beaks. They begun to shoot them with the stones until their bodies grew blisters and thus killed them with it. Before that no such thing was seen as blisters or that kind of birds before that day or afterward.' He (the Imam) said, 'Those of them who were left on that day left until they reached *Hadara Mawt* which is a valley near Yemen. Allah sent a flood which drowned them all.' He (the Imam) said, 'No water was ever seen in that valley before that day for fifteen years.' He (the Imam) said, 'For this reason it is called *Hadara Mawt* (death arrived).'"

The potter and the farmer in-laws

H 14493, h 45

Muhammad ibn Yahya has narrated from Ahmad ibn Muhammad ibn 'Isa from ibn Faddal from 'Abd Allah ibn Bukayr and Tha'labah ibn Maymun and Ali ibn 'Uqbah from Zurarah from 'Abd al-Malik who has narrated the following:

"Once, words were exchanged between abu Ja'far, *'Alayhi al-Salam*, and the children of al-Hassan, *'Alayhi al-Salam*. It came to my notice and I went to visit Abu Ja'far, *'Alayhi al-Salam*, to speak to him (the Imam) about it. He (the Imam) said, 'You must wait instead of stepping among us. Our case with our cousins is like the case of a man in banu Israel who had two daughters. He gave one of them in marriage to a farmer and the other one to a potter. He then went to visit the wife of the farmer and asked about their condition. She said, "My husband has prepared a large plantation and if Allah allows the sky to rain then we will be the most prosperous family in banu Israel." He then visited the wife of the potter and asked her about their condition. She said, "My husband has prepared a large amount of pottery, if Allah holds the sky back from raining we will be the most prosperous family in banu Israel." He returned home saying, 'O Lord, You are for them (to help).' Our case is similar to their case.'"

Cure for gases and pain

H 14494, h 46

Muhammad ibn Ahmad has narrated from ibn Mahbub from Jamil ibn Salih from Darih who has narrated the following:

"I once heard abu 'Abd Allah, *'Alayhi al-Salam*, when reading certain recitations for the protection of one of his children, say this. 'I swear you, O air, O pain or whatever you are, to the oath by which 'Amir al-Mu'minin, Ali, and the Messenger of Allah, *O Allah grant compensation to Muhammad and his family worthy of their services to Your cause*, sought protection against Jinn of the valley of al-Sabrah. They accepted and obeyed. You must accept, obey and leave my son so and so son of my daughter so and so in this hour, in this very hour.'" (The mention of Jinn is a reference to the case of the encounter of unbeliever Jinn with the Holy Prophet, during an armed expedition against banu Mustalaq. That Hadith is narrated in the book al-Irshad by Shaykh al-Mufid according to the footnote of the Arabic text)

Hadith of the Holy Prophet, *'Alayhi al-Salam,* a good advice . . .

H 14495, h 47
Muhammad ibn Yahya has narrated from Ahmad ibn Muhammad ibn Faddal from ibn Sinan from abu al-Jarud who has narrated the following:

"Abu Ja'far, *'Alayhi al-Salam,* has said that the Messenger of Allah, *O Allah grant compensation to Muhammad and his family worthy of their services to Your cause,* has said, 'One who misses someone and searches for him in his absence, himself is missed (by others for his being a caring person). One who does not prepare himself to bear patience in misfortunes of the eon (time) he fails. One who troubles people is troubled and one who then leaves them alone is not left alone.' It was then asked, 'What then must I do, O Messenger of Allah?' He (the Messenger of Allah) replied, 'Lend them from your dignity for the day of your poverty and need.'"

Usurpation of the donkey of the Imam . . .

H 14496, h 48
It is narrated from the narrator of the previous Hadith from Ahmad from al-Barqiy from Muhammad ibn Yahya from Hammad ibn 'Uthaman who has narrated the following:

"Musa ibn 'Isa was in his house which overlooked the place for Sa'y (near al-Ka'bah) when he saw abu al-Hassan, Musa, *'Alayhi al-Salam,* coming from Marwah on a mule. Ibn Hayyaj then commanded a man from Hamadan who was very close to him to hold the rein of the mule and claim it. He went and got hold of the rein of the mule and claimed that the mule belonged to him. Abu al-Hassan, *'Alayhi al-Salam,* moved from the saddle, dismounted the mule, told his slaves to take the saddle and allow him to take the mule. He said, 'The saddle also is mine.' Abu al-Hassan, *'Alayhi al-Salam,* said to him, 'You speak lies because we have proof that the saddle belongs to Muhammad ibn Ali. We bought the mule not very long ago and you know it.'"

The tax collector harasses the Imam

H 14497, h 49
It is narrated from Ahmad ibn Muhammad from Muhammad ibn Murazim from his father who has narrated the following:

"When abu 'Abd Allah, *'Alayhi al-Salam,* left abu Ja'far, al-Mansur in al-Hirah (a city near al-Kufa, Iraq), he (the Imam) left in the hour that he (the Imam) was allowed to leave. He (the Imam) arrived in al-Salihin (a town near Baghdad) in the beginning of the night. A tax collector on the road stopped him (the

Imam). He would not allow him to go. He (the Imam) tried to convince him but he refused. Musadif and I were with him (the Imam). Musadif said, 'I pray to Allah to keep my soul in service for your cause, he is like a filthy dog that has troubled you and I am afraid he may turn you back. I do not know what abu Ja'far, al-Mansur may do. If you grant us permission, Murazim and I can strike his neck and throw him in the canal.' He (the Imam) said, 'Hold it, O Musadif.' He (the Imam) continued asking him to allow him to go until most of the night was gone. Then he allowed him (the Imam) to leave. He (the Imam) said, 'O Murazim, is this better or what you said?' I replied, 'This is better, I pray to Allah to keep my soul in service for your cause.' He (the Imam) said, 'A man moves away from a smaller degree of humiliation but it leads him to bigger one.'"

Kindness of the Imam to his servant

H 14498, h 50
It is narrated from the narrator of the previous Hadith from Ahmad ibn Muhammad from al-Hajjal from Hafs ibn abu 'A'isha who has narrated the following:
"Abu 'Abd Allah, *'Alayhi al-Salam*, once sent a slave for an errand but he delayed and abu 'Abd Allah, *'Alayhi al-Salam*, went looking for him and found him sleeping. He (the Imam) sat near his head fanning to comfort him and when he woke up abu 'Abd Allah, *'Alayhi al-Salam*, said, 'O so and so it is not fair. You sleep day and night. The night is for you to rest and during the day you must work for us.'"

Allah has not placed anything good in opposition to *Ahl al-Bayt, 'Alayhim al-Salam*

H 14499, h 51
It is narrated from the narrator of the previous Hadith from Ahmad ibn Muhammad from Ali ibn al-Hakam from Hassan [from] abu Ali who has narrated the following:
"I once heard abu 'Abd Allah, *'Alayhi al-Salam*, say, 'You must not mention our secrets opposite to what we publicly say or what we say in public opposite to our secret issues. It is sufficient for you to say what we say and remain silent about what we remain silent. You have seen that Allah, most Majestic, most Glorious, has not placed anything good in people's opposing us. Allah, most Majestic, most Glorious, says, "Those who oppose His command must stay cautious about being afflicted by mischief or painful suffering."'" (24:63)

Hadith of the physician

H 14500, h 52
Muhammad has narrated from Ahmad ibn Muhammad from Ali ibn al-Hakam from Ziyad ibn abu al-Hallal who has narrated the following:
"Abu Ja'far, *'Alayhi al-Salam*, has said that Musa, *'Alayhi al-Salam*, asked, 'O Lord, where from is pain?' Allah said, 'It comes from Me.' Musa, asked, 'Where from is the cure?' Allah said, 'It comes from Me.' Musa then said,

'What do Your servants do with physicians?' Allah said, 'They just comfort their souls thereby.' That day physicians were called endeavoring.'"

Diseases and the body

H 14501, h 53
It is narrated from the narrator of the previous Hadith from Ahmad from ibn Faddal from ibn Bukayr from abu Ayyub who has narrated the following:
"Abu 'Abd Allah, *'Alayhi al-Salam*, has said, 'Every illness runs to the body waiting for the command to work on it.' In another Hadith it is said, 'except fever because it works as it comes.'"

Cure with wheat

H 14502, h 54
It is narrated from the narrator of the previous Hadith from Ahmad ibn Muhammad from 'Abd al-'Aziz ibn al-Muhtadiy from Yunus ibn 'Abd al-Rahman from Dawud ibn Zurbiy who has narrated the following:
"Once I became ill in al-Madinah very seriously and abu 'Abd Allah, *'Alayhi al-Salam*, had received information about my illness. He (the Imam) wrote to me, 'It has come to my knowledge that you have an illness. You should buy one *Sa'* (a certain unit of measurement) of wheat, then lie down on your back. Pour it on your chest and say, "O Lord, I ask You through Your name with which people in need ask You to remove their suffering. You give him domination on the land and designate him as your deputy over your creatures, O Allah, grant compensation to Muhammad and his family worthy of their services to Your cause. O Allah, grant me good health and recovery from this illness." Then sit straight, collect the wheat around you, then say what you had just said, distribute it among the destitute people; one mud (a certain measurement) to each destitute person and say the same recitation which you have just read.' Dawud has said, 'I followed the instruction and I found myself as if untied from the entanglement of the rope and more than one person had done so. They had benefitted thereby.'"

Hadith of 'On what is the fish'

H 14503, h 55
Muhammad ibn Ahmad has narrated from ibn Mahbub from Jamil ibn Salih Aban ibn Taghlib who has narrated the following:
"I once asked abu 'Abd Allah, *'Alayhi al-Salam*, about the earth and on what it is standing. He (the Imam) said, 'It stands on a fish.' I then asked, 'On what is the fish resting?' He (the Imam) said, 'It is on water.' I then asked, 'On what is water standing?' He (the Imam) said, 'It is on a rock.' I then asked, 'On what is the rock?' He (the Imam) said, 'It is on the horn of a gliding smooth bull.' I then asked, 'On what is the bull.' He (the Imam) said, 'It is on the moisture.'" I then asked, 'On what is the moisture?' He (the Imam) said, 'It is difficult and the knowledge of scholars wanders about it.'"

Creation of the Earth

H 14504, h 56

Ali ibn Ibrahim has narrated from his father from ibn abu 'Umayr from Jamil ibn Darraj from Zurarah who has narrated the following:

"One of the two Imam, (abu Ja'far or abu 'Abd Allah), *'Alayhi al-Salam*, has said, 'Allah, most Majestic, most Glorious, created the earth, then made salty water flow on it for forty mornings and sweet water for forty mornings until it joined and became mixed. He then took a handful in His hand and turned it all intensely, then made it in two groups. From each group a bunch of particles emerged, one bunch and group to the garden (paradise) and one to the fire.'"

Hadith of dreams and proof of divine authority for the people of a given time

H 14505, h 57

Certain persons of our people have narrated from Ali ibn al-'Abbas from al-Hassan ibn 'Abd al-Rahman who has narrated the following:

"Abu al-Hassan, *'Alayhi al-Salam*, has said, 'Dreams did not exist in the past in the beginning of the creation. It came into being later.' I then asked, 'What is the reason for that?' He (the Imam) said, 'Allah, most Majestic, most Glorious, sent a messenger to the people of his time and he called them to worship Allah. They said, 'If we worship Him, then what we will get for it? You do not have more wealth than we do and your tribe also is not stronger than our tribe.' He said, 'If you follow me Allah will admit you in the garden (paradise) and if you disobey me Allah will send you to the fire.' They asked, 'What are the garden (paradise) and the fire?' He explained it for them and they asked, 'When will we go there?' He said, 'This will happen when you die.' They said, 'We see our dead people turn into bones and dust.' They became worse in their rejecting and insults toward him. Allah, most Majestic, most Glorious, then invented for them the ability to dream. They came to him and informed him about what they had seen and what they did not know about it. He told them that Allah, most Majestic, most Glorious, wants to establish His argument against you. This is how your spirits are. When you die, even though your bodies will decay, the spirits will face suffering until the bodies are raised.'"

Dreams of believing people

H 14506, h 58

Ali ibn Ibrahim has narrated from his father from ibn abu 'Umayr from Hisham ibn Salim who has narrated the following:

"I once heard abu 'Abd Allah, *'Alayhi al-Salam*, say, 'The opinion and dream of a believing person in the latter portions of time is a seventieth of prophethood.'"

Question of the Holy Prophet . . .

H 14507, h 59

Muhammad ibn Yahya has narrated from Ahmad ibn Muhammad from Mu'ammar ibn Khallad who has narrated the following:

"Abu al-Hassan al-Rida', *'Alayhi al-Salam*, has said that the Messenger of Allah, *O Allah grant compensation to Muhammad and his family worthy of their services to Your cause*, in the morning would ask his companions, 'Is there any glad news?' He meant thereby dreams.'"

About the words of Allah '. . . glad news for them . . .'

H 14508, h 60

It is narrated from the narrator of the previous Hadith from Ahmad ibn Muhammad from ibn Faddal from abu Jamilah from Jabir who has narrated the following:

"Abu Ja'far, *'Alayhi al-Salam*, has said that a man once asked the Messenger of Allah, *O Allah grant compensation to Muhammad and his family worthy of their services to Your cause*, about the meaning of the words of Allah, most Majestic, most Glorious, '. . . will receive glad news both in this life and in the life hereafter. . .' (10:64) He (the Messenger of Allah) said, 'It is a reference to the good dreams of a believing person which give him glad news in this world.'"

Three kinds of dreams

H 14509, h 61

Ali ibn Ibrahim has narrated from his father from ibn abu 'Umayr from Sa'd ibn abu Khalaf who has narrated the following:

"Abu 'Abd Allah, *'Alayhi al-Salam*, has said, 'Dreams are of three kinds: One is a glad news from Allah for a believing person, a caution against Satan and muddled and mixed up dreams.'"

True or false dreams

H 14510, h 62

A number of our people have narrated from Ahmad ibn Muhammad ibn Khalid from his father from al-Nadr ibn Suwayd from Durust ibn abu Mansur from abu Basir who has narrated the following:

"I once asked abu 'Abd Allah, *'Alayhi al-Salam*, saying, 'I pray to Allah to keep my soul in service for your cause, dreams come from the same place, then how is it that certain ones are true and others are false?' He (the Imam) said, 'What you said is right. However, the false dreams are different. A man may see in the beginning of the night during the domination of rebels and sinful ones which is only one's imaginations, it is false and contradicting and there is nothing good in it. The true dreams are the ones, which take place after the two-thirds of the night are passed which is just before dawn when the angels arrive. Such dreams are true and do not go wrong, if Allah so wills, unless one is Junub (without wudu because of sexual activities) or has gone to sleep without *Tahur* (cleansing) and without speaking in real sense of Allah, most Majestic, most Glorious, in which case it contradicts and delays on its owner.'"

Hadith of the winds

H 14511, h 63

Muhammad ibn Yahya has narrated from Ahmad ibn Muhammad ibn 'Isa from al-Hassan ibn Mahbub from ibn Ri'ab and Hisham ibn Salim from abu Basir who has narrated the following:

"I once asked abu Ja'far, *'Alayhi al-Salam*, about the four kinds of winds; the North, the South, the Morning and *al-Dabur*. I said that people say that the North is from the garden (paradise); the South is from the fire. He (the Imam) said, 'Allah, most Majestic, most Glorious, has armies of winds with which He punishes whomever He wants of those who disobey Him. Every kind of wind has a guard-angel. When Allah, most Majestic, most Glorious, wants to punish a people with a certain kind of punishment He sends inspiration to the guard-angel for that wind with which He wants to punish. The guard commands it and it then becomes excited like a lion.' He (the Imam) said, 'Every wind has a name. Have you not heard the words of Allah, most High, ". . . We sent on them a wind which was *Sarsar*, on the day of continued wickedness." (54:19) He called one kind as 'Barren wind', (51:41), '. . . a wind with painful suffering in it.' (46:24) He has called it as, '. . . in it there was hurricane with fire in it which burnt.' (2:266) Besides, there are the other winds which He has mentioned whereby He punishes those who disobey Him.' He (the Imam) said, 'Allah, most Majestic, most Glorious, has other kinds of winds. The winds of mercy are that which are impregnating (plants) and other kinds which spread before blessings, that which stirs up clouds for rain, that which holds the cloud between the sky and earth, the winds that condense the clouds to rain by the permission of Allah of which are the winds which Allah has counted in His book. The four winds, the North, the South, the Morning and *al-Dabur* are names of guard-angels for the winds. When Allah wants the North to blow He commands the angel whose name is the North then he descends on Bayt al-Haram (the Sacred House), stands on the Shami corner and flaps his wings, then the wind of the North spreads as Allah wants in the land and sea. When Allah wants to send the South, He commands the guard-angel, whose name is the South. He descends on Bayt al-Haram (the Sacred House), stands on the Shami corner and flaps his wings, then the south wind blows in the land and sea as Allah wills. When Allah wants to send the Morning wind, He commands the guard-angel whose name is the Morning. He descends on Bayt al-Haram (the Sacred House), stands on the Shami corner and flaps his wings, then the Morning wind spreads in the land and sea. When Allah wants to send al-*Dabur* wind, He calls the guard-angel whose name is *al-Dabur*. He descends on Bayt al-Haram (the Sacred House), stands on Shami corner and flaps his wings, then *al-Dabur* wind spreads in the land and sea.' Abu Ja'far, *'Alayhi al-Salam*, then said, 'Have you not heard the saying, 'The wind of the north, the wind of the south, the wind of the morning and the wind of al-*Dabur*?' In the possessive case it refers to the guard-angels.'"

Winds are the blessings or torments of Allah

H 14512, h 64

It is narrated from the narrator of the previous Hadith from Ahmad ibn Muhammad from ibn Mahbub from 'Abd Allah ibn Sinan from Ma'ruf ibn Kharrabuz who has narrated the following:

"Abu Ja'far, '*Alayhi al-Salam*, has said that Allah, most Majestic, most Glorious, has winds of blessings as well as winds for punishment. If Allah wants He can make the winds which are punishment turn into that which are blessings.' He (the Imam) said, 'He does not turn that which is for blessing into that which is for punishment.' He (the Imam) said, 'It has never happened that He grants mercy to a people who obey Him and their obedience should become a misfortune for them except after their turning from His obedience to disobedience. This is how it happened to the people of Yunus. When they believed, Allah granted them mercy after His designating punishment for them and had approved it, then He compensated it with mercy and turned the approved punishment on them to mercy. It was diverted from them when it was sent on them and it had overwhelmed them but they pleaded before Him.' He (the Imam) said, 'The barren wind is the wind of punishment. It does not impregnate anything of the womb or plants and it is the wind which comes out from underneath the seventh earth from where never any wind had come out except on the people of 'Ad when Allah became angry on them. He commanded the keepers to take from it of the size of a ring.' He (the Imam) said, 'It rebelled against the keepers and came out of the amount equal to the nostril of a bull, expressing anger on the people of 'Ad.' He (the Imam) said, 'The keepers cried to Allah, most Majestic, most Glorious, because of it and said, 'O Lord, it has rebelled against our command and we are afraid that those who are not disobedient may become destroyed and those who establish your towns.' He (the Imam) said, 'Allah, most Majestic, most Glorious, sent Jibril to it who faced it with his both wings, returned it to its place and said to it, 'Come out on those about whom you are commanded.' He (the Imam) said, 'It came out on those against whom it was commanded, destroyed the people of 'Ad and those who were present with them.'"

Cure for anxiety, sadness, poverty and illness

H 14513, h 65

Ali ibn Ibrahim has narrated from his father from al-Nawfaliy from al-Sakuniy who has narrated the following:

"Abu 'Abd Allah, '*Alayhi al-Salam*, has said that the Messenger of Allah, *O Allah grant compensation to Muhammad and his family worthy of their services to Your cause*, has said, 'One with whom blessings increase must increase his speaking of Allah. He must say *Tahmid*, (all praise belongs to Allah); and one whose sadness and concerns increase, must increase saying, 'There is no means and no power except the means and power of Allah, most High, most Great'; his poverty will go away from him.' He (the Imam) said that once the Holy Prophet did not see a man from al-Ansar (people of al-Madinah) for a while and asked, 'Why were you absent?' He replied, 'It is because of poverty, O Messenger of

Allah, and prolonged illness.' The Messenger of Allah, *O Allah grant compensation to Muhammad and his family worthy of their services to Your cause*, said, 'Can I teach you words that on your saying them your poverty will go away from you as well as your illness?' He said, 'Yes, O Messenger of Allah, please do so.' He (the Messenger of Allah) said, 'In the morning and evening say, 'There are no means and no power except the means and power of Allah [most High, most Great]. I have placed my trust in the living one who never dies, and all praise belongs to Allah who has not taken any children and does not have any partner in the dominion, who does not need any supporter against weakness, who is indeed the most powerful.' The man has said that he had not said it for more than three days before which his poverty and illness had gone away from him.'"

Meaning of relatives

H 14514, h 66
Muhammad ibn Yahya has narrated from Ahmad ibn Muhammad ibn 'Isa from Ali ibn al-Hakam from 'Isma'il ibn 'Abd al-Khaliq who has narrated the following:

"I once heard abu 'Abd Allah, *'Alayhi al-Salam*, asking abu Ja'far al-Ahwal, when I was listening, 'Did you go to Basrah?' He replied, 'Yes, I went to Basra.' He (the Imam) asked, 'How was people's promptness to accept this matter (*Wilayah*, leadership with divine authority and power of *'A'immah*)? He replied, 'By Allah it is very little, they have done it but they are very few.' He (the Imam) said, 'You must approach the young ones because they are quicker to all good things.' He (the Imam) said, 'What do people of Basrah say about the verse of al-Quran, '. . . say, "I do not ask of you any compensation for it (preaching Islam) except that you must love (my) relatives (family)."' (42:23) I then said, 'I pray to Allah to keep my soul in service for your cause, they say that it is about the relatives of the Messenger of Allah, *O Allah grant compensation to Muhammad and his family worthy of their services to Your cause*.' He (the Imam) said, 'They have spoken a lie. It was revealed about us especially, about *Ahl al-Bayt*, Ali, Fatimah, al-Hassan and al-Husayn, the people of the Cloak, *'Alayhim al-Salam*.'"

Hadith of the man of al-Sham

H 14515, h 67
It is narrated from the narrator of the previous Hadith from Ahmad ibn Muhammad from al-Husayn ibn Sa'id from Muhammad ibn Dawud from Muhammad ibn 'Atiyyah who has narrated the following:

"Once a man from the people of al-Sham of their scholars came to abu Ja'far, *'Alayhi al-Salam*. He said, 'O abu Ja'far, I have come to ask you certain questions and my search has tired me to find one who can interpret it. I have asked three kinds of people about it and every kind has said something different from the others about it.' Abu Ja'far, *'Alayhi al-Salam*, asked, 'What is the question?' He said, 'I want to ask you about the first creature that Allah created of His creatures. Certain ones whom I asked said that it was destiny, others said that it was the Pen and others said that it was the Spirit.' Abu Ja'far, *'Alayhi al-*

Salam, said, 'They have not said anything. I tell you that Allah, most Blessed, most High, existed and there was nothing. He was Glorious and no one was there before His being Glorious as He has said, 'Allah, your Lord, is free of all defects, the Lord of Glory above and beyond what they say.' (37:180) He was the creator before the creatures. If the first thing that He created of His creatures was something from something then it goes on without end forever eternally, Allah with something. However, He existed and nothing else other than Him existed. He then created the thing from which are all things and that thing is water from which things are. He made the relation of everything to water and has made no lineage for water to which it can be ascribed. He created the wind and then made it to dominate over the water and it opened the center of the water until it produced foam as much as He wanted to produce foam. From that foam, He created a white and clean land without any cracks or holes, climbing up or down and without tree. He then rolled it and placed it on the body of water until smoke was produced from water as much as Allah wanted to be produced. From that smoke He created a clear and clean sky without any crack and hole and that is in His words, '. . . the sky that He built, and raised its ascent and leveled, made its night dark and its brightness to come out.' (79:27-29) He (the Imam) said, 'There was no sun, moon, stars or cloud. He then rolled it and placed it on earth, then related two creatures. He raised the sky as is in His words; most Glorious is whose mention. '. . . thereafter He spread the earth.' He says that He spread it.' The man from al-Sham then said that the words of Allah, most High, '. . . have the unbelievers not seen that the sky and earth were a piece and We slashed them apart?' (21:29) Abu Ja'far, *'Alayhi al-Salam*, said, 'Perhaps you think they were stuck together then one was slashed from the other?' He replied, 'Yes, that is true.' Abu Ja'far, *'Alayhi al-Salam*, said, 'You must ask forgiveness from your Lord. The words of Allah, most Majestic, most Glorious, 'They were a piece', means that the sky was one piece without rain, the earth was a piece without growing any grain. When Allah, most Blessed, most High, created the creatures, spread there all kinds of animals He opened the sky with water and the earth with plants.' The man from al-Sham said, 'I testify that you are of the children of the Prophets and your knowledge is from their knowledge.'"

Everything was water

H 14516, h 68
Muhammad has narrated from Ahmad ibn Muhammad, from ibn Mahbub from al-'Ala' ibn Razin from Muhammad ibn Muslim from al-Hajjal from al-'Ala' from Muhammad ibn Muslim who has narrated the following:

"Abu Ja'far, *'Alayhi al-Salam*, has said, 'Everything was water and His throne was on the water. Allah commanded the water, thus a fire began to blaze. He commanded the fire, it extinguished from which a smoke began to rise with which Allah created the skies, and He created the earth from ashes. Thereafter the water and fire quarreled as well as the air. The water said that it was the greatest army of Allah, the air said that it was the greatest army of Allah and the fire said that it was the greatest army of Allah.' Allah, most Majestic, most Glorious, sent revelation to the air that said, 'You are my greatest army.'"

Hadith of gardens and camels

H 14517, h 69

Ali ibn Ibrahim has narrated from his father from ibn Mahbub from Muhammad ibn Ishaq al-Madaniy who has narrated the following:

"Abu Ja'far, *'Alayhi al-Salam*, has said that the Messenger of Allah, *O Allah grant compensation to Muhammad and his family worthy of their services to Your cause*, was asked about the meaning of the words of Allah, most Majestic, most Glorious, '. . . on the day when We will raise the pious ones as delegates.' (19:85) He (the Messenger of Allah) said, 'O Ali, the delegation will not arrive without riding. They will be the people who remained pious before Allah and Allah loved them, gave them special treatment and agreed with their deeds so He called them the pious ones.'

"He (the Messenger of Allah) then said to him, 'O Ali, by the One who opens the seed and carves the fetus into shape that they will come out of their graves. The angels will greet them with the camels of glory, saddled with saddles of gold, decorated with crystals and rubies, with a covering of brocade, of silk brocade, with a purple braided muzzle whereby they fly to the Resurrection. Each man will be accompanied by one thousand angels in front, right and on their left who will lead them until they arrive at the gate of the greatest garden (paradise). At the gate of the garden (paradise), there is a tree. Under the shadow of one such tree, one thousand people can find enough room. On the right side of that tree, there is a fountain, which is purified. They will drink from that fountain whereby Allah will clean their heart from envy and the hairs fall off their skin. This is mentioned in the words of Allah, most Majestic, most Glorious, ". . . Their Lord will provide them with a drink of pure wine." (76:21) It will be from that pure and clean fountain.'

"He (the Messenger of Allah), said, 'Thereafter they will turn to another fountain on the left of the tree to take Ghusl (bath) and it is the fountain of life after which they will never die.' He (the Messenger of Allah), said, 'Thereafter they will be stopped in front of the Throne and they will remain safe from misfortunes, illness, heat and cold forever.' He (the Messenger of Allah) said that the Omnipotent, most Majestic is whose mention, will say to the accompanying angels, 'Lead My friends to the garden (paradise) and do not make them stand in line with the rest of the creatures, My happiness with them has made My mercy obligatory for them. How will I want to make them stand up with the people of good and bad deeds?' He (the Messenger of Allah) said, 'The angels then will lead them to the garden (paradise). When they arrive at the gate of the greatest garden (paradise) the angels will knock at the ring and it will reach every Hawra' whom Allah, most Majestic, most Glorious, has prepared for His friends in the garden (paradise). They receive the glad news on hearing the ringing of the ring and they say to each other that friends of Allah have arrived. They open the gate and they enter the garden (paradise). Their pairs of al-Hur and human beings will look at them and greet them saying, "We were very anxious to see you." The friends of Allah will say the same thing to them.'

"Ali, *'Alayhi al-Salam*, then said, 'O Messenger of Allah, inform us about the meaning of the words of Allah, most Majestic, most Glorious, ". . . chambers upon which chambers are built." (39:20) With what kind of materials these chambers are built O Messenger of Allah?' He (the Messenger of Allah) said, 'O Ali, Allah, most Majestic, most Glorious, has built those chambers for His friends with crystals, rubies, green jewels with ceilings of gold interwoven with silver. Every chamber has one thousand doors of gold. There are one thousand guard–angels, one for every door. There are raised furnishings in those chambers one over the other of silk and silk brocades of different colors, with fillings of musk, camphor and ambergris. Allah, most Majestic, most Glorious, has said, ". . . there are raised furnishings." (56:34) When a believing person is admitted in his dwelling in the garden (paradise), a crown of dominion will be placed on his head for honor. He will be made to wear garments of gold, silver, ruby and crystals arranged with designs as a garland under the crown.'

"He (the Messenger of Allah) said, 'He will be dressed with seventy garments of silk of many colors, with many designs of weaving with gold, silver, pearl and red rubies. It is mentioned in the words of Allah, most Majestic, most Glorious, ". . . they will be dressed in it with bracelets of gold and pearls and their dress will be of silk." (22:23) When a believing person sits on his bed it vibrates in joy and when the dwellings for friend of Allah settle in the gardens of (paradise) the guard-angel asks permission to offer him congratulations for the honor Allah, most Majestic, most Glorious, has granted to him. The servants of the believing person of male and female say, "You must wait; he is leaned against his throne and his pair al-Hawra' is getting ready, so you must wait for the friend of Allah." He (the Messenger of Allah) then said, 'His pair, al-Hawra' comes out from the tent, walks to him with servants around her dressed in seventy dresses, woven with rubies, pearl and green jewels which is made of musk and ambergris and a crown of honor on her head, a pair of shoes of gold interlaced with ruby and pearl, with shoelaces of red ruby. When she nears the friend of Allah he readies to stand up for her in happiness but she says, "O friend of Allah, this is not the day of becoming tired and suffering, so do not stand up. I am for you and you are for me." He (the Messenger of Allah) said, 'They then embrace each other for five hundred years of the years of this world without tiring on the part of anyone of them.'

"He (the Messenger of Allah) said, 'When he feels tired to a certain degree without being disheartened he looks at her neck with a necklace embroidered with red ruby. He finds a tablet at the center of pearl with a writing on it that says, "You O friend of Allah are my beloved and I, al-Hawra' am your beloved, my soul is devoted to you and your soul is devoted to me." Then Allah sends to him one thousand angels who congratulate him for his coming to the garden (paradise) and marry him with al-Hawra'.' He (the Messenger of Allah) then said, 'They then reach the first door of his gardens (paradise) and say to the guard-angel at the gate of his gardens to ask for permission from the friend of Allah; Allah has sent us to him to congratulate him. The guard-angel says, "You must wait until I inform the guard to inform him about you."' He (the Messenger of Allah) then said, 'The angel goes to the guard and there is a distance of three gardens. The angel reaches at the gate and says to the guard that at the gate of the courtyard there are one thousand angels whom the Lord of the worlds, most Blessed, most High, has sent to congratulate the friend of Allah and they have asked me to ask permission for them. The guard then says, "It is great (difficult) for me to give permission to anyone because he is with his pair, al-Hawra'.'''

"He (the Messenger of Allah) then said that between the guard and the friend of Allah there are two gardens.' He (the Messenger of Allah) then said, 'The guard then goes to the supervisor and says that at the gate of the courtyard there are one thousand angels whom the Lord of glory has sent to congratulate the friend of Allah. They ask permission so I ask permission for them. The supervisor then goes to the servants and says to them, "The messengers of the Omnipotent are at the gate of the courtyard and they are one thousand angels sent by Allah to congratulate the friend of Allah so you must inform him about them.'

"He (the Messenger of Allah) then said, 'They inform him and he gives permission to the angels who visit the friend of Allah when he is in the chamber which has one thousand doors and at every door there is a guard-angel. When the angels receive permission to visit the friend of Allah every guard-angel opens the door which the angel guards, then the supervisor admits every visiting angel through one door of the chamber.' He (the Messenger of Allah) then said, 'They then convey the message of the Omnipotent, most glorious, most Majestic and this is mentioned in the words of Allah, most High, ". . . the angels enter for them through every door [of the doors of the chamber] saying, 'we offer you greeting of peace' . . . to the end of the verse."' (13:23).

"He (the Messenger of Allah) then said, 'It is mentioned in the words of Allah, most Majestic, most Glorious, ". . . when you look you see bounties and a great kingdom." (76:20) It stands for the friend of Allah and in the condition he is, of honor, bounties, the great and vast kingdom. The angels as messengers of Allah, most Majestic, most Glorious, ask permission [to visit] him and do not go to him without his permission. It is a great and magnificent kingdom.' He (the Messenger of Allah) then said, 'Canals flow under their dwellings as it is mentioned in the words of Allah, most Majestic, most Glorious, ". . . canals flow beneath them." (18:31) The easy to reach fruits which is mentioned in the words of Allah, most Majestic, most Glorious, ". . . near over them their shadows and easy to be picked fruits." (76:14) It is because of being so near to them the believing person picks up whichever he desires of the fruits with his mouth when he is leaning and the varieties of the fruits that say to the friend of Allah, "O friend of Allah, eat me before that one."'"

"He (the Messenger of Allah) then said, 'Every believing person in the garden (paradise) has many gardens with and without trellises, with canals of wine, water, milk and honey running therein. When the friend of Allah asks for his meal whatever he desires is brought for him without causing any disdain to his desires.' He (the Messenger of Allah) then said, 'He then meets his friend in seclusion and they visit each other enjoying the bounties of the garden (paradise) in extended shadow similar to the one between dawn and sunrise and finer than this. The believing men each one has an al-Hawra' pair and four wives of the human beings. The believing person spends one hour with al-Hawra', one hour with a human being wife and one hour alone on the throne leaning and looking to each other. A beam of light covers the believing man when he is on his throne and he asks his servants, "What is this shining beam of light? Perhaps the Omnipotent is glancing at me." His servants say, "Holy that He is, Holy that He is, glorious is the glory of Allah, in fact, it is al-Hawra' of your women whom you have not yet met. She is looking over you from her tent and longing for you. She is ready for you and loves to meet you and when she saw you leaning on your bed she smiled to you with excitement wishing to see you and the beam of light that you saw and the light that covered you is from the whiteness of her teeth, due to its cleanness, clarity and fineness."' He (the Messenger of Allah) then said, 'The friend of Allah then says, "You must give her permission to come down to me." One thousand servants hurry to her as well as one thousand female servants with the glad news. She then comes down from her tent to him dressed in seventy garments woven with gold and silver with a garland of pearls, rubies and green jewels, colored with musk and ambergris of many colors. The marrow of her leg shows from behind seventy layers of garments with a height of seventy yards and the width between her two shoulders is ten yards. When she comes close to the friend of Allah the servants move forward with trays of gold and silver with pearls, rubies and green jewels in them, which they spread on her. Then she embraces him and he embraces her and no one of them feels weary.'

"He (the narrator) has said that abu Ja'far, 'Alayhi al-Salam, then said, 'The gardens mentioned in the book are the garden of Eden, the garden of Firdaws, the garden of al-Na'im and the garden of al-Ma'wa'.' He (the Imam) said, 'Allah, most Majestic, most Glorious, has other gardens that surround these gardens and a believing person can have of the gardens whatever he likes where he enjoys as he wishes. When a believing person wants something he only says, "You are free of all defects, O Lord." When he says it the servants hurry to him with whatever he desires without his asking them for anything or his commanding them. This is mentioned in the words of Allah, most Majestic, most Glorious, ". . . their call therein is 'You are free from all defects, O Lord,' and their greeting is peace," (10:10) meaning on the part of the servants. Their last words are, "All praise belongs to Allah, Cherisher of the worlds." (10:10) It means that after their enjoying any of the items of enjoyment like carnal relations, food and drink they praise Allah, most Majestic, most Glorious, after they finish. The words of Allah that say, '. . . for them there is an amount of known sustenance.' He (the Imam) said, 'It means that the servants know and they bring it to the friends of Allah before they ask them for it. About the words of Allah, most Majestic, most Glorious, ". . . fruits and they are gracious," he (the Imam) said, 'It means that they in the garden (paradise), do not desire anything but that they are honored with it.'"

Seventy aspects of their (*'A'immah's*) words

H 14518, h 70

Al-Husayn ibn Muhammad al-Ash'ariy has narrated from Mu'alla' ibn Muhammad from al-Washsha' from Aban ibn 'Uthman from abu Basir who has narrated the following:

"It was said to abu Ja'far, *'Alayhi al-Salam*, when I was with him, that Salim ibn abu Hafsah and his companions narrate from you that you speak in seventy ways (not consistent). He (the Imam) said, 'What does Salim want from me? Does he want that I bring the angels? By Allah the Prophets did not do so and Ibrahim, *'Alayhi al-Salam*, said, "I do not feel well." (37:89) He did not have any illness and he did not speak a lie. Ibrahim said, ". . . the big one among them has done it." (21:63) It had not done it and he did not speak a lie. Yusuf *'Alayhi al-Salam*, said, ". . . O camel men you are thieves." (12:70) By Allah they had not stolen anything and he did not speak a lie.'" (This Hadith speaks of Quranic proof of lawfulness of *Taqiyah*)

Hadith of abu Basir with the woman

H 14519, h 71

Aban has narrated from abu Basir who has narrated the following:

"Once I was sitting with abu 'Abd Allah, *'Alayhi al-Salam*, when the mother of Khalid who was cut off by Yusuf ibn 'Amr asked permission to see him (the Imam). Abu 'Abd Allah, *'Alayhi al-Salam*, said, 'Do you like to hear her words?' I said, 'Yes, I like to hear.' He (the Imam) gave her permission and made me sit with him on the same furnishing as his furnishing. She then came and spoke and she was a very eloquent woman. She asked him (the Imam) about the two of them. He (the Imam) said, 'Do you consider them as your *Waly* (leader with divine authority and power)?' She said, 'Can I then say to my Lord when I meet Him that you commanded me to consider them as my *Waly* (leader with divine authority and power)?' He (the Imam) said, 'Yes, you can do so.' She then said, 'This one sitting on the furnishing with you commands me to denounce them and Kathir al-Nawa' commands me to consider them as my *Waly* (leader with divine authority and power). Which one of these two is better and more beloved to you?' He (the Imam) said, 'This one by Allah is more beloved to me than Kathir al-Nawa' and his people. This one argues and says, "Those who do not judge according to what Allah has revealed are unbelievers." (5:44) ". . . those who do not judge according to what Allah has revealed are unjust." (5:45) ". . . those who do not judge according to what Allah has revealed are sinful ones."'" (5:47)

People hostile to *'A'immah*

H 14520, h 72

Muhammad ibn Yahya has narrated from Ahmad ibn Muhammad ibn 'Isa from al-Hassan ibn Ali from ibn Faddal from Ali ibn 'Uqbah from 'Umar ibn Aban from 'Abd al-Hamid al-Wabishiy who has narrated the following:

"I once said to abu Ja'far, *'Alayhi al-Salam*, that we have a neighbor who commits all the unlawful matters and even does not perform *Salat* (prayer), not to speak of other issues. He (the Imam) said, *'Tasbih* (Allah is free of all defects) and is the most Great. I can tell who is worse than this.' I said, 'Please do so.' He (the Imam) said, 'One who is hostile to us is worse than him. The servant (of Allah) before whom *Ahl al-Bayt* is mentioned if he then feels tender hearted, the angels wipe his back, his sins all are forgiven unless he commits a sin that takes him out of belief, his intercession is accepted but not about one who is hostile to us. A believing person can intercede for his neighbors and for those who have good deeds. He can say, "O Lord, my neighbor refrained from troubling people", thus he intercedes for him. Allah, most Blessed, most High, says, 'I am your Lord, and the right one to compensate for you.' He admits him in the garden (paradise) and those who have good deeds. The least amount of people for whom a believing person can intercede is thirty people and at that time people of the fire say, ". . . there is no one to intercede for us and we do not have a good friend.'" (26:100-101)

Disrespect of a believing person

H 14521, h 73

Muhammad ibn Yahya has narrated from Muhammad ibn al-Husayn from Muhammad ibn 'Isma'il ibn Bazi' from Salih ibn 'Uqbah abu Harun who has narrated the following:

"Abu Ja'far, *'Alayhi al-Salam*, once said to a group of people, when I was with him (the Imam), 'What is the matter with you that you take us lightly?' One man from Khurasan stood before him (the Imam) and said, 'We seek refuge with Allah against taking you lightly or any of your commands.' He (the Imam) said, 'Yes, you are one of those who take me lightly.' He said, 'I seek refuge with Allah against taking you lightly.' He (the Imam) said, 'Woe is on you, did you not hear so and so when we were near Juhfah, saying to you, 'Give me a ride for a mile, by Allah I have become tired.' By Allah, you did not raise your head for him and you took him lightly. One who takes a person, believing in us, lightly has ignored and taken respect for Allah, most Majestic, most Glorious, lightly.'"

The words of 'Abd al-Rahman with Abu 'Abd Allah, *'Alayhi al-Salam*

H 14522, h 74

Al-Husayn ibn Muhammad al-Ash'ariy has narrated from Mu'alla' ibn Muhammad from al-Washsha' from Aban ibn 'Uthman from 'Abd al-Rahman ibn abu 'Abd Allah who has narrated the following:

"I once said to abu 'Abd Allah, *'Alayhi al-Salam*, 'Allah, most Majestic, most Glorious, has granted us a favor by making us to know His Oneness. He has granted us a favor by making us to acknowledge Muhammad, *O Allah grant compensation to Muhammad and his family worthy of their services to Your cause*, as the messenger. He then has granted us a favor by making us to love you *Ahl al-Bayt* and denounce your enemies. We thereby want only to be saved from the fire.' He (the narrator) has said, 'I felt tender hearted and wept.' Abu 'Abd Allah, *'Alayhi al-Salam*, then said, 'Ask me, by Allah, anything you ask. I will give the answer.' He (the narrator) has said that 'Abd al-Malik ibn 'A'yan then said, 'I have not heard him (the Imam) saying as such to any creature before you.' I then asked, 'Tell me about the two men.' He (the Imam) said, 'They did injustice to us and took our right (mentioned) in the book of Allah, most Majestic, most Glorious, denied Fatimah, *'Alayha al-Salam*, the legacy of her father and their injustice continues to this day.' He (the narrator) has said that he (the Imam) - pointed behind – they (the two) threw the book of Allah behind them."

In praise of Hassan ibn Thabit

H 14523, h 75

Through the same chain of narrators as that of the previous Hadith, the following is narrated from Aban from 'Uqbah ibn Bashir al-Asadiy from al-Kumayt ibn Zayd al-Asadiy who has narrated the following:

"I once visited abu Ja'far, *'Alayhi al-Salam*, and he (the Imam) said, 'By Allah, O Kumayt, if we had an asset with us we would have given to you thereof. However, there is for you what the Messenger of Allah, *O Allah grant compensation to Muhammad and his family worthy of their services to Your cause*, said to Hassan ibn Thabit. "The holy spirit continues to be with you as long as you defend us." I then asked, 'Please tell me about the two men.' He (the Imam) took the pillow and folded it into two in front of his chest then said. 'By Allah, O Kumayt, all the blood even of the amount of cupping that is spilled, all assets taken without right, all stones turned away from other stones are upon the neck of the two of them (they will be held responsible)."'

The words of 'Umar to Ali, *'Alayhim al-Salam*

H 14524, h 76

Through the same chain of narrators as that of the previous Hadith, the following is narrated from Aban ibn 'Abd al-Rahman from ibn abu 'Abd Allah from abu al-'Abbas al-Makkiy who has narrated the following:

"I once heard abu Ja'far, *'Alayhi al-Salam*, say that 'Umar once met Ali, *'Alayhi al-Salam*, and said, 'Why is it that you read this verse of the al-Quran, ". . . which of you has been afflicted by insanity." (68:6) and apply it to me and my friend?' He (the Imam) has said that Ali, *'Alayhi al-Salam*, said, 'If you like I can inform you about a verse which is revealed about banu 'Umayyah, ". . . have you decided to spread destruction in the land when you take hold of the government and cut off good relations with relatives"' (47:22) He said, 'You have spoken a lie. Banu 'Umayyah maintains better relations with relatives than you do, but you refuse to do anything other than animosity toward banu Taym, banu 'Adi and banu 'Umayyah."'

About the words of Allah '. . . those who change the bounties of Allah'

H 14525, h 77

Through the same chain of narrators as that of the previous Hadith, the following is narrated from Aban ibn 'Uthman from al-Harth al-Nasriy who has narrated the following:

"I once asked abu Ja'far, *'Alayhi al-Salam,* about the meaning of the words of Allah, most Majestic, most Glorious, '. . . those who changed the bounty of Allah because of their disbelief.' (14:28) He (the Imam) asked, 'What do you say about it?' I then said, 'We say that it applies to the two sinful groups, banu 'Umayyah and banu al-Mughirah.' He (the Imam) said, 'It, by Allah, is about all of Quraysh. Allah, most Blessed, most High, has addressed His Holy Prophet, *O Allah grant compensation to Muhammad and his family worthy of their services to Your cause,* and said, "I gave excellence to Quraysh over the Arabs and completed my bounty on them. I sent to them my messenger but they changed my bounty because of disbelief and took their people into destruction.""""

About the words of Allah 'Leave them alone; you are not blamed'

H 14526, h 78

Through the same chain of narrators as that of the previous Hadith, the following is narrated from Aban from abu Basir who has narrated the following:

"Abu Ja'far, and abu 'Abd Allah, *'Alayhim al-Salam,* have said, 'When people called His Messenger a liar, Allah, most Blessed, most High, wanted to destroy the people of the earth except Ali, *'Alayhi al-Salam,* which is mentioned in His words, ". . . leave them alone and you are not to be blamed." (51:54) He, then, because of al-Bada' granted mercy to the believing people then said to His Holy Prophet, *O Allah grant compensation to Muhammad and his family worthy of their services to Your cause,* ". . . speak (remind them); reminding benefits the believing people."""" (51:55)

Conditions of the Day of Judgment

H 14527, h 79

A number of our people have narrated from Sahl ibn Ziyad from al-Hassan ibn Mahbub from ibn Ri'ab from abu 'Ubayd al-Hadhdha' from Thuwayr ibn abu Fakhtah who has narrated the following:

"I once heard Ali ibn al-Husayn, *'Alayhi al-Salam,* speak in the Masjid of the Messenger of Allah, *O Allah grant compensation to Muhammad and his family worthy of their services to Your cause.* He (the Imam) said, 'My father narrated to me that he heard his father, Ali ibn abu Talib, *'Alayhi al-Salam,* speak to people saying, "When it will be the Day of Judgment Allah, most Blessed, most High, will raise people from their graves, naked, empty handed, without hairs on their head and beard all on one ground. They will be driven by light and gathered by darkness until they stop on a stage of the day of resurrection where they climb one on the other and they will be stopped from moving forward. Their breathing will become difficult and they will perspire a great deal, their condition will become difficult and they will cry loudly." He (the Imam) said, "This will be the first frightening scene of the Day of Judgment. The Omnipotent will look at them from above His throne in the shadow of the angels and command an angel to announce, 'O crowd of creatures, remain quiet and listen to the announcer of the Omnipotent.'" He (the Imam) said that they all would hear those in front as well as those behind. Their voice will break at that time, their eyes anxious, they will tremble in fear, their hearts will feel choked and they will raise their heads to the direction of the voice, subdued toward the caller." He (the Imam) said, 'At that time the unbelievers will say, "This is a difficult day."' He (the Imam) said, 'The Omnipotent, most Majestic, most Glorious, the fairest Judge will then say, "I am Allah, there is no other deity beside Me. I am the fairest Judge. No injustice will be done to anyone of you today. I will judge among you with my justice and balance. No injustice will be done today before Me to anyone. Today I will make justice available for the weak against the stronger ones. The rights of those who had suffered wrong will be taken back from the unjust ones except that the wrongly taken rights will be taken back by compensating from the good deeds and bad deeds and I will grant reward for the good deeds. No one can cross this stage today before Me and an unjust person or one who has a usurped asset with him except the usurped asset, which its owner waives. I will grant him the reward for it and take it for him at the time of accounting. All creatures, you must take hold of it and ask for your losses from those who had done injustice to you in the world. I am the witness over you and I am a sufficient witness."' He (the Imam) said, 'They will recognize each other and take hold of it at the opportunity. No one remains without holding to those who had done injustice to them in this world.' He (the Imam) said, 'They will wait as long as Allah wants. Their condition will become difficult, their perspiration will increase as well as their sadness and their voices will rise with severe crying. They will wish for release instead of asking for taking back their rights from those who had done injustice to them.' He (the Imam) said, 'Allah, most Majestic, most Glorious, observes their difficulties and then an announcer announces for Allah, most Blessed, most High, which all of them will hear, those in front as well as those behind. It will say, "O creatures, remain quiet for the call of Allah, most Blessed, most High, and listen. Allah, most Blessed, most High, says to you, 'I am generous, if you want to gift to each other you can do so and if you do not gift I will take your rights back for you.'"' He (the Imam) said, 'They become happy because of their difficult condition and the congestion of their place and the crowd.' He (the Imam) said, 'Certain ones among them give their rights as gift in the hope for relief and others remain and say, "O Lord, injustice to us is greater than being given as gift."' He (the Imam) said, 'An announcer will then call from the front of the throne saying, "Where is Ridwan, the keeper of the garden (paradise) of al-Firdaws."' He (the Imam) said, 'Allah, most Majestic, most Glorious, will command him to show a castle of al-Firdaws garden (paradise) which is made of silver with all its buildings and servants.' He (the Imam) said, 'On the ground of the castle servants will appear.' He (the Imam) said, 'Then an announcer from Allah, most Blessed, most High, will announce saying, "O the community of creatures, raise your heads and look to this castle."' He (the Imam) said, 'They will raise their heads and all of them will wish to have it.' He (the Imam) said, 'The announcer will call from Allah, most Blessed, most High, saying, "O community of creatures this is for those who forgive a believing person."' He (the Imam) said, 'They will all forgive except a very few. Allah, most Majestic, most Glorious, will say, "Today no unjust person can go to My garden and no unjust can bypass My fire to (paradise). No Muslim will remain without his rights being secured in his favor during the accounting process. O creatures remain ready for accounting."' He (the Imam) said, 'They will be allowed to move to the next stage, dispelling one another until they arrive at the ground and the Omnipotent, most Blessed, most High, is on the throne. With the book of records published, the balance set, the Prophets and witnesses who are the *'A'immah* (respectively) will testify against the people of his time to whom he had said what Allah, most Majestic, most Glorious, had commanded to say and called to the path of Allah.' He (the narrator) has said that at that time a man from Quraysh asked, 'What happens if something is usurped from a Muslim by a pagan who has no good deeds, and about what he will get from him?' He (the Imam) said, 'If the unjust has no good deeds, the oppressed may have bad deeds which will be taken from his side and will be placed on the one who had done injustice to him.""

Those who love *Ahl al-Bayt*, *'Alayhim al-Salam*

H 14528, h 80

Abu Ali al-Ash'ariy has narrated from Muhammad ibn 'Abd al-Jabbar from al-Hassan ibn Ali from ibn Faddal from Tha'labah ibn Maymun from abu 'Umayyah, Yusuf ibn Thabit ibn abu Sa'idah who has narrated the following:

"When they visited abu 'Abd Allah, *'Alayhi al-Salam*, they said, 'We love you because of your nearness to the Messenger of Allah, *O Allah grant compensation to Muhammad and his family worthy of their services to Your cause*, and because of your rights that Allah, most Majestic, most Glorious, has made obligatory. We do not love you for any worldly reason, which can benefit us. We love you just for the sake of Allah and for the matters of the hereafter so that the religion of a man among us is established properly.' Abu 'Abd Allah, *'Alayhi al-Salam*, said, 'You have spoken the truth. You have spoken the truth.' He (the Imam) then said, 'Those who love us will be with us or come with us on the Day of Judgment like this,' he (the Imam) joined his two index fingers. He (the Imam) then said, 'By Allah, a man may fast the day, stand up for *Salat* (prayer) during the night. If he will go before Allah, most Majestic, most Glorious, without belief in *Wilayah* (divine authority and power) of *Ahl al-Bayt*, he will go before Him when He is not happy with him or He will be angry with him.' He (the Imam) then said, 'This is because of the words of Allah, most Majestic, most Glorious, ". . . what denied their spending an acceptance was nothing else except that they rejected Allah and His Messenger, and they did not come for *Salat* (prayer) except lazily and they did not spend (for the cause of Allah) except with dislike. Thus, their assets must not attract you as well as their children because Allah wants to make them suffer thereby in this world and remove their souls as being unbelievers."' (9:54-55) He (the Imam) then said,

87

'Just as bad acts will not have bad effect on belief, in the same way good acts will be of no benefit with disbelief.' He (the Imam) then said, 'You must remain as worshipping Allah alone. The Messenger of Allah, *O Allah grant compensation to Muhammad and his family worthy of their services to Your cause*, worshipped Allah alone. He called people but they did not accept his call. The first one who accepted his call was Ali ibn abu Talib, *'Alayhi al-Salam*. The Messenger of Allah, *O Allah grant compensation to Muhammad and his family worthy of their services to Your cause*, said about him, 'To me you are like Harun was to Musa except that there will be no Prophet after me.'"

Is perfection in good food and body?

H 14529, h 81

Ali ibn Ibrahim has narrated from Muhammad ibn 'Isa ibn 'Ubayd from Yunus who has narrated the following:

"Once abu 'Abd Allah, *'Alayhi al-Salam*, said to 'Abbad al-Basriy al-Sufiy, 'Woe is on you, O 'Abbad, placing restraint on your belly and genitals have deceived you. Allah, most Majestic, most Glorious, says in His book, ". . . O believing people remain pious before Allah and speak the firmly established word, then your deeds will come out properly." (33:70) You must take notice that Allah will not accept any of your deeds until you speak the truth and just words.'"

The five *al-Haram* (the Sacred areas) of Allah on Earth

H 14530, h 82

Yunus has narrated from Ali ibn Shajarah who has narrated the following:

"Abu 'Abd Allah, *'Alayhi al-Salam*, has said, 'Five issues are al-Haram (sacred) to Allah, most Majestic, most Glorious, in His land. The sacredness of the Messenger of Allah, *O Allah grant compensation to Muhammad and his family worthy of their services to Your cause*, the sacredness of the family of the Messenger of Allah, the sacredness of the book of Allah, most Majestic, most Glorious, the sacredness of al-Ka'bah and the sacredness of the believing person.'"

When a believing man becomes forty years old

H 14531, h 83

A number of our people have narrated from Ahmad ibn Muhammad from ibn abu Najran from Muhammad ibn al-Qasim from Ali ibn al-Mughirah who has narrated the following:

"I once heard abu 'Abd Allah, *'Alayhi al-Salam*, say, 'When a believing person becomes forty years old, Allah keeps him safe from three kinds of diseases: leprosy, vitiligo and madness. When he becomes fifty years old Allah, most Majestic, most Glorious, makes his presenting an account about his deeds light. When he becomes sixty years old, Allah grants him acceptance of his repentance. When he becomes seventy years old, the inhabitants of the sky love him. When he becomes eighty years old, Allah, most Majestic, most Glorious, commands to write down his good deeds and delete his bad deeds. When he becomes ninety years old Allah, most Blessed, most High, forgives his past and present sins and he is listed as the captive of Allah on earth.' In another Hadith it is said that when he becomes one hundred years old it then is the weakest part of life.'"

A believing person has the chance

H 14532, h 84

Muhammad ibn Yahya has narrated from Ahmad ibn Muhammad ibn 'Isa from Ali ibn al-Hakam from Dawud ibn Sayf from abu Basir who has narrated the following:

"Abu 'Abd Allah, *'Alayhi al-Salam*, has said that a man has the opportunity (to receive forgiveness) up to forty years of age. When he becomes forty years old Allah, most Majestic, most Glorious, sends revelation to the two angels with him to be stern and stringent with him to save and write down all of his deeds, more or less, small or large.'"

Permission to run away from plague

H 14533, h 85

Ali ibn Ibrahim has narrated from his father from ibn abu 'Umayr from Hammad ibn 'Uthaman from al-Halabiy who has narrated the following:

"I once asked abu 'Abd Allah, *'Alayhi al-Salam*, about the plague which may exist in one area of the city and a man moves to another area or out of the city to another place. He (the Imam) said, 'It is not harmful to do so. The Messenger of Allah, *O Allah grant compensation to Muhammad and his family worthy of their services to Your cause*, prohibited it because of a hill in front of the enemy when a plague affected people of that area. They began to move away, thus the Messenger of Allah, *O Allah grant compensation to Muhammad and his family worthy of their services to Your cause*, said, 'Running away from it is like running away during advancing on the enemy.' It was due to his dislike of evacuating the strategic location."

There is no escape from three things

H 14534, h 86

Ali has narrated from his father from ibn abu 'Umayr from abu Malik al-Hadramiy from Hamzah ibn Humran who has narrated the following:

"Abu 'Abd Allah, *'Alayhi al-Salam*, has said, 'There are three things from which no one, even a Prophet and those of lower rank, remain safe: thinking in temptation about the creation, omens and envy, except that a believing person does not use them in practical life.'"

H 14535, h 87

Muhammad ibn Yahya has narrated from Ahmad ibn Muhammad ibn 'Isa from al-Husayn ibn Sa'id from al-Qasim ibn Muhammad al-Jawhariy from Ali ibn abu Hamzah who has narrated the following:

"Abu Ibrahim, *'Alayhi al-Salam*, once said to me, 'I am having a fever for seven months and my son had a fever for twelve months and it increases on us. Have you realized that it does not cover the body? Sometimes it is in the upper part of

89

the body and sometimes it is in the lower part of the body.' I then said, 'I pray to Allah to keep my soul in service for your cause, if you grant me permission I can narrate the Hadith of abu Basir from your grandfather about his having fever that he would use cold water to bring it lower. He would use two clothes, one in cold water and one on him, exchange them, and say loudly, 'O Fatimah, daughter of Muhammad!' He (the Imam) would say it so loud that people at the door could hear him.' He (the Imam) said, 'You have spoken the truth.' I then said, 'I pray to Allah to keep my soul in service for your cause, have you still not found a medicine for fever?' He (the Imam) said, 'We have not found any medicine for it except prayer and cold water. I had fever and Muhammad ibn Ibrahim sent a physician for me. He brought a medicine that caused vomiting, and I did not like it because if I vomit, it hurts my joints.'"

Supplication and charms

H 14536, h 88

Al-Husayn from Muhammad al-Ash'ariy has narrated from Muhammad ibn Ishaq al-Ash'ariy from Bakr ibn Muhammad al-Azdiy who has narrated the following:

"Abu 'Abd Allah, *'Alayhi al-Salam*, has said, 'Once the Messenger of Allah, *O Allah grant compensation to Muhammad and his family worthy of their services to Your cause*, had a fever. Jibril *'Alayhi al-Salam*, came and read a protective recitation. 'In the name of Allah, read this protective recitation, O Muhammad, in the name of Allah, I seek cure for you. In the name of Allah, I seek cure for you from every illness that makes you tired. In the name of Allah, Allah grants you cure. In the name of Allah, you can take it in good health. In the name of Allah, the Beneficent, the Merciful, I do not swear by the places of the stars. You will be cured by the permission of Allah.' Bakr has said, 'I asked him (the Imam) about the recitation for fever and he (the Imam) narrated this to me.'"

Supplication against being choked

H 14537, h 89

Abu Ali al-Ash'ariy has narrated from Muhammad ibn Salim from Ahmad ibn al-Nadr from 'Amr ibn Shamir from Jabir who has narrated the following:

"Abu 'Abd Allah, *'Alayhi al-Salam*, has said that the Messenger of Allah, *O Allah grant compensation to Muhammad and his family worthy of their services to Your cause*, has said, 'If one says, "In the name of Allah, the Beneficent, the Merciful. There is no means and no power except the means and power of Allah, most High, most Great", three times, Allah will make it a protection for him against ninety-nine kinds of misfortune of which the least serious is death because of suffocation.'"

In the battle of 'Uhud

H 14538, h 90

Humayd ibn Ziyad has narrated from al-Hassan ibn Muhammad al-Kindiy from Ahmad ibn al-Hassan al-Mithamiy from Aban ibn 'Uthman from Nu'man al-Raziy who has narrated the following:

"Abu 'Abd Allah, *'Alayhi al-Salam*, has said that on the day of 'Uhud people in defeat ran away from the Messenger of Allah, *O Allah grant compensation to Muhammad and his family worthy of their services to Your cause*, and he (the Messenger of Allah) became extremely angry.' He (the Imam) said that when he (the Messenger of Allah) became angry perspiration like pearls would drop down from his forehead. He looked around and Ali, *'Alayhi al-Salam*, was on his side. He (the Messenger of Allah) said, 'Join the sons of your father with those who have run in defeat away from the Messenger of Allah.' He (the Imam) said, 'O Messenger of Allah. You are an example for me which I must follow.' He (the Messenger of Allah) then said, 'Help me against these.' He (the Imam) attacked and struck the first one whom he encountered from them. Jibril *'Alayhi al-Salam*, said, 'O Muhammad, this is cooperation and help.' He (the Messenger of Allah), said, 'He is from me and I am from him.' Jibril, said, 'I am from both of you, O Muhammad.' Abu 'Abd Allah, *'Alayhi al-Salam*, has said that the Messenger of Allah, *O Allah grant compensation to Muhammad and his family worthy of their services to Your cause*, looked to Jibril and saw him on a chair of gold between the sky and earth saying, 'There is no sword except Dhulfaqar and there is no young man except Ali.'"

The honorable and disgraceful events of the Arabs

H 14539, h 91

Humayd ibn Ziyad has narrated from 'Ubayd ibn Ahmad al-Dihqan from Ali al-Hassan al-Tatriy from Muhammad ibn Ziyad ibn 'Isa Bayya'a al-Sabiriy from Aban ibn 'Uthman who has said that narrated to me Fudayl al-Barjamiy who has narrated the following:

"I was in Makkah and Khalid ibn 'Abd Allah was the governor. He was in Masjid al-Haram (the Sacred Masjid) near Zamzam and he said, 'Call Qatadah for me.' An old man with a red head and beard came and I went near to listen. Khalid said, 'O Qatadah, tell me what was the most honorable event in the Arab people, the most majestic one and the most humiliating event.' Qatadah, said, 'May Allah keep you well, O Amir, ruler, I can tell you about the most honorable event in the Arab people, the most majestic one and the most humiliating event. It all was in one event. Khalid said, 'Woe is on you, how all of it can be in one event?' He said, 'Yes, may Allah keep the Amir well.' Khalid said, 'What is it?' He said, 'It was the event of Badr.' Khalid asked, 'How is that?' He said, 'It was the most honorable event in Arab people because Allah, most Majestic, most Glorious, honored Islam and its people, it is the most majestic event because Allah granted majesty to Islam and its people and it was the most humiliating event for the Arab people because Quraysh was killed and the Arab people were humiliated.' Khalid said, 'You have spoken a lie by Allah, there was no one more majestic than Arab people on that day. Woe is on you, Qatadah, read for me of their poetry.' He said, 'Abu Jahl came out on that day with a banner so that his place could be seen. He had a red turban on his head with a golden shield in his hand saying: "Even the recalcitrant war cannot take revenge on me. I am like the camel that is only two years old after reaching the peak of its strength and for this kind of thing my mother has given birth to me." Khalid said, 'The enemy of Allah has spoken a lie. The son of my brother was better than him, that is Khalid ibn Walid and his mother was Qushayriyah. Woe is on you, O Qatadeh, who is the author of this line, "I keep my promise and defend my status." He said, 'May Allah keep the Amir well. This was not on that day. It was said on the day of' 'Uhud when Talhah ibn abu Talhah came out asking for a duel but no one went for the challenge. He then said, 'You think that with your swords you send us to the fire and we send you with our swords to the garden (paradise), allow someone to come to me and send me with his sword to the fire and I send him with my sword to the garden (paradise).' Ali ibn abu Talib, *'Alayhi al-Salam*, went out and he said, "I am the son of the owner of two ponds, 'Abd al-Muttalib and Hashim who fed the needy in the year of famine. I keep my promise and defend my status."' Khalid, the condemned one, said, 'He has spoken a lie, by my life, by Allah, abu Turab was not as such.' The old man then said, 'O Amir, governor allow me to leave.' He (the narrator) has said that the old man left opening the way through the crowd with his hands saying, 'A heretic by the Lord of al-Ka'bah, he is a heretic by the Lord of al-Ka'bah.'"

Hadith of Adam, *'Alayhi al-Salam*, with the tree

H 14540, h 92

Ali ibn Ibrahim has narrated from his father from al-Hassan ibn Mahbub from Muhammad ibn Fudayl from abu Hamzah who has narrated the following:

"Abu Ja'far, *'Alayhi al-Salam*, has said that Allah, most Blessed, most High, made an agreement with Adam, *'Alayhi al-Salam*, that he must not go near the tree. When the time which was in the knowledge of Allah about his eating from the tree came, he forgot and ate from it as it is mentioned in the words of Allah, most Majestic, most Glorious, 'We had commanded Adam (certain matters). He forgot Our commandment and We did not find in him the determination (to fulfill Our commandments).' (20:115) When Adam, *'Alayhi al-Salam*, ate from the tree he was made to descend to earth. Habil with his sister were born as twins and Qabil with his sister were born as twins. Adam, *'Alayhi al-Salam*, issued a command that required Habil and Qabil to offer an offering. Habil owned sheep and Qabil was a farmer. Habil offered a sheep and Qabil offered from his farm what was not ripe. The offering of Habil was accepted but the offering of Qabil was not accepted as it is mentioned in the words of Allah, most Majestic, most Glorious, '(Muhammad), tell them the true story of the two sons of Adam (Abel and Cain). Each one of them offered a sacrifice. The sacrifice of one of them (Abel) was accepted but not that of the other (Cain) . . .' (5:27) The offering had to be consumed by the fire. Qabil decided to build a house of fire, it was the first one that he built as the house of fire, and he said, 'I will worship this fire until my offering is accepted.' Also Satan, kept away from mercy by Allah, came to him - his relation with the children of Adam, *'Alayhi al-Salam*, is like blood that runs in their veins – and said to him, 'O Qabil, the offering of Habil was accepted but your offering was not accepted. If you leave him alive, his descendents will express superiority over your children and will say that they are the children of one whose offering was accepted. You must kill him so there will be no one left behind him to express superiority over your children.' He killed him and Qabil returned to Adam, *'Alayhi al-Salam*, who asked, 'O Qabil, where is Habil?' He replied, 'You can find him where we offered offerings.' Adam, *'Alayhi al-Salam*, went to search and found him killed. Adam, *'Alayhi al-Salam*, said, 'Condemned is the land that accepted the blood of Habil.' Adam, *'Alayhi al-Salam*, wept for Habil for forty nights. Adam, *'Alayhi al-Salam*, then asked his Lord for a son. A son was born and he named him Hibbatu Allah because Allah, most Majestic, most Glorious, granted him with his sister as twins. When the time of the Prophet-hood of Adam, *'Alayhi al-Salam*, ended and his days became complete Allah, most Majestic, most Glorious, sent him revelation. It said, 'O Adam, your Prophet-hood is complete and your days have ended, so you must leave the knowledge which is with you, the faith, the magnificent name, the legacy of knowledge, the vestige of the knowledge of Prophet-hood in a successor from your descendents. It must remain with them to the Day of Judgment and do not leave the earth without a scholar from whom my religion can be learned as well as obedience to Me, whereby salvation for those who will be born from your time to the time of Noah be provided.' He (Adam) gave to him (Hibbatu Allah) the glad news about Noah, *'Alayhi al-Salam*. He said, 'Allah, most Blessed, most High, will raise a Prophet whose name is Noah and he will call to Allah, most Majestic, most Glorious, but his people will reject his call and Allah will destroy them by flood.' Between him and Noah, there were ten generations of Prophets and executors of the will of Prophets altogether. Adam, *'Alayhi al-Salam*, made a will to Hibbatu Allah that said, 'Whoever of you will meet him you must follow and acknowledge him because he will save you from drowning.' Adam, *'Alayhi al-Salam*, became ill with the illness because of which he died and he sent for Hibbatu Allah and said to him, 'If you meet Jibril or an angel convey my greeting of peace to him and say, "O Jibril, my father asks you to gift him of the fruits of the garden (paradise)."'Jibril said, 'O Hibbatu Allah, your father has died and we have descended to perform *Salat* (prayer) for him so turn back.' He turned back and found Adam, *'Alayhi al-Salam*, has passed away. Jibril showed him how to give him Ghusl (bath). He gave him the Ghusl (bath) and the body was ready for *Salat* (prayer). Hibbatu Allah said to Jibril, 'Lead the *Salat* (prayer) for Adam, *'Alayhi al-Salam*.' Jibril said, 'Allah, most Majestic, most Glorious, commanded us to do *Sajdah* (prostration) for your father, Adam, *'Alayhi al-Salam*, when he was in the garden (paradise); so we are not to lead any of his children.' Hibbatu Allah then led the *Salat* (prayer) for his father and Jibril with an army of angels behind him. He said thirty times *Takbir* (Allah is great beyond description). Jibril commanded to remove twenty-five *Takbir* – today the *Sunnah* among us is five times *Takbir*. Over the people of Badr nine or seven times *Takbir* were said – Thereafter when Hibbatu Allah buried his father, Qabil came to him and said, 'O Hibbatu Allah, I saw that my father favored you with knowledge which he did not give to me. It is the knowledge with which your brother Habil prayed and his offering was accepted. I killed him so that he cannot have any children to claim superiority over my children and say that they are the children of one whose offering was accepted and you are the children of one whose offering was not accepted. If you show the knowledge that is given to you by your father, I will kill you just as I killed your brother, Habil.' So Hibbatu Allah and his children remained afraid with the knowledge, belief, the magnificent name, the legacy of the Prophet-hood, the vestige of the knowledge of Prophet-hood until Noah *'Alayhi al-Salam*, was sent and the will of Hibbatu Allah appeared, when they looked at the will of Adam, *'Alayhi al-Salam*. They found Noah, *'Alayhi al-Salam*, and accepted his faith, followed him and acknowledged him.

"Adam, *'Alayhi al-Salam*, had made a will to Hibbatu Allah to pay proper attention to the will in the beginning of every year and make that day a festival for themselves. They were waiting for Noah and the time of his coming. In the same way, it has come in the will of every Prophet. This continued until Allah sent Prophet Muhammad, *O Allah grant compensation to Muhammad and his family worthy of their services to Your cause*. They recognized Noah with the knowledge, which was with them as it is mentioned in the words of Allah, most Majestic, most Glorious, '. . . We sent Noah to his people. . .' (7:59, 11:25, 29:14). Between Adam, *'Alayhi al-Salam*, and Noah there were Prophets who were hiding; there is no mention of them in al-Quran. They are not named as those who were not hiding are mentioned of the Prophets *'Alayhim al-Salam*. There are the words of Allah, most Majestic, most Glorious, mentioning them. '. . . messengers whom We have spoken of before and messengers of whom We have not spoken of to you.' (4:164) It means that Allah has not mentioned those who were hiding as He has mentioned those who were not hiding of the Prophets, *'Alayhim al-Salam*.

"Noah, *'Alayhi al-Salam*, lived for one thousand less five hundred years with his people. No one shared with him in his Prophet-hood but he came to a people who rejected the Prophets, *'Alayhim al-Salam*, who were between him and Adam, *'Alayhi al-Salam*, as it is mentioned in the words of Allah, most Majestic, most Glorious, '. . . the people of Noah rejected the messengers.' (26:105) They were the ones who lived between Noah and Adam, *'Alayhi al-Salam*, '. . . your Lord is majestic and merciful.' (26:191) When the time of Noah was complete as well as his Prophet-hood, Allah, most Majestic, most Glorious, sent him revelation. It asked him, "Leave the knowledge with him, the belief, the magnificent name, the legacy of the knowledge, the vestige of knowledge of Prophet-hood in his successor of his descendents. It is because I never cut them off (the Holy items) as I did not cut them off from the houses of the Prophets, *'Alayhim al-Salam*, which existed between you and Adam, *'Alayhi al-Salam*. I do not leave the earth without a scholar on it through whom My religion is learned, My obedience is learned and thereby is the salvation of those who are born between the passing away of a Prophet until the coming of another Prophet." Noah gave the glad news of Hud to Sam, *'Alayhi al-Salam*. In the time between Noah and Hud, there were Prophets and Noah said that Allah would send a Prophet who is called Hud. He will call his people to Allah, most Majestic, most Glorious, but they will reject him and Allah, most Majestic, most Glorious, will destroy them by wind. Those of you who will meet him must believe in him and follow him.

"Allah, most Majestic, most Glorious, will save them from the punishment, which will be inflicted upon them by the wind. Noah, *'Alayhi al-Salam*, commanded his son Sam to pay attention to this will in the beginning of every year and observe that day a day of festivity for them. They then paid attention to that which was with them of knowledge, belief, the magnificent name, the legacy of knowledge and the vestige of Prophet-hood. They found Hud, *'Alayhi al-Salam*, about whom Noah had given the glad news. They accepted his belief, followed him, acknowledged him and they were saved from the punishment by the wind and it is mentioned in the words of Allah, most Majestic, most Glorious, '. . . to 'Ad we sent their brother Hud,' (7:65) also in the words of Allah, most Majestic, most Glorious, '. . . 'Ad rejected the messengers, when their brother Hud said to them to remain pious', (26:123-124) and in the words of Allah, most Blessed, most High, '. . . Ibrahim made the will about it to his sons Ya'qub', (2:132) and His words, '. . . We granted to him Ishaq and Ya'qub. We granted guidance to both of them', [to keep it in his family], We had granted guidance to Noah before,' (6:84) to keep it in his family. The offspring of Prophets, *'Alayhim al-Salam*, who lived before Ibrahim commanded [accepted the faith of] Ibrahim, *'Alayhi al-Salam*. In the period between Ibrahim and Hud, there lived other Prophets. They are mentioned in the words of Allah, most Majestic, most Glorious. '. . . the people of Lot were not far away from you.' (11:89) There are also His words, majestic is whose mention, '. . . then Lot accepted his faith and said, "I seek refuge with my Lord", and in the words of Allah, most Majestic, most Glorious, '. . . and Ibrahim when he said to his people to worship Allah and remain pious before Him is better for you [if you know it].' (29:26). Between every two Prophets, there lived ten, nine or eight other Prophets. They all were Prophets who all faced what Noah, *'Alayhi al-Salam*, had faced and what Adam, Hud, Salih, Shu'ayb and Ibrahim *'Alayhim al-Salam*, had faced until it was the time of Yusuf son of Ya'qub, *'Alayhima al-Salam*. After Yusuf, it went to the grandsons, his brothers, until it (the legacy of the Prophets) went to Musa, *'Alayhi al-Salam*. There were other Prophets between Yusuf and Musa, *'Alayhima al-Salam*. Allah then sent Musa and Harun, *'Alayhima al-Salam*, to Pharaoh, Haman and Qarun. Thereafter, he sent other messengers continuously. 'Whenever a messenger came to his people they rejected him and We made those people follow one another, facing destructions and turned them into mere stories.' (23:44) Banu Israel killed, a Prophet, or two contemporary Prophets, or four until they perhaps in one day killed seventy-one Prophets and the show for their killing was arranged in the end of the day.

"When the Torah was revealed to Musa, *'Alayhi al-Salam*, it gave the glad news of the coming of Muhammad, *O Allah grant compensation to Muhammad and his family worthy of their services to Your cause*. Between Yusuf and Musa, *'Alayhima al-Salam*, there were other Prophets. Musa had made a will for Usha' son of Nun, *'Alayhi al-Salam*, and he was the young man whom Allah, most Majestic, most Glorious, has mentioned in His book. The Prophets continued giving glad news about the coming of Muhammad, *O Allah grant compensation to Muhammad and his family worthy of their services to Your cause*. It is mentioned in the words of Allah, most High, '. . . they [Jews and Christians]

95

find it written [the description of Muhammad, *O Allah grant compensation to Muhammad and his family worthy of their services to Your cause,*] with them [in the Torah and the Injil]. He will command them to do good deeds and prohibit them from committing evil deeds.' (7:157) This is how it is mentioned in the words of Allah, most Majestic, most Glorious, '. . . giving the glad news of the coming of a messenger whose name is Ahmad.' (61:6) Musa, and 'Isa, *'Alayhima al-Salam,* gave the glad news of the coming of Muhammad, *O Allah grant compensation to Muhammad and his family worthy of their services to Your cause,* just as the Prophets, *'Alayhim al-Salam,* gave the glad news of the coming of the other Prophets. It continued until it came to Muhammad, *O Allah grant compensation to Muhammad and his family worthy of their services to Your cause.* When Muhammad, *O Allah grant compensation to Muhammad and his family worthy of their services to Your cause,* completed his Prophet-hood and his days, Allah, most Blessed, most High, sent him revelation. It said, 'O Muhammad, your Prophet-hood is complete and your days as well. You must leave the knowledge, which is with you, belief, the magnificent name, the legacy of knowledge and the vestige of Prophet-hood in your family with Ali ibn abu Talib, *'Alayhi al-Salam.* I do not cutoff the knowledge which is with you, belief, the magnificent name, the legacy of knowledge and the vestige of Prophet-hood from your descendents as I did not do so with the families of the Prophets who lived between you and your father Adam, *'Alayhi al-Salam,* as is mentioned in the words of Allah, most Blessed, most High, '. . . Allah selected Adam, Noah, Ibrahim and the family of 'Imran over all the people of the worlds. They were descendents from each other and Allah is hearing and all-knowing.' (3:33-34). Allah, most Blessed, most High, does not turn knowledge into ignorance. He has not left Himself to seek help from His other creatures, not even to an angel of close position or a Prophet messenger; however, He has sent a messenger from His angels and told him to say so and so. He commanded them to do what He loves and prohibited from what He dislikes. He explained to them the affairs of His creatures with knowledge. He taught that knowledge, the knowledge of the Prophets and the chosen ones of the Prophets, brothers, the descendents who were from each other as is mentioned in the words of Allah, most Blessed, most High, '. . . We had given the book and wisdom to Ibrahim and We had given them a great dominion.' (4:54)

"The 'book' stands for Prophet-hood, 'wisdom' is a reference to the Prophets of wisdom of the chosen ones and the great dominion refers to *'A'immah* of guidance of the chosen ones and all of them are of the descendents who were from one another. The scholars are those with whom Allah has placed the remaining task and with them is the end, the preservation of the covenant until the end of the world; the scholars, those in control of the affairs, interpretation of knowledge and for those who provide guidance. Such is the task of the chosen ones, the messengers, the Prophet, and people of wisdom, *'A'immah* of guidance, the successors (people who possess divine authority), who are friends of Allah, most Majestic, most Glorious, the interpreters of the knowledge of Allah, the people of the vestige of the knowledge of Allah in the descendents who are from each other of the chosen ones after the Prophets, *'Alayhim al-*

Salam, of the fathers, brothers, and descendents of the Prophets. Those who seek protection with the excellence they reach to their knowledge and achieve salvation by helping them.

"Those who place the task of friends of Allah, most Majestic, most Glorious, (people who possess divine authority) and people of interpretation of His knowledge in people other than the chosen ones of the *Buyut* of (houses) of the Prophets, *'Alayhim al-Salam*, they have opposed the command of Allah, most Majestic, most Glorious. They have placed the ignorant ones in the place of the friends of Allah (people who possess divine authority) and in those who pretend without guidance from Allah, most Majestic, most Glorious, who think that they are people of interpretations of the knowledge of Allah. They have rejected Allah and His Messenger, disregarded the executor of his will, *'Alayhi al-Salam*, obedience to him and have not placed excellence of Allah where Allah, most Blessed, most High, had placed. They fell in error and misled their followers. They will have no argument and divine authority on the Day of Judgment.

"Divine authority and good argument rests in *Ale* (people of) Ibrahim, *'Alayhi al-Salam*, as is mentioned in the words of Allah, most Blessed, most High, 'We gave to *Ale* (people of) Ibrahim the book, the wisdom, Prophet-hood and a great dominion.' (4:54) Good argument and authority is with the Prophets, *'Alayhim al-Salam*, and with the people of houses of the Prophets until the Day of Judgment because the book of Allah speaks of it. It according to the command of Allah is one from another which He has placed on people as is mentioned in the words of Allah, most Blessed, most High, '. . . in the houses which Allah has commanded to be raised.' (24:36) The 'houses' mentioned here stand for the houses of the Prophets, messengers, people of wisdom and *'A'immah* of guidance. This is the foundation of the firm ring of belief by which salvation was found by those who were saved before you and with this those who follow *'A'immah* of guidance will find salvation as is mentioned in the words of Allah, most Blessed, most High, in His book, '. . . We gave guidance to Noah before and to the descendents of Dawud, Sulayman, Ayyub, Yusuf, Musa and Harun and this is how We reward the people of good deeds, as well as Zachariah, John, Jesus and Ilyas were of the virtuous ones, also 'Isma'il, Yasa', Yunus and Lot to whom We granted excellence over the worlds.'

"From their fathers, descendents and brothers We chose and guided them to the right and straight path. These were the ones to whom We gave the book, the wisdom and Prophet-hood. Those who disbelieved them must take notice that We have designated for it (guidance) a people who do not disbelieve it.' (6:84-87) He has designated the excellent from his *Ahl al-Bayt* (people of his family), brothers and descendents, as is mentioned in the words of Allah, most Blessed, most High. '. . . if your followers disbelieve, (a reference to (39:7) which says, 'if they disbelieve; Allah is needless of the worlds) I have designated your *Ahl al-Bayt* (family) as keepers of the belief with which I have sent you and they will never disbelieve it. I will not allow the belief with which I have sent you to vanish from your *Ahl al-Bayt* who are the scholars of your followers, and those who possess My authority and knowledge after you and the people of interpretation of the knowledge in which there is nothing untrue or sin or burden or aggression or showing off. On this foundation, the task of this nation is based.'

"Allah, most Majestic, most Glorious, has purified *Ahl al-Bayt* of His Prophet, *'Alayhim al-Salam*, and has asked the people to love his (Holy Prophet's) *Ahl al-Bayt* as payment for his preaching to them guidance. He established *Wilayah* (divine authority and knowledge) with them and designated them as executors of the will and as His beloved ones permanently in his followers. O people, you must learn a lesson from what I have said and the way Allah, most Majestic, most Glorious, has placed His *Wilayah* (divine authority and knowledge), obedience to Him, His love, the interpretation of His knowledge and His good arguments (people who possess divine authority and knowledge). You must accept it and with it seek protection, you will find salvation and it will be your good argument before your Lord, most Majestic, most Glorious. *Wilayah* (divine authority and knowledge) of Allah, most Majestic, most Glorious, cannot be reached without them. If one follows it, it then becomes obligatory for Allah to honor him and save him from punishment and one who comes before Allah, most Majestic, most Glorious, without what He has commanded him to do it then is obligatory for Allah, most Majestic, most Glorious, to bring him low and subject him to punishment.'"

Hadith Nafi' *Mawla* of 'Umar with Abu Ja'far, *'Alayhi al-Salam*

H 14541, h 93

A number of our people have narrated from Ahmad ibn Muhammad ibn Khalid from al-Hassan ibn Mahbub from abu Hamzah Thabit ibn Dinar al-Thumaliy and abu Mansur from abu al-Rabi' who has narrated the following:

"We performed al-Hajj with abu Ja'far, *'Alayhi al-Salam*, in the year in which Hisham ibn 'Abd 'Abd al-Malik also performed al-Hajj. Present with him at that time also was Nafi', *mawla* of 'Abd Allah ibn 'Umar al-Khattab. Nafi' looked to abu Ja'far, *'Alayhi al-Salam*, at the corner of the House where people had gathered around him (the Imam). He (Nafi') asked, 'O Amir al-Mu'minin, who is this man around whom people have become crowded?' He replied, 'He is the Prophet of the people of al-Kufah. This is Muhammad ibn Ali.' He said, 'You just wait. I will ask him such questions that only a Prophet or the son of a Prophet or the executor of the will of a Prophet can answer.' He said, 'Go and ask, perhaps you can disgrace him.' Nafi' came until he leaned on the people so he could see abu Ja'far, *'Alayhi al-Salam*, from a higher place. He said, 'O Muhammad ibn Ali, I have read the Torah, the Injil, Zabur and al-Furqan and I have learned its lawful and unlawful matters and I have come to ask you certain question which no one other than a Prophet, or son of a Prophet can answer.' Abu Ja'far, *'Alayhi al-Salam*, raised his head and said, 'You can ask whatever you like.' He asked, 'How many years was the period of time between Jesus and Muhammad, *O Allah grant compensation to Muhammad and his family worthy of their services to Your cause?'* He (the Imam) asked, 'Do you like the answer according to your words or my words?' He said, 'Answer me according to both of them.' He (the Imam) said, 'According to my words it was five hundred years but according to your words it was six hundred years.'

"He then said, 'Tell me about the meaning of the words of Allah, most Majestic, most Glorious, to His Prophet, '. . . ask those whom We sent before you of our messengers if We had made Lords other than the Beneficent to be worshipped.' (43:45) Who did Muhammad, *O Allah grant compensation to Muhammad and his family worthy of their services to Your cause,* ask when there was a period of five hundred years between him and Jesus?' Abu Ja'far, *'Alayhi al-Salam,* then read this verse, 'Free of all defect is One who took His servant on journey during a night from Masjid al-Haram (the Sacred area) to the distant Masjid, the surroundings of which We have blessed to show him of Our signs.' (17:1) Allah, most Blessed, most High, showed certain signs to Muhammad, *O Allah grant compensation to Muhammad and his family worthy of their services to Your cause,* when He took him on a journey to Bayt al-Maqdis. Allah, most Majestic, most Glorious, raised all the Prophets and messengers of earlier generations and the latter generations as well. He then commanded Jibril, *'Alayhi al-Salam,* who said Adhan even and Iqamah even times and said, 'Come to the best of deeds.' Muhammad, *O Allah grant compensation to Muhammad and his family worthy of their services to Your cause,* then led the *Salat* (prayer) and when he completed he asked, 'To what do you testify and what did you worship?' They replied, 'We testify that only Allah deserves worship, He is One and has no partners and we testify that you are the messenger of Allah. Upon this He has made a covenant with us and our confirmation.'

"Nafi' then said, 'You have spoken the truth, O abu Ja'far. Tell me about the meaning of the words of Allah, most Majestic, most Glorious, '. . . do the unbelievers not see that the skies and earth were together and We slashed them both.' (21:30) He (the Imam) said, 'When Allah, most Blessed, most High, made Adam, *'Alayhi al-Salam,* to descend to earth the skies were parched, meaning that it did not send any rain, the earth was parched, meaning that it did not grow anything. When Allah, most Majestic, most Glorious, accepted the repentance of Adam, *'Alayhi al-Salam,* He commanded the sky to send drops of rain through the cloud; then He commanded it to allow its openings to allow the rainfall and then He commanded the earth to grow trees that produced fruits and opened up with canals. That was its being parched and slashed.'

"Nafi' said, 'You have spoken the truth, O child of the Messenger of Allah. Tell me about the meaning of the words of Allah, most Majestic, most Glorious, '. . . on the day when the earth will be changed into another earth and the skies,' (14:48) which earth will be changed on that day?' Abu Ja'far, *'Alayhi al-Salam,* said, 'It will be the earth which will remain as bread whereof people will eat until Allah, most Majestic, most Glorious, will complete examining the accounts of people.' Nafi' said, 'They will be busy (with other issues) instead of eating.' Abu Ja'far, *'Alayhi al-Salam,* asked him this. 'Where is their business more intense on that day, will it be in the fire or somewhere else?' Nafi' replied, 'It will be in the fire.' He (the Imam) said, 'By Allah nothing will make them busy except that when they will ask for food they will be fed with al-Zaqqum and when they ask for drink they will be given boiling water to drink.' Nafi' said, 'You have spoken the truth, O child of the Messenger of Allah. Only one more question remains.' He (the Imam) said, 'What is it?' Nafi' said, 'Tell me about Allah, most Blessed, most High, When was He?' He (the Imam) said, 'Woe is on you, when was He not? Therefore, I can tell you when He was. Free of all defects is He who is eternal and forever, One, Omnipotent who does not have any companion and children.' He (the Imam) then said, 'O Nafi' answer me when I ask you about something.' He asked, 'What is it?' He (the Imam) asked, 'What do you say about the people of al-Nahrawan? If you say that 'Amir al-Mu'minin killed them for a truthful cause', you become an apostate; if you say, ''Amir al-Mu'minin killed them for a false cause', you will become an unbeliever.' He then turned around saying, 'You are the most knowledgeable person indeed and in all truth.' He went to Hisham who asked, 'What did you do?' He said, 'You must leave me alone. This by Allah, is the most knowledgeable of the people in all truth and he is a child of the Messenger of Allah, *O Allah grant compensation to Muhammad and his family worthy of their services to Your cause*, in all truth and his people deserve to take him as a Prophet.'"

Hadith of Christians from al-Sham with al-Baqir, *'Alayhi al-Salam*

H 14542, h 94

It is narrated from the narrator of the previous Hadith from 'Isma'il ibn Aban from 'Umar ibn 'Abd Allah al-Thaqafiy who has narrated the following:

"Hisham ibn 'Abd al-Malik once summoned abu Ja'far, *'Alayhi al-Salam*, to al-Sham from al-Madinah. He provided him (the Imam) accommodation and he (the Imam) would sit with people in their gathering. One day when he (the Imam) was with a group of people who asked questions, he (the Imam) looked at the Christians who were entering in the mountain. He (the Imam) asked, 'What do they have there in the mountain? Do they have a festivity today?' They replied, 'No, O child of the Messenger of Allah, but they come to visit one of their scholars every year on this day. He comes out for them. They ask him questions about what they want, and about what takes place in that year.' Abu Ja'far, *'Alayhi al-Salam*, asked, 'Does he have knowledge?' They replied, 'He is the most knowledgeable person. He has met the companions of disciples of Jesus, *'Alayhi al-Salam*.' He (the Imam) said, 'Can we go there?' They said, 'It is up to you, O child of the Messenger of Allah.' Abu Ja'far, *'Alayhi al-Salam*, masked his face with his clothe, went with his companions and mixed with people until they reached the mountain. Abu Ja'far, *'Alayhi al-Salam*, sat among the Christians with his people and the Christians brought a furnishing with pillows. They then went inside, brought him out and covered his eyes with a blindfold as if they were the eyes of a serpent. He then addressed abu Ja'far, and asked, 'O Shaykh, are you one of us or from the forgiven nation?' Abu Ja'far,

'Alayhi al-Salam, replied, 'I am from the forgiven nation.' He then asked, 'Are you of their scholars or of the ignorant ones of them?' He (the Imam) said, 'I am not of their ignorant ones.' He asked, 'Can I ask you or you want to ask me?' Abu Ja'far, *'Alayhi al-Salam*, replied, 'You can ask me.' The Christian man said, 'O Christians, a man from the followers of Muhammad says that I can ask him questions. He is full of answers.' He then said, 'O servant (of Allah), tell me about the hour which is not part of the day or part of the night.' Abu Ja'far, *'Alayhi al-Salam*, said, 'That is the hour between dawn to sunrise.' The Christian man then said, 'If it is not part of the day or night, then what is it?' Abu Ja'far, *'Alayhi al-Salam*, said that it is of the hours of the garden (paradise) in which our patients feel well.' The Christian man said, 'Can I ask you or you want to ask me.' Abu Ja'far, *'Alayhi al-Salam*, said, 'You can ask me.' The Christian man said, 'O community of Christians, he is full of answers.' He asked, 'Why is it that people of the garden (paradise) eat but do not excrete feces, give me a worldly example.' Abu Ja'far, *'Alayhi al-Salam*, answered, 'It is the child in the womb of her mother who eats what the mother eats but does not release any feces.' The Christian man said, 'Did you not say that you are not of the scholars?' Abu Ja'far, *'Alayhi al-Salam*, said, 'I said that I am not of their ignorant ones.' The Christian man said, 'Can I ask you or you want to ask me?' Abu Ja'far, *'Alayhi al-Salam*, said, 'You can ask me.' The Christian man said, 'O community of Christians, by Allah, I will ask him a question which will make him stuck as a donkey becomes stuck in the mud.' He (the Imam) said, 'You can ask what you like.' The Christian man said, 'Tell me about the case of a man who went to bed with his wife who became pregnant with twins who were born in one and the same hour and they died in one, the same hour and they were buried in one grave. One of them lived for one hundred fifty years and the other lived for fifty years. Who were they?' Abu Ja'far, *'Alayhi al-Salam*, said, 'They were 'Uzayr and 'Uzrah. Their mother became pregnant with them as you mentioned and gave birth as you mentioned. 'Uzayr and 'Uzrah lived for so and so years then Allah, most Blessed, most High, made 'Uzayr to die and he remained dead for one hundred years. He then brought him back to life. He lived with 'Uzrah for fifty years and they both died in one and the same hour.' The Christian man said, 'O community of Christians, I have not seen with my eyes anyone more knowledgeable than this man. Do not ask me for anything as long as he is in al-Sham. Take me back.' He was returned to his cave and the Christians returned with abu Ja'far, *'Alayhi al-Salam*.'"

Hadith of Abu al-Hassan Musa, *'Alayhi al-Salam* to Ali ibn Suwayd

H 14543, h 95

A number of our people have narrated from Sahl ibn Ziyad, from 'Isma'il ibn Mehran, from Muhammad ibn Mansur al-Khuza'iy, from Ali ibn Suwayd, and Muhammad ibn Yahya, from Muhammad ibn al-Husayn, from Muhammad ibn 'Isma'il ibn Bazi', from his uncle Hamzah ibn Bazi', from Ali ibn Suwayd and al-Hassan ibn Muhammad, from Muhammad ibn Ahmad al-Nahdiy, from 'Isma'il ibn Mehran, from Muhammad ibn Mansur, from Ali ibn Suwayd who has narrated the following:

"I wrote to abu al-Hassan, Musa, *'Alayhi al-Salam*, when he was in prison, a letter in which I asked him (the Imam) about his condition and many questions. The answer did not come for several months. Then he (the Imam) wrote to me and this is a copy of the answer:

"(I begin) in the name of Allah, the Beneficent, the Merciful. All praise belongs to Allah, most High, most Great, through whose greatness and light the hearts of believing can see and because of His greatness and light the ignorant ones become His enemies, through His greatness and light those in the skies and those on earth seek to establish the relation by using their different deeds and opposing religions. There are the right ones and those who are mistaken, lost and guided, those who can hear and deaf, seeing and blind wandering. All praise belongs to Allah whose religion Muhammad, *O Allah grant compensation to Muhammad and his family worthy of their services to Your cause*, has defined and described. Thereafter, you are of the people to whom Allah has given a special position with *Ale* (family of) Muhammad, because of protecting the love, which attracts you to His religion. (It is also because of) that He has inspired you with awareness and insight in matters of your religion. You give preference to them and ask your questions from them. You have written to ask me of the issues about which I was in a fearful condition. I was able to withhold them. When the domination of the tyrants ended and the domination of the owner of great dominion came (time of his martyrdom) in the form of departing and leaving the blameworthy world to its transgressing people against their Creator I found that I could explain what you have asked me. I am afraid that confusion may come upon our weak Shi'ah because of their ignorance. So fear Allah, most Glorious and inform about it only those who deserve it and be cautious against your becoming a means against the executors of the will or provoking against them through publicizing what I have entrusted you with and exposing what I have asked you to hide and you will never do so if Allah so wills. The first thing that I want to reach you is that I want to inform you of my death in these nights without being horrified or regretting or complaining about what is to happen of the matters that Allah, most Majestic, most Glorious, has determined and has made inevitable. You must get hold of the firm ring of *Ale* (family of) Muhammad and the formidable ring of the Executors of the Will one after other Executor of the Will. You must submit to them and agree with what they say and not to seek the religion of those who are not of your Shi'ah.

"You must not love their religion because they are treacherous ones who betrayed Allah and His Messengers, betrayed their trust and you know how they betrayed their trust. They were entrusted with the book of Allah but they changed its meaning in exchange for other meanings instead of that with which they were entrusted. The people who possessed divine authority and knowledge were shown to them but they turned away from them. Allah made them to taste hunger and fear because of what they had done. You have asked about the two men who usurped the assets of a man, which he spent for the poor and the destitute and those who deplete their supplies on a journey and in the way of Allah. When they usurped his asset, they did not stop for that much until they made him to carry that asset to their homes. When they secured it, then they made themselves as the person in charge of its spending and they reach the level of disbelief in doing so. By my life, they had played hypocrisy before as rejection against Allah, most Majestic, most Glorious, and His words, by considering His Messenger as deriding and they are rejecters, condemned by Allah, His angels and all people. By Allah, nothing entered in the heart of any of them of belief from the time of their coming out of their condition. It did not increase anything but doubt for them. They were deceitful, doubting and hypocrites until the angels of penalty took them away to the place of failure in the permanent dwelling. You have asked about those who were present with that man when they were usurping his assets and placed on his shoulder when certain ones knew but denied. They are of the first apostates of this nation; Allah, His angels and all people, condemn them.

"You have asked about the level of our knowledge. It is of three levels. One is about the past, about future and about that which is coming into being. That which is about the past is interpreted, that which is about future is written down and that which is about what is coming into being is placed in the hearts. It is knocked in the ears, that are the best and excellent form of our knowledge, and there is no Prophet after our Prophet, Muhammad, *O Allah grant compensation to Muhammad and his family worthy of their services to Your cause.*

"You have asked about the mothers of their children and about their marriage and their divorce. The mothers of their children are prostitutes to the Day of Judgment, their marriage is without guardian and divorce without waiting period. Those who come in our call then his belief destroys his misguidance, his certainty destroys his doubt. You have asked about their *Zakat*. In *Zakat*, you have more right. We have made it lawful for you and for those who are of your people, wherever they may be. You have asked about the weak ones. The weak ones are those with whom one cannot argue (because they cannot understand it) and do not know the difference. If he knows the difference then he is not weak. You have asked about testimony in their favor. You must testify (present a testimony) for the sake of Allah, most Majestic, most Glorious, even if it (testimony) is against your own-self, parents and relatives, or (if testimony is needed) between you and them. If you fear for your brother of injustice then it is not applicable. Call to the condition (religion) of Allah, most Majestic, most Glorious, to know us if you have hope in being accepted. You must not seek protection by means of showing off. Accept *Wilayah* (divine authority and knowledge) of *Ale* (family) of Muhammad and do not say about what has reached to you from us or is ascribed to us as false even though you may know something against it from us, because you do not know why we said it and how we explained it. You must have faith in what I inform you and must not publicize what we have held back from you of good issues. Of the obligation toward your brother is not to hold back from him anything, which benefits him in this life or in the hereafter. You must not be envious toward him even if he does bad things, you must accept his invitation when he calls, do not leave him to his enemies of the people even if he is closer to him than you are, and visit him when he is ill. Cheating is not of the moral manners of the believing people, causing trouble, betrayal, arrogance, using indecent words, committing indecent acts or commanding to do such things. When you see the deformed Arab man with an army heavily (in a large number) moving, then you can expect coming of the glad news for you and for your Shi'ah, the believing ones. When the sun appears, then you must raise your eye to the sky and see what Allah, most Majestic, most Glorious, has done to the criminal ones. I have explained for you a few items in general sense. O Allah, I beg You to grant compensation to Muhammad and his family worthy of their services to your cause, the people of goodness.'"

The rare hadith about abu Dharr

H 14544, h 96
Humayd ibn Ziyad has narrated from al-Husayn ibn Muhammad ibn Sama'ah from Muhammad ibn Ayyub and Ali ibn Ibrahim has narrated from his father all from Ahmad ibn Muhammad from ibn abu Nasr from Aban ibn 'Uthman from abu Basir who has said the following:

"Abu 'Abd Allah, *'Alayhi al-Salam*, has said that once abu Dharr came to the Messenger of Allah, *O Allah grant compensation to Muhammad and his family worthy of their services to Your cause*, and said, 'O Messenger of Allah, I have begun to dislike al-Madinah. If you grant me permission, my nephew and I like to move to Muzaynah (name of a place).' He (the Messenger of Allah) said, 'I am afraid, Arab horsemen may attack you, kill your nephew and you will come to me battered badly, then stand before me leaning against your staff and say, "My nephew is killed, and the cattle are taken away."' He said, 'O Messenger of Allah it (moving) will be good if Allah so wills.' The Messenger of Allah, *O Allah grant compensation to Muhammad and his family worthy of their services to Your cause*, granted him permission. He, his nephew, and his wife left. Shortly thereafter horse men of banu Farazah, among whom there was 'Uyaynah ibn Hesn, attacked them, took away their cattle, his wife who was from banu Ghifar and killed his nephew. Abu Dharr then came in a difficult condition until he stood before the Messenger of Allah, *O Allah grant compensation to Muhammad and his family worthy of their services to Your cause*, badly wounded, leaned on his staff and said, 'Allah and His Messenger spoke the truth. The cattle are taken away, my nephew is killed and I am standing leaning on my staff.' The Messenger of Allah, *O Allah grant compensation to Muhammad and his family worthy of their services to Your cause*, then called out the Muslims for help and they went to find them. They brought the cattle back and killed a few of the pagans.'"

Armed expedition of Dhat al-Riqa'

H 14545, h 97
Aban has narrated from abu Basir who has narrated the following:

"Abu 'Abd Allah, *'Alayhi al-Salam*, has said that during the armed expedition of Dhat al-Riqa' the Messenger of Allah, *O Allah grant compensation to Muhammad and his family worthy of their services to Your cause*, disembarked under a tree on the edge of the valley. A flooding that took place caused a cut off between him (the Messenger of Allah) and his companions. One of the pagans saw it when Muslims were standing on the edge of the valley waiting for the flood to subside. A man among the pagans said to his people, 'I will kill Muhammad.' He went and attacked the Messenger of Allah, *O Allah grant compensation to Muhammad and his family worthy of their services to Your cause*, and said, with sword in his hand, 'O Muhammad, who can save you?' He (the Messenger of Allah) said, 'My Lord and your Lord saves me.' Jibril, *'Alayhi al-Salam*, uprooted him along with his horse. He fell down on his back. The Messenger of Allah, *O Allah grant compensation to Muhammad and his family worthy of their services to Your cause*, stood up, took the sword, stepped on his chest and said, 'Who saves you from me, O Ghurth (his name was Ghurth)?' He said, 'Your generosity and grace can save me, O Muhammad.' He (the Messenger of Allah) then allowed him to go, and the man said, 'By Allah, you are better than me and more honorable.'"

Allah does not accept any deed without loving *Ahl al-Bayt*, *'Alayhim al-Salam*

H 14546, h 98

Ali ibn Ibrahim has narrated from his father from al-Qasim ibn Muhammad [and Ali ibn Muhammad from al-Qasim ibn Muhammad] from Sulayman ibn Dawud al-Minqariy from Hafs ibn Ghiyath who has narrated the following:

"Abu 'Abd Allah, *'Alayhi al-Salam*, has said, 'If you can keep yourselves unknown, you should do so. You must not feel bad if people did not praise you. You must not feel bad if you are spoken ill of among people when you are praised before Allah, most Blessed, most High. 'Amir al-Mu'minin, Ali, *'Alayhi al-Salam*, would say, "There is nothing good in the world except for two kinds of people. It is good for a man who increases his good deeds every day and a man who is ready to face his death with repentance, but how can he find repentance? By Allah, even if he keeps performing *Sujud* (prostrations) so much that his neck is cut off, still Allah, most Majestic, most Glorious, will not except any deed from him without his accepting our *Wilayah* (divine authority and knowledge). Whoever acknowledges our right, and keeps his hope for reward through us, then agrees with one-half of a *mud* (a certain measurement) of food every day, with any amount of clothes enough to cover his privacy, with a shack over his head, despite this, by Allah, they are afraid.

"They are deeply concerned and love to have that much of their share from the world as Allah, most Majestic, most Glorious, has described them saying, '. . . those who bring what was given to them but still their hearts are afraid.' (23:60) What is it that they bring? They by Allah, bring obedience to us with love and *Wilayah* (divine authority and knowledge), despite this they are afraid that it may not be accepted from them. By Allah, their fear is not because of doubt in their belief but they are afraid of having shortcomings in loving and obeying us.' He (the Imam) then said, 'If you are able not to go out from your home, you should do so, because in going out of your house it is obligatory on you not to backbite, not to lie, not to envy, not to show off, pretend or make evil plans.' He (the Imam) then said, 'The monastery of a Muslim is his home where he keeps his eyes away from unlawful matters as well as his tongue, his self and his genitals. Whoever recognizes the bounties of Allah by his heart, he becomes deserving more from Allah, most Majestic, most Glorious, before he expresses his thanks for it by his tongue. Whoever begins to feel that he is better than others, he then is of the arrogant ones.' I then said to him (the Imam), 'What happens if he feels to be better than others because of good health when he sees the others as committing sins?' He (the Imam) said, 'It is far away. Perhaps what he has committed is forgiven and you are kept on hold to present your accounts. Have you not read the story of the magicians of Musa, *'Alayhi al-Salam*?' He (the Imam) then said, 'How many are the arrogant ones because of what Allah has granted them and how many are those who are gradually covered (forgiven) by Allah and how many are those who are deceived because of the praises of people for him!' He (the Imam) then said, 'I have hope for the salvation of those who recognize our rights among this nation except for one out of three: a ruler who is unjust, one who follows his desires and one who commits sins openly.'

"He (the Imam) then read this verse, '. . . say to them, "If you love Allah, then follow me, Allah will love you . . .' (3:31) He (the Imam) then said, 'O Hafs, love is better than fear.' He (the Imam) then said, 'One who loves the world has not loved Allah and has taken people other than us as *Waliy* (people who possess divine authority and knowledge). Whoever recognizes our rights and loves us has loved Allah, most Blessed, most High.' A man then wept. He (the Imam) then asked, 'Why do you weep (as a hypocrite)? Even if all the inhabitants of the skies and earth come together to plead before Allah, most Majestic, most Glorious, to save you from the fire and take you to the garden (paradise) they cannot intercede for you, [if you have a living heart, you will be the one most fearing from Allah, most Majestic, most Glorious, in that condition].' He (the Imam) said, 'O Hafs, you must always remain behind and not in front. O Hafs, the Messenger of Allah, *O Allah grant compensation to Muhammad and his family worthy of their services to Your cause*, has said, "One who fears Allah, his tongue becomes speechless."' He (the Imam) then said, 'Once when Musa ibn 'Imran was giving advice to his people, a man stood up and tore down his shirt. Allah, most Majestic, most Glorious, sent a revelation to Musa ibn 'Imran. It said, "Tell him not to tear down his shirt, but he must open his heart for Me."' He (the Imam) then said, 'Once Musa ibn Imran passed by a man of his companions when he was in *Sajdah* (prostration). He came back after completing his work and found him in *Sajdah* (prostration) in the same condition. Musa said, "If what you need was in my hand I would have given it to you." Allah, most Majestic, most Glorious, sent revelation that said, "O Musa, even if he remains in *Sajdah* (prostration) until his neck falls apart, I will not accept from him until he turns to what I love."'

The most beloved thing to the Messenger of Allah, *O Allah grant compensation to Muhammad and his family worthy of their services to Your cause*

H 14547, h 99

Ali ibn Ibrahim has narrated from his father from ibn abu 'Umayr from Hisham ibn Salim and others who has narrated the following:

"Abu 'Abd Allah, *'Alayhi al-Salam*, has said, 'There was nothing more beloved to the Messenger of Allah, *O Allah grant compensation to Muhammad and his family worthy of their services to Your cause*, than remaining hungry and fearful for the sake of Allah.'"

Zuhd (restraint from worldly pleasures) of the Holy Prophet

H 14548, h 100

A number of our people have narrated from Sahl ibn Ziyad and Abu Ali al-Ash'ariy has narrated from Muhammad ibn 'Abd al-Jabbar all from ibn Faddal from Ali ibn 'Uqbah from Sa'id ibn 'Amr al-Juhfiy from Muhammad ibn Muslim who has narrated the following:

"I one day visited abu Ja'far, *'Alayhi al-Salam*, when he (the Imam) was eating while leaning against something. Otherwise, he (the Imam) would say that it is undesirable. I kept looking at him (the Imam) and he (the Imam) called me for food. When he completed, he (the Imam) said, 'O Muhammad, perhaps you see that the Messenger of Allah, *O Allah grant compensation to Muhammad and his family worthy of their services to Your cause*, was never seen by any eye eating while leaning against something, from the time Allah sent him to the day he left this world.' He (the Imam) then said to himself saying, 'No by Allah, no eye had seen him eating while leaning against something, from the day Allah sent him to the day he left this world.' He (the Imam) then said, 'O Muhammad, perhaps you may think that he (the Messenger of Allah) ate bread of wheat to his fill for three continuous days from the day Allah sent him to the day he left this world.' He (the Imam) addressing himself said, 'No, by Allah he did not eat to his fill bread of wheat for three continuous days from the day Allah sent him to the day he left this world. I do not say that he could not find any bread. He would give up to one hundred camels to one man and if he wanted to eat, he was able to eat. Jibril *'Alayhi al-Salam*, three times brought to him the keys to the treasures of the earth and gave him the choice, without any reduction in his reward from Allah, most Blessed, most High, in what Allah has prepared for him for the Day of Judgment, but he chose to remain humble before Allah, most Majestic, most Glorious. He never said, 'I do not have it,' when asked for something. If it was not available, he said that it would come (and we will give you). He (the Messenger of Allah) never gave anything, trusting Allah, but that he delivered it to the beneficiary even if it was the garden (paradise), he delivered it for the sake of Allah to him with his own hand.' He (the Imam) said, 'In the case of your companion ('Amir al-Mu'minin, Ali, *'Alayhi al-Salam*) he would sit like a slave and eat like a slave, feed people bread of wheat and meat, but he would return to his home to eat bread with oil. If he (the Imam) would buy a shirt of al-Sanbalaniy (name of a place), he would ask his slave to choose the better one and he would use the remaining. If his sleeves exceeded his fingers, he would cut the excess; if its length exceeed his ankles, he would cut it off. He when having the choice for doing one of two things for the sake of Allah, he chose the one which was more difficult for his body. He ruled people for five years but he did not place one brick on the other to build something for himself or separate a flock of cattle for himself and did not leave behind any legacy, black or white except seven hundred dirham of his gifts with which he wanted to hire a worker for his family. No one could work as hard as he did, even Ali ibn al-Husayn, *'Alayhim al-Salam*, after reading one of the books of Ali, *'Alayhi al-Salam*, would place it on the ground and say, 'Who can bear to do this?'"

Zuhd of the Holy Prophet, and his humility

H 14549, h 101

A number of our people have narrated from Sahl ibn Ziyad from Ahmad ibn Muhammad from ibn abu Nasr from Hammad ibn 'Uthaman who has narrated the following:

"Ali ibn al-Mughirah narrated to me that he had heard abu 'Abd Allah, *'Alayhi al-Salam*, say, 'Jibril, *'Alayhi al-Salam*, came to the Messenger of Allah, *O Allah grant compensation to Muhammad and his family worthy of their services to Your cause*, to give him choices and made a gesture for remaining humble; he would give good advice. The Messenger of Allah would eat like a slave and sit like a slave to remain humble before Allah, most Blessed, most High. At the time of his death, Jibril brought to him the key of the treasures of the world. He said, "These are the keys of the treasures of the world which your Lord has sent to you so you can have all that the earth carries without any reduction in what belongs to you." The Messenger of Allah, *O Allah grant compensation to Muhammad and his family worthy of their services to Your cause*, said, "In the company of the Friend, the most High (Instead, I want to be in the company of Allah).""""

Zuhd of the Holy Prophet

H 14550, h 102

Sahl ibn Ziyad has narrated from ibn Faddal from Ali ibn 'Uqbah from 'Abd al-Mu'min al-Ansariy who has narrated the following:

"Abu 'Abd Allah, *'Alayhi al-Salam*, has said that the Messenger of Allah, *O Allah grant compensation to Muhammad and his family worthy of their services to Your cause*, has said. 'Batha' and Makkah of gold were offered to me. I said, "O Lord, I like to satisfy myself with food one day and remain hungry the next day; when I am satisfied I thank You and appreciate and when hungry, I pray to You and speak of (remember) You.""""

Hadith of Jesus son of Mary, *'Alayhima al-Salam*

H 14551, h 103

Ali ibn Ibrahim has narrated from his father from Ali ibn Asbat who has narrated the following:

"*'A'immah*, *'Alayhim al-Salam*, have said that Allah, most Majestic, most Glorious, giving advice to Jesus, *'Alayhi al-Salam*, said. 'O Jesus, I am your

Lord and the Lord of your ancestors. My name is one, I am one, only one who alone has created all things and everything is of my making, and all things return to Me.

"O Jesus, you are *al-Masih* by My permission and you can create from clay something like a bird by My permission and you can bring the dead back to life by My words. So remain interested in Me as well as afraid. You cannot find any refuge from Me except with Me. O Jesus, I advise compassionately with mercy until My guardianship is established on you by your asking, then comes happiness from Me. You are blessed as a grown-up as well as when you were small. Testify that you are My servant, son of my female servant. Make room for Me in your soul like your own concerns and keep speaking of Me for your next life. Seek nearness to Me by means of optional *Salat* (prayer) and place your trust with Me; I will be sufficient for you, and do not place your trust in anything other than Me so I then ignore you.

"O Jesus, bear patience in misfortune, accept the fate, be like My happiness in you; if my happiness is obeyed, then I am not disobeyed. O Jesus, keep My remembrance alive by your tongue and My love must exist in your heart. O Jesus, wake up during the neglectful hours and strengthen for Me subtle wisdom. O Jesus, be interested, fearful and make your heart to die with concern and anxiety. O Jesus, examine the night to pursue My happiness and keep your day thirsty for the day of your need with Me. O Jesus, compete in good deeds with your best and you will be known with goodness wherever you go.

"O Jesus, judge among My servants with My advice and maintain My justice among them; I have sent to you that which is a cure for the chests and for the sickness from Satan. O Jesus, do not sit with those who are seduced. O Jesus, speak the truth. Whoever of the creatures has believed in Me has become humble and concerned and whoever becomes concerned about Me keeps hope in my reward. Bear witness that he is safe from My penalty as long as he has not changed or has altered my *Sunnah*. O Jesus, son of the virgin, weep for your soul. Do so like the one who says farewell to his family, who hates the world, leaves it for its people, and has become interested in what is with his Lord. O Jesus, along with it remain soft speaking, offer the greeting of peace clearly, remain awake when the eyes of virtuous people remain sleeping, remain cautious about the hereafter and the severe quake, the horrors of the Day of Judgment when family, children and asset will be of no benefit. O Jesus, apply the kohl of sadness to your eyes when people of falsehood laugh. O Jesus, remain humble and patient. Tuba, (a tree in the garden (paradise)) is for you if you achieve what is promised to those who bear patience. O Jesus, depart from the world day by day and taste that which has lost its taste. I speak the truth. For you is only this day and this hour. Depart from the world with an amount of supplies, which will be sufficient. The rough (clothes) and tasteless (food) should be sufficient in this life; you have seen what becomes of it and whatever you take is written and how you have consumed.

"O Jesus, you will be questioned, so be kind to the weak just as I am kind to you and do not dominate the orphan. O Jesus, you must weep for yourself in private, move your feet to the places of *Salat* (prayer) and allow Me to hear your pleasurable speaking, because My favor to you is good.

"O Jesus, consider how many nations I have destroyed because of the sins from which I have saved you. O Jesus, you must treat the weak with friendliness, raise your tired eye to the sky and pray to Me; I am close to you. Do not pray to Me unless you are pleading before Me and your concern is one concern; if you pray to Me as such, I answer your prayer. O Jesus, I am not happy with giving the world as reward to those who were before you or penalty for those whom I want to punish. O Jesus, you will die but I live. From Me is your sustenance, with Me is the time of you death, to Me is your destination and with Me is your account. Ask Me and do not ask anyone other than Me. Your prayer must be good so also will be My answer. O Jesus, how large is the number of human beings and how few is the number of those who bear patience! Trees are many but good trees are very little, so you must not be deceived by the good appearance of the tree until you taste its fruit. O Jesus, the rebellious disobedient must not deceive you who consumes My sustenance and worships someone other than Me; then he prays to Me in hardships and I answer his prayer; then he goes back to his bad deeds, rebels against Me and exposes himself to My anger. I swear by Myself that I will get hold of him such that he will not escape to any refuge from Me. Where can he run from My sky and earth?

"O Jesus, say to the unjust Israelites not to pray to Me when filthy earnings are in their lap and idols in their homes. I have sworn to answer those who pray to Me and make My answer to them a condemnation until they disperse. O Jesus, many times I give them a longer time and seek through goodness their coming back from their neglect from which they do not come back. The words come out of their mouths but their hearts do not hear them. They expose themselves to My anger and seek nearness to the believing by showing themselves as loving Me. O Jesus, in both private and in public one must be one and the same and so also your heart and your eye. Hold back your heart and tongue from unlawful matters and keep your eyes away from that which is of no benefit. Many times one look of an onlooker plants lust in his heart and leads him to the pond of destruction. O Jesus, be merciful and compassionate, be as you like people to be toward you, recall death very often, depart the family and do not play uselessly because it destroys its companion. Do not remain neglectful; neglectful people are far away from Me, remember and speak of Me with virtuous deeds so that I speak of you.

"O Jesus, repent and return to Me after sin. You must remind the repenting of Me. You must believe in Me, seek nearness to the believing through Me and command them to pray to Me. You must remain on your guard of the prayer of the oppressed because I have taken an oath on Myself to open a door for him of the doors of the sky to accept and that I must answer him even after a certain period. O Jesus, you must take notice that an evil companion is hated and an evil close associate destroys. You must take notice of one you can take as a close associate and choose for yourself believing brothers. O Jesus, return to Me with repentance because sins are not excessively great for Me to forgive and I am the most merciful of the merciful ones. Work for yourself when there is time before the time of your death and before others do not do such good acts. Worship Me for the day, which will be as one thousand years that you count, in which I will reward and recompense in multiples and that sins ruin its owners. Prepare supplies for yourself during the respite and compete in virtuous deeds. Many gatherings disperse and its people are neighbors of the fire.

"O Jesus, restrain from mortals that discontinue and step on the dwellings of those who lived before you, call them and quietly speak to them but you will not sense anything from them so learn a lesson from their condition. You must take notice that you will soon join them along with those who join. O Jesus, say to those who rebel against Me in disobedience and act in opposition to expect My penalty and wait for the coming of My destruction upon them and My joining them with the destroyed ones. Tuba (the tree in the garden (paradise)) is for you, O son of Mary, Tuba (the tree in the garden (paradise)) is for you, O son of Mary, if you accept and adopt the discipline of your Lord who is compassionate to you with compassion. From Him is the initiation of the bounties to honor and He is for you in hardship. O Jesus, you must obey Him; it is not lawful to disobey Him. I advised you as I had advised those before you and I Am the witness thereof. O Jesus, I have not honored any creature like My religion and I have not granted any bounty like My mercy. O Jesus, wash with water what is apparent of you and cure what is hidden with good deeds; you are returning. O Jesus, I gave you what I have granted to you as extra without impurity and have asked a loan from you for yourself and you acted stingily against it (your soul) to render it for destruction.

"O Jesus, you must beautify with religion, love the destitute, walk on earth gently and perform *Salat* (prayer) on all locations; they are clean. O Jesus, fasten your belt; every oncoming is near. Read My book when you are clean and allow Me to hear a sad voice. O Jesus, there is nothing good in an enjoyment that does not last very long and the life whose owner will soon vanish. O son of Mary, if your eye can see what I have prepared for My virtuous friends your heart will melt. Your soul will come out for being attracted to such blessings. No house is like the house in the hereafter where your neighbors are fine people. They are the people whose visitors are the angels of closest positions to Allah. They are the ones who come on the Day of Judgment safe from its horrors. It is the house where the bounties do not change and their people do not vanish.

"O son of Mary, compete for it with those who compete; it is the yearning of the hopeful ones. Its look is beautiful. Tuba (the tree in the garden (paradise)) is for you, O son of Mary, if you are of those who work for it along with your ancestors, Adam, and Ibrahim *'Alayhima al-Salam*, in the garden (paradise) of bounties and you must not seek anything in exchange for it or to replace it. This is how I deal with the pious ones. O Jesus, you must flee to Me with those who flee away from the blazing fire with shackles and penalties without any happiness, and grief does not leave their place. It is a piece like the piece of a dark night, those who are rescued from it succeed and those who remain are destroyed. It is the dwelling of tyrant, violent oppressor, rude, crude people and every arrogant boastful person. O Jesus, it is the worst house and the worst dwelling. It is the house of the unjust ones. I caution you against it and you must accept My expertise. O Jesus, you must remain watchful about Me as always you were and testify that I have created you. That you are My servant, I gave you your shape and sent you to the earth. O Jesus, two tongues in one mouth is not proper as well as two hearts in one chest and it also is the case with minds. O Jesus, do not wake up disobedient and you must not find awareness in a playful way; you must hold back your soul from lustful feelings and penalties. Every lustful feeling takes you away from Me. You must depart it and you must know that for Me you are like a trusted messenger, so you must remain cautious about Me. You must take notice that the world will deliver you before Me and I take your delivery with My knowledge. Thus, you must remain of a humble soul when you remember Me, with a heart showing reverence when speaking of Me, fully awake when neglectful ones remain asleep.

"O Jesus, this is My advice to you and My preaching to you, so take it from Me and I am the Cherisher of the worlds. O Jesus, when My servant bears patience with Me the reward for his deeds are before Me and I am sufficient to take revenge from those who disobey Me, then where do the unjust run away from Me? O Jesus, speak in a fine manner and remain knowledgeable and learning. O Jesus, keep sending good deeds to Me so that its mention remains with Me and take hold to My advice; it is cure for the hearts. O Jesus, you must not feel safe when you plot, from My plans and do not forget in the worldly private conditions to speak of Me. O Jesus, hold your soul accountable for checks-and-balances in matters of returning to Me to recompense for workers who will receive their reward and I Am the best to return to. O Jesus, you became a creature by My word and I made Mary to give birth to you by my command, which was sent to her, through my spirit, Jibril the trusted one among my angels until you stood on earth living and walking and it all was in my knowledge before. O Jesus, Zachariah is like your father and the guardian of your mother. He visited her in the ark, the place of worship and found food with her. Your fellow Yahya (John) is like you of My creatures whom I gave to his mother during her old age without sufficient power in her, whereby I wanted to manifest My dominating power and manifest with you My power. The most beloved of you is the more obedient one of you to Me and of more intense fear from Me.

"O Jesus, wake up and do not despair of comfort from Me and say *Tasbih* (Allah is free of all defects) along with those who do so and with fine words speak of My Holiness. O Jesus, when the forelocks of the servants are in My grip and their going and coming take place in My land why do they disbelieve Me? They ignore My bounties and become friend with My enemy, thus are the unbelievers destroyed.

"O Jesus, the world is a filthy prison but it seems beautiful, as you can see, to the tyrants who slaughter each other for it. You must remain aware of the world; everything of its bounties must vanish and its bounties are but very little.

"O Jesus, ask for Me near your pillow; you can find Me and pray to Me lovingly; I Am most efficient to hear among those who hear and answer the prayers of those who pray to Me.

"O Jesus, have fear of Me and make My servants to have fear of Me so that if the sinful ones continue blindly in their deeds, they will not be destroyed without knowledge about Me.

"O Jesus, remain frightened of Me as you remain afraid of beasts and of the death that approaches you. I have created all of this and you all must have fear of Me.

"O Jesus, the kingdom belongs to Me and it is in My hand and I Am the king. If you obey Me, I will admit you in my garden (paradise) in the neighborhood of the virtuous ones.

"O Jesus, when I become angry with you, the happiness of those who are happy with you will not benefit, and if I Am happy with you, the anger of those who are angry with you cannot harm you.

"O Jesus, speak of Me in your soul, I will speak of you with Myself. Speak of Me in your community and I will speak of you in a gathering, which is better than the community of human beings.

"O Jesus, pray to Me like a sad drowning person who has no helper.

"O Jesus, do not swear by Me falsely; so My throne will shake in anger. The world is short-lived but has long yearnings and with Me is the house, which is better than what you accumulate.

"O Jesus, what will you do when I will bring out the book that will speak in all truth and you will testify to the secrets that you hid and the deeds that you had done?

"O Jesus, say to the unjust Israelites, 'You have washed your faces and have made your hearts filthy. Are you trying to deceive Me or are you daring against Me? You apply fragrance for the people of the world and your inside to Me is like a stinking carrion and you are like dead people.' O Jesus, say to them, 'Trim your fingernails from unlawful earnings, make your ears deaf against hearing indecent words, come to Me with your hearts; I do not want your figures and shape.'

"O Jesus, feel happy with good deeds; with it I Am happy and weep with sins; it is disgrace. Do not do to others what you do not like to be done to you. If your right cheek is slapped, then turn your left cheek; and seek nearness to Me with love for your striving and stay away from the ignorant ones.

"O Jesus, remain humble with the people of good deeds, take part in it with them, bear witness thereof and say to the unjust ones of the Israelites, 'O associates of evil association and sitting on evil, if you do not desist I will metamorphose you into apes and pigs.'

"O Jesus, say to the unjust ones of the Israelites that wisdom weeps because of being away from Me and you, with laughs, abandon (Me), has My disowning you come upon you or do you have assurance of amnesty from My torments or do you want to expose yourselves to My punishment? I swear by Myself that I will leave you as a lesson to learn thereof for the coming generations.

"I then advise you, O son of Mary, the virgin, about the master of the messengers, My beloved who is Ahmad, owner of the red camel and the moon-like face, bright with light, of clean heart, stern in war, My beloved and honorable. He is the mercy for the worlds and the master of the children of Adam, *'Alayhi al-Salam*, on the day he will meet Me. The most honorable among the previous ones to Me and nearest to Me of the messengers, the one who is from Arab people, *'Ummy*, (unlettered, would have not attended commonly run schools) follower of My religion, who remains patient for My sake, strives against the pagans with his hand for my religion. You must inform the Israelites about him and command them to acknowledge him and believe in him, follow him and support him.

"Jesus asked, 'My Lord, who is he that if I make him happy You become happy?' He replied, 'He is Muhammad, the Messenger of Allah to all people. He is the nearest of all to Me and of the most readily available intercession among them. Tuba (the tree in the garden (paradise)) is for him as a Prophet and Tuba (the tree in the garden (paradise)) is for his followers who will come in My presence following his path. People of the earth praise him and people of the sky ask forgiveness for him. He is the blessed, trusted one, the clean and fine and the best remainder (successor) with Me. He will live in the last portion of time. When he will come, I will allow the sky to allow its haversack open and the earth to produce its blossom until they see blessings and I will make a blessing whatever he will place his hand on. He will have many spouses but very few children. He will live in Bakkah, the place of the foundation of Ibrahim.

"O Jesus, his religion is clean of falsehood (upright), his al-Qiblah (al-Ka'bah) is of the land of Yemen and he is of My party and I Am with him. Tuba (the tree in the garden (paradise)) is for him, al-Kawthar, (the pond) is for him, and the great position in the garden (paradise) of Eden is for him where the most honorable ones live and he will leave this world as a martyr. For him is a pond which is greater than Bakkah to the rising of the sun of exquisite sealed beverage, where there are utensils like stars and cups like the sand of earth. It is sweet; there is every kind of drink and taste of all kinds of fruits in the garden (paradise).

Whoever drinks thereof never becomes thirsty again and this is because of My giving excellence to him during the time of a lapse of Prophets between you and him. His secrets are like his apparent condition and his words are his deeds. He does not command people to do anything without himself doing it first. His religion is Jihad (hard work) in difficult times and in peacetime; many lands surrender before him and the ruler of Rome will yield before him. He is for the religion of Ibrahim. He says, 'In the name of Allah, the Beneficent, the Merciful' before having food, expresses greeting of peace and performs *Salat* (prayer) when people are sleeping. He performs five times *Salat* (prayer) everyday consecutively and calls for *Salat* (prayer) like the calling of the army by a slogan. He commences it with *Takbir* (Allah is great beyond description) and ends it with greeting of peace. He keeps his feet in line just as the angels keep their feet in line and his heart and head show reverence toward Me. Light is in his chest, truth is on his tongue and he is with the truth wherever he is. His beginning is from an orphan, wanders for a period about what is wanted from him. His eyes sleep but not his heart. He possesses intercession and with his followers, the Day of Judgment will commence. My hands are on their hand and those who turn back will do so against their own selves; and those who stand by their covenant, I will stand by My covenant with the garden (paradise). So command the unjust ones of the Israelites not to wipe out his books and change his *Sunnah*. They must read *Salam* (the phrase of offering greeting of peace) for him. He in the matter has high status and significant task.

"O Jesus, whatever brings you closer to Me I have shown you; and whatever takes you away from Me, I have prohibited you, you must seek to follow such guidance for your soul.

"O Jesus, the world appears sweet and I have employed you (to work for Me) so remain cautious against things about which I have warned you and the matters which I have given to you as gifts.

"O Jesus, you must look to your deeds like a sinful servant who makes mistakes, and do not look at others' deeds like the Lord. Live in the world with restraint and do not become attracted so that you are destroyed.

"O Jesus, you must think, contemplate and look around in the land to see how the end of the oppressive people was. O Jesus, whatever I say is advice, all of My words to you are true, and I am the clear truth, so it is truth that I speak. If you disobey Me after that I have informed, you will not find anyone other than Me to help and support you.

"O Jesus, make your heart humble, showing reverence for Me and look to those who are lower than you and do not look to those who are above you. You must take notice that the head of every sin and slip is the love for the world so you must not love it; I do not love it.

"O Jesus, make your heart to be fine for Me and speak of Me very often in private and you must take notice that My happiness gaze toward Me so you must be living in it and not dead.

"O Jesus, you must not take anyone as My partner and you must remain cautious about Me and do not be deceived by good health. You must not allow your soul to become attracted to the world. It is like a vanishing shadow. What comes forward of it is like what moves back. Thus, compete in virtuous deeds, with your all-out effort and be with the truth wherever it is even if you are cut or burn with fire. Do not disbelieve Me after that you have come to know, so do not become like the ignorant ones because a thing remains with a thing (ignorant remains with ignorant).

"O Jesus, you must shed tears for Me from your eyes and make your heart show reverence to Me.

"O Jesus, plead before Me in difficult conditions; I rescue those who are in difficult condition, answer the helpless and I am the most Merciful of the merciful ones.'"

About the words of Allah '. . . in that the people of hell dispute among them'

H 14552, h 104

Muhammad ibn Yahya has narrated from Ahmad ibn Muhammad from Ali ibn al-Hakam from Mansur ibn Yunus from 'Anbasah who has narrated the following:

"Abu 'Abd Allah, *'Alayhi al-Salam*, has said that when people of the fire settle they miss you and will not see anyone of you. They will say to each other, 'Why is it that we do not see the men whom we counted as evil ones? We mocked at them. Are our eyes deceived about them?' (38:62-63) He (the Imam) said, 'This is what is mentioned in the words of Allah, most Majestic, most Glorious, ". . . this is a truth about which people in fire dispute each other." (38:64) He (the Imam) said, 'They dispute about you over what they had been saying in the world.'"

Hadith of Iblis (Satan)

H 14553, h 105

Abu Ali al-Ash'ariy has narrated from Muhammad ibn 'Abd al-Jabbar from Safwan from Ya'qub ibn Shu'ayb who has narrated the following:

"Abu 'Abd Allah, *'Alayhi al-Salam*, once asked, 'Who is of most intense animosity toward you?' I replied, 'I pray to Allah to keep my soul in service for your cause, everyone.' He (the Imam) asked, 'Do you know why that, O Ya'qub is?' I replied, 'I do not know, I pray to Allah to keep my soul in service for your cause.' He (the Imam) said, 'It is because Satan invited them and they accepted, commanded them and they obeyed; but he invited you and you did not accept, commanded you but you did not obey him so he provokes people against you.'"

If one sees a disturbing dream

H 14554, h 106

Ali ibn Ibrahim has narrated from his father from ibn abu 'Umayr from Mu'awiyah ibn 'Ammar who has narrated the following:

"Abu 'Abd Allah, *'Alayhi al-Salam*, has said that if one dreams of something which he dislikes, he should change his position from as he was sleeping. He should then say, 'Whispering is from Satan to sadden the believing people. He cannot harm them in anything except by the permission of Allah'; then say, 'I seek protection by means of that with which the angels of Allah of close position, Prophets, messengers and His virtuous servants seek protection against the evil of what I have seen and against the evil of Satan, the one condemned to be stoned.'"

The Holy Prophet teaches a prayer to Fatimah, *'Alayhima al-Salam*

H 14555, h 107

Muhammad ibn Yahya has narrated from Ahmad ibn Muhammad and Ali ibn Ibrahim has narrated from his father all from ibn Mahbub from Harun from ibn Mansur al-'Abdiy from abu al-Ward who has narrated the following:

"Abu Ja'far, *'Alayhi al-Salam*, has said that the Messenger of Allah, *O Allah grant compensation to Muhammad and his family worthy of their services to Your cause*, said to Fatimah, *'Alayha al-Salam*, about the dream that she had seen, to say, 'I seek protection by means of that with which the angels of Allah, with closeness to Him, Prophets, the messengers and His virtuous servants seek protection against the evil of what I have seen in this night. I seek protection against any evil in it that may affect me or anything that I dislike'; then turn to your left three times (spew out three times).'"

Hadith of holding the soul accountable

H 14556, h 108

Ali ibn Ibrahim has narrated from his father and Ali ibn Muhammad all from al-Qasim ibn Muhammad from Sulayman ibn Dawud al-Minqariy from Hafs ibn al-Bakhtariy ibn Ghiyath who has narrated the following:

"Abu 'Abd Allah, *'Alayhi al-Salam*, has said, 'If one of you wants that whenever he may ask anything from his Lord, He will give it to him; he must give up all hope of receiving any help from anyone of the people; and his only hope must remain with Allah, Majestic is Whose name. When Allah, most Majestic, most Glorious, finds this in his heart, He grants him whatever he asks. You must examine your souls before you can count on it. On the Day of Judgment there will be fifty stations or stages; in each one people will be stopped for one thousand years.' He (the Imam) then read this verse, ". . . on the day which is equal to one thousand years of the kind you count."'" (32:5)

Saturday and Tuesday

H 14557, h 109

Through the same chain of narrators as that of the previous Hadith, the following is narrated from Hafs who has narrated the following:

"Abu 'Abd Allah, *'Alayhi al-Salam*, has said, 'If one wants to travel, he should travel on Saturday; even if a stone is displaced from a mountain on a Saturday Allah, most Majestic, most Glorious, returns it to its place. If one's needs become difficult for him he should begin to pursue it on a Tuesday because Allah softened the iron for Dawud on this day.'"

The condition of people on Day of Judgment

H 14558, h 110

Through the same chain of narrators as that of the previous Hadith, the following is narrated from Hafs who has narrated the following:

"Abu 'Abd Allah, *'Alayhi al-Salam*, has said, 'The condition of people on the Day of Judgment will be like the condition of arrows in a bag, placed tightly next to each other. The only space for everyone will be the space for his feet and he will not be able to move here or there.'"

Prostration of Abu 'Abd Allah, *'Alayhi al-Salam*

H 14559, h 111

Through the same chain of narrators as that of the previous Hadith, the following is narrated from Hafs who has narrated the following:

"I once saw abu 'Abd Allah, *'Alayhi al-Salam*, pass through the gardens of al-Kufah until he reached a palm tree. He made wudu near that tree and performed Ruku' (bowing down on one's knees) and *Sajdah* (prostration) and I counted in his *Sajdah* (prostration) five hundred times *Tasbih* (Allah is free of all defects). Then he leaned against that palm tree and read certain prayers; then said, 'O abu Hafs it, by Allah, is the palm tree about which Allah, most Majestic, most Glorious, told Mary, *'Alayha al-Salam*, "Shake the tree, fresh dates will fall down for you."'" (19:25)

Worthlessness of the worldly life

H 14560, h 112

Hafs ibn al-Bakhtariy has narrated from the following:

"Abu 'Abd Allah, *'Alayhi al-Salam*, has said that Jesus, *'Alayhi al-Salam*, has said, 'To get supplies for both this and the hereafter is difficult. Whenever you extend your hand for the supplies of this world, a sinful hand is already there before you however, for the supplies of the next world you will not find any helper to help you.'"

Despicability of a believing person's complaint before an unbeliever

H 14561, h 113

Muhammad ibn Yahya has narrated from Ahmad ibn Muhammad from ibn Mahbub from Yunus ibn 'Ammar who has narrated the following:

"I once heard abu 'Abd Allah, *'Alayhi al-Salam*, say, 'If a believing person stands in need for something and he takes his complaint and need before an unbeliever or one who opposes his religion it is like complaining against Allah, most Majestic, most Glorious, before His enemies. If a believing person takes his complaint and need before a believing person it is like one who takes his complaint before Allah, most Majestic, most Glorious.'"

The tree of al-Kharnubah and Sulayman, *'Alayhi al-Salam*

H 14562, h 114

Ibn Mahbub has narrated from Jamil ibn Salih from al-Walid ibn Sabih who has narrated the following:

"Abu 'Abd Allah, *'Alayhi al-Salam*, has said that Allah, most Majestic, most Glorious, sent revelation to Sulayman ibn Dawud, *'Alayhima al-Salam*, that said, 'The sign for the coming of your death is a tree that will grow in Bayt al-Maqdis called al-Kharnubah.' He (the Imam) said that Sulayman one day looked and saw the tree of al-Kharnubah had grown in Bayt al-Maqdis, and he asked it, 'What is your name?' It replied, 'My name is al-Kharnubah.' He (the Imam) said that Sulayman turned back to the place of his *Salat* (prayer) and stood there leaning on his staff and his spirit was taken away in the hour. He (the Imam) said that Jinn and man continued serving him striving to obey his command as before. They thought that he was alive and not dead. They could see him in the mornings and evenings standing still until the woodworm carved his staff, which then broke, and Sulayman fell to the ground. As you hear the words of Allah, most Majestic, most Glorious, '. . . when he fell down the Jinn found that if they knew the unseen they would not remain in suffering, humiliated.' (34:14)

The words of the pagans with the Holy Prophet, *'Alayhi al-Salam*

H 14563, h 115

Ibn Mahbub has narrated from Jamil ibn Salih from Sadir who has narrated the following:

"Abu Ja'far, *'Alayhi al-Salam*, has said, 'Jabir ibn 'Abd Allah narrated to me that the pagans when passing by the Messenger of Allah, *O Allah grant compensation to Muhammad and his family worthy of their services to Your cause*, around the House would bend down and cover their head with their clothes. They did it so that the Messenger of Allah would not see them. Allah, most Majestic, most Glorious, then revealed this verse, '. . . they bend down their middle part to hide from him; even when they cover He knows what they hide and what they make public.'" (11:5)

The creation of the garden (paradise) before hell

H 14564, h 116

Ibn Mahbub has narrated from abu Ja'far al-Ahwal from Salam ibn al-Mustanir who has narrated the following:

"Abu Ja'far, '*Alayhi al-Salam*, has said that Allah, most Majestic, most Glorious, created the garden (paradise) before creating the fire, obedience before disobedience, mercy before wrath, good before evil, the earth before the sky, life before death, the sun before the moon and the light before darkness.'"

About the words of Allah 'He created the Heavens and Earth in six days'

H 14565, h 117

It is narrated from the narrator of the previous Hadith from 'Abd Allah ibn Sinan who has narrated the following:

"I once heard abu 'Abd Allah, '*Alayhi al-Salam*, say that Allah created good on a Sunday and He did not want to create evil before the good. On Sunday and Monday, He created the earths, and their sustenance on Tuesday. He created the skies on Wednesday and on Thursday, and their sustenance on Friday as is mentioned in the words of Allah, most Majestic, most Glorious, 'He created the skies and earth and all that are between them in six days.'" (32:4)

In praise of Zurarah ibn 'Ayun

H 14566, h 118

Ibn Mahbub has narrated from Hanan and ibn Ri'ab from Zurarah who has narrated the following:

"I once asked abu Ja'far, '*Alayhi al-Salam*, about the meaning of the words of Allah, most Majestic, most Glorious, 'I will sit for them on your straight path. Then I will come to them from their front, behind, right and left and You will not find most of them giving thanks.' (7:17) Abu Ja'far, '*Alayhi al-Salam*, said, 'O Zurarah, he (Satan) is determined against you and your people and about the others his task is complete and he is finished with them.'"

Excellence of Shi'ah and Yahaya ibn Sabur

H 14567, h 119

Muhammad ibn Yahya has narrated from Ahmad ibn Muhammad ibn Khalid and al-Husayn ibn Sa'id all from al-Nadr ibn Suwayd from Yahya ibn 'Imran al-Halabiy from 'Abd Allah ibn Muskan from Badr ibn al-Walid al-Khath'amiy who has narrated the following:

"Yahya ibn Sabur came to abu 'Abd Allah, '*Alayhi al-Salam*, to say farewell to him (the Imam). Abu 'Abd Allah, '*Alayhi al-Salam*, said, 'By Allah, you are on the truth and those who oppose you are on something other than the truth. By Allah, I have no doubt about the garden (paradise) for you and I hope that Allah will make your eyes delightful very soon.'"

Excellence of Shi'ah

H 14568, h 120

Yahya al-Halabiy has narrated from 'Abd Allah ibn Muskan from abu Basir who has narrated the following:

"I once asked him (the Imam), *'Alayhi al-Salam*, 'I pray to Allah to keep my soul in service for your cause, is one who rejects this *'Amr Wilayah* (guardianship with divine authority of *'A'immah* over the creatures) against me like one who rejects you?' He (the Imam) said, 'O abu Muhammad, whoever rejects this *'Amr* against you is like rejecting the Messenger of Allah, *O Allah grant compensation to Muhammad and his family worthy of their services to Your cause*, and rejecting Allah, most Blessed, most High. O abu Muhammad, one who dies [from you] on this *'Amr* is a martyr.' I then asked, 'Is it so even if he dies on his bed?' He (the Imam) said, 'Yes, by Allah, even if he dies on his bed, he is alive and receives sustenance from his Lord.'"

Excellence of Shi'ah and advice of Abu 'Abd Allah, *'Alayhi al-Salam*

H 14569, h 121

Yahya al-Halabiy has narrated from 'Abd Allah ibn Muskan from Habib who has narrated the following:

"I heard abu 'Abd Allah, *'Alayhi al-Salam*, say, 'O yes, by Allah, no one among people is more beloved to me than you are. People have walked on various kinds of paths, certain ones follow their own opinion, others follow their desires and still others follow narrations; but you have taken hold of a matter, which has an origin (a principle). You must restrain yourselves from worldly attractions, work hard, attend funerals, visit the people during their illness and you must attend with your people the *Masajid* (plural of *Masjid*) for *Salat* (prayer). Is it not a shameful thing that one's neighbor would recognize one's rights but one does not recognize his rights?'"

Excellence of Shi'ah and reproach of their opposition

H 14570, h 122

It is narrated from the narrator of the previous Hadith from ibn Muskan from Malik al-Juhniy who has narrated the following:

"Abu 'Abd Allah, *'Alayhi al-Salam*, once said to me, 'O Malik, will you not be happy if you perform *Salat* (prayer), pay *Zakat* and stay away from sins then enter the garden (paradise)? O Malik, there is no nation who follows an Imam in this world but that they will come on the Day of Judgment when he will condemn them and they will condemn him, except you and those who are of a similar condition. O Malik, whoever of you dies with belief in this *'Amr*, *Wilayah* (divine authority and knowledge of *'A'immah*), is a martyr like the one who strikes with his sword in the way of Allah.'"

One who dies without knowing his Imam

H 14571, h 123
Yahya al-Halabiy has narrated from Bashir al-Kunasiy who has narrated the following:
"I once heard abu 'Abd Allah, *'Alayhi al-Salam*, say, 'You have maintained the required relation, and they have cut it off; you have loved, and people have hated, you have acknowledged, but people have rejected. It is the truth. Allah designated Muhammad, *O Allah grant compensation to Muhammad and his family worthy of their services to Your cause*, as a servant before designating him as a Prophet. Ali, *'Alayhi al-Salam*, was a well wishing servant for the sake of Allah, most Majestic, most Glorious. He gave good advice and Allah, most Majestic, most Glorious, loved him. Our right in the book of Allah is clearly (stated). For us is the best of the assets and for us is *Anfal* (assets captured during the war), Allah has made obedience to us obligatory and you follow them (*'A'immah*) and because of not recognizing them people are not excused.

"The Messenger of Allah, *O Allah grant compensation to Muhammad and his family worthy of their services to Your cause*, has said, 'If one dies without knowing who his Imam is, he has died as a pagan.' You must obey and you have seen the companions of Ali, *'Alayhi al-Salam*. He (the Imam) then said, 'The Messenger of Allah, *O Allah grant compensation to Muhammad and his family worthy of their services to Your cause*, during his illness because of which he passed away said, "Call for me my beloved one." The two (female ones) sent for their fathers and when they came he (the Messenger of Allah) turned his face away, from them and said, "You must call my beloved one for me." They said, "He (the Messenger of Allah) saw us, had he (the Messenger of Allah) meant us he would have spoken to us." They then sent for Ali, *'Alayhi al-Salam*. When he (Ali) came, he bent over him (the Messenger of Allah) and he (the Messenger of Allah) kept speaking and speaking to him until their meeting was complete. The two of them met him and asked, "What did he (the Messenger of Allah) say to you?" He (Ali) replied, "He (the Messenger of Allah) spoke to me about one thousand chapters of knowledge from each chapter of which one thousand chapters open up."'"

The Messenger of Allah would not return from the same road

H 14572, h 124
A number of our people have narrated from Sahl ibn Ziyad from al-Haytham ibn abu Masruq al-Nahdiy from Musa ibn 'Umar ibn Bazi' who has narrated the following:
"I once said to al-Rida', *'Alayhi al-Salam*, people narrate that when the Messenger of Allah, *O Allah grant compensation to Muhammad and his family worthy of their services to Your cause*, would walk on a road, he then return by a different road. Did he (the Messenger of Allah) do as is narrated?' He (the Imam) said, 'Yes, and I also do so many times.' He (the Imam) then said, 'O yes, this is more helpful for your sustenance.'"

Rebutting the backbiting

H 14573, h 125

Sahl ibn Ziyad has narrated from Yahya ibn al-Mubarak from 'Abd Allah ibn Jabalah from Muhammad ibn al-Fudayl who has narrated the following:

"I once said to abu al-Hassan, al-Awwal, *'Alayhi al-Salam,* 'I pray to Allah to keep my soul in service for your cause, about one of our brothers (in belief) I hear something which I dislike and I ask him about it. He denies it. Very reliable people have told me about it.' He (the Imam) said to me, 'O Muhammad, reject your hearing and eyes about your brothers (in belief) even if you are told upon fifty oaths (by fifty people). If he says something to you, you must acknowledge it and reject them (reporters). You must not publicize anything against him which may disgrace him whereby his magnanimity, his sense of honor is destroyed and you will become of those about whom Allah has said in His book, '. . . those who publicize indecent matters about the believing people will suffer a painful suffering.'" (24:18)

Hadith about one who is born in Islam

H 14574, h 126

Sahl ibn Ziyad has narrated from Ya'qub ibn Yazid from 'Abd Rabbihi ibn Rafi' from al-Habab ibn Musa who has narrated the following:

"Abu Ja'far, *'Alayhi al-Salam,* has said, 'One who is born in Islam as a free person, he is an Arab. Those who have a treaty and kept their treaty they are *mawla* (slave) of the Messenger of Allah, *O Allah grant compensation to Muhammad and his family worthy of their services to Your cause,* and those who accept Islam willingly are immigrants.'"

Three instances of good fortune

H 14575, h 127

Ali ibn Ibrahim has narrated from Harun ibn Muslim from Mas'adah ibn Sadaqah who has narrated the following:

"Abu 'Abd Allah, *'Alayhi al-Salam,* has said that the Messenger of Allah, *O Allah grant compensation to Muhammad and his family worthy of their services to Your cause,* has said, 'One who lives in the mornings and evenings with three things, the worldly bounties are complete for him. It is he who lives in the mornings and evenings in good health physically, with peace and safety in his soul and has enough for basic necessities of life. If he has the fourth one also then the bounties of both this and the hereafters are complete for him and that is al-Islam.'"

Allah has told people Who He Is

H 14576, h 128

It is narrated from the narrator of the previous Hadith from Harun ibn Muslim from Mas'adah who has narrated the following:

"Abu 'Abd Allah, has narrated from his father, *'Alayhi al-Salam*, who once said, when a man spoke to him in a lengthy manner. He (the Imam) said, 'O man, you despise statements and consider it insignificant. You must take notice that when Allah, most Majestic, most Glorious, sent His Messengers He did not send them with gold and silver but He sent them with statements and Allah, most Majestic, most Glorious, has made Himself known by means of statements, indications and signs.'"

Allah has made a powerful over another powerful

H 14577, h 129

Through the same chain of narrators as that of the previous Hadith, the following is narrated:

"He (the Imam), *'Alayhi al-Salam*, has said that the Holy Prophet, *O Allah grant compensation to Muhammad and his family worthy of their services to Your cause*, has said, 'Whatever Allah, most Majestic, most Glorious, has created, He has made another creature to dominate it. When Allah, most Blessed, most High, created the lower ocean, it moved its waves and tides and said that nothing can overpower it. He then created the earth and made it to spread on the ocean and it became humble.' He (the Imam) said that the earth then expressed pride and said that nothing is able to overpower it. He then created the mountains and established them on its back like pegs so that it cannot move away with whatever on it. It then became humble and calmed down. The mountains then expressed pride. They tried to increase in height and length saying that nothing was able to overpower them. He then created iron, which cut it down, and then they calmed down and became humble. Iron then acted arrogantly against the mountains and said that nothing can overpower it. He created the fire, which melted it down, thus iron also became humble. The fire then blazed and flamed in pride saying that no one is able to overpower it. He then created the water, which extinguished the fire, and it became humble. Water then acted in arrogance saying that nothing is able to overpower the water. He then created the wind, which scattered its waves and moved its contents in the bottom, which blocked its channels, thus water became humble. The wind then acted in arrogance saying that nothing is able to overpower the wind. He then created man who planned, plotted and built shelters so the wind became humble. Thereafter man rebelled saying that no one is able to overpower human beings. Allah then created death, which overpowered him so human beings also became humble. Thereafter death expressed pride and Allah, most Majestic, most Glorious, said, 'Do not be proud; I will slaughter you between the two groups, people of the fire and people of the garden (paradise) and will never give you life again, regardless, if you keep hope or fear.' He (the Imam) also said that forbearance overpowers anger, mercy overcomes resentment and charity overcomes sins. Abu 'Abd Allah, *'Alayhi al-Salam*, has said, 'There are many such similar conditions where one thing overcomes the other.'"

Advice of the Holy Prophet, *'Alayhi al-Salam*

H 14578, h 130

It is narrated from the narrator of the previous Hadith from Harun ibn Muslim from Mas'adah ibn Sadaqah who has narrated the following:

"Abu 'Abd Allah, *'Alayhi al-Salam*, has said that once a man came to the Messenger of Allah, *O Allah grant compensation to Muhammad and his family worthy of their services to Your cause*, and asked to advise him. The Messenger of Allah, *O Allah grant compensation to Muhammad and his family worthy of their services to Your cause*, asked, 'Will you follow my advice if I give you advice?' He said it three times. Every time the man said, 'Yes, O Messenger of Allah I will do so.' The Messenger of Allah then said, 'My advice is that when you like to do something you must think about its consequences; if it is proper then proceed but if it is error then stay away from it.'"

The commandment of the Holy Prophet, about having kindness for three things

H 14579, h 131

Through the same chain of narrators as that of the previous Hadith, the following is narrated:

"The Holy Prophet, *O Allah grant compensation to Muhammad and his family worthy of their services to Your cause*, has said, 'You must treat with kindness a person who is humiliated after enjoying glory, a poor person after his enjoying wealth and a scholar who is wasted in the time of ignorant people.'"

Prohibition on spying

H 14580, h 132

Through the same chain of narrators as that of the previous Hadith, the following is narrated:

"I one day heard abu 'Abd Allah, *'Alayhi al-Salam*, say to his people, 'One who comes to you with love, you must not criticize him for his faults. You must not allow him to continue in a sin to which he yields; such thing is not of the manners of the Messenger of Allah, *O Allah grant compensation to Muhammad and his family worthy of their services to Your cause*, or of the manners of his friends.' Abu 'Abd Allah, *'Alayhi al-Salam*, has said that the best legacy of fathers for their children is discipline and not wealth; wealth goes away and discipline remains.' Mas'adah has said that discipline means knowledge. Abu 'Abd Allah, *'Alayhi al-Salam*, has said, 'If you are given two days to live, use one of them to learn discipline (good moral manners) which you can use for help on the day of your death.' He then was asked, 'What kind of help is that?' He (the Imam) said, 'It is good planning for what you leave behind and control it.' Abu 'Abd Allah, *'Alayhi al-Salam*, once wrote to a man as follows:

In the name of Allah, the Beneficent, the Merciful

"Thereafter, the hypocrite does not like and is not interested in something which has made the believing persons fortunate. A fortunate person learns from the good advice for piety even if the advice is meant to be for others.'"

Temporary marriage

H 14581, h 133
Ali ibn Ibrahim has narrated from his father from Ali ibn Asbat who has said that certain persons of his people narrated from Muhammad ibn Muslim who has narrated the following:

"Abu Ja'far, *'Alayhi al-Salam*, once said to me, 'O ibn Muslim, people are show offs except you (all). It is because you have kept secret what Allah, most Majestic, most Glorious, loves and have made public what people love. People have made public what angers Allah, most Majestic, most Glorious, and they have kept secret what Allah, most Blessed most High, loves. He has become kind to you (all) so He has made *Mut'ah* for you to serve you in place of drinks.'

The stipulation al-Rida' *'Alayhi al-Salam* with Ma'mun

H 14582, h 134
A number of our people have narrated from Sahl ibn Ziyad from Mu'ammar ibn Khallad who has narrated the following:

"Abu al-Hassan al-Rida', *'Alayhi al-Salam*, once said to me that M'amun once said to him (the Imam), 'O abu al-Hassan, I wish you write to those who obey you in this area because their relation with us is destroyed.' I said to him, 'O 'Amir al-Mu'minin, if you fulfill for me I will fulfill for you. I have come in the issue in which I am now upon the condition that I will not issue any command or prohibition, appoint or cause anyone to resign. My coming in this issue has not increased for me any bounties. I was in al-Madinah and my letter was effective in the east and west. I would ride my donkey and pass through the streets of al-Madinah. There was no one more glorious than me and no one of them asked me for anything that I could provide but that I provided for him.' He (Ma'mun) then said, 'I will fulfill my side of the condition for you.'"

Of the rights of Muslims

H 14583, h 135
Ali ibn Ibrahim has narrated from his father from al-Nawfaliy from al-Sakuniy who has narrated the following:

"Abu 'Abd Allah, *'Alayhi al-Salam*, has said that the Messenger of Allah, *O Allah grant compensation to Muhammad and his family worthy of their services to Your cause*, has said. 'It is a right on a Muslim to inform his brothers (in belief) when he wants to go on a journey. It is a right on his brothers (in belief) to visit him when he comes back.'"

Two unknown bounties

H 14584, h 136
Through the same chain of narrators as that of the previous Hadith, the following is narrated:

"The Holy Prophet, *O Allah grant compensation to Muhammad and his family worthy of their services to Your cause*, has said, 'There are two issues in which most people are tempted: They are good health and opportunity.'"

Prohibition on exposing oneself for accusation

H 14585, h 137

Through the same chain of narrators as that of the previous Hadith, the following is narrated:

"'Amir al-Mu'minin, Ali, *'Alayhi al-Salam*, has said, 'One who exposes himself to a possibility of being accused, he must not blame those who may think about him pessimistically. If one keeps his secret a secret, goodness remains in his hands.'"

The kind of canal in the garden (paradise)

H 14586, h 138

Al-Husayn Muhammad al-Ash'ariy has narrated Mu'alla' ibn Muhammad from Muhammad ibn Jumhur from Shadhan who has narrated the following:

"Abu al-Hassan, Musa, *'Alayhi al-Salam*, has said, 'My father said to me that in the garden (paradise) there is a canal called Ja'far. On its right bank there is a white pearl in which there are one thousand castles and in every castle there is a castle for Muhammad and *Ale* (family) of Muhammad, *O Allah grant compensation to Muhammad and his family worthy of their services to Your cause*. On its left bank there is yellow pearl in which there are one thousand castles and in every castle there is a castle for Ibrahim and *Ale* (family) Ibrahim, *'Alayhim al-Salam*.'"

Victory is in protecting al-Islam

H 14587, h 139

Muhammad ibn Yahya has narrated from Ahmad ibn Muhammad ibn 'Isa from Ali ibn al-Hakam from Hisham ibn Salim who has narrated the following:

"Abu 'Abd Allah, *'Alayhi al-Salam*, has said, 'No two groups of falsehood confront each other but that the one which is of better consequences for the people of Islam succeeds.'"

The nature of the hearts

H 14588, h 140

It is narrated from the narrator of the previous Hadith from Ahmad from Ali ibn Hadid from certain persons of his people who has narrated the following:

"Abu 'Abd Allah, *'Alayhi al-Salam*, has said, 'The hearts are built to love those who benefit them and hate those who harm them.'"

Good advice of Ali ibn Al-Husayn, *'Alayhima al-Salam*

H 14589, h 141

Muhammad ibn abu 'Abd Allah has narrated from Musa ibn 'Imran from his uncle from al-Husayn ibn 'Isa ibn 'Abd Allah from Ali ibn Ja'far who has narrated the following:

"Abu al-Hassan, Musa, *'Alayhi al-Salam*, has stated this Hadith: 'Once, my father held my hand and said, 'Son, my father Muhammad ibn Ali, *'Alayhi al-Salam*, once held my hand just as I am holding your hand. He said that his father, Ali ibn al-Husayn, *'Alayhi al-Salam*, held his hand and said, "Son, do good to everyone who asks you to do it for him. If he deserves it you then have found the right person; if he is not deserving, you are the deserving person. If a man rebukes you when on your right side then turns to your left side and apologizes you must accept his apology.'"

Everything was water

H 14590, h 142

Muhammad ibn Yahya has narrated from Ahmad ibn Muhammad from ibn Mahbub from al-'Ala' ibn Razin from Muhammad ibn Muslim and al-Hajjal from al-'Ala' from Muhammad ibn Muslim who has narrated the following:

"Abu Ja'far, *'Alayhi al-Salam*, has said that everything was water and His throne was on the water. Allah, most Majestic, most Glorious, commanded the water and lit a fire. He then commanded the fire, it extinguished and smoke rose from its being extinguished. Allah, most Majestic, most Glorious, then created the skies thereof. Allah, most Majestic, most Glorious, created the earth from ashes. Then the water, the fire and the wind disputed among themselves. The water said, 'I am the great army of Allah.' The fire said, 'I am the great army of Allah.' The wind said, 'I am the great army of Allah.' Allah then sent revelation that said, 'The wind is My great army.'"

Hadith of Zaynab the fragrance seller

H 14591, h 143

Muhammad ibn Yahya has narrated from Ahmad ibn Muhammad from 'Abd al-Rahman ibn abu Najran from Safwan from Khalaf ibn Hammad from al-Husayn ibn Zayd al-Hashimiy who has narrated the following:

"Once Zaynab, the fragrance seller, *(al-Hawla')* came to the women and daughters of the Holy Prophet, *O Allah grant compensation to Muhammad and his family worthy of their services to Your cause*. She would sell fragrance to them. The Holy Prophet, *O Allah grant compensation to Muhammad and his family worthy of their services to Your cause*, came while she was with them. He said, 'When you come our homes smell good.' She said, 'Your home with your own fragrance smells much better than what I sell, O Messenger of Allah.' He (the Messenger of Allah) said, 'When you sell you must do it good and without mixing impurities; it is more pious and more protective for the asset.' She said, 'O Messenger of Allah, I do not come to sell anything, but I come to ask you about the greatness of Allah, most Majestic, most Glorious.' He (the Messenger of Allah), said, 'The glory of Allah is indeed glorious. I will tell you about a few things of His greatness.' He (the Messenger of Allah) then said, 'This earth with all that is on it compared with that which is lower than this looks like a ring thrown in a vast wilderness. These two along with what is on them compared to the size of the one below them look only like a ring thrown in a vast wilderness, and the third . . . until to the seventh one below . . . and he (the Messenger of

Allah) read this verse, '. . . He created seven skies and the same number of earths.' (65:12) The seven earths with all that is in and on them are over the back of the rooster where they look like a ring thrown in a vast wilderness. The rooster has two wings: one in the east and one in the west; its two legs are in the center. The seven, the rooster with all that is on and in it all are on the boulder where they look like a ring thrown in a vast wilderness. The boulder with all that is in it and all that is on it is on the back of the fish where they look like a ring thrown in a vast wilderness. All seven, the rooster, the boulder, the fish with all that is in it and all are on the dark ocean where they look like a ring thrown in a vast wilderness. The seven, the rooster, the boulder, the fish and the dark ocean are on the moving air where they look like a ring thrown in a vast wilderness. The seven, the rooster, the boulder, the fish, the dark ocean and the moving air are on *al-Thara'* where they look like a ring thrown in a vast wilderness. He (the Messenger of Allah) then read this verse, '. . . to Him belongs all that is in the skies, in the earth and all that is between them and all that is under *al-Thara'*.' (20:6) Then the news from *al-Thara'* is cutoff. The seven, the rooster, the boulder, the fish, the dark ocean, the moving air and *al-Thara'* with all that is in it and all that is on it compared to the size of the first sky look like a ring thrown in a vast wilderness. All these and the sky of the world with all that is on it and all that is in it compared to the size of that which is above it look like a ring thrown in a vast wilderness. The two skies and all that is in them and all that is on them before that which is above them look like a ring thrown in a vast wilderness. The three with all that is in them and all that is on them before the fourth look like a ring thrown in a vast wilderness,' until he (the Messenger of Allah) explained up to seven skies. 'All these with all that is in them and all that is on them before the protected ocean from the people of the earth look like a ring thrown in a vast wilderness. All these with all that is in them and all that is on them and the protected ocean from the people of the earth before the mountains of hail look like a ring thrown in a vast wilderness.' He (the Messenger of Allah) read this verse, '. . . He sends from the sky from the mountains which are of hail.' (24:43) 'These seven, the protected ocean and the mountains of hail before the air in which the hearts wander look like a ring thrown in a vast wilderness. These seven, the protected ocean, the mountains of hail and the air before barriers of light look like a ring thrown in a vast wilderness. These seven, the protected ocean, the mountains of hail, the air, the barriers of light before *al-Kursiy* look like a ring thrown in a vast wilderness.' He then read this verse, '. . . His *Kursiy* contains the skies and the earth and protecting them does not cause Him any fatigue, He is most High, most Great.' (2:255) 'These seven, the protected ocean, the mountains of hail, the air, the barriers of light and *al-Kursiy* before the Throne look like a ring thrown in a vast wilderness.' He (the Messenger of Allah) then read this verse, '. . . the Beneficent has domination over the Throne.' (20:5) In the narration of al-Hassan 'barrier is before the air before which the hearts wander.'"

Hadith of the man who hosted the Messenger of Allah, *O Allah grant compensation to Muhammad and his family worthy of their services to Your cause,* in al-Taef

H 14592, h 144

Ali ibn Ibrahim has narrated from his father from ibn Mahbub from Jamil ibn Salih from Yazid al-Kunasiy who has narrated the following:

"Abu Ja'far, *'Alayhi al-Salam,* has said that once before Islam, the Messenger of Allah, *O Allah grant compensation to Muhammad and his family worthy of their services to Your cause,* stayed with a man in Taef who served him (the Messenger of Allah) well. When Allah sent Muhammad, *O Allah grant compensation to Muhammad and his family worthy of their services to Your cause,* to people the man was asked, 'Do you know who is he whom Allah, most Majestic, most Glorious, has sent to people?' He replied, 'No, I do not know.' They told him, 'He is Muhammad ibn 'Abd Allah, the orphan brought up by abu Talib. He is the one who stayed with you in Taef on such and such day and you served him well.' He (the Imam) said that the man came to the Messenger of Allah, *O Allah grant compensation to Muhammad and his family worthy of their services to Your cause,* offered greeting of peace and accepted Islam. He then asked, 'Do you know me, O Messenger of Allah?' He (the Messenger of Allah) asked, 'Who are you?' He replied, 'I am the owner of the house where you stayed in Taef in the time of ignorance on such and such day and I served you well.' The Messenger of Allah, *O Allah grant compensation to Muhammad and his family worthy of their services to Your cause,* said, 'You are welcome. What can I do for you?' He said, 'I ask you to give me one hundred sheep along with its shepherd. The Messenger of Allah, *O Allah grant compensation to Muhammad and his family worthy of their services to Your cause,* commanded to give him what he had asked for. He (the Messenger of Allah) then said to his companions, 'Why could this man not ask me like what the old woman of banu Israel had asked from Musa, *'Alayhi al-Salam*?' They asked, 'What did the old woman of banu Israel ask from Musa?' He (the Messenger of Allah) said, 'Allah, most Majestic, most Glorious, commanded Musa to carry the bones of Yusuf from Misr (Egypt) before his leaving for the holy land in al-Sham. Musa then asked about the grave of Yusuf, *'Alayhi al-Salam,* and an old man came and said that if anyone knows his grave, it must be so and so female. Musa, *'Alayhi al-Salam,* then sent for her and she said, 'Yes, I know his grave.' He said, 'Show me and you can have whatever you like to ask for.' She said, 'I will show you only under my command.' He said, 'You can have the garden (paradise).' She said, 'No, it must be under my command on you.' Allah, most Majestic, most Glorious, sent revelation to Musa that said, 'Do not consider it a great thing if you leave it in her command.' Musa then said, 'It is under your command and I agree.' She said, 'My command is that I must be with you of the same position as your position and place in the garden (paradise) on the Day of Judgment.' The Messenger of Allah, *O Allah grant compensation to Muhammad and his family worthy of their services to Your cause,* said, 'Why did he not ask me what the old woman of banu Israel had asked.'"

The rights of the family of Muhammad, *'Alayhi al-Salam*, are obligatory

H 14593, h 145

Ali ibn Ibrahim has narrated from his father from ibn Mahbub from 'Abd Allah ibn Sinan who has narrated the following:

"I once heard abu 'Abd Allah, *'Alayhi al-Salam*, say, 'A woman of al-Ansar (people of al-Madinah) who very often visited us (*Ahl al-Bayt*) out of concern for our well-being and love, one day came face to face with 'Umar ibn al-Khattab who asked, 'Where do you want to go, O old woman of al-Ansar?' She replied, 'I want to visit *Ale* (family) Muhammad, to offer them greeting of peace, renew my allegiance with them and abide by their rights.' 'Umar said to her, 'Woe is on you, today they have no right on you and on us. It was only in the time of the Messenger of Allah, *O Allah grant compensation to Muhammad and his family worthy of their services to Your cause*. Today they have no right and you must return. She then turned back and went to 'Umm Salamah who asked her, 'What made you to come so late?' She replied, 'I met 'Umar ibn al-Khattab' and she told her about what he had said to her. 'Umm Salamah said, 'He has spoken a lie. Abiding by the rights of *Ale* (family) Muhammad is still obligatory on the Muslims today and until the Day of Judgment.'"

About the words of Allah '. . . they give glad news to those who have not joined them...'

H 14594, h 146

Ibn Mahbub has narrated from al-Harith ibn Muhammad ibn al-Nu'man from Burayd al-'Ijliy who has narrated the following:

"I once asked abu Ja'far, *'Alayhi al-Salam*, about the meaning of the words of Allah, most Majestic, most Glorious, '. . . they will receive glad news about those who have not yet joined them thereafter that there is nothing for them to fear and feel grieved.'(3:170) He (the Imam) said, 'They, by Allah are our Shi'ah. When their spirits arrive in the garden (paradise) they receive welcome with honor from Allah, most Majestic, most Glorious; they will come to know with certainty that they were on the right path and have followed the religion of Allah, most Majestic, most Glorious. They will receive the glad news about those who have not yet joined them of their brothers (in belief) after them of the believing people that there is not anything against them to fear or feel grieved.'"

About the words of Allah '. . . therein are beautiful...'

H 14595, h 147

It is narrated from the narrator of the previous Hadith from ibn Mahbub from abu Ayyub from al-Halabiy who has narrated the following:

"I once asked abu 'Abd Allah, *'Alayhi al-Salam*, about the meaning of the words of Allah, most Majestic, most Glorious, '. . . better and beautiful ones will be there, in the garden (paradise).' (55:70) He (the Imam) said, 'They will be the virtuous and believing female who had acknowledge (*Wilayah* (divine authority and knowledge *'A'immah*).' I then asked, 'The reserved Hur in the tents.' (55:72) He (the Imam) said, 'They will be al-Hur like sealed eggs, reserved who live in the tents of ruby and coral. Every tent with four doors and on every door seventy al-Kawa'ib (newly growing breasts) ones and veiled who come as honor from Allah, most Majestic, most Glorious, every day and bring glad news for the believing people.'"

Three hundred sixty constellations of the sun

H 14596, h 148

'Ali ibn Ibrahim and a number of our people have narrated from Sahl ibn Ziyad all from Muhammad ibn 'Isa from Yunus from abu al-Sabbah al-Kinaniy from Asbagh ibn Nabatah who has narrated the following:

"'Amir al-Mu'minin, Ali, *'Alayhi al-Salam*, has said that the sun has three hundred sixty *burj* (constellations), every one of them is like an Arabian island. Every day it comes down on one of them when it disappears, it reaches below the throne and remains in *Sajdah* (prostration) until the next day; then it turns to its rising location with two angels who hail, applaud with it when its face is toward the people of the sky. They make it toward the people of the earth. Had its face been to the people of the earth the earth would burn and all that is on it, because of intense heat. The meaning of its *Sujud* (prostrations) is mentioned in the words of Allah, most Perfect, most High, '. . . have you not considered that all that is in the skies and on earth perform *Sajdah* (prostration) before Allah, like the sun, the moon, the stars, the mountains, the tree, the animals and many people.'" (22:18)

Prohibition of Abu Ja'far, *'Alayhi al-Salam*

H 14597, h 149

A number of our people have narrated from Salih ibn abu Hammad from 'Isma'il ibn Mehran from those who narrated to him from Jabir ibn Yazid who has narrated the following:

"Muhammad ibn Ali, *'Alayhi al-Salam*, narrated for me seventy Hadith which I have never spoken of with anyone and will never narrate them to anyone. When Muhammad ibn Ali, *'Alayhi al-Salam*, passed away, it became heavy on my neck and my chest became constricted. I visited abu 'Abd Allah, *'Alayhi al-Salam*, and said, 'I pray to Allah to keep my soul in service for your cause, your father narrated to me seventy Hadith of which not even one Hadith has come out of my mouth to anyone and he commanded me to keep them secret. It is heavy on my neck and my chest has become constricted. What do you command me?' He (the Imam) said, 'O Jabir, if your chest has become constricted, then allow them to come out in the wilderness. Dig a ditch then hang your head in it and you must say, "Muhammad ibn Ali narrated to me such and such things" then fill it up; the earth will keep your secret.' Jabir has said, 'I followed his instruction and it became lighter on me than I felt before.' A number of our people have narrated from Sahl ibn Ziyad from 'Isma'il ibn Mehran a similar Hadith.'"

Prohibition on sitting with the sinners

H 14598, h 150

A number of our people have narrated from Sahl ibn Ziyad from Safwan ibn Yahya from al-Harith ibn al-Mughirah who has narrated the following:

"Abu 'Abd Allah, *'Alayhi al-Salam*, has said, 'I hold the innocent ones among you responsible because of the sins of the sick (the sinful) ones. Why must I not do so, when something which defames you and myself reaches you from a man and you sit with them, speak to them and a passerby passes thereby saying, 'They are worse than he is.' If you hear, something from him, which you dislike, you must express intense dislike and prohibit them. It will be better for you and for me.'"

People are of three kinds

H 14599, h 151

Sahl ibn Ziyad has narrated from 'Amr ibn 'Uthman from 'Abd Allah ibn al-Mughirah from Talhah ibn Zayd who has narrated the following:

"About the meaning of the words of Allah, most Blessed, most High, '. . . when they forgot the issue of which they were reminded, We rescued those who prohibit committing evil.' (7:165) Abu 'Abd Allah, *'Alayhi al-Salam*, has said, 'They were of three kinds of people. Those who carried commands and commanded others: they found salvation, those who carried out commands but did not command others: they metamorphosed into particles, and those who did not carry commands and did not command others: they were destroyed.'"

Letter of Abu 'Abd Allah, *'Alayhim al-Salam*, to Shi'ah

H 14600, h 152

It is narrated from the narrator of the previous Hadith from Ali ibn Asbat from al-'Ala' ibn Razin from Muhammad ibn Muslim who has narrated the following:

"Abu 'Abd Allah, *'Alayhi al-Salam*, wrote to Shi'ah as follows: 'The ones among you with the ability (elders) to speak and reason must show kindness to and prohibit the ignorant ones among you, and those who seek leadership, otherwise, you will all be affected by my condemnation.'"

Religion has two governments

H 14601, h 153

Muhammad ibn abu 'Abd Allah and Muhammad ibn al-Hassan all have narrated from Salih ibn abu Hammad from abu Ja'far al-Kufiy from a man who has narrated the following:

"Abu 'Abd Allah, *'Alayhi al-Salam*, has said, 'Allah, most Majestic, most Glorious, has made the world into two governments; the government of Adam, *'Alayhi al-Salam*, and the government of Satan. The government of Adam, *'Alayhi al-Salam*, is the government of Allah, most Majestic, most Glorious. Allah, most Majestic, most Glorious, may want to be worshipped openly. He then makes the government of Adam, *'Alayhi al-Salam*, dominant. When He wants His being worshipped secretly, it is the government of Satan. The propagator of what Allah has willed to remain covered is a defector from religion.'"

Hadith of people on the Day of Judgment

H 14602, h 154

A number of our people have narrated from Sahl ibn Ziyad from Muhammad ibn Sinan from 'Amr ibn Shamir from Jabir who has narrated the following:

"Abu Ja'far, *'Alayhi al-Salam*, once said to me, 'O Jabir on the Day of Judgment Allah, most Majestic, most Glorious, will gather together all the people of the early and the later generations to settle complaints and disputes. The Messenger of Allah, and 'Amir al-Mu'minin, Ali, *'Alayhima al-Salam*, will be called. The Messenger of Allah will dress in a green garment, which will light up the east and the west. 'Amir al-Mu'minin, Ali, *'Alayhi al-Salam*, will dress in the same way. The Messenger of Allah will also dress in a flowery dress, which will light up whatever is between the east and the west, and 'Amir al-Mu'minin, Ali, *'Alayhi al-Salam*, will dress in the same way. They will then climb up in that dress. Thereafter we will be called and the accounting of the people will be given to us. We, by Allah, will admit people of the garden (paradise) in the garden (paradise) and people of the fire in the fire. Thereafter the Prophets, *'Alayhim al-Salam*, will be called and they will form two rows before the Throne of Allah, most Majestic, most Glorious, until we complete the accounting of the people. When people of the garden (paradise) will enter in the garden (paradise) and people of the fire will enter in the fire, the Lord of glory will send Ali, *'Alayhi al-Salam*, to deliver them to their dwellings in the garden (paradise) and settle them with their spouses. Ali, *'Alayhi al-Salam*, by Allah is the one who will settle the people of the garden (paradise) in marriages with their spouses and no one else beside him (the Imam) has such honor from Allah, most Majestic, most Glorious, and an excellence which He has granted to him as a favor. He by Allah will send the people of the fire to the fire and he is the one who will lock the gates of the garden (paradise) because the doors of the garden (paradise) are up to him and the doors of the fire are up to him.'"

When love is not helpful

H 14603, h 155

Ali ibn Ibrahim has narrated from Salih ibn al-Sindiy from Ja'far ibn Bashir from 'Anbasah who has narrated the following:

"I once heard abu 'Abd Allah, *'Alayhi al-Salam*, say, 'You must mix and live with the people; if your loving Ali and Fatimah, *'Alayhim al-Salam*, will not benefit you in private and in secrecy, it will not benefit you in public.'"

Undesirability of naming children Ali or Fatimah

H 14604, h 156

Ja'far has narrated from 'Anbasah who has narrated the following:

"Abu 'Abd Allah, *'Alayhi al-Salam*, has said, 'You must maintain caution about speaking of Ali and Fatimah, *'Alayhim al-Salam*, because there is nothing more hateful to them than speaking of Ali and Fatimah, *'Alayhim al-Salam*.'"

When Allah decides to destroy a government

H 14605, h 157

Ja'far has narrated from 'Anbasah from Jabir who has narrated the following:

"Abu Ja'far, *'Alayhi al-Salam*, has said, 'When Allah, most Majestic, most Glorious, wants to destroy the government of a people He commands the band (the orbit) to move faster.'"

Words of Sulayman ibn Khalid to Abu 'Abd Allah, *'Alayhi al-Salam*

H 14606, h 158

Ja'far ibn Bashir has narrated from 'Amr ibn 'Uthman from abu Shabal who has narrated the following:

"Once, Sulayman ibn Khalid and I visited abu 'Abd Allah, *'Alayhi al-Salam*. Sulayman ibn Khalid said, 'The Zaydiy sect, has become known, tried and is famous among people and those on earth as followers of Muhammad and they are more beloved to them than you are; in such case if you can bring them closer to you, you should do so.' He (the Imam) said, 'O Sulayman ibn Khalid, if these dimwitted ones want to bar us from our knowledge and lead to their ignorance, then they are not welcome. They are not accepted; but if they listen to what we say and wait for our *'Amr* (the rise of al-Qa'im with divine authority and knowledge), then it is not harmful.'"

One suffering from sorrow bears more patience

H 14607, h 159

A number of our people have narrated from Sahl ibn Ziyad from ibn Mahbub from those whom he has mentioned who has narrated the following:

"Once during a funeral procession the stripe of the shoes of abu 'Abd Allah, *'Alayhi al-Salam*, came off and a man brought his stripe for him (the Imam). He (the Imam) said, 'Hold to the stripe of your shoes; it is more proper for the mourners to bear patience.'"

Benefits of cupping

H 14608, h 160

Sahl ibn Ziyad has narrated from ibn Faddal from those whom he has mentioned who has narrated the following:

"Abu 'Abd Allah, *'Alayhi al-Salam*, has said, 'Cupping from the head is as beneficial, against all illness, as rainfall is to the parched land, except death. He (the Imam) (to show the place) used his *Shibr* (commonly said to be the distance from the tip of thumb to the tip of the small finger with the palm wide open) on his eyebrows to wherever the thumb reached. He (the Imam) said, 'Up till here.'"

Why a believer is called a believer

H 14609, h 161

Muhammad ibn Yahya has narrated from Ahmad ibn Muhammad from Marwak ibn 'Ubayd from Rifa'ah who has narrated the following:

"Abu 'Abd Allah, *'Alayhi al-Salam*, once said, 'Do you know, O Rifa'ah, why a believing person is called a believing person?' I replied, 'No, I do not know.' He (the Imam) said, 'It is because he believes (seeks amnesty with) in Allah, He then allows His amnesty to include him.'" (The word *'Iman'* 'belief' in Arabic also means amnesty and safety)

One hostile to *'A'immah* is careless in worship

H 14610, h 162

A number of our people have narrated from Sahl ibn Ziyad from ibn Faddal from Hanan who has narrated the following:

"Abu 'Abd Allah, *'Alayhi al-Salam*, has said, 'A person hostile to *'A'immah* of *Ahl al-Bayt* is not concerned if he performs *Salat* (prayer) or commits fornication. This verse is revealed about them, ". . . working and hostile (to *'A'immah* of *Ahl al-Bayt*)) will feel the heat of the hot fire."'" (88:3-4)

One who does not love Ali, *'Alayhi al-Salam*

H 14611, h 163

Sahl ibn Ziyad has narrated from Ya'qub ibn Yazid from Muhammad ibn Murazim and Yazid ibn Hammad all from 'Abd Allah ibn Sinan as I think who has narrated the following:

"Abu 'Abd Allah, *'Alayhi al-Salam*, has said, 'One who is not a friend of Ali, *'Alayhi al-Salam*, may come to the Euphrates where there is water on his both sides in a crystal clear, large body. He fills up his palm and says, 'In the name of Allah', then in the end says, *'Tahmid*, (all praise belongs to Allah)', it is blood spilled or like the flesh of pigs.'"

In praise of Zayd ibn Ali

H 14612, h 164

Ali ibn Ibrahim has narrated from his father from ibn abu 'Umayr from a man whom he has mentioned from Sulayman ibn Khalid who has narrated the following:

"Abu 'Abd Allah, *'Alayhi al-Salam*, asked me, 'What did you do with my uncle, Zayd?' I replied, 'They guarded him when people dispersed, we took his body and buried him at the bank of the Euphrates. In the morning, the equestrians searched for his body. They found it and burned it.' He (the Imam) said, 'Why did you not tie something heavy like iron to him and throw him in the Euphrates? Allah has granted him compensation and condemned his killers.'"

Destruction of Banu 'Umayyah

H 14613, h 165

A number of our people have narrated from Sahl ibn Ziyad from al-Hassan ibn Ali al-Washsha' from those whom he has mentioned who has narrated the following:

"Abu 'Abd Allah, *'Alayhi al-Salam*, has said that Allah, most Majestic, most Glorious, gave permission for the destruction of banu 'Umayyah only seven days after their burning Zayd.'"

Allah protects one who protects His friend

H 14614, h 166

Sahl ibn Ziyad has narrated from Mansur ibn al-'Abbas from those whom he has mentioned from 'Ubayd ibn Zurarah who has narrated the following:

"Abu 'Abd Allah, *'Alayhi al-Salam*, has said, 'Allah, most Majestic, most Glorious, protects one who protects His friend.'"

People's coming and accounts are with them (*'A'immah*)

H 14615, h 167

Sahl ibn Ziyad has narrated from ibn Sinan from ibn Sa'dan from Sama'ah who has narrated the following:

"Once I was sitting with abu al-Hassan, al-Awwal, *'Alayhi al-Salam*, when people in the middle of the night were performing tawaf. He (the Imam) said, 'O Sama'ah, to us is the coming of these creatures and on us is their accounting. Whatever sins they have between themselves and Allah, most Majestic, most Glorious, we deem it necessary on Allah to leave for us. He accepts it (our decision) from us. Whatever is between them and people we then ask them to give it to us as a gift. They accept it and Allah, most Majestic, most Glorious, will reward them for it.'"

In praise of Salman and abu Dharr

H 14616, h 168

Sahl ibn Ziyad has narrated from Mansur ibn al-'Abbas from Sulayman al-Mustraiq from Salih al-Ahwal who has narrated the following:

"I once heard abu 'Abd Allah, *'Alayhi al-Salam*, say, 'The Messenger of Allah, *O Allah grant compensation to Muhammad and his family worthy of their services to Your cause*, formed a brotherhood between Salman and abu Dharr and set a condition on abu Dharr not to disobey Salman.'"

The obligation of keeping away from sinners

H 14617, h 169

Sahl ibn Ziyad has narrated from ibn Mahbub from al-Khattab ibn Muhammad from al-Harith ibn al-Mughirah who has narrated the following:

"Abu 'Abd Allah, *'Alayhi al-Salam*, once met me on the road of al-Madinah and asked, 'Who is he, is he Harith?' I replied, 'Yes, I am Harith.' He (the Imam) said, 'I hold your knowledgeable ones responsible for the sins of your dimwitted ones.' He then passed by. I visited him (the Imam), asked for permission, went inside (the house), and said, 'You met me and said, "I hold your knowledgeable people responsible for the sins of your dimwitted ones." It has made me feel as if a great matter is upon me.' He (the Imam) said, 'Yes, what prevents you, upon hearing something from one of your people which you dislike and it causes troubles for us, to go to him, reproach, and reprove him and speak to him clear words.' I said, 'I pray to Allah to keep my soul in service for your cause, what happens if they do not obey us and accept from us?' He (the Imam) said, 'In such case stay away from them and avoid going to their gatherings.'"

Allah punishes six for six things

H 14618, h 170

Sahl ibn Ziyad has narrated from Ibrahim ibn 'Uqbah from Sayabah ibn Ayyub and Muhammad ibn al-Walid and Ali ibn Asbat in a marfu' manner from 'Amir al-Mu'minin, Ali, *'Alayhi al-Salam*, who has narrated the following:

"Allah punishes six classes of people because of six things. He will punish Arabs because of prejudice, the landlords because of arrogance, the rulers because of injustice, the scholars of fiqh because of envy, the merchants because of cheating and the villagers because of ignorance.'"

The most beloved to the Messenger of Allah

H 14619, h 171

Ali ibn Ibrahim has narrated from his father from ibn abu 'Umayr from Hisham and others who has narrated the following:

"Abu 'Abd Allah, *'Alayhi al-Salam*, has said, 'There was nothing more beloved to the Messenger of Allah, *O Allah grant compensation to Muhammad and his family worthy of their services to Your cause*, than living in fear and hunger for the sake of Allah, most Majestic, most Glorious.'"

Manners of Ali, *'Alayhi al-Salam*

H 14620, h 172

Ali has narrated from his father and Muhammad ibn 'Isma'il has narrated from al-Fadl ibn Shadhan from all from ibn abu 'Umayr from 'Abd al-Rahman ibn al-Hajjaj and Hafs ibn al-Bakhtariy and Salamah Bayya' al-Sabiry who has narrated the following:

"Abu 'Abd Allah, *'Alayhi al-Salam*, has said that Ali ibn al-Husayn, *'Alayhi al-Salam*, once took the book of Ali, *'Alayhi al-Salam*, and looked in it, then said, 'Who is able to bear it, who is able to bear?' He would then follow it. When he stood for *Salat* (prayer), his color changed until it showed on his face. 'No one was able to bear what Ali, *'Alayhi al-Salam*, did, of his sons after him, save Ali ibn al-Husayn, *'Alayhi al-Salam*.'"

Manners of Ali, *'Alayhi al-Salam*, and his restraint from unlawful matters

H 14621, h 173

Muhammad ibn Yahya has narrated from Ahmad ibn Muhammad from Ali al-Nu'man from ibn Muskan from al-Hassan al-Sayqal who has narrated the following:

"I once heard abu 'Abd Allah, *'Alayhi al-Salam*, say, 'A friend of Ali, *'Alayhi al-Salam*, does not eat anything except lawful things because his friend would do so. The friend of 'Uthman does not care if it is lawful or not; his friend was such.' He (the Imam) then spoke of Ali, *'Alayhi al-Salam*, and said, 'O yes, by the one who took his soul that he did not eat anything unlawful from the world in small or large quantities until he departed the world. Whenever facing two issues of obedience to Allah he took the more difficult one for his body. Whenever the Messenger of Allah faced a difficult task, he would send him (the Imam) for it due to his confidence in him. No one of this nation had been able to bear a deed like the deeds of the Messenger of Allah, *O Allah grant compensation to Muhammad and his family worthy of their services to Your cause*, after him except Ali, *'Alayhi al-Salam*. He worked like a man who was as if he sees the garden (paradise) (before his very eyes). He (the Imam) freed one thousand slaves from his own assets that he had earned by the work of his two hands and making his forehead perspire for the sake of Allah, most Majestic, most Glorious, and seeking safety from the fire. His food consisted of vinegar and oil and his sweet was dates if he could find them. His clothes were of cotton. If his clothes had anything extra he would it cut off with a scissor.'"

Undesirability of eating hot food

H 14622, h 174

Abu Ali al-Ash'ariy has narrated from Muhammad ibn 'Abd al-Jabbar from al-Hassan ibn Ali from Yunus ibn Ya'qub from Sulayman Khalid from 'Amil (worker) of Muhammad ibn Rashid who has narrated the following:

"I once was present at the time of the dinner of Ja'far ibn Muhammad, *'Alayhi al-Salam*, during the summer. The tablespread was brought with bread in it and a bowl of broth with meat, hot like boiling. He placed his hand in it and found it to be hot. He pulled his hand back saying, 'I seek refuge with Allah against the fire, I seek refuge with Allah against the fire. We cannot bear this, then how can we bear the fire?' He kept saying so until it was possible to use the bowl and we also ate with him (the Imam). The table spread was then taken away and he (the Imam) said, 'O boy, bring us something.' A tray of dates was then brought. I extended my hand and it was dates. I said, 'I pray to Allah to keep you well, this is the season of grapes and fruits.' He (the Imam) said, 'It is dates.' He (the Imam) then said, 'Take this and bring us something.' Dates were brought and I extended my hand, it was dates and I said, 'It is dates.' He (the Imam) said, 'It is fine.'"

Of the manners of the Holy Prophet, *'Alayhi al-Salam*

H 14623, h 175

Muhammad ibn Yahya has narrated from Ahmad ibn Muhammad from Ali ibn al-Hakam from Mu'awiyah ibn Wahab who has narrated the following:

"Abu 'Abd Allah, *'Alayhi al-Salam*, has said that the Messenger of Allah, *O Allah grant compensation to Muhammad and his family worthy of their services to Your cause*, never ate when leaning against something. He practiced such manners, from the time Allah, most Majestic, most Glorious, sent him as His Messenger, until the time he departed this world. He showed humbleness before Allah, most Majestic, most Glorious, and his knees were not seen in a gathering. He never, when shaking hands with people, pulled his hand before the other man did. The Messenger of Allah, *O Allah grant compensation to Muhammad and his family worthy of their services to Your cause*, never recompensed anyone with bad things as Allah, most Blessed, most High, has said, '. . . repel what is evil with that which is good.' (23:96) He (the Messenger of Allah) followed it and did not deny anyone asking for help. If he had something, he gave, otherwise, he said, 'Allah will make it available.' He never gave anything on the responsibility of Allah but that Allah granted it to him even if he gave the garden (paradise) Allah, most Majestic, most Glorious, granted it in his favor.' He (the Imam) said, 'His brother (Ali ibn abu Talib) after him, by the one who took his soul, never ate anything unlawful from this world until he departed this world. Whenever he faced two tasks to fulfill for the sake of Allah, most Majestic, most Glorious, he undertook the more difficult one for his body. He freed one thousand slaves for the sake of Allah, most Majestic, most Glorious, from the earnings of his own hands. No one other than him could bear doing the kind of work that the Messenger of Allah, *O Allah grant compensation to Muhammad and his family worthy of their services to Your cause*, did. By Allah, every time the Messenger of Allah faced a difficult task he sent him for such task because of his confidence in him. When the Messenger of Allah, *O Allah grant compensation to Muhammad and his family worthy of their services to Your cause*, sent him with his banner, Jibril fought on his right and Michael on his left. He would not come back without victory by the help of Allah, most Majestic, most Glorious.'"

Manners of Fatimah, *'Alayha al-Salam*

H 14624, h 176

A number of our people have narrated from Sahl ibn Ziyad from Ahmad ibn Muhammad from ibn abu Nasr from Hammad ibn 'Uthaman from Zayd ibn al-Hassan who has narrated the following:

"I once heard abu 'Abd Allah, *'Alayhi al-Salam*, say, ''Amir al-Mu'minin, Ali, *'Alayhi al-Salam*, was most similar to the Messenger of Allah, *'Alayhi al-Salam*, in consumption of food and in behavior. He ate bread with oil and fed people bread and meat.' He (the Imam) said, 'Ali, *'Alayhi al-Salam*, brought water and firewood. Fatimah, *'Alayha al-Salam*, prepared flour, dough, bread and stitched. Her face was the best of faces among people and her cheeks looked like two roses, O Allah grant compensation to her, to her father, her husband and her children the purified ones.'"

All the Prophets were brave people

H 14625, h 177
Sahl ibn Ziyad has narrated from al-Rayyan ibn al-Salt from Yunus in a marfu' manner who has narrated the following:
"Abu 'Abd Allah, '*Alayhi al-Salam*, has said that Allah, most Majestic, most Glorious, has never sent a Prophet without a black, clear gallbladder (a reference to intense anger for the sake of Allah) and Allah has not sent any Prophet without making them to acknowledge *al-Bada'* (changing of Allah's plan).'"

Scaring the camel of the Messenger of Allah

H 14626, h 178
Sahl has narrated from Ya'qub ibn Yazid from 'Abd al-Hamid from those whom he has mentioned who has narrated the following:
"Abu 'Abd Allah, '*Alayhi al-Salam*, has said, 'When they tried to frighten the she-camel of the Messenger of Allah, *O Allah grant compensation to Muhammad and his family worthy of their services to Your cause*, the she-camel said. 'By Allah, I would never move one foot after the other even if they cut me piece by piece.'"

Would that we were a caravan like the family of Ya'qub, *'Alayhi al-Salam*

H 14627, h 179
Ali ibn Ibrahim has narrated from his father A number of our people have narrated from Sahl ibn Ziyad from Ya'qub ibn Yazid all from Hammad ibn 'Isa from Ibrahim ibn 'Umar from a man who has narrated the following:
"Abu 'Abd Allah, '*Alayhi al-Salam*, has said, 'I pray that our journey will soon end like the journey of *Ale* (family) Ya'qub, '*Alayhi al-Salam*, when Allah will issue His judgment about us and His creatures.'"

Words of wisdom that please Allah

H 14628, h 180
Sahl ibn Ziyad has narrated from Ya'qub ibn Yazid from 'Isma'il ibn Qutaybah from Hafs ibn 'Umar from 'Isma'il ibn Muhammad who has narrated the following:
"Abu 'Abd Allah, '*Alayhi al-Salam*, has said that Allah, most Majestic, most Glorious, says, 'I do not accept every word of wisdom. I only accept his wish and concern. If his wish and concern is in what I agree, I turn it into glorification and *Tasbih* (Allah is free of all defects).'"

About the words of Allah 'We will show them our signs. . .'

H 14629, h 181

Sahl ibn Ziyad has narrated from ibn Faddal from Tha'labah' ibn Maymun from al-Tayyar who has narrated the following:

"About the meaning of the words of Allah, most Majestic, most Glorious, 'We will soon show them Our signs in the horizons and in their souls until truth becomes clear to them,' (41:53) abu 'Abd Allah, *'Alayhi al-Salam*, has said, 'It stands for being sucked in the land, metamorphosed and being stoned.' I then asked about, 'until truth becomes clear to them.' He (the Imam) said, 'Leave that aside. That stands for reappearance of al-Qai'm with divine authority and power.'"

Obedience and disobedience to Ali, *'Alayhi al-Salam*

H 14630, h 182

Sahl has narrated from Yahya ibn al-Mubarak from 'Abd Allah ibn Jabalah from Ishaq ibn 'Ammar and ibn Sinan and Sama'ah from abu Basir who has narrated the following:

"Abu 'Abd Allah, *'Alayhi al-Salam*, has said that the Messenger of Allah, *O Allah grant compensation to Muhammad and his family worthy of their services to Your cause*, has said, 'Obedience to Ali, *'Alayhi al-Salam*, is humility; and disobedience to him is disbelief in Allah.' It was asked, 'How can obedience to Ali, *'Alayhi al-Salam*, become humility and disobedience to him disbelief in Allah?' He (the Messenger of Allah) said, 'Ali, *'Alayhi al-Salam*, deals with you according to the truth; if you obey him, you will become humble; if you disobey him, it is disbelief in Allah.'"

In praise of Shi'ah and in reproach of their opposition

H 14631, h 183

It is narrated from the narrator of the previous Hadith from Yahya al-Mubarak from 'Abd Allah ibn Jabalah from Ishaq ibn 'Ammar or a person other than him who has narrated the following:

"Abu 'Abd Allah, *'Alayhi al-Salam*, has said, 'We are banu Hashim, our Shi'ah are al-Arab and other people are al-A'raab (illiterate Arabs).'"

Quraysh, Arabs and Romans

H 14632, h 184

Sahl has narrated from al-Hassan ibn Mahbub from Hanan from Zurarah who has narrated the following:

"Abu 'Abd Allah, *'Alayhi al-Salam*, has said, 'We are Quraysh, our Shi'ah are al-Arab and other people are Roman giants.'"

The Book that al-Qa'im (the one who rises with divine authority and power) will show

H 14633, h 185

Sahl has narrated from al-Hassan ibn Mahbub from certain persons of his people who has narrated the following:

"Abu 'Abd Allah, *'Alayhi al-Salam*, has said, 'It is as I see al-Qa'im, *'Alayhi al-Salam*, on the pulpit in al-Kufah with a gown on him and he takes out a sealed letter from the pocket of his gown, then opens and reads it to people. They then run away like frightened sheep. No one remains except the principals. He then speaks in a certain language, thus no one finds any refuge until they return to him and I know the language (the speech) that he speaks.'"

Wisdom is a missing property of the believers, which he grabs when he finds it

H 14634, h 186

Sahl has narrated from Bakr ibn Salih from ibn Sinan from 'Amr ibn Shamir from Jabir who has narrated the following:

"Abu 'Abd Allah, *'Alayhi al-Salam*, has said, 'Wisdom is the straying animal of the believing people; wherever one of you can find it, you must take it.'"

Asha'ath ibn Qays and his Children

H 14635, h 187

Sahl ibn Ziyad has narrated from Ya'qub ibn Yazid or others from Sulayman Katib from Ali ibn Yaqtin from those whom he has mentioned who has narrated the following:

"Abu 'Abd Allah, *'Alayhi al-Salam*, has said that al-Ash'ath ibn Qays took part in murdering 'Amir al-Mu'minin, Ali, *'Alayhi al-Salam*, his daughter took part in murdering al-Hassan, *'Alayhi al-Salam*, and Muhammad his son took part in murdering al-Husayn, *'Alayhi al-Salam*.'"

Tenderheartedness when listening to recitation of al-Quran

H 14636, h 188

Ali ibn Ibrahim has narrated from Salih ibn al-Sindiy from Ja'far ibn Bashir from Sabbah al-Hadhdha' from abu 'Usamah who has narrated the following:

"I once became a travel-mate of abu 'Abd Allah, *'Alayhi al-Salam*, and he (the Imam) asked me to read. I then read a chapter from al-Quran. He (the Imam) felt tender-hearted and wept. He said, 'O abu 'Usamah, you must take good care of your hearts by speaking of Allah, most Majestic, most Glorious, and remain on your guard against what is induced in your heart. It comes in the heart many times and in many hours of doubt of the morning in which there is no belief or disbelief in it (the heart). When it is like old rug or disintegrating bone. O abu 'Usamah, is it not true that at certain times when you search in your heart you do not remember anything good or bad and you do not know where it is?' I replied, 'Yes, it happens to me and I see that it happens to people.' He (the Imam) said, 'Yes, no one is clear thereof.' He (the Imam) said, 'When that happens then speak of Allah, most Majestic, most Glorious, and remain on your guard against what is induced (in your heart). If He wills good for a servant He induces belief and if He wills bad for a servant He induces other things.' I then asked, 'What are other things, I pray to Allah to keep my soul in service for your cause?' He (the Imam) said, 'When He wills disbelief He induces disbelief.'"

Advice of Abu 'Abd Allah, *'Alayhi al-Salam*

H 14637, h 189

A number of our people have narrated from Ahmad ibn Muhammad ibn 'Isa from Ali ibn al-Hakam from Zayd al-Shahham from 'Amr ibn Sa'id ibn Hilal who has narrated the following:

"I once said to abu 'Abd Allah, *'Alayhi al-Salam*, 'I can hardly see you for many years, so advise me with something which I must follow.' He (the Imam) said, 'I advise you to remain pious before Allah, you must remain truthful in your words, restrain from sins and work hard. You must take notice that hard work without restraint from sins is of no benefit. You must never yearn and cherish in your soul to have what those above you have. What Allah, most Majestic, most Glorious, has said, to His Messenger is sufficient reason to accept this fact; ". . . you must not allow their wealth and children to attract you." (9:55) Allah, most Majestic, most Glorious, has also said, ". . . you must not keep looking (yearning for) to what We have granted them such as their wives and blossoms of the worldly life." (20:131) If you felt afraid in something then you must recall the manner of the living of the Messenger of Allah, *O Allah grant compensation to Muhammad and his family worthy of their services to Your cause*. His sustenance consisted of barley bread and his *Halwa*, sweet dish, consisted of dates and he used palm tree twigs for firewood. If you face a hardship, you must recall the hardships that the Messenger of Allah, *O Allah grant compensation to Muhammad and his family worthy of their services to Your cause*, faced. The creatures never faced any hardship as he (the Messenger of Allah), *O Allah grant compensation to Muhammad and his family worthy of their services to Your cause*, did.'"

Advice of the Messenger of Allah, *'Alayhi al-Salam*

H 14638, h 190

A number of our people have narrated from Sahl ibn Ziyad from ibn Mahbub from al-Hassan ibn al-Sariy from abu Maryam who has narrated the following:

"Abu Ja'far, *'Alayhi al-Salam*, has said, 'I heard Jabir ibn 'Abd Allah al-Ansari say, 'One day the Messenger of Allah, *O Allah grant compensation to Muhammad and his family worthy of their services to Your cause*, passed by when we were in our club (*Nadi*) and he was on his camel. It was during his return from his farewell al-Hajj. He (the Messenger of Allah) came nearby, offered greetings of peace and we responded likewise. He then said, 'Why is it that I see love of the worldly matters has overpowered people so much that they feel as if death is written upon the others only and following the truth is made obligatory on others only. It seems as if they have never heard anything about the news of the death of the people before them, while in fact their path is the

144

path of the people who have set on their journey. Very shortly they are to return to those people whose graves have become their homes. They consume their legacy and think that they live forever after those people are gone. Never ever can such a thing happen. The later generations do not learn a lesson from the earlier generations. They have ignored and forgotten all about the advice in the book of Allah. They feel safe from all evil consequences of bad deeds, from the coming of calamity and the aftermath of an incident. Tuba (the tree in the garden (paradise)) is for those who because of their fear from Allah, most Majestic, most Glorious, have ignored fearing the people. Tuba is for those who because of their own fault have ignored looking into the faults of the believing brothers (in belief). Tuba (the tree in the garden (paradise)) is for those who remain humble before Allah, most Majestic, most Glorious, hold back from what is made lawful for me without disregarding my way of life, give up the worldly blossoms without deviating from my *Sunnah* and follow the chosen ones of my descendents after me. It (Tuba) is for those who remain away from the people of arrogance, pride with great interest in the worldly matters, who involve in heresy against my *Sunnah* and from those who act on something other than my *Sunnah*. Tuba is for those believing people who earn an asset without committing sins, do not spend it in sins but take good care of the destitute people thereby. Tuba is for those who deal with people within the best moral discipline, assist them and turn away from their evil deeds. Tuba is for those who spend moderately and donate the extra, who hold back their words from meaninglessness and their acts from indecency.'"

Words of wisdom from *'A'immah, 'Alayhim al-Salam*

H 14639, h 191

Al-Husayn Muhammad al-Ash'ariy has narrated from Mu'alla' ibn Muhammad in a marfu' manner, from certain people of wisdom the following:

"He (a certain person of wisdom) has said, 'The people who need the most to wish that all people become rich are the stingy people, because if all people become rich no one will ask the stingy people to give away anything. The ones who need the most to wish that all people became free of all faults are the ones who are filled with faults because if all people become free of faults no one will look into their faults. The ones who need the most to wish that all people became forbearing ones are the dimwitted ones who need to be ignored for their dimwittedness. On the contrary stingy people wish that all people become poor, people filled with faults wish that all people become sinful and the sinful ones wish that all people become dimwitted ones, because in poverty people become needy to the stingy ones, in moral corruption one searches to find faults and in dimwittedness recompense is by means of sins.'" (Fortunately the above is not Hadith)

Prohibition on complaining before the opposition

H 14640, h 192

A number of our people have narrated from Ahmad ibn Muhammad ibn Khalid from al-Qasim ibn Yahya from his grandfather al-Hassan ibn Rashid who has narrated the following:

"Abu 'Abd Allah, *'Alayhi al-Salam*, once said to me, 'If you ever face a difficult condition do not complain against it before those who are opposed to your belief. You must mention it before one of your brothers (in belief); you will not lose one of the four facts; financial assistance or help for a social position or an accepted prayer or an advice with a good opinion.'"

A sermon of 'Amir al-Mu'minin, Ali, *'Alayhi al-Salam*

H 14641, h 193

Ali ibn al-Husayn al-Mu'addab and others have narrated from Ahmad ibn Muhammad ibn Khalid from 'Isma'il ibn Mehran from 'Abd Allah ibn abu al-Harith al-Hamadaniy from Jabir who has narrated the following:

"Abu Ja'far, *'Alayhi al-Salam*, has said that (once) 'Amir al-Mu'minin, Ali, *'Alayhi al-Salam*, delivered a sermon. He said, 'All praise belongs to Allah who brings low and takes high, who harms and benefits, who is generous vastly and glorious is whose praise, true are whose names, who encompasses the unseen and all that is significant in minds, who has placed death among His creatures with justice and has granted them life as a favor. He gives life, causes death. He has determined the sustenance, which He has established by His knowledge in measures and made them firm by His plans; He was all knowing and seeing. He is eternal without mortality and lives forever without end. He knows all that is in the earth and all that is in the sky and all that is between them and under *al-Thara'* (a certain level of physical cosmic realm).

"I praise Him with His purest praise which is treasured with the praise with which His angels praise Him as well as the Prophets. I praise Him in a manner of praising which cannot be enumerated, no time-span precedes it and no one can praise as such. I believe in Him, place my trust with Him, ask Him for guidance, consider Him sufficient support, ask Him to determine for me what is good and pray to Him to be happy with me. I testify that only Allah deserves worship, He is one and has no partners and I testify that Muhammad is His servant and Messenger whom He has sent with guidance and true religion to make it dominant over all other religions even though the pagans dislike. O Allah, (You must) grant compensation to Muhammad and his family worthy of their services to Your cause.

"O people, you must take notice that the world is not a house for you to settle and to remain therein. You are only like a caravan who has disembarked for a rest until the morning and then to depart for the journey, who have begun the journey very light and left for the journey very light. They did not find a way to separate themselves from the journey or a way to return to what they left behind. They are taken seriously that they must be moved (to death). They work hard (for the worldly things), rely on it, thus do not prepare themselves (for death)

146

until they are taken by their throat and are sent to the dwelling of the people about whom the pen is already dried up (their worldly accounts closed) and of many of whom no news or traces are left behind. Their stay in the world was short and their being dispatched to the hereafter was quick, so you reside in their towns, travel on their footprints and you are made to move unmistakably forward without any confusion or fatigue. Your days are tiring because of work and your nights take your spirits away. In the morning, your case is like their case and you just simply walk on the path that they walked. Thus, the worldly life must not deceive you; you are only travelers who have disembarked wherein death is about to descend. Death shoots at you its arrow and its moving means pass your news to the dwelling of rewards, punishment, compensation and accounting.

"May Allah grant mercy to the man who is concerned about his Lord. He avoids sins. He disputes against his desires, rejects his yearning, a man who has harnessed his soul by means of piety, kept in the rope for fear from his Lord, led to obey by the harness and has stopped by its rein from committing sins. He raises his eyes toward the place of return, expects every now and then approaching of his death, thinks all the time, remains awake for a long time, turns away from the world, disheartened about it and works hard for the next life with seriousness. He is a man who has taken patience as his stumper to safety, piety as his sufficient supplies and the medicine for his illness. He has learned a lesson and has considered himself to be as one of those who have left, thus he has abandoned the world and people. He learns for understanding and steadfastness and the memory of returning is settled in his heart. He has rolled up his furnishings, separated himself from his pillow, stood ready on his limbs and has entered in his turning condition with anxiety and concern about Allah, most Majestic, most Glorious. He alternates between his palms and face (for *Sujud* (prostrations) and raises his hands for prayer. He does it with humbleness, secretly to his Lord, his tears flow and his heart is restless. With tears pouring down, his muscles tremble for fear from Allah, most Majestic, most Glorious, his interest in what is with Allah is great but his fear from Him is intense. He is happy with bare necessities, he expresses without hiding and is content with the minimum of that which he knows (when answering a question).

"Such are the trusts of Allah in His lands through whom He defends His servants. If one of them swears by Allah, most Glorious, he stands by his oath; if he calls against someone, Allah provides him help. He listens to him when he speaks to Him secretly and answers his prayer when he prays. Allah has placed good consequences with piety and the garden (paradise) for its people as a dwelling. Their prayer in it is the best of prayers, "You are free of all defects O Lord" and their prayer for their guardian for what He has granted them, their last prayer is, "all praise belongs to Allah, Lord of the worlds.""

A sermon of 'Amir al-Mu'minin, Ali, *'Alayhi al-Salam*

H 14642, h 194

Ali ibn Ibrahim has narrated from his father from al-Hassan ibn Mahbub from Muhammad ibn al-Nu'man or others who has narrated the following:

"Abu 'Abd Allah, *'Alayhi al-Salam,* has identified this sermon to be one of the sermons of 'Amir al-Mu'minin, Ali, *'Alayhi al-Salam,* on Friday.

'All praise belongs to Allah. He is the owner of all praise and its guardian, the end of praise and its proper destination. He is the Initiator and inventor, the Glorious, the most Great, the Majestic, the Honorable. He is the only one for magnanimity, the single one for granting bounties, and the dominant through His glory. He prevails through His might, protects through His power, and overwhelms through His measures. He is the most High over all things through His omnipotence; the most praised one because of His favor and generosity. He is the one with extra when granting favors and copious benefits, the one who expands sustenance, whose bounties are plentiful. We praise Him for His bounties and apparent blessings with a praise of the weight of greatness of His glory, which can fill the measure of His bounties and His magnanimity. I testify that only Allah deserves worship, He is one and has no partners who existed as being the first and foremost and in His being eternal with full domination. All creatures are submissive before His oneness, Lordship and His eternity and acknowledge His being everlasting. I testify that Muhammad, *O Allah grant compensation to Muhammad and his family worthy of their services to Your cause,* is His servant and Messenger, the chosen one from among His creatures. He chose him with His knowledge, selected for His revelation and trusted him for His secret. He is happy with him for His creatures. He has assigned him for His great command, as a light for His principles of His religion and the program of His path and for the opening to His revelation. He (the Messenger of Allah) is a means, a step, a ladder for the door of His mercy. He sent him in the time of the lapse of the messengers and the guides to knowledge. He sent him in the time of differences of cultures, misguidance from the truth, ignorance about the Lord, rejection of Resurrection and warning. He sent him to all people and as a mercy for all the worlds with a gracious book, which He has made excellent, detailed, explained, clarified, fortified and protected against the coming of falsehood, from the front and behind it. It is the revelation from the most Wise and praised one. In it He has given examples, mentioned signs so that they may have understanding. He has made certain things lawful in it, other things unlawful and has established a system of laws for His servants as matters of good excuses and warnings so that people will not have any reason against Allah after His sending messengers and so that it can serve as a fact of proper notification for the worshipping people. He preached His message and strived hard in His way, worshipped Him until the time of his death, *O Allah grant compensation to Muhammad and his family worthy of their services to Your cause,* with great deal of peace.

'Servants of Allah, I advise you and I advise myself to remain pious before Allah who initiated all things with His knowledge and to Him they all move tomorrow for the day of return. In His hand are its destruction and your destruction, expiration of your days, the destruction of your appointed time and the ending of your duration. It will shortly end and vanish before you and before us as it expired for those before you. Servants of Allah, you must make your efforts and striving in this world to provide supplies in its short days for the long days of the hereafter. This is the home of work and the hereafter is the home of settling down and reward. You must keep aside thereof because deceived is one who is deceived by this world. You must never count on the world in matters of attaching one's hopes and interest to it, love it, have confidence in it and become fascinated thereby. It must not be more than what Allah, most Majestic, most Glorious, has said about it, "The worldly life is like water that We send from the sky. With it plants of earth and what people and cattle eat mix, until the earth takes its beauty and decoration. Its people think that they have full control on it but our command comes in the night or during the day and We turn it into harvested things as nothing existed the day before. This is how We explain our signs for the people of understanding." (10:24). Even though when one may gain a dress in this world, he inherits a lesson, and no one wakes up in the morning in peace but that he is afraid of misfortune or change of a bounty or loss of good health. When death is still behind it and it is just the beginning of the horror of standing before the Just Ruler who gives reward to every soul for whatever it has done. ". . . So that He will recompense the doers of evil deeds for what they have done and reward those who have done good deeds with goodness." (53:31) You must remain pious before Allah, most Majestic, most Glorious, and hasten to the happiness of Allah and to acting in obedience to Him by all the matters, which lead to His happiness; He is near and answers prayers. May Allah make you and us of those who act toward His love and avoid His displeasure.

'Thereafter, the best speech, the best story, the best advice and most beneficial reminder is the book of Allah, most Majestic, most Glorious. Allah, most Majestic, most Glorious, has said, "When al-Quran is recited you must remain silent; perhaps you will receive mercy." (7:204) I seek refuge with Allah against Satan, condemned to be stoned. In the name of Allah, the Beneficent, the Merciful "I swear by al-'Asr that human beings are in loss except the believing people who do good deeds and advise each other with truth and advise with patience." (103:1-3)

Allah and His angels say, "*O Allah grant compensation to Muhammad and his family worthy of their services to Your cause*," O believing people, you must also say, "*O Allah grant compensation to Muhammad and his family worthy of their services to Your cause*," with a great degree of peace and safety. O Lord, O Allah I beg You to grant compensation to Muhammad and his family worthy of their services to Your cause. Bless Muhammad and *Ale* (family of) Muhammad, be compassionate with Muhammad and *Ale* (family of) Muhammad, grant peace to Muhammad and *Ale* (family of) Muhammad like the most excellent compensation, blessing, mercy, compassion and peace that You had granted to

Ibrahim and *Ale* (family of) Ibrahim; You are praiseworthy and glorious. O Allah I request You to grant Muhammad the means, the nobility, the excellence, and the gracious position. O Allah make Muhammad and *Ale* (family of) Muhammad the greatest, among all the creatures, of nobility on the Day of Judgment, the nearest to You in position, most respected before You, on the Day of Judgment, in prestige, of the most excellent ones before You in rank and shares of blessings. O Lord, grant Muhammad the noblest standing, gift him with peace and intercession of al-Islam. O Lord, join us with him, without failure, suffering loss, regretting, or being changed, O Lord, of truth; Amin.'

"He then sat down for a short time then stood up and said, 'All praise belongs to Allah, who is the most deserving to be concerned about and praised, the best before whom one must remain pious and worshipping, who has the utmost priority to be spoken of with greatness and glory. We praise Him for the greatness of His self-sufficiency, copiousness of His grants, apparentness of His bounties and goodness of His trials. We believe in His guidance the light of which does not become extinguished, whose sublimity cannot fully be stated and whose ring (to hold to for support) does not become weak. We seek refuge with Allah against the evil of doubt, darkness of mischief and ask from Him forgiveness for accumulating sins and seek protection with Him against wickedness of deeds and detestable hopes, attacks of the horrors, the association with the people of doubt, agreement with what the sinful ones do on earth without any right. O Lord, forgive us and the believing male and female, living or dead whom You have made to die in the religion of Your Prophet, *O Allah grant compensation to Muhammad and his family worthy of their services to Your cause*. O Lord, accept their good deeds, ignore their evil deeds and send on them mercy, forgiveness and happiness. Forgive the living ones of the believing people, male and female who believe in Your oneness and acknowledge Your messenger, hold to Your religion, fulfill their obligations, follow Your Prophet, maintain Your *Sunnah*, consider Your lawful matters lawful and Your unlawful matters unlawful, fear Your penalty, keep hope in Your reward, remain friend of Your friends and hostile to Your enemies. O Lord, accept their good deeds, ignore their evils deeds, admit them in Your mercy among Your virtuous servants, O Lord, of the Truth; Amin.'"

For every believer there is a guard from Allah

H 14643, h 195

Al-Husayn Muhammad al-Ash'ariy has narrated from Mu'alla' ibn Muhammad al-Hassan ibn Ali al-Washsha' from Muhammad ibn al-Fudayl from abu Hamzah who has narrated the following:

"I once heard abu Ja'far, *'Alayhi al-Salam*, say, 'For every believing person there is an *al-Hafiz* (protector) and an *al-Sa'ib*.' I then asked, 'What is *al-Hafiz* and *al-Sa'ib*, O abu Ja'far?' He (the Imam) said, '*Al-Hafiz* is from Allah, most Blessed, most High, for guardianship which protects a believing person wherever he is. *Al-Sa'ib* is the glad news of Muhammad, *O Allah grant compensation to Muhammad and his family worthy of their services to Your cause*, with which Allah, most Blessed, most High, gives glad news to a believing person wherever and in whatever condition he is.'"

Mixing with people

H 14644, h 196
A number of our people have narrated from Sahl ibn Ziyad from al-Hajjal from Hammad from al-Halabiy who has narrated the following:
"Abu 'Abd Allah, *'Alayhi al-Salam*, has said, 'When you blend with people you inquire about them, when you inquire about them you will hate them.'"

People are like mines

H 14645, h 197
Sahl has narrated from Bakr ibn Salih in a marfu' manner who has narrated the following:
"Abu 'Abd Allah, *'Alayhi al-Salam*, has said, 'People are mines like the mines of gold and silver; those who had an origin in the time of ignorance, they have their origin in Islam also.'"

Hadith about al-Zawra' (name of a place) and that which is killed there

H 14646, h 198
Sahl ibn Ziyad has narrated from Bakr ibn Salih from Muhammad ibn Sinan from Mu'awiyah ibn Wahab who has narrated the following:
"Once, abu 'Abd Allah, *'Alayhi al-Salam*, read as an example a line of poetry, which is composed by ibn abu 'Aqib: 'In al-Zawra' eighty thousand of them will be slaughtered in a middle of the day battle like camels slaughtered as offering animals'- others have pronounced it al-Buzzal. He (the Imam) then asked, 'Do you know al-Zawra'?' I replied, 'Yes, I pray to Allah to keep my soul in service for your cause, they say that it is Baghdad.' He (the Imam) said, 'No, that is not it.' He (the Imam) then asked, 'Have you gone to al-Ray?' I replied, 'Yes, I have seen it.' He (the Imam) then asked, 'Have you seen the animal market?' I replied, 'Yes, I have seen it.' He (the Imam) asked, 'Have you noticed the black mountain on the right of the road? That is al-Zawra'. Eighty thousand of the children of so and so will be killed there, each one suitable for Khilafat (successor ruler).' I then asked, 'I pray to Allah to keep my soul in service for your cause, who will kill them?' He (the Imam) said, 'Children of *'Ajam* (non-Arab) will kill them.'"

About the words of Allah 'those who on hearing the signs of Allah do not act as blindly'

H 14647, h 199
Ali ibn Muhammad has narrated from Ali ibn al-'Abbas from Muhammad ibn Ziyad from abu Nasr who has narrated the following:
"I once asked abu 'Abd Allah, *'Alayhi al-Salam*, about the meaning of the words of Allah, most Majestic, most Glorious, '. . . those who when reminded of the

signs of their Lord, do not fall on them in a deaf and blind manner.' (25:73) He (the Imam) said, 'The converts are not skeptics.'"

About the words of Allah 'permission will not be given to them...'

H 14648, h 200

It is narrated from the narrator of the previous Hadith from Ali from 'Isma'il ibn Mehran from Hammad ibn 'Uthaman who has narrated the following:

"About the meaning of the words of Allah, most Blessed, most High, '. . . permission will not be given to them to present their excuse,' (30:57) abu 'Abd Allah, *'Alayhi al-Salam*, has said, 'Allah is glorious, Just and Great. Why will He not give them permission to present their excuse? In fact, it will happen after they fail to present any acceptable excuse.'"

About the words of Allah 'those who are pious before Allah...'

H 14649, h 201

Ali has narrated from Ali ibn al-Husayn from Muhammad al-Kunasiy who has said that narrated to us in a marfu' manner the following:

"About the meaning of the words of Allah, most Majestic, most Glorious, '. . . for those who remain pious before Allah, He provides a way out (to safety) and gives them sustenance from unexpected sources,' (65:3) abu 'Abd Allah, *'Alayhi al-Salam*, has said, 'These are a people from our Shi'ah who are weak. They do not have the means that can take them to us. They hear our Hadith and find light (of guidance) in our knowledge. A group of them who are stronger travel, spend their asset and bear tiredness until they come to us, listen to our Hadith, then they narrate it to them who listen and preserve them, but these ones lose them. Those are the ones for whom Allah, most Majestic, most Glorious, provides a way out to safety and gives them sustenance from unexpected sources.'

"This is about the meaning of the words of Allah, most Majestic, most Glorious. '. . . Have you heard the story of the overwhelming? . . .' (88:1) abu 'Abd Allah, *'Alayhi al-Salam*, has said, 'It is a reference to those who cheat the Imam.' About '. . . it will not help them to gain weight or satisfaction from hunger' he (the Imam) said, 'It will not benefit them and will not make them free of needs. Going inside will not benefit them and sitting down will not make them free of needs.'"

Those who planned to takeover, usurp *Khilafah*

H 14650, h 202

It is narrated from the narrator of the previous Hadith from Ali ibn al-Husayn from Ali ibn abu Hamzah from abu Basir who has narrated the following:

"About the meaning of the words of Allah, most Majestic, most Glorious, '. . . There is not a single place wherein any secret counsel can take place between any three people without Allah being the fourth, nor five people without His being the sixth, nor any gathering of more or fewer people, wherever it may be, without His being with them. On the Day of Judgment, He will tell them about their deeds. Allah has the knowledge of all things. (58:7) Abu 'Abd Allah, *'Alayhi al-Salam*, has explained it.

"He (the Imam) said, 'This was revealed about so and so, abu 'Ubaydah al-Jarrah, 'Abd al-Rahman ibn 'Awf, Salim *mawla* of abu Hudhayfah and al-Mughirah ibn Sha'bah when they wrote the document, the accord and concurrence that when Muhammad will pass away, his successor must not be allowed forever to come from banu Hashim and Prophet-hood. Allah, most Majestic, most Glorious, then revealed this verse about them.' I then asked about the meaning of the words of Allah, most Majestic, most Glorious, 'If the unbelievers persist in their disbelief, We shall also persist in punishing them. (43:79) Do they think that We do not hear their secrets and whispers? We certainly can hear them and Our Messengers who are with them, record it all. (43:80)'

"He (the Imam) said, 'These two verses were revealed about them on that day.' Abu 'Abd Allah, *'Alayhi al-Salam*, then said, 'You perhaps think that it (day when the letter was written) was similar to the day al-Husayn, *'Alayhi al-Salam*, was murdered (because of this plot the murder took place). This is how it was in the knowledge of Allah, most Majestic, most Glorious, of which the Messenger of Allah, *O Allah grant compensation to Muhammad and his family worthy of their services to Your cause*, was informed that when the document was written, al-Husayn was murdered and the domain moved out of banu Hashim, it all had happened.'

"I then asked about the meaning of the words of Allah, '. . . if two group of believing people fight each other, you must make peace between them; and if one group rebelled against the other then you must fight against the rebellious ones, until they come to obey the command of Allah. If they comply then make peace between them with justice.' (49:9) He (the Imam) said, 'The two groups is the explanation of the day of al-Basrah and they are people of this verse. They rebelled against 'Amir al-Mu'minin, Ali, *'Alayhi al-Salam*. It was obligatory on him (the Imam) to fight them until they were eliminated. They must have complied with the command of Allah and if they did not comply, it then was obligatory on him (the Imam) according to revelation from Allah not to hold back the sword until they complied and returned under their command because they had pledged allegiance willingly and without being forced. It was the rebellious group as Allah, most Blessed, most High, has explained. It was obligatory on 'Amir al-Mu'minin, Ali, *'Alayhi al-Salam*, to bring justice among them as victory over them was achieved just as the Messenger of Allah, *O Allah grant compensation to Muhammad and his family worthy of their services to Your cause*, kept justice in the case of the people of Makkah. He did them the favor of granting amnesty. What 'Amir al-Mu'minin, Ali, *'Alayhi al-Salam*, did with the group in al-Basrah after he achieved victory over them was exactly the same as the Prophet did in the case of the people of Makkah, without any difference.'

"I then asked, '. . . the town which is turned upside down.' (53:53) He (the Imam) said that it is a reference to the people of al-Basra. I then asked, '. . . the towns to which their messengers came with clear proofs, were turned upside down...' (9:70) He (the Imam) said, 'They were the people of Lot. Their town was turned upside down on them.'"

Certain companions' harassing Salman Farsi

H 14651, h 203

Ali ibn Ibrahim has narrated from 'Abd Allah ibn Muhammad ibn 'Isa from Safwan ibn Yahya from Hanan who has narrated the following:

"I heard my father narrating from abu Ja'far, *'Alayhi al-Salam*, who has said that once Salman was sitting with a group of people of Quraysh in the Masjid and they began to speak about their lineage and boast about their ancestors until they reached Salman. 'Umar ibn al-Khattab said to him, 'Tell me who are you, who was your father and what is your origin.' He said, 'I am Salman ibn 'Abd Allah. I was lost but Allah guided me through Muhammad, *O Allah grant compensation to Muhammad and his family worthy of their services to Your cause.* I was poor but Allah made me self-sufficient through Muhammad, *O Allah grant compensation to Muhammad and his family worthy of their services to Your cause.* I was a slave; Allah set me free through Muhammad, *O Allah grant compensation to Muhammad and his family worthy of their services to Your cause.* This is my ancestral line and social status.' He (the Imam) said, 'The Messenger of Allah, *O Allah grant compensation to Muhammad and his family worthy of their services to Your cause*, came out when Salman was speaking to them. Salman then said, 'O Messenger of Allah, I met these people and sat with them. They began to speak about their ancestors and boast about them until it was my turn and 'Umar ibn al-Khattab asked, "Who are you, what is your origin and social status?"'"

"The Holy Prophet, *O Allah grant compensation to Muhammad and his family worthy of their services to Your cause*, asked, 'What did you say, O Salman?' He replied, 'I said that my name is Salman ibn 'Abd Allah. I was lost but Allah guided me through Muhammad, *O Allah grant compensation to Muhammad and his family worthy of their services to Your cause.* I was poor but Allah made me self sufficient through Muhammad, *O Allah grant compensation to Muhammad and his family worthy of their services to Your cause.* I was a slave; Allah set me free through Muhammad, *O Allah grant compensation to Muhammad and his family worthy of their services to Your cause.* This is My ancestral line and social status.' The Messenger of Allah, *O Allah grant compensation to Muhammad and his family worthy of their services to Your cause*, said, 'O community of Quraysh, the social status of a man is his religion, his manhood is his moral discipline and his origin is his reason, his intellect. Allah, most Majestic, most Glorious, has said, 'We have created you male and female, made you in nations and tribes so that you can recognize each other. The most honorable among you in the sight of Allah most certainly is the one who is most pious. . .' (49:13)

"The Holy Prophet, *O Allah grant compensation to Muhammad and his family worthy of their services to Your cause*, then said to Salman, 'No one of these have any excellence over you except by means of being pious before Allah, most Majestic, most Glorious. If you remain more pious then you are a more excellent person.'"

Equitable practice of 'Amir al-Mu'minin, *'Alayhi al-Salam*

H 14652, h 204

Ali ibn Ibrahim has narrated from his father from ibn abu 'Umayr from 'Abd al-Rahman ibn al-Hajjaj from Muhammad ibn Muslim who has narrated the following:

"Abu 'Abd Allah, *'Alayhi al-Salam*, has said that when Ali, *'Alayhi al-Salam*, undertook the administration of the Muslim nation, he climbed on the pulpit, praised Allah and spoke of His glory. He then said, 'I by Allah will not reduce anything of your assets captured during a war as long as I have one palm tree left in al-Madinah. You must speak the truth to yourselves. Do you think that when I deny myself, I will give you anything (extra)?' He (the Imam) has said that 'Aqil then stood up and said, 'By Allah, will you allow me to be equal to that black man in al-Madinah?' He (the Imam) said, 'Sit down, and is there no one besides you to speak? You have no priority over him except by means of being more pious.'"

Advice of the Messenger of Allah, *'Alayhi al-Salam*

H 14653, h 205

A number of our people have narrated from Sahl ibn Ziyad from ibn Mahbub from ibn Ri'ab from abu 'Ubaydah who has narrated the following:

"Abu Ja'far, *'Alayhi al-Salam*, has said that the Messenger of Allah, *O Allah grant compensation to Muhammad and his family worthy of their services to Your cause*, once stood on al-Safa' and said, 'O banu Hashim, O banu 'Abd al-Muttalib, I am the Messenger of Allah to you. I am compassionate to you. I am responsible for my deeds and every man is responsible for his deeds. You must not say that Muhammad is from us so we will enter wherever he will enter. No, by Allah, I have no friends from you or others, O banu 'Abd al-Muttalib, except the pious ones; otherwise, I will not recognize you on the Day of Judgment when you will come carrying this world on your backs and people will come with the hereafter on their backs. I have hereby presented my argument so that you will not have any good reason to raise objections against me. I have clarified it between myself and you and between myself and Allah, most Majestic, most Glorious.'"

The dream of Abu Ja'far, *'Alayhi al-Salam*

H 14654, h 206

A number of our people have narrated from Ahmad ibn Muhammad ibn Khalid, from his father from al-Nadr ibn Suwayd from al-Halabiy, from ibn Muskan from Zurarah who has narrated the following:

"Abu Ja'far, *'Alayhi al-Salam*, has said, 'I saw as if I am on the top of a mountain and people climb to me from all sides until they became many trying to reach higher. Then people began to fall off the mountain from all sides and no one of them remained except a small group. They did the climbing five times. Every time people fell but that small group remained and Qays ibn 'Abd Allah ibn 'Jalan was among the small group.' He (the Imam) thereafter lived only for five years.'"

Angels Give *Ghusl* (bath) to Abu Ja'far, *'Alayhi al-Salam*

H 14655, h 207

It is narrated from the narrator of the previous Hadith from Ahmad ibn Muhammad from ibn abu Nasr from Hammad ibn 'Uthaman who has narrated the following:

"Abu Basir has narrated to me that he heard abu 'Abd Allah, *'Alayhi al-Salam*, say it. He (the Imam) said, 'A man who lived few miles away from al-Madinah saw a dream in which he was told, "You must leave for the city to perform *Salat* (prayer) for abu Ja'far, *'Alayhi al-Salam*, the angels are washing his body in al-Baqi'." The man came and found out that abu Ja'far, *'Alayhi al-Salam*, had passed away.'"

About the words of Allah '…at the brink of fire'

H 14656, h 208

Ali ibn Ibrahim has narrated from Ahmad ibn Muhammad ibn Khalid from his father who has narrated the following:

"It is about the meaning of the words of Allah, most Majestic, most Glorious, '. . . you were at the brink of the fire and He saved you thereof [through Muhammad].' (3:103) Abu 'Abd Allah, *'Alayhi al-Salam*, has said, 'This is, by Allah, how it was brought by Jibril *'Alayhi al-Salam*, to Muhammad, *O Allah grant compensation to Muhammad and his family worthy of their services to Your cause*.'"

About the words of Allah, 'you cannot achieve any goodness. . .'

H 14657, h 209

Zabayan who has narrated the following:

"About the meaning of the words of Allah, 'You will never achieve virtuous matters until you spend from whatever you love.' (3:92) Abu 'Abd Allah, *'Alayhi al-Salam*, has said, 'You must read it as '. . . all that you love.'"

About the words of Allah 'Were We to write upon them…'

H 14658, h 210

It is narrated from the narrator of the previous Hadith from his father from Ali ibn Asbat from Ali ibn abu Hamzah from abu Basir who has narrated the following:

"It is about the meaning of the words of Allah. Abu 'Abd Allah, *'Alayhi al-Salam*, has read as follows, '. . . had We made it obligatory on them to kill themselves [submit themselves to Imam totally] or move out of your towns [for His happiness] they would not do so except a very few of them. If people [opposing] did what they were advised to do, it would have been better for them and more strengthening (for their faith).' (4:66) It is also about this verse, '. . . then they did not find in their souls any obstacle about your judgment [in the issue of *Waliy*, governing authority] and submitted themselves [to obey Allah] in total submission.'" (4:64)

About the words of Allah 'those are the ones whose hearts are known to Allah'

H 14659, h 211

Ali ibn Ibrahim has narrated from Ahmad ibn Muhammad ibn Khalid from his father from abu Janadah al-Saluliy, companion of the Messenger of Allah, *O Allah grant compensation to Muhammad and his family worthy of their services to Your cause*, who has narrated the following:

"Abu al-Hassan, al-Awwal, *'Alayhi al-Salam*, has explained the meaning of the words of Allah, most Majestic, most Glorious, as follows. ' . . . Allah knows very well about what is in the hearts of these people, so disregard them [because the word of misfortune has already been decreed for them as well as punishment], give them good advise and say clear words to their souls.'" (4:63)

Allah does not make obedience to *'Ulil 'Amr* obligatory, then allow to oppose them

H 14660, h 212

Ali ibn Ibrahim has narrated from his father from ibn abu 'Umayr from 'Umar ibn 'Udhaynah from Burayd ibn Mu'awiyah who has narrated the following:

"Abu Ja'far, *'Alayhi al-Salam*, has read the meaning of the words of Allah, most Majestic, most Glorious, as follows, '. . . you must obey Allah, the Messenger and people who possess authority among you,' (4:59) [if you fear disputes on an issue then turn to Allah, to the Messenger and to those among you who possess authority]. He (the Imam) then said, 'How would He command them to obey them and then allow them to dispute them. He only has addressed thereby those to whom it is said, 'Obey Allah and obey the Messenger.'" (It is a reference to dispute among the people and not between the people and the three authorities, dispute against the Imam is not permissible)

People of Salih, *'Alayhi al-Salam*

H 14661, h 213

Ali ibn Ibrahim has narrated from his father from al-Hassan ibn Mahbub from abu Hamzah who has narrated the following:

"Abu Ja'far, *'Alayhi al-Salam*, has said that the Messenger of Allah, *O Allah grant compensation to Muhammad and his family worthy of their services to Your cause*, asked Jibril, *'Alayhi al-Salam*, 'How did the punishment for the people of Salih, *'Alayhi al-Salam*, take place?' He replied, 'O Muhammad, Salih was sent to his people when he was a sixteen year old boy. He lived with them until he became one hundred twenty years old and they still did not accept his faith. They had seventy idols, which they worshipped instead of Allah, most Majestic, most Glorious. When he saw this among them he said, "O my people, I was sent to you when I was sixteen years old and now I am one hundred twenty years old. I ask you for two things. If you like, you can ask me to ask my Lord to give whatever you want at this hour, or I ask you to ask your idols to give me what I want; and if they answered I will move away from you; I have disappointed you and you have disappointed me." They said, "What you have said is fair, O Salih." They prepared for the day that they were to move out. They went out with their idols on their backs then they brought their food and drink, which they ate and drank. When they completed they called, "O Salih, ask." He then asked their elder, "What is the name of this?" They said, "It is so and so." Salih said, "O so and so answer." It did not answer. Salih asked, "Why does he not answer?" They said, "Ask another one." He then called all of them one by one by their names and they did not answer. They then turned to their idols and said, "Why do you not answer Salih?" They did not answer them. They said, "You must move away from us for an hour so we can speak to our idols." They then removed their furnishings and clothes, placed their face on the soil, spread soil on their heads and said to their idols that if you did not answer Salih today you will be disgraced." They then called Salih and said, "O Salih, ask them." He called them and they did not answer. He said to them, "O my people, it is midday now and your idols have not answered. You ask me so I ask my Lord and He will answer you in this hour." Seventy people of their elders and distinguished ones among them said, "O Salih, we ask you if your Lord answers we follow you and all people in the town will pledge allegiance to you." Salih said, "Ask whatever you want." They said, "Come with us to this mountain." The mountain was nearby. He went with them and when they reached the mountain they said, "O Salih, ask your Lord to make a camel that is red, blond, covered with hairs and friendly come out for us from this mountain in this hour with a distance of a mile between its two sides." Salih said, "You have asked what is very great and heavy for me but it is very easy for my Lord, Allah, most Majestic, most Glorious." Salih asked Allah, most Blessed, most High, and the mountain opened up because of which their sanity almost fell apart when they heard it. The mountain then began to shake, very severely, as if a woman in labor. Then its head showed which came out from the opening. When its neck was complete it began to chew its cud. Then the rest of its body came out, then it stood up straight on the ground. When they saw it they said, "O Salih your Lord has answered very quickly. Pray to Him to bring out its young." He then asked Allah, most Majestic, most Glorious, about it, it threw it out, and they gathered around it. He asked, "O people, is there anything else left?" They said, "No, allow us to go to our people and inform them about what we have seen so they accept the faith." They returned but not all seventy reached the people before sixty-four of them became apostates. They said it is magic and lies. They went to the crowd. Only six said that it is true and the crowd said that it is lies and magic. They came back in that condition and out of six one more doubted and he was of those who injured the camel.'" Ibn Mahbub has said that I narrated this Hadith to one of our people called Sa'id ibn Yazid and he told me that he has seen the mountain from which the camel came out which is in al-Sham. He said, 'I have seen the mark of the camels scratching the mountain and another mountain one mile away from it.'"

People of Thamud

H 14662, h 214
Ali ibn Muhammad has narrated from Ali ibn al-'Abbas from al-Hassan ibn 'Abd al-Rahman from Ali ibn abu Hamzah from abu Basir who has narrated the following:

"I once asked abu 'Abd Allah, *'Alayhi al-Salam*, about the meaning of the words of Allah, most Majestic, most Glorious, 'People of Thamud said that (Our) warning was a lie. They said, "They said, 'Should we follow only one person among us. We shall be clearly in error and in trouble (if we do so). (54:24) How is it that he has received guidance? In fact, he is the most untruthful and arrogant person.'" (54:25) Abu 'Abd Allah, *'Alayhi al-Salam*, has said, 'This is the way they rejected Salih. Allah, most Majestic, most Glorious, has never destroyed a nation until He sent to them before the destruction the messengers to present before them authoritative argument. Allah sent Salih to them who called them to Allah but they did not accept; instead, they acted insolently saying, "We will not believe you unless you bring out of this rock a friendly camel." The rock was that which they held with greatness, worshipped it and offered offering in the beginning of each year when they gathered near the rock. They said, "If you are a messenger and Prophet as you say you are, then pray to your Lord to bring out from this solid rock a friendly she-camel." Allah brought out what they had asked for from it. Then Allah, most Blessed, most High, sent revelation to him that said, "O Salih, say to them that Allah has assigned a share of the water for this camel. One day you will use the water and one day the camel will use the water." On the day that was for the camel, it would drink the water and they used the milk of the camel. All of them, the small and grown up ones, consumed the milk. After the night in the morning, they would use the water and the camel would not use any water. They lived as such as long as Allah wanted. They then turned violent against Allah and certain ones of them went to the others saying, "You must destroy this camel so we can live with ease. We do not agree with a share of water for it and only one day for us." They then asked for one who could destroy the camel for a certain amount of payment. A red, blond, blue-eyed man who was born out of wedlock whose father no one knew called Qudar came. He was one of the evil wicked ones with misfortune on them. They assigned a certain amount of payment for him. When the camel moved to the water, which it used, he allowed it to drink and when coming back he sat in ambush on its path and hit it with the sword once, which did not do anything. He then hit it again and killed it. It fell on the ground on its side; its young ran away and climbed the mountain. It cried several times to the sky. The people of Salih came, all of them, without anyone left behind and all of them took part in hitting the camel. They distributed the meat among themselves and they all ate from its meat. When Salih saw it he came to them and said, "O people, what made you to do this, why did you disobey your Lord?" Allah, most Blessed, most High, sent revelation to Salih, *'Alayhi al-Salam*, that said, "Your people committed terror and a sin by killing the she-camel that I raised for them as authoritative proof against them which was not harmful to them. Instead it had great benefit for them, so say to them that I am about to send torment on them if they did not repent and return from their transgression within three days. If they repent I will accept it and I will prevent it from coming on them. If they did not repent and return, I will send on them torment on the third day." Salih went to them and said, "O my people, I am the messenger of your Lord to you and He says that if you repent, return and ask forgiveness He will forgive you, turn to you and accept your repentance." When he said this to them they turned to be more insolent and filthy than ever before. They said, "O Salih, bring on us whatever threat you have if you are truthful." He said, "My people, tomorrow your faces will become yellow, on the second day your faces will become red and on the third day they will become black." On the first day then their faces became yellow and they went to each other saying, "What Salih had said has come on us" but the insolent ones among them said, "Do not listen to what Salih says and we will not accept his words even if it is great." On the second day, their faces turned red; certain ones among them went to the others and said that what Salih had said has come on us. The insolent ones said, "Even if we all are destroyed we will not listen to Salih and will not abandon our gods which our forefathers have worshipped." They did not repent and did not return. On the third day, their faces turned black and they went to each other saying, "O people, what Salih had said has come on us." The insolent ones said, "Yes, what Salih had said has come on us." In the middle of the night Jibril, *'Alayhi al-Salam*, came with a high pitch sound that tore their ears, split their hearts and cracked their livers. During the three days they had applied Hunut (camphor), prepared their shroud and they knew that punishment was about to come. They all died in one blinking of an eye, the small and grown up ones. Nothing was left of them, such as camels, cattle or anything else but that Allah destroyed them all. They remained in their towns and beds dead. Allah then along with the high pitch sound sent fire from the sky which burnt them all and this was their story.'"

Words of Farwah from Abu Ja'far, *'Alayhi al-Salam*

H 14663, h 215

Humayd ibn Ziyad has narrated from al-Hassan ibn Muhammad al-Kindiy from more than one person of our people from Aban ibn 'Uthman from al-Fudayl ibn al-Zubayr who has narrated the following:

"Farwah narrated to me that I mentioned something of their issue and abu Ja'far, *'Alayhi al-Salam*, said, 'They battered you because of 'Uthman for eighty years knowing well that he was unjust; what will happen if you mentioned their two idols, O Farwah?'"

Question of a Man from Abu Ja'far, *'Alayhi al-Salam*

H 14664, h 216

Muhammad ibn Yahya has narrated from Ahmad ibn Muhammad from al-Husayn ibn Sa'id from Ali ibn al-Nu'man from 'Abd Allah ibn Muskan from Sadir who has narrated the following:

"Once we were with abu Ja'far, *'Alayhi al-Salam*, and we mentioned what people had done after their Prophet, *O Allah grant compensation to Muhammad and his family worthy of their services to Your cause*, and their humiliating 'Amir al-Mu'minin, Ali, *'Alayhi al-Salam*. One man from the people said, 'I pray to Allah to keep you well, where was the strength of banu Hashim and the number of their people?' Abu Ja'far, *'Alayhi al-Salam*, said, 'People remaining of banu Hashim were Ja'far and Hamzah who passed away, only two weak people, new Muslims, Abbas and Aqil were left with him and they were of al-Tulaqa' (the freed ones). Had Hamzah and Ja'far been present with them they would not reach where they reached; had they (people) seen them (Hamzah and Ja'far) they would not jeopardize their soul.'"

Cure for certain illnesses

H 14665, h 217
Muhammad ibn Yahya has narrated from Ahmad ibn Muhammad ibn 'Isa from 'Abd Allah ibn al-Mughirah from 'Isma'il ibn Muslim who has narrated the following:

"Abu 'Abd Allah, *'Alayhi al-Salam*, has said, 'If one may feel weakness, headache or urine blockage, he can place his hand on the troubled area. One then can say, 'Settle down; I settle you down by the One for whom all that is in the night and in the day has settled and who is (the strongest in) hearing and all-knowing.'"

Determination is in the heart . . .

H 14666, h 218
Muhammad ibn Yahya has narrated from Ahmad ibn Muhammad ibn 'Isa from Ahmad ibn Muhammad from ibn abu Nasr and al-Hassan ibn Ali ibn Faddal from abu Jamilah who has narrated the following:

"Abu 'Abd Allah, *'Alayhi al-Salam*, has said, 'Determination is in the heart, kindness and harshness is in the liver and bashfulness is in the lung.' In another Hadith from abu Jamilah it is said that the dwelling place of reason is the heart.'"

Cure for certain illnesses

H 14667, h 219
A number of our people have narrated from Sahl ibn Ziyad from Ali ibn Hassan from Musa ibn Bakr who has narrated the following:

"Once a boy complained before abu al-Hassan, *'Alayhi al-Salam*, and he (the Imam) asked about him and it was said that he has spleen trouble. He (the Imam) said, 'Feed him leek for three days.' We then fed him leek and he excreted blood; then he was completely cured.'"

Cure for weakness of the stomach

H 14668, h 220
Muhammad ibn Yahya has narrated from more than one person from Muhammad ibn 'Isa from Muhammad ibn 'Amr ibn Ibrahim who has narrated the following:

"I once asked abu Ja'far, *'Alayhi al-Salam*, and complained before him about weakness of my stomach. He (the Imam) said, 'You should drink al-Haza' (an herb similar to leek) with cold water.' I followed the instruction and felt as I liked.'"

Cure for gases. . .

H 14669, h 221
Muhammad ibn Yahya has narrated from Ahmad ibn Muhammad ibn 'Isa from Bakr ibn Salih who has narrated the following:

"I once heard abu al-Hassan, al-Awwal, *'Alayhi al-Salam*, say this. 'To cure an illness because of *al-Rih* (air or inflammation) or *al-Haam* (a kind of illness) and coldness in the joints, one can take a handful of fenugreek and a handful of dry fig. Soak them in water and cook them in a pan, then filter and allow it to cool: then drink every other day until you drink a total amount of one bowlful of the preparation.'"

Cure for the back

H 14670, h 222
A number of our people have narrated from Ahmad ibn Muhammad ibn Khalid from Muhammad ibn Ali from Noah ibn Shu'ayb from those whom he has mentioned who has narrated the following:

"Abu al-Hassan, *'Alayhi al-Salam*, has said, 'If one finds a change in his reproductive fluid, pure buttermilk and honey is useful for him.'"

Cupping on Tuesday

H 14671, h 223
Al-Husayn Muhammad has narrated from Mu'alla' ibn Muhammad from Muhammad ibn Jumhur from Humran who has narrated the following:

"Abu 'Abd Allah, *'Alayhi al-Salam*, once asked, 'On what kinds of issue people have differences?' I replied, 'They think that cupping on Tuesday is more proper.' He (the Imam) asked, 'What do they say about it?' I replied, 'They think it is the day of blood.' He (the Imam) said, 'What they have said is right, thus it is more proper not to stir it in its day. Do they not know that on Tuesday there is an hour that if it coincides with one's bleeding, it goes on until he dies or what Allah wills.'"

Cupping on Wednesday

H 14672, h 224
A number of our people have narrated from Sahl ibn Ziyad from Ya'qub ibn Yazid from a man of al-Kufah from abu 'Urwah brother of Shu'ayb or from Shu'ayb al-'Aqarqufiy who has narrated the following:

"I once visited abu al-Hassan, al-Awwal, *'Alayhi al-Salam*, when he had applied cupping on a Wednesday in prison. I said, 'People say that this is the day in which cupping causes vitiligo.' He (the Imam) said, 'Only those whose mothers become pregnant with them during *Hayd* (menses) fear from such illness.'"

Cupping on Friday at *Zawal* (declining of the sun toward the west at noontime)

H 14673, h 225

Muhammad ibn Yahya has narrated from Muhammad ibn al-Husayn from Muhammad ibn 'Isma'il from Salih ibn 'Uqbah from Ishaq ibn 'Ammar who has narrated the following:

"Abu 'Abd Allah, *'Alayhi al-Salam*, has said, 'Do not apply cupping on Friday at noon time; if one applies cupping on Friday at noon time and if something happens to him he should not blame anyone except himself.'"

Medicines are four

H 14674, h 226

Muhammad ibn Yahya has narrated from Ahmad ibn Muhammad ibn 'Isa from al-Hassan ibn Ali from abu Salmah from Mu'attib who has narrated the following:

"Abu 'Abd Allah, *'Alayhi al-Salam*, has said, 'There are four kinds of medicines (ways for treatment of an illness); sniffing thyme, cupping, lime and enema.'"

Cure for coughing

H 14675, h 227

Ali ibn Ibrahim has narrated from his father from ibn abu 'Umayr from 'Umar ibn 'Udhaynah who has narrated the following:

"Once, a man complained before abu 'Abd Allah, *'Alayhi al-Salam*, against coughing when I was present. He (the Imam) said, 'Take in your palm a certain amount of lovage and a similar amount of sugar; then swallow it dry for one or two days.' Ibn 'Udhaynah has said, 'I thereafter met the man and he said, "I only used it once and coughing went away."'"

Cure for phlegm

H 14676, h 228

Muhammad ibn Yahya has narrated from Ahmad ibn Muhammad ibn 'Isa from Sa'id Junah from a man who has narrated the following:

"Abu 'Abd Allah, *'Alayhi al-Salam*, has said, 'Musa ibn 'Imran complained before his Lord, most High, against moisture and wetness. Allah, most High, commanded him to take myrobalan, bulaylij (an Indian medicine) and fulvous, prepare them in dough with honey then take it.' Abu 'Abd Allah, *'Alayhi al-Salam*, then said, 'This is what you call al-Tariyfil.'"

There is no cure in unlawful medicine

H 14677, h 229

Muhammad ibn Yahya has narrated from Ahmad ibn Muhammad ibn Khalid from Muhammad ibn Yahya from brother of al-'Ala' from 'Isma'il ibn al-Hassan al-Mutabbib who has narrated the following:

"I once said to abu 'Abd Allah, *'Alayhi al-Salam*, 'I am an Arab man. I know about medicine and Arabic medicine. I do not accept gifts.' He (the Imam) said, 'It is not unlawful.' I then said, 'We allow the wound to gush out and iron it with fire.' He (the Imam) said, 'It is not unlawful.' I then said, 'We make the patients drink of these poisons, al-Asmahiqun and al-Ghariqun (agaric).' He (the Imam) said, 'It is not unlawful.' I then said, 'Perhaps the patient dies.' He (the Imam) said, 'Even if he dies.' I said, 'We make them drink wine.' He (the Imam) said, 'There is no cure in unlawful things. The Messenger of Allah, *O Allah grant compensation to Muhammad and his family worthy of their services to Your cause*, complained against an ailment and 'A'ishah said, 'You have pleurisy.' He (the Messenger of Allah), said, 'Allah, most Majestic, most Glorious, is honorable and He does not make me suffer from pleurisy.' He (the Imam) said, 'He (the Messenger of Allah) commanded to apply Aloe.'"

Permission to cut veins

H 14678, h 230
Ali ibn Ibrahim has narrated from his father from ibn abu 'Umayr from Yunus ibn Ya'qub who has narrated the following:
"I once asked abu 'Abd Allah, *'Alayhi al-Salam*, about the case of a man who drinks medicine and cuts a vein which may benefit him or kill him. He (the Imam) said, 'He can cut a vein and drink the medicine (it is not unlawful).'"

Benefits of cupping . . .

H 14679, h 231
Ahmad ibn Muhammad al-Kufiy has narrated from Ali ibn al-Hassan ibn Ali ibn Faddal from Muhammad ibn 'Abd al-Hamid from al-Hakam ibn Miskin from Hamzah al-Tayyar who has narrated the following:
"I once was with abu al-Hassan, *'Alayhi al-Salam*, and he (the Imam) noticed me moaning. He (the Imam) asked, 'What has happened to you?' I replied, 'My tooth aches.' He (the Imam) said, 'You should have applied cupping.' I applied cupping, it calmed down, and I informed him (the Imam) about it. He (the Imam) said, 'Draining a certain amount of blood and licking a certain amount of honey is the best medicine with which people can seek treatment.' I then asked, 'What is a *Muz'ah* of honey?' He (the Imam) said, 'It is licking honey.'"

Medicine for a toothache

H 14680, h 232
A number of our people have narrated from Sahl ibn Ziyad from Bakr ibn Salih from Sulayman ibn Ja'far al-Ja'fariy who has narrated the following:
"I once heard abu al-Hassan, Musa, *'Alayhi al-Salam*, say, 'To cure a toothache, you can take colocynth, peel it, then extract its oil. If the tooth has cavities, use drops, apply cotton, place it inside the cavity and lie down on your back. Use for three nights. If it is not a cavity but is painful and smells, then use drops in the ear of the side of the tooth for several nights, two drops each time or three drops; it will be cured by the permission of Allah.' I heard him (the Imam) say this. 'For the pain in the mouth and bleeding which comes from the teeth, blisters and redness in the mouth, take fresh colocynth which has become yellow. Place a mold of clay on it, then make a hole on top of it. Insert a knife in it and stir it

slowly and gently; then pour certain amount of vinegar of dates, which is sour. Then place it on fire to boil intensely; then one should take an amount that his finger can pick up and apply it on the spot, then gargle with vinegar. He can pour it in a bowl of glass or Bastuqah (a bowl) and refill with vinegar; the older it become, it becomes the better, by the will of Allah.'"

About astronomy

H 14681, h 233

A number of our people have narrated from Ahmad ibn Muhammad ibn Khalid from ibn Faddal from al-Hassan ibn Asbat from 'Abd al-Rahman ibn Sayabah who has narrated the following:

"I once said to abu 'Abd Allah, *'Alayhi al-Salam*, 'I pray to Allah to keep my soul in service for your cause. People say that study of astronomy is not lawful but it is very attractive to me; however, if it is harmful to my religion then I do not need anything that can harm me in my religion. If it is not harmful to my religion, by Allah, I like it and I like to study astronomy.' He (the Imam) said, 'It is not as they say it is. It is not harmful to your religion.' He (the Imam) then said, 'You study something from which a great deal is not available and a small amount of it is not beneficial. Your calculation is about the rise of the moon.' He (the Imam) then asked, 'Do you know how many minutes are between Jupiter and Venus?' I replied, 'No, by Allah, I do not know.' He (the Imam) then asked, 'How many minutes are between Venus and the moon?' I replied, 'No, I do not know.' He (the Imam) asked, 'Do you know how many minutes are there between the sun and Virgo?' I replied, 'No, by Allah, I have never heard about it from any astronomer.' He (the Imam) then asked, 'How many minutes are there between Virgo and the protected tablet?' I replied, 'No, by Allah, I have never heard about it from any astronomer.' He (the Imam) said, 'Between each of these to the other one is sixty or seventy minutes'; doubt is from 'Abd al-Rahman. He (the Imam) then said, 'O 'Abd al-Rahman, this is a calculation. If a man calculates and falls on it (succeeds with accuracy) he will know the location of a single reed, which is in the middle of a marsh, the number of reeds to its left and right, behind it and the number of what is in front of it until not even a single piece of the reeds of the marsh will remain unknown to him.'"

About 'No contagiousness of disease. . .'

H 14682, h 234

Muhammad ibn Yahya has narrated from Ahmad ibn Muhammad ibn 'Isa from al-Hassan ibn Mahbub who has said that al-Nard ibn Qarwash al-Jammal who has narrated the following:

"I once asked abu 'Abd Allah, *'Alayhi al-Salam*, about the case of camels with itches and scabies, if I must separate it from the others for fear of spreading and perhaps one needs to whistle so that it drinks water. Abu 'Abd Allah, *'Alayhi al-Salam*, said this. 'Once a desert Arab came to the Messenger of Allah, *O Allah grant compensation to Muhammad and his family worthy of their services to Your cause.* He said, "O Messenger of Allah, I find the sheep, cow, she-camel for a small price with scabies and I dislike buying it for fear of its spreading to my camels and sheep." The Messenger of Allah, *O Allah grant compensation to*

Muhammad and his family worthy of their services to Your cause, asked, 'O desert Arab, who made the first infecting agent?' He (the Messenger of Allah) then said this. 'In Islam there is nothing like, *al-'Adwa'* (contagiousness), omens, *Hammah* (ghost), bad luck, *Safar* (a pre-Islamic ritual associated with the second mouth of Islamic calendar). There is nothing like breastfeeding after weaning, becoming a desert Arab after migration (to religion), fasting in the form of remaining speechless for one day and one night, divorce before marriage, setting free of a slave before owning and remaining an orphan after becoming mature.'"

(Contagiousness of disease or the Arabic word *al-'Adwa'* in pre-Islamic belief and culture had a different meaning. They believed that every disease has a ghost and an independent entity without media, moves wherever it wants thus 'there is no *al-'Adwa"* (contagiousness) means there is no such ghost). (*Hammah* meant that the ghost of one-killed stays around crying for revenge until it is revenged for.)

About omens

H 14683, h 235
Ali ibn Ibrahim has narrated from his father from 'Abd Allah ibn al-Mughirah from 'Amr ibn Hurayth who has narrated the following:
"Abu 'Abd Allah, *'Alayhi al-Salam*, has said, 'An omen is how one places it. If one takes it lightly, it then is light; but if one takes it seriously, it can become intense and if one considers it nothing, then it is nothing.'"

Expiation for an omen

H 14684, h 236
Ali ibn Ibrahim has narrated from his father from al-Nawfaliy from al-Sakuniy who has narrated the following:
"Abu 'Abd Allah, *'Alayhi al-Salam*, has said that the Messenger of Allah, *O Allah grant compensation to Muhammad and his family worthy of their services to Your cause*, has said, 'The expiation (remedy) for an omen is placing one's trust with Allah.'"

The story of the thousand who moved out of their homes

H 14685, h 237
A number of our people have narrated from Sahl ibn Ziyad from ibn Mahbub from 'Umar ibn Yazid and others from certain ones of them from abu 'Abd Allah, and others from abu Ja'far, *'Alayhim al-Salam*, who has narrated the following:
"About the meaning of the words of Allah, most Majestic, most Glorious, '. . . consider those who left their towns in thousands for fear of death and Allah told them to die, then He brought them back to life,' (2:243) he (the Imam) said, 'These were people from certain cities of al-Sham numbering seventy thousand homes. Plague would take place among them every now and then. Therefore, when they would find a sign of it, the rich ones would leave the city because of

their strength; the poor and weak ones remained because of their weakness so death would take place on a greater number among the ones who remained and less among those who left. The ones who remained said, "If we had left the city we would suffer fewer deaths." Those who left the city said, "Had we not left the city we would suffer more deaths." Therefore, they decided that next time when a sign of coming of plague is found they all must leave the city. When they found the sign of it coming they all left to get away from plague for fear of death; so they moved in the land as long as Allah willed. They then passed by a ruined city from which its inhabitants had moved and plague had destroyed them. They disembarked there with comfort. Allah told them to die altogether; they all died in the same hour and turned into ashes that were visible. It was on the road of bypassers who collected the ashes and placed them in one place. One Prophet of the Israelite Prophets called Hizqael passed by and saw the bones. He wept and shed tears and said, "O Lord, if You like You can bring them back to life in this hour as you made them to die, so they can establish the land and reproduce your servants who will worship you with those who worship You of Your creatures." Allah, most Blessed, most High, then sent revelation to him that asked, "Do you really like it to happen?" He replied, "Yes, O Lord, I like their coming back to life." Allah, most Majestic, most Glorious, then sent him revelation that said, "Say so and so." He then said what Allah, most Majestic, most Glorious, had commanded him to say – Abu 'Abd Allah, *'Alayhi al-Salam*, said that it was the great name – when Hizqael said that word he then looked at the bones flying one to the other and they turned alive. They looked to each other saying, *Tasbih* (Allah is free of all defects), *Takbir* (Allah is great beyond description) and *Tahlil*, (no one deserves worship except Allah). Hizqael said at that time, "I testify that Allah has power over all things."' 'Umar ibn Yazid has said that abu 'Abd Allah, *'Alayhi al-Salam*, then said, 'This verse was revealed about them.'"

Did Ya'qub know that Yusuf is alive?

H 14686, h 238

Ibn Mahbub has narrated from Hanan ibn Sadir who has narrated the following:

"I once asked abu Ja'far, *'Alayhi al-Salam*, to inform me about the words of Ya'qub *'Alayhi al-Salam*, to his sons as quoted in the al-Quran, '. . . go and search for Yusuf and his brother,' (12:87) did he know that he was alive when he was absent for twenty years? He (the Imam) said, 'Yes, he knew that he was alive.' I then asked, 'How did he know it?' He (the Imam) said, 'He prayed in the morning before dawn and asked Allah, most Majestic, most Glorious, to send the angel of death to him. Beryal, the angel of death, came to him and asked, "What do you want, O Ya'qub?" He said, "Tell me if you take the spirits one by one or all together?" He replied, "I take them one spirit by spirit." He then asked, "Did you come across the spirit of Yusuf among the spirits?" He replied, "No, I have not come across his spirit." Thus Ya'qub learned that he is alive and at that time said to his sons, ". . . go and search for Yusuf and his brother."'"

About the words of Allah 'blind and speechless. . .'

H 14687, h 239

Muhammad ibn Yahya has narrated from Ahmad ibn Muhammad ibn 'Isa, from al-Husayn ibn Sa'id from Muhammad ibn al-Haseen, from Khalid ibn Yazid al-Qummiy from certain persons of his people who has narrated the following:

"This is about the meaning of the words of Allah, most Majestic, most Glorious, '. . . they thought that no mischief will take place. . .' (5:71) Abu 'Abd Allah, *'Alayhi al-Salam*, has said, 'It was when the Holy Prophet, *O Allah grant compensation to Muhammad and his family worthy of their services to Your cause*, was among them. '. . . they turned blind and deaf,' when the Messenger of Allah, *O Allah grant compensation to Muhammad and his family worthy of their services to Your cause*, passed away. '. . . then Allah forgave them,' when 'Amir al-Mu'minin, Ali, *'Alayhi al-Salam*, took control of their administration. '. . . they turned blind and deaf again,' and remained so to this day.'"

About the words of Allah 'condemned are the unbeliever Israelites. . .'

H 14688, h 240

A number of our people have narrated from Sahl ibn Ziyad from ibn Mahbub from ibn Ri'ab from abu 'Ubaydah al-Hadhdha' who has narrated the following:

"It is in explanation of the meaning of the words of Allah, most Majestic, most Glorious, '. . . the unbelievers of the Israelites were condemned by the tongue of Dawud and Jesus, son of Mary.' (5:78) Abu 'Abd Allah, *'Alayhi al-Salam*, has said, 'They were metamorphosed into pigs by the tongue of Dawud and into apes by the tongue of Jesus, son of Mary.'"

About the words of Allah 'they do not call only you a liar. . .'

H 14689, h 241

Muhammad ibn Yahya has narrated from Ahmad ibn Muhammad from al-Husayn ibn Sa'id from al-Nadr ibn Suwayd from Muhammad ibn abu Hamzah from Ya'qub ibn Shu'ayb from 'Imran ibn Mitham who has narrated the following:

"Abu 'Abd Allah, *'Alayhi al-Salam*, has said that once a man read before 'Amir al-Mu'minin, Ali, *'Alayhi al-Salam*, '. . . they will not consider you a liar but the unjust ones reject the signs of Allah.' (6:33) He (the Imam) said, 'Yes, by Allah, they considered him a liar but it was not noticed, 'they will not consider you a liar' means they will not bring a falsehood whereby to consider your truth as lies.'"

The story of ibn abu Sarh . . .

H 14690, h 242

Abu Ali al-Ash'ariy has narrated from Muhammad ibn 'Abd al-Jabbar from Safwan ibn Yahya from ibn Muskan from abu Basir who has narrated the following:

"I once asked one of the two Imam, (abu Ja'far or abu 'Abd Allah), *'Alayhim al-Salam*, about the meaning of the words of Allah, most Majestic, most Glorious,

'. . . Who are more unjust than those who ascribe lies to Allah or say that Allah has sent them revelations when nothing had been sent to them. . .' (6:93) He (the Imam) said, 'It was revealed about ibn abu Sarh whom 'Uthman later appointed as his agent for Egypt. The Messenger of Allah, *O Allah grant compensation to Muhammad and his family worthy of their services to Your cause*, on the day of the conquest of Makkah along with certain others pronounced him as condemned to death. He was one (of those) who would write for the Messenger of Allah, *O Allah grant compensation to Muhammad and his family worthy of their services to Your cause*. When, '. . . majestic and wise,' was revealed, he wrote it as 'all knowing and wise' and the Messenger of Allah, *O Allah grant compensation to Muhammad and his family worthy of their services to Your cause*, said, 'You must leave it the way it is revealed and do not change, even though Allah indeed is 'all knowing and wise.' He, ibn abu Sarh, would say to the hypocrites, 'I say to myself something similar to whatever comes (is revealed) and he does not ask me to change.' Allah, most Blessed, most High, then revealed about him this verse.'"

About the words of Allah 'Fight them until there is no more paganism'

H 14691, h 243

Ali ibn Ibrahim has narrated from his father from ibn abu 'Umayr from 'Umar ibn 'Udhaynah from Muhammad ibn Muslim who has narrated the following:

"I once asked abu Ja'far, *'Alayhi al-Salam*, about the meaning of the words of Allah, most Majestic, most Glorious, '. . . you must fight them until mischief (disbelief) is no more and religion is (followed) all for Allah.' (8:39) He (the Imam) said, 'The case to which this verse applies has not come yet. The Messenger of Allah, *O Allah grant compensation to Muhammad and his family worthy of their services to Your cause*, has granted them permission (for paying taxes as Jews and Christians or ransom as a pagan) for his own need and the need of his companions. If the case to which this applies had come into being, he (the Messenger of Allah) would not accept from them; instead they had to fight until Allah alone was worshipped and paganism banished.'"

Abbas and 'Aqil on the day of Badr

H 14692, h 244

Ali ibn Ibrahim has narrated from his father from ibn abu 'Umayr from Mu'awiyah ibn 'Ammar who has narrated the following:

"About the meaning of the words of Allah, most Majestic, most Glorious, '. . . O Prophet, say to the captives in your hands, "If Allah finds goodness in your hearts He will give you goodness for what is taken from you and forgive you,"' (8:70) Abu 'Abd Allah, *'Alayhi al-Salam*, has said that it was revealed about al-'Abbas, Aqil and al-Nawfil.' He (the Imam) said that the Messenger of Allah, *O Allah grant compensation to Muhammad and his family worthy of their services to Your cause*, on the day of Badr had prohibited the killing of anyone from banu Hashim and abu al-Bakhtariy. They were taken as captives. He (the

Messenger of Allah) sent Ali, *'Alayhi al-Salam*, and said to him to look and find who of banu Hashim is there.' He (the Imam) said, 'Ali, *'Alayhi al-Salam*, passed by Aqil ibn abu Talib, may Allah make his face honorable, and exchanged sharp words with him. Aqil said to him, 'Son of my mother, Ali, O yes, by Allah you have seen my difficult position.' He (the Imam) said that he returned to the Messenger of Allah, *O Allah grant compensation to Muhammad and his family worthy of their services to Your cause*. He said, 'This is abu al-Fadl in the hand of so and so and this is Aqil in the hand of so and so and Nawfil ibn al-Harith in the hand of so and so.' The Messenger of Allah, *O Allah grant compensation to Muhammad and his family worthy of their services to Your cause*, stood up until he went near Aqil and said, 'O abu Yazid, abu Jahl is killed.' He said, 'So you will not dispute about Tihamah.' He (Aqil) said, 'If you have not weakened the people, you must tie their hands so they cannot run away.' He (the Imam) said al-'Abbas was brought and it was said to him, 'Pay ransom for yourself and for the son of your brother.' He said, 'O Muhammad, you must allow me to ask Quraysh to release me.' He (the Messenger of Allah) said, 'You must pay from what you have left with the mother of al-Fadl. You has said to her, "If something happened to me then spend it on your children and on yourself."' He then said, 'Son of my brother, who told you about it?' He (the Messenger of Allah) replied, 'Jibril came to me from Allah, most Majestic, most Glorious, and told me about it.' He said swearing, 'No one knows about it except me and mother of al-Fadl. I testify that you are the Messenger of Allah.' He (the Imam) said, 'All the captives returned as pagans except al-'Abbas, Aqil and Nawfil, May Allah make their faces honorable. This verse was revealed about them, '. . . say to those who are captives in your hands that if Allah finds goodness in your hearts . . .'" (8:70)

About the words of Allah '...do you think providing water for al-Hajj...'

H 14693, h 245

Abu Ali al-Ash'ariy has narrated from Muhammad ibn 'Abd al-Jabbar from Safwan ibn Yahya from ibn Muskan from abu Basir who has narrated the following:

"About the meaning of the words of Allah, most Majestic, most Glorious, '. . . have you considered providing water for people performing al-Hajj and maintaining al-Haram (the Sacred) Masjid equal to believing in Allah, the Day of Judgment and fighting the enemy for the cause of Allah (all equal)? They are not equal in the sight of Allah,' (9:19) one of the two Imam, (abu Ja'far or abu 'Abd Allah), *'Alayhim al-Salam*, has said that it was revealed about Hamzah, Ali, Ja'far, al-'Abbas and Shaybah who expressed pride because of providing water for the people performing al-Hajj and maintaining the al-Ka'bah. Allah, most Majestic, most Glorious, revealed the above verse. Ali, *'Alayhi al-Salam*, Hamzah and Ja'far, may Allah grant them peace were those who believed in Allah and the Day of Judgment, struggled for the cause of Allah and are not equal before Allah (to those who did not fight).'"

Allah's preference of Ali, *'Alayhi al-Salam*

H 14694, h 246

Muhammad ibn Yahya has narrated from Ahmad ibn Muhammad ibn 'Isa from al-Hassan ibn Mahbub from Hisham ibn Salim from 'Ammar al-Sabatiy who has narrated the following:

"I once asked abu 'Abd Allah, *'Alayhi al-Salam*, about the meaning of the words of Allah, most Majestic, most Glorious, '. . . when a human being suffers harm and injuries he prays to his Lord repentantly before Him.' (39:8)

"He (the Imam) said, 'It was revealed about abu al-Fasil who said that the Messenger of Allah, *O Allah grant compensation to Muhammad and his family worthy of their services to Your cause*, was a magician. When he experienced hardship or illness, he turned to Allah repentantly with prayers for what he had said about the Messenger of Allah. When his difficulties were over, after receiving bounties, he would forget his prayers before, that is his repentance before Allah, most Majestic, most Glorious, because of what he said against the Messenger of Allah, *O Allah grant compensation to Muhammad and his family worthy of their services to Your cause*, that he called him a magician. Thus Allah, most Majestic, most Glorious, has said, '. . . enjoy your disbelief for a little time; you are of the people of the fire.' (39:8) It means that you can enjoy your influence on people without any right from Allah, most Majestic, most Glorious, and from the Messenger of Allah, *O Allah grant compensation to Muhammad and his family worthy of their services to Your cause*.'

"Abu 'Abd Allah, *'Alayhi al-Salam*, then said that Allah, most Majestic, most Glorious, then has turned to Ali, *'Alayhi al-Salam*. He has informed him about his condition and his excellence before Allah, most Blessed, most High. He has said, '. . . is the one who prays during the night in *Sajdah* (prostration) and standing fearful of the hereafter with hope in the mercy of his Lord, and those who know that [Muhammad is the Messenger of Allah] equal to those who do not know [that Muhammad is the Messenger of Allah. Instead they say that he is a magician], only people of reason have understanding.' (39:9) Abu 'Abd Allah, *'Alayhi al-Salam*, said, 'This is the meaning of this verse by means of interpretation, perceptively, O 'Ammar.'"

About the words of Allah 'two just people among you'

H 14695, h 247

Ali ibn Ibrahim has narrated from his father from ibn abu 'Umayr from Hammad ibn 'Uthaman who has narrated the following:

"I once read before abu 'Abd Allah, *'Alayhi al-Salam*, a phrase from al-Quran, '. . . and two just people of you. . .' (5:95) he (the Imam) said, 'It is 'one who possesses justice among you' and it is of what the scribes have missed.'"

171

About the words of Allah '...do not ask about certain matters...'

H 14696, h 248

A number of our people have narrated from Sahl ibn Ziyad from Ahmad ibn Muhammad from ibn abu Nasr from a man who has narrated the following:

"Abu Ja'far, *'Alayhi al-Salam*, has explained the meaning of the words of Allah. '. . . do not ask about certain things, [which have not become apparent for you] if they become apparent to you, they will make you feel bad.'" (5:101)

About the words of Allah '...the words of your Lord are complete...'

H 14697, h 249

Ali ibn Ibrahim has narrated from Ahmad ibn Muhammad ibn Khalid al-Barqiy from his father from Muhammad ibn Sinan from Muhammad Marwan who has narrated the following:

"Abu 'Abd Allah, *'Alayhi al-Salam*, read, '. . . the [beautiful] words of your Lord are complete in truth and justice.' (6:115) I said, 'I pray to Allah to keep my soul in service for your cause, we read it as, '. . . the words of your Lord are complete in truth and justice.' He (the Imam) said, 'There is 'beautiful' in it.'"

About the words of Allah 'We determine about the Israelites...'

H 14698, h 250

A number of our people have narrated from Sahl ibn Ziyad from Muhammad ibn al-Hassan ibn Shammun from 'Abd Allah ibn 'Abd al-Rahman al-Asamm from 'Abd Allah ibn al-Qasim al-Batal who has narrated the following:

"About the meaning of the words of Allah, most High, '. . . We have determined about banu Israel in the book that they will cause destruction in the land twice.' (17:4) [Abu 'Abd Allah, *'Alayhi al-Salam*, has said that it is a reference to the murder of Ali, *'Alayhi al-Salam*. It is also about shooting on al-Hassan, *'Alayhi al-Salam*] '. . . that you will rise in a high great uprising.' [He (the Imam) said that it is a reference to the killing of al-Husayn, *'Alayhi al-Salam*] '. . . When their first chance comes,' [is a reference to the support for finding compensation for the blood of al-Husayn, which was spilled] '. . . We will send against you Our servants who possess intense power. They will search around in the towns.' [It is a reference to the coming of a people whom Allah will send before the rise and reappearance of al-Qa'im with divine authority and power. He will not leave any case involved in the murder of *Ale* (family of) Muhammad, without being brought to justice]. '. . . It was a promise that must come true.' [It is a reference to reappearance of al-Mahdi with divine authority and power] '. . . then We will turn your chance against them.' (17:4-6) [It is a reference to the coming of al-Husayn, *'Alayhi al-Salam*. He will come with seventy people of his companions all in white golden protective helmets. They will come with two faces to show people that he is al-Husayn ibn Ali, *'Alayhi al-Salam*, who has come so that no believing one will doubt. That he is not Dajjal or Satan, when al-Qa'im is with them. When recognition will become verified in the hearts of the believing people that he is al-Husayn, *'Alayhi al-Salam*, death will approach al-Qa'im. He, al-Husayn, ibn Ali, *'Alayhim al-Salam*, will be the one to undertake his Ghusl (bath), shroud, Hunut and placing him in his grave; no Executor of the Will is succeeded except by another Executor of the Will.]'"

'Uthman's exiling abu Dharr

H 14699, h 251

Sahl has narrated from Muhammad ibn al-Hassan from Muhammad ibn Hafs al-Tamimiy who has said that narrated to me abu Ja'far al-Khath'amiy who has said the following:

"When 'Uthman sent abu Dharr in exile to al-Rabadhah, 'Amir al-Mu'minin, Ali, al-Hassan, al-Husayn, *'Alayhim al-Salam*, Aqil, and 'Ammar ibn Yasar, may Allah make their faces honorable, escorted him. At the time of saying farewell 'Amir al-Mu'minin, Ali, *'Alayhi al-Salam*, said, 'O abu Dharr, you expressed anger for the sake of Allah, most Majestic, most Glorious. You must keep your hope with the one for whom you were angered. The people feared from you about their worldly gains. You were afraid from them about your religion so they exiled you from what is doomed for destruction. They have placed you under a trial of hardship. By Allah, even if the sky and earth close up on a servant, if he is pious before Allah, most Majestic, most Glorious, He will make a way out for him from his hardship. So no other thing must keep you comfortable save the truth and no other thing must frighten you except falsehood.'

"Thereafter Aqil spoke saying, 'O abu Dharr, you know that we love you and we know that you love us. You have protected for us what people have lost except just a few and your reward is with Allah, most Majestic, most Glorious. For this reason, they have exiled and have sent you away. Your reward is with Allah, most Majestic, most Glorious, you must remain pious before Allah, take notice that your asking for ease from hardship is impatience and your impatience for good health is despair, so ignore despair and impatience and say, "Allah is sufficient for me and He is the best representative."'

"Thereafter al-Hassan, *'Alayhi al-Salam*, spoke. He said, 'O uncle, the people have done to you what you can see and Allah, most Majestic, most Glorious, watches from up high. You must keep the memories of the world away from you by means of the memories of departing it. You must leave such memories for the intensity of the ease and comfort that will come thereafter, bear patience until you meet your Prophet, *O Allah grant compensation to Muhammad and his family worthy of their services to Your cause*, when he will be happy with you, by the will of Allah.'

"Thereafter al-Husayn, *'Alayhi al-Salam*, spoke saying, 'O uncle, Allah, most Blessed, most High, has the power to change what you see and He deals with the affairs every day. The people denied you their world and you denied them your religion. How little is it that you need from what they have denied you and how badly they need what you have denied them! You must bear patience; goodness is patience, patience is of honor and you must keep away from impatience because impatience does not make you self-sufficient.'

"Thereafter, 'Ammar, may Allah make his face honorable, spoke saying, 'O abu Dharr, may Allah will make lonely those who have made you lonely and frighten those who have frightened you. By Allah, no other thing stops people from speaking the truth except their relying on the world and their love of the worldly things. People obey the crowd and domination is for those who overpower others. These ones have called people to their world. They have obeyed them and have bestowed their religion upon them, so they have lost their world and the hereafter and that is a clear loss.

"Thereafter abu Dhar, may Allah make his face honorable, spoke. He said, 'May Allah grant you peace and blessings. I pray to Allah to keep my soul and the souls of my father and mother in service for your cause. These faces, when I see them, they remind me of the Messenger of Allah, *O Allah grant compensation to Muhammad and his family worthy of their services to Your cause.* I do not have any interest in al-Madinah except with you. My presence in the neighborhood became heavy on 'Uthman. It was heavy on Mu'awiyah in al-Sham until he made me to travel to a town and I asked him to send me to al-Kufah, but he thought that he is afraid for the affairs of his brother, his agent there, being destroyed among people in al-Kufah. By Allah, he is sending me to a town where I will not see a human being or hear any one's humming. I by Allah, do not want to have any companion except Allah, most Majestic, most Glorious; I do not feel lonely with Allah. Allah beside whom no one deserves worship is sufficient for me, with Him I place my trust, He is the Lord of the great throne, *O Allah grant compensation to Muhammad and his family worthy of their services to Your cause.*'"

The rightful and the wrongful. . .

H 14700, h 252

Abu Ali al-Ash'ariy has narrated from Muhammad ibn 'Abd al-Jabbar from ibn Faddal and al-Hajjal all from Tha'labah from 'Abd al-Rahman ibn Muslimah al-Jaririy who has narrated the following:

"I once said to abu 'Abd Allah, *'Alayhi al-Salam* that they scold and reject us and we say that there will be a loud voice twice. They ask, 'How can you recognize the right from the wrong if they will be there?' He (the Imam) asked, 'What is your answer?' I said, 'We do not reply.' He (the Imam) said tell them, 'All those who believe in it (coming of the two loud voices) before will recognize and acknowledge it. Allah, most Majestic, most Glorious, says, ". . . are those who guide to the truth more deserving to be followed or those who cannot guide unless themselves are guided right, what is the matter with you that you judge the way you judge?"'" (10:35)

Two callers at both ends of the day

H 14701, h 253

It is narrated from the narrator of the previous Hadith from Muhammad ibn Faddal and al-Hajjal from Dawud ibn Farqad who has narrated the following:

"A man from al-'Ajaliyah had heard this Hadith: 'A caller will call, "So and so son of so and so (al-Qa'im (the one who rises with divine authority and power) and his followers are the successful ones" in the beginning of the day. Another caller will call in the end of the day saying, "'Uthman and his followers are the successful ones." He said, 'The caller in the beginning of the day informs about the (falsehood) of the caller in the end of the day.' The man said, 'We do not know which one is truthful and which one is false.' He (the Imam) said, 'Those who believe in it (coming of the loud voice) on the same basis confirm and acknowledge it before the call is made. Allah, most Majestic, most Glorious, has said, ". . . are those who guide to the truth more deserving to be followed or those who cannot guide unless themselves are guided right, what is the matter with you that you judge the way you judge?"'" (10:35)

Differences among the Abbasides

H 14702, h 254

Ali ibn Ibrahim has narrated from his father from ibn Mahbub from Ishaq ibn 'Ammar who has narrated the following:

"Abu 'Abd Allah, *'Alayhi al-Salam*, has said, ' You will not see what you love to see until children of so and so differ among themselves until people feel greedy and the word (unity) turns into disunity and the Sufyaniy appears.'"

Hadith of the out-loud calling

H 14703, h 255

Ali ibn Ibrahim has narrated from his father from ibn abu Najran and others from 'Isma'il ibn Sabbah who has narrated the following:

"I heard a Shaykh mention from Sayf ibn 'Amirah, who has said, 'I was with abu al-Dawaniq and I heard him say and initiating it himself, "O Sayf ibn 'Amirah it is necessary that a caller will call in the name of a man from the children of abu Talib."' I asked, 'Does any one of the people narrate it?' He replied, 'By the one in whose hand is my soul that my own ears heard it from him (abu Ja'far, *'Alayhi al-Salam*), who said that it is necessary that a caller will call in the name of a man.' I then said, 'O 'Amir al-Mu'minin, I have never heard anything similar to it.' He then said to me, 'O Sayf, if that happens we will be the first to accept him, because he is one of the sons of our uncle.' I then asked, 'From which one of your uncles?' He said, 'A man from children of Fatimah, *'Alayha al-Salam*.' He then said, 'O Sayf, had I not heard abu Ja'far, Muhammad ibn Ali say it, even if all the people of the earth narrated I would not accept it from them, but he is Muhammad ibn Ali, *'Alayhi al-Salam*.'"

The story of abu Dawaniq

H 14704, h 256

Ali ibn Ibrahim has narrated from his father from ibn Mahbub from Ali ibn abu Hamzah from abu
Basir who has narrated the following:

"I once was sitting with abu Ja'far, *'Alayhi al-Salam*, in the Masjid when Dawud
ibn Ali, Sulayman ibn Khalid and abu Ja'far, 'Abd Allah ibn Muhammad, abu
al-Dawaniq came in and sat in an area of the Masjid. It was said to them that
Muhammad ibn Ali, is here, so Dawud ibn Ali and Sulayman ibn Khalid stood
up to come to him (the Imam), but abu al-Dawaniq remained in his place. They
offered greeting of peace to abu Ja'far, *'Alayhi al-Salam*, who said to them,
'What prevented your tyrant from coming to me?' They then presented excuses
for him before him (the Imam). Abu Ja'far, Muhammad ibn Ali, *'Alayhim al-
Salam*, then said, 'O yes, by Allah, very shortly before the passing of many days
and nights he will dominate what is between its two regions. Thereafter, after
men will strengthen his backing and then the necks of men will become
subservient before him, then he will have strong domain.' Dawud ibn Ali then
asked, 'Will our domain come before your dominion?' He (the Imam) said,
'Yes, O Dawud, your domination will be before our sovereignty and your
control before the rise of our authority.' Dawud then said, 'Allah keeps you
well, is there a time limit for it?' He (the Imam) said, 'Yes, O Dawud, by Allah,
if banu 'Umayyah dominate for one day, you will dominate twice as much; if
they dominate for one year you will dominate for twice as much, thereafter
children will seize and control it from you just as children grab the ball. Dawud
ibn Ali then stood up from the meeting before abu Ja'far, *'Alayhi al-Salam*,
rejoicing to inform abu al-Dawaniq about it. When they both moved, he and
Sulayman ibn Khalid, abu Ja'far, *'Alayhi al-Salam*, called them back. He (the
Imam) said, 'O Sulayman, the people will have enough room in their domination
as long as they do not spill unlawfully a blood from us' – He (the Imam) pointed
to his chest – 'when they spill such blood, then inside of the earth will be better
for them than their living on its back. On such day, there will be no one to help
them on earth or in the sky to accept their excuse. Thereafter Sulayman ibn
Khalid left and informed abu al-Dawaniq who then came to abu Ja'far, *'Alayhi
al-Salam*, offered him greeting of peace, then mentioned what Dawud and
Sulayman ibn Khalid had told him. He (the Imam) said, 'Yes, O abu Ja'far, your
government will come before our government and your control before our
authority. Your control will be intense and hard and without ease with a lengthy
duration. By Allah, if banu 'Umayyah dominate for one day you will do twice as
long, if they dominate for one year you will do for twice as long and thereafter
children will seize its control from you as they grab the ball, did you
understand?' He (the Imam) then said, 'You will continue with vigorous
domination and comfort as long as you will not unlawfully spill a blood from us
and when you do so, Allah, most Majestic, most Glorious, will become angry
with you. He will remove your domination, control and achievement and Allah,
most Majestic, most Glorious, will make a servant of His blind (disgraceful)
servants who is not (physically) more blind than *Ale* (family of) abu Sufyan, by

whose hand you will be uprooted and in the hands of his companions', then he discontinued the conversation.'"

Destruction of Abbasides from where it began

H 14705, h 257

Ali ibn Ibrahim has narrated from his father from ibn abu 'Umayr from al-Mufaddal ibn Mazyad who has narrated the following:

"I once said to abu 'Abd Allah, *'Alayhi al-Salam*, in the days of 'Abd Allah ibn Ali that they (al-'Abbasi rulers) have faced differences among them. He (the Imam) said, 'Ignore it, their destruction will come from where their success had come.'"

(Success of al-'Abbasi dynasty came from the east by the help of abu Muslim Khurasani to over throw banu 'Umayyah, and Halaku (of Mangolia) also came from the east, same place as abu Muslim, to destroy al-'Abbasi dynasty. This is of the news about the unseen; al-Kafi was compiled in the beginning of al-'Abbasi dynasty).

Two signs before the rise of al-Qa'im (the one who rises with divine authority and power), *'Alayhi al-Salam*

H 14706, h 258

A number of our people have narrated from Sahl ibn Ziyad from Ahmad ibn Muhammad from ibn abu Nasr from Tha'labah' ibn Maymun from Badr al-Khalil al-Azdiy who has narrated the following:

"Once I was sitting with abu Ja'far, *'Alayhi al-Salam*, and he (the Imam) said this. 'There will be two signs before reappearance of al-Qa'im with divine authority and power, which has never taken place from the time Adam, *'Alayhi al-Salam*, descended to earth. There will be a sun [solar] eclipse in the middle of the month of Ramadan and a moon [lunar] eclipse in the end of the month of Ramadan.' A man then said, 'O child of the Messenger of Allah, sun eclipse happens in the end of a month and moon eclipse happens in the middle of the month.' Abu Ja'far, *'Alayhi al-Salam*, said, 'I know what you said but they are two signs which had never taken place from the time Adam, *'Alayhi al-Salam*, descended to earth.'"

Excellence of Shi'ah

H 14707, h 259

Ali ibn Ibrahim has narrated from his father from ibn abu 'Umayr from 'Amr ibn abu al-Miqdam who has narrated the following:

"I once heard abu 'Abd Allah, *'Alayhi al-Salam*, say, 'My father and I once went until we were between the grave and the pulpit (of the Holy Prophet) when a group of Shi'ah was there. He (the Imam) offered them greeting of peace then said, 'I by Allah love your scents and your spirits, but you must help me in this by restraint from sins and by working hard. You must take notice that our *Wilayah* (guardianship with divine authority and knowledge) cannot be achieved without restraint from sins and hard work. Whoever of you follows a servant of Allah, he must act as he (the leader) does. You are the Shi'ah of Allah and you are the helpers of Allah, you are the first and foremost of the earlier generations and the foremost of the later generations, the foremost in the world and the foremost in the hereafter to the garden (paradise). We have taken the responsibility of admitting you in the garden (paradise) on guarantee from Allah, most Majestic, most Glorious, and on guarantee from the Messenger of Allah, *O Allah grant compensation to Muhammad and his family worthy of their services to Your cause.*

"By Allah, on the ranks, stages of the garden (paradise) the majority are your spirits. You must compete in achieving excellent ranks. You are people of goodness and your women are women of goodness. Every believing female is an al-Hawra' 'Ayna' and every believing man is a friend of a believing man. 'Amir al-Mu'minin, Ali, *'Alayhi al-Salam*, said to Qanbar, 'O Qanbar, you can receive glad news, convey the glad news to others and enjoy the glad news. By Allah, the Messenger of Allah, *O Allah grant compensation to Muhammad and his family worthy of their services to Your cause*, passed away when he was extremely unhappy with his followers except al-Shi'ah.

It is a fact that everything has a glory, the glory of Islam is al-Shi'ah.

It is a fact that everything has a pillar and support, the pillar of Islam is al-Shi'ah.

It is a fact that everything has a peak; the peak of Islam is al-Shi'ah.

It is a fact that everything has nobility; the nobility of Islam is al-Shi'ah.

It is a fact that everything has a master, the master of the gatherings is the gathering of al-Shi'ah.

It is a fact that everything has an Imam; the Imam of the land is the land where al-Shi'ah live.

By Allah, had no one of you existed not a nest could have ever been seen. By Allah, had there been no one of you on earth, Allah would not make it pleasant for those who oppose you and they would not find goodness. There is nothing in the world and in the hereafter as their share. To those who are hostile to *'A'immah*, even if they worship and work hard, this verse applies, ". . . hostile working, feels the heat of the hot fire." (88:3-4) Everyone who is hostile to *'A'immah* and yet works hard his deeds scatter like dust. Our al-Shi'ah speak with the light of Allah, most Majestic, most Glorious. Those who oppose them speak by accident (if anything meaningful). By Allah no one of the servants of Allah among our al-Shi'ah sleeps but that Allah, most Majestic, most Glorious, raises his spirit to the sky to bless it. If it is the time for his death, He keeps it in treasuries of mercy and in the gardens of paradise under the shadow of His throne. If the time of his death is later, He sends him with trusted angels back to his body from which it was taken out so it lives there again. By Allah, those of you who perform al-Hajj and al-'Umrah are special before Allah, most Majestic, most Glorious. Your poor are of the rich people and your rich people are people of contentment. Allah has invited you to His religion and you have accepted His call.'"

Excellence of Imami Shi'ah

H 14708, h 260

A number of our people have narrated from Sahl ibn Ziyad from Muhammad ibn al-Hassan ibn Shammun from 'Abd Allah ibn 'Abd al-Rahman from 'Abd Allah ibn al-Qasim from 'Amr ibn abu al-Miqdam who has narrated the following:

"Ibn abu al-Miqdam has narrated a similar Hadith from abu 'Abd Allah, *'Alayhi al-Salam*, with the following addition: 'It is a fact that everything has its purest essence; the purest essence of the children of Adam, *'Alayhi al-Salam*, is Muhammad and *Ale* (family of) Muhammad, *O Allah grant compensation to Muhammad and his family worthy of their services to Your cause*, we and our Shi'ah after us. How good it is and how close to the throne of Allah, most Majestic, most Glorious, are our Shi'ah and how good is what Allah will do for them on the Day of Judgment! By Allah, if people would not consider it very great (exaggeration) or arrogance enter in them, the angels offer them greeting of peace first. By Allah, if any servant of Allah from our Shi'ah reads al-Quran standing in his *Salat* (prayer), for every letter there are one hundred good deeds. If he reads in a sitting position, for each letter there are fifty good deeds for him and for his reading in other condition for each letter there are ten good deeds for him, and for one of them who remains silent there is the reward of one who reads al-Quran of those who oppose it (al-Quran). There is the reward for those who fight for the cause of Allah, for you, by Allah, when sleeping on your bed. For you, by Allah, in your *Salat* (prayer) there is the reward like those who stand in line to fight for the cause of Allah. You, by Allah, are the ones about whom Allah, most Majestic, most Glorious, has said, ". . . We remove from their chest everything of malice so they sit as brothers facing each other." (15:47) Our Shi'ah are a people with four eyes; two eyes in their head and two eyes in their hearts; it is a fact that all people are as such except that Allah, most Majestic, most Glorious, has opened your eyes and has turned their eyes blind.'"

The Complaints of 'Abd Allah, *'Alayhi al-Salam*, before Allah

H 14709, h 261

Muhammad ibn Yahya has narrated from Ahmad ibn Muhammad ibn 'Isa from Ali ibn al-Hakam from Mansur ibn Yunus from 'Anbasah ibn Mus'ab who has narrated the following:

"I heard abu 'Abd Allah, *'Alayhi al-Salam*, say, 'I complain before Allah, most Majestic, most Glorious, against my loneliness and restlessness among the people of al-Madinah until you come and I see you and receive comfort. I wish this tyrant (ruler) will give me permission to find a fort in al-Taef where I will live and you with me. I will be able to guarantee him that from our side no harm will ever come out.'"

Kumayt and his poems in praise of *Ahl al-Bayt*

H 14710, h 262
Muhammad ibn Yahya has narrated from Ahmad ibn Muhammad ibn 'Isa from Ali ibn al-Hakam from Mansur ibn Yunus from 'Anbasah ibn Mus'ab who has narrated the following:

"Once, al-Kumayt read of his poetry: 'Allah has made my love pure, so in pulling my bow to increase tension I do not exceed the proper limit and my arrows do not proceed aimless.' Abu 'Abd Allah, *'Alayhi al-Salam*, said, 'You must not say 'I do not exceed the proper limit' instead say, 'I insist on pulling to tension my bow all the way but my arrows do not proceed aimless or waver.'" ('my love pure' is a reference to his love for *Ahl al-Bayt*)

The story of Sufyan . . . and severity of *Taqiyah*

H 14711, h 263
Sahl ibn Ziyad has narrated from Muhammad ibn al-Husayn from abu Dawud al-Mustariq from Sufyan ibn Mus'ab al-'Abdiy who has narrated the following:

"I once visited abu 'Abd Allah, *'Alayhi al-Salam*, and he (the Imam) said, 'Call 'Umm Farwah to come and listen what is done to her grandfather.' She came and sat behind the curtain.' He (the Imam) then said, 'Now you may read for us.' I then began to read, 'O Farwah, be generous to allow your flooding tears to come down your face.' She sobbed and so also did other women.' Abu 'Abd Allah, *'Alayhi al-Salam*, then said, 'The door, watch the door.' People of al-Madinah gathered at the door. Abu 'Abd Allah, *'Alayhi al-Salam*, said that a child in our family fainted because of which the women cried.'"

The Messenger of Allah informs of his controlling the treasuries of Kisra . . .

H 14712, h 264
Sahl ibn Ziyad from Ahmad ibn Muhammad from ibn abu Nasr from Aban ibn 'Uthman from certain persons of his people who has narrated the following:

"Abu 'Abd Allah, *'Alayhi al-Salam*, has said that when the Messenger of Allah, *O Allah grant compensation to Muhammad and his family worthy of their services to Your cause*, was digging the ditch they reached a rock. The Messenger of Allah, *O Allah grant compensation to Muhammad and his family worthy of their services to Your cause*, took the pickax from 'Amir al-Mu'minin, Ali, *'Alayhi al-Salam*, or from Salman, may Allah be pleased with him, and hit the rock which split into three parts. The Messenger of Allah, *O Allah grant compensation to Muhammad and his family worthy of their services to Your cause*, said, 'With this hit the treasures of Kisra (Persian king) and Qaysar (Roman king) is opened up for me.' One of them said to his friend, 'He promises us of the treasures of Kisra' and Qaysar while no one of us is able to go out for a rest room.'"

Al-'Azib winds

H 14713, h 265

Muhammad ibn Yahya has narrated from Ahmad ibn Muhammad ibn 'Isa from abu Yahya al-Wasitiy from certain persons of our people who has narrated the following:

"Abu 'Abd Allah, *'Alayhi al-Salam*, has said, 'Allah, most Blessed, most High, has a wind called al-Azib. If it is sent of the amount of the nostril of a bull, it can scatter all that is between the earth and the sky; and it is the wind called 'South.'"

The Messenger of Allah prays for rain

H 14714, h 266

Ali ibn Ibrahim has narrated from Salih ibn al-Sindiy from Ja'far ibn Bashir from Zurayq abu al-'Abbas who has narrated the following:

"Abu 'Abd Allah, *'Alayhi al-Salam*, has said that people came to the Messenger of Allah, *O Allah grant compensation to Muhammad and his family worthy of their services to Your cause*. They said, 'O Messenger of Allah, our towns are suffering from drought for years; so pray for us before Allah, most Blessed, most High, to send for us rain. The Messenger of Allah, *O Allah grant compensation to Muhammad and his family worthy of their services to Your cause*, asked for the pulpit, which was brought out, and people gathered. The Messenger of Allah climbed on the pulpit and prayed. He (the Messenger of Allah) commanded people to say Amen. Shortly Jibril came and said, 'O Muhammad, inform the people that your Lord has promised to make it rain on such and such day and in such and such hour. People kept waiting for that day and that hour until it was that hour. Allah, most Majestic, most Glorious, stirred a wind which spread cloud and which draped the sky which allowed the rain to pour down. The same people came to the Messenger of Allah, *O Allah grant compensation to Muhammad and his family worthy of their services to Your cause*, and said, 'Pray to Allah to stop the rain; we are about to drown.' People gathered and the Holy Prophet, *O Allah grant compensation to Muhammad and his family worthy of their services to Your cause*, prayed and commanded people to say Amen along with his prayer. One man said, 'O Messenger of Allah, we cannot hear what you say.' He told them to say, 'O Lord, make it to rain around us and not on us. O Lord, make it fall in the valleys, on the plants and trees and on the pasture. O Lord, make it a blessing and do not make it to cause suffering.'"

Lightening requires rain

H 14715, h 267

Ja'far ibn Bashir has narrated from Ruzayq who has narrated the following:

"Abu 'Abd Allah, *'Alayhi al-Salam*, has said, 'Lightening does not take place in the night or day unless it is raining.'"

Where are clouds

H 14716, h 268

Muhammad ibn Yahya has narrated from Ahmad ibn Muhammad ibn 'Isa from al-Husayn ibn Sa'id from ibn al-'Arzamiy in a marfu' manner who has narrated the following:

"'Amir al-Mu'minin, Ali, *'Alayhi al-Salam*, was asked, 'Where does the cloud live?' He (the Imam) replied, 'It lives in dense trees, on sea shores to which it descends and when Allah, most Majestic, most Glorious, wants to send it, He sends a wind which stirs it and then assigns angels to hit it with old cloths and that is lightening. It then rises.' He (the Imam) then read this verse, 'Allah is the one who sends the winds which stir the cloud; then We drive it to a dead town . . .' (35:9) The name of the angel is al-Ra'd (thunder)."

(Old cloths is a reference to the process by which lightening takes place just like living of the cloud in the trees which is a reference to moisture and humidity.)

A truthful tongue purifies deeds

H 14717, h 269

A number of our people have narrated from Sahl ibn Ziyad from Ahmad ibn Muhammad from ibn abu Nasr from Muthanna' al-Hannat and Muhammad ibn Muslim who have narrated the following:

"Abu 'Abd Allah, *'Alayhi al-Salam*, has said, 'One whose tongue is truthful, his deeds are pure; one whose intention is good Allah, most Majestic, most Glorious, increases his sustenance and one who makes his favor to his family good Allah makes him to live longer.'"

Good advice of the Holy Prophet, *'Alayhi al-Salam*

H 14718, h 270

Hassan ibn Muhammad al-Hashimiy who has said that narrated to me my father Ahmad ibn Muhammad, from Ahmad ibn Muhammad ibn 'Isa who has narrated the following:

"Ja'far ibn Muhammad, from his father from his grandfather from Ali, *'Alayhim al-Salam*, has narrated the following: The Messenger of Allah, *O Allah grant compensation to Muhammad and his family worthy of their services to Your cause*, has stated this Hadith: 'Allah, most Blessed, most High, says to the children of Adam, *'Alayhi al-Salam*, "If your eyes dispute with you about something which I have made unlawful, you must take notice that I have helped you with two covers. You can cover them and do not look. If your tongue may dispute with you about something, which I have made unlawful, then you must take notice that I have helped you with two covers with which you can cover it and do not speak. If your genital organs dispute with you about something which I have made unlawful, then you must take notice that I have provided for you two covers with which you can cover it and do not commit anything unlawful.'"

If three things are found in a person, then there is no hope for goodness from him

H 14719, h 271

Ali ibn Ibrahim has narrated from his father from Ali ibn Asbat from a mawla of banu Hashim who has narrated the following:

"Abu 'Abd Allah, *'Alayhi al-Salam*, has said that there are three things which on being found in someone, not anything good can be expected from him. One of them is one's failure to feel embarrassed because of a fault, one's failure to be afraid and anxious about his relation toward Allah in an unseen condition and one's failure to remain attentive about good and bad when he becomes an old person.'"

If a respected person of a people comes to you

H 14720, h 272

Abu Ali al-Ash'ariy has narrated from Muhammad ibn 'Abd al-Jabbar from al-Hajjal who has narrated the following:

"I once asked Jamil ibn Darraj if the Messenger of Allah, *O Allah grant compensation to Muhammad and his family worthy of their services to Your cause*, has said, 'When a noble person of a people comes, you must treat him honorably.' He replied, 'Yes, that is true,' I then asked, 'What is being a noble?' He replied, 'I asked abu 'Abd Allah, *'Alayhi al-Salam*, and he (the Imam) said, 'It is one who is wealthy.' I then asked, 'What is al-Hasab (social standing)?' he replied, 'It is one who does good deeds by means of his wealth and other means.' I then asked, 'What is honor?' he replied, 'It is piety.'"

More severe . . . is the poverty. . .

H 14721, h 273

Ali ibn Ibrahim has narrated from his father from al-Nawfaliy from al-Sakuniy who has narrated the following:

"Abu 'Abd Allah, *'Alayhi al-Salam*, has said that the Messenger of Allah, *O Allah grant compensation to Muhammad and his family worthy of their services to Your cause*, has stated this Hadith: 'Sadness of women is most intense, separation because of death is the most distant separation. More difficult than this is a poverty because of which one expects help from someone but he does not give anything.'"

Hadith of Yajuj and Majuj (Gog and Magog)

H 14722, h 274

Al-Husayn from Muhammad al-Ash'ariy has narrated from Mu'alla' ibn Muhammad from Ahmad ibn Muhammad from ibn 'Abd Allah from ibn al-'Abbas ibn al-'Ala' from Mujahid from ibn 'Abbas who has narrated the following:

"'Amir al-Mu'minin, Ali, *'Alayhi al-Salam* was asked about creatures. He (the Imam) said, 'Allah has created one thousand and two hundred on land and one thousand and two hundred in the ocean. Men are of seventy kinds. All men are from Adam, *'Alayhi al-Salam*, except Gog and Magog.'"

Three levels of people

H 14723, h 275

Al-Hassan ibn Muhammad al-Ash'ariy from Mu'alla' ibn Muhammad from al-Hassan ibn Ali al-Washsha' from Muthanna' from abu Basir who has narrated the following:

"Abu 'Abd Allah, *'Alayhi al-Salam*, has said, 'People are of three categories. One category is from us and we are from them. One category beautifies itself with us and one category's members consume each other in our name.'"

Signs of relief

H 14724, h 276

It is narrated from the narrator of the previous Hadith from Mu'alla' from al-Washsha' from 'Abd al-Karim ibn 'Amr from 'Ammar ibn Marwan from al-Fudayl ibn Yasar who has narrated the following:

"Abu Ja'far, *'Alayhi al-Salam*, has said that when poverty and need will increase and people deny one another, at that time expect the command of Allah, most Majestic, most Glorious, (reappearance of al-Qa'im with divine authority and power). I then asked, 'I pray to Allah to keep my soul in service for your cause, I have understood the need and poverty. What is the meaning of 'people's denying one another'?' He (the Imam) said, 'A man from you goes to his brother (in belief) and asks for a need but he looks at him with a face which is other than the face with which he would look at him before and speaks to him with a tongue which is other than the one with which he spoke before.'"

Sustenance and dimwittedness

H 14725, h 277

A number of our people have narrated from Sahl ibn Ziyad from Ahmad ibn Muhammad ibn Khalid from Muhammad ibn Ali from 'Ubayd ibn Yahya from Muhammad ibn al-Hassan from Ali ibn al-Husayn from his father who has narrated the following:

"Sustenance is assigned to dimwittedness, deprivation is assigned to reason and suffering is assigned to patience.'"

The story of the brother of 'Adhafir

H 14726, h 278

A number of our people have narrated from Sahl ibn Ziyad from Muhammad ibn 'Abd al-Hamid al-'Attar from Yunus ibn Ya'qub from 'Umar brother of 'Adhafir who has narrated the following:

"A man gave me six or seven hundred dirhams for abu 'Abd Allah, *'Alayhi al-Salam*, and it was in my bag. On my arrival in al-Hafirah (a place in Iraq), I found my bag was torn and all of its contents were gone. I informed the agent in the city and he said, 'Are you the one whose bag is torn and its contents are gone?' I replied, 'Yes, that is correct.' He said, 'When we will arrive in al-Madinah come to us so we can replace it for you.'

"When I arrived in al-Madinah I went to visit abu 'Abd Allah, *'Alayhi al-Salam*, and he said, 'O 'Umar, was your bag torn and your goods were gone?' I replied, 'Yes, that is correct.' He (the Imam) said, 'What Allah has given you is better than what is taken from you. Once a she-camel that belonged to the Messenger of Allah, *O Allah grant compensation to Muhammad and his family worthy of their services to Your cause*, was lost and people said, "He informs us about the sky and does not know about his she-camel." Jibril then came and said, "O Muhammad, your she-camel is in such and such valley with its noseband tangled around such and such tree." He (the Imam) said that he climbed on the pulpit, praised Allah and spoke of his glory, then said, "O people, you have spoken a great deal about the she-camel that belonged to me and about me. O yes, what Allah has given to me is better than what He has taken from me. O yes, my camel is in so and so valley with its noseband tangled around such and such tree." The people rushed and found it just as the Messenger of Allah, *O Allah grant compensation to Muhammad and his family worthy of their services to Your cause*, had informed them.' He (the Imam) then said, 'Go to the agent of al-Madinah to acquire from him what he has promised you; it is something that Allah has invited you to and you had not demanded from him.'"

Explanation of the words of abu Dharr

H 14727, h 279

Sahl has narrated from Muhammad ibn 'Abd al-Hamid from Yunus from Shu'ayb al-'Aqarqufy who has narrated the following:

"I once asked abu 'Abd Allah, *'Alayhi al-Salam*, about something which is narrated from abu Dharr, may Allah be pleased with him, who has said, 'There are three things which people dislike but I like them. I love death, I love poverty and I love test and trials.' He (the Imam) said, 'It is not the way they narrate it. He meant to say, "Death in obedience to Allah is more beloved to me than living in disobedience to Allah, trials and test in obedience to Allah is more beloved to me than good health in disobedience to Allah, and poverty in obedience to Allah is more beloved to me than being rich in disobedience to Allah."'"

The dream which the Messenger of Allah, *'Alayhi al-Salam,* saw

H 14728, h 280

Sahl ibn Ziyad has narrated from Muhammad ibn 'Abd al-Hamid from Yunus from Ali ibn 'Isa al-Qammat from his uncle who has narrated the following:

"I once heard abu 'Abd Allah, *'Alayhi al-Salam*, say, 'Jibril *'Alayhi al-Salam*, once came to the Messenger of Allah, *O Allah grant compensation to Muhammad and his family worthy of their services to Your cause*, and found him sad and depressed. He asked, 'O Messenger of Allah, what is the matter that I see you sad and depressed?' He (the Messenger of Allah) replied, 'Last night I saw a dream.' He then asked, 'What kind of dream was it?' He (the Messenger of Allah) replied, 'I saw banu 'Umayyah climb on the pulpits and climb down.' He said, 'I swear by the One who has sent you in all truth that I do not know anything about it.' Jibril ascended to the sky; then Allah made him to descend down with a verse of the al-Quran and he offered him condolences by His words, '. . . consider if We make them enjoy for many years, then comes to them what they were warned with, thereafter what they enjoyed will not benefit them at all.' (26:206-208) Allah, most Majestic, most Glorious, subsequently, revealed His words about the people. '. . . We have revealed al-Quran in the night of al-Qadr. What do you think the night of al-Qadr is? The night of al-Qadr is better than one thousand months. . .' (97:2-5) Allah, most Majestic, most Glorious, has made the night of al-Qadr for His Messenger better than one thousand months.'" (The reign of banu 'Umayyah lasted for a thousand months.)

About the words of Allah 'the opposition must remain fearful'

H 14729, h 281

Sahl has narrated from Muhammad ibn 'Abd al-Hamid from Yunus from 'Abd al-A'la' who has narrated the following:

"I once asked abu 'Abd Allah, *'Alayhi al-Salam*, about the meaning of the words of Allah, most Majestic, most Glorious, '. . . you must remain cautious about those who oppose His command because of the descending of misfortune on them or a painful torment.' (24:63) He (the Imam) said, 'It is a reference to misfortune in one's religion or an injury for which Allah will not grant any reward.'"

Hadith of 'Abd al-'A'la'

H 14730, h 282

Sahl ibn Ziyad has narrated from Muhammad ibn Yunus from servants (of Allah) al-A'la' who has narrated the following:

"I once said to abu 'Abd Allah, *'Alayhi al-Salam*, 'Your Shi'ah has developed hatred toward each other and reproach, if you consider it, I pray to Allah to keep my soul in service for your cause.' He (the Imam) said, 'I was thinking to write a letter (a book) to them so that no two of them will dispute against each other.' I said, 'Today we need such a letter more than ever.' He (the Imam) then said, 'This can never overcome the trouble between Marwan and ibn Dharr.' I then thought that he (the Imam) does not agree to write anything. I then left and went to 'Isma'il and said, 'I mentioned the disputes among Shi'ah to your father and their hatred toward each other. He (the Imam) said that he was thinking to write a letter (a book) after which no two will have any disputes between them about me.' He ('Isma'il) asked, 'Is it about what Marwan and ibn Dharr have said?' I replied, 'Yes, that is correct.'

"He said, 'O 'Abd al-A'la', you have a right on us and we have a right on you; but you are not quicker about our rights on you than we are about your rights on us.' He then said, 'I will consider it.' He then said, O 'Abd al-A'la', what can go wrong, if a people whose belief is one, who go to one man and follow one man, if they stop disputing against each other about him and refer to him for solution?' O 'Abd al-'A'la', it is not proper for a believing person. It is not proper if his brother (in belief) has advanced to a rank of the ranks of the garden (paradise), to pull him back. It is not proper to pull him back from his position where he is, and it is not proper for this other one to push his chest back who has not reached him but that he should help him to join him and ask forgiveness from Allah.'"

(It seems that the words of 'Isma'il end with his question, 'Is it about what Marwan and ibn Dharr have said?' Thereafter it is the Imam and 'Abd al-A'la' perhaps in another meeting with him (the Imam))

Differences among the followers of Musa *'Alayhi al-Salam*

H 14731, h 283

Muhammad ibn Yahya has narrated from Ahmad ibn Muhammad ibn 'Isa from ibn Mahbub from Jamil ibn Salih from abu Khalid al-Kabuliy who has narrated the following:

"It is about the meaning of the words of Allah: 'Allah tells a parable in which there is a company of horrific querulous people and only one of them is well disciplined. Can they be considered as equal? Only Allah deserves all praise. In fact, most of them do not know.' (39:29) Abu Ja'far, *'Alayhi al-Salam*, has said, 'The querulous ones are because the first one gathers the different ones in his leadership but they condemn and denounce each other. The well disciplined man is the first in the matters of his right as well as his Shi'ah, followers.' He (the Imam) then said, 'The Jews after Musa, *'Alayhi al-Salam*, turned into seventy-one sects of which one is in the garden (paradise) and seventy are in the fire. The Christians after Jesus, *'Alayhi al-Salam*, turned into seventy-two sects of which one is in the garden (paradise) and seventy one are in the fire. This nation, after its Prophet, *O Allah grant compensation to Muhammad and his family worthy of their services to Your cause*, turned into seventy-three sects of which seventy-two are in the fire and one is in the garden (paradise). Of the seventy-three sects, thirteen of them who claim to have come under our *Wilayah* (divine authority and knowledge) and love twelve of them are in the fire and only one is in the garden (paradise) and sixty of the other people are in the fire.'"

Government of falsehood lives longer

H 14732, h 284

It is narrated from the narrator of the previous Hadith from Ahmad ibn Muhammad from ibn Mahbub from 'Abd Allah ibn Sinan who has narrated the following:

"Abu 'Abd Allah, *'Alayhi al-Salam*, has said, 'The government of falsehood continues to last for a longer time and the government of the truth appears for a very short time.'"

When is relief for Shi'ah

H 14733, h 285

It is narrated from the narrator of the previous Hadith from Ahmad ibn Muhammad from ibn Mahbub from Ya'qub al-Sarraj who has narrated the following:

"I once asked abu 'Abd Allah, *'Alayhi al-Salam*, 'When the Shi'ah will have the glad news?' He (the Imam) said, 'It is when the children of al-'Abbas will dispute among themselves about their authority. Those who had no interest show interest in them. The Arabs leave their reign loose, everyone who has a spur raises it. Al-Shamiy rises, al-Hasaniy moves and the owner of this 'Amr, al-Qa'im reappears with divine authority and power from al-Madinah to Makkah with the legacy of the Messenger of Allah, *O Allah grant compensation to Muhammad and his family worthy of their services to Your cause.*' I then asked, 'What are the legacy of the Messenger of Allah, *O Allah grant compensation to Muhammad and his family worthy of their services to Your cause?*' He (the Imam) said, 'It is the sword of the Messenger of Allah, his coat of arm, his turban, his gown, his staff, his banner, his helmet and his saddle. He arrives in Makkah; then he takes the sword out of its sheath, wears the coat of arm, hoists the banner, dresses up in the gown and the turban, picks up the staff in his hand, asks Allah for permission, then certain ones of his friends come, then al-Hasaniy comes and informs him of the news. Al-Hasaniy then hurries up to come out but people of Makkah attack him, kill him and send his head to al-Shamiy. At that time the owner of this 'Amr, al-Qa'im with divine authority and power reappears. People pledge allegiance to him and follow him. Al-Shamiy at that time sends an army to al-Madinah. Allah, most Majestic, most Glorious, will destroy them before reaching it and at that time all of the children of Ali will flee from al-Madinah to Makkah and join the owner of this 'Amr, al-Qa'im who will proceed to Iraq and send an army to al-Madinah whose people will accept the belief. They will return to al-Madinah.'"

People of abu al-Khattab denounced by Abu Ja'far *'Alayhi al-Salam*

H 14734, h 286
A number of our people have narrated from Ahmad ibn Muhammad from ibn Mahbub from Malik ibn 'Atiyyah from certain persons of the companions of abu 'Abd Allah, *'Alayhi al-Salam*, who has narrated the following:

"Once abu 'Abd Allah, *'Alayhi al-Salam*, came to us very angry, saying, 'I just went out and certain black ones came to me shouting, *'Labbayka* (here I am O Lord, to obey your command) O Ja'far ibn Muhammad, *Labbayka* (here I am O Lord, to obey your command).' I then returned right back to where I had left, to my home, afraid and dismayed because of what they said until I performed *Sajdah* (prostration) in my place for *Sajdah* before my Lord, rubbed my face in humility of my soul and denounced before Him what they were yelling. Had Jesus, son of Mary passed the limit that Allah had set about him, he would have remained deaf without being able ever to hear, blind thereafter without being ever to see and remained speechless without being able to speak ever thereafter. May Allah condemn abu al-Khattab and kill him with iron.'"

(Companions of abu al-Khattab believed that Ja'far ibn Muhammad was a deity)

People are of three kinds

H 14735, h 287

It is narrated from the narrator of the previous Hadith from Ahmad ibn Muhammad from ibn Mahbub from Jahm ibn abu Juhaymah from certain Mawaliy of abu al-Hassan, *'Alayhi al-Salam*, who has narrated the following:

"A servant of abu al-Hassan, Musa, *'Alayhi al-Salam*, was a man from Quraysh so he began to speak of Quraysh and Arab. Abu al-Hassan, *'Alayhi al-Salam*, said, 'You can leave that alone. People are of three kinds: 'Arabi, Mawla' and al-'Ilj. We are Arab, our Shi'ah are Mawali and those who are not as we are al-'Ilj (faithless giants).' He then said, 'You say this O abu al-Hassan, then where is Afkhad (tribes or larger families) of Quraysh and Arab?' He (the Imam) said, 'It is how as I just said.'"

Al-Qa'im (the one who rises with divine authority and power), *'Alayhi al-Salam,* and people hostile to *'A'immah*

H 14736, h 288

It is narrated from the narrator of the previous Hadith from Ahmad ibn Muhammad from ibn Mahbub from al-Ahwal from Salam ibn al-Mustanir who has narrated the following:

"I once heard abu Ja'far, *'Alayhi al-Salam*, say this. 'When al-Qa'im will reappear with divine authority and power, belief will be proposed to all people hostile to *'A'immah*. If they did not accept it in the true sense, their necks will be struck down or they must agree to pay taxes as other taxpayers do, tie a belt around their midsection and move out of the cities to country sides.'"

A great deal of words without deeds

H 14737, h 289

Al-Husayn ibn Muhammad al-Ash'ariy has narrated from Ali ibn Muhammad ibn Sa'id ibn Ghazwan from Muhammad ibn Bunan from abu Maryam who has narrated the following:

"Abu Ja'far, *'Alayhi al-Salam*, has said that once my father when his companions were present said, 'Who among you can feel happy to hold a piece of burning charcoal in his palm, then squeeze it until it is extinguished?' People expressed fear and thought of it as torturous. I then stood up and asked, 'Father, do you command me to do it?' He (the Imam) said, 'I did not address you thereby; you are from me and I am from you. I addressed these ones.' He (the Imam) said that he (the Imam) repeated it three times; and then said, 'How plentiful are words and how little are the deeds! People of deeds are very few indeed, people of deeds are very few. O yes, we certainly know both the people of deeds and the people of words. It is not that we are blind about you but we examine your reports and write your traces.' He (the Imam) then said, 'By Allah, it was as if the earth shook them in extreme embarrassment and they perspired profusely, no one of them could raise his eyes from the ground. When he (the Imam) saw their condition he (the Imam) then said, 'May Allah grant you mercy, my intention was no other thing except good. The garden (paradise) is of degrees and ranks, the ranks and degrees of the people of deeds are not available to the people of words and the ranks and degrees of the people of words are not available for others.' He (the Imam) said that by Allah, it seemed as if they were released from chains and fetters.'"

If Shi'ah is refined only words remain

H 14738, h 290
Through the same chain of narrators as that of the previous Hadith, the following is narrated from Muhammad ibn Sulayman from Ibrahim ibn 'Abd Allah al-Sufiy who has narrated the following:

"Musa ibn Bakr al-Wasitiy has said that abu al-Hassan, *'Alayhi al-Salam*, once said to me this: 'If my Shi'ah (followers) are examined for a differentiation, I can only find as such by the words of their mouth. If I put them to the test, I will find them only as deviating from my manners and discipline. If I select from them I will find only one out of one thousand and if I sift them thoroughly, no one will remain except those who are for me. They for a long time have, when leaning on the pillows, been saying, 'We are Shi'ah of Ali, *'Alayhi al-Salam.*' Shi'ah (followers of *'A'immah*) are only those whose deeds verify their words.'"

About the conceited people

H 14739, h 291
Humayd ibn Ziyad has narrated from al-Hassan ibn Muhammad al-Kindiy from Ahmad ibn al-Hassan al-Mithamiy from Aban ibn 'Uthman from 'Abd al-A'la' mawla Ale Sam who has narrated the following:

"I once heard abu 'Abd Allah, *'Alayhi al-Salam*, say, 'On the Day of Judgment the beautiful woman who seduced people because of her beauty will be brought for judgment. She will say, 'You made my physical form good and attractive, thus I became involved in what I did.' Then Maryam will be shown to her. She then will be asked, 'Are you more beautiful or is she (Mary) more beautiful? We made her beautiful but she was not seduced.' Then the man of attractive physical form who seduced will be brought and he will say, 'O Lord, You made me of an attractive physical form so I became involved with women as I did.' Then Yusuf will be shown to him. He will be asked, 'Are you more attractive or this one? We created him physically attractive but he did not become seduced.' The person put to test and trial will be brought who because of test and trial had become involved in mischief and he will say, 'O Lord, You made my test and trial intense and it involved me in mischief.' Ayyub will be shown to him. He will be asked this. 'Did he undergo more intense test and trial or did you? He was tested but he did not become involved in mischief.'"

Freedom and security are complete life

H 14740, h 292
Through the same chain of narrators as that of the previous Hadith the following is narrated from Aban ibn 'Uthman from 'Isma'il al-Basriy who has narrated the following:

"I once heard abu 'Abd Allah, *'Alayhi al-Salam*, say, 'Can you sit in a place then speak and say whatever you like, denounce whoever you like to denounce and love and choose as your guardians whomever you like?' I replied, 'Yes, that is correct.' He (the Imam) then said, 'That is the life the way it should be.'"

May Allah bless one who makes us loveable to people

H 14741, h 293

Humayd ibn Ziyad from al-Hassan ibn Muhammad from Wuhayb ibn Hafs from abu Basir who has narrated the following:

"I once heard abu 'Abd Allah, *'Alayhi al-Salam*, say, 'May Allah grant kindness to a servant who convinces people about our being loveable ones and does not make them to hate us. O yes, by Allah, if they narrate the beautiful ones of our words, they will become more honorable with it and no one can stitch anything to them. In fact one of them hears the word and drops ten from himself (which destroys the beauty of our words).'"

About the words of Allah 'those who bring what is brought to them'

H 14742, h 294

Wuhayb has narrated from abu Basir who has narrated the following:

"I once asked abu 'Abd Allah, *'Alayhi al-Salam*, about the meaning of the words of Allah, most Majestic, most Glorious, '. . . those who bring that which was brought to them with fearful hearts.' (23:60) He (the Imam) said, 'It (their fearfulness) is due to their (need for) intercession and their hope; they are afraid for their deeds being rejected if they had not obeyed Allah, most Majestic, most Glorious, but they hope that it (their good deeds) will be accepted from them.'"

People calling to falsehood soon find followers

H 14743, h 295

Wuhayb ibn Hafs has narrated from abu Basir who has narrated the following:

"There is no one who calls to misguidance but that he finds followers and an audience."

Undesirability of separating the table of the black people

H 14744, h 296

A number of our people have narrated from Ahmad ibn Muhammad from 'Abd Allah ibn al-Salt from a man from people of Balkh who has narrated the following:

"I was present with al-Rida', *'Alayhi al-Salam*, during his journey to Khurasan. One day he (the Imam) asked for food and the table spread was made ready. He gathered all of his Mawali who were of black people as well as others. I then said, 'I wish you had told them to arrange a separate table spread for them.' He (the Imam) said, 'Wait, Allah, most Blessed, most High, is one, the mother is one, the father is one and the rewards are proportionate to the deeds.'"

The chemistry of the body is of four elements

H 14745, h 297

Muhammad ibn Yahya has narrated from Ahmad ibn Muhammad from ibn Sinan who has narrated the following:

"I once heard abu al-Hassan, *'Alayhi al-Salam*, say, 'The nature of the bodies has four conditions. Certain amount of it is air without which a soul cannot live and its flow that removes from the body illness and rancidness, the land, which produces dryness, the heat, and food from which blood is produced. Have you not considered that food goes to the stomach which digests it and softens then cleans it from which the nature takes what is pure for blood, then the residue goes down as well as water and it generates mucus.'"

About the words of a man 'May Allah grant you goodness'

H 14746, h 298

Muhammad ibn Yahya has narrated from Ahmad ibn Muhammad from al-Husayn ibn Yazid al-Nawfaliy from al-Husayn ibn 'A'yan, brother of Malik ibn 'A'yan who has narrated the following:

"I once asked abu 'Abd Allah, *'Alayhi al-Salam*, about the meaning of a man's saying to another man. 'May Allah give you good reward.' Abu 'Abd Allah, *'Alayhi al-Salam*, said, 'In the garden (paradise) there is a canal and its source is from al-Kawthar, the source of al-Kawthar is from the foot of the throne on which are the houses of executors of the wills and their followers. On both banks of that canal girls grow. Whenever one is picked up, a new one grows and they are named after that canal which is mentioned in the words of Allah, most Majestic, most Glorious, Allah, '. . . therein there are khayrat (goodness beautiful ones).' (55:70) When a man says to his friend, 'May Allah give you Khayr (meaning 'khayrat' just mentioned) (good reward) he intends to mention such dwellings which Allah, most Majestic, most Glorious, has prepared for His chosen ones and for the select ones of His creatures.'"

On the banks of a canal in the garden (paradise) *Hur* grows

H 14747, h 299

It is narrated from the narrator of the previous Hadith from Ahmad ibn Muhammad from ibn abu 'Umayr from al-Husayn ibn 'Uthman from abu Basir who has narrated the following:

"Abu 'Abd Allah, *'Alayhi al-Salam*, has said, 'In the garden (paradise) there is a canal. On the banks of this canal, *Hur* grows. When a believing person passes by one of them, if he likes then picks up one and Allah, most Majestic, most Glorious, makes another one grow at that place.'"

Hadith of *al-Qibab* (domes)

H 14748, h 300

Muhammad ibn Yahya has narrated from Ahmad ibn Muhammad from al-Washsha' from 'Abd Allah ibn Sinan from abu Hamzah who has narrated the following:

"Abu Ja'far, *'Alayhi al-Salam*, one night, when I was with him, when looking in the sky said, 'O abu Hamzah, this is the doom of our father Adam, *'Alayhi al-Salam*. Allah, most Majestic, most Glorious, beside this has thirty-nine other domes in which there are creatures who have not disobeyed Allah even for a blinking of an eye.'"

Allah has many *Qibab*

H 14749, h 301

It is narrated from the narrator of the previous Hadith from Ahmad ibn Muhammad from abu Yahya al-Wasitiy from 'Ajlan abu Salih who has narrated the following:

"Once a man came to abu 'Abd Allah, *'Alayhi al-Salam,* and asked saying, 'I pray to Allah to keep my soul in service for your cause, is this the dome of Adam, *'Alayhi al-Salam*?' He (the Imam) said, 'Yes, but Allah has many other dooms. O yes, behind your west, this one, there are thirty-nine wests of white earth full of creatures who find light thereby. They have not disobeyed Allah, most Majestic, most Glorious, even for a blinking of an eye and they do not know if Adam, *'Alayhi al-Salam,* is created or not but they denounce so and so and so and so.'"

One who patches his clothes

H 14750, h 302

Ali ibn Muhammad has narrated from Salih ibn abu Hammad from Yahya ibn al-Mubarak from 'Abd Allah ibn Jabalah from Ishaq ibn 'Ammar who has narrated the following:

"Abu 'Abd Allah, *'Alayhi al-Salam,* has said, 'If one stitches his shoes, patches up his clothes and carries his asset, he then has denounced arrogance.'"

Abu 'Abd Allah, *'Alayhim al-Salam,* denounces people of abu al-Khattab

H 14751, h 303

It is narrated from the narrator of the previous Hadith from Salih from Muhammad ibn 'Uramah from ibn Sinan from al-Mufaddal ibn 'Umar who has narrated the following:

"Once al-Qasim al-Sharikiy, Najm ibn Hutaym, Salih ibn Sahl and I were in al-Madinah and we debated on the issue of Lordship. Certain ones among us said to the others, 'Why do we speak about it when we are near him (the Imam) and we are not in the condition of *Taqiyah* (fearfulness) so allow us to go before him (the Imam).' We then moved and by Allah, we had not reached the door that he (the Imam) had already come out without shoes and gown with every hair on his head standing straight. He (the Imam) was saying, 'No, O Mufaddal, no, O al-Qasim, O Najm, no, in fact they are honorable servants of Allah and they do not speak a word before Him and by His command they work.'" (Salih ibn Sahl considered abu 'Abd Allah, *'Alayhi al-Salam,* as the Lord.)

A helper of Satan is called *tamrikh*

H 14752, h 304

It is narrated from the narrator of the previous Hadith from Salih from Ali ibn al-Hakam from Aban ibn 'Uthman who has narrated the following:

"Abu 'Abd Allah, *'Alayhi al-Salam,* has said, 'Satan has a helper called Tamrih. When night comes it fills between the two palpitating creatures (to induce temptation among them).'"

The words of the lizard

H 14753, h 305
It is narrated from the narrator of the previous Hadith from Salih from al-Washsha' from Karram from 'Abd Allah ibn Talhah who has narrated the following:

"I once asked abu 'Abd Allah, *'Alayhi al-Salam*, about the lizard. He (the Imam) said, 'It is filth and it is a metamorphosed creature. If you kill it you must take a Ghusl (bath).' He (the Imam) then said, 'My father was sitting in al-Hijr with another man talking to him that a lizard howled with its tongue. My father asked the man, 'Do you know what this lizard is saying?' he replied, 'I have no knowledge of what it says.' He (the Imam) said, 'It says, "By Allah, if you speak of 'Uthman in reproach I will reproach Ali until he moves from here."' My father said, 'Every dead of banu 'Umayyah metamorphoses into a lizard.' He (the Imam) then said, 'When 'Abd al-Malik ibn Marwan died he metamorphosed into a lizard and disappeared from the eyes of those with him among whom his sons were there. They felt it as great loss and they did not know how to manage it. They decided to find a trunk and carve it in the shape of a man, dressed it with an iron coat of arms then wrapped it in shrouds. No one of the people learned about it except his children and I.'"

Allah sent Muhammad, *'Alayhi al-Salam*, as a Mercy . . .

H 14754, h 306
It is narrated from the narrator of the previous Hadith from Salih from Muhammad ibn 'Abd Allah ibn Mehran from 'Abd al-Malik ibn Bashir from 'Aytham ibn Sulayman from Mu'awiyah ibn 'Ammar who has narrated the following:

"Abu 'Abd Allah, *'Alayhi al-Salam*, has stated this Hadith. 'If one of you wishes for al-Qa'im (the one who rises with divine authority and power) he must do so when in good health (healthy belief); Allah sent Muhammad, *O Allah grant compensation to Muhammad and his family worthy of their services to Your cause*, as mercy and He will send al-Qa'im for reprisal.' (The Holy Prophet did not force anyone to accept his religion but al-Qa'im will clean the earth of disbelief.)'"

The one most similar to Musa, *'Alayhi al-Salam*

H 14755, h 307
It is narrated from the narrator of the previous Hadith from Salih from Muhammad ibn 'Abd Allah from 'Abd al-Malik ibn Bashir who has narrated the following:

Abu al-Hassan, al-Awwal, *'Alayhi al-Salam*, has said, 'Al-Hassan, *'Alayhi al-Salam*, was the most similar person to Musa ibn 'Imran, *'Alayhi al-Salam*, from his head to his midsection and al-Husayn, *'Alayhi al-Salam*, was most similar to Musa ibn 'Imran, *'Alayhi al-Salam*, from his midsection to his feet.'"

The height of Adam and Eve

H 14756, h 308

Ali ibn Ibrahim has narrated from his father from al-Hassan ibn Mahbub from Muqatil ibn Sulayman who has narrated the following:

"I once asked abu 'Abd Allah, *'Alayhi al-Salam*, about how tall was Adam, *'Alayhi al-Salam*, when he came to earth? In addition, how tall was Eve, *'Alayha al-Salam*?' He (the Imam) said, 'We have found in the book of Ali ibn abu Talib, *'Alayhi al-Salam*, that when Allah, most Majestic, most Glorious, sent Adam, *'Alayhi al-Salam*, and his spouse to earth his legs were on the twin part of al-Safa' and his head in the horizon of the sky. He complained about heat from the sun. So Allah, most Majestic, most Glorious, sent revelation to Jibril to pinch him somehow to make him seventy grain, or arm of his own grain, tall as well as Eve to make her thirty-five grain, or arm of her own grain, tall.'"

(The word grain or arm which is the translation of the Arabic word Dhira' which according to Arabic dictionary means an arm's length and several other meanings like grain, particles and so on. Thus, the meaning of Hadith is not clear, so it falls in the mutashabeh category)

The rule for one who finds his father enslaved in the pre-Islamic era

H 14757, h 309

It is narrated from the narrator of the previous Hadith from his father from ibn Mahbub from abu Ayyub from al-Harith ibn al-Mughirah who has narrated the following:

"I once asked abu 'Abd Allah, *'Alayhi al-Salam*, about the case of a man whose father had become a captive in pre-Islamic times and he did not know about it until after several generations of slaves of his ancestors in Islam and then he was set free. He (the Imam) said, 'He must be related to his slave fathers, thereafter he is counted of the tribe from which his father was, if his father was known. He can inherit from them and they inherit him.'"

Allah has given three qualities to a believer

H 14758, h 310

Ibn Mahbub has narrated from abu Ayyub from 'Abd al-Mu'min Ansari who has narrated the following:

"Abu Ja'far, *'Alayhi al-Salam*, has said that Allah, most Blessed, most High, has given believing persons three qualities: He has given them honor in this and the next world, success in this and in the next world and has placed fear from them in the hearts of the unjust ones.'"

Three things are of the prestige of believers

H 14759, h 311

Ibn Mahbub has narrated from 'Abd Allah ibn Sinan who has narrated the following:

"I once heard abu 'Abd Allah, *'Alayhi al-Salam*, say, 'Three things are of the honor and beauty for a believing person in this and in the next world. One is performing *Salat* (prayer) in the end of the night, having no hope in what is in the hands of people. The third issue is his accepting *Wilayah* (divine authority and knowledge) of *Ale* (family of) Muhammad, *O Allah grant compensation to Muhammad and his family worthy of their services to Your cause.*' He (the Imam) said, 'Three evil things caused hardships for the best of the creatures. One was abu Sufyan who fought the Messenger of Allah, *O Allah grant compensation to Muhammad and his family worthy of their services to Your cause*, with hatred. Mu'awiyah who fought Ali, *'Alayhi al-Salam*, with hatred and Yazid ibn Mu'awiyah the condemned one who murdered al-Husayn ibn Ali, *'Alayhim al-Salam*, and treated him with animosity until he killed him (Al-Husayn, *'Alayhi al-Salam*).'"

The three worst things that affect the best creatures of Allah

H 14760, h 312
Ibn Mahbub has narrated from Malik ibn 'Atiyyah from abu Hamzah al-Thumaliy who has narrated the following:

"Ali ibn Al-Husayn, *'Alayhi al-Salam*, has said, 'There is no status for a person of Quraysh or an Arab except because of humility, there is no grace except because of piety and there is no deed without intention, and there is no worship without *fiqh* (knowledge of Shari'ah). It is a fact that the most hated of people in the sight of Allah is one who follows the *Sunnah* of an Imam but does not follow him in his (Imam's) deeds.'"

Yazid ibn Mu'awiyah enslaves people of Quraysh

H 14761, h 313
Ibn Mahbub has narrated from abu Ayyub from Burayd ibn Mu'awiyah who has narrated the following:

"I once heard abu Ja'far, *'Alayhi al-Salam*, say, 'Once Yazid ibn Mu'awiyah entered al-Madinah intending to perform al-Hajj. He then sent for a man from Quraysh who came to him and Yazid asked, 'Do you acknowledge that you are my slave? If I want, I can sell you or I can keep you as my slave if I so wanted? He said, 'By Allah, O Yazid, you are not more honorable than me in Quraysh in status, and your father was not more excellent than my father in the time of ignorance and in Islam; and you are not more excellent than me in religion or in good deeds, so how can I acknowledge what you ask me to acknowledge?' Yazid then said, 'If you do not acknowledge, by Allah, I will kill you.' He said, 'If you kill me, it is not greater than your killing of al-Husayn ibn Ali, *'Alayhim al-Salam*, grandson of the Messenger of Allah, *O Allah grant compensation to Muhammad and his family worthy of their services to Your cause.* He (Yazid) commanded, then he was killed.'"

Hadith of Ali ibn al-Husayn, *'Alayhima al-Salam*, with Yazid

"He then sent for Ali ibn al-Husayn, *'Alayhim al-Salam*, and said to him (the Imam) whatever he had said to the man of Quraysh. Ali ibn al-Husayn, *'Alayhim al-Salam*, said, 'Is it not the case that if I did not acknowledge what you ask me to acknowledge you will kill me as you killed the man yesterday?' Yazid, may Allah condemn him, said, 'Yes, that is correct.' Ali ibn Al-Husayn, *'Alayhim al-Salam*, said, 'I then acknowledge what you ask me to acknowledge as a coerced slave. You can keep or sell me as you like.' Yazid, may Allah condemn him, said, 'You deserve to be spared and it does not reduce your nobility and honor.'"

Rejecting one verse of al-Quran is rejecting the whole Quran

H 14762, h 314

Al-Husayn from Muhammad al-Ash'ariy has narrated from Ali ibn Muhammad ibn Sa'id from Muhammad ibn Salim ibn abu Salmah from Muhammad ibn Sa'id ibn Ghazwan who has narrated the following:

"'Abd Allah ibn al-Mughirah narrated, 'I once said to abu al-Hassan, *'Alayhi al-Salam*, that I have two neighbors, one is hostile to *'A'immah* and the other is Zaydiy and I must associate with them so which one can I associate with?' He (the Imam) said, 'They are the same. One who rejects a verse of the book of Allah he has thrown Islam behind his back and he is like rejecting the whole al-Quran, Prophets and the messengers.' He (the Imam) then said, 'He is hostile to you and Zaydiy is hostile to us.'"

Prohibition on sitiing in a meeting where an Imam is abused

H 14763, h 315

Muhammad ibn Sa'id has narrated from al-Qasim ibn Muhammad ibn 'Urwah from 'Ubayd ibn Zurarah from his father who has narrated the following:

"Abu Ja'far, *'Alayhi al-Salam*, has stated this Hadith: 'One may sit in a gathering where one of *'A'immah* is insulted. If he is able to retaliate but does not do so, Allah, most Majestic, most Glorious, dresses him with the dress of lowliness in this world, will make him suffer in the hereafter and takes away from him what He has granted him of our recognition.'"

Worship without *Wilayah* is not accepted

H 14764, h 316

Abu Ali al-Ash'ariy has narrated from Muhammad ibn 'Abd al-Jabbar from ibn Faddal from Ibrahim son of brother of abu Shabal from abu Shabal who has narrated the following:

"Abu 'Abd Allah, *'Alayhi al-Salam*, once initiated a conversation with me. He (the Imam) said, 'You have loved us when people have hated us, you have acknowledged us when people have rejected us, you have maintained good relations with us when people have been unjust to us. Thus, Allah has made your living like our living and your dying like our dying. O yes, by Allah, the only thing between a man and Allah's granting delight to his eyes is the reaching of his soul to this place' - he (the Imam) pointed to his throat and pulled the skin.

He (the Imam) then repeated it and he was not happy until he swore for me and said, 'I swear by Allah, besides whom no one deserves worship that my father, Muhammad ibn Ali, *'Alayhim al-Salam*, narrated this to me, O abu Shabal. Are you not happy to perform *Salat* (prayer) which will be accepted and they perform *Salat* (prayer) which will not be accepted, you pay *Zakat* which will be accepted and they pay *Zakat* which will not be accepted? Will you not be happy to perform al-Hajj, which will be accepted by Allah, most Majestic, most Glorious and they perform al-Hajj, which will not be accepted? By Allah, *Salat* (prayer) is not accepted except your *Salat* (prayer), payment of *Zakat* is not accepted except your *Zakat* and there is no al-Hajj except your al-Hajj. You must maintain piety; you are in peace and return the trust safely. When people will be differentiated at that time, every nation will go to their desires and you will go with the truth as long as you remain obedient to us. Is it not the case that judges, rulers and people of questions (fatwa) are from them?' I replied, 'Yes, that is correct.' He (the Imam) then said, 'You must remain pious before Allah, most Majestic, most Glorious; you cannot listen to all the people. People have gone here and there but you are holding to what Allah, most Majestic, most Glorious, is holding. Allah, most Majestic, most Glorious, has chosen Muhammad, *O Allah grant compensation to Muhammad and his family worthy of their services to Your cause*, from His servants. Thus, you have chosen what Allah has chosen; so you must remain pious before Allah and return the trust safely to blacks and whites even if he is a Harawriy (a sect) or a Shamiy (people of Syria).'"

Deeds are not accepted without *Wilayah*

H 14765, h 317

A number of our people have narrated from Sahl ibn Ziyad from ibn Faddal from Ibrahim son of brother of abu Shibl from abu Shibl who has narrated a similar Hadith as the previous Hadith.

Deeds are not accepted without *Wilayah*.

H 14766, h 318

Suhayb ibn Ziyad has narrated from Muhammad ibn Sinan from Hammad ibn abu Talhah from Mu'adh ibn Kathir who has narrated the following:

"I once looked at the station (Arafat) with a great number of people there. Then I went near abu 'Abd Allah, *'Alayhi al-Salam*, and said, 'There are a great number of people at the station.' He (the Imam) turned his eyes, turned them around among the people and said to me, 'Come close, O abu 'Abd Allah, it is hay which waves bring from all places. No, by Allah, there is no al-Hajj except your al-Hajj, no, by Allah, Allah does not accept from anyone other than you.'"

Hadith of the mother of Khalid and abu Basir

H 14767, h 319

Al-Husayn from Muhammad al-Ash'ariy has narrated from Mu'alla' ibn Muhammad from al-Hassan ibn Ali al-Washsha' from ibn 'Uthman from abu Basir who has narrated the following:

"Once I was sitting with abu 'Abd Allah, *'Alayhi al-Salam*, when the mother of Khalid who was cut off by Yusuf ibn 'Amr asked permission to see him (the

Imam). Abu 'Abd Allah, *'Alayhi al-Salam*, said, 'Do you like to hear her words?' I said, 'Yes, I like to hear.' He (the Imam) gave her permission and made me sit with him on the same furnishing as his furnishing. She then came and spoke and she was a very eloquent woman. She asked him (the Imam) about the two of them. He (the Imam) said, 'Do you consider them as your *Waly* (leader with divine authority and power)?' She said, 'Can I then say to my Lord when I meet Him that you commanded me to consider them as my *Waly* (leader with divine authority and power)?' He (the Imam) said, 'Yes, you can do so.' She then said, 'This one sitting on the furnishing with you commands me to denounce them and Kathir al-Nawa' commands me to consider them as my *Waly* (leader with divine authority and power). Which one of these two is better and more beloved to you?' He (the Imam) said, 'This one by Allah, is more beloved to me than Kathir al-Nawa' and his people. This one argues and says, "Those who do not judge according to what Allah has revealed are unbelievers." (5:44) ". . . those who do not judge according to what Allah has revealed are unjust." (5:45) ". . . those who do not judge according to what Allah has revealed are sinful ones."'" (5:47) (The text of this Hadith is the same as the narrators are different.)

Words of Fatimah, *'Alayha al-Salam*

H 14768, h 320

It is narrated from the narrator of the previous Hadith from Mu'alla' from al-Hassan from Aban from abu Hashim who has narrated the following:

"Ali, *'Alayhi al-Salam*, was taken out of his home at that time Fatimah, *'Alayhi al-Salam*, also came out. She had placed the shirt of the Messenger of Allah, *O Allah grant compensation to Muhammad and his family worthy of their services to Your cause*, on her head, holding the hands of her two sons and said, 'What have I done to you, O abu Bakr, that you want to make my sons orphans and myself a widow. By Allah, had it not been a bad and harmful thing, I would have spread my hairs and cried before my Lord for help.' A man among the people then said, 'What do you want from him?' She then took his hand and left with him.'"

(The man perhaps addressed abu Bakr for fear from the falling of misfortune on them because of her plea before Allah.)

Prayer of Fatimah, *'Alayha al-Salam*

H 14769, h 321

Aban has narrated from Ali ibn 'Abd al-'Aziz from 'Abd al-Hamid al-Ta'iy who has narrated the following:

"Abu Ja'far, *'Alayhi al-Salam*, has said, 'By Allah, had she spread her hairs they all would have died.'"

One born out of wedlock receives his reward

H 14770, h 322

Aban has narrated from ibn abu Ya'fur who has narrated the following:

"Abu 'Abd Allah, *'Alayhi al-Salam*, has said, 'One who is born out of wedlock must be asked to work; if he does good or bad deeds, he is rewarded accordingly.'"

Nicknames of Marwan and his father

H 14771, h 323

Aban has narrated from 'Abd al-Rahman ibn abu 'Abd Allah who has narrated the following:

"I once heard abu 'Abd Allah, *'Alayhi al-Salam*, say that once the Messenger of Allah, *O Allah grant compensation to Muhammad and his family worthy of their services to Your cause*, came out of his chamber when Marwan and his father were listening to his conversations. He (the Messenger of Allah) said, 'The lizard is the son of the lizard.' From that day on they narrate that the lizard listens to conversations.'"

The birth of Marwan and the words of 'A' ishah

H 14772, h 324

Aban has narrated from Zurarah who has narrated the following:

"I once heard abu Ja'far, *'Alayhi al-Salam*, say, 'When Marwan was born they brought him to the Messenger of Allah, *O Allah grant compensation to Muhammad and his family worthy of their services to Your cause*, for prayer and they sent him to 'A'ishah to pray for him. When she went close to him she said, 'Take the lizard, son of lizard, away from me.' Zurarah has said, 'I do not know except that he said, "He (The Messenger of Allah) condemned him (Marwan)."'"

'Umar belies Ali, *'Alayhi al-Salam*

H 14773, h 325

Aban has narrated from 'Abd al-Rahman ibn abu 'Abd Allah from abu al-'Abbas al-Makkiy who has narrated the following:

"I once heard abu Ja'far, *'Alayhi al-Salam*, say that 'Umar once met Ali, *'Alayhi al-Salam*, and said, 'Why is it that you read this verse of al-Quran, ". . . which of you (believing or unbelieving group) has misfortune (insanity)," (68:6) and apply it to me and my friend.' He (the Imam) has said that Ali, *'Alayhi al-Salam*, said, 'If you like I can inform you about a verse which is revealed about banu 'Umayyah, ". . . have you decided to spread destruction in the land when you take hold of the government and cut off good relations with relatives?" (47:22) He said, 'You have spoken a lie. Banu 'Umayyah maintains better relations with relatives than you do, but you refuse to do anything other than animosity toward banu Taym, banu 'Adi and banu 'Umayyah.'"

Standing under the first drop of rain

H 14774, h 326

Ali ibn Ibrahim has narrated from Harun ibn Muslim from Mas'adah ibn Sadaqah who has narrated the following:

"Abu 'Abd Allah, *'Alayhi al-Salam*, has said that Ali, *'Alayhi al-Salam*, would stand under the sky when it rained, his hairs, beard and clothes would get wet. It was said, 'O 'Amir al-Mu'minin, come in the shelter, under the shelter.' He (the Imam) replied, 'This water has newly come from near the throne (the domain and knowledge of Allah).' He (the Imam) then began to speak saying, 'Under the throne of Allah is an ocean in which there is water which (helps) the food for animals to grow. When Allah, most Majestic, most Glorious, wants to grow whatever He wants due to His kindness, He inspires it to rain from the sky to sky until it comes to the sky of the land in the cloud. The cloud is like a sifter, Allah then inspires the wind to shake the clouds and melt into water, then take it to so and so place to rain, which may turn into flooding and so on. It sends the rain on them as it is ordered. With every drop of rain, one angel comes down until the angel places it where it is supposed to fall. The number of drops are counted and weighed except the rain of a storm, which is not counted. Also, the flood of the time of Noah, *'Alayhi al-Salam*, which just kept pouring without weighing and without the count of numbers.' Abu 'Abd Allah, *'Alayhi al-Salam*, narrated to me that his father has narrated from 'Amir al-Mu'minin, Ali, *'Alayhim al-Salam*. He has narrated from the Messenger of Allah, *O Allah grant compensation to Muhammad and his family worthy of their services to Your cause*, who has said that Allah, most Majestic, most Glorious, has made the cloud to send the rain. It is as if it comes through the sifting tool. It melts the coolness into water to come down harmlessly unlike large pieces of hail which can become torturous as a penalty from Allah, most Majestic, most Glorious, when He wants to afflict whoever of His servants He wants to afflict.' The Messenger of Allah, *O Allah grant compensation to Muhammad and his family worthy of their services to Your cause*, has said, 'You must not wink (point out) to the rain or to the crescent; it is detestable in the sight of Allah.'"

The letter of 'Amir al-Mu'minin, *'Alayhi al-Salam,* to ibn Abbas

H 14775, h 327

A number of our people have narrated from Sahl ibn Ziyad from Ali ibn Asbat in a marfu' manner who has narrated the following:

"'Amir al-Mu'minin, *'Alayhi al-Salam*, once wrote to ibn Abbas. 'Thereafter, (you should take notice) that something which one can never miss makes him happy, or causes him sadness that which never comes in his reach even though one strives very hard to achieve it. Therefore, you should become happy for the good deeds that you have sent forward, a judgment or a word. You should become sad for that which you have neglected of such issues. You must leave alone what you have missed of the worldly matters and must not become very sad about it. You must not become very delighted because of what you have gained of the worldly matters. You must consider the issue of the hereafter very important. With Salam.'"

Excellence of Shi'ah and advice of Abu Ja'far, *'Alayhi al-Salam*

H 14776, h 328

Sahl ibn Ziyad has narrated from al-Hassan ibn Ali from Karram from abu al-Samit who has narrated the following:

"Abu 'Abd Allah, *'Alayhi al-Salam*, has said, 'My father and I once went until we were between the grave and the pulpit (of the Holy Prophet) when a group of Shi'ah was there. He (the Imam) offered them greeting of peace; then said, 'I by Allah love your scents and your spirits, but you must help me in this by restraint from sins and by hard work. You must take notice that what is with Allah can only be achieved by hard work and restraint from sin. Whoever of you follows a servant of Allah, he must act as he (the leader) does. O yes, by Allah, you follow my religion and the religion of my ancestors, Ibrahim and 'Isma'il. If those people follow those people's religion you must help me in it (your religion) by restraint from sins and hard work.'"

When al-Qa'im (the one who rises with divine authority and power), *'Alayhi al-Salam*, will Rise. . .

H 14777, h 329

Abu Ali al-Ash'ariy has narrated from al-Hassan ibn Ali al-Kufiy from al-'Abbas ibn 'Amir from Rabi' ibn Muhammad al-Musliy from abu al-Rabi' al-Shamiy who has narrated the following:

"I once heard abu 'Abd Allah, *'Alayhi al-Salam*, say, 'When our al-Qa'im (the one who rises with divine authority and power) will rise, Allah will extend the hearing and seeing (powers) of our Shi'ah, thus, they will not need a postal system. He will speak to them and they will hear him and look at him (the Imam) when he is in his place.'"

One who seeks advice from Allah . . .

H 14778, h 330

A number of our people have narrated from Sahl ibn Ziyad from 'Uthman ibn 'Isa from Harun ibn Kharijah who has narrated the following:

"Abu 'Abd Allah, *'Alayhi al-Salam*, has said, 'If one asks Allah to choose for him what is good and agrees with what Allah has done for him, Allah inevitably chooses for him what is good.'"

Words of 'Amir al-Mu'minin, *'Alayhi al-Salam*, to Juwayrah

H 14779, h 331

Sahl ibn Ziyad has narrated from Dawud ibn Mehran from Ali ibn 'Isma'il al-Mithamiy from a man from Juwayriyah ibn Mushar who has narrated the following:

"Once I ran after 'Amir al-Mu'minin, Ali, *'Alayhi al-Salam*, and he said, 'O Juwayriah, the dimwitted ones are destroyed only because of the shoes running behind them. What has brought you here?' I replied, 'I have come to ask you about three things: nobility and high rank, kindheartedness and reason (power of understanding).' He (the Imam) said, 'Nobility and rank is what high authority provides, kindheartedness is establishing a means of living, and reason is to remain pious before Allah.'"

Why the sun is hotter than the moon

H 14780, h 332

Sahl ibn Ziyad has narrated from Ali ibn Hassan from Ali ibn abu al-Nawar from Muhammad ibn Muslim who has narrated the following:

"I once asked abu Ja'far, *'Alayhi al-Salam*, saying, 'I pray to Allah to keep my soul in service for your cause, why the sun has more heat than the moon does?' He (the Imam) said, 'Allah has created the sun from the light of fire and purity of water, one layer of this and one layer of that up to seven layers, then He dressed it with the dress of fire. For this reason it is hotter than the moon.' I then asked I pray to Allah to keep my soul in service for your cause, what about the moon?' He (the Imam) said, 'Allah, most Blessed, most High, created the moon from the brightness of the light of the fire and purity of water, one layer of this and one layer of that up to seven layers, then He dressed it with a dress of water: thus it is cooler than the sun.'" (Wording is in general terms according to today's perceptions)

With established truth one does not live in doubts

H 14781, h 333

A number of our people have narrated from Ahmad ibn Muhammad ibn Khalid from certain persons of our people from Muhammad ibn al-Haytham from Zayd abu al-Hassan who has narrated the following:

"I once heard abu 'Abd Allah, *'Alayhi al-Salam*, say, 'One who has an established reality does not stay with heaped up doubts. He does not stop until he knows the end goal, seeks to learn about newly emerging issues from the one who speaks for the owner of the legacy. You must find out what it is that you are ignorant of and what it is that you have denied and by what means (*'A'immah*) you recognized what you understood if you are of the believing people.'"

Truth defeats falsehood

H 14782, h 334

It is narrated from the narrator of the previous Hadith from his father from Yunus ibn Ibrahim in a marfu' manner who has narrated the following:

"Abu 'Abd Allah, *'Alayhi al-Salam*, has said, 'No falsehood is able to face the truth without being defeated, and it is because of the words of Allah, most Majestic, most Glorious, '. . . in fact We throw the truth on falsehood and it invalidates the falsehood which is to vanish.'" (21:18)

All relation except what al-Quran has approved is heresy

H 14783, h 335

It is narrated from the narrator of the previous Hadith from his father in a mursal manner who has narrated the following:

"Abu Ja'far, *'Alayhi al-Salam*, has said this: 'You must not accept anyone as your confidant other than Allah, otherwise, you will not remain a believing person. All means, ancestral links, nearness of relatives, confidants, heresy and doubts will cut off and vanish like dust settled on a smooth rock that easily washes away by a pouring rainfall, except what al-Quran has established.'"

'A'immah are the source of all goodness

H 14784, h 336

Ali ibn Muhammad ibn 'Abd Allah has narrated from Ibrahim ibn Ishaq from 'Abd Allah ibn Hammad from ibn Muskan who has narrated the following:

"Abu 'Abd Allah, *'Alayhi al-Salam*, has said, 'We are the origin of all goodness and from our branches are all virtuous matters. Belief in the Oneness of Allah is a virtuous matter. Performing *Salat* (prayer) is a virtuous matter as well as fasting, holding back one's anger, and forgiving someone's bad deeds. Kindness to poor ones is a virtuous matter and so are maintaining good relations with the neighbors and to acknowledge the excellence of virtuous people. Our enemies are the origin of all evil and of their branches are all indecent and loathsome acts. Of such matters are speaking lies, stinginess, tale bearing, cutting off of good relations with relatives, consuming unlawful interests and the assets of orphans without any right and transgressing against the limits (laws) of Allah, engaging in indecent acts, the apparent and hidden ones, committing fornication, theft and other matters of equally hideous nature. If one calls himself of our followers but is attached to the branches of our enemies, he has spoken a lie.'"

The virtuous plan of living

H 14785, h 337

It is narrated from the narrator of the previous Hadith and others and from Ahmad ibn Muhammad ibn Khalid from 'Uthman ibn 'Isa ibn Najih who has narrated the following:

"Abu 'Abd Allah, *'Alayhi al-Salam*, once said to a man, 'You must remain content with what Allah has granted to you, do not look to what others have, and do not wish for what you cannot achieve. Those who remain content are satisfied, and those who do not remain content do not feel satisfied. You must achieve your share of the next life.' Abu 'Abd Allah, *'Alayhi al-Salam*, has said, 'The most beneficial among things for a man is his finding his own faults before everything else, and the most expensive matter is hiding poverty, the least beneficial matter is advice to one who does not accept and association with a greedy person. The most comforting matter is cutting off of hope from people.' He (the Imam) said, 'You must not behave as exasperated and ill-mannered, you must humble your soul by bearing with those who oppose you, who are above you, and who are more excellent than you. You must acknowledge his excellence so you do not oppose him. If one does not acknowledge others excellence, he is conceited by his own opinion.' He (the Imam) said to a man, 'You must take notice that there is no honor for one who is not humble before Allah, most Blessed, most High, and there is not a high rank for one who does not express humility before Allah, most Majestic, most Glorious.' He (the Imam) said to a man, 'You must firmly establish the affairs of your hereafter as the worldly people firmly establish their worldly matters. The world is designed as testimony for recognizing thereby the unseen of the matters of the hereafter. So you must recognize the hereafter thereby and you must not look at the world for any reason other than to learn a lesson thereby.'"

Advantageous advice

H 14786, h 338

A number of our people have narrated from Sahl ibn Ziyad and Ali ibn Ibrahim has narrated from his father all from ibn Mahbub from Hisham ibn Salim who has narrated the following:

"I once heard abu 'Abd Allah, *'Alayhi al-Salam*, say this to Humran ibn 'Ayan. 'O Humran, you must look at those who are lower than you in (financially) capabilities, and you must not look to those above you in (such) capabilities. It is of greater contentment for you with your designated share and makes you more deserving to receive more favors from your Lord. You must take notice that working less but all the time with certainty is better in the sight of Allah, most Majestic, most Glorious, than a great deal of work without certainty. You must take notice that no form of restraint from sin is more beneficial than keeping away from what Allah has made unlawful, restraint from harming the believing people and back-biting them. No life is more pleasant than living with excellent moral manners and no asset is more beneficial than contentment with a less but sufficient amount and no ignorance is more harmful than conceit.'"

People are similar to people and al-Nasnas

H 14787, h 339

Ibn Mahbub has narrated from 'Abd Allah ibn Ghalib from his father from Sa'id ibn al-Musayyib who has narrated the following:

"I once heard Ali ibn al-Husayn, *'Alayhi al-Salam*, say, 'A man came to 'Amir al-Mu'minin, Ali, *'Alayhi al-Salam*, and asked, "Tell me, if you know, about people, those who are like people and about al-Nasnas." 'Amir al-Mu'minin, Ali, *'Alayhi al-Salam*, said, "O al-Husayn, answer the man." Al-Husayn, *'Alayhi al-Salam*, said this: "The answer to your words 'Tell me about people' is that we are the people according to the words of Allah, most Blessed, most High, in His book. ". . . then leave as 'the people leave,'" (2:199) the Messenger of Allah, *O Allah grant compensation to Muhammad and his family worthy of their services to Your cause*, left with the people. The answer to your words 'those who are like people' is that such people are our Shi'ah. They are our *mawaliy*. They are from us according to what Ibrahim *'Alayhi al-Salam*, has said, '. . . those who follow me are from me.' (14:36). The answer to your words 'al-Nasanas' is that they are al-Sawad al-'A'zam (the great crowd)" he made a hand gesture to people then said, ". . . they are nothing but cattle, in fact, worse because of falling in misguidance."'" (25:44)

The question of Sadir from Abu Ja'far, *'Alayhi al-Salam*

H 14788, h 340
Ali ibn Ibrahim has narrated from his father from Hanan ibn Sadir Ahmad ibn Muhammad from Muhammad ibn Yahya has narrated from Ahmad ibn Muhammad from 'Isma'il ibn Hanan from Hanan ibn Sadir from his father who has narrated the following:

"I once asked abu Ja'far, *'Alayhi al-Salam*, about the two of them. He (the Imam) said, 'O abu al-Fadl, do not ask me about them. By Allah, no one of us has died without resentment toward them and every one of us today resents them. Our grown up ones make a will for the smaller ones about it. They usurped our right and denied our share of the gains. They were the two who imposed their control on us and impaired Islam so much that it can never be repaired until al-Qa'im will reappear with divine authority and power and our speaker will speak.' He (the Imam) then said, 'O yes, by Allah, when al-Qa'im will reappear with divine authority and power and our speaker will speak, their affairs that they had hidden will be disclosed and what they showed will vanish. By Allah, whatever suffering and trouble that we, *Ahl al-Bayt* face is because of the foundation that they had established, thus, may the condemnation of Allah, the condemnation the angels and all people fall up on them!'"

People after the Holy Prophet, turned to heresy except three people

H 14789, h 341
Hanan has narrated from his father who has narrated the following:

"Abu Ja'far, *'Alayhi al-Salam*, has said, 'People after the Holy Prophet, turned back except three.' I then asked, 'Who were the three?' He (the Imam) said, 'They were, al-Miqdad ibn al-Aswad, abu Dharr al-Ghifariy and Salman al-Farisiy, may Allah grant them mercy and blessings. After a short while few people recognized.' He (the Imam) said, 'These were the corner stones and they did not vote until 'Amir al-Mu'minin, Ali, *'Alayhi al-Salam*, was brought by force to vote. This is mentioned in the words of Allah, most High, '. . . Muhammad is only the messenger before whom the messengers lived. If he dies or is killed will you then turn backwards? If you turn backwards, it can never harm Allah in anything save that Allah will soon grant good reward to those who are thankful.'" (3:144)

Words of the Holy Prophet, on the day of Victory

H 14790, h 342
Hanan has narrated from his father who has narrated the following:

"Abu Ja'far, *'Alayhi al-Salam*, has said this: 'The Messenger of Allah, *O Allah grant compensation to Muhammad and his family worthy of their services to Your cause*, on the day of the conquest of Makkah climbed on the pulpit to speak. He said, "O people, Allah has removed from you the haughtiness of the time of ignorance and boasting about the ancestors. O yes, by Allah, you are from Adam, *'Alayhi al-Salam*, and Adam is from clay. By Allah, the best of the servants of Allah is one who remains pious before Him. Arabic is not a father; it is a speaking tongue. One who is short in deeds, his ancestor cannot take him anywhere. O yes, by Allah, if a blood was spilled in the time of ignorance or a feud existed – feud is enmity – it now is under my foot until the Day of Judgment.'"

Repentance of the children of Ya'qub, *'Alayhi al-Salam*

H 14791, h 343
Hanan has narrated from his father who has narrated the following:

"I once asked abu Ja'far, *'Alayhi al-Salam*, about the children of Ya'qub, *'Alayhi al-Salam*, if they were Prophets. He (the Imam) said, 'No, they were not Prophets but they were grandsons of the children of Prophets who did not pass away without repentance and remembering what they had done; and the two old men (shaykhayn) passed away without repenting or remembering what they had done to 'Amir al-Mu'minin, Ali, *'Alayhi al-Salam*. May Allah, angels and all people condemn them.'"

Prayer of Sulayman, *'Alayhi al-Salam,* for rain

H 14792, h 344
Hanan has narrated from abu al-Khattab Ahmad ibn Muhammad from the virtuous servant of Allah, *'Alayhi al-Salam*, who has narrated the following:

"The virtuous servant of Allah has said that in the time of Sulayman people faced a severe famine. They complained before him and asked him to pray for rain. He (the Imam) said that Sulayman said to them, 'When I will perform the morning *Salat* (prayer), I will come with you.' When he performed the morning *Salat* (prayer) he went and they went with him. On the way he came across an ant with its hands raised to the sky and the two legs on the ground; it said, 'O Lord, I am a creature of your creatures and we cannot live without sustenance from You, so do not destroy us because of the sins of the children of Adam, *'Alayhi al-Salam*.' Sulayman said to his people, 'You must return to your homes; you will have water because of the others.' He (the Imam) said, 'That year they had so much water the like of which they had never seen before.'"

Allah has people of good fortune and the wicked ones

H 14793, h 345
A number of our people have narrated from Sahl ibn Ziyad from Musa ibn Ja'far from 'Amr ibn Sa'id from Khalaf ibn 'Isa from abu 'Ubayd al-Mada'iniy who has narrated the following:

"Abu Ja'far, *'Alayhi al-Salam*, has said, 'Allah, most High, has such servants who are blissful and affluent. They live and people live in their shelter and they are like rainfall. Allah, most Majestic, most Glorious, has other kinds of servants who are condemned and detested. They live badly and people cannot live in their shelter. They are like locusts that on falling upon things destroy them all together.'"

Signature of Ali al-Rida', 'Alayhim al-Salam, for Fadl ibn Shadhan

H 14794, h 346

Al-Husayn from Muhammad and Muhammad ibn Yahya all have narrated from Muhammad ibn Salim ibn abu Salmah from al-Hassan ibn Shadhan al-Wasitiy who has narrated the following:

"I once wrote to abu al-Hassan al-Rida', 'Alayhi al-Salam, and complained against the cruelty of the people of al-Wasit and their attacks on me. There was an 'Uthmaniy group who tried to cause troubles for me. He (the Imam) wrote the answer in his own handwriting, 'Allah, most Blessed, most High, has made a covenant with His friends to bear patience in the government of falsehood. Therefore, you must bear patience with the decree of your Lord. When the master of the creatures (al-Qa'im (the one who rises with divine authority and power)) will rise, they will say, "Woe is on us! Who has moved us from our sleeping place (the grave)? This is what the Beneficent had warned about and the messengers have been proved truthful.'" (36:51)

Excellence of knowing about Allah

H 14795, h 347

Muhammad ibn Salim ibn abu Salmah has narrated from Ahmad ibn al-Rayyan from his Jamil ibn Darraj who has narrated the following:

"Abu 'Abd Allah, 'Alayhi al-Salam, has said, 'If people had known the excellence of recognizing Allah, most Majestic, most Glorious, they would not extend their eyes to what He has granted to His enemies of the blossoms of the worldly life and its bounties. The world would seem less important than what they walk on. Instead, they would enjoy their recognizing Allah, most Majestic, most Glorious, in happiness like the happiness of those who live forever in the garden (paradise) with the friends of Allah. Recognizing Allah, most Majestic, most Glorious, provides comfort in all frightening conditions, good company in all times of loneliness, light for all kinds of darkness, strength in all kinds of weakness and cure for all kinds of illness.' He (the Imam) then said, 'Before you there lived people who were killed, burned, cut in pieces with a saw, the earth narrowed down on them and grew tight despite its vastness; but all such hardships could not turn them away from their belief or frighten them or make them express impatience because of the suffering brought on them. They caused them such exasperating conditions for no reason other than their belief in Allah, most Majestic, most Praiseworthy. You must pray to your Lord to grant you such ranks as their ranks and bear patience in the hardships of the eons, so that you can achieve what they had achieved.'"

About the creation of flies

H 14796, h 348

Muhammad ibn Yahya has narrated from Ahmad ibn Muhammad ibn 'Isa from Sa'id ibn Junah from certain persons of our people who has narrated the following:

"Abu 'Abd Allah, *'Alayhi al-Salam*, has said, 'Allah, most Majestic, most Glorious, has not created anything smaller than a gnat. There is a bug called al-Jirjis which is smaller than gnat and what we call al-Wala' is smaller than al-Jirjis. It has everything that an elephant has but it surpassed the elephant by two wings.'"

About the meaning of the words of Allah 'O believers you must answer Allah'

H 14797, h 349

Muhammad ibn Yahya has narrated from Ahmad ibn Muhammad ibn 'Isa from Muhammad ibn Khalid and al-Husayn ibn Sa'id all from al-Nadr ibn Suwayd from Yahya al-Halabiy from 'Abd Allah ibn Muskan from Zayd ibn al-Walid al-Khath'amiy from abu al-Rabi' al-Shamiy who has narrated the following:

"I once asked abu 'Abd Allah, *'Alayhi al-Salam*, about the meaning of the words of Allah, most Majestic, most Glorious, '. . . O believing people, answer the call of Allah and the messenger when He calls you to an issue that provides you life.' (8:24) He (the Imam) said, 'It was revealed about *Wilayah* (divine authority and knowledge) of Ali, *'Alayhi al-Salam*.' I then asked about the meaning of the words of Allah, '. . . no leaf falls off but that He knows it or a grain that is in the dark parts of the earth and there is no wet or dry thing but that it is in the clear book.' (6:59) He (the Imam) said, 'The 'leaf' stands for a miscarried child, 'grain' stands for a child, 'dark parts of the earth' stands for the womb, 'wet' stands for the people who live and 'dry' stands for the people who die and all of it is in the clear Imam.' I then asked him (the Imam) about the meaning of the words of Allah, most Majestic, most Glorious, '. . . say to them to travel in the land and see how was the end and consequences of those who lived before you.' (30:42) He (the Imam) said, 'It means that you must look in al-Quran to learn how the end of those who lived before was and the report which is provided for you.' I then asked about the meaning of the words of Allah, '. . . you can pass by them in the morning and in the night. Why do you then not consider?' (37:137-138) He (the Imam) said, 'You pass by them (their stories) in al-Quran. You must read what Allah, most Majestic, most Glorious, has stated about them as their news.'"

You must hold to the original . . .

H 14798, h 350

It is narrated from the narrator of the previous Hadith from ibn Muskan from a man from the people of mountain whose name he has not mentioned who has narrated the following:

"Abu 'Abd Allah, *'Alayhi al-Salam*, has said, 'You must take hold of the original and be on your guard against the newly invented matters which have no covenant, trust, responsibility and agreement. Be on your guard against the people whom you trust the most about yourself because people are the enemies of bounties.'"

Leaving a dead body with something heavy in water

H 14799, h 351

Yahya al-Halabiy has narrated from abu al-Mustahal from Sulayman ibn Khalid who has narrated the following:

"Abu 'Abd Allah, *'Alayhi al-Salam*, once asked me, 'What made you to place the body of Zayd where you did?' I replied, 'It was because of three things; one was because very few people were left with us. We were eight people only. The other thing was that we were afraid of the coming of dawn when it exposed us. The third thing was that it was his resting place (by his choice or fate).' He (the Imam) asked, 'How far from the Euphrates was the place where you placed him?' I replied, 'It was a distance of throwing a stone.' He (the Imam) then said, '*Tasbih* (Allah is free of all defects), I wish you had tied something heavy to him, then thrown him into the Euphrates. It would have been better.' I then said, 'I pray to Allah to keep my soul in service for your cause, we could not have done it.' He (the Imam) asked, 'What was your belief the day you went to fight for Zayd?' I replied, 'We were the believing people.' He then asked, 'Who was your enemy?' I replied, 'They were unbelievers.' He (the Imam) said, 'I find in the book of Allah, most Majestic, most Glorious, ". . . O believing people, when you come face to face in fighting with the unbelievers, the necks must be struck down until they are weakened, then it is to tie down firmly to grant favors or for ransom until the war lays down its burden.' (47:4) You, however, first evacuated your captives. *Tasbih* (Allah is free of all defects); you could not walk with justice - not even for one hour.'"

The Holy Prophet, *'Alayhi al-Salam,* did not face what the other Holy Prophets, *'Alayhim al-Salam,* faced

H 14800, h 352

Yahya al-Halabiy has narrated from Harun ibn Kharijah from abu Basir who has narrated the following:

"Abu 'Abd Allah, *'Alayhi al-Salam*, has said that Allah, most Majestic, most Glorious, exempted your Prophet from facing such hardships from his followers like those which other Prophets faced because of their followers, but He placed it on us.'"

Were those who fought the Holy Prophet worse or those who fought 'Amir al-Mu'minin

H 14801, h 353

Yahya has narrated from 'Abd Allah ibn Muskan from Durays who has narrated the following:

"Once, people argued before abu Ja'far, *'Alayhi al-Salam*. Certain ones said, 'The war which Ali, *'Alayhi al-Salam*, fought was against a kind of people more evil than those against whom the Messenger of Allah, *O Allah grant compensation to Muhammad and his family worthy of their services to Your cause*, fought. Others said that the wars that the Messenger of Allah, *O Allah grant compensation to Muhammad and his family worthy of their services to Your cause*, fought were against a kind of people more evil than those against whom Ali, *'Alayhi al-Salam*, fought. Abu Ja'far, *'Alayhi al-Salam*, heard them and asked, 'What are you saying?' They replied, 'We pray to Allah to keep you well, we argued about the wars that the Messenger of Allah, *O Allah grant compensation to Muhammad and his family worthy of their services to Your cause*, fought and the wars that Ali, *'Alayhi al-Salam*, fought. Certain ones among us said that the kind of people who fought against Ali were more evil and others said that the kind of people who fought the Messenger of Allah, *O Allah grant compensation to Muhammad and his family worthy of their services to Your cause*, were more evil.' Abu Ja'far, *'Alayhi al-Salam*, then said, 'No, the war of Ali, *'Alayhi al-Salam*, was against the kind of people who were more evil.' I then asked, 'I pray to Allah to keep my soul in service for your cause, is the war of Ali, *'Alayhi al-Salam*, against the kind of people more evil than the war of the Messenger of Allah, *O Allah grant compensation to Muhammad and his family worthy of their services to Your cause*?' He (the Imam) said, 'Yes, and I will inform you about it. The enemies of the Messenger of Allah, *O Allah grant compensation to Muhammad and his family worthy of their services to Your cause*, were those who had not acknowledged Islam, and those who fought against Ali, *'Alayhi al-Salam*, acknowledged Islam, then rejected it.'"

About the words of Allah 'We gave him his wife . . .'

H 14802, h 354

Yahya ibn 'Imran has narrated from Harun ibn Kharijah from abu Basir who has narrated the following:

"About the meaning of the words of Allah, most Majestic, most Glorious, '. . . We brought back to life his family and likewise with them.' (21:84) I asked abu 'Abd Allah, *'Alayhi al-Salam*, 'His children were brought back to life; how can it be likewise their number?' He (the Imam) said, 'He brought back to life his children who had died before because of their natural death also, and they were of likewise number as those who had died on that day.'"

About the words of Allah 'Their faces will become dark...'

H 14803, h 355

Yahya al-Halabiy has narrated from al-Muthanna from abu Basir who has narrated the following:

"About the meaning of the words of Allah, most Majestic, most Glorious, '. . . Their faces will become dark as if covered by the pitch-black darkness of night.' (10:27) Abu 'Abd Allah, *'Alayhi al-Salam*, has said, 'Inside the house during the night is darker than the outside; and that is how their darkness is more darkness.'"

The conquest after the Messenger of Allah, *'Alayhi al-Salam*

H 14804, h 356

Al-Husayn Muhammad has narrated from Mu'alla' ibn Muhammad from al-Washsha' from Aban ibn 'Uthman from al-Harith ibn al-Mughirah who has narrated the following:

"I heard 'Abd al-Malik ibn 'A'yan asking abu 'Abd Allah, *'Alayhi al-Salam*, and continued asking until he said, 'People then are destroyed.' He said, 'Yes, by Allah, O ibn 'A'yan all people are destroyed.' I then asked, 'All those in the east and all in the west?' He (the Imam) said, 'It is because they were opened (conquered) through misguidance, yes, by Allah, they were destroyed except three.'" (Three is a reference, according to footnote, to al-Miqdad, abu Dharr and Salman.)

A servant of Allah does not deserve faith without three qualities

H 14805, h 357

Muhammad ibn Yahya has narrated from Muhammad ibn al-Husayn, from Ishaq ibn Yazid from Mehran, from Aban ibn Taghlib and 'Iddah who have said the following:

"Once we were sitting with abu 'Abd Allah, *'Alayhi al-Salam*, and he (the Imam) said, 'A servant does not deserve to have the reality of belief until he loves death more than his loving the worldly life, illness more than good health, poverty more than richness. Are you as such?' They replied, 'No, by Allah, we pray to Allah to keep our souls in service for your cause.' They all sensed failure, and despair filled their hearts. When he (the Imam) observed their condition he asked, 'Will any of you agree to live as long as he lives and then die with a belief other than this belief (religion of *Ahl al-Bayt*) or likes to die with this belief?' They said, 'It is to die with this belief (religion of *Ahl al-Bayt*) which we have at this hour.' He (the Imam) said, 'If that is the case, then I see that you love death more than life.' He (the Imam) then said, 'Will anyone of you like to live as long as he will live without any illness and pain until his death with a belief other than this *'Amr* (religion of *Ahl al-Bayt*)?' They replied, 'No, O child of the Messenger of Allah.' He (the Imam) then said, 'If that is the case, then I see that you like illness more than you like good health.' He (the Imam) then said, 'Will anyone of you like to have everything on which the sun shines but he has a belief other than this belief (religion of *Ahl al-Bayt*)?' They replied, 'No, O child of the Messenger of Allah.' He (the Imam) then said, 'If that is the case, then I see that you love poverty more than being rich.'"

If one loves someone he must act like him

H 14806, h 358

Muhammad ibn Yahya has narrated from Ahmad ibn Muhammad from al-Hassan ibn Ali from Hammad al-Lahham who has narrated the following:

"Abu 'Abd Allah, *'Alayhi al-Salam*, has said that his father, *'Alayhi al-Salam*, said to him, 'Son, if you oppose me in deeds you will not be with me tomorrow in the dwelling.' He (the Imam) then said, 'Allah, most Majestic, most Glorious, refuses to make friendship between two people, who oppose each other in their deeds, and bring them all in the same dwelling on the Day of Judgment. No, by the Lord of al-Ka'bah, this will not happen.'"

There is no guidance without *'A'immah*

H 14807, h 359

Al-Husayn from Muhammad al-Ash'ariy has narrated from Mu'alla' ibn Muhammad from al-Washsha' from Muhammad ibn al-Fudayl from abu Hamzah who has narrated the following:

"I once heard abu Ja'far, *'Alayhi al-Salam*, say, 'No one of this nation follows the religion of Ibrahim *'Alayhi al-Salam*, except we and our Shi'ah. No one of this nation who found guidance has found it through any other source except us and no one who is misled is misled except because of (hostility toward) us.'"

Allah is gracious, He does not punish for what is not in one's control

H 14808, h 360

Ali ibn Ibrahim has narrated from his father from ibn abu 'Umayr from Ali ibn 'Atiyyah who has narrated the following:

"I once was with abu 'Abd Allah, *'Alayhi al-Salam*, when a man asked him (the Imam) about a man who does something because of anger and yet will Allah hold him responsible? He (the Imam) said, 'Allah possesses the entire honor, thus He does not tie down His servant (because of something which is beyond his control).' In the copy of this Hadith from abu al-Hassan, al-Awwal, *'Alayhi al-Salam*, it is said, 'Allah does not cause to restlessness to His servant.'"

Before the Messenger of Allah deeds of his followers are presented

H 14809, h 361

Ali has narrated from his father from ibn abu 'Umayr from Muhammad ibn abu Hamzah and from more than one person who has narrated the following:

"Abu 'Abd Allah, *'Alayhi al-Salam*, has said that the Messenger of Allah, *O Allah grant compensation to Muhammad and his family worthy of their services to Your cause*, has said, 'In my life there is good for you and in my death there is good for you.' He (the Imam) then said that people asked, 'We know about your life, O Messenger of Allah, but what is for us in your death?' He (the Messenger of Allah) said, 'About what is in my life Allah, most Majestic, most Glorious, has said, ". . . Allah would not to punish them when you are among them . . ." (8:33) and what is in my death for you is that your deeds will be presented before me and I will ask forgiveness for you.'"

Claim to be the Imam without qualification

H 14810, h 362

Ali ibn Ibrahim has narrated from his father from ibn abu 'Umayr from Hisham ibn Salim who has narrated the following:

"Abu 'Abd Allah, *'Alayhi al-Salam*, has said, 'Whoever claims that he possesses this *'Amr* (*Wilayah*, divine authority and knowledge) must be rejected; it is such a lie that even Satan needs it (such a lie)."

Ali ibn al-Husayn's visiting his Father, *'Alayhima al-Salam*

H 14811, h 363

Ali ibn Muhammad has narrated from Salih ibn abu Hammad from Ali ibn al-Hakam from Malik ibn 'Atiyyah from abu Hamzah who has narrated the following:

"The first time that I came to know Ali ibn al-Husayn, *'Alayhim al-Salam*, was when I saw a man came through the Bab al-Fil. He then performed four Rak'at *Salat* (prayer). I followed him until he came to the well of *Zakat*, which is near the house of Salih ibn Ali where two she-camels were secured and there was a black slave with the she-camels. I asked, 'Who is this man?' He replied, 'He is Ali ibn al-Husayn, *'Alayhim al-Salam*.' I went close, offered greeting of peace, and said, 'What brings you to the town where your father and grandfather were killed?' He replied, 'I visited my father and performed *Salat* (prayer) in this Masjid. There is the direction of my journey (toward al-Madinah).' O Allah grant compensation to him (the Imam) worthy of his services to your cause."

About the words of Allah 'those who are killed unjustly'

H 14812, h 364

It is narrated from the narrator of the previous Hadith from Salih from al-Hajjal from certain persons of his people who has narrated the following:

"I once asked abu 'Abd Allah, *'Alayhi al-Salam*, about the meaning of the words of Allah, most Majestic, most Glorious, '. . . for one who is killed unjustly We have made an authority for his guardian, so killing (the murderer) is not excessive.' (17:33) He (the Imam) said, 'It is about al-Husayn, *'Alayhi al-Salam*. If the entire inhabitants of the earth (who take part in or condone his murder) are killed for him it is not excessive.'"

The reason for earthquakes

H 14813, h 365

It is narrated from the narrator of the previous Hadith from Salih from certain persons of his people from 'Abd al-Samad ibn Bashir who has narrated the following:

"Abu 'Abd Allah, *'Alayhi al-Salam*, has said, 'The fish that carries the earth once whispered to itself (in pride) that it is carrying the earth by its power. Allah, most Blessed, most High, sent a fish, smaller than the length of the distance between the tips of the thumb to the tip of small finger and bigger than the distance between the tips of the thumb to the tip of the index finger when stretched open, which entered in its gale. It fainted and remained in that condition for forty mornings. Allah, most Majestic, most Glorious, due to His compassion and mercy took it out. When Allah, most Majestic, most Glorious, wants an earthquake to take place He sends that fish to that fish and when it sees it, it trembles and an earthquake takes place.'"

(One aspect of the above Hadith reminds that a tremendous event like an earthquake is because of the will and knowledge of Allah)

Restlessness of the Earth and the gesture of 'Amir al-Mu'minin, *'Alayhi al-Salam*

H 14814, h 366

It is narrated from the narrator of the previous Hadith from Salih from Muhammad ibn Sinan from ibn Muskan from abu Bakr al-Hadramiy from Tamim ibn Hatim who has narrated the following:

"Once we were with 'Amir al-Mu'minin, Ali, *'Alayhi al-Salam*, that an earthquake took place. He (the Imam) made a hand gesture and said, 'Calm down. What is the matter with you?' He (the Imam) then turned to us and said, 'Had it been that quake about which Allah, most Majestic, most Glorious, has informed us (in al-Quran Chapter 99) it would answer me but it was not that quake.'"

The garden (paradise) is for those who love Shi'ah

H 14815, h 367

Abu Ali al-Ash'ariy has narrated from Muhammad ibn 'Abd al-Jabbar from Safwan ibn Yahya from abu al-Yasa' from abu Shabal who has narrated the following:

"Safwan has said, 'I do not know except that I heard it from abu Shibl, saying that Abu 'Abd Allah, *'Alayhi al-Salam*, has said, 'One who loves what you believe in he enters the garden (paradise) even if he does not say what you say.'"

Sermon of 'Amir al-Mu'minin, *'Alayhi al-Salam*

H 14816, h 368

Muhammad ibn Yahya has narrated from Ahmad ibn Muhammad ibn 'Isa from al-Hassan ibn Mahbub from Muhammad ibn al-Nu'man abu Ja'far al-Ahwal from Salam al-Mustanir who has narrated the following:

"Abu Ja'far, *'Alayhi al-Salam*, has said that after the story between 'Amir al-Mu'minin, Ali, *'Alayhi al-Salam*, Talhah, al-Zubayr and 'A'ishah ended in al-Basrah, he (the Imam) climbed on the pulpit. He (the Imam) praised Allah, spoke of His glory and prayed for the Messenger of Allah, *O Allah grant compensation to Muhammad and his family worthy of their services to Your cause*, then said, 'O people, the world is green and sweet-looking. It lures people with lust, desires, and beautifies itself for them with the immediate matters. By Allah, it deceives those who establish hope in it and betrays those who maintain expectations about it. Certain people will receive the worldly legacy, which is nothing other than regret and sorrow. They advance toward it, competing with others to gain it, and express jealousy, transgression against religious people and people of excellence. It is injustice in animosity and aggression with happiness (to themselves) but not for much gain. By Allah, there is no nation that lived in the thickness of honor and the bounties of Allah in the worldly life, continued piety, obedience to Allah and appreciated the bounties of Allah, their condition as such never changed suddenly except after they changed themselves. They deviated from obedience to Allah, committed sinful deeds, lacked conservitism, neglected vigilance toward Allah, most Majestic, most Glorious, and took their thanksgiving for the bounties of Allah lightly. Allah, most Majestic, most Glorious, says in His book, ". . . Allah does not change the condition of a people unless they change what is in their souls. When Allah decides to afflict a people with suffering then there is no escape there-from and there is no one other than Allah as their guardian." (13:11) If disobedient people, who accumulate sins, remain cautious against the vanishing of the bounties of Allah, the coming of the wrath of Allah, the changing of good health that He has provided, were to become certain that it is from Allah, most Majestic, most Glorious, because of what their hands have gained, it would help them. Thus, they change and repent, plead before Allah, most Majestic, most Glorious, with sincerity of their intentions and acknowledge that they have sinned. They confess that their deeds are evil. He will ignore them in the matters of all of their sins, reduce their penalties for all of their slips and return to them the entire honor and bounties. Then He will reform their affairs about whatever He had granted to them and that, which is destroyed and spoiled with them. You, O people, must remain pious before Allah, in the true sense, realize fear of Allah, most Majestic, most Glorious, and make your certainty (of belief) pure. Repent and return to Him from the evil deeds that Satan had enticed you to commit in the form of fighting *Waliy* of your *'Amr* (people who possess divine authority and knowledge), people of knowledge after the Messenger of Allah, *O Allah grant compensation to Muhammad and his family worthy of their services to Your cause.* You must repent and express regret in matters of cooperations that you offered to cause differences, scatter the affairs and destroy the issues of peace among people. Allah, most Majestic, most Glorious, accepts repentance, forgives sins and knows what you do.'"

The star of 'Amir al-Mu'minin, *'Alayhi al-Salam*

H 14817, h 369

A number of our people have narrated from Sahl ibn Ziyad from al-Hassan ibn Ali ibn 'Uthman who has narrated the following:

"Abu 'Abd Allah, al-Mada'iniy narrated to me from abu 'Abd Allah, *'Alayhi al-Salam*, who has said that Allah, most Majestic, most Glorious, created a star in the seventh al-Falak (planetary group, system). He created it of cold water. The other six stars, which are moving are made from hot water. That is the star of the Prophets and the executor of the will, the star of 'Amir al-Mu'minin, Ali, *'Alayhi al-Salam*, which commands to move out of the world, exercise restraint from sins, commands to use the soil as furnishings, bricks as the pillow, use rough textured clothes and to eat tasteless food. Allah has not created any other star closer to Allah, most High, than that star.'"

Interpretation of certain dreams

H 14818, h 370

Al-Husayn ibn Ahmad ibn Hilal has narrated from Yasar al-Khadim who has narrated the following:

"I once said to abu al-Hassan al-Rida', *'Alayhi al-Salam*, 'I saw in my dream a cage with seventeen bottles in it. The cage suddenly fell and all the bottles broke.' He (the Imam) said, 'If your dream comes true, a man from my family will rise for power and will achieve domination for seventeen days, then he will die.' Muhammad ibn Ibrahim rose in al-Kufah with abu al-Saraya and stayed for seventeen days, then died.'"

Imam al-Rida', *'Alayhi al-Salam*, proclaims himself as Imam

H 14819, h 371
It is narrated from the narrator of the previous Hadith from Ahmad ibn Hilal Muhammad ibn Sinan who has narrated the following:

"I once said to abu al-Hassan al-Rida', *'Alayhi al-Salam*, in the days of Harun, 'You have proclaimed yourself *Waliy* of *'Amr* (guardian with divine authority and knowledge) by sitting on the seat of your father when the sword of Harun drips blood.' He (the Imam) said, 'The words of the Messenger of Allah, *O Allah grant compensation to Muhammad and his family worthy of their services to Your cause*, have made me so daring which he said, 'If abu Jahl can take one hair from my head then you must testify that I am not a Prophet.' I say to you that if Harun can take one hair from my head, then you must testify that I am not an Imam.'"

The story of the slave-girl of Zubayr

H 14820, h 372
It is narrated from the narrator of the previous Hadith from Ahmad from Zur'ah from Sama'ah who has narrated the following:

"Once a man from children of 'Umar al-Khattab tried to molest the girl of a man from the family of 'Aqil; and she said, 'This 'Umariy troubled me.' He then said to her to promise him and make him enter the corridor. She did so. He came down hard, killed him and threw his body on the road. The Bakries, 'Umaries and 'Uthmanies gathered and said, 'There is no match for our man. We will kill no one for him other than Ja'far ibn Muhammad. No one else has killed our man.'

"Abu 'Abd Allah, *'Alayhi al-Salam*, had gone to Quba' (name of a place). I met him (the Imam) and informed him (the Imam) about the reason people had gathered against him (the Imam). He (the Imam) said, 'You can just ignore them.' When he (the Imam) came and they saw him (the Imam) they attacked him (the Imam) (verbally) saying, 'No one has killed our man except you and we will not apply revenge against anyone else other than you.' He (the Imam) said, 'You must allow a group of you to speak to me.' A group of people stood aside from among them. He (the Imam) held their hands and took them inside the Masjid. They came out saying, 'Abu 'Abd Allah, Ja'far ibn Muhammad is our Shaykh, we seek refuge with Allah against accusing him of doing such a thing or to have commanded for such a thing.'

"They then dispersed. I went with him (the Imam) and asked, 'I pray to Allah to keep my soul in service for your cause, how quickly they became happy after their being angry so much?' He (the Imam) said, 'Yes, I called them and told them, 'You must hold it or I will bring out the document.' I then asked, 'What kind of document is it, I pray to Allah to keep my soul in service for your cause?' He (the Imam) said, 'The mother of al-Khattab was a slave-girl of al-Zubayr, son of 'Abd al-Muttalib. Nufayl seduced her and made her pregnant. Al-Zubayr pursued him but he fled to Taef. Al-Zubayr followed him and Thaqif saw him and asked, 'O abu 'Abd Allah, what are you doing here?' He told them that your Nufayl has seduced my slave-girl.' He fled to al-Sham and al-Zubayr followed him when going there for his trade. He went to the king of al-Dumah (a fort between al-Madinah and al-Sham) who said, 'O abu 'Abd Allah, I need your help.'

"He said, 'O king, how can I help you?' The king said, 'You have withheld the son of a man from your people and I like that you return him to his father.' Al-Zubayr said, 'Allow him to come so I can see and recognize him.' In the next day, al-Zubayr visited the king. When the king saw him, he laughed. Al-Zubayr asked, 'What has made you to laugh O king?' The king replied, 'I do not think this man is born from an Arab woman, because when he saw you he could not control his stomach gases but kept releasing.' Al-Zubayr said, 'O king when I will go to Makkah I will try to comply with your request.' When al-Zubayr returned, he (Nufayl) had appealed before all tribes of Quraysh to convince al-Zubayr to return the son of Nufayl (al-Khattab born from the slave-girl of al-Zubayr) to him (Nufayl) but he refused. He (Nufayl) then appealed before 'Abd al-Muttalib for the same reason and he said, 'There is something between me and al-Zubayr. Consider what he has done to my son so and so (al-'Abbas) but you can go and speak to him with fairness to make him agree.'

"Al-Zubayr then said to them, 'Satan has a dominion. The son of this man is the son of Satan and do not trust him to lead us as our leader. He must not come before us. Bring him to me through the door of Masjid. I want to heat up a piece of iron to set marks on his face and form a binding document on him and his father not to come before us (to lead) in a gathering or issue commands on our children or throw arrows with us.' He (the Imam) said, 'They agreed, marked his face with iron and formulated a document about it. That document is with us. I told them that if you did not desist I could make that document public. It contains disgraceful matters that apply to you.'

"A *mawla* of the Messenger of Allah, died without leaving behind any heirs. A dispute took place between the children of al-'Abbas and abu 'Abd Allah, *'Alayhi al-Salam*, about the legacy of the deceased. In that year Hisham ibn 'Abd al-Malik performed al-Hajj. He sat between them to settle the dispute. Dawud ibn Ali said, 'It is in our guardianship.' Abu 'Abd Allah, *'Alayhi al-Salam*, said, 'It is under my guardianship.' Dawud ibn Ali (to please Hisham) said, 'Your father fought Mu'awiyah.' Abu 'Abd Allah, *'Alayhi al-Salam*, said this: 'You must take notice that when you say, 'My father fought Mu'awiyah', the share of your father was a greater share after which he fled with his embezzlement.' He (the Imam) then said, 'Tomorrow I will place a collar around your neck like a pigeon.' Dawud ibn Ali said, 'The words you spoke are not more valuable than a piece of the dropping of a camel in the valley of al-Arzaq.' He (the Imam) said, 'That is a valley in which you and your father have no right. "Hisham said, 'Tomorrow I will sit between you for a settlement.' The next day abu 'Abd Allah, *'Alayhi al-Salam*, went with a document in a bag of cotton and Hisham sat for settlement. Abu 'Abd Allah, *'Alayhi al-Salam*, then placed the document before him. After reading the document, he asked for Jandal al-Khuza'iy, and 'Ukkashah al-Damriy, two old people who had lived in the time of ignorance. He threw the document before them asking if they recognized the handwriting. They said, 'We recognize the handwriting. It is in the handwriting of al-'As ibn 'Umayyah, and this is the handwriting of so and so for so and so of Quraysh and this is the handwriting of Harb ibn 'Umayyah.' Hisham said, 'O abu 'Abd Allah, I see that you have the handwritings of my ancestors with you.' He (the Imam) said, 'Yes, that is correct.' He (Hisham) said, 'My judgment is in your favor, O abu 'Abd Allah and it is under your guardianship.'

"He (the Imam) came out and said, 'If the scorpion comes back we are there and the sole of the shoe is ready for it.' I then asked, 'What was the document all about, I pray to Allah to keep my soul in service for your cause?' He (the Imam) said, 'Nuthaylah was a slave-girl of the mother of al-Zubayr, abu Talib and 'Abd Allah. 'Abd al-Muttalib made her to give birth to his son so and so (al-'Abbas). Al-Zubayr said, 'This slave-girl belongs to us because we inherited from our mother and your son, this is our slave. He appealed before the tribes of Quraysh to convince al-Zubayr to return his son. He (al-Zubayr) said, 'I agree with the condition that your son, this one will not move ahead of us in a gathering or throw arrows with us.' He recorded it in a document with witnesses to confirm the agreement and that was the document.'"

People of the right are Shi'ah

H 14821, h 373
Al-Husayn from Muhammad has narrated from Muhammad ibn Ahmad al-Nahdiy from Mu'awiyah ibn Hakim from certain persons of his people from 'Anbasah ibn Bijad who has narrated the following:

"It is an explanation of the meaning of the words of Allah, most Majestic, most Glorious. '. . . as for those who are of the people of the right hand, greeting of peace is offered to you from the people of the right hand.' (56:90-91) Abu 'Abd Allah, *'Alayhi al-Salam*, has said that the Messenger of Allah said to 'Amir al-Mu'minin, Ali, *'Alayhi al-Salam*, 'They are your Shi'ah with whom your sons will remain unharmed from being murdered.'"

Allegiance of Ali to the Holy Prophet, *'Alayhima al-Salam*

H 14822, h 374

Narrated to us Yahya from Ahmad ibn Muhammad ibn 'Isa from al-Hassan ibn Ali from Safwan from Muhammad ibn Ziyad ibn 'Isa from al-Husayn ibn Mus'ab who has narrated the following:

"Abu 'Abd Allah, *'Alayhi al-Salam*, has stated this Hadith. ''Amir al-Mu'minin, Ali, *'Alayhi al-Salam*, has said, "I pledged allegiance with the Messenger of Allah, *O Allah grant compensation to Muhammad and his family worthy of their services to Your cause*. The pledge required that I must remain with him, in hardships, in ease, in freedom and in being restricted until Islam increased and found thickness." He (the Imam) said, 'Ali, *'Alayhi al-Salam*, made them (the Shi'ah) to pledge such allegiance with him and to defend Muhammad and his descendents against all that they dispel from themselves and their children, and I also made them to pledge such allegiance with me. Thus, there were those who remained safe and there were those who were destroyed.'"

The Story of *Ale* (family) Dharih and their Belief

H 14823, h 375

It is narrated from the narrator of the previous Hadith from Ahmad ibn Muhammad from abu Yahya al-Wasitiy from certain persons of our people who has narrated the following:

"Abu 'Abd Allah, *'Alayhi al-Salam*, has said, 'Behind Yemen there is a valley called valley of Barahut. The inhabitants of that valley are only black snakes and owls of the birds. In that valley there is a well. It is called Balhut. To this valley, the spirits of the pagans come and go in the mornings and evenings where they drink of pus for water. Behind that valley there live a people called Dharih. When Allah sent Muhammad, *O Allah grant compensation to Muhammad and his family worthy of their services to Your cause*, a calf that belonged to them cried and hit with its tail, saying, "O *Ale* (family of) Dharih, – in a clear voice – a man has come in Tihamah who calls to testimony of *Tahlil*, (no one deserves worship except Allah)." They said, "For what reason Allah has made this calf to speak?"' He (the Imam) said that it cried for the second time. They decided to build a ship (boat) which they did and seven people embarked in it with supplies as Allah placed in their hearts; then they hoisted its sails and made it to sail in the sea. They sailed in it until they reached Jaddah. They then went to the Holy Prophet, *O Allah grant compensation to Muhammad and his family worthy of their services to Your cause*, who said to them, 'You are from Dharih and the calf has cried among you.' They said, 'Yes, that is true. Instruct us about the religion and the book.' The Messenger of Allah, *O Allah grant compensation to Muhammad and his family worthy of their services to Your cause*, instructed them about the religion. He instructed them about the book, *Sunnah*, obligations and laws as he had brought from Allah, most Majestic, most Glorious, and appointed a man from banu Hashim to go with them, so there are no differences among them until this day.'"

Hadith of the night journey

H 14824, h 376

Ali ibn Ibrahim has narrated from his father from Ahmad ibn Muhammad from ibn abu Nasr from Aban ibn 'Uthman from Hadid who has narrated the following:

"Abu 'Abd Allah, *'Alayhi al-Salam*, has said that when the Messenger of Allah, *O Allah grant compensation to Muhammad and his family worthy of their services to Your cause*, was taken during his night journey, in the morning he told people about his story. They asked to describe for them Bayt al-Maqdis. He (the Imam) said that he (the Messenger of Allah) began to describe it for them but as his journey was in the night, he was not clear in his description, thus, Jibril came and said, 'Look here.' He looked, then described it for them when looking at it. Then he described the caravan of their camels, which moved between them and al-Sham and then he said, 'This is the caravan of camels of banu so and so, which will arrive at sunrise led by a brownish or red camel.' He (the Imam) then said that Quraysh sent a man on horseback to turn the caravan back. He (the Imam) said that it arrived at sunrise. Qurt ibn 'Abde 'Amr said, 'I regret that I am not young (strong enough to punish you), when you think that you went to Bayt al-Maqdis and returned in the same night.'"

Hadith of the migration and abu Bakr

H 14825, h 377

Humayd ibn Ziyad has narrated from Muhammad ibn Ayyub from Ali ibn Asbat from Hakam ibn Miskin from Yusuf ibn Suhayb who has narrated the following:

"Abu 'Abd Allah, *'Alayhi al-Salam*, has said this. 'I once heard abu Ja'far, *'Alayhi al-Salam*, say that the Messenger of Allah, *O Allah grant compensation to Muhammad and his family worthy of their services to Your cause*, once turned to abu Bakr in the cave and said this: "Calm down, Allah is with us," when he was trembling restlessly. When the Messenger of Allah, *O Allah grant compensation to Muhammad and his family worthy of their services to Your cause*, saw his condition he said, "Do you want that I show you my companions and supporters in their gatherings, speaking to each other; show to you Ja'far and his friends sail in the sea?" He replied, "Yes, please do so." The Messenger of Allah, *O Allah grant compensation to Muhammad and his family worthy of their services to Your cause*, wiped his hand over his eyes and he looked at his supporters speaking and looked at Ja'far, *'Alayhi al-Salam*, and his friends in the sea sailing. He at that time thought that he was a magician.'"

Hadith of Suraqah ibn Malik

H 14826, h 378

Ali ibn Ibrahim has narrated from his father from ibn abu 'Umayr from Mu'awiyah ibn 'Ammar who has narrated the following:

"Abu 'Abd Allah, *'Alayhi al-Salam*, has said that the Messenger of Allah, *O Allah grant compensation to Muhammad and his family worthy of their services to Your cause*, moved out of the cave toward al-Madinah, when Quraysh had assigned one hundred camels as reward for anyone who captured him (the

Messenger of Allah). Suraqah ibn Malik ibn al-Ju'shum was one of those who were searching for him. He caught up with the Messenger of Allah, *O Allah grant compensation to Muhammad and his family worthy of their services to Your cause*, who said, 'O Lord, protect me against the evil of Suraqah by whatever means You like.' The legs of his horse sank in the soil. He folded his foot, then ran and said, 'O Muhammad, I realize that what has happened to the legs of my horse is from you. Pray to Allah to release my horse. I swear by my life that if I will not benefit you, I will not harm you either. The Messenger of Allah, *O Allah grant compensation to Muhammad and his family worthy of their services to Your cause*, prayed and Allah, most Majestic, most Glorious, released his horse. He came back in pursuit after the Messenger of Allah, *O Allah grant compensation to Muhammad and his family worthy of their services to Your cause*, until he did it three times, each time the Messenger of Allah prayed and the earth held the legs of his horse. When, for the third time, his horse was released, he said, 'O Muhammad, this is my camel before you with my slave. If you need her for riding or milk her take from it, and this is an arrow from my arrow-pack as a token. I go back and turn away those who search for you.' He (the Messenger of Allah) said, 'We do not need any of your things.'"

Conditions of the Shi'ah in the absence of the Imam

H 14827, h 379
A number of our people have narrated from Ahmad ibn Muhammad from ibn abu Najran Muhammad ibn Sinan from abu al-Jarud who has narrated the following:

"Abu Ja'far, *'Alayhi al-Salam*, has said, 'You will not see the one for whom you are waiting, until you become like al-Muwat (dead) goat who is not a matter of any kind of worry for the lion. The lion can then cut from whichever part of its body it wants; you will not have any high position to rise or supporter to seek support thereby.'"

Conditions of the Shi'ah in the absence of the Imam

H 14828, h 380
It is narrated from the narrator of the previous Hadith from Ali ibn al-Hakam from ibn Sinan from abu al-Jarud a similar Hadith.

"I asked 'Ali ibn al-Hakam, 'What is al-Muwat of goats?' He said, 'It is that which has become equal and none has any preference over the others.'"

In praise of Zayd ibn Ali; the rise of Sufyani as a sign of the rise of al-Qa'im, *'Alayhi al-Salam*

H 14829, h 381
Ali ibn Ibrahim has narrated from his father from Safwan ibn Yahya from 'Is ibn al-Qasim who has narrated the following:

"I once heard abu 'Abd Allah, *'Alayhi al-Salam*, say, 'You must remain pious before Allah Who is One and has no partners. You must look to your souls. By Allah, a man who has sheep, if he finds that there is a man who knows more about sheep than the one dealing with his sheep, he removes that and brings the one who is more knowledgeable about his sheep. By Allah, if you had two souls to use one for an experiment in a fight and the other one remained you would then work according to the result of the experiment. However, one has only one soul. If it goes it then is gone as well as repentance. You deserve to choose for your souls. If the one from us comes then you must see for what reason you are moving. Do not say that Zayd moved. He was a scholar, a truthful person and he did not call to himself. He called to al-Rida', from *Ale* (family of) Muhammad, *O Allah grant compensation to Muhammad and his family worthy of their services to Your cause.* If he were to succeed, he would have complied with what he had told you. He moved against a strong ruler to break him down. The one who rises from us today for anything, he calls you to al-Rida', from *Ale* (family of) Muhammad, *O Allah grant compensation to Muhammad and his family worthy of their services to Your cause.* We hold you to bear witness that we do not agree with him when he disobeys us today; and there is no one with him but if he rises with the banners and flags, then he has more reason not to listen to us except that descendents (certain ones) of Fatimah may gather around him. By Allah, your *Waliy* (guardian with divine authority and knowledge) is the one who is accepted by consensus. If it is in the month of Rajab, then you must go in the name of Allah, most Majestic, most Glorious, if you like to delay to the month of al-Sha'ban it is not harmful, and if you like to fast at home it perhaps is more strengthening for you. The appearance of Sufyani for you is a sufficient sign.'"

Prohibition to rise before al-Qa'im

H 14830, h 382

Ali ibn Ibrahim has narrated from his father from Hammad ibn 'Isa from Rib'iy in a marfu' manner who has narrated the following:

"Ali ibn al-Husayn, *'Alayhim al-Salam*, has said, 'By Allah, no one from us will rise before al-Qa'im will reappear with divine authority and power, except that his condition will be like that of a bird flying from the nest before its wigs are able to lift it in the air. Therefore, children (predators) pick it up and play with it.'"

The command to remain at home before the rise of Sufyani

H 14831, h 383

A number of our people have narrated from Ahmad ibn Muhammad from 'Uthman ibn 'Isa from Bakr ibn Muhammad from Sadir who has narrated the following:

"Abu Ja'far, *'Alayhi al-Salam*, once said, 'O Sadir, stay in your home and remain there, keep calm until the night makes it calm. When you learn that al-Sufyaniy has moved then travel to us even if you have to do it on foot.'"

Cure for fever

H 14832, h 384

Muhammad ibn Yahya has narrated from Ahmad ibn Muhammad ibn 'Isa from Ali ibn al-Hakam from Kamil ibn Muhammad from Muhammad ibn Ibrahim al- Ju'fiy who has narrated the following:

"My father narrated to me saying, 'I visited abu 'Abd Allah, *'Alayhi al-Salam*, and he (the Imam) asked, "Why is it that I see you grave-faced?"' I replied, 'I have fever of al-Rib''. He (the Imam) then said, 'Why do you not benefit from the blessed and fine medicine? Powder sugar and mix it with water, then drink before breakfast and in the evening.' I followed the instruction and the fever did not come back.'"

Cure for pain with sugar

H 14833, h 385

It is narrated from the narrator of the previous Hadith from Ahmad ibn Muhammad from al-Hassan ibn Ali ibn al-Nu'man from certain persons of our people who has narrated the following:

"I once complained before abu 'Abd Allah, *'Alayhi al-Salam*, because of pain. He (the Imam) said, 'When you want to go to bed take two pieces of sugar.' I followed the instruction and I completely recovered. I spoke to a physician about it who was an expert person in our town. He asked, 'From where has abu 'Abd Allah, *'Alayhi al-Salam*, learned it? This is of our treasured knowledge; however, he has books he may have found it in his books.'"

Cure for fever with al-Quran and sugar

H 14834, h 386

It is narrated from the narrator of the previous Hadith from Ahmad ibn Muhammad from Ja'far ibn Yahya al-Khuza'iy from al-Husayn ibn al-Hassan from 'Asem ibn Hamid ibn Yunus from a man who has narrated the following:

"Abu 'Abd Allah, *'Alayhi al-Salam*, once asked a man, 'How do you treat your people suffering from fever?' He replied, 'I pray to Allah to keep you well, it is the bitter medicine, like Basfa'ij and al-Ghafis and so on.' He (the Imam) said, *'Tasbih* (Allah is free of all defects) the One who can cure with bitter is also able to cure with sweet.' He (the Imam) said, 'When one of you may suffer from fever he must take a clean bowl, place one and a half (lump of) sugar in it, then read what he knows of al-Quran, then place it under the stars with a piece of iron on it. In the morning pour water on it, soak it with his hand, then drink it. In the second night increase one more sugar which become two sugars and one half, on the third night increase one more sugar (lump) which become three and a half sugar.'"

Excellence of *Bismi Allah* (in the name of Allah)

H 14835, h 387

Ahmad ibn Muhammad al-Kufiy has narrated from Ali ibn al-Hassan ibn Ali from 'Abd al-Rahman ibn abu Najran fn Harun who has narrated the following:

"Once abu 'Abd Allah, *'Alayhi al-Salam*, said to me, 'They have denied (the expression) 'In the name of Allah, the Beneficent, the Merciful.' They by Allah, have denied the best of the names. When entering his house the Messenger of Allah, *O Allah grant compensation to Muhammad and his family worthy of their services to Your cause*, when Quraysh gathered around him would say, 'In the name of Allah, the Beneficent, the Merciful' loudly, raising his voice. Quraysh then turned back and fled. Allah, most Majestic, most Glorious, then revealed, '. . . when you speak of your Lord, in al-Quran, alone they turn back on their heels in hatred.' (17:46)

Abu 'Abd Allah, *'Alayhi al-Salam,* expressed frustration because of the behavior of Arabs

H 14836, h 388

It is narrated from the narrator of the previous Hadith from 'Abd al-Rahman ibn abu Najran from abu Harun al-Makfuf who has narrated the following:

"Abu 'Abd Allah, *'Alayhi al-Salam,* on mentioning the Messenger of Allah, *O Allah grant compensation to Muhammad and his family worthy of their services to Your cause,* would say, 'I pray to Allah to keep my soul and the souls of my father, mother, my people and my tribe in service for his cause. It is very strange of the Arabs. They do not raise us on their heads when Allah, most Majestic, most Glorious, says, ". . . you were at the brink of the pit of the fire but he rescued you thereof." (3:103) Because of the Messenger of Allah, *O Allah grant compensation to Muhammad and his family worthy of their services to Your cause,* they were rescued.'"

About the words of Allah 'to Allah belongs the kingdom'

H 14837, h 389

It is narrated from the narrator of the previous Hadith from Ibrahim ibn abu Bakr ibn abu Sammak from Dawud ibn Farqad from 'Abd al-A'la' Mawla Ale (family) Al-Sham who has narrated the following:

"I once asked abu 'Abd Allah, *'Alayhi al-Salam,* about the meaning of the words of Allah, '. . . Say, "O Lord, You are the owner the kingdom, You give to whomever You want and take it away from whomever You want." (3:26) Has Allah not given banu 'Umayyah the kingdom?' He (the Imam) said, 'It is not as you think it is. Allah, most Majestic, most Glorious, gave the kingdom to us but banu 'Umayyah took it away like the case of a man who owns clothes but another man takes them away. It then does not belong to the one who has taken it away.'"

About the words of Allah 'Allah brings the dead earth back to life'

H 14838, h 390

Muhammad ibn Ahmad ibn al-Salt has narrated from 'Abd Allah ibn al-Salt from Yunus from al-Mufaddal ibn Salih from Muhammad al-Halabiy who has narrated the following:

"I once asked abu 'Abd Allah, *'Alayhi al-Salam,* about the meaning of the words of Allah, most Majestic, most Glorious, '. . . you must take notice that Allah brings the earth back to life after its death.' (57:17) He (the Imam) said, 'It means justice after tyranny.'"

Dhulfaqar came from the sky

H 14839, h 391

Muhammad ibn Yahya has narrated from Ahmad ibn Muhammad ibn 'Isa from Ali ibn Muhammad ibn 'Ushaym from Safwan ibn Yahya who has narrated the following:

"I once asked al-Rida', *'Alayhi al-Salam*, about the sword of the Messenger of Allah, *O Allah grant compensation to Muhammad and his family worthy of their services to Your cause*, Dhulfaqar. He (the Imam) said, 'Jibril, *'Alayhi al-Salam*, brought it from the sky and its ring was made of silver.'"

Hadith of Noah, *'Alayhi al-Salam*, on the Day of Judgment; Ja'far and Hamzah

H 14840, h 392

Muhammad ibn Yahya has narrated from Ahmad ibn Muhammad ibn Khalid from al-Qasim ibn Muhammad from Jamil ibn Salih from Yusuf ibn abu Sa'id who has narrated the following:

"I once was with abu 'Abd Allah, *'Alayhi al-Salam*, and he (the Imam) said to me, 'When it will be the Day of Judgment, Allah, most Blessed, most High, will raise all creatures, among them Noah, *'Alayhi al-Salam*, will be the first to have been called and it will be asked, "Did you preach?" He will reply, "Yes, I preached." It will be asked, "Who testifies in your favor?" He will say, "Muhammad 'Abd Allah, *O Allah grant compensation to Muhammad and his family worthy of their services to Your cause*, testifies."' He (the Imam) said, 'Noah, *'Alayhi al-Salam*, will then come out and people walk until they come to Muhammad, *O Allah grant compensation to Muhammad and his family worthy of their services to Your cause*. He will be like a large amount of musk with Ali, *'Alayhi al-Salam*, along with him as it is mentioned in the words of Allah, most Majestic, most Glorious, ". . . when they saw him happy the faces of the unbelievers turned troubled." (67:27) Noah, *'Alayhi al-Salam*, will say to Muhammad, *O Allah grant compensation to Muhammad and his family worthy of their services to Your cause*, "O Muhammad, Allah, most Blessed, most High, asks me if I preached. I replied, 'Yes, I did,' but He asked, "Who testifies in your favor?" I said, "Muhammad, *O Allah grant compensation to Muhammad and his family worthy of their services to Your cause*, testifies." He (Muhammad) will say, "O Ja'far, O Hamzah, go and testify in his favor that he had preached."' Abu 'Abd Allah, *'Alayhi al-Salam*, then said, 'Ja'far and Hamzah are witnesses in favor of the Prophets *'Alayhim al-Salam*, in support of their preaching.' I then asked, 'I pray to Allah to keep my soul in service for your cause, where will Ali, *'Alayhi al-Salam*, be?' He (the Imam) said, 'His rank is greater than that.'"

The Holy Prophet, *'Alayhi al-Salam*, looked to his people in an equitable manner

H 14841, h 393

Narrated to me Muhammad ibn Yahya has narrated from Ahmad ibn Muhammad from 'Umar ibn 'Abd al-'Aziz from Jamil who has narrated the following:

"Abu 'Abd Allah, *'Alayhi al-Salam*, has said that the Messenger of Allah, *O Allah grant compensation to Muhammad and his family worthy of their services to Your cause*, when sitting among his companions would distribute his glances on all of them in equal measure by looking at this then on that one and so on.'"

The Messenger of Allah did not speak to people from the depth of his reason

H 14842, h 394

It is narrated from the narrator of the previous Hadith from Ahmad ibn Muhammad from ibn Faddal from certain persons of our people who has narrated the following:

"Abu 'Abd Allah, *'Alayhi al-Salam*, has said that the Messenger of Allah, *O Allah grant compensation to Muhammad and his family worthy of their services to Your cause*, never spoke to anyone according to the depth of his own power of reason. The Messenger of Allah, *O Allah grant compensation to Muhammad and his family worthy of their services to Your cause*, has said, 'We, the community of the Prophets, are commanded to speak to people according to the depth and level of their power of reasoning.'"

Permission to use words with hidden meanings, irony

H 14843, h 395

Muhammad ibn Yahya has narrated from Ahmad ibn Muhammad and a number of our people have narrated from Sahl ibn Ziyad all from ibn Mahbub from Malik ibn 'Atiyyah who has narrated the following:

"I once said to abu 'Abd Allah, *'Alayhi al-Salam*, 'I am a man from Bajilah and I follow the religion of Allah, most Majestic, most Glorious, that you are my leader with divine authority and knowledge. Certain ones who do not know me ask, "Who are you?" I reply, 'I am a man from Arab, then from Bajilah.' Is there anything sinful in such answer if I did not say that I am of the *mawaliy* (followers) of banu Hashim?' He (the Imam) said, 'No, is your heart and desire not determined to accept us as your *Waliy* (guardian with divine authority and knowledge)?' I replied, 'Yes, that is the condition of my mind.' He (the Imam) said, 'There is nothing wrong if you said that you are from Arab which you are in lineage, gifts, number and social status. You in religion and the contents of religion with which you follow the commands of Allah, most Majestic, most Glorious, in the matters of obeying us and learning His guidance from us are of our friends who accept our *Wilayah* (divine authority and knowledge), you are from us and to us is your direction.'"

Shi'ah as their disciples, with love and respect

H 14844, h 396

Narrated to us ibn Mahbub from abu Yahya Kawkab al-Dam who has narrated the following:

"Abu 'Abd Allah, *'Alayhi al-Salam*, has said that the disciples of Jesus were his Shi'ah and our Shi'ah are our disciples. Our disciples are more obedient to us than the disciples of Jesus were. Jesus said to his disciples, '. . . who is ready to help me for the cause of Allah.' By Allah, no one of the Jews helped him or fought for his cause. However, our Shi'ah have continued, from the time Allah, most Majestic, most Glorious, took His Messenger, *O Allah grant compensation to Muhammad and his family worthy of their services to Your cause*, from this world, to help us. They fight for our cause, suffer for us by being burned, tortured and exiled in the land, may Allah grant them good reward from us with the best of rewards. 'Amir al-Mu'minin, Ali, *'Alayhi al-Salam*, has said, 'By Allah, if I cut the noses of those who love us with the sword, they will not become angry with us. By Allah, if I get close to our enemies and present to them an abundance of wealth, they will not have any love for us.'"

About the meaning of the words of Allah 'Rome is defeated. . .'

H 14845, h 397

Ibn Mahbub has narrated from Jamil ibn Salih from abu 'Ubaydah who has narrated the following:

"I once asked abu Ja'far, *'Alayhi al-Salam*, about the meaning of the words of Allah, most Majestic, most Glorious, 'Alif, Lam, Mim. Rome is defeated in the nearby land.' (30:1-2) He (the Imam) said, 'O abu 'Ubaydah, it has an interpretation which no one besides Allah and those who are firmly established in knowledge of *Ale* (family of) Muhammad, *O Allah grant compensation to Muhammad and his family worthy of their services to Your cause*, knows. When the Messenger of Allah, *O Allah grant compensation to Muhammad and his family worthy of their services to Your cause*, migrated to al-Madinah, Islam was supported to become strong. He (the Messenger of Allah) wrote to the king of Rome a letter with a messenger and called him to accept Islam. He (the Messenger of Allah) wrote a letter to the king of Persia and asked him to accept Islam and sent a messenger to him. The king of Rome treated the letter of the Messenger of Allah, *O Allah grant compensation to Muhammad and his family worthy of their services to Your cause*, with greatness and respected His Messenger. The king of Persia, however, affronted the letter of the Messenger of Allah, *O Allah grant compensation to Muhammad and his family worthy of their services to Your cause*, tore his letter in pieces and insulted His Messenger. At that time, the king of Persia was fighting the king of Rome and the Muslims loved that the king of Rome defeated the king of Persia. The side of the king of Rome seemed more hopeful for them than the side of the king of Persia. When the king of Persia defeated the king of Rome, the Muslims disliked it and felt sad. Allah, most Majestic, most Glorious, then revealed a book (a verse) about it which we read. "Alif, Lam, Mim. Rome is defeated in the nearby land [defeated by the Persians], the nearby land [which is al-Sham (Syria) and its surroundings] they [the Persians] after their victory over [the Rome] will soon be defeated [by the Muslims] in few years. To Allah belongs the matter before and thereafter and on that day the Muslims will rejoice because of the help of Allah Who helps whomever He, most Majestic, most Glorious, wants." When the Muslims fought and conquered it the Muslims became happy for the help of Allah, most Majestic, most Glorious.'

"I then asked, 'Has Allah, most Majestic, most Glorious, not said, ". . . in few years" but many years passed in the time of the Messenger of Allah, *O Allah grant compensation to Muhammad and his family worthy of their services to Your cause*, as well as the rule of abu Bakr. The believing people defeated the Persians during the ruler of 'Umar.' He (the Imam) said, 'Did I not say that it has applications and interpretations and –al-Quran – O abu 'Ubaydah has abrogating and abrogated (duplicate and duplicated). Have you not heard the words of Allah, most Majestic, most Glorious, ". . . to Allah belongs the matter before and thereafter?" It means that it (the say) depends on His wish and will to delay what is to come first or bring forward what is to come later until the determination becomes inevitable. Help arrives in such time for the believing people and for this reason is use of the words of Allah, most Majestic, most Glorious, ". . . on that day the believing people become happy because of the help from Allah. He helps whomever He wants." that is the day when the determination becomes inevitable with help.'"

Invalidation of claims of *Khilafat* by abu Bakr

H 14846, h 398

Ibn Mahbub has narrated from 'Amr ibn abu al-Miqdam from his father who has narrated the following:

"I once said to abu Ja'far, *'Alayhi al-Salam. 'Ammah*, (common) people think that allegiance to abu Bakr as people came together was because Allah, most Majestic, most Glorious, agreed and Allah would not bring mischief among the followers of Muhammad, *O Allah grant compensation to Muhammad and his family worthy of their services to Your cause*, after him. Abu Ja'far, *'Alayhi al-Salam*, then said, 'Have they not read the book, has Allah not said, "Muhammad is only a Messenger. There lived other Messengers before him. Should (Muhammad) die or be slain, would you then turn back to your pre-Islamic behavior? Whoever does so can cause no harm to Allah. Allah will reward those who give thanks."' (3:144) I then said, 'They interpret it in another way.' He (the Imam) said, 'Has Allah, most Majestic, most Glorious, not informed about nations before them who created differences among themselves after the coming of clear proofs, as He has said, ". . . We gave clear proofs to Jesus, supported him with the Holy Spirit. Had Allah wanted people after him would not fight after the coming of the clear proofs but they created differences; certain ones among them believed and certain others disbelieved. Had Allah wanted they would not fight each other, but Allah does whatever He wants." (2:253) This shows that the companions of Muhammad, *O Allah grant compensation to Muhammad and his family worthy of their services to Your cause*, create differences among themselves of whom certain ones believe and others become unbelievers.'"

Sajdah (prostrations) of Abu 'Abd Allah, *'Alayhi al-Salam*

H 14847, h 399

It is narrated from the narrator of the previous Hadith from Hisham ibn Salim from 'Abd al-Hamid ibn abu al-'Ala' who has narrated the following:

"I once entered al-Haram, the Sacred Masjid and a *mawla* of abu 'Abd Allah, *'Alayhi al-Salam*, was there; so I went to him to ask about abu 'Abd Allah, *'Alayhi al-Salam*, but he (the Imam) was there in *Sajdah* (prostration). I waited for a long time and his *Sajdah* (prostration) became very long. I then stood up, said many Rak'ats of *Salat* (prayer), and completed but he was still in *Sajdah* (prostration). I asked his *mawla* as to since when he was in *Sajdah* (prostration). He said, 'He was in *Sajdah* (prostration) before we came.' When he (the Imam) heard my voice he raised his head and said, 'O abu Muhammad, come close to me.' I then went close to him (the Imam) and offered to him greeting of peace. He heard a voice behind him and asked, 'What are these loud voices?' I replied, 'These are the Murji'ah, al-Qadriah and al-Mu'tazilah people.' He (the Imam) said, 'The people want (to speak to) me so allow us to move from here.' I stood up with him (the Imam) and when they saw him, (the Imam) they stood up and moved to him (the Imam). He (the Imam) said, 'Hold it and remain away from me, do not bother me and expose me to the Sultan; I am not a Mufti for you.' He then held my hand, left them and moved.

"When we left the Masjid, he then said to me, 'O abu Muhammad, by Allah, if Satan would make *Sajdah* (prostration) for Allah, most Majestic, most Glorious, after his sin and showing arrogance, for the life of the world that *Sajdah* (prostration) would not benefit him. Allah, most Majestic, most Glorious, would not accept it until he performed *Sajdah* (prostration) for Adam, *'Alayhi al-Salam*, as Allah, most Majestic, most Glorious, had commanded him to do.

"So also is this disobedient nation who is struck by mischief after its Prophet, *O Allah grant compensation to Muhammad and his family worthy of their services to Your cause.* They have abandoned the Imam whom their Prophet, *O Allah grant compensation to Muhammad and his family worthy of their services to Your cause,* had appointed for them. Allah, most Blessed, most High, will not accept their deeds. Nothing of their deeds is raised until they go before Allah as He has commanded them and accept the *Wilayah* (divine authority and knowledge) of the Imam about whose *Wilayah* they are commanded to acknowledge. They must enter through the door that Allah, most Majestic, most Glorious, and His Messenger, *O Allah grant compensation to Muhammad and his family worthy of their services to Your cause,* have opened for them. "O abu Muhammad, Allah has made obligatory five obligations on the followers of Muhammad, *O Allah grant compensation to Muhammad and his family worthy of their services to Your cause*: Of such obligations is *Salat* (prayer), fasting, al-Hajj, and accepting our *Wilayah* (divine authority and knowledge). He has exempted them in certain matters of the four kinds of obligations but He has not exempted any Muslim in anything about accepting our *Wilayah* (divine authority and knowledge). No, by Allah, there is no exemption in it.'"

(Example of such exemptions is shorter *Salat* (prayer) on a journey as well fasting and so on. . .)

For every government Allah has set a time

H 14848, h 400
A number of our people have narrated from Ahmad ibn Muhammad ibn Khalid from 'Uthman ibn 'Isa from abu Ishaq al-Jurjaniy who has narrated the following:
"Abu 'Abd Allah, *'Alayhi al-Salam*, has said, 'Allah, most Majestic, most Glorious, has set a time limit of nights, days, years and months for the domination of the rulers. If they behave with justice among people Allah, most Majestic, most Glorious, commands the companion of al-Falak (the path) to delay in its movement, which increases their days, nights, years and months. If they tyrannize people and behave unjustly among them, Allah, most Blessed, most High, commands the companion of al-Falak (the course) to move it faster to shorten their nights, days, years and months when Allah, most Majestic, most Glorious, has completed the number of the nights and months.'"

Where is wind from

H 14849, h 401
Abu Ali al-Ash'ariy has narrated from certain persons of his people from Muhammad ibn al-Fudayl from al-'Arzamiy who has narrated the following:
"I once was with abu 'Abd Allah, *'Alayhi al-Salam*, in al-Hijr near al-Ka'bah under the drain-shoot when a man was disputing with another man. One was saying to the other one, 'By Allah, you do not know from where the winds blow' and he kept saying it many times, Abu 'Abd Allah, *'Alayhi al-Salam*, then said, 'Do you know it?' He replied, 'No, but I hear people say so.' I then asked abu 'Abd Allah, *'Alayhi al-Salam*, 'I pray to Allah to keep my soul in service for your cause, from where does the wind blow?' He (the Imam) then said, 'The wind is imprisoned under al-Shamiy corner. When Allah, most Majestic, most Glorious, wants to allow something to come out of there, like the South, then it is South, or North then it is North, or Saba', then it is Saba', or Dabur then it is Dabur. He (the Imam) then said, 'Of the proof of this is that you see this corner moving all the time in winter, summer, and night and days.'"

No other (creature) are more than angels

H 14850, h 402
A number of our people have narrated from Sahl ibn Ziyad and Ali ibn Ibrahim has narrated [from his father] all from ibn Mahbub from Dawud al-Riqqiy who has narrated the following:
"Abu 'Abd Allah, *'Alayhi al-Salam*, has said, 'No other creatures of Allah are as numerous as the angels are. Every night seventy thousand angels descend to perform tawaf around the Sacred House, for the night and it also happens every night.'"

Angels are of three kinds

H 14851, h 403
Narrated to us ibn Mahbub from 'Abd Allah ibn Talhah in a marfu' manner who has narrated the following:

"The Holy Prophet, *O Allah grant compensation to Muhammad and his family worthy of their services to Your cause*, has said, 'Angels are of three parts: One part has two wings, one part has three wings and one part has four wings.'"

In the garden (paradise) there is a canal in which Jibril immerses his wing

H 14852, h 404

Maysarah from al-Hakam ibn Utaybah who has narrated the following:

"Abu Ja'far, *'Alayhi al-Salam*, has said, 'In the garden (paradise) there is a canal in which Jibril dives every morning, then comes out and quivers. Allah, most Majestic, most Glorious, then from every drop creates one angel.'"

The greatness of the creation of certain angels

H 14853, h 405

It is narrated from the narrator of the previous Hadith from certain persons of his people from Ziyad al-Qandiy from Durust ibn abu Mansur from a man who has narrated the following:

"Abu 'Abd Allah, *'Alayhi al-Salam*, has said that Allah, most Majestic, most Glorious, has an angel. From one loop of his ear to his shoulder there is a distance of a five hundred year flight of a bird.'"

The rooster of Allah

H 14854, h 406

Al-Husayn Muhammad has narrated from Mu'alla' ibn Muhammad from al-Washsha' from Muhammad ibn al-Fudayl who has narrated the following:

"Abu Ja'far, *'Alayhi al-Salam*, has said, 'Allah, most Majestic, most Glorious, has a rooster. One leg of this rooster is on the seventh earth, with its neck fixed under the throne and its wings in the air. When it becomes midnight or the second third of the night toward the end of the night, it flips its wings and crows, "Free of all defects and most Holy is our Lord, Allah, the Dominant, the clear truth. No one deserves worship beside Him, the Lord of the angels and the spirit." Then the roosters flip their wings and crow.'"

About cupping

H 14855, h 407

Muhammad ibn Yahya has narrated from Ahmad ibn Muhammad ibn 'Isa from al-Hajjal from Tha'labah' ibn Maymun from 'Ammar al-Sabatiy who has narrated the following:

"Abu 'Abd Allah, *'Alayhi al-Salam*, once asked, 'What do they say from your side about cupping?' I replied, 'They think it is better before breakfast instead of after food.' He (the Imam) said, 'No, after food more blood flows and it is more strengthening for the body.'"

Apply cupping

H 14856, h 408

It is narrated from the narrator of the previous Hadith from ibn Mahbub from 'Abd al-Rahman ibn al-Hajjaj who has narrated the following:

"Abu 'Abd Allah, *'Alayhi al-Salam*, has said, 'Read verse two hundred fifty five of chapter two; then apply cupping any day you like. Give charity and commence your journey any day you like.'"

Medicine agitates

H 14857, h 409

Muhammad ibn Yahya from Muhammad ibn al-Hassan from Mu'awiyah ibn al-Hakim who has narrated the following:

"I heard 'Uthman al-Ahwal say, 'I heard abu al-Hassan, *'Alayhi al-Salam*, say, "Every medicine agitates the illness and there is nothing more beneficial for the body than holding back the hand except for what one needs.""

Fever can be reduced

H 14858, h 410

It is narrated from the narrator of the previous Hadith from Ahmad ibn Muhammad from Muhammad ibn Khalid in a marfu' manner who has narrated the following:

"Abu 'Abd Allah, *'Alayhi al-Salam*, has said, 'Fever can be reduced by cupping, enema and vomiting.'"

Dust settles on...

H 14859, h 411

A number of our people have narrated from Ahmad ibn Muhammad ibn Khalid from Muhammad ibn Ali from Hafs ibn 'Asem ibn Hamid from Sayf al-Tammar from abu al-Murhif who has narrated the following:

"Abu Ja'far, *'Alayhi al-Salam*, has said, 'Dust settles on those who cause it to rise and it destroys al-Mahadir.' I then asked, 'I pray to Allah to keep my soul in service for your cause, what is al-Mahadir?' He (the Imam) said, 'It is those who make a big haste. They only want those who oppose them.' He (the Imam) then said, 'O abu al-Murhif, if they want you to suffer a calamity, Allah, most Majestic, most Glorious will make them suffer by a certain kind of entanglement.' Abu Ja'far, *'Alayhi al-Salam*, marked the ground then said, 'O abu al-Murhif,' - I replied, 'Here I am, to obey your command, - 'Do you think that a people who have restricted themselves for Allah, most Majestic, most Glorious, He will not make a way out for them? Yes, by Allah, Allah certainly makes a way out for them.'"

Letter of abu Muslim

H 14860, h 412

Muhammad ibn Yahya has narrated from Muhammad ibn al-Husayn from 'Abd al-Rahman ibn abu Hashim from al-Fadl al-Katib who has narrated the following:

"Once I was with abu 'Abd Allah, *'Alayhi al-Salam*, when the letter of abu Muslim came. He (the Imam) said, 'There is no answer from us to your letter. You must leave because it seems we are secretly speaking to each other.' He (the Imam) then said, 'What is it that you speak secretly about, O Fadl, Allah, most Majestic, most Glorious, does not hurry because of the haste of the servants. Removing a mountain from its place is easier than dislodging a government for which the appointed time is not complete. He (the Imam) then said, 'There are so and so' . . . until he (the Imam) counted to seven persons of the sons of so and so (al-'Abbas). I then asked, 'What is the sign between us and you, I pray to Allah to keep my soul in service for your cause?' He (the Imam) said, 'The earth will continue with its inhabitants until al-Sufyaniy moves. When al-Sufyaniy appears then you must answer our call,'- saying it three times- 'It is inevitable.'"

The case of Iblis

H 14861, h 413
Abu Ali al-Ash'ariy has narrated from Muhammad ibn 'Abd al-Jabbar from Ali ibn Hadid from Jamil ibn Darraj who has narrated the following:

"I once asked abu 'Abd Allah, *'Alayhi al-Salam*, about the case of Iblis (Satan) if he was an angel or if he was in charge of anything of the sky. He (the Imam) said, 'He was not of the angels and he was not in charge of anything in the sky, due to his lacking gracefulness.' I then went to al-Tayyar and informed him about what I had heard; but he refused to agree, saying, 'How can he not be of the angels and Allah, most Majestic, most Glorious, says, ". . . when We commanded the angels to perform *Sajdah* (prostration) for Adam, *'Alayhi al-Salam*, they did so except Iblis." (18:50) Al-Tayyar then visited him (the Imam) and asked when I was there. He said, 'I pray to Allah to keep my soul in service for your cause, considering the words of Allah, most Majestic, most Glorious, ". . . O believing people . . ." in more than one passage addressed to believing people, does it also include the hypocrites? He (the Imam) said, 'Yes, hypocrites are included, the misguided and all who acknowledged the apparent call.'"

Assigning *Salat* (prayer)

H 14862, h 414
It is narrated from the narrator of the previous Hadith from Ali ibn Hadid from Murazim who has narrated the following:

"Abu 'Abd Allah, *'Alayhi al-Salam*, has said that once a man came to the Messenger of Allah and said, 'O Messenger of Allah, *O Allah grant compensation to Muhammad and his family worthy of their services to Your cause*, can I perform *Salat* (prayer) and assign certain portions of it for you?' He (the Messenger of Allah) said, 'That is good.' He then said, 'O Messenger of Allah, can I assign one half of my *Salat* (prayer) for you?' He said, 'That is more excellent.' He then said, 'O Messenger of Allah, can I perform *Salat* (prayer) and assign all of it for you?' The Messenger of Allah, *O Allah grant compensation to Muhammad and his family worthy of their services to Your*

234

cause, said, 'In such case Allah is sufficient support for you in all matters that are important to you of the world or of the hereafter.' Abu 'Abd Allah, *'Alayhi al-Salam*, then said, 'The duty and responsibility that Allah placed on His Messenger, He did not place on anyone else of His creatures. He commanded him (the Messenger of Allah) to rise alone and all by himself among all people even if he could not find a group to fight in his favor. He has not commanded so to anyone else, of His creatures before or after him. He (the Imam) then read this verse, '. . . you must fight in the way of Allah and do not command anyone else other than yourself.' (4:84) He (the Imam) then said, 'Allah takes for him (the Messenger of Allah) what He takes for Himself. Allah, most Majestic, most Glorious, has said, ". . . one who brings one good deed receives tenfold reward." (6:160) He has made asking compensation from Allah for the Messenger of Allah, *O Allah grant compensation to Muhammad and his family worthy of their services to Your cause*, equal to ten good deeds.'"

Light in the darkness of earth

H 14863, h 415

It is narrated from the narrator of the previous Hadith from Ali ibn Hadid from Mansur ibn Ruh from Fudayl al-Sa'igh who has narrated the following:

"I once heard abu 'Abd Allah, *'Alayhi al-Salam*, say, 'You, by Allah, are the light in the darkness of earth. By Allah, the inhabitants of the sky look to you in the darkness of the earth as you look to the shining star in the sky. Certain ones of them say to the others, "O so and so, it is strange, how so and so has found this *'Amr* (*Walayah* (guardianship of *'A'immah* with divine authority) and has knowledge?" It is the words of my father, *'Alayhi al-Salam*, "It is not strange how those who are destroyed are destroyed but it is amazing those who are saved, how they are saved!"'"

Moon is in al-'Aqrab

H 14864, h 416

A number of our people have narrated from Ahmad ibn Muhammad ibn Khalid from Ali ibn Asbat from Ibrahim ibn Muhammad ibn Humran from his father who has narrated the following:

"Abu 'Abd Allah, *'Alayhi al-Salam*, has said, 'If one travels or gets married when the moon is in al-'Aqrab (Scorpio) he will not see goodness.'"

A donkey and a mule

H 14865, h 417

It is narrated from the narrator of the previous Hadith from ibn Faddal from 'Ubays ibn Hisham from 'Abd al-Karim ibn 'Amr from al-Hakam ibn Muhammad ibn al-Qasim who had heard 'Abd Allah ibn 'Ata' who has narrated the following:

"Abu Ja'far, *'Alayhi al-Salam*, once said, 'Go and prepare two stumpers, a donkey and a mule. I prepared a donkey and a mule and brought to him (the Imam) the mule, knowing that he (the Imam) liked that one out of the two. He (the Imam) asked, 'Who commanded you to bring this mule for me?' I replied, 'I have chosen this for you.' He (the Imam) said, 'Did I command you to choose for me?' He (the Imam) then said, 'The more likeable of carry-animals to me are donkeys.'

"I then brought the donkey for him and prepared the mounting step for him (the Imam) until he sat on the saddle and said, "All praise belongs to Allah who has guided us with Islam, taught us al-Quran, and favored us with Muhammad, *O Allah grant compensation to Muhammad and his family worthy of their services to Your cause.* 'Glory belongs to Him who has made it subservient to us when we would not have been able to do so ourselves. (43:13) To our Lord we shall all return. (43:14)'"""

"He moved and I moved along with him (the Imam) until we reached another place and I said to him that it is time of *Salat* (prayer), I pray to Allah to keep my soul in service for your cause. He (the Imam) said, 'This is the valley of ants; *Salat* (prayer) cannot be performed here.' We reached another place and I said to him the same thing. He (the Imam) said, 'It is a salty land. *Salat* (prayer) cannot be performed here.' He then disembarked by his own choice. He (the Imam) then said to me, 'Have you performed *Salat* (prayer) or optional *Salat* (prayer)?' – Uncertainty is from the narrator – I said, 'This is the *Salat* (prayer) which people of Iraq call *Salat* (prayer) at noon time.' He (the Imam) said, 'Those who perform *Salat* (prayer) are the Shi'ah of Ali, ibn abu Talib, *'Alayhi al-Salam*, and it is the *Salat* (prayer) of those who most often return to Allah.' He performed *Salat* (prayer) and so did I. I then held the saddle step for him and he (the Imam) said what he had said at the beginning of the journey. He (the Imam) then said, 'O Lord, condemn al-Murji'ah; they are our enemies in this world and in the hereafter.' I then asked, 'I pray to Allah to keep my soul in service for your cause, what reminded you of al-Murji'ah?' He (the Imam) said, 'I just thought about them.'"

Dealing with abu Lahab

H 14866, h 418

Muhammad ibn Yahya has narrated from Ahmad ibn Muhammad ibn 'Isa from ibn abu 'Umayr and Ali ibn Ibrahim has narrated from his father from ibn abu 'Umayr from al-Husayn ibn abu Hamzah who has narrated the following:

"Abu 'Abd Allah, *'Alayhi al-Salam*, has said that when Quraysh decided to murder the Holy Prophet, *O Allah grant compensation to Muhammad and his family worthy of their services to Your cause*, they said, 'How do we deal with abu Lahab?' 'Umm Jamil said, 'I will keep him occupied and ask him to remain with me until morning.' When it was the next morning and the pagans prepared themselves against the Holy Prophet, *O Allah grant compensation to Muhammad and his family worthy of their services to Your cause*, abu Lahab and his woman woke up and they were drinking. Abu Talib called Ali, *'Alayhi al-Salam*, and said, 'Son, go to your uncle abu Lahab and ask him to open the door; if he responded then go inside his home: but if he did not respond, then force the door to break it. Go inside and say to him, "My father says to you, 'If a man's uncle is his eye (master) among the people he is not humiliated.'"' He (the Imam) said that 'Amir al-Mu'minin, Ali, *'Alayhi al-Salam*, went and found the door locked. He knocked at it but he did not open. He then forced the door, broke it and went inside. When abu Lahab saw him he asked, 'What has happened to you, O son of my brother?' He said that my father said to you, 'If a man's uncle is his master (eye) among the people he is not humiliated.' He said, 'Your father has spoken the truth. What is happening, O son of my brother?' He replied, 'The son of your brother is being killed but you are eating and drinking.' He then jumped and took his sword but 'Umm Jamil held him back. He raised his hand and slapped on her face, which made her eye pop out. She later died blind. Abu Lahab went out with his sword. When Qurash saw him, they found anger on his face. They asked, 'What is the matter with you, O abu Lahab?' He said, 'I pledged allegiance with you against the son of my brother and you want to kill him. I swear by al-Lat and al-'Uzza' I am thinking to become a Muslim then you will see what I will do.' They apologized and he returned.'"

Day of Badr

H 14867, h 419

It is narrated from the narrator of the previous Hadith from Aban from Zurarah who has narrated the following:

"Abu 'Abd Allah, *'Alayhi al-Salam*, has said that on the day of Badr, Satan was showing the Muslims as very little in number in the eye of the pagans and the number of the pagans very large in the eyes of the Muslims. Jibril attacked him with the sword and he fled from him saying, 'O Jibril I am being given time, I am being given time' until he fell in the sea.'" Zurarah has said, 'I asked abu Ja'far, *'Alayhi al-Salam*, what for was he afraid when he was given time?' He (the Imam) said, 'He was afraid for certain parts of his sides being cutoff.'"

War of the confederated

H 14868, h 420

Ali ibn Ibrahim has narrated from his father from Ahmad ibn Muhammad from ibn abu Nasr from Hisham ibn Salim from Aban ibn 'Uthman from those who narrated to him who has narrated the following:

"Abu 'Abd Allah, *'Alayhi al-Salam*, has said this: 'The Messenger of Allah, *O Allah grant compensation to Muhammad and his family worthy of their services to Your cause*, stood on the mound where Masjid of al-Fath is. It was during the war of confederated tribes, in a dark and cold night and said, "Who is ready to go to bring us news about them (the enemy) and the garden (paradise) will be his reward?" No one responded. He (the Messenger of Allah) repeated it again but no one made any move. Abu 'Abd Allah, *'Alayhi al-Salam*, made a hand gesture, saying, "The people did not want it. They wanted something better than the garden (paradise)." He then asked, "Who is this?" He replied, "It is Hudhayfah." He (the Messenger of Allah) asked, "Did you not hear me all night and did not speak, come close." Hudhayfah stood up saying, "This cold and miserable condition, I pray to Allah to keep my soul in service for your cause, stopped me from answering you." The Messenger of Allah, *O Allah grant compensation to Muhammad and his family worthy of their services to Your cause*, said, "Go until you can hear them and bring their news for me." When he left, the Messenger of Allah, *O Allah grant compensation to Muhammad and his family worthy of their services to Your cause*, prayed, "O Lord, protect him from his front, behind, right and left sides until You return him safely." The Messenger of Allah, *O Allah grant compensation to Muhammad and his family worthy of their services to Your cause*, told him, "O Hudhayfah, do not speak anything until you will come to me." He took his sword and bow and his shield. Hudhayfah has said, "I moved but I did not feel any misery or cold. I passed by the door of the ditch which was seized by the believing and unbelieving people." When Hudhafah left, the Messenger of Allah, *O Allah grant compensation to Muhammad and his family worthy of their services to Your cause*, pleaded before Allah. "O the One who responds to the pleading of the agonized ones, O the One who answers the helpless ones, please dispel my concerns, sadness and agony as You see my condition and the condition of my companions." Jibril came to him and said, "O Messenger of Allah, Allah, most Majestic, most Glorious, has heard your words and prayer and He has answered you and has taken good care of you against fear from your enemies." The Messenger of Allah, *O Allah grant compensation to Muhammad and his family worthy of their services to Your cause*, then bowed down on his knees, spread his hands and allowed his eyes to shed tears. He then said, "Thanks are due to You, thanks to You for granting me mercy and to my companions." The Messenger of Allah, *O Allah grant compensation to Muhammad and his family worthy of their services to Your cause*, then said, "Allah, most Majestic, most Glorious, sent upon them a wind from the sky of the earth with sand in it and a wind from the fourth sky with pebbles in it." "Hudhayfah has said, "I left and saw people had lit fire in many places. Then the first army of Allah arrived with sand and it left nothing of their fire without being extinguished, tents and spears that were blown away so much so that they were protecting themselves by using their shield against the blowing sand and we could hear the sound of the sand striking against their shield." Hudhayfah then sat between two pagan men but Satan stood up in the form of a respectable man among the pagans and said, "O people you have camped near this magician and liar man. You have not lost anything in the matters related to him. It is not a good year, hoofs and cloven footed animals are destroyed; so you can return but every one of you must look who is sitting next to you." Hudhayfah has said that I then turned to the man on my right, tapped him with my hand and asked, "Who are you?" He replied, "I am Mu'awiyah." I then turned to the man on my left and asked, "Who are you?" He replied, "I am Suhayl ibn 'Amr." Hudhayfah has said that then the greater army of Allah came, abu Sufyan moved to his stumper and called among Quraysh, "You must find safety, find safety." Talhah al-Azdiy said, "Muhammad has increased your injuries." He then moved to his stumper and called among banu Ashja', "You must move to find safety, move to safety." 'Uyaynah ibn Hafs did a similar thing, then al-Harth ibn 'Awf al-Muzniy did likewise, then al-Aqra' ibn Habis moved similarly and the confederated tribes all moved. Hudhayfah returned to the Messenger of Allah, *O Allah grant compensation to Muhammad and his family worthy of their services to Your cause*, and informed him of the news.

Abu 'Abd Allah, *'Alayhi al-Salam*, then said, 'It was similar to the Day of Judgment.'"

Ali ibn al-'Abbas

H 14869, h 421
Ali ibn Ibrahim has narrated from his father from ibn Mahbub from Hisham al-Khurasaniy from al-Mufaddal ibn 'Umar who has narrated the following:

"I once was with abu 'Abd Allah, *'Alayhi al-Salam*, in al-Kufah in the days when Ali ibn al-'Abbas had come. We then arrived at al-Kunasah. He (the Imam) said, 'This is where they crucified my uncle, Zayd, may Allah grant him mercy.' He (the Imam) then passed until he reached the arcade of oil sellers, which is at the end of the market of the saddle sellers. He (the Imam) then dismounted and said, 'This is the place of the first al-Kufah Masjid which was marked by Adam, *'Alayhi al-Salam*, and I do not like to enter it riding.' I then asked, 'Who was the one who changed his markings?' He (the Imam) said, 'The first thing was the flood at the time of Noah, *'Alayhi al-Salam*, thereafter people of Kisra' and Nu'man, then others changed it, after them was Ziyad ibn abu Sufyan.' I then asked, 'Was there a Masjid in the time of Noah, *'Alayhi al-Salam*?' He (the Imam) said, 'Yes, O Mufaddal, Noah and his people lived at a distance of one day's journey from Euphrates to the west of al-Kufah. Noah, *'Alayhi al-Salam*, was a carpenter. Allah, most Majestic, most Glorious, then made him a Prophet and chose him in nobility. Noah was the first one who made a ship that moved on the water.' He (the Imam) said, 'Noah, *'Alayhi al-Salam*, lived one thousand years less five hundred among his people calling them to Allah, most Majestic, most Glorious, but they mocked and laughed at him. When he saw this from them he prayed against them saying, "O Lord, do not leave on earth of the unbelievers any dwelling town. If You leave them they will mislead your servants and they will reproduce no one except sinners and unbelievers." (71:26-27) Allah, most Majestic, most Glorious, then sent him revelation that said, "Build a ship, the Ark, make it large and quickly." Noah, *'Alayhi al-Salam*, then built the Ark in Masjid of al-Kufah with his own hands. He brought the wood until he finished it.' Al-Mufaddal has said that Hadith of abu 'Abd Allah, *'Alayhi al-Salam*, discontinued at noon time. Abu 'Abd Allah, *'Alayhi al-Salam*, stood for *Salat* (prayer), performed al-Zuhr and al-'Asr *Salat* (prayer), then returned from Masjid, turned to his left and pointed with his hand to the place of the houses of the perfume sellers which is the place of the house of ibn Hakim and that is the Euphrates today. He (the Imam) then said to me, 'O Mufaddal, this is where the people of Noah had fixed their idols, the Yaghuth, Ya'uq and Nasr.' He then moved until he rode his stumper. I then asked saying, 'I pray to Allah to keep my soul in service for your cause, how long did it take Noah, *'Alayhi al-Salam*, to build his Ark?' He (the Imam) said, 'It took him two *dawrs*.' I then asked, 'How long is a *dawr*?' He (the Imam) said, 'It is eight years.' I then said, 'al-'Ammah, (non-Shi'ah) say that it took him five years to build the Ark.' He (the Imam) said, 'No, that was not the case, Allah says, ". . . and our *al-Wahy* (and quickly)." (11:37, 23:27) I then asked him (the Imam) about the meaning of the words of Allah, most Majestic, most Glorious, '. . .

until our command came and the oven gushed forth water.' (11:40, 23:27) Where was it and how was it? He (the Imam) said, 'The oven was in the house of his old believing woman behind al-Qiblah (direction of (al-Ka'bah)) of the Masjid on the right side.' I said, 'That place today is the corner of al-Fil gate.' I then asked, 'Was it the first place from which water gushed forth?' He (the Imam) said, 'Yes, that is correct. Allah, most Majestic, most Glorious, liked to see the people of Noah become a sign. Then Allah, the most Blessed, the most High, sent rain on them and it flooded all over. The Euphrates flooded and all fountains. Allah, most Majestic, most Glorious, drowned all of them but He saved Noah and those who were with him in the Ark.' I then asked, 'For how long did Noah remain in the Ark before the water dried up and they came out?' He (the Imam) said, 'They remained in it for seven days and their nights. It circled around the House seven times, then it stopped on al-Judiy which is Euphrates of al-Kufah.' I then asked, 'Is the Masjid of al-Kufah old?' He (the Imam) said, 'Yes, it was the place for the *Salat* (prayer) of the Prophets. The Messenger of Allah, *O Allah grant compensation to Muhammad and his family worthy of their services to Your cause*, performed *Salat* (prayer) in it when he was taken for the night journey to the sky and Jibril said to him, "O Muhammad, this is Masjid of your father Adam, *'Alayhi al-Salam*, and the place of *Salat* (prayer) of Prophets. So disembark and perform *Salat* (prayer) there. He disembarked and performed *Salat* (prayer)." Jibril, *'Alayhi al-Salam*, ascended thereafter with him to the sky.'"

Noah, *'Alayhi al-Salam*, completed the ark

H 14870, h 422

Ali ibn Ibrahim has narrated from his father from Ahmad ibn Muhammad from ibn abu Nasr from Aban ibn 'Uthman from abu Hamzah al-Thumaliy from abu Razin al-Asadiy who has narrated the following:

"'Amir al-Mu'minin, Ali, *'Alayhi al-Salam*, has said, 'When Noah, *'Alayhi al-Salam*, completed the Ark and there was a time set for the destruction of his unbelieving people between him and his Lord that the oven must gush forth water. It began to gush out water and his woman said, "The oven has gushed forth water." He went to it and sealed it and water stopped. He then embarked whoever wanted to embark and took out whoever wanted to disembark. He then went to his seal and removed it. Allah, most Majestic, most Glorious, says, ". . . We opened the doors of the sky with pouring water. We made the earth to allow its fountains to flow with water and the waters met for a commandment that was determined and decreed, We carried him on something made of boards and nails."' (54:11-13) He (the Imam) said, 'The carpentry work took place in the middle of your Masjid - which is reduced in size – that measured seven hundred yards of his yards.'"

The woman of Noah

H 14871, h 423

Muhammad ibn Yahya has narrated from Ahmad ibn Muhammad from al-Hassan ibn Ali from certain persons of his people who has narrated the following:

"Abu 'Abd Allah, *'Alayhi al-Salam*, has said that the woman of Noah, *'Alayhi al-Salam*, came to him when he was building the Ark and said, 'Water is coming out of the oven.' He then went there quickly, placed a lid on it and sealed it with his seal. The water stopped. When he completed the Ark he went to remove the seal as well as the lid, then water began to gush out.'"

Religion of Noah

H 14872, h 424

Ali ibn Ibrahim has narrated from his father from Ahmad ibn Muhammad from ibn abu Nasr from Aban ibn 'Uthman from 'Isma'il al-Ju'fiy who has narrated the following:

"Abu Ja'far, *'Alayhi al-Salam*, has said that the religion of Noah, *'Alayhi al-Salam*, required to worship Allah alone with oneness and purity and denouncing belief in partners (for Him). It is the *fitrah* (the clay) on which people are designed. Allah formed a covenant with Noah, *'Alayhi al-Salam*, with the Prophets, *'Alayhim al-Salam* to worship Allah, most Blessed, most High, and not to consider anything as His partner. He commanded them to perform *Salat* (prayer), command others to do good and prohibit them from committing sins, accept the lawful and unlawful issues. He did not sanction on him laws of penalties and inheritance. This was his Shari'ah. Noah *'Alayhi al-Salam*, lived one thousand years less five hundred years, calling them in private and in public; but when they refused and showed hard headedness he then prayed, '. . . O Lord, I am defeated, so grant me help.' (54:10) Allah, most Majestic, most Glorious, sent him revelation, '. . . no one among your people will ever believe besides those who have believed, so do not feel bad about what they do.' (11:36) For this reason Noah, *'Alayhi al-Salam*, said, '. . . they will not reproduce anyone other than sinful unbelievers.' (71:27) Allah, most Majestic, most Glorious, sent him revelation that said, '. . . build an Ark in Our sight.'" (23:27)

Noah, *'Alayhi al-Salam*, was planting

H 14873, h 425

It is narrated from the narrator of the previous Hadith from his father and Muhammad ibn Yahya has narrated from Ahmad ibn Muhammad all from al-Hassan ibn Ali from 'Umar ibn Aban from 'Isma'il al-Ju'fiy who has narrated the following:

"Abu 'Abd Allah, *'Alayhi al-Salam*, has said that when Noah, *'Alayhi al-Salam*, was planting the seeds people passed by; they laughed and mocked him saying, 'He has become a planter.' When they became tall and thick trees, he cut them down, and then carved them. They said, 'He has become a carpenter.' He then put them together to build a ship. They passed by, laughed and mocked him saying, 'He has become a sailor in dry land,' but he completed the work.'"

The size of the ark of Noah

H 14874, h 426

Ali has narrated from his father from ibn Mahbub from al-Hassan ibn Salih al-Thawriy who has narrated the following:

"Abu 'Abd Allah, *'Alayhi al-Salam*, has said that the length of the Ark of Noah was one thousand two hundred arms' length, its width was eight hundred arms' length and its height was eight arms' length. It was of the size of the space between al-Safa' and al-Marwah. It circled around the House seven times, then it settled on al-Judiy.'"

Noah, *'Alayhi al-Salam*, carried eight pairs

H 14875, h 427

Muhammad ibn abu 'Abd Allah has narrated from Muhammad ibn al-Husayn from Muhammad ibn Sinan from 'Isma'il al-Ju'fiy and 'Abd al-Karim ibn 'Amr and 'Abd al-Hamid ibn abu al-Daylam who has narrated the following:

"Abu 'Abd Allah, *'Alayhi al-Salam*, has said that Noah, *'Alayhi al-Salam*, carried eight pairs (of living things) in the Ark as Allah, most Majestic, most Glorious, has said, '. . . eight pairs; two of sheep, two of goat, two of camels and two of cows.' (6:143) There were two pairs of sheep. It was of domesticated sheep of the kind people maintain. The other pair was of the mountain and wild sheep, which is lawful for hunting. There were two pairs of goats, one domesticated and the other pair was of the deer kind, which are wild ones that live in the wilderness. Of camel, there were two pairs, one pair of Arabic camel and the other kind was al-Bukhatiy. Of cows there were two pairs, one kind domesticated and the other kind was of the wild cows and every good kind of wild birds as well as domesticated ones, then the earth submerged in water.'"

Water rose by fifteen arms' length in height

H 14876, h 428

Muhammad ibn Yahya has narrated from Ahmad ibn Muhammad from al-Hassan ibn Ali from Dawud ibn Yazid from those whom he has mentioned who has narrated the following:

"Abu 'Abd Allah, *'Alayhi al-Salam*, has said that water rose by fifteen arms' length high above every mountain and every flat land.'"

Noah, *'Alayhi al-Salam*, lived for. . .

H 14877, h 429

A number of our people have narrated from Ahmad ibn Muhammad from Ali ibn al-Hakam from certain persons of our people who has narrated the following:

"Abu 'Abd Allah, *'Alayhi al-Salam*, has said that Noah, *'Alayhi al-Salam*, lived for two thousand and three hundred years of which eight hundred and fifty years was before his preaching as a Prophet. One thousand less five hundred years he lived among his people as the Prophet and five hundred years after disembarking the Ark in which time he built cities and settled his children in the towns. Thereafter the angel of death came to him when he was in the sun. He offered him greeting of peace and Noah, *'Alayhi al-Salam*, responded and asked, 'What brings you here, O angel of death?' He replied, 'I have come to take your soul away.' He said, 'Will you allow me to move in the shadow?' He said, 'Yes, you can do so.' He moved in the shadow and said, 'O angel of death, all the time that

I lived in the world feels to me like my moving from the sun to the shadow. Go ahead to complete your assignment.' He took away his soul *'Alayhi al-Salam.'"*

Noah, *'Alayhi al-Salam*, lived for . . .

H 14878, h 430

Muhammad ibn abu 'Abd Allah has narrated from Muhammad ibn al-Husayn from Muhammad ibn Sinan fn 'Isma'il ibn Jabir and 'Abd al-Karim ibn 'Amr and 'Abd al-Hamid ibn abu al-Daylam who has narrated the following:

"Abu 'Abd Allah, *'Alayhi al-Salam*, has said that Noah, *'Alayhi al-Salam*, lived for five hundred years after the flood. Then Jibril came to him and said, 'O Noah, your Prophet-hood is complete as well as your days. So look to the great name, the legacy of knowledge and the vestige of the knowledge of Prophet-hood, which is with you. You must give it to your son, Sam because I do not leave the earth without a scholar through whom obedience to Me is learned. Through him, My guidance to serve as means of salvation between the times of departing of one Prophet to the coming of the other Prophet remains available. I do not leave the people without My authority among them who calls people to Me and guides them to My path and who has the knowledge of My commandments. I have decided to make a guide for every people through whom the fortunate ones find guidance, so that he can serve as My authority and argument against the mischievous ones.' He (the Imam) said, 'Noah, *'Alayhi al-Salam*, gave the great name, the legacy of knowledge and the vestige of the knowledge of Prophet-hood to Sam. Haam and Yafath did not have the knowledge that could benefit anyone.' He (the Imam) said, 'He gave the glad news about the coming of Hud, *'Alayhi al-Salam*, and commanded them to obey him. He also commanded them to open the will every year to look into it (study) and make it a festival day for themselves.'"

People fabricate. . .

H 14879, h 431

Ali ibn Muhammad has narrated from Ali ibn al-'Abbas from al-Hassan ibn 'Abd al-Rahman from 'Asem ibn Humayd from abu Hamzah who has narrated the following:

"I once said to abu Ja'far, *'Alayhi al-Salam*, that certain persons of our people fabricate against those who oppose us and accuse them.' He (the Imam) said to me, 'Restraint from such involvement against them is more polite and graceful.'

"He (the Imam) then said, 'By Allah, O abu Hamzah, 'People, all of them except our Shi'ah, are sons of transgressors (adultery).' I then asked, 'How can I substantiate it?' He (the Imam) said, 'O abu Hamzah, the book of Allah which is revealed explains it. Allah, most Blessed, most High, has assigned three shares for us, *Ahl al-Bayt* in all of *al-Fay'* (assets seized from the enemy). He, most Majestic, most Glorious, has said, ". . . you must take notice that whatever amount you gain of anything, one-fifth of it belongs to Allah, the Messenger, the relatives, the orphans, the destitute and those who deplete their supplies on a journey." (8:41) We are the owners of one-fifth and whatever is gained from the enemy. We have made it (our shares in what people gain and assets taken from the enemy) unlawful to all people except our Shi'ah.

"By Allah, O abu Hamzah, whatever of the land is conquered, or any one-fifth is deducted or taxes imposed, collected and charged is unlawful to those who receive it, in the form of matrimonial issues or assets. When the truth will become dominant, a man then will love to sell his own beloved soul for the cheapest price and a man of them will seek to pay all of his belonging as ransom to rescue his soul, but they cannot materialize any of such desires. They by force have removed us and our Shi'ah from our rights without any good reason, right and valid argument.' I then asked him (the Imam) about the meaning of the words of Allah, most Majestic, most Glorious, '. . . do they expect for us anything except one of the two good things?' (9:52) He (the Imam) said, 'It is death in obedience to Allah or to end up in the time when al-Qa'im will reappear with divine authority and power. We expect for them, despite the difficult conditions we go through, that Allah will afflict them with a suffering by His power.' He (the Imam) said, 'It is metamorphosed' or by our hands which is 'being killed'. Allah, most Majestic, most Glorious, has said to His Prophet, *O Allah grant compensation to Muhammad and his family worthy of their services to Your cause*, '. . . wait and we also wait with you.' It is waiting for the coming of affliction upon their enemies.'"

Explanation of the words of Allah. . .

H 14880, h 432
Through the same chain of narrators as that of the previous Hadith, the following is narrated:
"It is an explanation of the meaning of the words of Allah, most Majestic, most Glorious, '. . . say, "I do not ask you for any compensation for it (teaching you the guidance of Allah) and I am not of the pretending ones." He is not for anything other than being a reminder for the worlds.' Abu Ja'far, *'Alayhi al-Salam*, said, 'He is 'Amir al-Mu'minin, Ali, *'Alayhi al-Salam*.' '. . . and you will learn the news about him after a certain amount of time.' (38:86-88) He (the Imam) said that it will take place in the time when al-Qa'im will reappear with divine authority and power.

"This is about the meaning of the words of Allah, most Majestic, most Glorious. '. . . We had given the book to Musa; then they created differences in it.' (11:110) He (the Imam) said, 'They created differences among themselves as this nation has done in the book. They will create such differences in the book which al-Qa'im will bring to them until a great number of people refuse to accept it, after he will present it before them. Then their necks will be struck down.'

"About the meaning of the words of Allah, most Majestic, most Glorious, '. . . was it not because of the definitive word He would have settled it among them. The unjust ones will suffer a painful punishment.' (42:21) He (the Imam) said,

'Had it not been because of what Allah, most Majestic, most Glorious, has said about them, al-Qa'im would not leave anyone of them alive.'

"About the meaning of the words of Allah, most Majestic, most Glorious, '. . . those who acknowledge the coming of the day of recompense,' (70:26) he (the Imam) said, 'It is when al-Qa'im will reappear with divine authority and power.'

"This is about the meaning of the words of Allah, most Majestic, most Glorious. '. . . Allah is our Lord, we were not pagans.' (6:23) He (the Imam) said, 'They intend thereby *Walayah* (guardianship of Ali, with divine authority and knowledge).'

"About the meaning of the words of Allah, most Majestic, most Glorious, '. . . say, "Truth has come and falsehood is banished."' (17:81) He (the Imam) said, 'When al-Qa'im will reappear with divine authority and power the government of falsehood will be banished.'"

When you read al-Quran . . .

H 14881, h 433

It is narrated from the narrator of the previous Hadith from Ali ibn al-Hassan from Mansur ibn Yunus from abu Basir who has narrated the following:

"I once asked abu 'Abd Allah, *'Alayhi al-Salam*, about the meaning of the words of Allah, most Majestic, most Glorious, '. . . when you read al-Quran ask Allah for protection against Satan, condemned to be stoned. He has no control over the believing people who place their trust with their Lord.'(16:98-99) He (the Imam) said, 'O abu Muhammad, by Allah, he (Satan) controls the body of the believing people but not their religion. He gained control over Ayyub, *'Alayhi al-Salam*, and changed his physical appearance but could not control his religion. He may gain control over the believing people's body but cannot gain control over their religion.' I then asked about the meaning of the words of Allah, most Majestic, most Glorious, '. . . his only control takes place on those who take him as thier guardians and the pagans.' (16:100) He (the Imam) said, 'In the case of pagans he controls their body as well as their religion.'"

Tawaf in the time of ignorance

H 14882, h 434

It is narrated from the narrator of the previous Hadith from Ali ibn al-Hassan from Mansur from Hariz ibn 'Abd Allah from al-Fudayl who has narrated the following:

"I once entered the Masjid al-Haram (the Sacred) with abu Ja'far, *'Alayhi al-Salam*, who was leaning on me and he (the Imam) looked at the people when we were at the gate of banu Shaybah. He (the Imam) said, 'O Fudayl, this is how they made *tawaf* in the time of ignorance when they did not recognize any truth or follow any religion. O Fudayl, look at them, falling on their face, may Allah condemn them, of the metamorphosed creatures fallen on their faces. He (the Imam) then read this verse, '. . . are those who walk fallen on their face better guided or those who walk straight on the right path,' (67:22) and said, 'It (path) is a reference to Ali, *'Alayhi al-Salam*, and the executors of the will.' He (the Imam) then read this verse, '. . . when they see him happy with high rank, the faces of unbelievers will become wicked looking and it will be said to them, "This is that to whom you were called."' (67:27) He (the Imam) said, 'This name (zulfah) is only for Ali, *'Alayhi al-Salam*, O Fudayl, no one else is named with this name except a fabricator and a liar to the day of al-Ba's (war) suffering. O yes, by Allah, O Fudayl, Allah, most Majestic, most Glorious, has no other people performing al-Hajj except you and He does not forgive the sins of anyone except your sins. He does not accept the deeds of anyone except your deeds. You are the ones to whom this verse applies, ". . . if you stay away from major sins which are prohibited We will expiate your evil deeds and admit you in a graceful dwelling." (4:31) O Fudayl, will you not be happy to perform *Salat* (prayer), pay *Zakat* and hold back your tongues then enter the garden (paradise)?' He (the Imam) then read this verse, '. . . have you not seen those to whom it is said, "Hold back your hands, perform *Salat* (prayer) and pay *Zakat*." (4:77) To you only by Allah this verse applies.'"

Allah does not love destruction

H 14883, h 435

A number of our people have narrated from Sahl ibn Ziyad from ibn Mahbub from Muhammad ibn Sulayman al-Azdiy from abu al-Jarud from abu Ishaq who has narrated the following:

"'Amir al-Mu'minin, Ali, *'Alayhi al-Salam*, has said, 'When he takes control (of the government) he spreads destruction in the land of the plantations and lives, [with his injustice and wicked behavior] and Allah does not love destruction.' (4:31)

Their guardians are Satan [idols]

H 14884, h 436

Sahl ibn Ziyad has narrated from ibn Mahbub from ibn Ri'ab from Humran ibn 'A'yan from narrated the following:

"Abu Ja'far, *'Alayhi al-Salam*, has said, '. . . Those who have disbelieved their guardians are Satan [idols].'" (2:257)

Who can intercede before Him

H 14885, h 437

Ali ibn Ibrahim has narrated from Ahmad ibn Muhammad from Muhammad ibn Khalid from Muhammad ibn Sinan from abu Jarir al-Qummiy – Muhammad ibn 'Ubayd Allah , in another copy, 'Abd Allah – who has narrated the following:

"Abu al-Hassan, *'Alayhi al-Salam*, has said, '. . . to Him belongs all that is in the sky and in the earth [and all that is between them and under al-Thara' (soil), who knows the unseen and the apparent, the Beneficent, the Merciful]. Who is he who can intercede before Him without His permission?'"

How much is *Ayat al-Kursi*

H 14886, h 438
Muhammad ibn Khalid has narrated from Hamzah ibn 'Ubayd from 'Isma'il ibn 'Abbad who has narrated the following:
"Abu 'Abd Allah, *'Alayhi al-Salam*, has said, '. . . they cannot encompass anything of His knowledge except for what He wants. . . . He is most High and most Great [all praise belongs to Allah, Cherisher of the worlds] and the two verses that follow.'" (2:255)

How to read certain verses

H 14887, h 439
Ahmad ibn Muhammad ibn 'Isa from al-Husayn ibn Sayf from his brother from his father am abu Bakr ibn Muhammad who has narrated the following:
"I heard abu 'Abd Allah, *'Alayhi al-Salam*, read this verse as, '. . . they were shaken [then they were shaken] while the messenger says . . .'" (2:214)

[Under the guardian-ship of Satan]

H 14888, h 440
Ali ibn Ibrahim has narrated from his father from Ali ibn Asbat from Ali ibn abu Hamzah from abu Basir who has narrated the following:
"Abu 'Abd Allah, *'Alayhi al-Salam*, has said, '. . . they followed what Satans followed [under the guardianship of Satan] against the kingdom of Sulayman.' (2:102) He (the Imam) also read, '. . . ask banu Israel, how many clear signs [of whom certain ones believed and certain others rejected, others confirmed and yet others changed] and those who change the bounties of Allah after that it has come to him, you must take notice that the penalty of Allah is stern.'" (2:211)

(Inside the square brackets in the above Ahadith are the words of the Imam as interpretations of the verse of the al-Quran)

Stop eating certain things

H 14889, h 441
Muhammad ibn Yahya has narrated from Ahmad ibn Muhammad ibn 'Isa from 'Abd al-Rahman ibn Hammad from Muhammad ibn Ishaq from Muhammad ibn al-Fayd who has narrated the following:
"I once said to abu 'Abd Allah, *'Alayhi al-Salam*, that when one of us becomes ill the physicians instruct him to stop eating certain things. He (the Imam) said, 'We, *Ahl al-Bayt*, do not stop him from eating anything except dates and we use apple and cold water to cure an illness.' I then asked, 'Why do you stop him from eating dates?' He (the Imam) said, 'It is because the Holy Prophet stopped Ali, *'Alayhi al-Salam*, in his illness from eating dates.'"

Stopping a person in his illness...

H 14890, h 442

It is narrated from the narrator of the previous Hadith from Ahmad from ibn Mahbub from ibn Ri'ab from al-Halabiy who has narrated the following:

"I once heard abu 'Abd Allah, *'Alayhi al-Salam*, say, 'Stopping a person in his illness from eating certain foods is not beneficial after seven days.'"

Reducing such foods is beneficial

H 14891, h 443

A number of our people have narrated from Ahmad ibn Muhammad ibn Khalid from 'Abd al-Karim from Musa ibn Bakr who has narrated the following:

"Abu al-Hassan, Musa, *'Alayhi al-Salam*, has said, 'Stopping a patient completely from eating certain foods in his illness, is not beneficial, only reducing such foods is beneficial.'"

Walking increases the illness

H 14892, h 444

Muhammad ibn Yahya has narrated from Ahmad ibn Muhammad ibn 'Isa from abu Yahya al-Wasitiy from certain persons of our people who has narrated the following:

"Abu 'Abd Allah, *'Alayhi al-Salam*, has said, 'Walking of a patient contrarily increases the illness. My father, *'Alayhi al-Salam*, in his illness needed to be carried on a piece of clothing for his wudu and so on because he (the Imam) said that walking for a patient has an adverse effect.'"

I saw in my dream . . .

H 14893, h 445

Ali ibn Ibrahim has narrated from his father from ibn abu 'Umayr from ibn 'Udhaynah who has narrated the following:

"Once, a man came to abu 'Abd Allah, *'Alayhi al-Salam*, and said, 'I saw in my dream that the sun was shining on my head but not on my body.' He (the Imam) said, 'You will gain a great matter, a shining light and a universal religion. Had it covered your body you would be submerged in it but it has covered your head. Have you not read, ". . . when he saw the sun shining, he said this is my Lord. . . . but when it disappeared, he [Ibrahim, *'Alayhi al-Salam*,] denounced it." (6:78) He said, 'I pray to Allah to keep my soul in service for your cause, they say that sun is a Khalifah (successor of the Holy Prophet) or a king.' He (the Imam) said, 'I do not see you can become a Khalifah and there was no king in your ancestors; however, what Khilafat is greater than religion and the light for which you can have hope to enter the garden (paradise)? They confuse it.' I then said, 'You have spoken the truth, I pray to Allah to keep my soul in service for your cause.'"

248

Sun shine on his feet . . .

H 14894, h 446

It is narrated from the narrator of the previous Hadith from a man who has narrated the following:

"About the case of a man who in his dream had seen the sun shine on his feet and not on his body, he (the Imam) said, 'He will gain plenty of things that the earth grows of wheat and dates which is lawful except that he must work hard for it as Adam, *'Alayhi al-Salam*, did.'"

When abu Hanifah was with him . . .

H 14895, h 447

Ali has narrated from his father from al-Hassan ibn Ali from abu Ja'far al-Sa'igh from Muhammad ibn Muslim who has narrated the following:

"Once I visited abu 'Abd Allah, *'Alayhi al-Salam*, when abu Hanifah was with him (the Imam). I said, 'I pray to Allah to keep my soul in service for your cause, I have seen a strange dream.' He (the Imam) said to me, 'You can explain it. The scholar for it is sitting here,' he made a gesture with his hand to abu Hanifah. I said, 'I saw in a dream that I entered my house and my wife came out. She broke a large number of walnuts and spread them on me. I was amazed because of this dream.' Abu Hanifah said, 'You are a man who disputes and argues against mean people about the legacy of your wife and after a tiring work you achieve from her what you need, by the will of Allah.' Abu 'Abd Allah, *'Alayhi al-Salam*, said, 'You have found it, by Allah, O abu Hanifah.' Abu Hanifah left and I said, 'I pray to Allah to keep my soul in service for your cause, I did not want this hostile person (to *'A'immah*) to interpret my dream.' He (the Imam) said, 'O ibn Muslim, Allah will not show you bad things. Their interpretation does not concur with our interpretation and our interpretation does not agree with their interpretations. The interpretation is not as he said it is.' I then said, 'I pray to Allah to keep my soul in service for your cause, you just said that he had found the interpretation. Then you swore. How has he missed the truth?' He (the Imam) said, 'I swore that he found it (meaning the misinterpretation but not the right one).' I then asked, 'What is the right interpretation?' He (the Imam) said, 'O ibn Muslim, you will find a *Mut'ah* (marriage for a certain period) and your wife will learn about it. She will tear down your new clothes because the shells are the clothes of the nut.' Ibn Muslim has said that, by Allah, his interpretation did not take more than a Friday morning to materialize. On a Friday morning I was sitting at the door that a girl passed by and I liked her. I commanded my slave and he brought her back inside my house. I formed a *Mut'ah* contract with her but my wife noticed my presence as well as her presence. She came in on us. The girl ran to the door but I remained inside. She tore down on me my new clothes that I used to wear on *'id* days.'

"Musa al-Zawwar al-'Attar came to abu 'Abd Allah, *'Alayhi al-Salam*, and said, 'O child of the Messenger of Allah, *O Allah grant compensation to Muhammad and his family worthy of their services to Your cause*, I have seen a dream which has terrified me. I saw my son-in-law who is dead embraced me and I am afraid that the time of my death may have come close.' He (the Imam) said, 'O Musa, expect death every morning and evening because it will approach us inevitably but embracing of the dead is longevity of the life of the living. What was the name of your son-in-law?' He replied, 'It was Husayn.' He (the Imam) said, 'Your dream means that you will live and visit the shrine of abu 'Abd Allah, al-Husayn, *'Alayhi al-Salam*. Whoever embraces one who is of the same name as al-Husayn, *'Alayhi al-Salam*, he visits him by the will of Allah.'"

I saw in a dream . . .

H 14896, h 448

'Isma'il ibn 'Abd Allah al-Qarashiy has narrated the following:

"Once a man came to abu 'Abd Allah, *'Alayhi al-Salam*, and said this. 'O child of the Messenger of Allah, *O Allah grant compensation to Muhammad and his family worthy of their services to Your cause*, I saw in a dream that I was moving out of al-Kufah to a place that I know. There was something in the shape of a man or a piece of wood carved as such on a wooden horse showing his sword and I was looking at him, terrified and frightened.' He (the Imam) said, 'You are a man who wants to slay another man because of his assets, have fear of Allah who has created you then causes you to die.' He said, 'I testify that you have received the knowledge and have interpreted it from its right source. I can inform you, O child of the Messenger of Allah, *O Allah grant compensation to Muhammad and his family worthy of their services to Your cause*, about your interpretation for me. A man of our neighbors came to me and displayed before me an asset and I thought to own it for a greatly reduced value because I knew that there is no other demand for it.' Abu 'Abd Allah, *'Alayhi al-Salam*, asked, 'Does your companion accept our *'Amr, Walayah* (guardianship of *'A'immah* with divine authority and knowledge) and denounce our enemy?' He replied, 'Yes, O child of the Messenger of Allah, *O Allah grant compensation to Muhammad and his family worthy of their services to Your cause*, he is a man of good understanding and strong religion. I repent before Allah, most Majestic, most Glorious, and before you because of my intention about him and about myself. Instruct me, O child of the Messenger of Allah, 'Had he been a *Nasib* (hostile to *'A'immah*) was slaying lawful?' He (the Imam) said, 'You must return the trust to the one who has entrusted you and has expected you to provide him with good advice, even if he is a killer of al-Husayn, *'Alayhi al-Salam*.'"

Supporting myself . . . and wept

H 14897, h 449

Muhammad ibn Yahya has narrated from Ahmad ibn Muhammad ibn 'Isa from al-Husayn ibn Sa'id from Fadalah ibn Ayyub from Sayf ibn 'Amirah from abu Bakr al-Hadramiy from 'Abd al-Malik ibn 'A'yan who has narrated the following:

"I once got up in the presence of abu Ja'far, *'Alayhi al-Salam*, supporting myself by my hand and wept.' He (the Imam) asked, 'What is the matter?' I replied, 'I had hoped that I will attend, when al-Qa'im will reappear with divine authority and power, with proper strength.' He (the Imam) said, 'Will you not be happy that your enemies kill each other and you remain safely in your homes? When that time comes, one of you will receive the strength of forty men with hearts like chunks of steel that if thrown on the mountains will uproot them. You are the keepers of the earth and the guards of its treasures.'"

When is victory and relief

H 14898, h 450

A number of our people have narrated from Ahmad ibn Muhammad ibn Khalid, from Muhammad ibn Ali, from 'Abd al-Rahman ibn abu Hashim, from Sufyan al-Jaririy, from abu Maryam Ansari, from Harun ibn 'Antarah from his father who has narrated the following:

"I have heard 'Amir al-Mu'minin, Ali, *'Alayhi al-Salam*, many times say, with his hands joined and fingers crisscrossed, 'My ease is my constraint and my constraint is my ease.' He (the Imam) then said, 'Destroyed are those who think it is now and rescued are those who wait for its coming soon who do not allow the pebbles to destabilize the anchor (of their belief). I swear by Allah in a true oath that after grief and sadness there is a marvelous victory (reappearance of al-Qa'im with divine authority and power).'"

How far is Qarqisah . . .

H 14899, h 451

Muhammad ibn Yahya has narrated from Ahmad ibn Muhammad from ibn Faddal from Ali ibn 'Uqbah from his father from Maysarah who has narrated the following:

"Abu Ja'far, *'Alayhi al-Salam*, once said, 'O Maysarah, how far is Qarqisah from you?' I replied, 'It is near the bank of Euphrates.' He (the Imam) said, 'O yes, there an event will take place the like of which has not happened from the time Allah, most Blessed, most High, created the skies and the earth and no such event will take place as long as the skies and earth will be there. It will be a feast for the birds. It will satisfy the beasts of earth and the birds of the sky where Qays will perish but no one will be called to help him.' From more than one person this is narrated and with an addition of, 'Come to the flesh of tyrants.'"

Any banner raised before...

H 14900, h 452

It is narrated from the narrator of the previous Hadith from Ahmad ibn Muhammad from al-Husayn ibn Sa'id from Hammad ibn 'Isa from al-Husayn ibn al-Mukhtar from abu Basir who has narrated the following:

"Abu 'Abd Allah, *'Alayhi al-Salam*, has said, 'Any banner raised before al-Qa'im will reappear with divine authority and power is the banner of Satan who worships things other than Allah, most Majestic, most Glorious.'"

Killing will take place . . . in Quraysh

H 14901, h 453

It is narrated from the narrator of the previous Hadith from Ahmad ibn Muhammad from Ali ibn al-Hakam from Hisham ibn Salim from Shihab ibn 'Abd Rabbihi who has narrated the following:

"Abu 'Abd Allah, *'Alayhi al-Salam*, once said to me, 'O Shihab, a great deal of killing will take place in a family of Quraysh, so much so that even if one of them is invited to accept Khilafah he will refuse.' He (the Imam) then said, 'O Shihab, do not think that I thereby intended my cousins these ones.' Shihab has said, 'I testify that he (the Imam) intended those people.'"

When people did what they did

H 14902, h 454

Humayd ibn Ziyad has narrated from al-Hassan ibn Muhammad al-Kindiy from more than one person from Aban ibn 'Uthman from al-Fudayl from Zurarah who has narrated the following:

"Abu Ja'far, *'Alayhi al-Salam*, has stated this Hadith. He (the Imam) said, 'When people did what they did and when they voted for abu Bakr, nothing stopped 'Amir al-Mu'minin, Ali, from calling to himself other than considering the condition of the people. It was for fear for them of turning to apostasy, leaving Islam to worship idols, abandoning the testimony that only Allah deserves worship, He is one and has no partners and to testify that Muhammad is His servant and Messenger. It was more beloved to him to leave them with what they had done as opposed to their turning to apostasy and leaving Islam. Destruction is for those who did what they did. Those who did not do so and just joined other people without proper knowledge and without animosity to 'Amir al-Mu'minin, Ali, *'Alayhi al-Salam*, it does not make them unbelievers or out of Islam. For this reason Ali, *'Alayhi al-Salam*, kept his cause to himself as he did and voted under duress when he did not find any supporter.'"

They turned to apostasy . . .

H 14903, h 455

Narrated to us Muhammad ibn Yahya has narrated from Ahmad ibn Muhammad ibn 'Isa from al-Husayn ibn Sa'id from Ali ibn al-Nu'man from 'Abd Allah ibn Muskan from 'Abd al-Rahim al-Qasir who has narrated the following:

"I once said to abu Ja'far, *'Alayhi al-Salam*, that people feel shocked when we say that they turned to apostasy.' He (the Imam) said, 'O 'Abd al-Rahim, people after the death of the Messenger of Allah, *O Allah grant compensation to Muhammad and his family worthy of their services to Your cause*, turned to the people of ignorance. Al-Ansar (people of al-Madinah) were isolated and their isolation was not in goodness. They voted for Sa'd expressing the slogans of the time of ignorance, 'O Sa'd you are the hope, your hairs look good and you are the champion.'"

Like those who followed Harun . . .

H 14904, h 456

Humayd ibn Ziyad has narrated from al-Hassan ibn Muhammad al-Kindiy from more than one person from certain persons of his people from Aban ibn 'Uthman from abu Ja'far al-Ahwal and al-Fudayl ibn Yasar from Zakaria al-Naqqad who has narrated the following:

"I once heard abu Ja'far, *'Alayhi al-Salam*, say that people after the Messenger of Allah, *O Allah grant compensation to Muhammad and his family worthy of their services to Your cause*, became like those who followed Harun *'Alayhi al-Salam*, and those who followed the calf. Abu Bakr called to vote but Ali, *'Alayhi al-Salam*, rejected (all things) except al-Quran, 'Umar called to vote for him but Ali, *'Alayhi al-Salam*, rejected except al-Quran, 'Uthman called to vote for him but Ali, *'Alayhi al-Salam*, rejected except al-Quran which he did not reject. Whoever rises, before the coming out of al-Dajjal, and calls to pledge allegiance with him (vote for him as the successor of the Messenger of Allah) he will find people who will vote for him and raise the banner of misguidance, and the owner of such banner will be a transgressor.'"

Hadith of abu Dharr, may Allah be pleased with him

H 14905, h 457

Abu Ali al-Ash'ariy has narrated from Muhammad ibn 'Abd al-Jabbar from 'Abd Allah ibn Muhammad from Salmah al-lu'lu'iy from a man who has narrated the following:

"Abu 'Abd Allah, *'Alayhi al-Salam*, once said, 'O yes, I can tell you how Salman and abu Dharr accepted Islam.' A man then hastefully said, 'I know how Salman became a Muslim. Tell me about how abu Dharr became a Muslim.' He (the Imam) said, 'Abu Dharr lived in the valley of Marr (a place one day's journey from Makkah), grazing sheep. Once a wolf approached his sheep from the right side but he drove it away with his cane, it then came from the left and he drove it away with his staff saying, 'I have not seen a wolf as filthy and evil as you are.' The wolf said, 'By Allah, more evil than me are people of Makkah. Allah, most Majestic, most Glorious, has sent a Prophet to them but they have rejected him and scolded him.'

"It struck the ears of abu Dharr. He said to his wife, 'Bring for me my supply bag, my tools and walking stick.' He then left for Makkah to find information about the news he had received from the wolf, until he arrived in Makkah during the hot hour of the day, tired and exhausted. He went to Zam Zam (the water fountain) because of thirst. He picked up a bucketful of water but it came out full of milk. He then said to himself, 'This by Allah shows that what the wolf had told and about the matter I have come here is right.' He drank the milk and then moved to a side of Masjid where he found a number of the people of Quraysh sitting in a circle. He sat nearby and found them reproaching the Holy Prophet, *O Allah grant compensation to Muhammad and his family worthy of their services to Your cause*, as the wolf had said. They continued speaking against the Holy Prophet, and reproaching him until abu Talib, toward the end of the day, came out. On seeing him, they said to each other, 'You must stop now, his uncle is coming.' Abu Dharr has said, 'They stopped reproaching and he continued speaking to them until the end of the day. Then he stood up to leave and I also moved behind him. He turned to me and asked, 'Say what you need?' I said, 'This Prophet who is sent to you.' He asked, 'What do you want from him?' I replied, 'I want to accept his religion, acknowledge his truthfulness, offer my soul in his services and obey whatever he will command me.' He asked, 'Will you do it?' I replied, 'Yes, I will do so.' He said, 'Come tomorrow at this time so I can send you to him.' I waited that night in the Masjid until the next day. I sat with those people and they spoke of the Holy Prophet, *O Allah grant compensation to Muhammad and his family worthy of their services to Your cause*, with reproach until abu Talib appeared and on seeing him they said to each other, 'You must stop; his uncle is coming.' He continued speaking to them until he stood up to leave. I followed him and offered him greeting of peace.

'He said, 'Say what you need.' I said, 'This Prophet who is sent to you.' He asked, 'What do you want from him?' I replied, 'I want to accept his religion, acknowledge his truthfulness, offer my soul in his services and obey whatever he will command me.' He asked, 'Will you do it?' I replied, 'Yes, I will do so.' He said, 'Come with me.'

"I followed him and he took me to a house where Hamzah, *'Alayhi al-Salam,* was sitting. I offered him greeting of peace and sat down. He asked, 'What do you need?' I said, 'This Prophet who is sent to you.' He asked, 'What do you want from him?' I replied, 'I want to accept his religion, acknowledge his truthfulness, offer my soul in his services and obey whatever he will command me.' He asked, 'Will you testify that only Allah deserves worship, and that Muhammad is His Messenger?' Abu Dharr has said, 'I testified.

'Hamzah took me to a house where Ja'far, *'Alayhi al-Salam,* was present. I offered him greeting of peace and sat down.' Ja'far, *'Alayhi al-Salam,* asked, 'What do you need?' I said, 'This Prophet who is sent to you.' He asked, 'What do you want from him?' I replied, 'I want to accept his religion, acknowledge his truthfulness, offer my soul in his services and obey whatever he will command me.' He asked, 'Will you testify that only Allah deserves worship, and that He has no partners and that Muhammad is His servant and Messenger?'

'I testified and he took me to a house where Ali, *'Alayhi al-Salam,* was present. I offered him greeting of peace and sat down. He asked, 'What do you need?' I said, 'This Prophet who is sent to you.' He asked, 'What do you want from him?' I replied, 'I want to accept his religion, acknowledge his truthfulness, offer my soul in his services and obey whatever he will command me.' He asked, 'Will you testify that only Allah deserves worship, and that Muhammad is His Messenger?'

'I testified, and he took me to a house where the Messenger of Allah, *O Allah grant compensation to Muhammad and his family worthy of their services to Your cause*, was present. I offered him greeting of peace and sat down. The

Messenger of Allah, *O Allah grant compensation to Muhammad and his family worthy of their services to Your cause*, asked, 'What do you need?' I said, 'This Prophet who is sent to you.' He asked, 'What do you want from him?' I replied, 'I want to accept his religion, acknowledge his truthfulness, offer my soul in his services and obey whatever he will command me.' He asked, 'Will you testify that only Allah deserves worship, and that Muhammad is His Messenger?' I said, 'I testify that only Allah deserves worship and I testify that Muhammad is His Messenger.'

'The Messenger of Allah, *O Allah grant compensation to Muhammad and his family worthy of their services to Your cause*, then said to me, 'O abu Dharr, go to your country and you will find that one of your cousins have died who has left no heirs behind except you. Take his legacy and stay with your family until our *'Amr* (religion) becomes victorious.' He (the Imam) said that he returned, took the asset of legacy and stayed with his family until the *'Amr* (religion) of the Messenger of Allah, *O Allah grant compensation to Muhammad and his family worthy of their services to Your cause*, received victory.' Abu 'Abd Allah, *'Alayhi al-Salam*, said, 'This was the story of abu Dharr and how he accepted Islam. The story of Salman is what you have heard.' He said, 'I pray to Allah to keep my soul in service for your cause, tell us the story of Salman.' He (the Imam) said, 'You have heard it.' He (the Imam) did not tell it because of bad manners of the man."

Thumamah ibn 'Uthal, captured

H 14906, h 458

Ali ibn Ibrahim has narrated from his father from Ahmad ibn Muhammad from ibn abu Nasr from Aban ibn 'Uthman from Zurarah who has narrated the following:

"Abu Ja'far, *'Alayhi al-Salam*, has said that a group of the horsemen of the Holy Prophet, *O Allah grant compensation to Muhammad and his family worthy of their services to Your cause*, had captured Thumamah ibn 'Uthal. The Messenger of Allah, *O Allah grant compensation to Muhammad and his family worthy of their services to Your cause*, had said, 'O Lord, make me dominant over Thumamah.' The Messenger of Allah, *O Allah grant compensation to Muhammad and his family worthy of their services to Your cause*, said to him, 'I give you three choices and you can choose one. I can eliminate you.' He said, 'In this case you have killed a great persona (a great chief).' 'I can release you in exchange for ransom.' He said, 'You will find me very expensive.' 'I can set you free as a favor.' He said, 'In this case you will find me grateful.' He (the Messenger of Allah) said, 'I set you free as a favor.' He said, 'I testify that only Allah deserves worship, and I testify that you, Muhammad are the Messenger of Allah, I had found you to be the Messenger of Allah but I did not want to testify when I was tied down.'"

When the Holy Prophet was born, a man came

H 14907, h 459

It is narrated from the narrator of the previous Hadith from Ahmad ibn Muhammad from Aban from abu Nasr who has narrated the following:

"Abu Ja'far, *'Alayhi al-Salam*, has said that when the Holy Prophet, *O Allah grant compensation to Muhammad and his family worthy of their services to Your cause*, was born, a man of the followers of the book came to a group of Quraysh. Among this group one was Hisham ibn al-Mughirah, al-Walid ibn al-Mughirah, al-'As ibn Hisham, abu Wajzah ibn abu 'Amr ibn 'Umayyah and 'Utbah ibn Rabi', and asked, 'Is a child born among you last night?' They replied, 'No, no child is born.' He then said, 'He then is born in Palestine. His name is Ahmad with a mole of blackish silk color. The destruction of the followers of the Bible will come through his hands. This has come to pass up on you, O Quraysh.' They dispersed and asked. They were told that a boy is born in the house of 'Abd Allah ibn 'Abd al-Muttalib. They searched and found the man. They told him that a boy, by Allah, is born in their community. He then asked if he was born before or after what he had said to them. They said that he was born before his telling to them about him. He then said that they must go to see the child. They went to his mother and asked her to show to them the child. She said, 'My child, by Allah, on falling on the ground did not fall like other children. On falling on the ground he supported himself with his hands, raised his head to the sky and looked to it. Thereafter a light came out from him and in its brightness I saw the castles of Busra' and I heard a caller in the air saying, "You have given birth to the master of the nation. When you give birth to him you must say, 'I protect him by the One against the evil of all jealous ones and name him Muhammad.'"' The man then asked her to show him to them. She showed him and he looked at him. He then looked on the other side on his mole (special) mark between his shoulders. He fainted and fell down. They took the child home to his mother and said, 'May Allah bless you with him.' When they came out the man had regained consciousness. They asked, 'Woe is on you, what happened to you?' He replied, 'Prophet-hood from banu Israel is gone to the Day of Judgment. This by Allah, will destroy them.' Quraysh became happy but when he saw them happy he said, 'Although you have become happy, by Allah, he will dominate you with a strong domination about which the people of the west and east will speak. Abu Sufyan would say, 'Will he dominate his city?'"

When Aminah went in labor. . .

H 14908, h 460

Humayd ibn Ziyad has narrated from Muhammad ibn Ayyub from Muhammad ibn Ziyad from Asbat ibn Salim who has narrated the following:

"Abu 'Abd Allah, *'Alayhi al-Salam*, has said that when Aminah went in labor for the birth of the Holy Prophet, *O Allah grant compensation to Muhammad and his family worthy of their services to Your cause*, Fatimah daughter of Asad, wife of abu Talib was there all the time to help her. They both in their astonishment asked each other, 'Did you see what I just saw?' They then asked each other, 'What did you see?' The other one answered, 'This light that shone between the east and west.' At that time abu Talib came and asked, 'What has happened and why are you astonished?' Fatimah informed him and he said, 'I can give you the glad news of the birth of a son from you who will be the executor of the will of this child.'"

'Who is he that can give a good loan . . .

H 14909, h 461
Muhammad ibn Ahmad has narrated from 'Abd Allah ibn al-Salt from Yunus and 'Abd 'Abd al-'Aziz ibn al-Muhtadiy from a man from who has narrated the following:
"It is about the meaning of the words of Allah, most Majestic, most Glorious, '. . . who is he that can give a good loan to Allah who will make it increase in multiples and grant him gracious reward?' (57:11) Abu al-Hassan, *al-Madi* (who passed away), *'Alayhi al-Salam*, has said, 'It (the good loan) is the compensation (khums) to the Imam in the government of the sinful ones.'"

Very proper for a believing person

H 14910, h 462
Yunus has narrated from Sinan ibn Tarif who has narrated the following:
"I once heard abu 'Abd Allah, *'Alayhi al-Salam*, say this. 'It is very proper for a believing person to have fear of Allah, most Blessed, most High. Such fear must be like one's fear of falling in the fire when he is on the brink of the fire and one must have great hope in Him as if he is of the people of the garden (paradise).' He (the Imam) then said, 'Allah is with the expectation of His servant. If he expects good from Him, it is good and if he expects bad, then it is bad.'"

A messenger from al-Madinah came . . .

H 14911, h 463
Muhammad ibn Yahya has narrated from Ahmad ibn Muhammad from ibn Sinan from 'Isma'il ibn Jabir who has narrated the following:
"Once I was with abu 'Abd Allah, *'Alayhi al-Salam*, when a messenger from al-Madinah came. He (the Imam) asked, 'Who is in your company?' He replied, 'I have no company.' He (the Imam) said, 'Had I seen you before leaving for the journey I would have made you to follow proper discipline.' He (the Imam) then said, 'One is Satan, two are two Satans, three are a company and four are friends.'"

Number of travel-mates is four . . .

H 14912, h 464
It is narrated from the narrator of the previous Hadith from Ahmad from al-Husayn ibn Sayf from his brother, Ali from his father who has said that narrated to him Muhammad ibn al-Muthanna who has said that narrated to him a man of banu Nawfil ibn 'Abd al-Muttalib who has narrated the following:

"Abu Ja'far, *'Alayhi al-Salam*, has said that the Messenger of Allah, *O Allah grant compensation to Muhammad and his family worthy of their services to Your cause*, has said, 'The most beloved number of travel-mates is four. If a people number above seven it becomes a great deal of noise.'"

Not to go on a journey alone . . .

H 14913, h 465

A number of our people have narrated from Ahmad ibn Muhammad ibn Khalid from his father from those whom he has mentioned who has narrated the following:

"Abu al-Hassan, Musa, *'Alayhi al-Salam*, has narrated from his father from his grandfather, *'Alayhim al-Salam*, who have said this. The Messenger of Allah, *O Allah grant compensation to Muhammad and his family worthy of their services to Your cause*, advised Ali, *'Alayhi al-Salam*. He said, 'You must not go on a journey alone; Satan is with one as well as with two but a little far. O Ali, if a man travels alone he is lost and two are two lost ones but three forms a group' – certain one of them (narrators) has said, 'it is travelers.'"

Travel with your sword . . .

H 14914, h 466

Ali ibn Ibrahim has narrated from his father from al-Qasim ibn Muhammad and Ali ibn Muhammad al-Qasaniy from Sulayman ibn Dawud from Hammad ibn 'Isa who has narrated the following:

"Abu 'Abd Allah, *'Alayhi al-Salam*, has said that it is in the advice of Luqman to his son, 'My son, you must travel with your sword, shoes, turban, tent, your water container, your needle, threads and your shoe stitching tools. You must supply yourself with medicines, which can benefit you and those with you. You must cooperate with your travel-mates unless it is in disobedience to Allah.'"

Fine supplies during a journey . . .

H 14915, h 467

Ali has narrated from his father from al-Nawfaliy from al-Sakuniy who has narrated the following:

"Abu 'Abd Allah, *'Alayhi al-Salam*, has narrated from his ancestors, *'Alayhim al-Salam*, who have said that the Messenger of Allah, *O Allah grant compensation to Muhammad and his family worthy of their services to Your cause*, has said, 'It is of the nobility of a man to have fine supplies during a journey.'"

Prepare fine supplies. . .

H 14916, h 468

Ali has narrated from his father from ibn abu 'Umayr from 'Abd Allah ibn Sinan who has narrated the following:

"Abu 'Abd Allah, *'Alayhi al-Salam*, has said that Ali ibn al-Husayn, *'Alayhim al-Salam*, for a journey to al-Hajj or al-'Umrah would prepare fine supplies, like almonds, sugar, fried flour mixed with beans and sweetened to prepare a broth (or use without such preparation).'"

Resemblance between Mu'alla' and I

H 14917, h 469
Ali ibn Ibrahim has narrated from his father from ibn abu 'Umayr from al-Walid ibn Sabih who has narrated the following:
"Once when I visited abu 'Abd Allah, *'Alayhi al-Salam*, he (the Imam) fetched me a piece of cloth and said, 'O Walid, fold it on its folding areas.' I stood up before him (the Imam) and abu 'Abd Allah, *'Alayhi al-Salam*, said, 'May Allah grant mercy to Mu'alla' ibn Khunays.' I then thought that he (the Imam) may have found resemblance between Mu'alla' and I in my standing before him (the Imam).' He (the Imam) then said, 'Woe is on the world, woe is on the world! The world is a house of trial, where Allah makes His enemies dominant over His friends, and after this there is the house which is not like this.' I then asked, 'I pray to Allah to keep my soul in service for your cause, where is that house?' He (the Imam) said, 'It is there' pointing with his hand to the ground.'"

In praise of Shi'ah

H 14918, h 470
Muhammad ibn Ahmad has narrated from 'Abd Allah ibn al-Salt from Yunus from those whom he has mentioned from abu Basir who has narrated the following:
"Abu 'Abd Allah, *'Alayhi al-Salam*, once said to me this: 'O abu Muhammad, Allah, most Majestic, most Glorious, has such angels who make sins drop from the backs of our Shi'ah as the wind makes the leaves to fall from trees in the fall season. It is as is said in the words of Allah, most Majestic, most Glorious, '. . . they say *Tasbih* (Allah is free of all defects) with the praise of their Lord and ask forgiveness for the believing people.' (40:7) By Allah, He has intended no one else other than you.'"

When Allah alone is mentioned

H 14919, h 471
Ali ibn Ibrahim has narrated from his father from ibn abu 'Umayr from 'Umar ibn 'Udhaynah from Zurarah who has said that abu al-Al-Khattab in his best condition narrated to me the following:
"I once asked abu 'Abd Allah, *'Alayhi al-Salam*, about the meaning of the words of Allah, most Majestic, most Glorious, '. . . when Allah alone is mentioned, the hearts of those who disbelieve in the hereafter shrink.' [He (the Imam) said that when Allah alone says to obey those whom Allah has commanded to be obeyed of *Ale* (family of) Muhammad], the hearts of those who do not believe in the hereafter shrink but when the people, obedience to whom Allah has not made obligatory, are mentioned they receive it as glad news.'" (39:45)

Adam received certain words

H 14920, h 472
Ali ibn Ibrahim has narrated from his father from ibn abu 'Umayr from Ibrahim Sahib al- Sha'ir from Kathir ibn Kalthamah who has narrated the following:

"About the meaning of the words of Allah, most Majestic, most Glorious, '. . . Adam received certain words from his Lord' (2:37) He (the Imam) said that he (Adam, *'Alayhi al-Salam*) said, 'Only Allah deserves worship, You are free of all defects, O Lord, I praise You. I have committed bad deeds and done injustice to my soul, so forgive me and You are the best in forgiving. No one deserves worship except You. O Lord, I praise You. I have committed bad deeds and have done injustice to my soul, forgive me, have mercy on me; You are the most Merciful of the merciful ones. Only Allah deserves worship, You are free of all defects. O Lord, I praise You. I have committed bad deeds and done injustice to my soul, accept my repentance; You accept repentance with Your mercy.' There is another Hadith about the words of Allah, most Majestic, most Glorious. '. . . Adam, received certain words from his Lord.' (2:37) In this Hadith he (the Imam) said, ' Adam, *'Alayhi al-Salam*, asked Him through the rights of Muhammad, Ali, al-Hassan, al-Husayn and Fatimah, *'Alayhim al-Salam*.'"

The kingdom of the skies . . .

H 14921, h 473

Muhammad ibn Yahya has narrated from Ahmad ibn Muhammad ibn 'Isa and Ali ibn Ibrahim has narrated from his father from ibn abu 'Umayr from abu Ayyub al-Khazzaz from abu Basir who has narrated the following:

"Abu 'Abd Allah, *'Alayhi al-Salam*, has said that when Ibrahim *'Alayhi al-Salam*, saw the kingdom of the skies and earth, he looked and saw a man committing fornication. He prayed against him and he died. He then saw another man committing fornication. He prayed against him and he also died until he prayed against three people who all died. Allah, most Majestic, most Glorious, sent him revelation that said, 'O Ibrahim, your prayer is acceptable. Do not pray against My servants because if I did not want I would not create them. I create My creatures of three kinds: of one kind is a servant who worships Me and does not consider anyone as My partner. Of another kind is a servant who worships someone other than Me but he is not able to escape from Me and I create a servant who worships someone other than Me but I bring out from him someone who worships Me.' He then saw a dead body on the shore, half in the water and half on land. Predators on land from one side and those in water from the other side consumed it. They then fought each other, then they consumed each other. Ibrahim, *'Alayhi al-Salam*, wondered about what he saw. He then appealed, '. . . O Lord, show me how You bring the dead back to life?' (2:260) He said, 'How do you bring back to life that which is reproduced of that which is consumed?' He asked, 'Have you not believed (in My power)?' He replied, 'Yes, I believe but it is to comfort my heart. That is, I want to see this as I see all other things.' He said, 'Take four birds, mix them, then place a part of the mixture on every mountain.' He cut, and mixed them, just as the dead body mixed in the predators, which consumed each other. He mixed them. '. . . place one part on every mountain then call them. They will come running to you.' He did it and when he called them they responded and the mountains were ten in number.'"

(Saturn) is a cold planet

H 14922, h 474

Ali ibn Ibrahim has narrated from his father from ibn Mahbub from Malik ibn 'Atiyyah from Sulayman ibn Khalid who has narrated the following:

"I once asked abu 'Abd Allah, *'Alayhi al-Salam*, about the case of cold and heat and about where from are they. He (the Imam) said, 'O abu Ayyub, al-Mirrikh (Mars) is a hot planet and Zuhal (Saturn) is a cold planet, when Mars is high Saturn is low which is in spring. They remain as such. With change in their position, the other one's position also changes. When Mars rises, one degree, Saturn falls one degree up to three months until Mars ends in height and Saturn ends with fall. Mars becomes bright and heat increases. When it is summer and the beginning of fall, Saturn begins to rise and Mars begins to fall. Saturn's rise ends and becomes bright in the beginning of winter and the end of fall thus cold increases. As this rises that one falls and as this falls that one rises. If in summer a day becomes cold it is because of the moon and if a day in winter is hot, it is because of the sun. This is the plan of the most majestic all knowing. I am the servant of the Lord of the worlds.'" (According to the footnote of the Arabic version, this does not contradict the coming of heat from the sun as well as Hadith 332 above, which speaks about the hot structure of the sun. It apparently is about the effect of the two above-mentioned planets on weather, which is not apparent, or that they are not the ones as are known today.)

If one loves you. . .

H 14923, h 475

A number of our people have narrated from Sahl ibn Ziyad from Ja'far ibn Muhammad al-Ash'ariy from 'Abd Allah ibn Maymun al-Qaddah who has narrated the following:

"Abu 'Abd Allah, *'Alayhi al-Salam*, has said that the Messenger of Allah, *O Allah grant compensation to Muhammad and his family worthy of their services to Your cause*, has said this. 'If one loves you, O Ali, and then dies he has completed his appointed time, and one who loves you but has not died, every time that the sun rises or sets it rises with his sustenance and belief' – in another copy it is said, 'with light'."

Epic trials and conditions

H 14924, h 476

Ali ibn Ibrahim has narrated from his father from al-Nawfaliy from al-Sakuniy who has narrated the following:

"Abu 'Abd Allah, *'Alayhi al-Salam*, has said that the Messenger of Allah, *O Allah grant compensation to Muhammad and his family worthy of their services to Your cause*, has said, 'There a time will come on my followers when their conscience will become filthy but their appearance will look good because of their greed for the world. They do not intend to receive what is with Allah, their Lord. Their religion will be a show-off and they will not have any fear. Allah will encompass all of them with a penalty from Him. They will pray like a drowning person but it will not be answered.'"

Hadith of jurists and scholars

H 14925, h 477

It is narrated from the narrator of the previous Hadith from his father from al-Nawfaliy from al-Sakuniy who has narrated the following:

"'Amir al-Mu'minin, Ali, *'Alayhi al-Salam*, has said, 'Jurists and scholars when writing (speaking) to each other were of three kinds of conditions without a fourth one. If one's aim is to have understanding and knowledge for the sake of the hereafter, Allah is sufficient support in what is important for one in this world. If it is to reform what is secret, and the privacy, then Allah, in such case, is sufficient support for him in his public affairs. If it is for the sake of reforming and improving what is between him and Allah, most Majestic, most Glorious, Allah, most Blessed, most High, improves in such case what is between him and the people.'"

Praise of abu Dharr

H 14926, h 478

Al-Husayn ibn Muhammad al-Ash'ariy has narrated from Mu'alla' ibn Muhammad from Ali ibn Asbat from Sa'dan ibn Muslim from certain persons of our people who has narrated the following:

"Abu 'Abd Allah, *'Alayhi al-Salam*, has said that there was a man in al-Madinah. He once entered the Masjid of the Messenger of Allah, *O Allah grant compensation to Muhammad and his family worthy of their services to Your cause*, and said this. 'O Lord, grant me comfort in my anxiety, company for my loneliness and a virtuous associate.' He then saw a man in a far corner of the Masjid. He offered him greeting of peace and asked, 'Who are you, O servant of Allah?' He replied, 'I am abu Dharr.' The man said, '*Takbir* (Allah is great beyond description, Allah is great beyond description).' Abu Dharr asked, 'Why do you say *Takbir* (Allah is great beyond description), O servant of Allah?' He replied, 'I entered the Masjid and prayed to Allah, 'O Lord, grant me comfort in my anxiety, company for my loneliness and a virtuous associate.' Abu Dharr then said, 'I must have said it more deservingly than you if you are such an associate. I heard the Messenger of Allah, *O Allah grant compensation to Muhammad and his family worthy of their services to Your cause*, say. "You and I will be on an island (hill) on the Day of Judgment, until people complete their accounting." However, you must move away from me, O servant of Allah, because the Sultan (government) has prohibited people from sitting with me (a curfew is imposed on me about meeting people)."

There will come a time on people . . .

H 14927, h 479

Ali ibn Ibrahim has narrated from his father from al-Nawfaliy from al-Sakuniy who has narrated the following:

"Abu 'Abd Allah, *'Alayhi al-Salam*, has said this. ''Amir al-Mu'minin, Ali, *'Alayhi al-Salam*, has said that the Messenger of Allah, *O Allah grant compensation to Muhammad and his family worthy of their services to Your cause*, has said, 'There will come a time on people when there will not remain anything of al-Quran except its writing. No other thing will remain of Islam except its name. They will hear about it but they will be the farthest from it. Their Masjids will be well built but they will be ruins in matters of guidance. The jurists of that time will be the worse jurists under the shadow of the sky. Mischief will come out from them and to them it will return.'"

Inherited pardoning . . .

H 14928, h 480

Al-Husayn ibn Muhammad al-Ash'ariy has narrated from Mu'alla' ibn Muhammad from Ali ibn Asbat from Muhammad ibn al-Husayn ibn Yazid who has narrated the following:

"I once heard al-Rida', *'Alayhi al-Salam*, in Khurasan say, 'We are the *Ahl al-Bayt* (family) who have inherited pardoning from *Ale* (family of) Ya'qub and gratefulness from *Ale* (family of) Dawud.'" He (the narrator) thought, 'In this Hadith there was another word which Muhammad had forgotten.' I said, 'Perhaps it is, ". . . and patience from *Ale* (family of) abu Ayyub."' He said, 'It seems proper.'

"Ali ibn Asbat has said, 'I said that because I heard Ya'qub ibn Yaqtin narrate from certain persons of our people that when abu Ja'far al-Mansur went to al-Madinah in the year when Muhammad and Ibrahim, sons of 'Abd Allah ibn al-Hassan, were killed, he spoke to his uncle 'Isa ibn Ali. He said, "O abu al-'Abbas, 'Amir al-Mu'minin has decided that trees of al-Madinah must be eliminated. Its fountains closed and it (the city) must be turned upside down." He said, "O 'Amir al-Mu'minin, your cousin Ja'far ibn Muhammad is around. You must send for him and ask him about this opinion." He sent for him (the Imam) and 'Isa informed him about the issue. He (the Imam) turned to him saying, "O 'Amir al-Mu'minin, Dawud, *'Alayhi al-Salam*, had received gratefulness, Ayyub was tried by patience and Yusuf forgave after becoming dominant, you must forgive; you are a descendent of these people."'"

"They pleaded with Allah for victory..."

H 14929, h 481

Muhammad ibn Yahya has narrated from Ahmad ibn Muhammad ibn 'Isa from al-Husayn ibn Sa'id from al-Nadr ibn Suwayd from Zur'ah ibn Muhammad who has narrated the following:

"About the meaning of the words of Allah, most Majestic, most Glorious, '. . . before they pleaded with Allah for victory over the unbelievers. . .' (2:89) abu 'Abd Allah, *'Alayhi al-Salam*, has said that the Jews had found in their books that the place to which Muhammad will migrate is between 'Ayr and 'Uhud, (names of two mountains around al-Madinah), so they moved to find it. They arrived at a mountain called Hadad and they said that Hadad and 'Uhud is the same. They scattered at that point. Certain ones of them disembarked at Tayma' others at Fadak and yet others at Khaybar (names of certain places). The ones who had disembarked at Tayma' wished to see their brethren. Once an Arab from Qays passed by and they hired from him (a camel) and he said, 'I will pass (travel) with you through 'Ayr and 'Uhud.' They said, 'When you arrive at that place then inform us about it.' When he arrived in the middle of the land of al-

Madinah, he said, 'This is 'Uhud and that is 'Ayr.' They disembarked from his camel and said, 'We have found what we were looking for, so we do not need your camel. You can go wherever you like.' They wrote to their brethren who were at Khaybar and Fadak, 'We have found the place. You must come to us.' They replied, 'We are settled and purchased assets here but we are not far from you. When that happens we will quickly come to you.' They then found assets in al-Madinah. When they became wealthy Tubba' learned about their wealth and he attacked them. They sought protection in their strongholds and he surrounded them (by his army) but they would feel tender-hearted about the weak ones of the people of Tubba' and at night they would throw to them dates and barley. Tubba' was informed about it who also felt tender-hearted about them so he granted them amnesty and they came down from their strong-holds to him. He said to them, 'I have liked your country and I intend to stay with you.' They said, 'You cannot do so because a Prophet will migrate to this place and no one else can do so until that happens.'

"He said, 'I will leave with you certain ones from my family so that when that happens they support and help him.' He left two tribes, al-'Aws and al-Khazraj. When they grew in number they would take away, the assets of the Jews and the Jews said to them, 'When Muhammad comes he will remove you away from our country and our assets.' Allah, most Majestic, most Glorious, sent Muhammad, *O Allah grant compensation to Muhammad and his family worthy of their services to Your cause.* Al-Ansar (people of al-Madinah) accepted his religion. However, the Jews refused to accept his religion and this is referred to in the words of Allah, most Majestic, most Glorious, '. . . before they pleaded with Allah for victory over the unbelievers but when he (the Messenger of Allah) came to them and they recognized him they turned to disbelief, thus, the condemnation of Allah is on those who disbelieve.'" (2:89)

"They pleaded with Allah for victory..."

H 14930, h 482

Ali ibn Ibrahim has narrated from his father from Safwan ibn Yahya from Ishaq ibn 'Ammar who has narrated the following:

"I once asked abu 'Abd Allah, *'Alayhi al-Salam*, about the meaning of the words of Allah, most Majestic, most Glorious. '. . . at one time, they pleaded with Allah for victory over the unbelievers but when he (the Messenger of Allah) came to them, they recognized him. However, they turned to disbelief; thus, the condemnation of Allah is on those who disbelieve.' (2:89) He (the Imam) said, 'There was a people between the time of Jesus and Muhammad, *O Allah grant compensation to Muhammad and his family worthy of their services to Your cause*, who warned the idol worshippers about the coming of the Holy Prophet. They said that a Prophet would come. He will destroy your idols and will do this and that against you but when the Messenger of Allah, *O Allah grant compensation to Muhammad and his family worthy of their services to Your cause*, came they refused to accept his religion.'"

Five signs of the rise of al-Qa'im

H 14931, h 483

Muhammad ibn Yahya has narrated from Ahmad ibn Muhammad ibn 'Isa from Ali ibn al-Hakam from abu Ayyub al-Khazzaz from 'Umar ibn Hanzalah who has narrated the following:

"I once heard abu 'Abd Allah, *'Alayhi al-Salam*, say, 'Before the time when al-Qa'im will reappear with divine authority and power, five signs will become apparent; one of which is a loud voice, the rise of al-Sufyaniy, the sinking, the assassination of a pure soul and al-Yamaniy.' I then asked, 'Can we join if someone from your *Ahl al-Bayt* (family) will rise before the coming of such signs?' He (the Imam) said, 'No, you must not do so.' The next day I read before him (the Imam) this verse, '. . . if We wanted We could have sent a sign on them from the sky and their necks remained subdued,' (26:4) and I asked if that is the loud voice.' He (the Imam) said, 'If that comes to pass the necks of the enemies of Allah, most Majestic, most Glorious, all become subdued.'"

Signs of the rise of al-Qa'im

H 14932, h 484

Muhammad ibn Yahya has narrated from Ahmad ibn Muhammad from ibn Faddal from abu Jamilah from Muhammad ibn Ali al-Halabiy who has narrated the following:

"I once heard abu 'Abd Allah, *'Alayhi al-Salam*, saying that the rising of disputes among banu al-'Abbas is inevitable, the call is inevitable and the coming of the time when al-Qa'im will reappear with divine authority and power is inevitable.' I then asked, 'How is the call?' He (the Imam) said, 'A caller from the sky will call in the beginning of the day, "O yes, Ali and his Shi'ah are the triumphant ones."' He (the Imam) said that in the end of the day a caller will call, 'O yes, 'Uthman and his Shi'ah are the triumphant ones.'"

(Jurist) of the people of Basrah

H 14933, h 485

A number of our people have narrated from Ahmad ibn Muhammad ibn Khalid from his father from Muhammad ibn Sinan from Zayd al-Shahham who has narrated the following:

"Once Qatadah ibn Di'amah visited abu Ja'far, *'Alayhi al-Salam*, and he (the Imam) asked, 'O Qatadah, are you the *faqih* (jurist) of the people of Basrah?' He replied, 'That is how they think.' Abu Ja'far, *'Alayhi al-Salam*, said, 'I am informed that you interpret al-Quran.' Qatadah, replied, 'Yes, I do so.' Abu Ja'far, *'Alayhi al-Salam*, then asked, 'Do you interpret with knowledge or with ignorance?' He replied, 'No, not with ignorance I interpret with knowledge.' Abu Ja'far, *'Alayhi al-Salam*, said, 'If you interpret with knowledge then you are what you are (supposed to be). Can I ask you a question?' Qatadah said, 'Yes, you can ask.' He (the Imam) said, 'Tell me about the meaning of the words of Allah, most Majestic, most Glorious about Saba', '. . . We determined in it the journey so you can travel in it during the nights and days in safety.' (34:18) Qatadah said, 'It is the one who leaves his home with lawful supplies, lawful means of transportation, lawfully hired means with the intention to visit the House. That person is safe until he returns to his family.'"

"Abu Ja'far, *'Alayhi al-Salam*, said, 'I ask you answer on oath by Allah. O Qatadah, can you believe that a person may leave his home with lawful supplies, lawful means of transportation, lawful hiring with the intention to visit this House. However, the bandits cut off his path, his supplies vanish and he suffers a beating to the point of his destruction?' Qatadah replied, 'Yes, that can happen.' Abu Ja'far, *'Alayhi al-Salam*, said, 'Woe is upon you, O Qatadah, if you have interpreted al-Quran by your own understanding you have destroyed yourself, if you have taken from people then you are destroyed and have destroyed others.

"Woe is on you O Qatadah, that (the person mentioned in the above verse) is one who leaves his home with lawful supplies. He leaves with lawful means of transportation and hiring with the intention to visit this House, recognizing our rights, with his heart inclined toward us. It is as Allah, most Majestic, most Glorious, has said, '. . . then make the hearts of people to incline toward them.' (14:37) It is not a reference to their bowing down toward the House. We, by Allah are the call of Ibrahim, *'Alayhi al-Salam*. Whoever's heart is inclined to us and has loved us his Hajj is accepted. Otherwise, it is not accepted. O Qatadah, if that is the case as I said it is, he is safe from the suffering in hell on the Day of Judgment.' Qatadah then said, 'I certainly, by Allah, will interpret as such.' Abu Ja'far, *'Alayhi al-Salam*, said, 'Woe is on you, O Qatadah, only those to whom al-Quran is addressed know it.'"

Description of hell

H 14934, h 486

Ali ibn Ibrahim has narrated from Muhammad ibn 'Isa from Yunus from Mufaddal ibn Salih from Jabir who has narrated the following:

"Abu Ja'far, *'Alayhi al-Salam*, has said that the Messenger of Allah, *O Allah grant compensation to Muhammad and his family worthy of their services to Your cause*, has said this. 'The trusted *Ruh* informed me that no one deserves worship except Allah. When all people will receive the command to stand up, all of the past and later generations, hell will be brought near. One hundred thousand angels of the extremely strong ones will hold it with one thousand harnesses. It will make crushing, shattering, exhalation, sobbing and braying sounds. It will sob and bray in a terrifying manner. If Allah will not move it away until accounting will end, all will be destroyed.

'After that, a neck will come out of it, which will encompass all creatures, the virtuous ones as well as the criminal ones. All of the creatures of Allah, including the angels and the Prophets will say, "O Lord, my soul, save my soul" but you will say O Lord, "My followers, O Lord, my followers." Thereafter the bridge will be placed on it. It will be thinner than a hair and sharper than a sword with three arches, (stages) the first one for trust and kindness, the second one for *Salat* (prayer) and the third one for the Cherisher of the worlds, other than whom no one deserves worship. They will receive the command to pass through but kindness and trust will stop them. If they pass them safely, *Salat* (prayer) will stop them. If they pass it safely, they will reach before the Cherisher of the worlds, most Majestic, most Glorious, as the words of Allah, most Blessed, most High, speak. ". . . your Lord maintains surveillance." (89:14) People will be on the bridge, certain ones hanging because of the slip of one of their feet and holding of the other foot and the angels around them saying, "O honorable, O forbearing, forgive, pardon, return with generosity and save." People will tumble on it like moths. If one is saved by the mercy of Allah, most Blessed, most High, he will look at it and say, "All praise belongs to Allah who saved me from you after despair, from His generosity, indeed our Lord is forgiving and appreciating.""

The companions of al-Qa'im are three hundred and some

H 14935, h 487

Ali ibn Ibrahim has narrated from his father from ibn abu 'Umayr from Mansur ibn Yunus from 'Isma'il ibn Jabir from abu Khalid who has narrated the following:

"It is an explanation of the meaning of the words of Allah, most Majestic, most Glorious. '. . . you must work hard to achieve goodness before others. Wherever you are Allah will bring you all together.' (2:148) Abu Ja'far, *'Alayhi al-Salam*, has said, 'Goodness stands for *Walayah* (guardianship of *'A'immah* with divine authority and knowledge),' and the words of Allah, '. . . wherever you are Allah will bring all' is a reference to the army of al-Qa'im (the one who rises with divine authority and power) who number three hundred and ten and something.' He (the Imam) then said, 'They, by Allah are the people of a limited number. They come together, by Allah, within one hour like the pieces of the cloud in a fall day.'"

We are afraid of vermin

H 14936, h 488

A number of our people have narrated from Ahmad ibn Muhammad from Ima'il ibn Bazi' from al-Mundhir ibn Hayfar from Hisham ibn Salim who has narrated the following:

I heard abu 'Abd Allah, *'Alayhi al-Salam*, say, 'You should travel during the cool hours.' I said, 'We are afraid of vermin.' He (the Imam) said, 'Even if you will be affected it is good for you because you will be safe.'"

The earth is wrapped up...

H 14937, h 489

Ali ibn Ibrahim has narrated from his father from al-Nawfaliy from al-Sakuniy who has narrated the following:

"Abu 'Abd Allah, *'Alayhi al-Salam*, has said that the Messenger of Allah, *O Allah grant compensation to Muhammad and his family worthy of their services to Your cause*, has said, 'You should travel during the night; during the night the earth is wrapped up (you can cover more distance).'"

How does it happen?

H 14938, h 490
A number of our people have narrated from Ahmad ibn Muhammad ibn Khalid from 'Isma'il ibn Mehran from Sayf ibn 'Amirah Ahmad ibn Muhammad from Bashir al-Nabbal from Humran ibn 'A'yan who has narrated the following:
"I once said to abu Ja'far, *'Alayhi al-Salam*, that people say, 'During the night the earth wraps around us.' How does it happen?' He (the Imam) said, 'This way'- while turning his clothes."

The earth wraps around...

H 14939, h 491
Ali ibn Ibrahim has narrated from his father from ibn abu 'Umayr from Hammad ibn 'Uthman who has narrated the following:
"Abu 'Abd Allah, *'Alayhi al-Salam*, has said that the earth wraps around (completes one round) in the end of the night."

No other day is more unfortunate. . .

H 14940, h 492
A number of our people have narrated from Ahmad ibn Muhammad ibn Khalid from 'Uthman ibn 'Isa from abu Ayyub al-Khazzaz who has narrated the following:
"Once we wanted to leave for a journey and we went to offer greeting of peace to abu 'Abd Allah, *'Alayhi al-Salam*, and he said, 'Have you tried to seek blessings on Monday?' We replied, 'Yes, that is what we have done.' He then said, 'No other day is more unfortunate for us then a Monday in which revelation stopped coming to us because of the passing away of our Prophet, *O Allah grant compensation to Muhammad and his family worthy of their services to Your cause.* You can leave for your journey on Tuesday.'"

Not fortunate during his journey...

H 14941, h 493
It is narrated from the narrator of the previous Hadith from Bakr ibn Salih from Sulayman al-Ja'friy who has narrated the following:
"Abu al-Hassan, Musa, *'Alayhi al-Salam*, has said this: 'For a traveler five things are not fortunate during his journey. One is a crow crowing from the right side, or spreading its tail. Another thing is the howling wolf that howls on one's face while sitting on its tail and oscillates its voice three times. Another such thing is the deer running from the right to the left, the crying owl, a woman with a gray hair on her forehead, and a donkey with pierced ears. If one senses a feeling in his soul because of such things he must say, 'I seek protection with You, O Lord, against the evil of what I find in my soul.' He (the Imam) said, 'He will be protected with it.'"

Beautified our Shi'ah with forbearance...

H 14942, h 494

Muhammad ibn Yahya has narrated from Salmah ibn al-Khattab from 'Abd Allah from Muhammad ibn Sinan from 'Abd Allah ibn al-Qasim from 'Amr ibn abu al-Miqdam who has narrated the following:

"Abu 'Abd Allah, *'Alayhi al-Salam*, has said, 'Allah, most Blessed, most High, has beautified our Shi'ah with forbearance and has covered them with knowledge. It is because of His knowledge of them before creating Adam, *'Alayhi al-Salam.*'"

Admits him in the garden...

H 14943, h 495

Abu Ali al-Ash'ariy has narrated from Muhammad ibn 'Abd al-Jabbar and a number of our people have narrated from Sahl ibn Ziyad all ibn Faddal from Tha'labah ibn Maymun from 'Umar ibn Aban from al-Sabbah ibn Sayabah who has narrated the following:

"Abu 'Abd Allah, *'Alayhi al-Salam*, has said, 'A man loves you but he does not know what you say (believe in); Allah, most Majestic, most Glorious, admits him in the garden (paradise). A man hates you and does not know what you say (believe in); Allah, most Majestic, most Glorious, throws him in the fire. A man among you finds the book of the records of his deeds full of good deeds without his doing any good deed.' I then asked, 'How can that happen?' He (the Imam) said, 'He passes by a people who reproach us but when they see him they say to each other, "You must stop; this man is of their Shi'ah". One of our Shi'ah passes by them and they wink at him and say things against him. Allah then writes for him good deeds and the book of the record of his good deeds become full without doing good deeds.'"

Instruction to visit each other

H 14944, h 496

A number of our people have narrated from Ahmad ibn Muhammad ibn Khalid from his father from abu Jahm from abu Khadijah who has narrated the following:

"Abu 'Abd Allah, *'Alayhi al-Salam*, once asked, me, 'How far is Basrah from you?' I replied, 'By water, if the wind is good, it is five days' journey and by land, it is eight days' journey.' He (the Imam) said, 'It is very close. You must visit and find out about each other's conditions. On the Day of Judgment every one must bring a witness to prove what his religion is.' He (the Imam) said, 'When a Muslim sees his brothers (in belief) it is life for his religion if he speaks of Allah, most Majestic, most Glorious.'"

People of the noble manners...

H 14945, h 497

Ali ibn Ibrahim has narrated from his father from Hammad ibn 'Isa from Rib'iy who has narrated the following:

"Abu 'Abd Allah, *'Alayhi al-Salam*, has said, 'No one of Arabs and non-Arabs love us except people of the noble manners and origins and no one hates us of these and those except filthy and of grafted origin.'"

News of the ark of the Israelites

H 14946, h 498

Muhammad ibn Yahya has narrated from Ahmad ibn Muhammad from Muhammad ibn Khalid and al-Husayn ibn Sa'id from al-Nadr ibn Suwayd from Yahya al-Halabiy from Harun ibn Kharijah from abu Basir who has narrated the following:

"About the meaning of the words of Allah, most Majestic, most Glorious, '. . . Allah has appointed Saul as a king for you. They said, "How can he dominate us when we deserve more to be king than he. [He (the Imam) said, 'He was not of the descendents of Prophets or of the kings], . . . Allah has chosen him as your ruler. . .' [He (the Imam) said that their Prophet then said], "As the evidence of his authority, he will bring to you the Ark, which will be a comfort to you from your Lord and a legacy of the household of Moses and Aaron. The angels will carry it. [Allah, most Majestic, most Glorious, then said], "Allah will test you with a river. Those who drink its water will not be of My people and those who do not even taste the water or who taste only some of it from within the hollow of their hand, will be My friends. They all drank the water except a few [who were three hundred and thirteen people. Certain ones of them filled their hands and certain ones did not drink and when they came out those who had filled up their hands] said, "We do not have the strength to fight against Goliath and his army." [Those who had not filled their hands said,] "How often, with Allah's permission, have small groups defeated the large ones?" Allah is with those who exercise patience.'" (2:249)

Evidence of his authority...

H 14947, h 499

It is narrated from the narrator of the previous Hadith from Ahmad ibn Muhammad from al-Husayn ibn Sa'id from Fadalah ibn Ayyub from Yahya al-Halabiy who has narrated the following:

"It is about the meaning of the words of Allah. 'As the evidence of his authority, he will bring to you the Ark, which will be a comfort to you from your Lord and a legacy of the household of Moses and Aaron, it will be carried by the angels.' (2:248) Abu Ja'far, *'Alayhi al-Salam*, has said, the angels carried it in the form of a cow.'"

"He will bring to you the Ark..."

H 14948, h 500

Ali ibn Ibrahim has narrated from his father from Hammad ibn 'Isa from Hariz from the one who narrated to him who has narrated the following:

"It is about the meaning of the words of Allah, most Blessed, most High, '. . . he will bring to you the Ark, which will be a comfort to you from your Lord and a legacy of the household of Moses and Aaron. It will be carried by the angels.'

Abu Ja'far, *'Alayhi al-Salam*, has said, 'It is a reference to the broken pieces of the slates with knowledge and wisdom (on them).'"

Sons of the Messenger of Allah

H 14949, h 501

A number of our people have narrated from Ahmad ibn Muhammad ibn Khalid from al-Hassan ibn Zarif from 'Abd al-Samad ibn Bashir from abu al-Jarud who has narrated the following:

"Abu Ja'far, *'Alayhi al-Salam*, once asked me, 'What do they say to you about al-Hassan and al-Husayn, *'Alayhim al-Salam*?' I replied, 'They reject our saying that they are children of the Messenger of Allah, *O Allah grant compensation to Muhammad and his family worthy of their services to Your cause.*' He (the Imam) then asked, 'What kind of reasoning do you show them to prove your point?' I replied, 'We refer them to the words of Allah, most Majestic, most Glorious, about Jesus, *'Alayhi al-Salam*, ". . . Noah received Our guidance before Abraham and so did his descendants: David, Solomon, Job, Joseph, Moses, and Aaron. Thus is the reward for the righteous people. (6:84) We also gave guidance to Zacharias, John, Jesus, and Elias, who were all pious people." (6:85) He (the Imam) asked, 'Then what do they say?' I replied, 'They say that sometimes children of the daughter are also called of one's children but they are not of his seed.' He (the Imam) then asked, 'Then what kind of reasoning do you show them to prove you point?' I replied, 'We refer them to the words of Allah, most Blessed, most High, to His Messenger, *O Allah grant compensation to Muhammad and his family worthy of their services to Your cause*, ". . . If anyone disputes (your prophesy) after knowledge has come to you, say, 'Allow each of us to bring our children, women, our people, and ourselves to one place and pray to Allah to condemn the liars among us.'" (3:61)

"He (the Imam) asked, 'What then do they say?' I replied, 'They say, 'In the Arabic language a man may call children of another man as, 'Our children.' Abu Ja'far, *'Alayhi al-Salam*, then said this. 'O abu al-Jarud, I will show proof in the book of Allah, most Blessed, most High. They were of the seed of the Messenger of Allah, *O Allah grant compensation to Muhammad and his family worthy of their services to Your cause*. No one except an unbeliever will reject it.' I then asked, 'Where is such proof, I pray to Allah to keep my soul in service for your cause?' He (the Imam) said, 'It is where Allah, most High, says, 'You are forbidden to marry your mothers, daughters, sisters. . . . You are forbidden to marry the wives of your sons who are from your seed. . . .' (4:23) O abu al-Jarud, you can ask, "Was it lawful for the Messenger of Allah, to marry their ex-wives? If they said, 'Yes', they have spoken a lie and have committed a sin. If they said, 'No', then they are his children from his seed.'"

On the day of 'Uhud, faced defeat...

H 14950, h 502

Muhammad ibn Yahya has narrated from Ahmad ibn Muhammad ibn 'Isa from Ali ibn al-Hakam from al-Husayn abu al-'Ala' al-Khaffaf who has narrated the following:

"When, people on the day of 'Uhud, faced defeat, they began to run away from the Holy Prophet, *O Allah grant compensation to Muhammad and his family worthy of their services to Your cause*. He (the Messenger of Allah) turned his face to them and kept saying, 'I am Muhammad and I am the Messenger of Allah, I am not killed and I have not died.' So and so looked at him and said, 'Even now he is mocking at us when we are defeated;' but Ali, *'Alayhi al-Salam*, remained with him along with Simak ibn Kharashah and abu Dujanah, may Allah grant him mercy. The Holy Prophet, called him and said, 'O abu Dujanah, you can also go; you have my permission to suspend your pledge of allegiance.

"Ali, however, is myself and I am he.' He turned around and sat before the Holy Prophet, *O Allah grant compensation to Muhammad and his family worthy of their services to Your cause*, wept and said, 'No, by Allah', he raised his head to the sky and said, 'No, by Allah, I will not suspend my pledge of allegiance with you. I have pledged allegiance with you, then to whom can I return? Must I return to my wife who will die or the children who also will die or to the house that will be destroyed, or the asset that will vanish and the time of death that is approaching?' He kept fighting until his wounds made him to feel heavy when he and Ali were shielding him (the Holy Prophet), *O Allah grant compensation to Muhammad and his family worthy of their services to Your cause*, one on each side. When he fell down, Ali, *'Alayhi al-Salam*, carried him and brought him before the Holy Prophet, *O Allah grant compensation to Muhammad and his family worthy of their services to Your cause*, and placed him before him (the Messenger of Allah).

"He asked, 'Did I keep my promise and pledge?' He (the Messenger of Allah) replied, 'Yes, you have kept your promise.' The Holy Prophet said good things about him. When people attacked him (the Messenger of Allah), *O Allah grant compensation to Muhammad and his family worthy of their services to Your cause*, from the right, Ali removed them from the right. They advanced from the left of the Holy Prophet, *O Allah grant compensation to Muhammad and his family worthy of their services to Your cause*. He continued until his sword broke into three pieces. He then came to the Holy Prophet, *O Allah grant compensation to Muhammad and his family worthy of their services to Your cause*, and threw it before him saying this is my sword which has broken.' On that day the Holy Prophet, *O Allah grant compensation to Muhammad and his family worthy of their services to Your cause*, gave Dha al-Faqar to him.

"When the Holy Prophet, *O Allah grant compensation to Muhammad and his family worthy of their services to Your cause*, saw him with his shaking legs because of excessive struggle in fighting, he raised his head to the sky. He (the Messenger of Allah) wept and said, 'O Lord, You have promised me that my religion will be victorious and if You will do so it will not cause You fatigue.' Ali, *'Alayhi al-Salam*, came to the Holy Prophet, *O Allah grant compensation to Muhammad and his family worthy of their services to Your cause*, and said, 'I hear a great deal of strong reverberation. I also hear someone saying, "Move forward, O Hayzum (name of the horse of Jibril)." Whenever I am about to hit someone he falls dead before I hit him.'

"He (the Messenger of Allah) said, 'These are Jibril, Michael, and Israfil among the angels.' Thereafter Jibril came and stood on the side of the Messenger of Allah, *O Allah grant compensation to Muhammad and his family worthy of their services to Your cause*, and said, O Muhammad, 'This is support.' He (the Messenger of Allah) said, 'Ali is from me and I am from Ali.' Jibril said, 'I am from both of you.' People were then defeated. The Messenger of Allah, *O Allah grant compensation to Muhammad and his family worthy of their services to Your cause*, said, 'O Ali, go with your sword. See to them if they are riding their camels and pulling their horses on the side, then it means that they are returning to Makkah but if you see them riding their horses and pulling their camels on their side then it means they are moving to al-Madinah.'

"Ali, *'Alayhi al-Salam*, went to them and found them on their camels. Abu Sufyan said, 'O Ali, What you want is happening. We are going to Makkah. Go to your friend.' Jibril, *'Alayhi al-Salam*, followed them. Whenever they heard the sound of the hoofs of his horse, they moved faster. He followed them. When they moved, they said to each other, 'The army of Muhammad is coming.' Abu Sufyan entered Makkah and informed them of the news. The shepherds and firewood collectors came and said, 'We saw the army of Muhammad. Whenever abu Sufyan embarked they disembarked, led by a man riding a blond hair horse following their traces. People of Makkah came to abu Sufyan and reproached him. The Holy Prophet, *O Allah grant compensation to Muhammad and his family worthy of their services to Your cause*, moved with Ali, *'Alayhi al-Salam*, carrying the banner and walking in front of him, when they arrived at the top of al-Qubah people saw him.

"Ali, *'Alayhi al-Salam*, called, 'O people, this is Muhammad. He is not dead or killed.' The speaker of the words who had said that he now is mocking at us when we are defeated said, 'This is Ali with the banner in his hand.' The Holy Prophet moved faster to them and the women of al-Ansar (people of al-Madinah) were in their courtyards and at the front of their doors. Men came out to him (the Messenger of Allah) closer, returning from their escape and flight. The women and the women of al-Ansar (people of al-Madinah) had cried, scratched their faces spread their hairs, pulled the hairs of their forehead and torn the sides of their clothing. They had deprived themselves of food because of sorrow for the Holy Prophet, *O Allah grant compensation to Muhammad and his family worthy of their services to Your cause*.

"When he saw them, he (the Messenger of Allah) said good things to them and commanded them to cover themselves and to go inside their homes. He (the Messenger of Allah) said, 'Allah, most Majestic, most Glorious, has promised to me that He will make His religion victorious over all other religions.' Allah revealed to Muhammad, *O Allah grant compensation to Muhammad and his family worthy of their services to Your cause*, 'Muhammad is only a messenger

273

before whom other messengers lived. If he dies or is killed, will you then return back upon your heels? Those who return back on their heels cannot harm Allah in anything.'" (3:144)

Expedition in al-Hudaybiyah

H 14951, h 503

Ali ibn Ibrahim has narrated from his father from ibn abu 'Umayr and others from Mu'awiyah ibn 'Ammar who has narrated the following:

"Abu 'Abd Allah, *'Alayhi al-Salam*, has said that when the Messenger of Allah, *O Allah grant compensation to Muhammad and his family worthy of their services to Your cause*, came out for the armed expedition in al-Hudaybiyah, it was in the month of Dhi al-Qa'dah. When he (the Messenger of Allah) arrived at the place at which he assumed the state of *Ihram* they, (people with him) also assumed the state of *Ihram* but carried their arms also. When they found that the pagans have sent to him Khalid ibn Walid to force him back, he said, 'Find a man who can take me through another road to Makkah.' A man from Muzinah or Juhaynah was found but he did not agree and he said, 'Find for me another man.'

"Another man from Muzaynah or Juhaynah was brought who explained it to him and he (the Messenger of Allah) agreed. He travelled with him until he arrived at al-'Aqabah. He (the Messenger of Allah) asked, 'Who can climb it so that Allah will make (his sins) drop as He made the sins of banu Israel drop when He said, ". . . enter the gate and do *Sajdah* (prostration). We will forgive your sins."' A group of the people of al-Ansar (people of al-Madinah) from the tribe of Aws and al-Khazraj numbering one thousand eight hundred then advanced. When they descended in al-Hudaybiyah, they found a woman with her son in a tent. Her son ran fleeing. When she found out that it is the Messenger of Allah, *O Allah grant compensation to Muhammad and his family worthy of their services to Your cause*, she called loudly, 'They are al-Sabi'un (name of a religious group), they will not harm you.' "When the Messenger of Allah, *O Allah grant compensation to Muhammad and his family worthy of their services to Your cause*, arrived he commanded her to give them a bucket of water. The Messenger of Allah, *O Allah grant compensation to Muhammad and his family worthy of their services to Your cause*, took the water, drank from it and washed his face. She took the extra and poured it in the well. That well continued with water until this day. The Messenger of Allah, *O Allah grant compensation to Muhammad and his family worthy of their services to Your cause*, left that area.

"The pagans sent to him Aban ibn Sa'id in a group of horsemen who was in front of them, then they sent al-Hulays who saw the animals for sacrifice grooming each other (without saddles and not for transportation but free for offering). He returned and did not go to the Messenger of Allah, *O Allah grant compensation to Muhammad and his family worthy of their services to Your cause*. He said to abu Sufyan, 'We did not make an agreement with you to prevent the offering animals from reaching where they are to reach.' Abu

Sufyan said, 'Keep quiet. You are only an Arab man.' He then said, 'You must allow Muhammad to do what he wants or I will rise with the 'Uhabish (a group of a people).' Abu Sufyan said, 'You must remain quiet until we make an agreement with Muhammad.' They sent 'Urwah ibn Mas'ud who had come to Quraysh about the case of the people who were killed by al-Mughirah ibn Sha'bah who had travelled with him from Taef. They were traders and he (al-Mughirah) had killed them. He (al-Mughirah) then came to the Messenger of Allah, *O Allah grant compensation to Muhammad and his family worthy of their services to Your cause*, with their assets. He (the Messenger of Allah) refused to accept their assets saying, 'It is treachery and we do not need it.' They (the pagans) sent him to the Messenger of Allah, and they said, 'O Messenger of Allah, this is 'Urwah ibn Mas'ud who respects sacrificial offerings.' He (the Messenger of Allah) told them to allow him to remain. They allowed him to remain and he asked, 'O Muhammad, what for have you come?' He (the Messenger of Allah) replied, 'I have come to make *tawaf* around the House, perform *Sa'y* (walking) between Safa' and al-Marwah, offer this camel as animal offerings and leave its flesh for you.'

"He said, 'By al-Lat and al-'Uzza', I do not think that a man like you should be prevented from doing what you have come for. Your people swear you to Allah and family relations not to enter their town without their permission, to cut off family relation and make their enemies daring against them.' The Messenger of Allah, *O Allah grant compensation to Muhammad and his family worthy of their services to Your cause*, said, 'I do intend to do it when I enter it (the town).' When 'Urwah ibn Mas'ud spoke to the Messenger of Allah, *O Allah grant compensation to Muhammad and his family worthy of their services to Your cause*, he held his beard and al-Mughirah was standing by. He hit his hand. He asked, 'Who is this O Muhammad?' He replied, 'He is the son of your brother al-Mughirah.' He said, 'O treachery! by Allah, I have come for no other reason but to clean up your mess.' He then returned to abu Sufyan and his friends and said, 'By Allah, I do not think a person like Muhammad should be turned back from what he has come for.'

"They then sent Sohail ibn 'Amr and Huwaytib ibn 'Abd al- 'Uzza'. The Messenger of Allah, *O Allah grant compensation to Muhammad and his family worthy of their services to Your cause*, commanded to spread the animals for sacrificial offering and they asked, 'What for have you come?' He (the Messenger of Allah) replied, 'I have come to make *tawaf* around the House, perform *Sa'y* (walking) between Safa' and al-Marwah, offer this camel as animal offerings and leave its flesh for you.' The two of them said, 'Your people swear you to Allah and to family relations not to enter their town without their permission, or to cut off family relations and make their enemies daring against them.' The Messenger of Allah, *O Allah grant compensation to Muhammad and his family worthy of their services to Your cause*, told them that it is necessary for him to enter Makkah. The Messenger of Allah, *O Allah grant compensation to Muhammad and his family worthy of their services to Your cause*, wanted to send 'Umar. He said, 'O Messenger of Allah, my tribe is small and you know

my position among them. "I think you must send 'Uthman ibn 'Affan to them.'"
The Messenger of Allah, *O Allah grant compensation to Muhammad and his
family worthy of their services to Your cause*, sent him to them and told him to
go to his people who believe and give them the glad news of what my Lord has
promised me about the conquest of Makkah. When 'Uthman left he met Aban
ibn Sa'id who made room for him by pushing the saddle back and allowed
'Uthman to ride with him who informed them and a skirmish took place among
them. Sohail ibn 'Amr remained before the Messenger of Allah, *O Allah grant
compensation to Muhammad and his family worthy of their services to Your
cause*, and 'Uthman sat in the army of pagans. The Messenger of Allah, *O Allah
grant compensation to Muhammad and his family worthy of their services to
Your cause*, asked the Muslims to pledge allegiance. He (the Messenger of
Allah) tapped his one hand against the other for 'Uthman. The Muslims said,
'How good is it for 'Uthman who has performed *tawaf* around the House, *Sa'y*
(walking) between Safa' and al-Marwah and has come out of the state of *Ihram*.'
The Messenger of Allah, *O Allah grant compensation to Muhammad and his
family worthy of their services to Your cause*, said, 'He must not have done so.'
When he came back and the Messenger of Allah asked if he had performed
tawaf around the House, he replied, 'I was not to perform *tawaf* around the
House when the Messenger of Allah, *O Allah grant compensation to
Muhammad and his family worthy of their services to Your cause*, has not
performed *tawaf*.' He then mentioned the story and his experience with
Quraysh.

"He (the Messenger of Allah) said to Ali, *'Alayhi al-Salam*, to write: 'In the
name of Allah, the Beneficent, the Merciful.' Sohail said, 'I do not know the
Beneficent, the Merciful, except that which is in Yamamah, but you must write
as we write, 'In your name O Lord.' He said, 'Write; this is a settlement made
by the Messenger of Allah and Sohail ibn 'Amr.' Sohayl then said, 'What for
then we fight you, O Muhammad?' He said, 'I am the Messenger of Allah and I
am Muhammad ibn 'Abd Allah.' The people said, 'You are the Messenger of
Allah.' He said, 'Write that this is a settlement between Muhammad ibn 'Abd
Allah.' People said, 'You are the Messenger of Allah.' In the statements it was
said that whoever from us comes to you, you must return him to us and that the
Messenger of Allah is not to force him in his religion and whoever from you
comes to us we will not return him to you.' "The Messenger of Allah, *O Allah
grant compensation to Muhammad and his family worthy of their services to
Your cause*, then said, 'We do not need them and that they must be allowed to
worship openly among you and without secrecy and that they can exchange gifts
from al-Madinah to Makkah.' There was no statement more blissful than this
(exchange of gifts) which helped Islam to almost dominate the inhabitants of
Makkah. Sohail ibn 'Amr then took hold of abu Jandal (his son who just had
become a Muslim and had escaped the pagans) and said, 'This is the first case to
which the agreement must be applied (my son, abu Jandal must be returned to
us).'

"The Messenger of Allah, *O Allah grant compensation to Muhammad and his family worthy of their services to Your cause*, said, 'Have I asked you to apply the agreement in my favor yet?' He (Sohail) said, 'You have not been treacherous, O Muhammad.' He (Sohail) then took abu Jandal, his son back. He (abu Jandal) said, 'O Messenger of Allah, will you hand me over to him?' He (the Messenger of Allah) said, 'I have not set any exception to the agreement so that I can keep you with me and he (the Messenger of Allah) prayed, 'O Lord, make a way out for abu Jandal from his difficulties.'"

'Come to you fed up with fighting...

H 14952, h 504
Ali ibn Ibrahim has narrated from his father from Ahmad ibn Muhammad from ibn abu Nasr from Aban from al-Fadl ibn al-'Abbas who has narrated the following:

"It is about the meaning of the words of Allah, most Majestic, most Glorious. '. . . or that they come to you fed up with fighting against you or their own people.' (4:90) Abu 'Abd Allah, *'Alayhi al-Salam*, has said that it was revealed about banu Mudlij. They came to the Messenger of Allah, *O Allah grant compensation to Muhammad and his family worthy of their services to Your cause*, saying, 'We are troubled on seeing you being the Messenger of Allah and we are not with you or with our people against you.' I then asked, 'What did the Messenger of Allah, *O Allah grant compensation to Muhammad and his family worthy of their services to Your cause*, do with them?' He (the Imam) said, 'He (the Messenger of Allah) asked to wait until he deals with the Arabs first, then call them to Islam and if they did not accept, he may go to war against them.'"

Jibril, Michael, Israfil and Karubil

H 14953, h 505
Muhammad ibn Yahya has narrated from Ahmad ibn Muhammad ibn 'Isa from ibn Faddal from Dawud ibn abu Yazid, who is Farqad, from abu Yazid al-Hammar who has narrated the following:

"Abu 'Abd Allah, *'Alayhi al-Salam*, has said that Allah, most Blessed, most High, sent four angels to destroy the people of Lot. They were Jibril, Michael, Israfil and Karubil, *'Alayhim al-Salam*. They visited Ibrahim, *'Alayhi al-Salam*, and they were wearing turbans. They offered him greeting of peace but he did not recognize them and he found them well formed. He said to himself that no one other than myself should serve them. He liked very much to serve guests. He prepared and brought for them a healthy roasted calf. He placed it before them, '. . . he noticed that their hands did not reach to it (the food) and he felt afraid of them.' (11:70) When Jibril, *'Alayhi al-Salam*, noticed it he removed his turban from his face and head. Ibrahim, *'Alayhi al-Salam*, recognized him and said, 'Is it you?' He replied, 'Yes, I am he.' His wife, Sarah, passed by and he gave her the glad news of the birth of Ishaq who is followed by Ya'qub.' She said what Allah, most Majestic, most Glorious, has quoted her saying and they answered as it is mentioned in the majestic book. Ibrahim, *'Alayhi al-Salam*, asked, 'What for have you come?' They replied, 'We have come to destroy the people of Lot.'

"He then asked them, 'Will you destroy them even if there are one hundred believing people?' Jibril, *'Alayhi al-Salam*, replied, 'No, we will not do so.' He then asked, 'What can happen if there are fifty people?' He replied, 'No, we will not destroy them.' He then asked, 'What happens if there are thirty believing people?' He replied, 'No, we will not destroy them.' He asked, 'What happens if there are twenty people?' He replied, 'No, we will not do so.' He then asked, 'What happens if there are ten people?' He replied, 'No, we will not destroy them.' He then asked, 'What happens if there are five people?' He replied, 'No, we will not do so.' He then asked, 'What happens if there is one believing person?' He replied, 'No, we will not do so.' He then said, 'But there is Lot among them.' They said, 'We know who is there. We will save him and his family except his wife who is of those who are gone.' They then left.' Al-Hassan, al-'Askari, abu Muhammad, has said, (according to footnote, 'this may or may not be a reference to the eleventh Imam *'Alayhi al-Salam*, I, the narrator, do not know whose words these are') except that he (Ibrahim, *Alayhi al-Salam*) wanted them to remain as it is mentioned in the words of Allah, most Majestic, most Glorious. '. . . he argues with us about the people of Lot.' (11:74) They went to Lot when he was in his farm near the city. They offered him greeting of peace and they had their turbans on them. When he saw them well formed with white turbans and white clothes he asked them, 'Do you want lodging?' They replied, 'Yes, we need lodging.' He led them and they followed him but he regretted his offering them lodging and said to himself, 'What will I do if my people will come to them and I know their behavior. He turned to them and said, "You are coming to the most evil creatures of Allah" and Jibril said that we are not in a hurry until there are three testimonies against them. Jibril said, 'This is one.' He went for a while then turned to them and said, 'You are coming to the most evil creatures of Allah.' Jibril said, 'This is the second testimony.' He continued until he reached at the gate of the city and he turned to them and said, 'You are coming to the most evil creatures of Allah.' Jibril said, 'This is the third testimony.' They then entered the city and when his wife saw them so well formed, she climbed on the roof, made a loud sound but they did not hear her. She then started a smoke. When they saw the smoke they came running to the door. She climbed down to them and told them that certain people have come with him the like of whom in beauty she has never seen. They went to the door to enter.

"When Lot saw them he stood up before them and said, 'My people, you must have fear of Allah and do not harass me because of my guests. Is there no man of understanding among you? These are my daughters who are cleaner for you.' He called to lawful matters but they said, 'You know that we have no right in your daughters and you know what we want. He then said, 'I wish I had enough power and strong support' Jibril, *'Alayhi al-Salam*, then said, 'If he only knew how much power he already had.' They spoke a great deal with him until they entered the house.' Jibril then called loudly, 'O Lot, allow them to come in.' When they went in the house Jibril pointed with his finger at them and their eyes were gone as it is mentioned in His words, '. . . We obliterated their eyes.' (54:38)

"Jibril then said, 'We are the messengers of your Lord. They cannot reach you. You must travel with your family during the night.' Jibril said to him, 'We are sent to destroy them.' He said, 'O Jibril, you must do it quickly.' He replied, 'The appointed time against them is the morning, is the morning not near?' He (the Imam) said that he commanded him to carry with him those with him except his wife. He (the Imam) said, 'Jibril then pulled it (the land) with his two wings from the seventh earth and raised it until the inhabitants of the sky of the world could hear the barking of their dogs and the crowing of their roosters. He then turned it upside down, and then rained down on it and on the city nearby, stones of baked clay.'"

Was better for this nation...

H 14954, h 506

Muhammad ibn Yahya has narrated from Ahmad ibn Muhammad from Muhammad ibn Sinan from abu Sabbah ibn 'Abd al-Hamid from Muhammad ibn Muslim who has narrated the following:

"Abu Ja'far, *'Alayhi al-Salam*, has said, 'By Allah, what al-Hassan ibn Ali, *'Alayhim al-Salam*, did was better for this nation than all things on which the sun shines. By Allah, this verse, '. . . consider those who were told to hold back their hands, perform *Salat* (prayer), pay *Zakat*,' (4:77) is a reference to obedience to the Imam. However, they wanted fighting (in the time of al-Hassan, *'Alayhi al-Salam*). When fighting was required to fight for al-Husayn, *'Alayhi al-Salam*, they said, 'O our Lord, why have You commanded us to fight? We wished You had delayed it for a short time we accepted your call and followed the messengers.' (4:77) They wanted to delay it until al-Qa'im will reappear with divine authority and power.'"

Astronomy, if it is real . . .

H 14955, h 507

Muhammad ibn Yahya has narrated from Salmah ibn al-Khattab and A number of our people have narrated from Sahl ibn Ziyad all from Ali ibn Hassan from Ali ibn 'Atiyyah al-Zayyat from Mu'alla' ibn Khunays who has narrated the following:

"I once asked abu 'Abd Allah, *'Alayhi al-Salam*, about astronomy, if it is real. He (the Imam) said, 'Yes, it is real. Allah, most Majestic, most Glorious, had sent al-Mushtary (Jupiter) to earth in the form of a man and took a non-Arab man took and he taught him astronomy until he (al-Mushtary) thought that he (the non-Arab man) had perfected it. He then asked, 'Look where is al-Mushtariy?' He replied, 'I do not see him in al-Falak (the group) and I do not know where he is?' He (the Imam) said that he then moved him away and held the hand of a man of al-Hind (India) and taught him until he thought that he had perfected it. He told him to look to al-Mushtariy and find where he is. He said, 'My calculation shows that you are al-Mushtariy.' He (the Imam) said that he made a loud sound and died but his people inherited his knowledge, thus knowledge is there.'"

(The Arabic footnote considers this Hadith a definitely forged Hadith without citing any other Hadith or al-Quran against it. Therefore, it is just his personal view. Other notes consider it one more Mutashabeh Hadith)

A family of al-Hind (India) know it

H 14956, h 508

Ali ibn Ibrahim has narrated from his father from ibn abu 'Umayr from Jamil ibn Salih from the one who narrated to him who has narrated the following:

"Once abu 'Abd Allah, *'Alayhi al-Salam*, was asked about astronomy. He (the Imam) said, 'No one except a family of al-Arab and a family of al-Hind (India) know it.'"

Before the rise of thee children of al-'Abbas

H 14957, h 509

Humayd ibn Ziyad has narrated from abu al-'Abbas 'Ubayd Allah ibn Ahmad al-Dihqan from Ali ibn al-Hassan al-Tatriy from Muhammad ibn Ziyad Bayy'a al-Sabiriy from Aban from Sabah ibn Sayabah from Mu'alla' ibn Khunays who has narrated the following:

"I took the letters of 'Abd al-Salam ibn al-Nu'aym, Sadir and those of more than one persons to abu 'Abd Allah, *'Alayhi al-Salam*, when the blackened one appeared (abu Muslim al-Marwaziy) before the rise of children of al-'Abbas. The letters said, 'We have determined that this *'Amr Wilayah* (divine authority and knowledge) must come to you. What then is your response?' He (the narrator) has said that he (the Imam) threw the letters on the ground and said, 'Fie on them. I am not the Imam for these people. Do they not know that only he eliminates al-Sufyaniy?'"

Houses of the Holy Prophet, *'Alayhi al-Salam*

H 14958, h 510

Aban has narrated from abu Basir who has narrated the following:

"I once asked abu 'Abd Allah, *'Alayhi al-Salam*, about the meaning of the words of Allah, most Majestic, most Glorious. '. . . in the houses which Allah has determined to be exalted.' (24:36) Abu 'Abd Allah, *'Alayhi al-Salam*, has said, 'It is the houses of the Holy Prophet, *O Allah grant compensation to Muhammad and his family worthy of their services to Your cause.*'"

The coat of arms of the Messenger of Allah, *'Alayhi al-Salam*

H 14959, h 511

Aban has narrated from Yahya ibn abu al-'Ala' who has narrated the following:

"I once heard abu 'Abd Allah, *'Alayhi al-Salam*, say, 'The coat of armsof the Messenger of Allah, *O Allah grant compensation to Muhammad and his family worthy of their services to Your cause*, called Dhat al-Fudul, had two rings of silver in front of it and two on its back.' He (the Imam) said, 'Ali, *'Alayhi al-Salam*, wore it on the day of Jamal (camel) (in Basrah, Iraq).'"

A belt of black and white color

H 14960, h 512

Aban has narrated from Ya'qub ibn Shu'ayb who has narrated the following:

"Abu 'Abd Allah, *'Alayhi al-Salam*, has stated this Hadith: 'On the day of Jamal, Ali, *'Alayhi al-Salam*, tied a belt of black and white color around his abdomen. Jibril had brought it from the sky and the Messenger of Allah, *O Allah grant compensation to Muhammad and his family worthy of their services to Your cause*, would tie it around his abdomen when wearing a coat of arms'"

When al-Miqdad was about to leave the world...

H 14961, h 513

Aban has narrated from Fudayl ibn Yasar who has narrated the following:

"Abu Ja'far, *'Alayhi al-Salam*, has said that 'Uthman once said to al-Miqdad, 'O yes, by Allah, you must desist or I will send you to your first Lord (kill you).' He (the Imam) said, 'When al-Miqdad was about to leave the world he said to 'Ammar, 'Say to 'Uthman that I have returned to my first Lord.'"

'Usamah was about to die

H 14962, h 514

Aban has narrated from al-Fudayl and 'Ubayd who has narrated the following:

"Abu 'Abd Allah, *'Alayhi al-Salam*, has said, 'When Muhammad ibn 'Usamah was about to die, banu Hashim went to visit him. He said to them, 'You are aware of my relations with you. I have a debt on me and I like that you guarantee to pay it on my behalf. Ali ibn al-Husayn, *'Alayhi al-Salam*, said, 'O yes, by Allah, I will pay one-third of your debts.' He remained quiet and they remained quiet. Ali ibn al-Husayn, *'Alayhim al-Salam*, then said, 'All of your debts are on me.' He (the Imam) said that Ali ibn al-Husayn, *'Alayhi al-Salam*, said, 'I could have accepted the responsibility for all of his debts in the first time but I did do so because I disliked that they may say, "He made the move before giving us a chance."'"

He left its rein...

H 14963, h 515

Aban has narrated from abu Basir who has narrated the following:

"Abu 'Abd Allah, *'Alayhi al-Salam*, has said that the camel of the Messenger of Allah, *O Allah grant compensation to Muhammad and his family worthy of their services to Your cause*, called al-Quswa' was such that whenever disembarked from, he left its rein on it and it moved among the Muslims. This man gave it something and the other gave it something until it became satisfied.' He (the Imam) said that once it entered its head in the tent of Samurah ibn Jundab. He picked up a stick and hit its head that caused an injury. It went to the Holy Prophet, and complained.'"

Every hour for one month

H 14964, h 516

Aban has narrated from a man who has narrated the following:

"Abu 'Abd Allah, *'Alayhi al-Salam*, has said that Maryam remained pregnant with Jesus, *'Alayhi al-Salam*, for nine hours, every hour for one month.'"

They have spoken a lie

H 14965, h 517

Aban has narrated from 'Umar ibn Yazid who has narrated the following:

"I once said to abu 'Abd Allah, *'Alayhi al-Salam*, that al-Mughirah (followers of al-Mughirah) say that this day is for the night that follows it. He (the Imam) said, 'They have spoken a lie. This day is for the night before it. People of Nakhlah on seeing the moon would say that al-Haram (the Sacred) month has begun.'"

Define them for us so we will know them

H 14966, h 518

Muhammad ibn Yahya has narrated from Ahmad ibn Muhammad ibn 'Isa from Ali ibn Salar abu 'Amrah from abu Maryam al-Thaqafiy from 'Ammar ibn Yasar who has narrated the following:

"Once when I was with the Messenger of Allah, *O Allah grant compensation to Muhammad and his family worthy of their services to Your cause*, he (the Messenger of Allah) said, 'The special Shi'ah (followers) who are pure are from us, *Ahl al-Bayt*.' 'Umar then said, 'O Messenger of Allah, define them for us so we will know them.' The Messenger of Allah, *O Allah grant compensation to Muhammad and his family worthy of their services to Your cause*, said, 'I just wanted to informed you about this fact.' The Messenger of Allah, *O Allah grant compensation to Muhammad and his family worthy of their services to Your cause*, then said, 'I am the guide to Allah, most Majestic, most Glorious, and Ali has supported the religion. The lighthouses of religion are *Ahl al-Bayt* and they are its light whereby brightness is sought.' 'Umar then said, 'O Messenger of Allah, what will happen if one's heart does not agree with it?' The Messenger of Allah, *O Allah grant compensation to Muhammad and his family worthy of their services to Your cause*, said, 'There is no heart placed where it is placed but that it either agrees or disagrees. One whose heart agrees with us, *Ahl al-Bayt*, he is saved, and one whose heart disagrees with us, *Ahl al-Bayt*, is destroyed.'"

Enemies for our sake

H 14967, h 519

Ahmad has narrated from Ali ibn al-Hakam from Qutaybah al-A'sha' who has narrated the following:

"I once heard abu 'Abd Allah, *'Alayhi al-Salam*, say, 'You have made your fathers, sons, and spouses as your enemies for our sake, your reward is with Allah, most Majestic, most Glorious. What you will most urgently need is what you will need when the soul reaches here' – he pointed to his throat."

We decided to meet in the house of Tahir

H 14968, h 520

It is narrated from the narrator of the previous Hadith from Ahmad ibn Muhammad from al-Hassan ibn Ali from Dawud ibn Sulayman al-Hammar from Sa'id ibn Yasar who has narrated the following:

"Once, al-Harith ibn al-Mughirah, al-Nasriy, Mansur, al-Sayqal and I asked permission to visit abu 'Abd Allah, *'Alayhi al-Salam*. We decided to meet in the house of Tahir, his *mawla* and we performed al-'Asr *Salat* (prayer), then we left to visit him (the Imam). We found him leaning against a bed near the ground and we sat around him. He (the Imam) then sat straight. He then stretched his legs on the ground, then said, 'All praise belongs to Allah who has taken people left and right, one sect is Murji'ah, one sect is Khawarij, one sect is Qadriah and you are called al-Turabiyah.' He (the Imam) then said to the one on his right. O yes, by Allah, He is only Allah who is One and has no partners and there is His Messenger and *Ale* (family of) His Messenger, *O Allah grant compensation to Muhammad and his family worthy of their services to Your cause*, and their Shi'ah, may Allah make their faces graceful and whatever is other than this is nothing. Ali, *'Alayhi al-Salam*, by Allah, had the greatest priority to the Messenger of Allah over all people.' He (the Imam) said it three times.'"

Angels of the skies of the world

H 14969, h 521

It is narrated from the narrator of the previous Hadith from Ahmad from Ali ibn al-Mastur al-Nakha'iy from those who have said the following:

"Abu 'Abd Allah, *'Alayhi al-Salam*, has stated this Hadith: 'The angels of the skies of the world, who find one, two or three people speak of the excellence of *Ale* (family of) Muhammad, *'Alayhi al-Salam*, tell each other. They say, 'Look at them, even though they are of such a small number, they speak of the excellence of *Ale* (family of) Muhammad, *'Alayhi al-Salam*', and other group of angels say, 'It is because of the generosity of Allah which He gives to whoever He wants, the generosity of Allah is great.'"

You must not overburden

H 14970, h 522

It is narrated from the narrator of the previous Hadith from Ahmad ibn Muhammad from Ali ibn al-Hakam from 'Umar ibn Hanzalah who has narrated the following:

"Abu 'Abd Allah, *'Alayhi al-Salam*, once said, 'O 'Umar, you must not overburden our Shi'ah. You must be kind to them because people do not bear what you bear.'"

Place them under our feet....

H 14971, h 523

Muhammad ibn Ahmad al-Qummiy has narrated from his uncle 'Abd Allah ibn al-Salt from Yunus ibn Ibrahim from 'Abd Allah ibn Sinan from al-Husayn al-Jammal who has narrated the following:

"About the meaning of the words of Allah, most Majestic, most Glorious, '. . . our Lord, show us those who misled us, of Jinn and men so we can place them under our feet to bring them low', (41:29) abu 'Abd Allah, *'Alayhi al-Salam*, has said, 'They are the two of them and so and so was a Satan.'"

"Our Lord, show us"

H 14972, h 524

Yunus has narrated from Sawrah ibn Kulayb who has narrated the following:

"This is about the meaning of the words of Allah, most Majestic, most Glorious, '. . . our Lord, show us those who misled us, of Jinn and men so we can place them under our feet to bring them low.' (41:29) Abu 'Abd Allah, *'Alayhi al-Salam*, said, 'O Sawrah, they by Allah, are those people' three times. By Allah, O Sawrah we are the treasurers of the knowledge of Allah in the sky and we are the treasurers of the knowledge of Allah on earth.'"

"Because they plan during the night..."

H 14973, h 525

Muhammad ibn Yahya has narrated from Ahmad ibn Muhammad ibn 'Isa from al-Husayn ibn Sa'id from Sulayman al-Ja'fariy who has narrated the following:

"This is about the meaning of the words of Allah, most Majestic, most Glorious, '. . . because they plan during the night such words with which Allah is not happy.' (4:108) I once heard abu al-Hassan, *'Alayhi al-Salam*, say, 'They by Allah are so and so and abu 'Ubayd al-Jarrah.'"

"They are those whose hearts are known"

H 14974, h 526

Ali ibn Ibrahim has narrated from his father from and Muhammad ibn 'Isma'il and others from Mansur ibn Yunus from ibn 'Udhaynah from 'Abd Allah ibn al-Najashiy who has narrated the following:

"This is about the meaning of the words of Allah, most Majestic, most Glorious, '. . . they are those whose hearts are known to Allah, so ignore them and advise them and say to them about their souls clear words.' (4:63) Abu 'Abd Allah, *'Alayhi al-Salam*, has said, 'By Allah, they are so and so.' '. . . We have sent the messengers who must be obeyed by the permission of Allah. If they do injustice to themselves then come to you and ask forgiveness from Allah and the Messenger also asks forgiveness for them they will find Allah forgiving and merciful.' (4:64) He (the Imam) said, 'It is a reference to the Holy Prophet, *O Allah grant compensation to Muhammad and his family worthy of their services to Your cause*, and Ali, *'Alayhi al-Salam*, and because of what they had done. If they come to you, O Ali, repenting and ask Allah to forgive them for what they have done and the messenger asks forgiveness for them they will find Allah forgiving and merciful. '. . . no, by Allah, they will not believe until they ask you for judgment about their dispute.' (4:65) Abu 'Abd Allah, *'Alayhi al-Salam*, has said, 'This is a reference to Ali, *'Alayhi al-Salam*. "They then do not find any obstacle in their heart to accept your judgment [through your words, O

Messenger of Allah, about the *Wilayah* (divine authority and knowledge) of Ali, *'Alayhi al-Salam*,] and totally submit' (4:65) [to the command of Ali, *'Alayhi al-Salam*].'"

"Dreams materialize . . ."

H 14975, h 527, 528

Muhammad ibn Yahya has narrated from Ahmad ibn Muhammad ibn 'Isa from ibn Faddal from al-Hassan ibn al-Jahm who has narrated the following:

"I once heard abu al-Hassan, *'Alayhi al-Salam*, say, 'Dreams materialize according to the way they are interpreted.' I then asked, 'I pray to Allah to keep my soul in service for your cause, certain persons of our people have narrated that the dream of the king was confused.' Abu al-Hassan, *'Alayhi al-Salam*, said, 'A woman at the time of the Messenger of Allah, *O Allah grant compensation to Muhammad and his family worthy of their services to Your cause*, saw a dream that the beam of her house broke. She went to the Messenger of Allah, *O Allah grant compensation to Muhammad and his family worthy of their services to Your cause*, and explained her dream. The Holy Prophet, *O Allah grant compensation to Muhammad and his family worthy of their services to Your cause*, said, 'Your husband will come as a virtuous person.' Her husband was absent and he came as the Holy Prophet, *O Allah grant compensation to Muhammad and his family worthy of their services to Your cause*, had said. Then her husband remained absent and she saw in her dream that the beam of her house broke. She came to the Holy Prophet, *O Allah grant compensation to Muhammad and his family worthy of their services to Your cause*, and explained her dream. He said, 'Your husband will come as a virtuous person.' He came as he had said. He remained absent for the third time and she saw in her dream that the beam of her house broke. She met a left-handed man and explained her dream to him. The bad man said, 'Your husband will die.' He (the Imam) said, 'This was reported to the Holy Prophet, *O Allah grant compensation to Muhammad and his family worthy of their services to Your cause*, who said, 'I wish he had interpreted it in a good sense for her.'"

The dream of a believing person

H 14976, h 529

A number of our people have narrated from Sahl ibn Ziyad and Ali ibn Ibrahim has narrated from his father from ibn Mahbub from 'Abd Allah ibn Ghalib from Jabir ibn Yazid who has narrated the following:

"Abu Ja'far, *'Alayhi al-Salam*, has said that the Messenger of Allah, *O Allah grant compensation to Muhammad and his family worthy of their services to Your cause*, would say, 'The dream of a believing person floats between the sky and earth over the head of its owner until he interprets it or someone else. When it is interpreted, it then holds to the earth. So you must not tell anyone about your dream except those who have good understanding.'"

A dream must not be stated . . .

H 14977, h 530

Muhammad ibn Yahya has narrated from Ahmad ibn Muhammad from Muhammad ibn Khalid from al-Qasim ibn 'Urwah from abu Basir who has narrated the following:

"Abu 'Abd Allah, *'Alayhi al-Salam*, has said that the Messenger of Allah, *O Allah grant compensation to Muhammad and his family worthy of their services to Your cause*, has said, 'A dream must not be stated before anyone except a believing person who is free of jealousy and transgression.'"

The ugliest of all people...

H 14978, h 531

Humayd ibn Ziyad has narrated from al-Hassan ibn Muhammad al-Kindiy from Ahmad ibn al-Hassan al-Mithamiy from Aban ibn 'Uthman from a man who has narrated the following:

"Abu Ja'far, *'Alayhi al-Salam*, has said that at the time of the Messenger of Allah, *O Allah grant compensation to Muhammad and his family worthy of their services to Your cause*, there was a man called Dhu al-Namerah who was the ugliest of all people and for this reason he was called Dhu al-Namerah. Once he came to the Holy Prophet, *O Allah grant compensation to Muhammad and his family worthy of their services to Your cause*, and said, 'O Messenger of Allah, tell me about what Allah, most Majestic, most Glorious, has made obligatory.' The Messenger of Allah, *O Allah grant compensation to Muhammad and his family worthy of their services to Your cause*, said, 'Allah has made seventeen *Rak'at Salat* (prayer) obligatory every day and night, fasting in the month of Ramadan, if you are at home in that month, performing al-Hajj if you are able to do so.' The Messenger of Allah explained it for him. He then said, 'I swear by the One who has sent you in all truth as a Prophet that I will not increase anything for my Lord beyond what He has made obligatory.' The Holy Prophet, *O Allah grant compensation to Muhammad and his family worthy of their services to Your cause*, asked, 'Why is that so, O Dhu al-Namerah?' He said, 'It is because He has created me as ugly as I am.' Jibril came to the Holy Prophet, *O Allah grant compensation to Muhammad and his family worthy of their services to Your cause*, and said, 'O Messenger of Allah your Lord, most Blessed, most High, says, "Will you be happy if I will raise you as beautiful as Jibril on the Day of Judgment?" The Messenger of Allah, *O Allah grant compensation to Muhammad and his family worthy of their services to Your cause*, said, 'O Dhu al-Namerah, this is Jibril who commands me to tell you that your Lord says, "Will you be happy if I will raise you as beautiful as Jibril?"' Dhu al-Namerah then said, 'I agree O Lord, I swear by Your Majesty that I will increase for You until you become happy.'"

Hadith of one who was brought back to life by Jesus, *'Alayhi al-Salam*

H 14979, h 532

Muhammad ibn Yahya has narrated from Ahmad ibn Muhammad ibn 'Isa from ibn Mahbub from abu Jamilah from Aban ibn Taghlib and others who has narrated the following:

286

"Once abu 'Abd Allah, *'Alayhi al-Salam*, was asked about the people whom Jesus, *'Alayhi al-Salam*, brought back to life if they ate, received sustenance, the period of time for which they lived thereafter and if they gave birth to children. He (the Imam) said, 'Yes, he had a very brotherly friend for the sake of Allah, most Blessed, most High, whom Jesus would visit. Jesus, *'Alayhi al-Salam*, remained absent from him for a while, then he went to visit and offer him the greeting of peace. His mother came and he asked for him. She replied, 'He has died, O Messenger of Allah.' He asked if she liked to see him.' She replied, 'Yes, I love to see him.' He said, 'Tomorrow I will come to bring him back to life for you by the permission of Allah, most Blessed, most High.' The next day he came and said to her to show him where his grave was. They went to his grave and Jesus, *'Alayhi al-Salam*, then prayed to Allah, most Majestic, most Glorious. The grave opened and her son came out alive. When she saw him, they both wept. Jesus, *'Alayhi al-Salam*, sympathized with them. He asked if he liked to remain with his mother in the world. He asked, 'O Prophet of Allah, with eating, a certain time or without eating, sustenance and time?' Jesus, *'Alayhi al-Salam*, asked, 'Do you want to live with eating, sustenance, time to live for twenty years, marriage and birth of children?' He replied, 'Yes, I agree.' He (the Imam) said, 'Jesus, *'Alayhi al-Salam*, gave him to his mother and he lived for twenty years, married and children were born to him.'"

"Those who enter it (Masjid al-Haram)..."

H 14980, h 533

Ibn Mahbub has narrated from abu Wallad and others from certain persons of our people who have narrated the following:

"It is about the meaning of the words of Allah, most Majestic, most Glorious. '. . . those who enter it (Masjid al-Haram (the Sacred) in deviation and injustice . . .' (22:25) Abu 'Abd Allah, *'Alayhi al-Salam*, has said, 'It is a reference to those who worship things other than Allah, most Majestic, most Glorious. Or they acknowledge the *Walayah* (guardianship) of people other than *'A'immah* (leaders who possess divine authority and knowledge), they have deviated with injustice and it is obligatory on Allah, most Blessed, most High, to make them taste a painful suffering.'"

"Those who are expelled..."

H 14981, h 534

Ibn Mahbub has narrated from abu Ja'far al-Ahwal from Salam ibn al-Mustanir who has narrated the following:

"This is about the meaning of the words of Allah, most Blessed, most High. '. . . those who are expelled from their homes in injustice just because they have said, "Our Lord is Allah."' (22:39) Abu Ja'far, *'Alayhi al-Salam*, has said this. 'It was revealed about the Messenger of Allah, *O Allah grant compensation to Muhammad and his family worthy of their services to Your cause*, Ali, Hamzah, Ja'far and al-Husayn, *'Alayhim al-Salam*.'"

What was the answer that you received?

H 14982, h 535

Ibn Mahbub has narrated from Hisham ibn Salim from Burayd al-Kunasiy who has narrated the following:

"I once asked abu Ja'far, *'Alayhi al-Salam*, about the meaning of the words of Allah, most Majestic, most Glorious, '. . . on the day when He will bring the messengers together and ask them, "What was the answer that you received?" They will say, 'We have no knowledge thereof.'" (5:109) He (the Imam) said, 'It has an explanation, that He asks, "What kind of answer did you receive about the executors of your will from your followers?" They will reply, 'We do not know about what they did to them after we died.'" (Messengers call their knowledge as no knowledge before the knowledge of Allah.)

Hadith of Islam of Ali, *'Alayhi al-Salam*

H 14983, h 536

Ibn Mahbub has narrated from Hisham ibn Salim from abu Hamzah from Sa'id ibn al-Musayyib who has narrated the following:

"I once asked Ali ibn al-Husayn, *'Alayhi al-Salam*, about how old Ali ibn abu Talib, *'Alayhi al-Salam*, was on the day he became a Muslim?' He (the Imam) said, 'Was he ever a non-Muslim?' The fact of the matter is that on the day Allah, most Majestic, most Glorious, commanded His Messenger to work as His Messenger, Ali was ten years old but he was not a non-Muslim. He believed in Allah, most Blessed, most High, and the Messenger of Allah, *O Allah grant compensation to Muhammad and his family worthy of their services to Your cause*, before all people by three years, in the form of performing *Salat* (prayer). The first *Salat* (prayer) that he (Ali) performed with the Messenger of Allah, *O Allah grant compensation to Muhammad and his family worthy of their services to Your cause*, consisted of two Rak'ats of al-Zuhr and it was as Allah, most Blessed, most High, had made it obligatory on those who became Muslims in Makkah. It was two and two Rak'ats. The Messenger of Allah, *O Allah grant compensation to Muhammad and his family worthy of their services to Your cause*, performed them two and two Rak'ats for ten years until he (the Messenger of Allah) migrated to al-Madinah and left Ali, *'Alayhi al-Salam*, as his successor for certain things which no one could do besides him (Ali).

"The Messenger of Allah, *O Allah grant compensation to Muhammad and his family worthy of their services to Your cause*, left Makkah on the first day of Rabi' al-'Awwal. It was on a Thursday after thirteen years from the day Allah had commanded him to work as His Messenger and he arrived in al-Madinah, twelve days after the beginning of the month of Rabi' al-Awwal at noon time. He disembarked in al-Quba', performed al-Zuhr as two Rak'ats and al-'Asr as two Rak'ats. He then stayed there waiting for Ali, *'Alayhi al-Salam*. He performed five *Salat* (prayer) of two Rak'ats each, every day. He had stayed with 'Amr ibn 'Awf. He stayed with him for ten days or so. They asked him if he wanted to stay with them so that they prepared for him a Masjid and home.

He answered, 'No, I am waiting for Ali ibn abu Talib and I have commanded him to meet me. I am not choosing a living place until he comes and he will arrive shortly by the will of Allah.'

"Ali, *'Alayhi al-Salam*, arrived when the Holy Prophet was with 'Amr ibn 'Awf. He disembarked. When Ali arrived then the Messenger of Allah, *O Allah grant compensation to Muhammad and his family worthy of their services to Your cause*, moved from Quba' to bani Salim ibn 'Awf. Ali was with him, on a Friday at noon time. He marked for a Masjid, marked its al-Qiblah (the direction of al-Ka'bah) and performed *Salat* (prayer) with them on Friday, two Rak'ats with two sermons; then on the same day he moved to al-Madinah on the camel which Ali, *'Alayhi al-Salam*, had brought with him who remained with him without separation and walked as he walked. Through every neighborhood of al-Ansar (people of al-Madinah) that the Messenger of Allah, *O Allah grant compensation to Muhammad and his family worthy of their services to Your cause*, passed they stood up for him, asked him to disembark and stay with them. He (the Messenger of Allah) said, 'You must allow the camel because it has the instruction where to go.

'The camel moved with the Messenger of Allah, *O Allah grant compensation to Muhammad and his family worthy of their services to Your cause*. He (the Messenger of Allah) had left its rein uncontrolled until it arrived at the place that you see.' He (the Imam) pointed with his hand to the door of the Masjid of the Messenger of Allah, *O Allah grant compensation to Muhammad and his family worthy of their services to Your cause*, where *Salat* (prayer) for dead people are performed. 'It stopped there and sat down, placing its neck on the ground. The Messenger of Allah, *O Allah grant compensation to Muhammad and his family worthy of their services to Your cause*, disembarked and abu Ayyub came forward quickly to hold his saddle and took it to his home. The Messenger of Allah disembarked as well as Ali, *'Alayhi al-Salam*, until his Masjid was built as well as his homes were built and the house for Ali, *'Alayhi al-Salam*. Then they moved to their homes.' Sa'id ibn al-Musayyib then asked Ali ibn al-Husayn, *'Alayhi al-Salam*, saying, 'I pray to Allah to keep my soul in service for your cause. Abu Bakr was with the Messenger of Allah, *O Allah grant compensation to Muhammad and his family worthy of their services to Your cause*, when he came to al-Madinah, when did he depart?' He (the Imam) said, 'The Messenger of Allah arrived in Quba' and he was waiting for Ali, *'Alayhi al-Salam*. Abu Bakr said, "Allow us to move to al-Madinah; people are very happy because of your arrival and they are waiting for the glad news, so allow us to go and not to stay here waiting for Ali. I do not think he can come before a month." "The Messenger of Allah, *O Allah grant compensation to Muhammad and his family worthy of their services to Your cause*, told him, "No, I will never do so and he will arrive very shortly. I do not want to move without my cousin, my brother for the sake of Allah, most Majestic, most Glorious, and the most beloved one to me in my family; he saved my life with his own life from the pagans." He (the Imam) said, 'Abu Bakr became angry and detested it. He felt jealous against Ali, *'Alayhi al-Salam*. It was his first time that he expressed hatred before the

Messenger of Allah, *O Allah grant compensation to Muhammad and his family worthy of their services to Your cause*, toward Ali, *'Alayhi al-Salam*. It was his first disagreement with the Messenger of Allah, *O Allah grant compensation to Muhammad and his family worthy of their services to Your cause*. He left until he arrived in al-Madinah and left the Messenger of Allah, *O Allah grant compensation to Muhammad and his family worthy of their services to Your cause*, in Quba' waiting for Ali, *'Alayhi al-Salam*.'

"I (the narrator) then asked Ali ibn al-Husayn, *'Alayhi al-Salam*, about when the Messenger of Allah, *O Allah grant compensation to Muhammad and his family worthy of their services to Your cause*, gave Fatimah, *'Alayha al-Salam*, in marriage to Ali, *'Alayhi al-Salam*' He (the Imam) said, 'It was in al-Madinah one year after migration and she was nine years old.' [See H 1, Ch. 1, h 1 in Behar al-Anwar, Volume 43, about the special rate of growth of Fatimah, *'Alayha al-Salam*] Ali ibn al-Husayn, *'Alayhi al-Salam*, then said, 'The only child born from Khadijah to the Messenger of Allah, *O Allah grant compensation to Muhammad and his family worthy of their services to Your cause*, in the nature of Islam was Fatimah, *'Alayha al-Salam* . Khadijah had died one year before migration and abu Talib died after the death of Khadijah one year later. When he lost both of them, the Messenger of Allah, *O Allah grant compensation to Muhammad and his family worthy of their services to Your cause*, disliked living in Makkah and felt great sadness so much so that he feared for his life because of unbelievers of Quraysh and he complained before Jibril *'Alayhi al-Salam*, about it.

'Allah, most Majestic, most Glorious, sent revelation to him to leave the town of unjust inhabitants and to migrate to al-Madinah; there is no helper for you in Makkah and you must fight the pagans. Then the Messenger of Allah, *O Allah grant compensation to Muhammad and his family worthy of their services to Your cause*, left for al-Madinah.' I then asked, 'When *Salat* (prayer) became obligatory for the Muslims as it is today?' He (the Imam) said, 'It happened in al-Madinah when his call spread in public and Islam became strong. Allah, most Majestic, most Glorious, has made *Jihad* (fighting for the cause of Allah) obligatory on the Muslims. Then the Messenger of Allah, *O Allah grant compensation to Muhammad and his family worthy of their services to Your cause*, increased the number of *Rak'ats* of *Salat* (prayer) by seven *Rak'ats*. He increased two *Rak'at* with al-Zuhr, two with al-'Asr, one with al-Maghrib, two with 'Isha' and left the morning *Salat* (prayer) as it was because of the quicker coming of the angels of the day from the sky and the ascending of the angels of the night to the sky. The angels of the day and the angels of the night attended the morning *Salat* (prayer) with the Messenger of Allah, *O Allah grant compensation to Muhammad and his family worthy of their services to Your cause*, and for this reason Allah, most Majestic, most Glorious, has said, '. . . the reading at dawn, because the reading at dawn is attended.' (17:78) The Muslims attended as well as the angels of the day and the angels of the night.'"

Hold back your tongue...

H 14984, h 537

Ali ibn Ibrahim has narrated from his father from ibn abu 'Umayr from *'Alayhi al-Salam*, who has narrated the following:

"Abu 'Abd Allah, *'Alayhi al-Salam*, has said, 'How easy it is to achieve what makes people happy with you! Just hold back your tongue from speaking against them.'"

I am not the one to deal with them

H 14985, h 538

Muhammad ibn Yahya has narrated from Ahmad ibn Muhammad ibn 'Isa and Abu Ali al-Ash'ariy has narrated from Muhammad ibn 'Abd al-Jabbar all from Ali ibn Hadid from Jamil ibn Darraj from Zurarah who has narrated the following:

"Once abu Ja'far, *'Alayhi al-Salam*, was in Masjid al-Haram (the Sacred) when banu 'Umayyah and their government was mentioned. Certain ones of his companions said, 'We hope you will be the one to deal with them and Allah, most Majestic, most Glorious, will make this cause dominant through your hand.' He (the Imam) said, 'I am not the one to deal with them and He will not want me to deal with them. The ones who will deal with them (banu 'Umayyah) are children born out of wedlock. Allah, most Blessed, most High, has not created any era from the time He created the skies and earth, of shorter years or days than their (banu 'Umayyah's) years and days. Allah, most Majestic, most Glorious, commands the angel in whose hand is the group (of planets and stars) to scroll it in a fast scrolling manner.'"

Closely associated...

H 14986, h 539

Ali ibn Ibrahim has narrated from his father from ibn abu 'Umayr from Hammad ibn 'Uthaman who has narrated the following:

"Abu 'Abd Allah, *'Alayhi al-Salam*, has stated this Hadith. 'Whoever becomes closely associated with the children of Mirdas (Abbas), they turn him to disbelief; those who keep away from them, are made poor; whoever shows them hostility, they kill him; those who fortify against them, they bring them down and those who run away from them, they find them until their government will end.'"

She is the daughter of the Prophet

H 14987, h 540

Ali ibn Ibrahim has narrated from his father from and Ahmad ibn Muhammad al-Kufiy from Ali ibn 'Amr ibn Ayman all from Muhsin ibn Ahmad ibn Mu'adh from Aban ibn 'Uthman from Bashir al-Nabbal who has narrated the following:

"Abu 'Abd Allah, *'Alayhi al-Salam*, has said that once when the Messenger of Allah, *O Allah grant compensation to Muhammad and his family worthy of their services to Your cause*, was sitting a woman came. He said welcome to her, held her hand and made her to sit down; then he said, 'She is the daughter of the

Prophet, whose people had neglected. Khalid ibn Sinan called them to the faith but they refused to believe. There was a fire called the fire of al-Hadathan that emerged every year and it consumed certain ones from among them. It came in a certain time. He said, 'If I returned this, will you then believe what I say?' They agreed. It came and he went, faced it with his clothes and turned it back then followed it up to the cave then entered the cave. They sat at the opening of the cave. They saw him as if he would never come out. He came out saying, 'This, this and all of this is from this. Banu 'Abas thought I can not come out while my forehead perspired.' He then asked if they believed in what he said. They replied, 'No, we will not believe.' He then said, 'I will die on such and such day, and when I die then you must bury me. A group of wild donkeys will come, led by a tailless one until they stand on my grave. You then must exhume my grave and ask me whatever you like.' When he died, they buried him and on that day, the wild donkeys came and gathered. They also came to exhume his grave, then they said, 'You did not believe in him in his lifetime, then how will you believe after his death? If you exhume him it will be damnation for you, so you must leave him alone; and they left him alone.'"

When people did what they did...

H 14988, h 541

Ali ibn Ibrahim has narrated from his father from Hammad ibn 'Isa from Ibrahim ibn 'Umar al-Yamaniy from Sulaym ibn Qays al-Hilaliy who has narrated the following:

"I heard Salman al-Farsiy, may Allah be pleased with him, say that when the Messenger of Allah, *O Allah grant compensation to Muhammad and his family worthy of their services to Your cause*, passed away and people did what they did. Abu Bakr, 'Umar and abu 'Ubayd al-Jarrah disputed against al-Ansar (people of al-Madinah). They argued against them based on the reasoning and arguments of Ali, *'Alayhi al-Salam*. They said, 'O community of al-Ansar (people of al-Madinah), the community of Quraysh has the priority over you (to become the successor of the Holy Prophet); the Messenger of Allah is from Quraysh, the immigrants are from Quraysh, Allah in His book has begun with them and has given them preference. The Messenger of Allah, *O Allah grant compensation to Muhammad and his family worthy of their services to Your cause*, has said, ''A'immah (leaders) are from Quraysh.' Salman has said, 'I then went to Ali, *'Alayhi al-Salam*, when he was giving Ghusl (bath) to the Messenger of Allah, *O Allah grant compensation to Muhammad and his family worthy of their services to Your cause*. By Allah, I informed him of what the people had done. I said that at this hour abu Bakr is on the *minbar* (pulpit) of the Messenger of Allah, *O Allah grant compensation to Muhammad and his family worthy of their services to Your cause*. By Allah, he does not become happy if they pledge allegiance to him with one hand. They must pledge allegiance to him with both hands, the right and left hand together.' He then asked, me, 'O Salman, do you know who was the first who pledged allegiance on the *minbar* (pulpit) of the Messenger of Allah, *O Allah grant compensation to Muhammad and his family worthy of their services to Your cause*?'

"I replied, 'I do not know except I know that in the *Zullah* (shadow) of banu al-Sa'idah when al-Ansar (people of al-Madinah) disputed the first one who pledged allegiance was Bashir ibn Sa'd and abu 'Ubayd al-Jarrah then 'Umar then Salim.' He (the Imam) said, 'I did not ask you about this. I asked, 'Who was the first to pledge allegiance when he climbed the *minbar* of the Messenger of Allah, *O Allah grant compensation to Muhammad and his family worthy of their services to Your cause*?' I replied, 'No, I do not know but I saw an old man leaning against his cane with a mark between his two eyes because of *Sajdah* (prostration) with intense *al-Tashmir* (business) climbed to him. He was the first one. He wept and said, 'All praise belongs to Allah who did not make me die before seeing you at this place. Extend your hand.' He extended his hand and he pledged allegiance to him then he climbed down and left the Masjid.' Ali, *'Alayhi al-Salam*, then asked, 'Do you know who he is?' I replied, 'No, but I disliked his words that sounded like expressing happiness for the death of the Messenger of Allah, *O Allah grant compensation to Muhammad and his family worthy of their services to Your cause*.'

"He (the Imam) said, 'That was Iblis, may Allah condemn him. The Messenger of Allah, *O Allah grant compensation to Muhammad and his family worthy of their services to Your cause*, told me about it, that Iblis and the heads of his companions saw the Messenger of Allah, *O Allah grant compensation to Muhammad and his family worthy of their services to Your cause*, appoint me for people on the day of Ghadire Khum by the command of Allah, most Majestic, most Glorious. He (the Messenger of Allah) told them that I had more authority over their souls than they themselves did and commanded that those present must inform those who were absent. Then Satans and the devils of Iblis moved to Iblis and said, 'This nation has received mercy and is protected. You and we have no way against them because they have recognized their Imam and their source of refuge after their Prophet.'

'Iblis, may Allah condemn him, then left very sad and depressed. The Messenger of Allah, *O Allah grant compensation to Muhammad and his family worthy of their services to Your cause*, told me that when he will pass away people will pledge allegiance with abu Bakr in the shadow of banu Sa'idah after their disputes. Then they will go to the Masjid and the first one to pledge allegiance on my *minbar* (pulpit) will be Iblis, may Allah condemn him, in the form of an old man who is *Mushammir* (busily at work). He will say so and so. Then he will leave and gather his Shayatin and his devils, then blow his nostrils and express excitement saying, 'You had thought that I will have no way against them. You can see how I have succeeded and what I have done to them. They abandoned the command of Allah, most Majestic, most Glorious, and obedience to Him and all that the Messenger of Allah, *O Allah grant compensation to Muhammad and his family worthy of their services to Your cause*, commanded them to obey.'"

(Satan) cried

H 14989, h 542

Muhammad ibn Yahya has narrated from Ahmad ibn Sulayman from 'Abd Allah ibn Muhammad al-Yamaniy from Misma' ibn al-Hajjaj from Sabah al-Hadhdha' from Sabah al-Muzniy from Jabir who has narrated the following:

"When the Messenger of Allah, *O Allah grant compensation to Muhammad and his family worthy of their services to Your cause*, held the hand of Ali, *'Alayhi al-Salam*, on the day of al-Ghadir, Iblis (Satan) cried. He cried in his army so badly that it made all of his army on land and in water to gather around him saying, 'O our master and guardian, what has made you so desperate? We had never heard you cry as frightened as this one.' He said to them, 'This Prophet has done something that if completed, Allah will never be disobeyed.' They said to their master, 'You were able to deal with 'Adam (quite well).' When the hypocrites said that he speaks of his desires, one of them said this to his friend. 'Can you see his eyes turn in his head like a mad person?' He meant thereby the Messenger of Allah, *O Allah grant compensation to Muhammad and his family worthy of their services to Your cause*. Satan then cried in excitement and his friends came together around him. He said, 'Did you know that I dealt with 'Adam before?' They replied, 'Yes, you dealt with him quite well.' He then said, ''Adam broke his promise but did not become an unbeliever in his Lord. These have broken their promise in addition to becoming unbelievers to the Messenger of Allah.' When the Messenger of Allah, *O Allah grant compensation to Muhammad and his family worthy of their services to Your cause*, passed away, people established someone other than Ali, *'Alayhi al-Salam*, in place of the Messenger of Allah, *O Allah grant compensation to Muhammad and his family worthy of their services to Your cause*. Iblis wore the crown of the king, set up a pulpit and sat on a cushion. He collected his foot soldiers as well as those riding; then said to them, 'You must rejoice because Allah will not be worshipped until the Day of Judgment.' Abu Ja'far, *'Alayhi al-Salam*, then read this verse of al-Quran, '. . . Iblis made his thoughts to come true about them and they followed him except a group of the believing people.' (34:20) Abu Ja'far, *'Alayhi al-Salam*, has said, 'The meaning of this verse materialized when the Messenger of Allah, *O Allah grant compensation to Muhammad and his family worthy of their services to Your cause*, passed away. The thinking of Iblis emerged when they said to the Messenger of Allah, *O Allah grant compensation to Muhammad and his family worthy of their services to Your cause*, that he speaks of his desire, Iblis then had a thought about them and they made his thoughts and conjectures to come true.'"

Last night I saw. . .

H 14990, h 543

Muhammad ibn Yahya has narrated from Ahmad ibn Muhammad ibn 'Isa from Ali ibn Hadid from Jamil ibn Darraj from Zurarah who has narrated the following:

"One of the two Imam, (abu Ja'far or abu 'Abd Allah), *'Alayhi al-Salam*, has said, 'Once in the morning the Messenger of Allah, *O Allah grant compensation to Muhammad and his family worthy of their services to Your cause*, felt sad and depressed. Ali, *'Alayhi al-Salam*, asked, 'What has happened, O Messenger of Allah, I see you feel sad and depressed?' He (the Messenger of Allah) replied, 'I am depressed because last night I saw that banu Taym, banu 'Adiy and banu 'Umayyah climb on my *minbar* (pulpit), this one and turn people backward. I then asked, 'O Lord, will this happen during my life time or after I die?' He said, 'It will happen after you die.'"

Had I not disliked . . .

H 14991, h 544
Jamil has narrated from Zurarah who has narrated the following:

"One of the two Imam, (abu Ja'far or abu 'Abd Allah), *'Alayhi al-Salam*, has stated this Hadith: 'The Messenger of Allah, *O Allah grant compensation to Muhammad and his family worthy of their services to Your cause*, has said, 'Had I not disliked one's saying that Muhammad sought the support of a people only to become victorious over his enemies, I would have struck down the necks of a great many people.'"

(Jesus) *'Alayhi al-Salam*, would say. . .

H 14992, h 545
A number of our people have narrated from Sahl ibn Ziyad from 'Ubayd Allah al-Dihqan from 'Abd Allah ibn al-Qasim from ibn abu Najran from ibn Taghlib who has narrated the following:

"Abu 'Abd Allah, *'Alayhi al-Salam*, has said that *al-Masih* (Jesus) *'Alayhi al-Salam*, would say the following: 'One who does not seek cure for an injured person's injuries is inevitably a partner of the one who has caused him injuries. The one who has caused injuries wants to destroy the injured person and the one who does not seek cure for the injuries of the injured does not want his well-being. When he does not want his well-being, he has inevitably wanted his destruction and so also is the case of speaking wisdom to those who do not deserve it, because you become ignorant and you must not withhold wisdom from those who deserve it otherwise, you have committed a sin. One of you must behave like a physician who cures an illness if he finds it proper for his medicine; otherwise, he holds it back.'"

We lived very affluently

H 14993, h 546
Sahl has narrated from 'Ubayd Allah from Ahmad ibn 'Umar who has narrated the following:

"Once Husayn ibn abu Fakhtah and I visited al-Rida', *'Alayhi al-Salam*, and I said, 'I pray to Allah to keep my soul in service for your cause, we lived very affluently; but the condition now has somewhat changed, so pray for us before Allah, most Majestic, most Glorious, to return those bounties to us.' He (the Imam) said, 'What do you want to be, do you want to live as kings? Will it make you happy to be like Tahir and Harthamah and you will live without what you have (of belief)?' I then said, 'No by Allah, it does not make me happy even if the whole world and all that is in it become full of gold and silver but I will live without what I have (of belief).' He (the Imam) then said, 'Who is then more affluent than you? You must express gratitude to Allah and Allah, most Majestic, most Glorious, says, ". . . If you give thanks I will increase." (14:7) He who is free of all defects and the most High has said, ". . . O family of Dawud, you must act in gratitude; very few of My servant are grateful." (34:13) You must think good about Allah; abu 'Abd Allah, *'Alayhi al-Salam*, would say, "One who thinks good about Allah, Allah is with his thoughts. One who is happy with a small amount of sustenance, Allah accepts a small amount of deeds from him; and one who agrees with small and lawful sustenance, his expenses become light and his family lives in bounties. Allah shows him his worldly illnesses and the cure for them. He takes him out of it safely to the dwelling of peace."' He (the narrator) has said that he (the Imam) then asked, 'What has ibn Qiyaman done?' I replied, 'By Allah, he would meet us in a good manner.' He (the Imam) then said, 'Do you know what prevented him from it?' He (the Imam) then read, '. . . still the building that they build is a doubt in their hearts except if their hearts are cut off.' (9:110) He (the Imam) then said, 'Do you know why ibn Qiyaman became confused?' I replied, 'No, I do not know.' "He (the Imam) said, 'He followed abu al-Hassan, *'Alayhi al-Salam*. He then came from his right, then from his left and he wanted to go to the Masjid of the Holy Prophet, *O Allah grant compensation to Muhammad and his family worthy of their services to Your cause.* Abu al-Hassan, *'Alayhi al-Salam*, noticed his behavior and said, 'What do you want? May Allah confuse you.' "He (the Imam) then said, 'Consider that if after the returning of Musa, *'Alayhi al-Salam*, they said, "If only you had appointed him we would follow him in his footprints" or those who said, "We will continue to remain holding back until Musa comes back."' I replied, 'No, it is those who said, "You appointed him and we followed him in his footprints."' He (the Imam) then said, 'From this kind of manner came ibn Qiyaman and those who agree with his words.' He (the narrator) has said that then he (the Imam) mentioned ibn al-Sarraj. He (the Imam) said, 'He confirmed the death of abu al-Hassan, *'Alayhi al-Salam*, by saying this in his will at the time of his death. "Whatever I leave behind, even my shirt on my neck, is for the heirs of abu al-Hassan, *'Alayhi al-Salam*." He did not say, "It is for abu al-Hassan, *'Alayhi al-Salam*." It is his acknowledgement. However, what is the benefit for him out of what he has said.' Then he (the Imam) remained quiet.'"

When you travel with a people

H 14994, h 547
Ali ibn Ibrahim has narrated from his father from al-Qasim ibn Muhammad from 'Isma'il ibn Dawud al-Minqariy from Hammad who has narrated the following:

"Abu 'Abd Allah, *'Alayhi al-Salam*, has said that luqman said to his son, 'When you travel with a people then seek a great deal of advice from people about their and your own affairs. You should smile at them quite well, be gracious in your supplies, and when they invite you, accept their invitation. When they ask you for help, you must help them and you must have the upper hand in three things.

You should remain quiet for a long time, offer more prayer and generosity of self with what is with you of the stumper or assets or supplies. If they ask you to testify for a right, you must testify for them. You must make your opinion serious when they ask you for advice. You must not decide until you establish and consider, do not answer in your advice until you stand up in your thoughts, sit down, sleep, eat and pray when you are still using your thoughts and your wisdom in the advice. One who does not refine his advice for one who asks for advice, Allah, most Blessed, most High, takes away his opinion and removes trust from him. If you see your companions move, then you must also walk with them. If you see them work on a certain thing, you must also work with them, if they give charity and give a loan you must also give with them, listen to one who is older than you, if they command you for something and ask you, you must say, 'Yes, I agree.' You must not say, 'No, I do not agree.' Saying no, is weakness and blamable. When you become confused on the way you must disembark; if you doubt about your intention you must hold and seek advice. When you see one person do not ask him about the road and do not ask him for direction because one person in the wilderness is doubtful, perhaps he is the eye (spy) of thieves and road robbers or the Satan that has caused you confusion. You must avoid two people also unless you see what is not seen, people of reason on seeing something with his eyes recognizes the truth and one witnessing sees what an absent person does not see. Son, when the time for *Salat* (prayer) comes then do not delay it for anything, seek comfort thereby; it is religion and maintaining good relation in the group even if it is on the point of iron (difficult condition). Do not sleep on your stumper because it quickly causes injuries on its back and it is not of the acts of the people of wisdom unless it is in a carriage in which you can stretch and relax your joints. When you are about to approach your destination then you must disembark from your stumper and begin to feed it before yourself. When you intend to disembark then you must find the best area of the land of color, soft soil and abundance of grass. After you disembark pray two Rak'at before you sit. When you need to use the rest room then move far away. When you embark then perform two Rak'ats *Salat* (prayer) and say farewell to the land where you are, offer it greeting of peace and to its inhabitants; every area has inhabitants in the form of angels. If you can, do not eat food before giving charity and you must read the book of Allah, most Majestic, most Glorious, as long as you are riding. You must say *Tasbih* (Allah is free of all defects) as long as you are working. You must pray as long as you are free and must not travel in the beginning of the night but you must travel in the end of the night, travel after midnight to the end of the night and you must not raise your voice during your travelling.'"

Debate me that Ali, *'Alayhi al-Salam,* killed. . .

H 14995, h 548

A number of our people have narrated from Ahmad ibn Muhammad ibn Khalid from al-Husayn ibn Yazid al-Nawfaliy from Ali ibn Dawud al-Ya'qubiy from 'Isa ibn 'Abd Allah 'Alawiy who has narrated the following:

"Al-'Usaydiy and Muhammad ibn Mubashshir narrated to me that 'Abd Allah ibn Nafi' al-Azraq had said the following: 'I wish I could find that there is someone between the two halves of it (earth) whom I can reach with stumpers and who can debate me that Ali killed the people of al-Nahrawan without being unjust to them: I will travel to meet such person.' He was asked, 'Even if he is of his (Ali's) children?' He said, 'Is there any scholar in his children?' It was said to him, 'This is the beginning of your ignorance. Can they remain without a scholar?' He then asked, 'Who is their scholar today?' It was said that he is Muhammad ibn Ali, ibn al-Husayn ibn Ali, *'Alayhi al-Salam*.' He (the narrator) has said that he then left with the robust ones of his companions until he arrived in al-Madinah and asked for permission to see abu Ja'far, *'Alayhi al-Salam*, who was informed that he is 'Abd Allah ibn Nafi'. He (the Imam) said, 'What has he to do with me? He denounces me and my father on both ends of the day all the time.' Abu Basir al-Kufiy then said. 'I pray to Allah to keep my soul in service for your cause. This man thinks that if he can find someone between the two poles of the earth where his stumper can reach and debate with him to prove that Ali, *'Alayhi al-Salam*, who killed people of al-Nahrawan did so but he was not unjust, he will travel to him (to hear his proof).' Abu Ja'far, *'Alayhi al-Salam*, then said, 'Do you think he has come to debate with me?' He replied, 'Yes, that is correct.' He (the Imam) said, 'O *Ghulam* (young boys) go out and unload his luggage and tell him to come to us tomorrow.'

"He (the narrator) has said that next day 'Abd Allah ibn Nafi' with his distinguished companions were ready and abu Ja'far, *'Alayhi al-Salam*, sent to all sons of immigrants and al-Ansar (people of al-Madinah) and called them to gather together. He (the Imam) himself then came in public in two clothes of distinct color and moved forward among the people distinctly bright looking and he (the Imam) said, 'All praise belongs to Allah who is the position giver of the positions, the quality giver of the qualities, the direction giver of the directions. All praise belongs to Allah who is never overcome by slumber or sleep. To Him belongs all that is in the skies and all that is in the earth . . . - to the end of the verse- I testify that only Allah deserves worship, He is One and has no partners and I testify that Muhammad is His servant and Messenger whom He chose and guided to the straight path. All praise belongs to Allah who has honored us with Prophet-hood and has particularly granted us *Wilayah* (divine authority and knowledge).

"O community of the children of immigrants and al-Ansar, whoever knows of the excellent merits of Ali ibn abu Talib, *'Alayhi al-Salam*, must stand up and narrate to us.' He (the narrator) has said that people stood and narrated and enumerated his (Ali's) merits and excellent qualities. 'Abd Allah said, 'I narrate these excellent merits from these people but disbelief took place after his appointing the two arbitrators.' They then mentioned of his excellent merits the Hadith of Khaybar. The Messenger of Allah had said, 'I will give the banner tomorrow to a man who loves Allah and His Messenger and Allah and His Messenger love him. He attacks (the enemy) but does not flee and he will not come back until Allah will make it a victory through his hands.'

"Abu Ja'far, *'Alayhi al-Salam*, then asked, 'What do you say about this Hadith?' He replied, 'It is true and there is no doubt about it but disbelief took place afterward.' Abu Ja'far, *'Alayhi al-Salam*, said, 'May your mother weep for your death. Tell me about Allah, most Majestic, most Glorious. The day that He loved Ali ibn abu Talib, *'Alayhi al-Salam*, did He know that he (Ali) will kill the people of al-Nahrawan or did He not know it?' Ibn Nafi' asked, 'Say it again.' Abu Ja'far, *'Alayhi al-Salam*, said, 'Tell me about Allah, most Majestic, most Glorious. The day that He loved Ali ibn abu Talib, *'Alayhi al-Salam*, did He know that he (Ali) will kill the people of al-Nahrawan or He did not know it?' He (the Imam) said, 'If you say that He did not know, you become an unbeliever.'" He (the narrator) has said that he said, 'He knew it.' He (the Imam) then asked, 'Allah loved Ali, *'Alayhi al-Salam*, to work in obedience to Him or work in disobedience to Him?' He replied, 'He (Allah) loved him (Ali) so that he will work in His obedience.' Abu Ja'far, *'Alayhi al-Salam*, then said, 'Stand up, you are reduced (defeated in the argument).' He stood up saying, 'Until the white thread becomes clear for you from the black thread of dawn. Allah knows where to place His Messenger-ship (who to delegate as His Messenger).'"

No one ... better than me in astronomy

H 14996, h 549

Ahmad ibn Muhammad and Ali ibn Muhammad all have narrated from Ali ibn al-Hassan al-Tamimiy from Muhammad ibn al-Khattab al-Wasitiy from Yunus ibn 'Abd al-Rahman from Ahmad ibn 'Umar al-Halabiy from Hammad al-Azdiy from Hisham al-Khaffaf who has narrated the following:

"Abu 'Abd Allah, *'Alayhi al-Salam*, once asked me, 'How is your insight in astronomy?' I replied, 'There is no one in Iraq better than me in astronomy.' He (the Imam) then asked, 'How is the rotation of al-Falak (the group, system) according to you?' He (the narrator) has said, 'I took off my hat and rotated it.' He (the Imam) said, 'If that is the case then what do you say about Banat al-Na'sha, al-Jady and al-Farqadayn (names of stars) which are not seen as rotating in any day of the eon in the case of al-Qiblah (al-Ka'bah)?' I then said, 'This is something that by Allah I do not know and I have not heard anyone of the calculators mention it.' He (the Imam) then asked, 'How many parts in light is al-Sakinah (name of a star) from Venus?' I said, 'This is a star about which I have never heard and I have not heard any of the people speak about it.' He (the Imam) said, '*Tasbih* (Allah is free of all defects), so you have dropped a star altogether.' He (the Imam) then asked, 'How many parts in light is Venus from the moon?' I replied, 'This is something which no one knows except Allah, most Majestic, most Glorious.' He (the Imam) asked, 'How many parts in light is the moon from the sun?' I replied, 'I do not know this.' He (the Imam) said, 'You have spoken the truth.' He (the Imam) asked, 'What about the two armies which face each other, both have calculators and each one calculates victory for his people and for his side; then they fight and one defeats the other; then where is the bad luck, misfortune?' I replied, 'No, by Allah I do not know this.' He (the

Imam) then said, 'You have spoken the truth. The origin of calculation is real but no one knows it except those who know the birth of all creatures.'"

Sermon of 'Amir al-Mu'minin, Ali, *'Alayhi al-Salam*

H 14997, h 550

Ali ibn al-Hassan al-Mu'addib has narrated from Ahmad ibn Muhammad ibn Khalid and Ahmad ibn Muhammad from Ali ibn al-Hassan al-Tamimiy all from 'Isma'il ibn Mehran who has narrated the following:

"'Abd Allah ibn al-Harith narrated to me from Jabir, from abu Ja'far, *'Alayhi al-Salam*, who has said that 'Amir al-Mu'minin, Ali, *'Alayhi al-Salam*, in Siffin addressed the people and delivered this sermon. He praised Allah, spoke of His glory and said, '*O Allah grant compensation to Muhammad and his family worthy of their services to Your cause.*' He then said, 'Thereafter, you must take notice that Allah, most High, has sanctioned my right on you as your *Waliye 'Amr* (guardian with divine authority and knowledge) and my status with which Allah, most Majestic, most Glorious, has placed me among you. Your rights upon me, similarly, are obligatory on me just as it is obligatory upon you to respect my rights. Right is the most beautiful thing to describe and of a great vastness in maintaining fairness. No other thing is applied in one's favor without being applied against him and it is not applied against him unless it is applied in his favor.

"The only case where it is applied for one and not against one is the case of Allah, most Majestic, most Glorious, purely and not in the case of His creatures. It is because He is powerful with full control over His creatures and because His justice is applied in all kinds of cases where His determination is applied. He, however, has sanctioned His right on His servants and they must obey Him for which He has designed expiation in the form of His good rewards due to His generosity, magnanimity and grace. He expands it with additional favor because of His being worthy of granting favors. Of His rights, one category is that which He has made obligatory on people on a mutual manner; when it becomes obligatory on one, it similarly requires the others to fulfill a similar obligation toward the other party.

"The greatest of such right is the right of the governing authority on those in his domain. There are the rights of those governed on the governing authority which is an obligation that Allah, most Majestic, most Glorious, has sanctioned on each one of them as part of the system which brings them together, it is the strength and glory of their religion and the safeguards for the preservation of the traditions of truth among them. Therefore, the governed cannot find well being without the righteous governing authority, and the governing authority cannot thrive without righteous governed people. When people respect the rights of the governing authority and the governing authorities respect the rights of the people, truth becomes strong among them. The programs of the system of religion function properly, the landmarks of justice find fairness, the traditions flow with smoothness, and then people live in a righteous time and in prosperity of life with hope in the continuity of the government, which turns the ambitions of the enemies into despair.

'However, when the governed overpower their *Waliye 'Amr* (guardian with divine authority and knowledge) and *Waliye 'Amr* seeks to dominate the governed then differences of opinions emerge. The desire to dominate through injustice becomes apparent and lawlessness in religion multiplies. The landmarks of traditions are then abandoned, then people act according to the desires, (noble) traces vanish, illnesses of the souls appear a great deal, neglect of great laws do not remain frightening and confronting the greatness of the formation of falsehood is not considered a noble task.

'In such case the virtuous ones weaken, the wicked ones gain strength, the lands face ruination and the punishable consequences from Allah, most Majestic, most Glorious, grow greater against the servants. Therefore, O people, allow us to cooperate in obeying Allah, most Majestic, most Glorious, maintaining His system of justice, to stand by the covenant with Him, act with fairness for Him in all of His rights; what is needed most urgently is to provide each other with good advice and proper cooperation. In the matters of compliance with the rights even though one may feel the greatest degree of desire to comply thereby for the pleasure of Allah, however, one cannot comply in full with the rights of the owner of the right. In matters of the rights of Allah, most Majestic, most Glorious, it is obligatory upon the servants to wish well and provide good advice with the utmost degree of hard work and efforts in cooperating to preserve the truth among them. In addition, there is no one, no matter how great his status in rights is, and how great his excellence in the right is, he is not free of want of cooperation which Allah, most Majestic, most Glorious, has placed on him. On the other hand there is no one, no matter how low the affairs have brought him and the eyes have gone in him cannot remain without helping and without being helped.

'People of excellence and meritorious condition and those of great bounties are in greater degree of want and all people are needy before Allah, most Majestic, most Glorious, in equal measures and degrees.'

"A man then answered from his army who was not recognized who he was and it is said that he was not seen in his army before or thereafter. He stood up and spoke of the glory of Allah, most Majestic, most Glorious, and of the matters in which He has placed them under the trial. He spoke of the favors, which He has granted to them of the obligations toward His right on them, and of confirmation of all that he had mentioned of the changing conditions with him and with them. He then said, 'You are our commander, and we are under your commands. Through you Allah, most Majestic, most Glorious, has taken us out of humiliation and with your honor, He has freed His servants from the fetters. You can choose for us, proceed with your choice, plan, and proceed with your plans because you are the truthful speaker, successful governing authority and the authorized dominant owner. We do not consider any form of disobedience to you as lawful and do not analogize our knowledge with your knowledge. Your status with us is great and your excellent merits in our souls are glorious.'

"'Amir al-Mu'minin, Ali, *'Alayhi al-Salam*, then responded to him as follows: 'It is of the right and truth that one in whose soul the glory of Allah has become great and His status majestic must see everything other than Him as small. The most deserving of those who are as such is the one to whom the bounties of Allah become great as well as His kind favors to him. Just as the bounty of Allah becomes great for someone, in the same way the right of Allah increases on him in greatness. Of the lowliest condition of the governing authorities before the virtuous people is when love of expressing pride on their (authorities') part becomes perceivable and they base their affairs on arrogance. I disliked that something in your thoughts may roam about my loving to rejoice listening to being praised. "I, all thanks are due to Allah, am not as such. Had I loved it (applauses), I would have abandoned it due to its lowering (in my soul) Allah, who is free of all defects, in what He is rightful in matters of greatness and magnanimity. Perhaps people consider praises as sweet after a trial. Therefore, you must not praise me with glorious praises; it may take my soul out of complying with my duty to Allah and for you in the remaining rights, which I have not complied with yet, and the obligations that I have not fulfilled which require completion.

'You must not speak to me the way people speak to tyrants. You must not keep in reserve what is kept before the hasteful rulers. You must not associate pretending with me. You must not think of me as feeling heavy in complying with a right about which I am told or feeling self-greatness and as unsuitable for me. One who thinks that compliance with a right about which he has received notice or a matter of justice, present before him as heavy, his acting, accordingly, becomes heavier on him. You must not withhold from me the word about a right or advice about justice. I in my soul am not above mistake and I do not feel safe in my deeds except if Allah suffices it for my soul. He suffices in matters on which He has greater control than I do. You and I are servants, slaves of the Cherisher besides whom there is no Lord and Cherisher. He owns of us what we do not own of ourselves. He has brought us out of the condition in which we existed to what is for our well-being. He changed us from being lost and misled to guidance and granted us understanding after blindness.'

"The man who had answered him before answered him again saying, 'You by Allah, deserve what you have said and, by Allah, more than what you have said. His bounties with us are such that we cannot fully express our appreciation for them. Allah, most Blessed, most High, has placed on you the burden of our guardianship and has given to you the authority to manage our social matters. You are our knowledge to find guidance and our leader whom we follow. All of your commands are progressive; all of your words are moral discipline. Our eyes in life have become delightful with you and our hearts have become joyful with you. Our understanding powers are amazed in describing your brilliant excellent merits. We do not say to you, 'O righteous Imam (leader) to purify you and do not cross the limits of fairness in speaking of your praise.' In our souls, we have no criticisms against your certainty or against the purity of your religion, so that we fear about your inventing in the bounties of Allah, most Blessed, most High, something tyrannical or behaving arrogantly. We say about you what we say to seek thereby nearness to Allah, most Majestic, most Glorious, by our offering you reverence and expanding it due to your excellent merits and to appreciate the greatness of your task. You must be considerate to yourself and to us but you must give preference over yourself and over us to Allah. We are obedient to you in whatever you command us and follow you in the affairs and in what is beneficial for us.'

"'Amir al-Mu'minin, Ali, *'Alayhi al-Salam*, then said, 'I ask you to bear witness before Allah against my soul because of your knowledge of my becoming the person in charge of your government and affairs. In a very short time, the place of resurrection will gather all of us together before Him for questioning about that in which we lived. Then we will testify against each other so you must not testify opposed to what you will see and witness tomorrow; nothing remains hidden from Allah, most Majestic, most Glorious, and nothing is permissible before Him except good advice from the heart in all matters.'

"The man then, - it is said that he after his words to 'Amir al-Mu'minin, Ali, *'Alayhi al-Salam*, was not seen again - with intense burst of emotion from his chest, wept which stopped him from speaking. His condition seemed like painful choking and it caused breakage in his voice due to the dangerousness of the looming tragedy (of his murder), the terrifying calamity in his (Imam Ali's) government. He praised Allah and spoke of His glory, then he complained before Him against the looming danger on him (Imam Ali), against the greatness of the danger and his facing humiliation in his lifetime, against the condition of the Islamic system damaged and corrupted, the upside down turning of its limits and the cutting off of his government. He then turned to implore before Allah, most Majestic, most Glorious. He expressed gratitude for His granting favors to him, dispelling suffering from him (the Imam) and he glorified Him with goodness.

"He said, 'O Lord, of the servants, O provider of calmness to the lands, our words can never properly speak of your favors, our admiration can never describe your acts and our glorification can never give an account of your beautiful trials. How can we say anything when through the bounties of Allah and through your hands the means of the worldly goodness has come in our hands? Is it not the case that for the lowliness of the lowly, you were a protection, and lived with disobedient rejecters in a brotherly manner?

"Through who else other than you and your *Ahl al-Bayt*, Allah, most Majestic, most Glorious, took us out of the terrifying dangers? Through who else other than you and your *Ahl al-Bayt* He dispelled from us the overwhelming hardships. Through whom else other than you, Allah supported the landmarks of our religion, reformed and established well-being of what the world had destroyed? Through you only after cruelty, our name came out in public for recognition. Prosperity in life for which our eyes were delighted came when you took charge of our government as a favor to us. With your hard work and tireless efforts, you made all of your promises to come true.

'You stood firmly by your covenants for us. You have been watching for those of us who became absent as well as the successor of *Ahl al-Bayt* for us. You have been the honor for the weak ones among us, the refuge for our poor ones and support for the great ones among us. Your justice brought us together in all affairs and your patience provided us greater room in the matters of the rights. You had been a source of comfort for us when we would see you and a source of serenity when we speak of you. What were the good deeds that you did not perform and what were the virtuous matters on which you did not act? If the issue about which we fear for you has been as such that, our efforts could change and our capabilities could defend, or that we could offer ransom for you with our souls or our children, we would gladly offer our souls and our children for you. We accept such danger to reduce it against you. We stand up with our utmost efforts to stand between you and the danger and to defend you against your enemies. Allah however, is the dominant power that cannot be barred, the majesty that does not go away and the Lord that cannot be defeated.

'If He obliges us by granting you good health, the mercy of saving you for us, exercises compassion to ease off your difficulties with your safety for us by keeping you safe among us, we will speak of Allah, most Majestic, most Glorious, in appreciation and gratitude. We speak of His greatness all the time, distribute half of our assets as charity, half of our slaves being set free and speak of Him humbly in our souls, we will be submissive before Him in all of our affairs. We pray that He will take you to His garden (paradise) and apply to you His determination. No one can dispel from you His decision and there will be no opposition in our hearts about what He will choose for you of what is with Him because of your condition. However, we will weep for the changing of the majesty of this government into weakness and its being consumed by this world as well as the next world after which we will not find for you any successor before whom we can present our complaints or a similar government for which we can maintain our hope.'"

Sermon of 'Amir al-Mu'minin, Ali, *'Alayhi al-Salam*

H 14998, h 551

Ali ibn Ibrahim has narrated from his father, Muhammad ibn Ali all from 'Isma'il ibn Mehran, Ahmad ibn Muhammad ibn Ahmad from Ali ibn al-Hassan al-Tamimiy, and Ali ibn al-Husayn, from Ahmad ibn Muhammad ibn Khalid, all from 'Isma'il ibn Mehran, from al-Mundhir ibn Jayfar, from al-Hakam ibn Zuhayr, from 'Abd Allah ibn Jarir al-'Abdiy from al-Asbagh ibn Nabatah who has narrated the following:

"Once 'Abd Allah ibn 'Umar, sons of abu Bakr and Sa'd ibn abu Waqqas came to 'Amir al-Mu'minin, Ali, *'Alayhi al-Salam*, asking for preferred positions in the government. He (the Imam) climbed on the pulpit and people turned their attention toward him. He (the Imam) then said, 'All praise belongs to Allah who

304

is the proprietor of all praise and the end of generosity. Description cannot confine Him and languages cannot define Him. He is not recognizable by means of goals. I testify that only Allah deserves worship, He is One and has no partners and I testify that Muhammad is His Messenger, *O Allah grant compensation to Muhammad and his family worthy of their services to Your cause*, the Prophet of guidance, the source of piety and the Messenger of the Lord, the most High. He came with truth from the truth to warn people by means of al-Quran, which is a light and enlightening proof. He warned by means of the clear book and passed away as the messengers of the past generations did.

'O people, men who had sunk in the worldly gains, who had gained real properties, made canals to flow, who rode most beautiful stumpers, dressed in the softest clothes, it became the point of disgrace and ignominy for them, if Allah will not forgive them. If I prevent such people from their indulgence in such conditions again and make them to live with what they deserve, thus, if they miss their past opportunities, they must not say that ibn abu Talib has deprived us and has barred us from receiving our rights.

'Allah is the best support against them. Those who face in *Salat* (prayer) our al-Qiblah (al-Ka'bah), consume the flesh of the animals we slaughter, believe in our Prophet, testify to the testimony of our belief and embrace our religion, we will apply the laws of al-Quran and the rules of Islam upon them. No one has any distinction over the others except because of piety. O yes, for the pious ones with Allah, most High, is the best of rewards, compensation and return in goodness. Allah, most Blessed, most High, has not made the world as reward for the good deeds of the pious people. What is with Allah is better for the virtuous people. People of the religion of Allah, you must consider and think about what you find in the book of Allah and what you leave with the Messenger of Allah, *O Allah grant compensation to Muhammad and his family worthy of their services to Your cause*. You must think if it is because of your hard work that you did in the way of Allah, or because of social status or ancestors or because of deeds or of obedience and restraint from sins. You must think about that in which you are interested. You must act quickly toward your dwellings –may Allah grant you mercy - about which you have received the command to establish, develop and build that, which does not face ruination but remains forever and never will diminish. The dwellings to which you have received invitations, encouragement to acquire, exhortation to establish interest therein and that He has kept the reward with Him for the good deeds.

'You must seek the completion of the bounties of Allah, most Majestic, most Glorious, by means of submitting yourselves to His determination and by appreciating His favors. One who is not happy with this is not one of our community and as the ones who like to come to us. A ruler judges according to the laws of Allah without any anxiety and such people are successful.' In another copy it is said, 'They have no anxiety because of this or any sadness.' He then said, 'I will discipline you with my whip with which I discipline my people, so you must not be frightened and if I will use my whip on you with which I apply the penalty as sanctioned by our Lord, you must not feel frightened. Do you want that I will strike you with my sword? I know what you want and what straightens your unevenness. However, I do not want to buy your well-being in exchange for my own destruction; however, Allah will make a people to dominate you and they will revenge for me from you, and in such case you will have no worldly things to enjoy or any hereafter to go to. May Allah do away with and crash down the people of the blazing fire."

When al-Qa'im will reappear...

H 14999, h 552

Muhammad ibn Yahya has narrated from Ahmad ibn Muhammad ibn 'Isa and Abu Ali al-Ash'ariy has narrated from Muhammad ibn 'Abd al-Jabbar all from Ali ibn Hadid from Jamil from Zurarah who has narrated the following:

"Once Humran asked abu Ja'far, *'Alayhi al-Salam*, saying, 'I pray to Allah to keep my soul in service for your cause, I wish you to explain for us when al-Qa'im will reappear with divine authority and power, so we enjoy its great happiness.' He (the Imam) said, 'O Humran, you have friends, brothers (in belief) and people whom you know. In the past, there was a man of the scholars who had a son who was not interested in the knowledge of his father and did not ask him about anything but he had a neighbor who came to him, asked question and acquired knowledge. When the time of the death of the scholar came, he called his son and said to him. 'Son, you have been refraining from the knowledge that I possessed, and your interest in it was very little, so you did not ask me about anything but my neighbor would come to me, ask questions, acquire knowledge from me and preserve it. If you will need anything you must go to him.' He introduced his neighbor to him; he died and left his son behind him. The king of that time then saw a dream and asked for the man. He was told that he has died. The king asked if he has left behind a son. He was told that he has left behind a son. The king said, 'You must bring him to me.' They sent for him and the boy said, 'By Allah, I do not know what for the king has called me and I do not have any knowledge, if he will ask me about something I will be disgraced. He then remembered what his father had told him about his neighbor. He went to the man who had acquired knowledge from his father and told him that the king has sent for him to ask him about something and that he does not know what he wants to ask him. 'My father had commanded me to come to you when I needed anything.' The man said, 'I know why he has sent for you. If I give the answer you must then share with me whatever Allah brings out for you.' He agreed on oath and confirmed that he must keep his promise and the boy agreed. He told the boy that the king will ask him about the dream that he has seen and it is about, 'What time is it.' 'You must tell him that it is the time of wolf.' The boy went to the king who asked him, 'Do you know why I have sent for you?' He said, 'You have sent for me to ask me about the dream that you have seen which says, 'What time is it?' The king said, 'You have spoken the truth. Tell me what time is it.' He told the king that it was the time of wolf. The king commanded to give him a certain amount of reward. The boy took the reward and went home but he refused to stand by his promise with his neighbor, saying to himself that he cannot deplete the asset before he dies and perhaps he will not need to ask him for anything as such again. He waited as long as Allah wanted. The king then saw a dream and sent his people to call him. He then regretted what he had done and said, 'By Allah, I have no knowledge by the help of which I can go to the king and I do not know what to do with the fellow neighbor to whom I have not been truthful and I did not keep my promise with him.' He then said, 'I must go to him in any case, apologize and swear; perhaps he may provide me the information I need.' He then went to him and said, 'I did what I did. I did not keep my promise about the matter between you and I and what I had received is scattered but I need your help and I swear to Allah that you must not allow me to fail and I guarantee that this time whatever I will receive it will be shared with you. The king has sent for me and I do not know what for has he sent for me.' He said, 'He wants to ask you about the dream that he has seen which says, 'What time is it.' You must say that it is the time of the ram.' He went to the king who asked, 'Do you know why I have sent for you?' He replied, 'It is because you have seen a dream and you want to ask me what time is it.' He said, 'You have spoken the truth. Tell me what time is it.' He said that it is the time of the ram.' He commanded to give him his reward. He took the reward and went home. He thought about it and his opinion told him to keep his promise with his fellow man or not to keep his promise. One time he said that he must keep his promise and then he said that he does not have to keep it. He then said, 'Perhaps I will not need him any more after this time forever'. Therefore, he decided not to share the reward with him once again. He then lived as long as Allah wanted.

"The king then saw a dream and sent for him. He regretted for what he had done to his fellow man and after twice breaking his promise did not know what he must do. He did not have the knowledge. He then decided to go to the man. He then went to him and swore before him to Allah, most Blessed, most High, asked him to teach him and inform him. This time he will keep his promise. He assured him and asked him not to leave him in that condition. 'I will not be untruthful this time and I will keep my promise,' he assured him. He said that the king has called him to ask him about his dream that he has seen which says, 'What time is it.' When he asks you about it say that it is the time of balance. He (the Imam) said, 'He went to the king and he asked, 'Do you know why I have called you?' He replied, 'Yes, you have called me to ask about what time is it.' He said, 'You have spoken the truth. Tell me what time is it.' He then said that it is the time of balance.' He commanded to give him the reward for him. He returned with the reward to his fellow man and placed it before him. He said, 'This is what I have received. We can divide it between the two of us.' The man of knowledge said, 'The first time it was the time of wolf and you were of the wolves, the second time was the time of the ram which thinks to do something but does not do it and so also were you thinking to keep your promise but did not do so. This time it was the time of balance in which you were in favor of keeping your promise. You can take your assets. I do not need anything thereof.' He returned it to him.'"

In matters of bravery

H 15000, h 553

Ahmad ibn Muhammad ibn Ahmad al-Kufiy has narrated from Ali ibn al-Hassan al-Tamimiy from Ali ibn Asbat from Ali ibn Ja'far who has narrated the following:

"Mu'attib or others narrated to me that 'Abd Allah ibn al-Hassan once sent a message to abu 'Abd Allah, *'Alayhi al-Salam*, that said, 'Abu Muhammad says that he is braver, more generous and more knowledgeable than you are.' Abu 'Abd Allah, then told His Messenger to say to him, 'In matters of bravery, by Allah, you did not have any stance by which your bravery or cowardice could be judged. In matters of generosity, in fact, it is taking something to place it where it rightfully belongs. In matters of knowledge you must take notice that your father Ali ibn abu Talib, *'Alayhi al-Salam*, freed one thousand slaves. If you are more knowledgeable then mention the names of only five of them.' The messenger returned, after informing him, came back and said that he says, 'You are a bookish man.' Abu 'Abd Allah, *'Alayhi al-Salam*, told him to say to him, 'O yes, by Allah, the books you are speaking of are the books of Ibrahim, Musa and Jesus, *'Alayhim al-Salam*, which I have inherited from my ancestors, *'Alayhim al-Salam*.'"

"Give the glad news..."

H 15001, h 554

Ali ibn Ibrahim has narrated from his father from Hammad ibn 'Isa from Ibrahim ibn 'Umar al-Yamaniy from those whom he has mentioned who has narrated the following:

"It is about the meaning of the words of Allah, most Majestic, most Glorious. '. . . give the glad news to those who have accepted belief that they have a truthful standing before their Lord.' (10:2) Abu 'Abd Allah, *'Alayhi al-Salam*, has said, it stands for the Messenger of Allah, *O Allah grant compensation to Muhammad and his family worthy of their services to Your cause*.'"

"Signs and warnings..."

H 15002, h 555

Muhammad ibn Yahya has narrated from Ahmad ibn Muhammad from Ali ibn al-Hakam from 'Abd Allah ibn Yahya al-Kahiliy who has narrated the following:

"It is about the meaning of the words of Allah, most Majestic, most Glorious. '. . . signs and warnings will not help those who do not believe.' (10:101) Abu 'Abd Allah, *'Alayhi al-Salam*, has said that when the Messenger of Allah, *O Allah grant compensation to Muhammad and his family worthy of their services to Your cause*, was taken for the night journey, Jibril came with Buraq (literally meaning electric, name of the stumper) which he rode and went to Bayt al-Maqdis. He met there whomever he met of his brethren, the Prophets, *'Alayhim al-Salam*, then returned home and told his companions about his visiting Bayt al-Maqdis and about his return in the same night and that Jibril had brought al-Buraq for him which he rode. As proof for this he said, 'I passed by the caravan of camels of abu Sufyan on the water of banu so and so, that they had lost a camel of red color and the people were looking for it.'

"They said to each other that he has passed by al-Sham when riding fast. You have seen al-Sham and you have knowledge thereof, so you can ask him about its markets, doors and business people. They asked, 'O Messenger of Allah, how is al-Sham and its markets?' Abu 'Abd Allah, *'Alayhi al-Salam*, has said that when they asked the Messenger of Allah, *O Allah grant compensation to Muhammad and his family worthy of their services to Your cause*, about something that he did not know it would become difficult for him until he could see it face to face. At such time Jibril came and said, 'O Messenger of Allah, *O Allah grant compensation to Muhammad and his family worthy of their services to Your cause*, this is al-Sham which I have raised for you.' The Messenger of Allah, *O Allah grant compensation to Muhammad and his family worthy of their services to Your cause*, paid attention and found it to be al-Sham, its doors, markets and business places. He then asked, 'Where are the ones who were asking about al-Sham?' They said, 'They are so and so.' The Messenger of Allah, *O Allah grant compensation to Muhammad and his family worthy of their services to Your cause*, answered them about all that they had asked but only very few of them accepted the faith and that is mentioned in the words of Allah, '. . . signs and warnings will not help those who do not believe.' (10:101) Abu 'Abd Allah, *'Alayhi al-Salam*, (expressed his concern and) said, 'We seek protection with Allah against disbelief in Allah and in His Messenger. We believe in Allah and in His Messenger, *O Allah grant compensation to Muhammad and his family worthy of their services to Your cause*.'"

'Uff (fie on you)" to his brother . . .

H 15003, h 556

Ahmad ibn Muhammad ibn Ahmad has narrated from Ali ibn al-Hassan al-Tamimiy from Muhammad ibn 'Abd Allah from Zurarah from Muhammad ibn al-Fudayl from abu Hamzah who has narrated the following:

"I once heard abu 'Abd Allah, *'Alayhi al-Salam*, saying, 'When a man says, "*'Uff* (fie on you)" to his brother (in belief) he comes out of his guardianship. When he says, "You are my enemy." one of them becomes an unbeliever because Allah, most Majestic, most Glorious, does not accept the deed of a believing person along with his reproaching a believing person. He does not accept a deed from a believing person when he is keeping bad feelings in him about a believing person. If the curtain can move away from before the people so they can see the connection between Allah, most Majestic, most Glorious, and a believing person, their necks become submissive before the believing people, their affairs become easy for them and obedience to them become easy. If they look at the deeds that Allah, most Majestic, most Glorious, has rejected they will say, "Allah, most Majestic, most Glorious, does not accept any deed."'"

"I heard him (the Imam) say to a Shi'ah man, 'You are fine and your women are fine. Every female believing person is a *Hawra'* and *'Ayna'* and every believing man is truthful.' He (the narrator) has said that I heard him (the Imam) say, 'Our Shi'ah are the closest of all creatures to the throne of Allah, most Majestic, most Glorious, on the Day of Judgment following us. Every Shi'ah who stands for

Salat (prayer) a number of angels equal to the number of those who oppose him in his belief surround him and pray for him in congregation until he completes his *Salat* (prayer), and those of you who fast will enjoy in the gardens of paradise. The angels service them until they break their fast.' I heard abu 'Abd Allah, *'Alayhi al-Salam*, state this Hadith. 'You are the people of the greeting of peace of Allah in safety and the people to whom Allah gives preference with mercy, the people of good opportunities with His protection for you and the people of calling to the obedience of Allah who will not face the task of presenting any account or face any fear and sadness. You are for the garden (paradise) and the garden (paradise) is for you. Your names with us are of the virtuous ones, the reforming ones and you are the people who are happy with Allah, most Majestic, most Glorious, because of His being happy with you. Angels are your brothers in goodness. When you work hard, they pray and when you become unaware, they work hard. You are the best of the creatures; your towns are the garden (paradise) for you and your graves are the garden (paradise) for you. For the garden (paradise) you are created and in the garden (paradise) are bounties for you and to the garden (paradise) you are moving.'"

Returned from Ethiopia...

H 15004, h 557

Ahmad ibn Muhammad ibn Ahmad has narrated from Muhammad ibn Ahmad al-Nahdiy from Muhammad ibn al-Walid from Aban ibn 'Uthman from al-Fudayl who has narrated the following:

"Abu Ja'far, *'Alayhi al-Salam*, has stated this Hadith: The Messenger of Allah, *O Allah grant compensation to Muhammad and his family worthy of their services to Your cause*, asked Ja'far, *'Alayhi al-Salam*, when he returned from Ethiopia, 'What did you see there that interested you the most?' he replied, 'It was when I saw a female with a heavy basket on her head. A man passing by bumped against her load that fell off her head. She sat down and said, 'Woe is upon you when the judge of all judges will sit on his chair to punish the oppressor for the suffering he has caused to the oppressed.' The Messenger of Allah, *O Allah grant compensation to Muhammad and his family worthy of their services to Your cause*, expressed astonishment.'"

Astronomer for Nimrod...

H 15005, h 558

Ali ibn Ibrahim has narrated from his father from ibn abu 'Umayr from Hisham ibn Salim from abu Ayyub al-Khazzaz from abu Basir who has narrated the following:

"Abu 'Abd Allah, *'Alayhi al-Salam*, has said that Azar, father of Ibrahim, *'Alayhi al-Salam*, was an astronomer for Nimrod who did not go out without his command. One night he looked in the stars and in the morning, he said to Nimrod, 'I have seen something very strange.' He asked, 'What is it?' He replied, 'I saw that a child will be born and in his hand our destruction will take place. Very soon he will be conceived by his mother.' He (the Imam) said that he was astonished and asked, 'Has any woman conceived with him?' He replied, 'No, that has not happened yet.' He (the Imam) said that he then barred women from men and he gathered all women in one city where no man could meet them privately. Azar went to bed with his wife and Ibrahim, *'Alayhi al-Salam*, was conceived by his mother. He thought he can be the one of his concern, he sent nurses to examine, and at that time, they could tell if there was anything in the womb. They examined but Allah, most Majestic, most Glorious, kept what was in the womb to the back. They said, 'We did not see anything in her womb.' Of the information that he had was that he will be burned in the fire but he did not have the knowledge that Allah, most Majestic, most Glorious, will rescue him. He (the Imam) said that when the mother of Ibrahim gave birth, Azar wanted to take him to Nimrod to be killed. His wife said to him, 'Do not take your son to Nimrod for being killed. Allow me to take him to a cave and leave him there until the time of his death comes. You must not become the one to kill your son.' He then agreed. He (the Imam) said that she took him to a cave, fed him milk and placed a rock on the opening of the cave, then left him there. Allah, most Majestic, most Glorious, made his sustenance in his thumb and he would suck and milk flow from it. He would grow in one day like children grow in one week and he grew in one week like other children grew in one month and in one moth he grew like others grew in one year. He remained there as long as Allah wanted.

"His mother said to his father, 'If you give me permission I will go to see the child.' He gave her permission. She went and found Ibrahim, *'Alayhi al-Salam*, his eyes shone like two lanterns. She took him and held to her chest, fed him, then went back home. Azar asked about him and she said, 'I buried him in the soil.' She waited and visited Ibrahim, *'Alayhi al-Salam*, from time to time, held him to her chest, fed him and returned back home. When he moved she came to him as before from time to time to do what she did before. One time when she wanted to leave, he took hold of her clothes and she asked, 'What is the matter?' He said, 'Take me with you.' She said, 'I must get permission from your father.' He (the Imam) said that the mother of Ibrahim, *'Alayhi al-Salam*, went to Azar and informed him of the story. He told her, 'Bring him to me, make him sit on the road and when his brothers pass by, bring him along with them. He will not be recognized.' He (the Imam) said that brothers of Ibrahim carved idols for sale and sold them in the market. He (the Imam) said that she went and brought him until she made him to sit on the road until his brothers passed by and he went home with them. When his father saw him, he began to feel love for him in his heart. He then lived as long as Allah wanted. He (the Imam) has said that one day when his brothers were carving idols Ibrahim picked the adze, took a piece of wood and carved an idol the like of which they had never seen before. Azar said to his mother, 'I hope we can receive goodness by the blessing of your son this one.' He (Ibrahim, *'Alayhi al-Salam*,) picked up the adze (that he wanted). He broke the idol that he had carved. His father expressed intense shock and asked him. 'Why did you break it?' Ibrahim, *'Alayhi al-Salam*, asked, 'What you want to do with it?' Azar said, 'We worship it.' Ibrahim then asked, 'Do you worship what you yourself carve?' Azar said to his mother, 'This is the one through whose hands our kingdom will be ruined.'"

Opposed his people and blamed...

H 15006, h 559

Ali ibn Ibrahim has narrated from his father from Ahmad ibn Muhammad from ibn abu Nasr from Aban 'Uthman from Hujr who has narrated the following:

"Abu 'Abd Allah, *'Alayhi al-Salam*, has said that Ibrahim, *'Alayhi al-Salam*, opposed his people and blamed them for their worshipping gods until he was brought before Nimrod who debated him. Ibrahim, *'Alayhi al-Salam*, said, 'My Lord is the one who brings the dead to life' and he (Nimrod) said, 'I also give life and cause to die.' Ibrahim, *'Alayhi al-Salam*, said, 'Allah brings the sun from the east; you then bring it up from the west if you can.' Thus the unbeliever was confounded and Allah does not guide the unjust people.' (2:258) Abu Ja'far, *'Alayhi al-Salam*, has said that Ibrahim *'Alayhi al-Salam*, reproved them for their gods. He then looked at the stars and said, '. . . I do not feel well.' (37:88-89) Abu Ja'far, *'Alayhi al-Salam*, has said that he by Allah, had no illness and he did not speak lies; (he was in the state of *Taqiyah*, fear for his life). When they moved away from him to attend their festivity, Ibrahim, *'Alayhi al-Salam*, entered the chamber of their gods and broke them all except the large one. He then placed the adze on its shoulder. They came back to their gods and looked at what had happened to them; they said, 'No one can dare to do and break them except the young man who reproved and denounced them.' They then did not find any other way more serious than killing him by fire. They collected firewood and made it plentiful until it was the day that he was to be burned. Nimrod and his army came out. A building was built for this purpose so that he could see how the fire would burn him. Ibrahim, *'Alayhi al-Salam*, was placed in catapult. The earth said, 'O Lord, there is no one on my back except him to worship You and he is burned in the fire.' The Lord said, 'If he will pray to me I will save him.'

Aban has mentioned that Muhammad ibn Marwan has narrated from those who narrated to him the following:

"Abu Ja'far, *'Alayhi al-Salam*, has said that the prayer of Ibrahim, *'Alayhi al-Salam*, on that day was, 'O the One [O the One, O Powerful] O powerful, O the One who has not given birth to anyone and is not born from anyone and there is no one like Him.' He then said, 'I have appointed Allah as my attorney, placed my trust in Allah.' The Lord, most Blessed, most High, then said, 'I am a sufficient helper for you.' He then said to the fire, 'Be cool and peaceful.' He (the Imam) said, 'The teeth of Ibrahim, *'Alayhi al-Salam*, shivered because of coolness until Allah, most Majestic, most Glorious, said, '. . . and peaceful to Ibrahim.' Jibril came. When he was speaking to Ibrahim in the fire, Nimrod said, 'If one chooses a god he must choose one like the God of Ibrahim.' He (the Imam) said that a great one of their great people said, 'I read something on the fire not to burn him.' He (the Imam) said that a blaze of fire then shot toward him until it burnt him down.' He (the Imam) said that Lot accepted his belief and left as immigrants to al-Sham along with him and Sarah.'"

A native of that town...

H 15007, h 560

Ali ibn Ibrahim has narrated from his father and A number of our people have narrated from Sahl ibn Ziyad all from al-Hassan ibn Mahbub from 'Abd al-Rahman ibn abu Ziyad al-Karkhiy who has narrated the following:

"I once heard abu 'Abd Allah, *'Alayhi al-Salam*, say that Ibrahim was born in Kuthiy Ruba' and his father was a native of that town. The mothers of Ibrahim and Lot were Sarah and Waraqah – in another copy it says Ruqiyah - were sisters, daughters of Lahij. Lahij was a Prophet, a Warner but not a messenger. Ibrahim, *'Alayhi al-Salam*, when young was born in the nature which Allah, most Majestic, most Glorious, had designed and created until He, most Blessed, most High, granted him guidance to His religion and chose him. He married Sarah daughter of Lahij and she was the daughter of his maternal aunt. Sarah owned a large number of cattle and a vast land. Her condition was good and Ibrahim, *'Alayhi al-Salam*, had owned all that belonged to her. He looked after the assets and the cattle increased as well as the farm so much so that in the land of Kuthiy there was no man wealthier than him. When Ibrahim, *Alayhi al-Salam*, broke the idols of Nimrod, he commanded to capture him and built a building that they filled with firewood. Ibrahim, *'Alayhi al-Salam*, then was thrown in the fire to burn. Then they kept it isolated until the fire was extinguished. They then went over the building and saw Ibrahim, *'Alayhi al-Salam*, safe and sound but the ropes with which he was tied down had burned. They informed Nimrod about it and he commanded them to send him in exile. That he must not allow him to take his cattle and assets. Ibrahim then argued against them saying that if you do not allow me to take my cattle with me then I have the right on you to return to me the time of my life that I have spent in your land. His case was brought before the judge of Nimrod who issued a judgment that said, 'Ibrahim must give to the people of Nimrod what he has earned in their land and that the people of Nimrod must return to Ibrahim the amount of his life that he has spent in their land. Nimrod was informed about it and he commanded to allow him to leave with his cattle and assets and that he must be exiled, otherwise, he will destroy your religion and harm your gods. They then exiled Ibrahim and Lot, *'Alayhima al-Salam*, to the land of al-Sham. Ibrahim, *'Alayhi al-Salam*, left with Lot who would not move away from them. He said to them, 'I am going to my Lord who will soon grant me guidance,' meaning Bayt al-Maqdis. 'Ibrahim, *'Alayhi al-Salam*, left with his cattle and assets. He built a coffin (a box) in which he placed Sarah with locks for the sake of safeguarding. They left until they were out of the domain of Nimrod and they entered in the domain of a man from al-Qibt (Coptic people) called 'Ararah. They passed by his tax collector who stopped them for collecting taxes. When they were there with the coffin the tax collector asked Ibrahim, *'Alayhi al-Salam*, to open the coffin for taxing. Ibrahim, *'Alayhi al-Salam*, said, 'Charge us whatever you like of gold or silver we will pay, but we will not open it for you.' The tax collector refused and said, 'You must open the coffin.' He (the Imam) said that Ibrahim, *'Alayhi al-Salam*, became angry, when Sarah appeared who was well formed physically with beauty. The taxman asked, 'What is the relation between you and this woman?' Ibrahim, *'Alayhi al-Salam*, said that she was his wife and daughter of his maternal aunt.' The taxman asked, 'What made you to hide her in this coffin?' Ibrahim, *'Alayhi al-Salam*, replied, 'It is because of the sense of protectionism and that people must not see her.' The taxman said, 'I will not allow you to go until I inform the king about you and her condition.' He (the Imam) said that he sent a messenger to the king and informed him. The king sent a messenger to take the coffin to him. They came to take it to the king and Ibrahim, *'Alayhi al-Salam*, said, 'I must stay with the coffin (box) as long as my soul is in my body.' They informed the king about it who commanded to take him with the coffin. They took Ibrahim, *'Alayhi al-Salam*, and the coffin and all that were with him to the king and the king said, 'Open the coffin.' Ibrahim, *'Alayhi al-Salam*, said, 'O king, there is my wife in it who is the daughter of my maternal aunt and I am ready to pay a ransom even if it will cost all that is with me but you must not open it.' He (the Imam) said that the king forced Ibrahim, *'Alayhi al-Salam*, to open the coffin. When he saw her, he could not control himself due to dimwittedness and stretched his hand to Sarah. Ibrahim turned his face away and because of fervor said, 'O Lord, keep his hand away from my wife and the daughter of my maternal aunt.' His hand could not reach her and could not return back to him. The king then asked, 'Is it your Lord who has done this to my hand?' He replied, 'Yes, He has done so, my Lord has fervor and He dislikes unlawful matters. He is the one who stopped you from doing what you wanted of unlawful act.' The king said, 'Pray to your Lord to return my hand to me and if he answered your prayer I will not bother about her.' Ibrahim, *'Alayhi al-Salam*, said, 'O Lord, return his hand to him so that he will stay away from my wife.' He (the Imam) said, 'Allah, most Majestic, most Glorious, returned his hand and the king turned to him with his eyes, then stretched his hand to her and Ibrahim, *'Alayhi al-Salam*, turned his face away because of fervor and said, 'O Lord, keep his hand away from my wife.' He (the Imam) said that his hand froze and could not reach her. The king then said to Ibrahim, *'Alayhi al-Salam*, 'Your Lord has fervor indeed. Pray to Him to return my hand and if he did I will not repeat.' Ibrahim, *'Alayhi al-Salam*, said, 'I will do so upon the condition that if you repeated then do not ask me to pray for you.' The king agreed and Ibrahim, *'Alayhi al-Salam*, prayed, 'O Lord, if he is truthful return his hand.' His hand then returned. When the king saw that kind of fervor and saw the sign in his hand he treated Ibrahim, *'Alayhi al-Salam*, with greatness, reverence, honor and remained cautious about him and said, 'You have amnesty from my side and all that is with you and you can go wherever you want to go but I have one wish.' Ibrahim *'Alayhi al-Salam*, asked, 'What is your wish?' He said, 'Allow me to give her a servant of Coptic woman to serve her who is beautiful and of good understanding.' He (the Imam) said that Ibrahim, *'Alayhi al-Salam*, allowed him to do so. He gave Hajar as a gift, who was the mother of 'Isma'il. Ibrahim, *'Alayhi al-Salam*, then moved with all that was with him. The king walked behind him for his greatness, respect and reverence. Allah, most Blessed, most High, revealed to Ibrahim, *'Alayhi al-Salam*, that said, 'Stop and do not walk before a dominating tyrant, when he is walking behind you but make him to walk before you and you walk behind him. Consider him great, revere him because he wants domination and it is necessary for the earth to have rulers, virtuous or not virtuous.' Ibrahim, *'Alayhi al-Salam*, stopped and said to the king, 'My Lord, has sent revelation to me at this hour to treat you with greatness and reverence and allow you to walk in front of me and that I must walk behind you for your majesty.' The king then asked, 'Has your Lord revealed this to you?' Ibrahim, *'Alayhi al-Salam*, replied, 'Yes, that is true.' The king said, 'I testify that your Lord is friendly, forbearing and honorable and you are attracting me to your religion.' He (the Imam) said that the king said farewell to him and Ibrahim moved until he arrived in al-Sham. When the birth of a son was delayed for Sarah, he said,'If you want, you could sell Hajar to me; Allah perhaps will give us a son to become our successor.' Ibrahim, *'Alayhi al-Salam*, bought Hajar from her and went to bed with her and 'Isma'il, *'Alayhi al-Salam*, was born.'"

H 15008, h 561

Ali ibn Ibrahim has narrated from his father from and Muhammad ibn Yahya has narrated from Ahmad ibn Muhammad ibn 'Isa from al-Husayn ibn Sa'id all ibn abu 'Umayr from Husayn ibn Ahmad al-Minqariy from Yunus ibn Zabayan who has narrated the following:

"I once said to abu 'Abd Allah, *'Alayhi al-Salam*, 'Why is it that these two men do not refrain from criticizing this man? He (the Imam) asked, 'Who is this man and who are these two men?' I then said, 'They are Hujr ibn Za'idah and 'Amir ibn Judha'ah against al-Mufaddal ibn 'Umar.' He (the Imam) then said, 'O Yunus I had asked them to desist and refrain from criticizing him but they did not do so. I then called them, asked, wrote to them and made it clear what I needed from them, but they did not desist, may Allah not forgive them. By Allah, there are many 'Azzah who are more true in his love than the two of them in whatever they maintain of my love, just as the poet has said: 'O yes, why did she not think that if I do not love whoever she loves I am not loving her.' By Allah, if they love me, they must have loved the one whom I love.'"

In the Masjid there is a circle...

H 15009, h 562

Muhammad ibn Yahya has narrated from Ahmad ibn Muhammad ibn 'Isa from Ali ibn al-Nu'man from al-Qasim Sharik al-Mufaddal who was a truthful man who has narrated the following:

"I once heard abu 'Abd Allah, *'Alayhi al-Salam*, say, 'In the Masjid there is a circle which exposes us to harm and exposes them as well. They are not from us and we are not of them. I go to hide and provide cover but they unveil my cover, may Allah unveil their cover. They say, 'He is the Imam (leader).' By Allah, I am not an Imam except for those who obey me; but those who disobey me, I am not their Imam. Why do they attach to my name? Why do they not refrain from pronouncing my name, by Allah? May Allah not gather me together with them in a house.'"

One of them was Talib ibn abu Talib...

H 15010, h 563
Muhammad ibn Yahya has narrated from Muhammad ibn al-Husayn from Safwan from Dharih who has narrated the following:

"Abu 'Abd Allah, *'Alayhi al-Salam*, has said that when Quraysh moved out to Badr and took with them the children of 'Abd al-Muttalib, one of them was Talib ibn abu Talib. They began to sing their slogan of pride. Talib ibn abu Talib disembarked to sing his slogan saying, 'O Lord, if they will make Talib to attack along with a group of horsemen, then make him to be with the defeated group, the group which is defeated without gaining anything they can capture from the other party.' Quraysh then said, 'He must be returned because he may cause our defeat.' In another Hadith from abu 'Abd Allah, *'Alayhi al-Salam*, it is narrated that he accepted Islam."

Fatimah, *'Alayha al-Salam*, came to one of the pillars. . .

H 15011, h 564
Humayd ibn Ziyad has narrated from al-Hassan ibn Muhammad al-Kindiy from Ahmad ibn al-Hassan al-Mithamiy from Aban ibn 'Uthman from Muhammad ibn al-Mufaddal who has narrated the following:

"I once heard abu 'Abd Allah, *'Alayhi al-Salam*, say that Fatimah, *'Alayha al-Salam*, came to one of the pillars in the Masjid and addressing the Holy Prophet, *O Allah grant compensation to Muhammad and his family worthy of their services to Your cause*, said, 'After you great differences have taken place. If you had been present the issue would not increase this much. We have missed you just as the land loses its drenching rain. Your nation is in disorder; you must bear witness and do not remain absent.'"

Ja'far was killed . . .

H 15012, h 565
Aban has narrated from abu Basir who has narrated the following:

"Abu 'Abd Allah, *'Alayhi al-Salam*, has said that once when the Messenger of Allah, *O Allah grant compensation to Muhammad and his family worthy of their services to Your cause*, was in the Masjid, all the heights were made low and all the low lands were made high before him. He (the Messenger of Allah) saw Ja'far, may Allah grant him eternal peace, fighting the unbelievers.' He (the Imam) said that Ja'far was killed and the Messenger of Allah, *O Allah grant compensation to Muhammad and his family worthy of their services to Your cause*, said, 'Ja'far is killed', whereupon he (the Messenger of Allah) felt a huge shooting pain in his abdomen."

Day of Hunayn

H 15013, h 566

Humayd ibn Ziyad has narrated from 'Ubayd Allah ibn Ahmad al-Dihqan from Ali ibn al-Hassan al-Tatriy from Muhammad ibn Ziyad Bayya' al-Sabiriy from 'Ajlan abu Salih who has narrated the following:

"I once heard abu 'Abd Allah, *'Alayhi al-Salam*, say, 'On the day of Hunayn forty people were killed by the hand of Ali, *'Alayhi al-Salam*.'"

With al-Buraq

H 15014, h 567

Aban has narrated from 'Abd Allah ibn 'Ata' who has narrated the following:

"Abu Ja'far, *'Alayhi al-Salam*, has stated this Hadith: 'Once Jibril, *'Alayhi al-Salam*, came to the Messenger of Allah, *O Allah grant compensation to Muhammad and his family worthy of their services to Your cause*, with al-Buraq which is smaller than a mule and bigger than a donkey. It is of anxious ears with eyes on its hoofs, one span of its step equal to the range of its eyesight. On reaching a mountain its hands became shorter and its legs longer but when climbing down its hands became longer and its legs became shorter and with its mane hanging toward the right side and two wings behind it.'"

The three who lagged behind

H 15015, h 568

Ali ibn Ibrahim has narrated from Salih ibn al-Sindiy from Ja'far ibn Bashir from Fayz ibn al-Mukhtar who has narrated the following:

"Abu 'Abd Allah, *'Alayhi al-Salam*, once asked, 'How do you read, '. . . and on the three who lagged behind . . .' (9:118) He (the Imam) said, 'If they remained behind (which is the meaning of the word Khullifu), they would have been considered obedient. However, they opposed, which is the meaning of the word Kh'alafu, which stand for 'Uthman and his two friends. O yes, they did not hear the sound of any hoof and banging of stones except that they said, 'It is coming on us' and on his two friends. Allah then made fear to dominate them until morning.'"

You must read al-Ta'ibun al-'Abidun

H 15016, h 569

Muhammad ibn Yahya has narrated from Ahmad ibn Muhammad from Ali ibn al-Hakam from Ali ibn abu Hamzah from abu Basir who has narrated the following:

"Abu Ja'far, *'Alayhi al-Salam*, has said, 'You read '. . . al-Ta'ibun al-'Abidun.' (9:112) He (the Imam) said, 'No, you must read al-Ta'ibin al-'Abidin . . .' He (the Imam) was asked about the reason for such recitation. He (the Imam) said, 'He bought from believing, repenting and worshipping ones. . .'" (This makes it to have the same condition as the believing ones in the beginning of the verse (9:111).)

H 15017, h 570

A number of our people have narrated from Sahl ibn Ziyad from Yahya ibn al-Mubarak from 'Abd Allah ibn Jabalah from Ishaq ibn 'Ammar who has narrated the following:

"This is about the meaning of the words of Allah, most Majestic, most Glorious. '. . . a messenger has come to you from among you to whom your suffering is difficult. He is protective for you and is compassionate and kind to the believing people.' (9:128) He (the Imam) said, 'It is '. . . a messenger has come to us from among us to whom our suffering is difficult, who is protective for us and is compassionate and kind to the believing people.'" (9:128) (The difference is a matter of the Tafsir (interpretation) of *Ahl al-Bayt, 'Alayhim al-Salam*)

"Allah sent down His comfort..."

H 15018, h 571

Muhammad ibn Ahmad has narrated from ibn Faddal from al-Rida', who has narrated the following:

"This is about the meaning of the words of Allah, most Majestic, most Glorious, '. . . Allah sent down His comfort on him [His Messenger] and supported him with an army which you did not see. . . .' (9:40) Al-Rida', *'Alayhi al-Salam*, has said, 'This is how we recite and in that sense it was revealed,' when I asked him (the Imam) about it."

You may feel grieved. . .

H 15019, h 572

Muhammad ibn Yahya has narrated from Ahmad ibn Muhammad from Muhammad ibn Khalid and al-Husayn ibn Sa'id from al-Nadr ibn Suwayd from Yahya al-Halabiy from ibn Muskan from 'Ammar ibn Suwayd who has narrated the following:

"This is about the meaning of the words of Allah, most Majestic, most Glorious. 'Perhaps you, (Muhammad), may by chance leave (untold) a part of that which is revealed to you. You may feel grieved. They say, "Why has a treasure not been sent to him or an angel is not sent down with him?"' (11:12) I heard abu 'Abd Allah, *'Alayhi al-Salam*, say this. 'When the Messenger of Allah, *O Allah grant compensation to Muhammad and his family worthy of their services to Your cause*, arrived in Qadid (name of a place), he said to Ali, *'Alayhi al-Salam*, "O Ali, I asked my Lord to make the guardianship between you and I. He did so, I asked my Lord to establish goodwill between you and I. He did so and I asked my Lord to make you the executor of my will. He did so and thereupon the two men of Quraysh said, 'By Allah one Sa' (a certain unit of measurement) of dates in a basket is more beloved to us than for what Muhammad asks his Lord. Why does he not ask his Lord to send an angel to support him against his enemy, or ask for a treasure to make him rich out of his poverty? By Allah, whatever he prays for, a true or a false thing, He answers his prayer.'" Then Allah, most Blessed, most High, revealed, 'Perhaps you, (Muhammad), may by chance leave (untold) a part of that which is revealed to you and feel grieved because they say, "Why has some treasure not been sent to him or an angel sent down with him?" You (Muhammad) are only a Warner and Allah is the guardian of all things.'"' (11:12)

"Made all people one..."

H 15020, h 573

Ali ibn Ibrahim has narrated from his father from ibn abu 'Umayr from 'Abd Allah ibn Sinan who has narrated the following:

"Once abu 'Abd Allah, *'Alayhi al-Salam*, was asked about the meaning of the words of Allah, most Majestic, most Glorious. '. . . had your Lord wanted He could have made all people one nation but they continue to differ with each other except those to whom your Lord grants mercy.' (11:118-119) He (the Imam) said, 'They were one nation then Allah sent Prophets to remove their excuses of having no guidance and divine authority among them.'"

"One who does a good deed..."

H 15021, h 574

Ali ibn Muhammad has narrated from Ali ibn al-'Abbas from Ali ibn Hammad from 'Amr ibn Shamir from Jabir who has narrated the following:

"This is about the meaning of the words of Allah, most Majestic, most Glorious. '. . . one who does a good deed We add to it for him more goodness.' (42:23) Abu Ja'far, *'Alayhi al-Salam*, has said that it is a reference to those who accept *Walayah* (guardianship of *'A'immah* with divine authority and knowledge) of *Ale* (family of) Muhammad. Their following such guidance adds to the *Walayah* (guardianship and divine authority) of the Prophets of the past and the believing people of the earlier generations. Their *Walayah* (guardianship with divine authority and knowledge) then reaches the *Walayah* (guardianship with divine authority) of Adam, *'Alayhi al-Salam*. It is mentioned in the words of Allah, most Majestic, most Glorious. '. . . one who does a good deed for him there is something better than that good deed.' (27:89) One for this reason will enter the garden (paradise) as Allah, most Majestic, most Glorious, has said. '. . . say, "Whatever reward I ask from you is for your own self."' (34:47). The Holy Prophet says, 'The reward that I ask from you in the form of the love besides which I do not ask from you for anything is for you through which you will find guidance and will be saved from suffering on the Day of Judgment.' For the enemies of Allah and friends of Satan, people of rejection and denial He has said, '. . . say, "I do not ask from you for any reward and I am not a pretending one."' (38:86) He says, 'I will be pretending if I ask you what you are not worthy of (I do not ask the hypocrites to love my family; it is useless).'

"The hypocrites then said to each other, 'Is it not enough for Muhammad that he has dominated us for twenty years and now in addition he wants to load his family on our necks?' Therefore, they said, 'Allah has not revealed it. It is nothing more than his own words that he speaks to raise his family over our necks. If Muhammad will be killed or die, we will remove his family from government and then we will never allow it to go back to them forever.' Allah, most Majestic, most Glorious, wanted to inform His Holy Prophet, *O Allah grant compensation to Muhammad and his family worthy of their services to Your cause*, of that which they were hiding in their chests secretly. Allah, most

Majestic, most Glorious, thus, has said in His book, '. . . do they say that he has fabricated it against Allah falsely? Had Allah wanted He could have sealed his heart,' (42:24) He says, 'Had I wanted I could have held back revelation from you so you could not speak of the excellence of your family, or about loving them.'

"Allah, most Majestic, most Glorious, has said, '. . . Allah deletes falsehood and establishes the truth through His words. [He says that truth is on the side of your family. It is *Walayah* (guardianship with divine authority and knowledge)]. He has full knowledge of all that is in the hearts.' (42:24) He speaks about what He has placed in their hearts of animosity towards your family, the injustice to them after your passing away as is mentioned in the words of Allah, most Majestic, most Glorious, '. . . the unjust secretly speak to each other and say, "Is it not true that he is only a human being like you? Do you then come to magic when you can see it?"' (21:3) There are the words of Allah, most Majestic, most Glorious. '. . . I swear by the star when it descends down.' [He has said that He swears by the passing away of Muhammad from this world]. He swears that your companion is not misled [in giving preference to his family] and has not transgressed. He does not speak out of his own desires [He (Allah) says that he does not speak of the excellence of his family out of his own desire but it is the words of Allah, most Majestic, most Glorious, '. . . it is but revelation that is revealed to him.' (53:1-4)

"Allah, most Majestic, most Glorious, has said this to Muhammad, *O Allah grant compensation to Muhammad and his family worthy of their services to Your cause*. '. . . say to them, "If I had with me what you want to happen quickly between you and I the matter would have been settled.' (6:58) He has said, 'If I inform you of what you hide in your chests about my death to happen quicker so you will do injustice to my family after me, your case will then be like what Allah, most Majestic, most Glorious, has said. '. . . it is like the case of one who kindles a fire. When his surroundings become bright . . .' (2:17) is a reference to His saying that the earth became bright by the light of Muhammad just as the sun brightens it. Allah has given the example of Muhammad, *O Allah grant compensation to Muhammad and his family worthy of their services to Your cause*, to be like the sun. The example of the executor of the will like the moon as is mentioned in the words of Allah, most Majestic, most Glorious. 'He has made the sun a source of light and the moon a brightness.' It is also in His words, '. . . a sign for them is the night from which We extract the day when they were in darkness.' (36:37) Also it is in the words of Allah, most Majestic, most Glorious, '. . . Allah removed their light and left them in darkness in which they cannot see.' (2:17) It is a reference to the passing away of Muhammad, *O Allah grant compensation to Muhammad and his family worthy of their services to Your cause*, from this world. After this darkness appeared then they did not see the excellence of *Ahl al-Bayt*.

"Allah, most Majestic, most Glorious, has said, '. . . if you call them to guidance they cannot listen and you see them look to you but they cannot see.' (7:198)

The Messenger of Allah, *O Allah grant compensation to Muhammad and his family worthy of their services to Your cause*, left the knowledge which was with him with the executor of the will as mentioned in the words of Allah, most Majestic, most Glorious, '. . . Allah is the light of the skies and earth.' (24:35) He says that He is the guide of the skies and earth like the knowledge that I have given and that is the light (My light) by which guidance is found like a niche in which there is a lantern. Niche is the heart of Muhammad, *O Allah grant compensation to Muhammad and his family worthy of their services to Your cause*, lantern is My light in which there is knowledge.

"In addition, there are His words. '. . . the lantern is in a glass' which He says I want to make you pass away. Therefore, you must leave that which is with you with the Executor of the Will just as a lantern is placed in a glass 'as if it is a brilliant star.' Thus, inform them of the excellence of Executor of the Will, 'it lights up from a blessed tree' and the origin of the blessed tree is Ibrahim, *'Alayhi al-Salam*, as mentioned in the words of Allah, most Majestic, most Glorious, '. . . the mercy and the blessings of Allah is upon you *Ale* (family of), *Ahl al-Bayt*; He is praiseworthy and glorious.' (11:73)

"It is in the words of Allah, most Majestic, most Glorious, '. . . Allah chose Adam, *'Alayhi al-Salam*, Noah, *Ale* (family of) Ibrahim, and *Ale* (family of) of 'Imran over the worlds. They were offspring of each other and Allah is hearing and knowledgeable.' (3:33-34) '. . . it is not from the east or from the west'. He says that you are not Jews who face during *Salat* (prayer) to the west. You are not Christians who turn their faces toward the east in *Salat* (prayer).

"You are followers of the religion of Ibrahim, *'Alayhi al-Salam*, as Allah, most Majestic, most Glorious, has said, '. . . Ibrahim was not a Jew or Christian, but he was an upright man, submitted to the will of Allah and he was not a pagan.' (3:67) "Also there is the words of Allah, most Majestic, most Glorious, '. . . its oil almost lights up even if no fire touches it. It is light upon light. Allah guides to His light whomever He wants.' He says that the example of your children who are born from you is like the oil which is extracted from olive.' Its oil almost lights up even if no fire touches it. It is light upon light. Allah guides to His light whomever He wants.' He says that they almost speak like the Prophets do, even though no angels come to them.'"

"We will soon show them our signs..."

H 15022, h 575

Abu Ali al-Ash'ariy has narrated from Muhammad ibn 'Abd al-Jabbar from al-Hassan ibn Ali from Ali ibn abu Hamzah from abu Basir who has narrated the following:

"I once asked abu 'Abd Allah, *'Alayhi al-Salam*, about the meaning of the words of Allah, most Majestic, most Glorious, '. . . We will soon show them our signs in the horizons and in their souls until it becomes clear that He is the truth.' (41:53) He (the Imam) said, 'He will show them in their souls metamorphoses and in the horizons their breaking down on them, then they will see the power of

Allah, most Majestic, most Glorious, in their souls and in the horizons.' I then asked about the meaning of, '. . . until it will become clear that He is the truth.' He (the Imam) said, 'When al-Qa'im will reappear with divine authority and power it will become clear that it is the truth from Allah, most Majestic, most Glorious, which the creatures must see.'"

The connection with them, *'Alayhi al-Salam,* is the connection of the eons

H 15023, h 576

Muhammad ibn Yahya and al-Husayn from Muhammad have all narrated from Ja'far ibn Muhammad from 'Abbad ibn Ya'qub from Ahmad ibn 'Isma'il from 'Amr ibn Kaysan from abu 'Abd Allah, al-Ju'fiy who has narrated the following:

"Abu Ja'far, Muhammad ibn Ali, *'Alayhi al-Salam,* once asked me, 'For how long is your *al-Ribat* (border guarding)?' I replied, 'Forty.' He (the Imam) said, 'Our *Ribat,* is the *Ribat* of eons (obedience to the Imam is permanent). One who keeps a stumper to serve in our *Ribat* he will receive twice as much as the weight of the stumper as long as he keeps it. One who keeps for us arms, he will receive equal to its weight as long as it is with him. You must not become restless for once, twice or three times or four times facing hardships because our case and your case is like the case of the Prophet of banu Israel to whom Allah, most Majestic, most Glorious, sent revelation to call his people to help in a war and that He will soon grant them victory. He brought them together from the tops of mountains and other places, then they moved to the war zone but without striking any spears or sword, they were defeated. Allah, most Blessed, most High, sent him revelation again to call his people to help in the war and that He will soon grant them victory. He gathered them together and then moved to the war zone but without striking of any sword or spears, they were defeated. Allah then sent him revelation to call his people to help in the war and that He will soon grant them victory. He called them and they said that you promised us support but you did not support us. Allah, most Blessed, most High, sent revelation that said, 'They must choose to help in the war or the fire.' He said, 'O Lord, helping in the war is more beloved to me than the fire.' He called them and three hundred and thirteen people answered his call; equal to the number of the people of Badr. They moved to the war zone but without striking any sword or spears: Allah, most Majestic, most Glorious, granted them victory.'"

Uprooted by the flu

H 15024, h 577

A number of our people have narrated from Sahl ibn Ziyad from Bakr ibn Salih and al-Nawfaliy and others in a marfu' manner who has narrated the following:

"Abu 'Abd Allah, *'Alayhi al-Salam,* has said that the Messenger of Allah, *O Allah grant compensation to Muhammad and his family worthy of their services to Your cause,* would not seek treatment by medicine because of the flu saying that in everyone there is a vein of leprosy which is uprooted by the flu.'"

Army of the army of Allah

H 15025, h 578

Muhammad ibn Yahya has narrated from Ahmad ibn Muhammad ibn 'Isa from ibn abu 'Umayr from Hisham ibn Salim who has narrated the following:

"Abu 'Abd Allah, *'Alayhi al-Salam*, has said that the Messenger of Allah, *O Allah grant compensation to Muhammad and his family worthy of their services to Your cause*, has said, 'The flu is an army of the army of Allah, most Majestic, most Glorious, which He sends on the illness to remove it.'"

There are two veins...

H 15026, h 579

Muhammad ibn Yahya has narrated from Musa ibn al-Hassan from Muhammad ibn 'Abd al-Hamid through the chain of his narrators in a marfu' manner who has narrated the following:

"Abu 'Abd Allah, *'Alayhi al-Salam*, has said that the Messenger of Allah, *O Allah grant compensation to Muhammad and his family worthy of their services to Your cause*, has said, 'In every child of Adam, *'Alayhi al-Salam*, there are two veins. One vein is in his head, which stirs leprosy, and one vein is in his body, which stirs vitiligo. When the vein which is in the head becomes excited Allah, most Majestic, most Glorious, makes flu to dominate until it makes it to flow out with the illness; and when the vein which is in the body becomes excited Allah sends pimples to make the illness flow out. If one of you finds flu or pimples he must praise and thank Allah, most Majestic, most Glorious, for good health.' He (the Imam) said, 'The flu is excess in the head.'"

Use these three items...

H 15027, h 580

Muhammad ibn Yahya has narrated from Ahmad ibn Muhammad ibn 'Isa from ibn Mahbub from a man who has narrated the following:

"Once, a man came to abu 'Abd Allah, *'Alayhi al-Salam*, and complained because of his eyes. He (the Imam) said, 'Why do you not use these three items: Aloe, Camphor and al-Murr (the gum or sap of a certain tree).'"

Apply Aloe...

H 15028, h 581

It is narrated from the narrator of the previous Hadith from Ahmad from ibn Mahbub from Jamil ibn Salih who has narrated the following:

"I once said to abu 'Abd Allah, *'Alayhi al-Salam*, 'We have a young girl who could see a star like a trail.' He (the Imam) said, 'Yes, and now she sees like a grain.' I said that her eye sight has become weak.' He (the Imam) said, 'She must apply Aloe, al-Murr (the gum or sap of a certain tree) and camphor in equal parts.' We applied it and it proved beneficial.'"

A package was brought for him...

H 15029, h 582

It is narrated from the narrator of the previous Hadith from Ahmad from Dawud ibn Muhammad from Muhammad ibn al-Fayd who has narrated the following:

"Abu 'Abd Allah, *'Alayhi al-Salam*, has said, 'Once I was with abu Ja'far, Mansur al-Dawaniqiy, that a package was brought for him. He opened it and looked at it, took out something and said, 'O abu 'Abd Allah, do you know what is it?' I asked, 'What is it?' He said, 'It is something which they bring from the back of Africa from Tanjah' or Tabnah' – doubt is from Muhammad. I then asked, 'What is it?' He said, 'There is a mountain from which every year a few drops fall and turn solid and it is very good for the whiteness in the eye. It is used as an eye powder and the whiteness goes away by the permission of Allah.' I then said, 'Yes, I know it and if you like I can tell you about its name and condition.' He (the Imam) said that he did not ask about its name and asked, 'What is its condition?' I said, 'This is a mountain on which a Prophet of the Prophets of banu Israel lived in exile from his people where he worshipped Allah. His people found about him and they killed him. The mountain weeps for him and these drops are from its tears. On the other side there is a fountain from which water flows night and day but it does not reach that eye fountain.'"

The eye powder of abu Ja'far, *'Alayhi al-Salam*

H 15030, h 583

Ali ibn Ibrahim has narrated from his father from ibn abu 'Umayr from Sulaym mawla Ali ibn Yaqtin who suffered from eye ache:

"Abu al-Hassan, *'Alayhi al-Salam*, wrote to him this note on his own initiation. 'What prevents you from using the eye powder of abu Ja'far, *'Alayhi al-Salam*, one part camphor of Rabahiy, one part Aloe of Asqutariy, powdered together and filtered through silk like the eye powder of al-Ithmid (antimony) once a month, which accelerates every illness away from the head and moves it out of the body.' He (the narrator) has said that he applied that eye powder and had no complaint until the time of his death.'"

Hadith of the Worshipper

H 15031, h 584

Muhammad ibn Yahya has narrated from Ahmad ibn Muhammad ibn 'Isa from Ali ibn al-Hakam from Muhammad ibn Sinan from those who narrated to him who has narrated the following:

"Abu 'Abd Allah, *'Alayhi al-Salam*, has said that in banu Israel there was a worshipper who had not committed anything of the worldly matters, because of which Satan snorted in despair; as such that all of his armies gathered around him. He asked, 'Who is for me against him (the worshipper)?' Certain ones among them came forward and said, 'I am for you against him.' He asked, 'How you will do it?' He said, 'I will move against him by means of women.' Satan said, 'You are a failure because he cannot be tempted by means of women.' Another one of his army came forward and said, 'I am for you against him.' Satan asked, 'How will you do it?' He replied, 'I will move against him by means of wine and enjoyable matters.' Satan said, 'This is not of such things.' Another one of his army came forward and said, 'I am for you against him.' Satan asked, 'How will you make it work?' He replied, 'I will move against him by means of good deeds.' Satan said, 'You, it seems, are the suitable one against him.' He moved where the worshipper lived and stood near him in prayer. The worshipper would go to sleep and rest but the Satan would never go to sleep or rest. The worshipping man blamed himself for his shortcomings in worship, belittled his deeds, and asked, 'O servant of Allah, by what means have you become so strong in worshipping and *Salat* (prayer)?' He did not answer. He repeated his question but he did not answer. He asked again, then he said, 'O servant of Allah, it is because I committed a sin, then I repented and when I recall that sin, it gives me strength in performing *Salat* (prayer).' He then said, 'Please tell me what kind of sin was it so that I can also do it, then repent and thereafter become strong in performing *Salat* (prayer).'

"He said, 'Go to the city and ask for so and so female prostitute, give her two dirham and benefit from her.' He then asked, 'How can I have two dirham and I do not know what two dirhams are.' The Satan picked up two dirhams from under his foot and gave them to him. He then left for the city in a worshipper's dress asking for the home of so and so prostitute. People gave him the direction, thinking that perhaps he wanted to give her good advice, so they showed him her home. He went to her, threw the two dirhams to her and asked her to come. She went with him to her home and told him to come in. She said, 'You have come to me in such a dress with which no one goes to someone like me. You must tell me about your story.'

"He then told her his story and she said, 'O servant of Allah, refraining from sin is easier then repenting and besides, everyone who seeks repentance does not find. This person (who has given you this idea) is a Satan who has come to you in the form of a worshipper. You can go back and see you will not find him there.' He returned and she died in that night. In the morning, a writing was found at her door. 'You must come to attend the funeral of so and so. She is of the people of the garden (paradise).' People had doubts and they waited for three days without arranging for her burial because of the doubt about her case. Allah, most Majestic, most Glorious, sent revelation to a Prophet, who as I know was no one else other than Musa ibn 'Imran, *'Alayhi al-Salam*, to go to so and so female to perform funeral *Salat* (prayer) for her and command people to perform *Salat* (prayer) for her as well. I have forgiven her and have made the garden (paradise) obligatory for her because of her making my so and so servant steadfast in his worship and her saving him from disobeying Me.'"

A deprived person...

H 15032, h 585

Ahmad ibn Muhammad [ibn Ahmad] has narrated from Ali ibn al-Hassan from Muhammad ibn 'Abd Allah ibn Zurarah from Muhammad ibn al-Fudayl from abu Hamzah who has narrated the following:

"Abu Ja'far, '*Alayhi al-Salam,* has said that in banu Israel there lived a worshipper who was a deprived person. Wherever he went, something had to happen to him. His wife spent for him everything that she had until nothing was left for them; so they remained one day starving. She gave him a roll of yarn saying, 'This is all that is left with me so you must try to sell it and buy something for us to eat.' He then left with the roll of yarn to sell. He found that the market was closed. He found two buyers who turned back. He then decided to go to the water for wudu and throw water on himself, then go home. He went to the sea where he found a fisherman had spread his net. He took it out and only one fish of a bad quality had remained with him. It had become soft and stinking. He asked him to sell that fish in exchange for that roll of yarn, which may benefit him in his net. He agreed. He took the fish, gave the roll of yarn to him and returned with the fish to his home. He informed his wife who took the fish to prepare for food. When she cut it open, a pearl appeared in it. She called her husband and showed the pearl to him. He took the pearl, went to the market and sold it for twenty thousand dirham, then returned home with the asset. He had just placed it at home that a beggar knocked at the door saying, 'O people of the house, give some charity to a destitute, may Allah grant you mercy.' The man called him in and he entered. He told him to pick up one of the two bags. He took one of them and left. His wife said, '*Tasbih* (Allah is free of all defects): when we had just become affluent he allowed one-half of it to go away.' As soon as she said it, the beggar knocked at the door and the man allowed him to come in. He entered and placed the sack back saying, 'Use them in good health. I am only an angel of the angels of your Lord. Your Lord wanted only to try you. He has found you a thankful person.' He then left."

A Sermon of 'Amir al-Mu'minin, Ali, '*Alayhi al-Salam*

H 15033, h 586

Ahmad ibn Muhammad has narrated from Sa'd ibn al-Mundhir ibn Muhammad from his father from his grandfather from Muhammad ibn al-Husayn from his father from his grandfather who has narrated the following:

"Others have also narrated this sermon through different chains of narrators who has mentioned that he (the Imam) delivered this sermon in Dhiqar (Iraq). He (the Imam) praised Allah and spoke of His glory. He (the Imam) then said, 'Thereafter, Allah, most Blessed, most High, sent Muhammad, *O Allah grant compensation to Muhammad and his family worthy of their services to Your cause,* in all truth to take His servants out of the worshipping of His creatures to His worship. Take them out from the covenants of His creatures to His covenant, from obedience to His creatures to His obedience and from the guardianship of His creatures to His own guardianship with glad news and warning. Therefore, he can call them to Allah by His permission as the shining lamp in the beginning and in return, in excusable case as well as in the case of warning, call them with judgment, differentiation and details, which He has established and distinctions that He has made; call them to Allah with al-Quran that He has explained so that the servants know their Lord after being ignorant about Him, affirm and acknowledge Him whence before they denied Him.

Therefore, he can prove His existence after that they had refused to accept. He has manifested Himself in His book without their seeing Him and showed them His forbearance how forbearing He is, showed them His pardoning how forgiving He is and showed them His power to prove how has He determined. He has frightened them of his domination and how He has created what He has created of signs, how has He deleted what He has deleted of the disobedient ones to set up examples and that how has He mowed down and destroyed by torments and how He has provided sustenance, guidance and favors. He has shown them His rules. He has established and has exercised patience so that those who want to hear can hear and see.

"Allah, most Majestic, most Glorious, sent Muhammad, *O Allah grant compensation to Muhammad and his family worthy of their services to Your cause*, for such task. After him there will come a time upon you. After me, no other thing will be more obscure than the truth, and no other thing will be more clear and apparent than falsehood. No other thing will be more abundant than lies against Allah, most Blessed, most High, and the Messenger of Allah, *O Allah grant compensation to Muhammad and his family worthy of their services to Your cause*. To the people of that time no other thing will remain worthless than the book when it is recited the way it must be recited in truth, and no asset will be more valuable, more sellable and more expensive than the book when it is presented with its meaning changed and misplaced. Among the servants and the towns there will be nothing more detestable than lawful matters and no other thing more popular than unlawful matters. No act will be considered more indecent and the penalty more severe than for guidance from misguidance (in religion). In that time the book and those who carry it will be thrown away. Memorizing it will be neglected. They will interpret it according to their desires, which they inherit from their ancestors, and act to change the meaning of al-Quran falsely in rejection.

"So they sell it for a very little and cheap price, even then they will be unwilling to buy it. Thus, the book and the people of the book at that time will remain castaway and exiled as two companions together on one road who will not find any shelter, but how good as two companions they are. Good for them and for the one for whom they work. The book and the people of the book in that time will live among the people but not among them, they will be with them but not with them; misguidance does not agree with guidance even if they are in one place. They (people) gather together to disagree and scatter the community. They (people of such. time) authorize for the running of their affairs and the affairs of their religion those among them who work evil plots and in unlawful matters, bribes and murder as if they are the *'A'immah* (leaders) of the book and the book (of Allah) is not their Imam (leader). Nothing of the truth will remain with them except its name and they will not know of the book except its writing and shape.

"An incoming comes when hearing of the laws of al-Quran but is not comforted when sitting until he goes out of the religion. One moves from the religion of one king to the religion of another king, from the guardianship of one king to the guardianship of another king. One moves from the obedience of one king to the obedience of another king, from the covenant with one king to the covenant with another king and Allah, most Blessed, most High, takes them step by step in a way which they do not realize. His plans are firmly established with hope and good expectations. It continues with them giving birth in disobedience and rule with injustice without the religion of Allah, most Majestic, most Glorious, and compensate but not for the sake of Allah.

"Their Masjid in that time will be well built in misguidance but in ruination of the matters of guidance [because of changing guidance in them]. Their readers and constructors will be the most failing ones of the creatures of Allah in His creation. Misguidance will emerge from them and to them it will return. Attending their Masjid and walking to them will be disbelief in Allah, most great except for those who walk to them with knowledge of the misguidance. Their Masjid because of their deed as such will remain in ruination in matters of guidance but well established in matters of misguidance. This will be the case because of the changes in the *Sunnah* of Allah and His laws being subjected to transgression. They will not call to guidance, distribute *al-Fay'*, will not keep their promise and they will call their dead in that condition a martyr, which is a matter of fabricating falsehood against Allah, rejection and considering ignorance sufficient in place of knowledge. Already and before such time, they have caused severe suffering to the virtuous ones with great intensity, calling their truthfulness about Allah as heresy and fabrications, applying penalty for bad deeds to the doing of good deeds.

"Allah, most Majestic, most Glorious, has sent a messenger from among you, to whom your suffering is extremely grave, who has an intense desire for your well being, very compassionate and kind to the believing people, *O Allah grant compensation to Muhammad and his family worthy of their services to Your cause.* He has sent to him a glorious book to which falsehood cannot approach from any direction and it is a revelation from the wise and the most praise-worthy One. It is a reading in Arabic language without confusion and crookedness so he can warn the living ones and so that the word (of Allah) will come to pass on the unbelievers. You must not allow the yearnings to mislead you and you must not consider your life never-ending. People before you were destroyed. They extended their yearnings and neglected the coming of the time of their death until the promised time descended upon them. In such time excuses were rejected, repentance time was no more and with it the crushing and penalty arrived.

"Allah, most Majestic, most Glorious, has already sent you warning and has distinguished for you the word, has taught you the *Sunnah*, explained to you the instruction and the pathways to remove the defects, exhorted to remember and has showed the way to safety. Those who act virtuously for the sake of Allah and follow His words of guidance as his guide, He shows him the way to what is well established and firm, grants him the opportunity to proper understanding, steadfastness, shows him the path of happiness with possible ease. Those under the protection of Allah are safe and well protected. His enemies are afraid and conceited. You must remain on your guard about your relation with Allah, most Majestic, most Glorious, through increased remembrance and remaining anxious about this matter by means of piety. You must seek nearness to Him by means of obedience to Him; He is near and answers (the prayers). Allah, most Majestic, most Glorious, has said, 'If My servant ask you about Me, I am near and answer the call of those who call when he calls, so they must ask for answer from Me and believe in Me to gain proper understanding.' (2:186) You must ask Allah for answers, believe in Him, and speak of Allah with greatness.

"It is not proper after recognizing the greatness of Allah to have a feeling of greatness about himself. The highness of those who know the greatness of Allah is in their humbleness before Him, and the dignity of those who know the glory of Allah is in their expressing lowliness before Allah and the safety of those who know the power of Allah is in their submitting themselves before His will. They then will not remain ignorant of their own soul after recognition and will not be misled after guidance. You must not flee from the truth like the fleeing of those in good health from those suffering from scabies and the fleeing of those in good health from those suffering from illness. You must take notice that you will not recognize good understanding until you recognize those who have abandoned it. You will not keep up with the covenant of the book until you recognize those who have disregarded it. You will not hold firmly to it (the book) until you recognize those who have thrown it behind their backs. You will not read the book the way it must be read until you recognize those who have changed its meanings. You will not recognize misguidance until you recognize guidance and you will not recognize piety until you recognize transgressors. When you recognize this, you recognize heresy and pretending. You will see the fabrications against Allah, against His Messenger and changing the meaning of His book. You will see how Allah has guided those whom He has guided. You must not allow those who do not have knowledge to keep you ignorant.

"The knowledge of al-Quran is understandable only to those who have sensed its taste. With knowledge he learned his ignorance and has made his eyesight seeing, his deafness as hearing, has found the knowledge of what he has lost, has gained life after being dead, has registered with Allah, most Majestic, most Glorious, good deeds, deleted with it bad deeds and has achieved thereby the happiness of Allah, most Blessed, most High. You must seek such knowledge from the proper people only. The people of such knowledge are special. They are the light with whom brightness is sought and 'A'immah (leaders) who are followed. They are the life of knowledge and death for ignorance. They are the ones whose judgment informs you of their knowledge and their remaining silent of their speaking and their appearance of their hidden facts. They do not oppose religion and they do not have differences in it. It is a truthful witness among them, and the silent speaker. It is of their status to bear witness in all truth and as truthful reporters who do not oppose the truth and do not have any difference in it. From Allah there is precedence about them and Allah, most Majestic, most

Glorious, has passed a truthful judgment about them. In this, there is a reminder for those who like to remember. You must understand the truth when you hear it with an understanding for practice and you must understand it but not just for the sake of narration and reporting. Narrators of books are many but those who practice are very few and Allah is the best supporter.'"

Mother of a sinner…

H 15034, h 587

A number of our people have narrated from Sahl ibn Ziyad from 'Umar ibn Ali from his uncle, Muhammad ibn 'Umar from ibn 'Udhaynah who has narrated the following:

"I once heard from 'Umar ibn Yazid his saying. 'Ma'ruf ibn Kharbudh narrated to him from Ali ibn al-Husayn, *'Alayhi al-Salam*, who has said the following. 'Woe is upon the mother of a sinner who continues arguing (to defend his sinning), woe is upon the mother of one who commits an indecent act and continues disputing. Woe is upon the mother of one who speaks a great deal but it is not about Allah, most Majestic, most Glorious.'"

Gray hair in his beard…

H 15035, h 588

Muhammad ibn Yahya has narrated from Ahmad ibn Muhammad ibn 'Isa and Ali ibn Ibrahim has narrated from his father all from Ahmad ibn Muhammad from ibn abu Nasr from Aban ibn 'Uthman from al-Hassan ibn 'Umarah from Nu'aym al-Quda'iy who has narrated the following:

"Abu Ja'far, *'Alayhi al-Salam*, has said that Ibrahim, *'Alayhi al-Salam*, one morning saw a gray hair in his beard and said, 'All praise belongs to Allah, Lord of the worlds Who has brought me this far and I have not disobeyed Him even for a blinking of an eye.'"

Glad news of being chosen…

H 15036, h 589

Aban ibn 'Uthman has narrated from Muhammad ibn Marwan from those who narrated to him who has narrated the following:

"Abu Ja'far, *'Alayhi al-Salam*, has stated this Hadith: 'When Allah, most Majestic, most Glorious, chose Ibrahim, *'Alayhi al-Salam*, as His friend, the glad news of being chosen by Allah as His special friend was brought to him by the angel of death in the form of a young white man dressed in two white clothes with water and oil dripping from his head. Ibrahim, *'Alayhi al-Salam*, entered the house but came face to face with him (the man) coming out of the house. 'Ibrahim, *'Alayhi al-Salam*, had a great fervor about his family. When going out for something, he would lock the door and take the keys with him. He, when returned, opened the door and saw a man standing as beautiful as a man can be. He took hold of his hand and asked, 'O servant of Allah, who allowed you to enter my house?' He replied, 'Its Lord allowed me to enter.' He said, 'Its Lord! Who has more right than I do, and then who are you?' He replied, 'I am the angel of death.' Ibrahim, *'Alayhi al-Salam*, was shocked and asked, 'Have you come to take away my spirit?' He replied, 'No, Allah has chosen a servant as

His special friend and I have come with this glad news for him.' He then asked, 'Who is he? Perhaps I can serve him until I die.' He replied, 'You are he.' He then went to Sarah, *'Alayha al-Salam*, and said, 'Allah, most Blessed, most High, has chosen me as His special friend.'"

Hadith with the angel

H 15037, h 590

Ali ibn Ibrahim has narrated from his father from ibn abu 'Umayr from Sulaym al-Farra' from those whom he has mentioned who has narrated the following:

"He has narrated from abu 'Abd Allah, *'Alayhi al-Salam*, a similar Hadith except that in his Hadith with the angel when he said, 'Its Lord has allowed me to enter, Ibrahim, *'Alayhi al-Salam*, recognized that he was the angel of death and asked, 'What has made you to descend?' He replied, 'I have come to give the glad news to a man whom Allah, most Blessed, most High, has chosen as His special friend.' Ibrahim, *'Alayhi al-Salam*, then asked, 'Who is this man?' The angel asked, 'What do you want from him?' Ibrahim *'Alayhi al-Salam*, said, 'I like to serve him all my life time.' The angel of death then said, 'You are he.'"

Travelling on a camel...

H 15038, h 591

Ali ibn Ibrahim has narrated from his father from al-Hassan ibn Mahbub from Malik ibn 'Atiyyah from abu Hamzah al-Thumaliy who has narrated the following:

"Abu Ja'far, *'Alayhi al-Salam*, has said that one day Ibrahim, *'Alayhi al-Salam*, went out travelling on a camel and passed by a wilderness of land where he saw a man standing in *Salat* (prayer) and his length causing a cut between the earth to the sky. His hairs were his clothe.' He (the Imam) said that Ibrahim stood there and was amazed. He then sat down waiting for him to complete his *Salat* (prayer). When it took him very long he moved him with his hand and said, 'Make it light, I want to ask you for something.' He then made it light and sat down with Ibrahim, *'Alayhi al-Salam*. Ibrahim asked, 'For whom do you perform *Salat* (prayer)?' He replied, 'I perform *Salat* (prayer) for the Lord of Ibrahim.' He then asked, 'Who is the Lord of Ibrahim?' He replied, 'He is the one who has created you and I.' Ibrahim, *'Alayhi al-Salam*, then said, 'You have amazed me and I like to become your brother for the sake of Allah. Where do you live so I can visit you when I want to meet and visit you?' He said that it is behind this hill - pointing with his hand to the sea – but the place of my *Salat* (prayer) is this place and you can find me here when you want by the will of Allah.' He (the Imam) said that the man then asked, 'Do you need me for something?' 'Ibrahim, *'Alayhi al-Salam*, said, 'Yes, I need you.' He asked, 'What for do you need me?' 'Ibrahim, *'Alayhi al-Salam*, said, 'I want that first you pray to Allah and I will say, 'Amen.' Then I pray and you say, 'Amen.' The man asked, 'What for should we then pray to Allah?' 'Ibrahim, *'Alayhi al-Salam*, said this. 'We must pray to Allah and plead before Him to forgive the believing people who have sinned.' The man said, 'No, we will not do so.' 'Ibrahim, *'Alayhi al-Salam*, asked, 'Why we should not pray?' He replied, 'I am praying to Allah for something for three years and my prayer is not yet answered. I feel shy before Allah, most Blessed, most High, to pray again until I learned that He has accepted my prayer.' 'Ibrahim, *'Alayhi al-Salam*, then asked, 'What for did you pray?' He said, 'One day I was performing *Salat* (prayer) here that a boy who was so wonderful with light shining from his forehead and two bunches of hair hanging down his back, drove by cows like being oiled and sheep that were so healthy. He amazed me and I asked, 'O wonderful boy, to who these cows and sheep belong?' He said, 'They belong to 'Ibrahim, *'Alayhi al-Salam*.' I then asked, 'Who are you?' he replied, 'I am 'Isma'il, son of Ibrahim, the special friend of Allah, most Majestic, most Glorious.' I asked Him to show me His special friend.' 'Ibrahim, *'Alayhi al-Salam*, then said, 'I am Ibrahim, the special friend of the Beneficent and that boy is my son.' The man then said, 'All praise belongs to Allah who has answered my prayer.' He then turned to 'Ibrahim, *'Alayhi al-Salam*, and embraced him and said, 'Now, you can stand up and pray and I will say Amen. 'Ibrahim, *'Alayhi al-Salam*, prayed for the believing male and female on that day and asked forgiveness for them from Allah and to be happy with them.' He (the Imam) said, 'The man then said Amen to his prayer.' Abu Ja'far, *'Alayhi al-Salam*, has said that the prayer of 'Ibrahim, *'Alayhi al-Salam*, reaches the sinful believing people of our Shi'ah up to the Day of Judgment.'"

'If you try to count the bounties of Allah...'

H 15039, h 592

Ali ibn Muhammad has narrated from certain persons of our people in a marfu' manner who has narrated the following:

"Ali ibn al-Husayn, *'Alayhi al-Salam*, would read this verse of al-Quran. '. . . if you try to count the bounties of Allah, you will not be able to enumerate them.' (16:18) He (the Imam) would say, *'Tasbih* (Allah is free of all defects). He has not made the duty of recognizing His bounties by His servants more than their recognizing their inability to know them fully. He has not made the ability of His servants to know and perceive His essence more than their knowledge of the fact that they cannot perceive Him in full. He, most Majestic, most Glorious, appreciates their recognizing the fact that they fall far short to recognize Him fully. He thus has made the recognition of falling short as an expression of their thanks giving just as He knows the knowledge of the people of knowledge that they cannot perceive Him fully. Thus, He has made it (such knowledge) their belief with knowledge on His part that He has expanded the expression and it (expression) cannot go any farther. No one of His servants is able to worship Him the way He must be worshipped. How can one who has no limit or quality be worshipped fully? Allah, most Blessed, most High, is by far high and exalted.'"

"Banu 'Umayyah was mentioned..."

H 15040, h 593

Muhammad ibn Yahya has narrated from Muhammad ibn al-Husayn from Ibrahim ibn abu Hashim from 'Anbasah ibn Bijad al-'Abid from Jabir who has narrated the following:

"Once we were with abu Ja'far, *'Alayhi al-Salam*, when the sultan (government) of banu 'Umayyah was mentioned. Abu Ja'far, *'Alayhi al-Salam*, said, 'No one escapes Hisham without being killed.' He (the narrator) has said that he (the Imam) mentioned his government to last for twenty years. He (the narrator) has said that we expressed shock. He (the Imam) then said, 'What is the matter with you! When Allah, most Majestic, most Glorious, wants to destroy a government of people He commands the angel to quicken the revolving of al-Falak (the group, the system) and then determines as He wills.' He (the narrator) has said that we mentioned these words to Zayd, *'Alayhi al-Salam*, and he said, 'I saw Hisham when the Messenger of Allah, *O Allah grant compensation to Muhammad and his family worthy of their services to Your cause*, was insulted before him, he did not reprove it and did not change it. By Allah, even if no one will help and support me except myself and my son, I will rise against him.'"

"(Government) which is not for him...."

H 15041, h 594

Through the same chain of narrators as that of the previous Hadith, the following is narrated from 'Anbasah Mu'alla' ibn Khunays who has narrated the following:

"Once I was with abu 'Abd Allah, *'Alayhi al-Salam*, that Muhammad ibn 'Abd Allah came and offered greeting of peace. Abu 'Abd Allah, *'Alayhi al-Salam*, was emotionally moved and his eyes became full with tears. I then asked, 'How is it that you treated him in a way that you would not do before?' He (the Imam) said, 'I was emotionally moved for him because he is ascribed to a matter (government) which is not for him, because I do not find his name in the book of Ali, *'Alayhi al-Salam*, as of the khulafa or Muluk, (rulers, successors) in this nation or of its kings.'"

People of the cave were old...

H 15042, h 595

Ali ibn Ibrahim has narrated in a marfu' manner who has narrated the following:

"Abu 'Abd Allah, *'Alayhi al-Salam*, once asked a man, 'Who is *al-Fata*' (young one) according to you?' He replied, 'He is a young man.' He (the Imam) said, 'No, *al-Fata*' is a believing man. The people of the cave were old people but Allah, most Majestic, most Glorious, called them al-Fityah (the young ones) because of their belief.'"

Distance of our journeys further apart...

H 15043, h 596

Muhammad has narrated from Ahmad ibn Muhammad from ibn Mahbub from Jamil ibn Salih from Sadir who has narrated the following:

"Once a man asked abu Ja'far, *'Alayhi al-Salam*, about the meaning of the words of Allah, most Majestic, most Glorious, '. . . they said, "Our Lord, make the distance of our journeys further apart," thus they wronged themselves.' (34:19) He (the Imam) said, 'They were a people whose towns were joined to each other and they could see each other, they had flowing canals and abundant wealth. They did not appreciate the bounties of Allah and changed their condition. Allah, most Majestic, most Glorious, sent upon them a roaring deluge which drowned their towns, their homes and destroyed their assets. It changed their garden into two gardens of bitter tamarisk and a few lotus trees. Allah, most Majestic, most Glorious, then said, '. . . We recompensed them as such because of their disbelief and We do not recompense as such except the ungrateful ones.'"

That is how we are and all praise belongs to Allah

H 15044, h 597

Al-Husayn ibn Muhammad al-Ash'ariy has narrated from Mu'alla' ibn Muhammad from al-Washsha' from abu Basir from Ahmad ibn 'Umar who has narrated the following:

"Once a man came to abu Ja'far, *'Alayhi al-Salam*, and said, 'You are the *Ahl al-Bayt* (the family) of mercy, Allah, most Blessed, most High, has chosen you for mercy.' Abu Ja'far, *'Alayhi al-Salam*, said, 'That is how we are and all praise belongs to Allah. We do not make anyone to enter into misguidance and we do not take anyone out of guidance to the worldly matters. The world will not end before Allah, most Majestic, most Glorious, will raise from our *Ahl al-Bayt* one who will act according to the book of Allah and will reject all the detestable matters among you.'"

This is the end of the book al-Rawdah of al-Kafi, which is the last book. All praise belongs to Allah, Lord of the worlds, *O Allah grant compensation to Muhammad and his family worthy of their services to Your cause*. I praise Allah who is free of all defects for His granting me the ability to complete this gracious book, in the form of correcting, with footnotes and recording. I thank Him, glorify Him for His great blessing and glorious work, He is generous and gracious.

CPSIA information can be obtained
at www.ICGtesting.com
Printed in the USA
BVHW020854030423
661648BV00029B/316